TEACHER PREP

**MERRILL
PRENTICE HALL**

Teacher Preparation Classroom

YOUR CLASS. THEIR CAREERS. OUR FUTURE. WILL YOUR STUDENTS BE PREPARED?

We invite you to explore our new, innovative and engaging Web site and all that it has to offer you, your course, and tomorrow's educators! Preview this site today at www.prenhall.com/teacherprep/demo. Just click on "go" on the login page to begin your exploration.

Organized around the major courses pre-service teachers take, the Teacher Preparation site provides media, student/teacher artifacts, strategies, research articles, and other resources to equip your students with the quality tools needed to excel in their courses and prepare them for their first classroom.

This ultimate on-line education resource will provide you and your students access to the following:

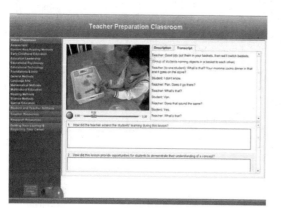

Online Video Library. More than 250 video clips—each tied to a course topic and framed by learning goals and Praxis-type questions—capture real teachers and students working in real classrooms.

Student and Teacher Artifacts. More than 200 student and teacher classroom artifacts—each tied to a course topic and framed by learning goals and application questions—provide a wealth of materials and experiences to help your students observe children's developmental learning.

Lesson Plan Builder. Step-by-step guidelines and lesson plan examples to support students as they learn to build high-quality lesson plans.

Articles and Readings. More than 500 articles from ASCD's renowned journal *Educational Leadership* are available. The site also includes Research Navigator, a searchable database of additional educational journals.

Strategies and Lessons. More than 500 research-supported instructional strategies appropriate for a wide range of grade levels and content areas.

Licensure and Career Tools. Resources devoted to helping your students pass their licensure exam; learn standards, law, and public policies; plan a teaching portfolio; and succeed in their first year of teaching.

HOW TO ORDER *TEACHER PREP* FOR YOU AND YOUR STUDENTS:

- For students to receive a *Teacher Prep* Access Code with this text, please provide your bookstore with ISBN 0-13-614929-4 when you **place** your textbook order. The bookstore **must** order the text with this ISBN to be eligible for this offer.

Upon ordering *Teacher Prep* for their students, instructors will be given a lifetime *Teacher Prep* Access Code. To receive your access code, please email: **Merrill.marketing@pearsoned.com** and provide the following information:

- Name and Affiliation
- Author/Title/Edition of Merrill text

FAMILIES, SCHOOLS, AND COMMUNITIES
Building Partnerships for Educating Children

FOURTH EDITION

CHANDLER BARBOUR
Towson University, Emeritus

NITA H. BARBOUR
University of Maryland, Baltimore County, Emerita

PATRICIA A. SCULLY
University of Maryland, Baltimore County

PEARSON

Merrill
Prentice Hall

Upper Saddle River, New Jersey
Columbus, Ohio

Library of Congress Cataloging-in-Publication Data

Barbour, Chandler.
    Families, schools, and communities: building partnerships for educating children/Chandler Barbour,
Nita H. Barbour, Patricia A. Scully. — 4th ed.
        p. cm.
    Includes bibliographical references and index.
    ISBN-13: 978-0-13-239282-2
    ISBN-10: 0-13-239282-8
1. Community and school—United States. 2. School environment—United States. 3. Students—United
States—Social conditions. 4. Education—Curricula—United States. 5. Child development—United States.
I. Barbour, Nita. II. Scully, Patricia A. III. Title.
    LC225.3.B27 2008
    371.19—dc22

                                                                            2007013720

Vice President and Executive
    Publisher: Jeffery W. Johnston
Publisher: Kevin M. Davis
Acquisitions Editor: Julie Peters
Editorial Assistant: Tiffany Bitzel
Production Editor: Linda Hillis Bayma
Production Coordination: Shelley L. Creager, Aptara Inc.
Design Coordinator: Diane C. Lorenzo

Photo Coordinator: Maria B. Vonada
Cover Designer: Ali Mohrman
Cover Image: SuperStock
Production Manager: Laura Messerly
Director of Marketing: David Gesell
Marketing Manager: Amy Judd
Marketing Coordinator: Brian Mounts

This book was set in Galliard by Aptara Inc. It was printed and bound by R.R. Donnelley & Sons Company. The cover was printed by R.R. Donnelley & Sons Company.

Photo Credits for Chapter Openers: Patricia A. Scully, pp. 1, 87; Corbis/Bettmann, p. 25; Shirley Zeiberg/PH College, pp. 57, 199; Amanda Weil, p. 117; Scott Cunningham/Merrill, pp. 141, 285; Steven Barbour, p. 165; Linda Coan O'Kresik/Bangor Daily News, p. 231; Karen D. Turner, p. 259; D. John McCarthy/U.S. Space Camp, p. 319.

Pearson Prentice Hall™ is a trademark of Pearson Education, Inc.
Pearson® is a registered trademark of Pearson plc
Prentice Hall® is a registered trademark of Pearson Education, Inc.
Merrill® is a registered trademark of Pearson Education, Inc.

Pearson Education Ltd.
Pearson Education Singapore Pte. Ltd.
Pearson Education Canada, Ltd.
Pearson Education–Japan

Pearson Education Australia Pty. Limited
Pearson Education North Asia Ltd.
Pearson Educación de Mexico, S.A. de C.V.
Pearson Education Malaysia Pte. Ltd.

10 9 8 7 6 5 4 3 2 1
ISBN-13: 978-0-13-239282-2
ISBN-10:   0-13-239282-8

*We dedicate this text edition to our family members, friends, and colleagues
who have helped us learn how important homes, schools, and communities have
been in our own lifetimes of learning.—CB/NHB*

*I dedicate this text edition to Mary Rivkin, my inspirational mentor, Mary Fryer
and Audrey Jewett, my dear colleagues, and Mary Rogers, my children's wonderful caregiver.
Thank you for your friendship and support through the years.—PS*

Preface

Late in 2006 the United States passed the 300 million population mark, and professional observers became more reflective on the status, the changes, and the future of the third largest country in the world. We all are aware of the rapid changes in economic matters, in globalization, in the cultural diversity about us, and in new technologies available to all. Of course, these factors present greater challenges and new opportunities for those of us in the social sciences and helping professions. Certainly our nation requires the best educational practices to cope with the 21st-century landscape.

Educators and social-services providers, as well as family members, community members, and caregivers of all kinds, are in the forefront for interpreting our emerging world for children. The responsibility for accomplishing this task is staggering, and we ask: How do we best prepare for our new challenges and at the same time maintain our forward thrust?

Interest in educational reform and renewal has surfaced periodically for generations in America, and in recent decades reform has been debated by political leaders. Renewal, repair, or reconsideration seems to be on everyone's mind, and criticism has become a constant in many communities. This places schools and educators in an uncomfortable arena at times, and many sense an urge to justify all actions and procedures.

In the 12 years since the first edition of this text, our recommendations for community and family collaboration with schools have widened, and acceptance in many schools appears high. The notion of collaboration can be seen often now in other areas of society: ecological and environmental planning, urban development issues, physical- and mental-health programs, as well as the many outreach programs that social-services agencies promote. We feel the concept of partnerships is growing rapidly in the United States, and groups—from small neighborhoods to our own Congress—are finding benefits in seeking better protocols. Continuing progress in these areas has implications for how we nurture, protect, and educate our children, however. Consider the following developments:

1. *Econonics and National Priorities*
   We find greater wealth in America today, but almost one fifth of our children live in poverty, and the inadequate health care for this population is even more alarming. Providing an adequate income for all families has become a topic for national discussion.

2. *Global Patterns*
   In America, globalization in our attitudes as well as in the manufacture of goods and services expands every month. Very few citizens can now maintain a parochial view point and focus only on local interests. Whether we are sympathetic to the notion or not, we all live within a global economy and communication network, which means that many of our actions and policies take on an international interest. All children must now think in world terms and be able to draw on a far more extensive array of resources, services, and ideas.

3. *Isolation in Our Society*
   Investigators find that our society is more isolated, despite merged interests and enhanced communication devices in the 21st century. More young Americans depend on virtual worlds for personal contacts, and their natural social networks are growing thinner. Ironically, a society that has encouraged citizens to communicate instantaneously with almost anyone on

the planet has the sobering responsibility for having removed those same persons from many family and collegial relationships. Social and emotional isolation is on the rise.

4. *Mass Media and Electronic Communication*
Mass media and electronic communication have created vast new opportunities and challenges for all citizens. The recent and rapid rise of the Internet has outdistanced all estimates, and it signals changes in the way Americans will communicate, purchase materials, and access information from now on. Although the benefits are extensive, electronic connections in our high-tech world have seized a great deal of time and attention from all young Americans. They are a boon for motivation, but the virtual worlds now open to youth must be associated in some way to our mainstream society.

5. *Governmental Oversight*
Governmental agencies, as well as most state governments, are displaying more interest in education and seek to play a more influential role. Some policies that have emerged in recent years include endorsement of voucher plans, support for religious agencies that seek connections with public education, and test-regulated indices for "successful" teaching. The effect of this governmental interest and role is perceived differently by educators and community leaders.

Although we are faced with new and sobering challenges, old demands are still evident in our postindustrial society. Cultural and ethnic diversity is expanding rapidly in the United States, and efforts to address the needs of exceptional children grow each year. Many authorities see gains in adjusting societal expectations for the greater diversity of America; others believe more is needed.

All these concerns point to a need to develop education agendas aimed at blending interests, using cooperation to the fullest, and identifying all resources possible for addressing children's educational needs. In addition, most authorities agree that major changes in the procedures and formats of many U.S. schools are needed as never before. For many, the greatest changes focus on drawing more partners into the management of children's formal education. A number of educational collaborations and partnership designs have spread across the United States and have served as effective bridges in many school districts. This text moves in a similar direction, and the authors support the designs that emphasize the benefits of collaboration among the many agencies and persons working with our children.

Children develop and learn at home, at school, and in the community. Their experiences may be positive or negative, but we all must acknowledge that the persons in these three social settings influence students' education from birth to adulthood. Because of this reality, we must look for the best ways to enable all community adults to remain involved and be contributors to children's experiences in positive ways.

A basic tenet of *Families, Schools, and Communities: Building Partnerships for Educating Children* is that schools will always be a primary venue for educating the young child, and educators must be in the forefront of any endeavor to bring about change. The authors stress that to accomplish the tasks at hand, however, all school districts must develop vibrant partnerships—uniting parents and community members with teachers in educating tomorrow's citizens. Schools are where the action will bloom, but respectful collaboration is the key to success.

Significant steps for improving children's education through collaboration are already being made in schools and communities across the United States. A growing number of research studies, controlled assessments, and personal accounts support new partnership approaches. The authors salute all these efforts. We maintain that most schools do not need to reconceptualize curricula or most of their current teaching practices. The big job now is to study and adapt the amazing examples that already exist.

NEW TO THE FOURTH EDITION

New and Expanded Topics. Building on the success of the third edition, we have used that material as a base but have rearranged some topics to give the text more coherence and usability. Users of this text and objective reviewers of our third edition have pointed out areas in need of amplification. Consequently, we have increased coverage of the following topics:

- Community and family diversity in American communities and homes
- Political involvement in schools and new federal directions
- Effects of media on socialization, learning, and communication
- Collaborative models and programs
- Social concerns: bullying and obesity problems
- Including children with disabilities in school and community (in a new Chapter 6)

Reflections. To increase the usability of the text content and to provide readers with chances to examine their attitudes and perceptions, we have inserted stimulating situations and questions within each chapter. Seven or eight boxed "Reflections" in each chapter are designed to help beginning professionals relate the text information and concepts to their personal situations and to sharpen critical-thinking skills. The reflections will extend and expand the "Suggested Activities and Questions" material that readers find at the end of each chapter.

Applications. To further connect theory and practice for readers, we added "Applying These Concepts to Your Work with Children and Families" near the close of each chapter. The practical and classroom-linked suggestions contained in these sections help readers apply the substance of the text directly to their work with children and help them examine their reactions to real-life events. These sections boost the demonstration aspects of the text and also encourage readers to evaluate their insights as they pursue the project suggestions.

Updated References, Resources, and Figures. Because research studies and findings are frequently expanded or replicated, we have also updated a large number of references. We have updated the Resources section in each chapter to include new publications, other media, and Web sites that we believe will have staying power. Updated figures and tables in each chapter synthesize information for the reader.

ORGANIZATION OF THIS TEXT

We feel it vital for pre-service and in-service teachers as well as other social-services providers to acknowledge the numerous influences on children's lives and how the structures of homes and communities affect children's learning in schools. We believe that by studying and analyzing this broader scope of curriculum, teachers in training and other professionals will recognize the crucial educative forces of family, peer group, and community.

The vignettes about children's experiences that are included in all the chapters, plus the model programs outlined in Chapter 12, serve to bring the text's messages closer to reality.

We begin this book with an overview of the powerful influences surrounding all young children in America. Together with this, we identify the three primary contexts of home life, school life, and community life and discuss how these social settings interplay to affect children's lives. Society does change, of course, and some forces influencing children have intensified in recent years. We categorize these influence patterns so that readers will gain a better perspective of what exists in the United States today.

Chapter 2 focuses on (a) how responsibilities for children's education emerged over time, (b) the range of philosophies and perspectives that have appeared in American education, and (c) how different ethnic groups in the United States have been affected educationally for more than three centuries. We look particularly at the uneven progress of collaborations associated with schoolwork.

Chapters 3 and 4 present information on U.S. family life, and we review various family patterns and clarify the different ways in which families function. This information helps prospective teachers grasp the range of situations that professionals encounter as they work with children in a diverse society. Our hope is that readers will appreciate our urging of more collaborations in light of this diversity.

Chapter 5 is devoted to the expansion of out-of-home care programs for the millions of pre-school-aged children as well as young school-aged children. Far more mothers have joined the American workforce and must now find adequate care for their preschool-aged children and their in-school children who need care during after-school hours. We discuss the various child-care arrangements and practices as well as the agency-directed preschool programs that a growing number of young children encounter.

Chapter 6 focuses on the need in both school and community for an inclusive program for children with disabilities. Ensuring the optimal growth and development of children with disabilities is a responsibility shared by their families, schools, and community agencies, and in this chapter we examine the issues from the perspectives of parents, teachers, and other professionals.

Chapter 7 examines the responsibilities and expectations society maintains for parents and professionals in educating and protecting children in the three social settings. In this section we point out the various educational assignments and expectations that each setting places on the others.

Chapters 8, 9, and 10 deal with curriculum in the three social settings. Curriculum surrounds children, and although we do not always take notice of it, much of what children learn comes from the world outside the classroom. The reader must recognize that all citizens are educators and that when teachers acknowledge this, an even greater potential for learning exists.

The last two chapters focus on the possibilities for collaboration among the three social settings. In Chapter 11, we offer many practical suggestions for ways teachers, parents, and others can work together. Chapter 12 examines the demanding and often difficult process of merging the efforts of people interested in collaboration. In this final chapter, we present seven successful models that demonstrate collaboration. We believe that these time-tested programs can provide a helpful template for agencies and communities seeking to marshall efforts to arrive at healthy partnerships.

Appendix I presents an extensive bibliography of children's books to help make the family, school, and community diversity presented in this text more realistic. This listing has been updated and expanded to include information on religious practices.

Appendix II presents the Code of Ethical Conduct that the NAEYC (National Association for the Education of Young Children) promulgates. The authors consider this a foundation for the text's thesis.

SPECIAL FEATURES

To assist instructors and students using this text, we have included several pedagogical aids.

Chapter Objectives, Implications, and Summaries. Concise statements of each chapter's main ideas serve as advance organizers for the content that follows. In addition, we have placed a brief section near the end of each chapter that urges the reader to reflect on and personalize the chapter information. These "Applying These Concepts to Your Work with Children and Families" sections are designed to increase understanding by relating text to self. A chapter summary reviews the highlights of the content in each chapter.

Vignettes. Stories of real-life events that we have encountered clarify many concepts throughout the text chapters. The children in the vignettes represent families from a wide range of ethnic and socioeconomic groups who live in a variety of geographic areas. These personal stories are all from our experiences (except the names used) and give a human connection to the chapter information and purpose.

Suggested Activities and Questions. Each chapter ends with questions and activities that give instructors another means to make the text applicable to their course outlines and to students' lives. For students, the activities will help apply concepts presented and will stimulate reflection and discussion on the reading as well as their own experiences.

Resources. No text can give comprehensive coverage to the diverse topics included here for either community workers or teacher candidates. All instructors will supplement this content with their specialized knowledge, particular readings, and projects. We present a framework that points to ways that material can be organized and processed. To underscore this point, we provide a number of resources in each chapter.

In addition to citing extensive references within the text and featuring tables and figures that encapsulate text content, we list particular titles at the end of each chapter to allow for a more thorough examination of the material. We also have included other resources: (a) up-to-date films and videos to provide another medium for the chapter concepts; (b) lists of key organizations and agencies that relate to the profession; and (c) selected Web sites that give current status reports for our chapter features.

Bibliography of Children's Literature. The selections in the children's book section (Appendix I) present valuable examples of children in different family arrangements learning in a variety of settings. This updated bibliography provides instructors as well as in-service teachers and other professionals with curriculum material to illuminate the chapter content. It will be particularly valuable for Chapters 3, 4, 5, 6, 8, 9, and 10.

Glossary. Because the text draws from sociology, psychology, human development, and anthropology as well as from pedagogy and curriculum content, we include a glossary to help readers with specialized terms.

SUPPLEMENTS

- Online Instructor's Manual—Available in the Instructor's Resource Center on **www. prenhall.com,** this downloadable supplement will extend activities, questions, and overviews from each chapter to provide professors with additional practical application.

- Online Test Bank—Available in the Instructor's Resource Center on **www.prenhall.com,** this downloadable supplement includes essay, multiple choice, and true/false test questions to assess student understanding of chapter concepts.

- Online PowerPoint Slides—Available in the Instructor's Resource Center on **www. prenhall.com,** this downloadable supplement can work in conjunction with the Online Instructor's Manual to provide professors with key summarizations of chapter content.

- TestGen—This computerized test management software on disc provides instructors with electronic access to Test Bank questions and the ability to customize exams. Request this product from your Prentice Hall sales representative.

- BlackBoard Cartridge and WebCT Cartridge—Available in the Instructor's Resource Center on **www.prenhall.com,** this downloadable supplement acts as a TestGen for online courses. These cartridges contain the converted Test Bank file for simple insertion into pre-existing online courses.

ACKNOWLEDGMENTS

Many people provided valuable assistance in gathering content and assembling this text. We would like to acknowledge particularly the following individuals: Janel, Jack, and Catherine Hino for unflagging support and encouragement; Nancy Berge for expert counsel about special education; Valerie Mekras for supplying background material and references on special-needs programs and photos for several sections; University of Maryland,

Baltimore County, colleague Debbie Bell for un-flagging encouragement; Audrey Jewett for providing materials and suggestions for examining topics in the text; and Greg Mekras and Belle Kuhn for supplying helpful photos to illustrate several sections.

Many thanks go to our professional colleagues, several classroom teachers, and several parents who generously supplied photos to illustrate our text. Library personnel at the University of Maine and at the University of Maryland, Baltimore County, have been patient, helpful, and supportive in filling numerous requests and supplying materials in a timely fashion.

We wish to thank Julie Peters, our editor at Merrill/Prentice Hall, for her guidance. We also thank Shelley L. Creager, our production editor at Aptara, and Robin C. Bonner, our copyeditor, for their many valuable contributions. Several individuals reviewed the third edition of this text and made valuable comments and suggestions to improve this fourth edition. We thank them here: Susan Matoba Adler, University of Illinois, Urbana–Champaign; Carol Katowitz, Ivy Tech Community College of Indiana; Judith A. Myers-Walls, Purdue University; Sharla Snider, Texas Woman's University; and Francine Stuckey, Eastern New Mexico University.

Brief Contents

Contents

Chapter 6
Including Children
with Disabilities   141

Chapter 7
Responsibility for Educating
and Protecting Children   165

Chapter 10
Curriculum of the Community   259

Chapter 11
Strategies for Working
Together   285

Chapter 12
Models for Parent–School–Community
Partnerships   319

NOTE: Every effort has been made to provide accurate and current Internet information in this book. However, the Internet and information posted on it are constantly changing, and it is inevitable that some of the Internet addresses listed in this textbook will change.

Home, School, and Community Influences on Children's Lives

There was a child went forth every day,

    And the first object he looked upon and received with wonder or pity or love or dread, that object he became,

    And that object became part of him for the day or a certain part of the day . . . or for many years or stretching cycles of years.

(Whitman, W., 1855, p. 90)

This beginning chapter highlights the many ways in which young children's learning, behaviors, and viewpoints are affected by family members, school personnel, members of the immediate community, and forces in the larger society. At one point in time, the family operated as the main socializing agent for children, but over the years, school and community influences have increased dramatically. Today, strong **collaboration** among the social settings is needed to resolve the challenging issues facing children in our increasingly diverse country. After reading this chapter, you will be able to

1. Discuss how the three social settings—home, school, and community, including peer groups and the media—affect children's perceptions and attitudes about learning and their success at school.

2. Explain how these three social settings have greater or lesser impact, depending on the child's age, stage of development, and the social context.

3. Identify some of the key issues facing children today and discuss how collaboration among the social settings is helping to address them.

4. Discuss the impact of professional development standards on preparing teachers and other professionals to work with families and the community more effectively.

5. Give examples of the impact that special interest groups can have on children's perceptions of their world and on their behavior.

Zach was waiting impatiently at the child-care center for his mother to pick him up. He looked in his "cubbie" for the big green fists—a gift from his father during last week's visit. Zach picked up the vibrating Incredible Hulk Hands from his backpack, where he had left them on arriving at the center, and approached Kelsey, also waiting for her mother. He grinned, and in his deepest voice, he said, "I'm warning you, if you don't tell me where you planted the bomb, I'm going to clobber you," and he lunged at Kelsey. "No, I won't tell. We'll all blow up," giggled Kelsey, entering into the play and holding up her fists to Zach. The children jabbed at each other, growling and hissing, until Zach accidentally struck Kelsey's head, and Kelsey began to cry. At that moment, Zach's mother and the teacher entered the room. The teacher, calming Kelsey, said to Zach's mother, "We don't allow aggressive play here at the center. I really wish you wouldn't let Zach bring toys like that."

In spite of Zach's attempt to explain what had happened, his tired mother, while she got ready to go out, informed him that he couldn't watch television that evening. When they reached home, she let Zach select Three Billy Goats Gruff *and* Max's Dragon Shirt *to read while he waited for his father to pick him up. When Tom, Zach's mother's boyfriend, arrived, Zach asked him to read. As Tom got to the first little goat crossing the bridge, Zach exclaimed, "Oh, let me read the troll part," and pulling the book closer, asked, "Is this where the troll speaks?"*

"Yeah, how did you know?" Tom exclaimed.

Zach replied, "Dad told me," and then, in a gruff, "pretend read" voice, demanded, "Who's that tramping on my bridge?" At each goat's passing, his voice got gruffer, and he clenched his fist as he told the goats he was going to eat them up. When the third goat passed, Tom, in character, gave Zach a gentle push, hugging and tickling him as the "goat" pushed the troll into the river. Zach giggled and said, "Let's read it again, and I'll be the goats this time." When Zach got to the third goat part, he butted Tom, who pulled Zach off the couch with him, "falling into the river." A bit of horseplay ensued. Zach then got up and said, "Now, let's read Max's Dragon Shirt. You know, I'm gonna ask my dad to buy me a dragon shirt like that. Isn't it wild?"

Children develop constantly, and as they do, they are affected by both genetic and environmental factors. Throughout the 20th century, researchers argued over the importance of each factor (**the nature–nurture controversy**) and attempted to determine which aspect exerted the greatest influence. Through the 1980s, most authorities credited social and environmental factors with exerting the most influence, but we have found far more appreciation of a **bidirectional process** since that time (Maccoby, 2002).

One feature often ignored in these debates is the important role children play in their own growth, a position underscored by **interactionist–constructionist** theories of development and extended by cultural context theories. Bronfenbrenner's **bioecological theory** maintains that there are multiple contexts (physical, mental, social, and historical) affecting a child's growth and development. The interactions between the child, other people, objects, and symbols in these contexts unleashes the child's genetic potential to produce many and varied changes (Gander, 2003). Although heredity may increase the likelihood that we will behave in certain ways, it does not cause us to actually do so. Brain research further supports this **transactional process of development** (Marcus, 2004). In the preceding vignette, you can see that Zach's development is being influenced by the ways in which he interacts with the experiences in his life.

Experiences of one kind or another bombard the **perceptual field** of any child, constantly influencing learning and development (Ridley, 2003), for better or worse. Zach's feelings and attitudes toward aggressive behavior, as well as his reading habits, are influenced by his interactions at school, at home, and in his community, as well as by what he witnesses through the media.

The messages children receive from their surroundings are not always consistent, but they still influence attitudes and values. One can't be sure,

for example, exactly what Zach is internalizing. It appears that his attitude toward reading is positive and that he is getting similar messages from those close to him. Reading appears to be fun; people answer his questions about the text and respond to his reactions to the story. Though his mother denied him television that day, she allowed him to select books to entertain himself.

The messages Zach receives about aggression, though, may not be as consistent. Zach's father buys him toys that represent aggression, but the **child-care center** bans them. In spite of the ban, his friend Kelsey seems to share in his "aggressive-acting behavior," at least until she is hurt. The mother attempts to reinforce the school's nonaggressive policy by forbidding television temporarily and by suggesting a more passive activity. Still, Zach finds acceptance of his need to express aggression by reenacting a story with his mother's friend and engaging in horseplay.

As a teacher or community worker, you cannot ensure that all the influences impacting children are positive, so you must be sensitive to the idea that children's learning will be affected both positively and negatively by many factors beyond your control. You must also be attuned to your own feelings and reactions, as these, too, affect children's growth. As you identify the strengths of **family,** media, and community influences, you should strive to build on these qualities. Figure 1–1 shows the relative influence on children of their home, school, and community experiences.

CHILDREN'S PERCEPTIONS AND ATTITUDES

Sociocultural theorists such as Lev Vygotsky suggest that parents, teachers, and community members play an essential role in helping to socialize children to the values and customs of the larger society (Trawick-Smith, 2006). For example, at early ages, children are aware of their family's and community's attitudes regarding education, other cultures, racial or religious groups, and roles that males and females play in society (Maeroff, 1999; Sadker & Sadker, 2005).

Figure 1–1   Social Setting Influences According to Age

Note: Percentages show the waking-hours experience of composite American children. The increasing influence of school and community relates to other factors in addition to age, for example, stage of development, location, family socioeconomic status, and extent of contact.
Source: Adapted from Berns, 2006; Douville-Watson & Watson, 2002; Woolfolk, 2000.

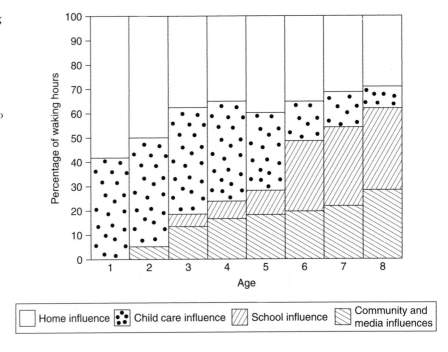

Attitudes determine what individuals attend to in a situation, how they perceive the situation, and even their response to the event. Children acquire certain attitudes by hearing words, observing actions, and surmising the feelings of significant others in their environment. These attitudes then become more firm when children are encouraged to express such beliefs. As children become aware of different values and beliefs, however, they may modify their attitudes and can even help to change those of adults. Through social interaction, both adults and children can influence each other's perceptions and attitudes.

Home Influence on Attitudes and Perceptions

Children's attitudes and perceptions emerging from home influences develop early. Family members communicate to even very young children how they feel about themselves and their neighbors and about their schools and community.

⟨⟩— Mrs. Kohl was astonished when her three-year-old, Brittany, spat at Mrs. Foster, an older woman living upstairs in their building. Mrs. Kohl didn't remember that the day before, when Mrs. Foster knocked at the apartment door, she had told her husband not to answer, saying, "I'm tired of the old hag coming around, nosing in our business, and always borrowing something. I feel like spitting, she annoys me so." When Brittany's mother took her to her room as punishment, the child said defiantly, "I spit. She old hag." ⟨⟩

At this point, it may be just Mrs. Foster that Brittany has antipathy for, but continued negative attitudes expressed by her parents and others toward older persons will affect the child's acceptance and attitude toward the presence of, interactions with, and the authority of older persons. If Mrs. Foster displays friendliness and kindness toward Brittany, however, she may modify the child's perception of her and perhaps influence Brittany's mother to feel differently, as well.

Parents' attitudes and feelings toward school will influence their children's feelings in a similar way. The annual Phi Delta Kappa/Gallup polls (Rose & Gallup, 2006) over the past quarter century show that on the whole, Americans value their local schools and have confidence in them.

Even very young children respond positively to books when significant adults engage them in literacy interactions.

Belle Kuhn

On the other hand, we find vast differences throughout the country in the faith that individuals have for schooling in general. Parents communicate this faith, or lack thereof, to their children and thus influence how their children react to their teachers, their learning experiences, and even attending school.

A few years later, Mrs. Kohl and her neighbor, Mrs. Reed, received letters stating that their daughters would be in Mrs. Owens's kindergarten. Reactions in the two households differed, and each affected the children's feelings about school. Mrs. Reed was delighted. Turning to her daughter, she said. "Oh, Sammie, you're going to love school! Mrs. Owens was my teacher, and you'll just love all the fun things you'll do in class."

Mrs. Kohl, on the other hand, felt quite different. She expressed her thoughts to her husband in her daughter's presence, "Rats, Brittany has that old Mrs. Owens. I was hoping she'd get the new young teacher." It was no wonder the two children reacted differently when they met at the bus stop on the first day of school. Samantha jumped up and down and grabbed Brittany's hand as she ran toward the stopped bus, saying, "Oh, we're going to have so much fun." Brittany, however, pushed her away and refused to get on the bus. No amount of cajoling from the adults could convince her that she should get on. Mrs. Kohl was forced to drive Brittany to school for

several days before the child would take the bus with her friend.

Initially, both children appear to be responding to their parental attitudes as they viewed and responded to schooling. It is also difficult to determine what caused the change in Brittany. School may have been fun, and she may have started to enjoy her teacher. Or, perhaps her peers influenced her thinking on "how one ought to go to school."

REFLECTION

The next time you are in a classroom when parents are picking up their children, ask the parents if their children have always enjoyed school. Do you note incidents that are similar to Brittany's? This will give you a glimpse of the parent-to-child linkage.

Parental attitudes, toward an interest and involvement in such issues as disposition toward work or reading provide models for children's interests and involvement. Coleman (1991) pointed out that children whose parents stress the importance of good work habits, punctuality, and task completion carry these traits over into their schoolwork and have greater academic success. Since Durkin's (1966) classic study of the commonality of influences on early readers, other studies relating to the effect of home environment and parental perceptions of **literacy development** indicate that parental attitudes toward and modeling of reading with young children are critical factors in children's development. Children respond more positively to books when they engage in a greater level of literacy interaction with adults and when the adults believe in the importance of these interactions (Clay, 1991; Hill-Clark, 2005; Leland & Kasten, 2002). Readers will find a fuller examination of parenting and its influence on children's development and learning in Chapter 4.

School Influence on Attitudes and Perceptions

Although the thesis is questioned by some (Harris, 2002; Rowe, 1994), most developmentalists agree that parental attitudes have a major effect on children's learning and acceptance of school (Borkowski, Ramey, & Stile, 2002). In turn, the attitudes of school personnel affect how children learn. Research by the Institute for Responsive Education on educators' attitudes toward low-income parents shows that many didn't expect low-income parents to be productive participants in their children's education and, in turn, those parents felt that their participation wouldn't have much effect, and therefore they often had negative attitudes toward the schools (Heleen, 1990). Children internalize these attitudes of mutual disrespect. Children's self-worth is diminished or enhanced as the children sense how school personnel view the lifestyle and culture of their families, and these attitudes can breed tolerance or intolerance for others.

In the following vignette, Camille and Helen reacted differently to a bus driver's careless words, but both were distressed.

Camille and Helen arrived at their homes upset over a comment their bus driver had made. There were empty cans on the bus, and the driver said, "Don't touch them cans. I just drove a bunch of Black kids on a trip,

and they aren't clean." Camille exclaimed to her mother, "But I ride the bus everyday. Does he think I'm not clean 'cause I'm Black?"

Helen's distress was similar, but from a different perspective. "We had to ride the bus after a bunch of Black kids today, and they left it dirty. Ugh!" Both Camille and Helen could have misinterpreted the bus driver's words, but their attitudes about self and others were affected by the driver's careless speech.

Teachers can't prevent what happened to Camille or Helen. They can only be alert to problems and provide an emotional climate that accepts all children regardless of their ethnic or social class standing. They must be cognizant of how their own words and actions can bring to pass the **self-fulfilling prophecies** noted long ago by Rosenthal and Jacobson (1968).

Rosenthal and Jacobson advance the notion that teachers' expectations of children result in self-fulfilling prophecies and that children whom teachers perceive to be capable and intelligent will do much better than will those children whom teachers do not perceive to be capable. In this classic study, first- and second-graders appeared to be most subjected to their teachers' attitudes. Studies conducted in the 1970s, 1980s, and 1990s continue to show that children are affected by their teachers' perceptions of them and react both behaviorally and academically according to their teachers' expectations (Gallego & Cole, 2001; Proctor, 1984).

In elementary school, girls are likely to do better academically than boys, but by the time students graduate from high school, boys score higher on **Scholastic Aptitude Tests (SAT)** (Sadker & Sadker, 2005). Young men do, however, have a greater high-school dropout rate than do young women, and men are the minority of students enrolled in higher education. Some researchers suggest that this happens because teachers treat boys and girls differently. Researchers have noted that as early as preschool, girls are inclined to select activities with more rules, guidelines, and suggestions for accomplishing the task, whereas boys tend to select activities that allow for more open-ended behavior. Because they are rewarded for such behavior, girls tend to become more compliant and boys become more assertive (Eccles, Wigfield, Harold, & Blumenfeld, 1993). As children progress through school, these reinforced behaviors get boys more attention, more opportunities for classroom discussion, and more specific guidelines as to the correctness of their responses. Girls are called on less often than are boys, are given less feedback on their responses, and are encouraged to listen rather than to participate. Girls tend to be praised for their neatness, whereas boys receive praise for academic contributions.

Consequently, some girls get the message that their academic responses are not as important as are those of boys (Butler, 2004). Because achievement in elementary school is often measured on tasks that required mastery skills, girls, who are reinforced for obeying the rules, can be expected to do better than boys, but as children progress and school success depends more on problem solving and assertiveness, boys, who been reinforced for more aggressive behavior, can be expected to outperform girls (Harris, 2004; Sadker & Sadker, 2005). Teachers who recognize that boys and girls may have different strengths and learning styles will avoid gender stereotyping, which shortchanges both girls and boys.

Because of their ethnically based preconceived expectations of performance, teachers also may discriminate against children of different ethnic and ability groups by treating them differently (Bartoleme & Macedo, 1997; Ogbu, 1994). Teachers are likely to give high achievers and majority-culture children more opportunities to respond, more praise, and more time to formulate a response. Teachers who perceive minority children to be low achievers do not expect them to know answers and do not give them as many opportunities or as much encouragement to respond. Such differential treatment over time lowers children's involvement in school and may prevent them from developing confidence in their abilities (Dilworth & Brown, 2001; Hrabowski, Maton, Greene, & Greif, 2002). A particularly troublesome outcome of this discrimination is the low numbers of men of color who attend postsecondary programs.

Schools can also become places of sanctuary for children both during the school day and in the extended hours, so many schools offer the community use of their buildings for recreational, athletic, and social activities (Maeroff, 1999). When the school building becomes a focal point of the community, and school personnel act as intermediaries between families and the community, the school can strengthen the ties between the two social settings.

Community Influence on Attitudes and Perceptions

Community influence on children's attitudes varies because of the different perspectives held by the organizations within a community and the interactions of individual citizens. Bronfenbrenner (1986, 1993) points out that a community's influence on children's growth and development will be from both **formal** and **informal community structures.** Influence from formal structures comes from political and social systems, health and recreational services, business enterprises, entertainment, and educational services. The informal structures are the social networks that each family establishes with people outside the home. Members of many communities hold common attitudes toward their local schools, as evidenced by communitywide political support for various activities, linkages established with other community organizations, and news coverage by local media.

It is difficult to measure the actual effect of community attitudes on student achievement, but we know that children quickly assimilate attitudes expressed by adults around them. Research suggests that a community's **social climate** and the personal relationships that children form within the community influence their attitudes about learning (Maeroff, 1999). For example, if school sports activities are highlighted in the media coverage and the teams get money for trips but the school librarian can't buy children's literature for the library, children soon get the message that being a good athlete is more important than being a good reader. When a community paper publishes the poems, stories, and artwork of local primary-school children, children understand that

Communities' influences on children's learning vary, but community programs, such as museums, zoos, and recreational services broaden children's perspectives.

Patricia A. Scully

the community values their academic achievements. Primary-school children are less likely to make such direct connections to community attitudes toward their schools, but they get excited about winning a pizza for reading a certain number of books. Eventually, they get a message that reading is important.

Business people often provide support for various school programs. Sometimes children witness that support and learn that important people value learning. When children hear the local grocer, businessperson, or politician comment on the positive qualities of teachers, they learn that others value the learning experiences these teachers provide.

REFLECTION

When you have a chance to solidify community connections, do it in the following ways:

1. By offering children's work for display in public places and commercial space.
2. By encouraging children to write thank-you notes to businesses that display their work.
3. By encouraging parents to acknowledge community support for school programs.

Peer Group Influence

In ways similar to the community, the peer group becomes an agency of **enculturation** and learning. Even very young children develop a sense of self from their perceptions of important people in their surroundings, including relatives, teachers, and peers. Socioeconomic status, ethnic identity, and parents' occupations affect how families view themselves and the process by which they socialize their children (Bornstein, 2002). Later, as children leave the home setting, their self-perception and socializing skills become influenced by how their peers view them.

When children move out from family to child-care centers, school, and the community at large, they begin to form attachments, and friendships emerge through their play. These relationships influence behavior. Even infants and toddlers are observed reacting to other infants by touching them, by crying when others cry, and later by offering nurturance or comfort. By about age three, early friendships begin to form and children's peers begin to have a more lasting influence (Parke, 1990).

Peer influence on behavior gradually becomes more dominant. Harris (1998, 2002) and Rowe

(1994) maintained that peer groups have an even stronger influence than that of parents, although that extreme position has been refuted by other researchers (Berk, 2005). Gradually, children discover that others can share their feelings or attitudes or have quite different ones. The perspectives of others will affect how children feel about their own families. Children usually have a "family" view of their own and of other cultures. So, when confronted with other perspectives, they often need to rethink their own viewpoints. It is often difficult for children to adjust to the idea that other families can function radically differently from their own and yet hold many of the same attitudes and beliefs and be equally nurturing and secure. The peer group serves as a barometer for children examining themselves and their feelings about self and family.

The peer group also influences development of children's socializing skills. These early friendships help children learn how to negotiate and relate to others, including their siblings and other family members. They learn from peers how to cooperate and socialize according to **group norms** and group-sanctioned modes of behavior. The peer group can influence what the child values, knows, wears, eats, and learns. The extent of this influence, however, depends on other situational constraints, such as the age and personality of children and the nature of the group (Harris, 1998; Hartup, 1983). Socialization is particularly important for children with disabilities, and it is the reason many programs include peers who are typically developing in special education programs or include children with disabilities in general education classrooms.

In its most acceptable form, the peer group is a healthy coming-of-age arbiter, by which children grasp negotiating skills and learn to deal with hostility and to solve problems in a social context. In its most destructive mode, the peer group can demand blind obedience to a group norm, which can result in socially alienated gangs with pathological outlooks (Perry, 1987).

Media Influence

Today, all members of our society are influenced both directly and indirectly by powerful media vehicles, including printed materials, television, sound recordings, and the Internet. Publicists, promoters, and sales personnel have at some point used all of these media to advocate what people should wear, what they should eat, and what values they should hold. Vivid colors and language tell us what is happening in the world and how to react to the events shown. Although much of our society's media seems dominated by superficial chitchat, hyped news events, and depictions of violence, it is also a source of education, humor, and nonviolent entertainment. Just remember that the effect of media will vary with a child's age and stage of development.

Most realize that although the different media forms can be used elegantly for mediated learning, their major objectives are entertainment and product promotion. In the following section, we discuss what we broadly term the entertainment industry in its role as a general, society-wide influence on young children. We first discuss two of its primary forms, print and television, and then treat other current media under the rubric of the industry in general.

Print Materials. The kind of books and other print media that children read and have read to them influences and supports their emotional, social, and intellectual development both directly and indirectly. Print materials, such as books, magazines, and newspapers, reach the child indirectly, through parents, caregivers, and teachers, and directly, such as when children participate in a library presentation or select particular publications to buy or borrow. The printed material made available to children implies the values of the home, school, and community (Aldridge & Kirkland, 2006).

Print media affect children's development indirectly through the publications their parents read. Books and magazines inform adults how to lead healthy and productive lives and proclaim the dangers of unhealthy practices. Advertising affects the types of clothing, food, and (especially) toys bought for children. Some toys engage children's imagination and are designed for groups of children playing together. Other toys are more suitable for children playing alone. Children's potential for social and intellectual development is affected by which type of toy adults are motivated to buy.

Studies on early literacy indicate that the amount and types of printed materials that adults have in the home, as well as how adults interact with these materials around children, affect the children's interest and literacy achievement (Desmond, 2001). From the books that adults read to children, children internalize attitudes, feelings, and biases about their own and other cultures. Zach, in the chapter's opening vignette, had a chance to express aggression in acceptable ways through *Three Billy Goats Gruff.* He was influenced in the kind of clothes he wanted by the story *Max's Dragon Shirt.* Books, like peers, provide children with a vision of their world that sometimes reaffirms their own lives and sometimes challenges their perspectives.

Television. Television's substantial impact on all growing children began in the 1950s with the proliferation of TV sets. Three generations of children have been raised with TV, and very different role models, interaction modes, and experiences are now visited on American youth. Today, more than 99% of American households contain at least one television set, and children start the viewing process early even before they reach 2 years of age. Conservative estimates are that preschool children watch nearly 3.5 hours of TV per day (Gentile & Walsh, 2002), and this average continues through age 18 (Singer & Singer, 2001). In the 21st century, however, television viewing is becoming somewhat diminished because of increased use of computer games and the Internet, and also because children now spend more time in child-care, school, and **after-school-care** programs.

Television influences children in direct proportion to both time spent viewing and the overall effect of what is viewed (American Academy of Pediatrics, 1990). Certainly, eating habits, family interactions, and use of leisure time are considerably influenced by television (Hewlett & West, 2005; Horgen, 2005; Winn, 2002). Commercials take up 12 to 14 minutes of every hour of television, and in that time, advertisers try to influence

viewers with all types of consumerism. Schools and parents are far behind advertisers in finding the most effective ways of using media.

Children are especially susceptible to electronic media, and televised advertising has a huge effect. Heavy viewers are drawn to the advertised products, including unhealthy food products, and they tend to eat more snack foods and be overweight. Social interactions are also affected: Heavy viewers hold more traditional sex-role attitudes, behave more aggressively, are less socially competent, and perform more poorly in school compared to light or nonviewers. (Arendell, 1997; Desmond, 2001).

Not all TV advertising is negative, of course. There have been efforts through TV to modify behaviors such as smoking, drunken driving, and poor nutritional habits (Van Evra, 2004). How children are affected by both positive and negative advertisements also depends on such factors as parent–child interactions, how children are disciplined, and even to some degree on social–economic factors (Strasburger & Wilson, 2002).

Advertising is not the only way in which television influences viewers. Two additional, concerns about the effects of television are the amount of violence, in both commercials and programs, and the amount of time children's television watching takes away from more creative and intellectual pursuits.

REFLECTION

Consider how much TV you watched while growing up and reflect on the positive and the negative influences that it had on how you worked, how you dressed, and what you ate. Is this influence on children more potent now?

Research on the impact of television viewing on academic achievement indicates that such influence is complex in nature. Television viewing takes time away from important social interactions, such as conversation, storytelling, imaginative play, and for primary-school children, the leisure reading that promotes literacy. We must remember, however, that the amount of viewing, the kind of programs watched, IQ, and socioeconomic status are all factors that affect children's attitude and achievement (Gunter, Harrison, & Wykes, 2003; Winn, 2002).

The Entertainment Industry. Almost all young children in the United States are exposed, on a daily basis, to entertainment and education delivered through other media besides print and television. Films (in theaters and on cassette or DVD), radio, sound recordings on compact disc and audiocassette, computer games, plus access to the Internet are the main sources.

The entire entertainment industry now has a tremendous influence on American society. Whereas a few movie stars, musicians, and sports figures were the entertainment models for generations during the 20th century, today, the visual and auditory stimuli of the new media bombard most homes and communities. Some of this exposure is educational, positive, and directed at an appropriate level for young children. A considerable amount of current fare, however, is violent in nature, is provocative, and is presented in ways unsuitable for children's level of maturity (DeGaetano, 2005; Levin, 2005). With the rapid expansion of electronic transmission devices, young people are exposed more than ever to both good and bad influences.

Producers and advertisers expand successful films and television shows by flooding sales counters with associated toys, clothing, and DVDs. Similar marketing comes from developers of video and computer games. These games influence individuals' values, compete for children's attention, and certainly reduce the amount of reflection and interaction time children have with both adults and peers (Singer & Singer, 2001). Although some maintain that such games are opportunities for children to "let off steam," others insist that there are better ways of achieving this goal.

In 2002, the U.S. Department of Commerce (2004) found that 74% of married couples with children had a home computer and that 87% of those maintained Internet access. In addition, over 90% of American elementary schools have Internet access. Meaning that the wonders and dangers of global electronic communication are available to a large majority of American children.

The Internet is now the world's largest source of information; it completely dwarfs even the world's renowned libraries. The amount of information is extraordinary for today's young people; it also carries great potential for misuse. For example, many primary-school-age children regularly "surf the 'Net'" and tell about their findings. Pornography is widely available to any child willing to misrepresent his or her age. Even more alarming are the steadily expanding hate-group Web sites, some of which are designed for children. Some help arrived with the Children's Online Privacy Protection Act of 1998, and Web-filtering software continues to appear on the market.

Internet filtering systems are a must to make Internet use in schools and homes safer. Web-Blocker is installed in many schools, and a 2003 Supreme Court decision permits such programs to be used by public libraries. CyberPatrol and Net Nanny are examples of useful filters for home computers. A filtering system is a resource that must be harnessed successfully by families, schools, and communities if its potential is to be productive (Hafner, 2002).

On the positive side, electronic media provide children with opportunities to practice skills, solve problems, create illustrations and graphs, and expand their knowledge base. For example, some primary-school children use the Internet to practice chess, send e-mail, and retrieve information from Internet bulletin boards. We can best assess the impact of these media on children's learning by observing how children use them.

When parents and other adults watch DVDs or television or use the computer with children, the children benefit more from the programs and the adults learn more about the children. Adults discover what children know and what interests or bores them. The adults may then act to enhance their children's learning. Adults may introduce children to the original stories from which the TV programs were adapted, helping them to learn to

When parents use the computer with children, the children benefit more and adults learn more about their children.

Joe Carini / PacificStock.com

make comparisons and develop better discrimination skills about stories and presentations. For children to be engaged in positive learning, it seems urgent that schools, parents, teachers, and other concerned individuals develop partnerships for interpreting and dealing with the products of both currently available media sources and those soon to appear in their communities (Murray, 1997; Paik, 2001). Helping children develop skills as critical consumers of media (Hesse & Lane, 2003) can help to reverse the negative influences of the media industry.

When Meringoff (1980) compared children's reactions to stories presented through television, books, and radio, children seemed to view television events as something not directly associated with themselves, but they appeared to personalize the events in books. Berns (2006) and Singer and Singer (2001) surmised that because the reader is more intimately involved in the book, it is a stronger socializing agent. However, the stronger personal influence of printed materials over television or the Internet could also reflect the manner in which the two are presented to children (Neuman, 1995). Young children first know about

books because someone reads to them and interacts with them about the story, whereas more often than not children are left to watch television or to use computer games by themselves. We know that children are socialized on how to react to books; thus, they get more personal meaning from them as they become readers themselves. Some researchers (Desmond, 2001; Neuman, 1997) suggest that when parents or other adults interact with children viewing television or using the computer, those children develop better interactive and processing skills.

The entertainment industry (Figure 1–2) influences the actions, dress codes, and values of many adults. It also captures and holds children's interests for a large part of each day. As a teacher or community worker, you must understand that this influence on children both enhances and inhibits their growth as human beings. You should not underestimate the effect of this influence but rather try to incorporate it into your teaching or advising so that children assimilate it in a healthy context with the rest of their education. For example, knowledge that children pick up from TV can be startling but relevant, and schools, communities,

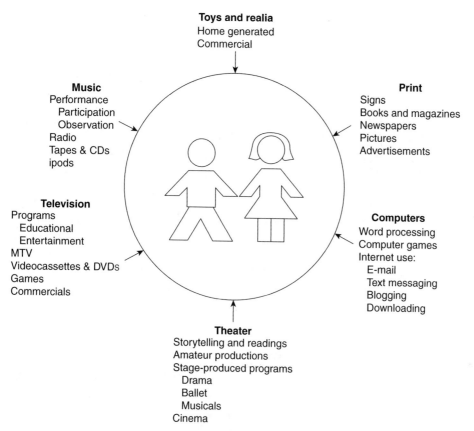

Figure 1–2   Media Influence on Children's Lives

and families may reinforce the unexpected learning in positive ways.

The teacher in Amanda's kindergarten class was introducing the letter–sound relationship of "J." When soliciting words children could recall, Mrs. Pineo got judge *from Juan. So she asked if anyone knew what* judge *meant. Children responded, "it's someone who would send you to jail if you did something wrong ... especially if you murdered someone, he'd be sure to send you to jail!" When asked how they knew this, the class as a whole replied, "It was on television!" That evening during dinner, Amanda announced to her family, "a judge would put you in jail if you did something really bad—like murder." The give and take of the subsequent table conversation between Amanda and her parents provided further clarification on how Amanda was assimilating information from school, the media, and home.*

One desirable outcome of our highly mediated world is that all people see and sense the diversity of individuals we have in modern American communities. As we view televised images of children playing in the streets of Guatemala, Canada, or Kazakhstan, we see them delighting in the same things that children in Seattle or Pittsburgh find desirable. Cultures across the world are borrowing steadily from each other and far more rapidly than previous generations. In *American Skin* (Wynter, 2002), a hopeful thesis on diversity is advanced for the **transracial** effect now found throughout the United States. Wynter makes a persuasive case for most Americans no longer reacting to racial and ethnic differences but adopting wholeheartedly the interesting and beneficial features of other cultural groups. This appears to be a positive departure from our society's background of **ethnocentrism.**

AGE LEVELS AND INFLUENCE

Community, home, school, peers, and media exert a greater or lesser influence on children's learning, depending on the age of the children concerned (note again Figure 1–1). Many theorists have described the stages in children's development from dependency to independence and have theorized how children learn. (See Table 2–1 in the following chapter for a review of selected theories.) In practice, parents, teachers, and community people rarely subscribe to one particular theory, but the decisions they make about children's learning will reflect a stronger belief in one viewpoint. As you develop strategies to promote **partnerships** for children's education, it is helpful to keep in mind that the perspective others may have on development may differ from your own.

The Early Years—Strong Home Influence

Early researchers such as Maslow (1970), Erikson (1963), and Piaget (1967) all emphasize the strong need for attachment and environmental support of infants and toddlers. Developing children require a physically and emotionally supportive environment in which their basic needs can be met. Infants must first develop trust in others so that they can explore their surroundings. According to Piaget, it is this exploration that enables them to construct knowledge about themselves and their world (Piaget, 1967).

Neuroscientists have discovered links between brain structure and brain activity, and brain research substantiates the notion that a child's knowledge develops because of an interactive process, beginning even as the brain develops before birth. Heredity may determine the framework of a developing child's brain, but researchers point out the many ways in which genes, environment, and infant responses interact to develop the connections between the brain cells that account for learning (Brynes, 2001; Pinker, 2002).

Because of this brain–environment interactive development, we can see that myriad events will affect growth, some positively and some negatively. Type of housing, presence of caregivers, and lifestyles associated with different homes influence children's lives in profound and dramatic ways. Some environments are extremely supportive and nurturing, whereas others are dominating, negligent, and even dysfunctional. For example, affectionate interactions, consistent practices, organized schedules, and high-quality nourishment bring support and security to young children (Carnegie Corporation, 1994). Such nurturing environments have secure caregivers who respond to their children by touching, cuddling, talking to, and reading with them. Most authorities agree that emotional support and interactions with the child provide building blocks for intellectual competence and language comprehension.

On the other hand, the trials of homelessness, highly mobile families, absentee parents, and poverty often mean that parents are unable to provide positive and secure environments. The lack of a responsive environment, which stems from the parents' own life experience, will affect a child's intellectual, social, and emotional competence. The young brain is quite resilient, however, and later stimulation or strong emotional bonds can help many children overcome some of the negative results of early deprivation (Bruer, 2002; Newberger, 1997).

Regardless of family configuration, American society expects all families to provide economic and emotional support for infants and toddlers. With more single-parent and dual-income parents, and fewer extended family members available to support them, families face many challenges in providing optimal care for their children. These issues will be discussed further in Chapters 4 and 5.

Preschool and Kindergarten Years—Increasing School Influence

As children develop a sense of autonomy, they need to learn the boundaries within which they can operate, and they must learn to identify new ones they will encounter as they separate from home. Bronfenbrenner's (1979, 1993) bioecological model accurately explains the transitions from the intimate **microsystem** of home to the **mesosystem** of outer linkages that come to bear on the developing child's perceptions and behavior. As parents give their children necessary support, they must also give them freedom to try things on their own.

As we noted, one's sense of self first develops in the home and then extends into the neighborhood, child-care center, and larger community. At school, the teacher and the children's peers begin to alter or reinforce this sense. Children modify their behavior in school in response to various rules and regulations and to perceived teacher and peer expectations. At the same time, significant others in the home setting continue to influence development as the early schoolers move from basic trust to **autonomy** and independence.

Many children have school-like experiences in their preschool years. For other children, school as a culture first comes into focus when they enter formal public or private elementary school. In the preschool years, children may encounter several different types of school-like experiences. Head Start programs, child-care centers, and nursery schools all demonstrate somewhat different philosophical orientations. Some programs seek to introduce children to school through a more structured curriculum, others try to extend the nurturance of the home, and still others combine facets of both. The current movement toward universal preschool for children is an indication of the growing awareness of the importance of this developmental stage. Although it is difficult to conduct rigorous studies to determine the influence

Children reenact behaviors of significant others in their play as they move toward autonomy and independence.

of different programs on developing children, we have evidence that quality preschool programs do have a lasting, positive effect on children's academic growth and on subsequent life-skill development (Campbell & Ramey, 1995; Weikart, 2004).

Primary Years—Growing Community Influence

Community influence appears early in children's lives and progresses steadily as children mature; refer again to Figure 1–1 to see that by the time a child turns eight, community impact is high. The effect of community depends, however, on how families use neighborhood resources. The nature of that effect is not simple; it derives from the many subsystems within the community (Bronfenbrenner, Moen, & Garbarino, 1984). For example, the family may live in a neighborhood that provides positive social and physical support or in an area where parents are afraid to take their children outside.

As children expand their horizons, the living conditions of the neighborhood and community give them experiences on which to build their linguistic, kinesthetic, artistic, spatial, and interpersonal skills. Children who can visit zoos, museums, libraries, business establishments, parks, and other natural settings are better equipped to deal with the many mathematical, scientific, social, and language concepts discussed in schools than are children who can't. Recent decades have produced a rich mix of cultural and ethnic diversity in many American communities—which contrasts starkly with the situation that existed in the mid-20th century. Inclusive schools, ethnically diverse neighborhoods, and **transcultural** events in most vicinities all produce a positive effect on young children.

Traditions, cultural values, community **mores,** opportunities for recreation, and other social and cultural activities all play a part in children's development. Experiences interacting with adults in clubs, sports, and art and music activities open up children to differences in communication styles and offer them a range of experiences. Coleman (1991) called this type of involvement with adults a child's **social capital** and stressed that this capital is as important as financial capital in determining school performance. Maeroff (1999) pointed out how childrern living in poverty may have fewer opportunities to participate in interactive incidents with different adults than those children who do not. Although socialization practices are learned at home, children who participate in community activities have greater opportunities to practice their negotiating, problem-solving, and intellectual skills. Steven, in the following vignette, begins to learn some of these important lessons.

Steven, in third grade, signed up for tae kwon do sessions but was unhappy because the instructor was "always criticizing" what he did. "I don't even know what I do wrong," he told his mother.

"And what do you do when he tells you something?" she asked.

"Oh, I get so mad, I just grit my teeth."

"Are you sure he never compliments you?"

"Uh, uh, hardly ever," pouted Steven.

"Well, want to try an experiment?" his mother suggested.

"The next time he even suggests something is good, smile at him and say, 'Oh, that really helps me know what I should be doing,' and just ignore the criticisms." Steven reluctantly agreed to give it a try.

Two weeks later, a jubilant Steven returned from a practice session saying, "Hey Mom, he really does tell me lots about what I'm doing right!" Whether Steven or the instructor changed behavior patterns isn't clear, but certainly Steven was learning new ways of working with adults so that he could profit from their instruction.

Positive interactions between community and family give a sense of security and well-being to all. This situation helps families provide the kind of nurturing that children need. Regrettably, not all communities provide healthy conditions for children. Community tolerance for gangs, illicit activities, or establishments with erotic content will have unhealthy and negative influences on children's growth and the experiences they have. Violence in the streets limits everyone's sense of security. Yet, even in neighborhoods besieged by poverty, extended family, churches, social and service organizations, and neighborhood groups can make a positive difference in children's lives and support and extend the work of families and schools (Ramsey, 2004).

REFLECTION

Think of the neighbors and workers in your childhood community and reflect on how they influenced your growing up. Did they influence how you saw school when you were in the primary grades? Did they make you feel safe in your area? How? Now compare this to the school community that you last visited. Any differences?

INFLUENCE OF SPECIAL-INTEREST GROUPS

In recent years, the United States has witnessed a steady increase in the number and potency of **special-interest groups** with agendas focused on political, environmental, gender equity, or school curriculum issues. Groups such as the Family Research Council, Common Cause, Children's Defense Fund, Action for Children's Television, and the various prochoice and anti-abortion groups are all organized to affect everything from legislative matters to informal controls on school procedures. These groups can have both direct and indirect influence on children's learning, depending on family, school, and community reactions to their efforts and objectives.

Although a number of special interest groups have a broadly conceived objective and have existed for many years, other citizen groups have a single objective and are ephemeral in nature. The single-issue group is frequently very successful in its endeavors because it focuses on an emotional issue that is newsworthy: One example is "Let's stop the building of more 'big box' stores in Newton." These groups die out quickly after a mission is accomplished.

Some groups have been formed by parents concerned about a particular educational issue affecting children. For instance, in 1968, Peggy Charren, concerned about the amount of violence in children's programs, organized a group of parents to form Action for Children's Television (ACT). The group lobbied for improved television programming and advertising during children's viewing time and worked to educate the public regarding television's positive and negative influences. The action resulted in the Children's Television Act of 1990.

Grassroots efforts by special-interest groups resulted in the special education legislation of the 1960s that improved education for all children. As children with disabilities were first mainstreamed into regular classrooms, curricula, classroom environments, and learning for all children expanded. Continued pressure by these special-interest groups has led to an examination of the effects of the laws and to the passing of additional legislation to better serve children with special needs.

The influence of special-interest groups is not always viewed as positive, however. Schott (1989) and Mahood (2000) noted that some conservative interest groups seek to effect legislation that would permit censoring of library books and dictating of particular elements in curricula. In many communities, both schools and libraries have been forced to remove from their shelves certain books deemed quality literature by literary critics because of the views of special-interest groups. One teacher was dismissed for focusing on Langston Hughes's poems, material that a special-interest group found racially inflammatory (Kozol, 1991).

At the local level, some religious groups have succeeded in banning Halloween activities and even traditional fairy tales that include supernatural events and characters. Other groups have successfully changed units of study in schools about Christmas and Hanukkah and banned community displays of the Nativity. Special-interest groups have positive influence when they act to initiate dialogue among parents and teachers as to the appropriateness of materials in schools. Their influence is negative when they seek to restrict children's access to humanity's best artistic, philosophical, and intellectual efforts and attempt to deny children's learning about different ethnic and cultural groups and other historical periods.

Federal Agencies as Special-Interest Groups

Although it is difficult to describe our federal government as a special-interest group, it does work that way at times. For more than one and a half centuries, our national leaders left education entirely to the individual states, and only Supreme Court action, on occasion, visited the school arena. In recent times, however, political administrations have become increasingly concerned about educational policy and practice because these have affected political goals and objectives.

Before the 1960s, President Lyndon Johnson began the federal incursion with the very ambitious **War on Poverty** program, which carried many implications for schools. Since that time, most administrations have deliberated about school problems, and they have seen fit to develop mandates and regulations and have used federal funding to stimulate action for one procedure or another. Enhancing legislation for science study is one example; promoting a voucher plan for selected groups is another; Goals 2000 (Educate America Act) was another; and a recent initiative is the **No Child Left Behind (NCLB) Act.**

Federal mandates have expanded and are often fitted to different political agendas that bear little relationship to the needs, cultural expectations, and developmental levels of children in various parts of the country. The danger of such an approach is that the broad sweep of a mandate limits the diversity and uniqueness of individuals and groups. When schools reflect the political agendas of national leaders rather than focus on teaching children to develop inquiring minds, our children are in danger of becoming docile followers. **Standardized tests** have become commonplace in our schools, and in recent years we see even greater use of tests because officials worry that achievement is eroding in many American classrooms (Meier, 2002a). Overreliance on tests, however, detracts from teacher oversight and opportunity to develop curricula keyed to the needs of particular children.

We need federal oversight and influence to promote certain programs that make life more productive and fair for children. Quality education is often cited as a dominant interest of the U.S. public, and most educators like to see our national government showing interest in schools, providing funds for programs, and acting as a partner in the huge task of educating young people. If these preferences are true, the government has a reason to be involved in supporting our schools and community efforts. Increasingly, however, critics are raising concerns about the narrow definitions of school accountability and academic success that have resulted from the increased federal involvement in education (Sacks, 2005).

Professional Associations as Special-Interest Groups

In recent years, the **National Association for the Education of Young Children (NAEYC)** and the Association for Childhood Education International (ACEI), two long-established and well-respected organizations devoted to children's education and well-being, have partnered with the National Council for the Accreditation of Teacher Education (NCATE) to develop professional standards for the initial licensure of early childhood and elementary teachers. Although these standards (which can be viewed in their entirety at www.naeyc.org and www.acei.org) emphasize the importance of prospective teachers understanding child development and curriculum, a key element in both sets of standards is the equal importance of teacher collaboration with families and communities.

For example, NAEYC Standard 2, Building Family and Community Relationships, underscores the importance of teachers developing respectful, reciprocal relationships with families and the communities within which the families reside. Standard 3, Observing, Documenting, and Assessing to Support Young Children and Families, stresses the need for a partnership between professionals and parents as essential for children's optimal development and learning. Standard 4a, Connecting with Children and Families, highlights the importance that teachers establish positive relationships with parents as the foundation for their work with children. The last standard, Standard 5, Growing as a Professional, puts emphasis on the teacher as a continuous, collaborative learner who serves as an advocate for children. The standard also accentuates the teacher's use of ethical guidelines (see Appendix A for a copy of the NAEYC Code of Ethical Conduct).

Like NAEYC, ACEI has several standards that relate directly to the importance of the relationship between elementary teachers, families, and communities. ACEI Standard 5.3, Collaboration with Families, affirms the significance of teachers establishing and maintaining partnerships with families to promote the intellectual, social, emotional, and physical growth of children. The standard urges teachers to use multiple strategies to engage families who may have diverse beliefs, traditions, values, and practices.

ACEI Standard 5.4, Collaboration with Colleagues and the Community, advocates for the teacher to be aware of the influence of the larger community environment on students' lives and learning and recommends that teachers collaborate with community organizations and utilize community resources to support children's learning.

Although all colleges and universities may not participate in the NCATE accreditation process, the standards set by NAEYC and ACEI resonate with teacher and parent educators. The ideas reflected in these standards are also echoed in the professional standards of other groups, such as social workers, curriculum specialists, and health workers in school settings. There is broad agreement that it is through partnerships between professionals, families, and communities that the best outcome for children can be achieved.

UNDERSTANDING AND COLLABORATION

Why is it important for you as beginning teachers, caregivers, or community workers to be knowledgeable of these influences that affect children's development? First, by understanding these influences, you will be able to recognize situations where children appear to be strongly affected. Then you can reinforce or give support for those events that exert positive influences on children. It is equally important to recognize and then offset the harmful influences. As suggested throughout this chapter and in remaining chapters, teachers and community workers have used particular strategies effectively to improve children's experiences.

As you work with children, you will use various media, engage children in group processes, and take children into the community to learn important concepts. Often, children will express very different responses to a learning situation that you provide. For example, Zach's teacher attempted to counter some of the influence of the home and peers by "not allowing" aggressive play in the school. The strategy may work well for this teacher, but other solutions may have, as well, such as having a discussion with both children and parents, noting where electronic toys may be acceptable. Such a discussion might have been productive in this situation. Profes-

sionals try to be attuned to children's and parents' responses. If you follow such a course, you will become more sensitive and adept at responding to children's development and needs.

As children enter the primary-school years, peers will exert a greater influence. When this influence is problematic and harmful, professionals will want to modify it. Counteracting negative peer influence is very difficult, however. Still, becoming aware of these influences gives you some background while you continue to show an accepting attitude and model positive interactions with all persons.

Your job is to provide the foundation for children's thinking skills, plus the development of competency in reading, writing, math, science, and social science concepts. Understanding the impact of both negative and positive influences on a child's learning makes your objectives and goals clearer as you plan for each student's learning.

At the present time, there are a number of issues related to children that particularly require collaboration between families, schools, and communities in order to affect positive change. We discuss some of these issues in the following sections.

Diversity

One of the challenges facing American schools today is educating the rapidly diversifying child population with a teaching force that remains largely White, middle-class, and female. Beginning teachers and community workers, regardless of their race or ethnic background, have a responsibility to increase their awareness of the beliefs and values of the families they serve. By continuously examining your own background and perspectives, you will become aware of your assumptions about families and children from various ethnic, social, and racial groups. As mentioned earlier in this chapter, your attitude toward and expectations of your students have a profound effect on their learning and school success. As a member of a school community, you will have the opportunity to get to know families as individuals. For some families, perhaps newly arrived in the United

States, the school will be an important link to the larger society, and as a professional in a school setting, you will have an essential role to play in helping children and families adjust to life in the United States.

REFLECTION

Become aware of your own attitudes toward the different families you find in schools and neighborhoods where you are involved. Increase your objectivity and professionalism by doing the following:

- Listening to their family stories about themselves.
- Helping them interpret school policies and regulations.
- Putting yourself in their shoes when considering complaints.
- Being willing to reassess children's work when you find new information.

Continued discrimination against certain groups and increased social stratification in the United States seems to fly in the face of the values of equality and justice that have been foundations of our democracy. You as an individual can only do so much to help overcome the inequities that exist as a result of poverty, race, and cultural differences, but you do have an obligation to provide the best education and support that you can to the children and families you serve. Chapters 3, 4, and 11 will address the issues of diversity and suggest ways to work successfully with families and communities of all kinds.

Childhood Obesity

The increasing concern about adult and childhood obesity reflects a worldwide health issue in many of the developed countries. Nowhere in the world, however, is the problem as grave as in the United States, where nearly one third of adults are classified as obese and almost two thirds are overweight, an increase of more than 20% since 1994

(Horgen, 2005). Childhood obesity is increasing at an even more alarming rate.

Although many approaches to fighting childhood obesity have focused on weight loss, increasing attention is being paid to the societal influences that seem to be leading children to gain weight in the first place. Television commercials for sugared cereals, candy, fast-food, soft drinks, and snack foods dominate children's programming. Internet sites use fast food and candy products as part of the plot or reward system. Administrators allow vending machines filled with soda and sugary and salty snacks in school buildings. Children are being targeted by food industries that use media figures, pop stars, and athletes to promote its products in ways that are difficult to avoid.

Obesity has strong negative effects on children's health, but there are also serious social, psychological, and economic ramifications (Lynn-Garbe & Hoot, 2004/05). At present, however, there is no national program to combat the obesity epidemic in the United States. Until there is, individual parents, professionals, schools, and communities will continue their grassroots efforts to increase exercise time and restrict unhealthy foods in schools. Advocates suggest that regulating advertising directed at children, prohibiting advertising in school, and promoting media literacy (Hesse & Lane, 2003) in children are necessary steps in the long-term solution of this difficult issue.

Tyranny of Tests

Changes in school curriculum fostered by the increasing reliance on high-stakes standardized tests, which may begin as early as kindergarten, has significantly decreased the amount of time for recess, physical education, and other opportunities for children to move about in school. This may be one factor in the rise in obesity, but the tightly focused, direct instruction that is increasingly replacing age-appropriate, play-based appropaches in prekindergarten and kindergarten (Hatch, 2005) may have other negative effects as well. Despite child development and brain development

Brain research emphasizes the value of play in all aspects of children's growth.

Patricia A. Scully

research that emphasizes the need for choice and the value of play in all aspects of children's growth (Olfman, 2005), many schools have moved away from constructivist models and toward prescribed curricula based on behaviorist theory. Chapters 8, 9, and 10 will provide more detailed information about the curricula of the home, school, and community.

APPLYING THESE CONCEPTS TO YOUR WORK WITH CHILDREN AND FAMILIES

As a teacher or community worker acting alone, you have minimal opportunity to change the attitudes, feelings, and biases of others that impinge on local classrooms. In collaboration with families and community members, however, you can make a greater impact on children's lives. As anthropologist Margaret Mead famously stated, "Never doubt that a small group of thoughtful, committed citizens can change the world; indeed, it's the only thing that ever has." Therefore:

1. Become aware of your own attitudes. Do you tend to favor the child from an affluent family? Are you patronizing when you work with poor children?

2. Note how you act toward the child, and consider how he or she responds to your actions.

3. Ask parents about their goals for their children and share your goals for the year—how are they in agreement.

4. Always be welcoming to all children and parents.

5. Be sure all children in your care have a spot in the limelight at some point.

6. As you prepare activities, provide for different ways that children can respond and be successful.

7. Praise all children at some point in an activity, but do it honestly.

SUMMARY AND REVIEW

Children are well or poorly educated, depending on many factors that both directly and indirectly influence what they learn and how they learn it. The attitudes, values, and interests that homes, schools, and communities have regarding children's learning can be in concert or in conflict. Young children are usually more strongly influenced by immediate or extended family attitudes, and primary-school-age children begin to be influenced by peer groups, media, and community mores and traditions. Teachers in many instances have no control over these factors and must study and be alert to their influence in order to provide appropriate education for children in their classrooms.

According to Coleman (1990), children need many types of support systems to grow into functioning adults. They need what he called human, financial, and social capital, which provide the nurturing and physical environment in which children learn to cope with their world. Children with little financial capital may still succeed if sufficient social and human resources are available to them. We find that families can compensate somewhat for lack of effective community and school influences on their children, and community and school personnel can exert influence and extend resources to compensate for missing family social resources. Schools, however, are far more effective in educating children when families, schools, and communities unite their efforts. When these three social settings recognize the influences on children's experience and work together in resolving conflicting issues undermining child development, the best possible circumstances result.

SUGGESTED ACTIVITIES AND QUESTIONS

1. List what you consider the major influences that guided your education. Are they different from those we have noted in this chapter? What influences did your classmates list? Discuss.

2. Watch a half hour of commercial children's television. Make note of all the commercials and the nature of each, and determine how much of the half hour is devoted to them. Identify what you believe could be the effect of these ads on young children. Discuss your conclusions with your classmates.

3. Interview a teacher in a local primary school and determine whether any special-interest group in-

fluences the decisions this person makes with regard to curricula. Do some groups exert positive pressure? If so, how does the teacher view the group's effect on children's learning? Do some exert negative pressures? If so, how does the person view these pressures as limitations on children's learning?

4. Discuss with a primary-school child a list of favorite books, movies, television shows, computer games, Web sites, and entertainers. Find out what the child likes or finds important about these choices. Ask whether the child wants to be like any of the people or characters, and why. How do you think the media to which the child is exposed has influenced these choices?

RESOURCES

Books

Irvine, J. J. (2003). *Educating teachers for diversity: Seeing with a cultural eye.* New York: Teachers College Press.

Jones, E., & Cooper, R. M. (2006). *Playing to get smart.* New York: Teachers College Press.

Singer, D. G., & Singer, J. L. (Eds.) (2001). *Handbook of children and the media.* Thousand Oaks, CA: Sage.

Trawick-Smith, J. (2006). *Early childhood development: A multicultural perspective* (4th ed.). Upper Saddle River, NJ: Merrill/Prentice Hall.

Films and Videos

A teacher's culture [Video, 30 min]. (2000). New York: Insight Media. Enables viewers to reflect on their own cultural beliefs and discusses need to treat all cultures with respect.

Beyond the standards movement: Defending quality education in an age of test scores [Video, 30 min]. (2000). Featuring Alfie Kohn, this video offers a powerful argument against the obsession with standardized tests and a case for the learning process.

Feed me! Kids and nutrition [Video or DVD, 20 min]. (2007). Focuses on the MyPyramid for kids and shows how it can be used to help children make the right dietary choices.

Your partners at home: Working with your students' parents [Video, 24 min]. (2003). New York: Insight Media. Shows how to build and maintain working relationships with parents.

Organizations

American Obesity Association
1250 24th St. NW
Washington, DC 20037
202-776-7111
http://www.obesity.org

Parents Television Council
707 Wilshire Blvd. #2075
Los Angeles, CA 90017
213-629-9255
www.parentstv.org

Children Now
1212 Broadway, 5th Floor
Oakland, CA 94612
510-763-2444
www.childrennow.org

National Institute on Media and the Family
606 24th Avenue South
Suite 606
Minneapolis, MN 55454
612-672-5437
www.mediafamily.org

Web Sites

http://www.learntobehealthy.org   A science learning site for educators that includes games and activities related to fitness and nutrition for children K–6.

http://www.lionlamb.org   A project designed to stop marketing violence to children.

http://www.newhorizons.org   New Horizons provides articles and resources on brain research and other educational innovations.

http://www.superkids.com   Reviews educational software for children.

Chapter 2

Historical and Philosophical Perspectives

History is the witness of the times, the light of truth, the life of memory, the mistress of life.

(Cicero, *de Oratore*)

In this chapter we examine the underlying beliefs of and the evolution of roles played by persons in the home, in the school, and in the community and discuss how they advance children's education. After reading this chapter you will be able to

1. Discuss the various beliefs about child development and the modes of instruction emanating from philosophical convictions that go back many generations.

2. Explain that historically, the family and the community have always played significant roles in children's education, but at different periods, each setting has had a more dominant position, with the school assuming leadership at the beginning of the 20th century.

3. Describe how parents, teachers, and community members have always worked together to some degree for children's benefit, although the idea of partnerships is a relatively new focus.

4. Identify how, in recent decades, the federal government has encouraged new procedures for parental involvement in children's education.

5. Discuss how, since the 1960s, programs for poor children, children with special needs, and children of differing ethnic backgrounds have focused on the importance of parents as an educating force.

6. Explain the growing importance for a curriculum emphasis on diversity in American schools, as our society becomes more multicultural and global engagements bring greater requirements to American life.

OVERVIEW OF PHILOSOPHICAL VIEWPOINTS

Historically, the philosophical ideas of society, together with political and sociological events, have influenced our underlying premises about children's educational development. Further, these ideas, which range from a conservative–academic approach to liberal progressivism, will influence the ways in which children are taught. As ideology and the political and social circumstances change, the type of relationship and dominant role that each of the three social settings has in the lives of children also changes. The following overview of some major philosophical theories presents the forces that influence how families, schools, and communities consider their roles (see Table 2–1, pp. 28–29).

Today's ideas regarding the purpose of education, how children learn, the best strategies for teaching them, and who should teach them have roots in early philosophical teachings. For example, we find in early Chinese society Confucius (552–479 B.C.) proclaiming that the basic aim of education was to teach individuals to become moral citizens capable of solving society's problems, to become good and productive citizens, and even to make good use of leisure time. These are important goals even today. For example, Goal 3 of Goals 2000 states (U.S.D.O.E., 1993b) that schools provide an education "so that all children learn to use their minds so they may be prepared for responsible citizenship."

The Greek philosopher Plato (470–347 B.C.), stated that education must train the spirit through music, the body through gymnastics, and the mind through philosophy, a notion not unlike today's view that education must encompass the "whole" child (physical, social, emotional, and intellectual). Aristotle (384–322 B.C.) insisted that the teacher must take into consideration the successive stages and rates of child development when considering what to teach individual children. Advocates of "**age-appropriate curriculum**" and "**individualized teaching**" do find commonality with some of Aristotle's precepts.

Today's variations in methods of instruction also have parallels in the writings of early philosophers. Confucius (552–479 B.C.) believed that the teacher was the **transmitter of knowledge** and students memorized this knowledge to be able to repeat any of it when needed. Socrates (470–399 B.C.), on the other hand, used the technique of **dialoguing with students** in order to stimulate his followers to discover and develop their own internal knowledge.

At present, some educators insist there be a **predetermined curriculum** that all children learn and be tested on periodically to show mastery. This is the academic or traditional program, and No Child Left Behind (NCLB) legislation supports this view. Others believe that educators should build on children's prior knowledge and interests to stimulate further learning.

The early 20th century theories on development tended to cluster around two contrasting views, known today as the **nature–nurture** (or genetics–environment) controversy. Brain research findings (Bruer, 1999; Dowling, 2004) have added new information on how genetics influence brain functioning and also on how development results as neophytes act on their environment. Some theorists (e.g., Piaget) propose that it is not either nature or nurture that explains development but an interactive–constructive perspective that more fully explains child development. Other authorities (e.g., Bronfenbrenner, 1979) maintain that although both environmental and biological factors influence development, one cannot understand the development of particular children without considering the cultural, historical, and ecological evidence around them.

The development of the Internet and the prospect of world cultures moving to a global society has precipitated different outlooks on educational needs. We find political perspectives now affect how we perceive education. Traditionally, America has been a society that supports individual accomplishments, but students in the 21st century need new skills and outlooks to relate to persons whose culture and language is very different from their own. By considering the values of the social rituals, the communal orientation, and the different responsibilities found in many cultures worldwide.

In the following section, we examine the evolution and status of the constrasting views that influence how we educate our children. Readers should recognize that political and social factors at any given time influence how schools and educational practices swing from one perspective to another.

John Locke (1632–1704) was an early advocate recognizing the importance of environmental influences on children's behavior. He believed that a child's mind was a blank slate and that stimuli from others and the environment controlled the child's development and learning. Following this, the behaviorists, such as John Watson (1878–1958) and B. F. Skinner (1904–1990), believed that children learned as a result of conditioning by adults, who provided stimuli and then rewarded correct responses. Children learned because their needs were satisfied (or not satisfied) by another person or because of environmental factors.

In contrast, Jean-Jacques Rousseau (1712–1778) viewed children as unfolding and developing according to an innate plan—the result of systematic and natural internal forces. Johann Pestalozzi (1746–1827) and Friedrich Froebel (1782–1852) formed schools and developed materials for children based on this naturalistic philosophy. They believed children learned through play and sensory experiences in the ever increasing stages of development. They also maintained children learned best when homes, schools, and communities were involved (Froebel, 1889). The first kindergartens of the 19th century in America were formed following these models, using specific materials designed to stimulate this sensory learning (Seefeldt & Barbour, 1998). These early Froebelian kindergarten materials changed when John Dewey (1859–1952) introduced his precepts on how children's thinking develops.

Dewey maintained that children develop concepts using their natural environment as they organize and manipulate the world around them. They form and test hypotheses of how things

Table 2–1   Perspectives of Major Theories of Child Development

Orientation	Nativism	Behaviorism	Interactionism
Basic premise	Based on Darwinian theory, *On the Origin of Species* (1859), that all organisms seek to enhance their chances of survival. Genetics or internal mechanisms as primary focus in children's development.	Environment as primary force in children's development.	Both internal mechanisms and environment are forces for child development.
Major contributors	G. Stanley Hall (1844–1929) Arnold Gesell (1880–1961)	J. B. Watson (1878–1958) B. F. Skinner (1904–1991)	Jean Piaget (1896–1980)
Stages of development	Developed sequences of characteristic behavior. Maturational readiness means that a child must develop to an appropriate point before training or teaching has an effect.	No stages. Learning happens as a result of conditioning. Classical conditioning and unconditional stimuli result in reflex response, which later becomes a learned response. Operant conditioning means a child learns as a result of receiving positive reinforcers or rewards.	Children develop by assimilating external stimuli and accommodating new stimuli to already existing structures. Sensorimotor stage (birth–2 yr), use of senses. Preoperational stage (2–7 yr), use of mental imagery. Concrete operations stage (7–11 yr), logical thinking occurs.
Meaning for parents and educators	Adult supports development and observes outward behaviors that would indicate readiness of learning.	Adult determines desired behavior and sets up strategies for reinforcing children when behaviors occur.	Adults provide a rich and stimulating environment that assists children in interacting with that environment as they construct their own knowledge.

happen and then evaluate and interpret the evidence they have discovered. Dewey proposed that children constantly test and hypothesize as they play and entertain themselves. A playful attitude, he maintained, keeps children motivated, and this motivation is what allows them to grow and learn (Dewey, 1910, 1944). Thus, the development of a child-initiated or play-oriented curriculum in early childhood settings stems from Rousseauian and

Deweyian ideas. In a related way, Arnold Gesell (1880–1961) documented children's growth, finding general developmental similarities and trends among children. He concluded that development is a result of laws and a sequence of maturation that is a continuous spiral. Gesell and his associates maintained that parents and teachers must permit the child's natural unfolding before learning can take place.

Table 2–1 (*Continued*)

Psychoanalytical (Psychological)		Social–Cultural Context
Sexual energy within humans as force for personality development		Environmental and biological factors affect human development, but cultural, sociological, and historical factors play an important part. Individual development depends on the relationship and interactions of all these elements
Sigmund Freud (1856–1939)	Erik Erikson (1902–1994)	Urie Bronfenbrenner (1917–2005) Lev Vygotsky (1896–1936)
Three structures: Id—instructive Ego—rational Superego—moral	Expanded on Freud's theories.	Multiple and distinct ecological systems affect development. The systems and all institutions within the systems interact and affect each other. Microsystems:
Oral stage (birth–1 yr), need for gratification from mouth. Anal stage (2–3 yr), need for gratification from the anal area. Phallic stage (4–5 yr), need for gratification from the genitals. Latency stage (middle years of repression of sexuality).	Basic trust (birth–1 yr), development of sense of inner goodness. Autonomy (2–3 yr), development of sense of self and pride of achievement. Initiative (3–5 yr) takes charge of activities. Industry (6 yr–puberty), becomes producer and user of things.	experiences and influences from school, family, peers, church, etc. Ecosystems: institutions that do not directly affect the child but indirectly affect the child's experiences—extended family, neighbors, mass media, etc. Macrosystem: overarching values, laws, customs of a particular culture or society. Metrosystem: the interconnections between these systems.
Adults provide the needed support so that children's instincts are satisfied, but not so much that children do not move appropriately from one stage to the next.		Adults are only one part of the influences that affect learning. Adults aware of influences can to some degree control these.

In the mid-1800s, Charles Darwin's (1809–1882) work on evolution and natural selection provided enormous momentum for the scientific study of children, and his theory supports principles in both the nature and nurture positions. Darwin's studies of his own children as well as studies of different species in the Galapagos Islands challenged the idea of a fixed nature for species. Development, he insisted, unfolds in a natural, dy-namic way, and all species adapt to their particular environments in order to enhance their chance of survival (Thomas, 2001).

A third view, often labeled the interactionist–constructivist view, has emerged in recent decades. Theorists with this orientation insist that both biological and environmental factors affect development in a reciprocal manner. As different theorists expanded this perspective throughout the 20th

Children develop concepts using
their natural environment as they
organize and manipulate the world
around them.

Greg Mekras

century, they focused on specific aspects of development. Jean Piaget (1896–1980), a cognitive theorist, proposed that children develop by assimilating and acting on stimuli, or information, from the environment and by accommodating new stimuli to already existing structures. He held that children construct their own understanding and knowledge, which changes only as they find inconsistencies in their environment and incorporate the new information to produce new insights or knowledge.

Another view recognizing both internal and environmental influences was advanced by Sigmund Freud (1856–1939) and his followers. Freud was the first psychologist to view human nature as all encompassing. He formed his views by studying his dreams and recollections of his childhood experiences and that of his patients. His psychoanalytical theory was mainly concerned with human emotional, motivational, and personality development, even though he recognized the biological, social, and intellectual aspect of development. He believed both the positive and negative aspects of **sexual energy** are the driving forces of human behavior. He viewed sexual energy as biologically determined, but that environmental factors do determine how this energy is invested and thus how children grow.

Erik Erikson (1902–1994), a follower of Freud, felt that sexual energy as the driving force of development was too limiting an explanation. Erikson identified eight **stages of development**, each with positive and negative attributes, and he insisted that cultural and social values affected how one progresses from one stage to another. For Erikson, there are **critical periods of development**, and for a person to develop normal patterns of behavior, the positive attributes at each stage need to be satisfied before the next stage can truly develop.

Theorists, of social–cultural context such as Lev Vygotsky (1896–1934) and Urie Bronfenbrenner (1917–2005), also regard development as being influenced in a reciprocal manner by both biological and environmental factors. They believe, however, that to understand development it is necessary to take into account the cultural and historical context in which development occurred. These theorists contend that there are many social systems with which a child interacts (e.g., family, school, neighborhood, community, and dominant beliefs in society), and it is a combination of these interactions that affects development. The theorists of social–cultural

Children have two spheres of operating. One is their ability to problem solve independently. The other is their problem-solving ability under the guidance of a more skilled adult.

David Kuhn

context have steered educators to a greater understanding and acceptance of the complexities of development.

Vygotsky stressed the importance of recognizing both the biological–physiologic and the cultural factors that influence a child's development. He insisted that it is the social interactions that children experience within their unique cultural and historical context that determines each child's unique developmental pattern.

In earliest development, Vygotosky believed that biological and maturational factors do influence a child's physical and intellectual development to a large degree. Later learning, he felt, was a result of children's independently acting on and interpreting their environment, and his theory shows that at that point, the varying social factors better explain the physical and mental changes in children's growth. For example, in one significant Russian study, Vygotsky (1978) shows that children interact in different ways with various adults and how these interactions progress over time determines the what and the how of a child's learning.

As children's development approaches the problem-solving stage, Vygotsky believed that children have two spheres of operation. One is the ability to problem solve independently; the other is their problem-solving ability under the guidance of a more skilled person. The difference between these two levels was labeled the **zone of proximal development** (Vygotsky, 1978).

In a similar fashion, Bronfenbrenner's theory examines the ecological systems that affect children's development. According to Bronfenbrenner, these interacting, interdependent social–ecological systems are the primary elements that differentiate and actualize the biological potential of children (Bronfenbrenner, 1979). In other words, the interplay between biology and ecology causes changes in the child, which in turn produce other changes. In addition, the theory holds that these cascading changes have an ever increasing effect, both positively and negatively, on a child's development.

Cognitive ability or intelligence is normally associated with theories of child development. It is impossible to present even a summary of the extensive literature dealing with human intelligence, but we urge readers to seek this information in educational psychology and child development texts such as Puckett & Black (2005), Trawick-Smith (2006), or McDevitt & Ormrod (2002). Readers will find the traditional early 20th-century views of Spearman, Terman, and Thorndike on the innate and unchanging nature of IQ (intelligence quotient) still supported in contemporary research and writing. Most educators and child development authorities, however, find the work of Howard Gardner (1993) and Robert Sternberg (1997), who present convincing evidence about multiple intelligencies, to be very useful. These last two authorities and their associates have convincing evidence that IQ does move beyond a single and static reasoning ability and does change with time and experience.

It should be clear that throughout history, theorists and researchers have stressed specific but different elements and aspects of development. All these theories, together with political and social events, have influenced how families, schools, and communities envision their roles in educating children throughout the generations. We believe students should maintain a perspective of human development that recognizes the contributions of various theorists. Providing a richer understanding of human growth and development, as well as a platform for decision making.

REFLECTION

As you reflect on the philosophy governing your work with children, remember these key points:

- Theorists, throughout history, have stressed different aspects of development and learning.
- The theories have influenced how families, schools, and communities over generations have seen their roles in educating children.
- Political and social events have a hand in highlighting particular theories.
- New professionals often find that a broad perspective on learning and development enriches their understanding.

HISTORICAL PATTERNS

Partnerships among homes, schools, and communities for children's education is a term of the 1980s, 1990s, and 2000s, yet throughout the history of the United States, we find connections among the functions of these three vital social settings. At different times, each, as an institution, has occupied a domi-

nant role in children's education, at the same time acknowledging the others as important forces in helping children to succeed in society.

In colonial times, the family was the major force for educating children, although the community exerted pressure on families not conforming to local codes of conduct. Later, as towns and villages developed, community leaders recognized that some families were not willing or able to educate their children successfully. Taking command in the later colonial period, community leaders gave needed support to families, developed laws concerning education, and eventually formed public schools to ensure that children met the community objectives.

In the late 1800s, as public schools developed into bureaucracies, professional educators moved to the forefront and took responsibility for overseeing schools and curricula. At the same time, the public mandated a more diverse curriculum, so teachers were required not only to teach academic skills but also to provide programs that would help children develop socially, physically, morally, and emotionally. At this time, when blue-collar jobs required increased technical skills, schools also became responsible for teaching vocational skills. In the later part of the 20th century, when only part of the school population succeeded in these extended schools, questions began to arise. Parents and communities became perplexed and displeased about lower success rates, and alienation often set in.

Beginning in the 1990s, a new trend for developing collaborations (stimulated by researchers, professional educators, and more recently by federal agencies) became a focus for parents, community leaders, and teachers. In this way, many people came to appreciate the truth of the African proverb, "It takes an entire village to educate a child." As you review the following historical overview of relationships among parents, communities, and schools, consider what happens to children as society changes.

In this chapter, we trace the changes and forces that have shaped our present educational condition in the United States with respect to the roles played in childhood education by families, communities, and schools from the dominant culture. We also consider attitude changes over the three centuries toward the children from minority cultures and other special populations. Naturally, all changes have affected the roles and responsibilities of the three institutions for the education of all children. Table 2–2 lists major American events affecting family–community–school relationships.

FAMILY AS A SIGNIFICANT EDUCATIONAL FORCE

From prehistoric cultures to modern society, the family has been the most important social setting for educating the child. In all societies, children must learn skills of survival, the rules and regulations of the society in which they live, and the values by which their society functions (Eitzen & Zinn, 2005; Sanderson, 1995). Children learn by following their elders' examples, through direct teaching of important skills by their elders, and by the oral communication of traditions, lore, attitudes, beliefs, and values (Bornstein, 2002).

The education that children received in the colonial period depended on economic status, ethnic background, child gender, and to some extent the section of the country in which the child lived. Early settlers for the most part were able to form cohesive family units that depended on one another for survival. Towns and villages, particularly in New England, were initially established around particular religious groups migrating from Europe. With their religious heritage, early colonists believed that children needed to learn not only the vocational skills necessary for survival but also particular codes of behavior and moral integrity. The more economically advantaged also valued reading and writing for their own children. It was a patriarchal society, and in most cases teaching was the responsibility of the home, with the father the dominant force. Parents, grandparents, and older siblings were the primary instructors. Fathers taught their sons skills needed to carry on the family vocation; mothers taught their daughters homemaking skills. In the intact homes, children had a profound appreciation and sense of family. They tended to understand their social roles in the family and the role their family played in the larger community (Fass & Mason, 2000; Zelizer, 1994).

Table 2–2   Events Affecting Family–Community–School Relationships

1600s	**Families Responsible for Children's Education**
1642	Massachusetts Bay School Law requires all families to teach children to read the Bible and the laws of the land.
1647	Old Deluder Satan Law requires every community of 100 or more to establish schools.
1700s	**Communities Responsible for Children's Education (national influence—state responsibility).**
1800s	**Educational Establishment Responsible for Children's Education**
1815	First Parent Program established in Portland, Maine.
1835	Massachusetts establishes first state board of education.
1852	Massachusetts establishes the first mandatory attendance law.
1867	U.S. Office of Education established.
1873	First public school kindergarten founded in St. Louis.
1888	Federation for Child Study founded.
1889	G. Stanley Hall establishes first child study center at Clark University for studying children and disseminating information to parents about child-rearing practices.
1896	*Plessy v. Ferguson* decision supports segregation.
1897	National Congress of Mothers founded (later became Parent–Teacher Association).

(Continued)

Table 2–2   (*Continued*)

Early 1900s	**Educational Establishment Responsible for Educating Parents as Well as Children**
1909	White House holds first conference on care of dependent children.
1912	Children's Bureau established in Washington, DC.
1916	First parents cooperative founded at the University of Chicago.
1920	Rehabilitation Act assists veterans of World War I to get job training.
1924	Immigration Act establishing national origins quota system.
1942–1945	Japanese American internment program.
Mid 1900s	**Parent and Community Involvement in School Policies**
1954	*Brown v. Board of Education* opens the way for desegregation of schools.
1956	Ford Foundation offers grant to New York City to train volunteers to work with teachers.
1964	Civil Rights Act mandating desegregation of schools paves the way for compensatory education acts, which required parental involvement in schools.
1965	Elementary and Secondary Education Act/Title I and Project Head Start/Chapter I.
1965	First **Bilingual Education** Act passed.
1967	Economic Opportunity Act follow-through programs begin.
1972	Home Start programs established.
1975	Public Law 94-142, Education for All Handicapped Children Act (amended in 1990 to Individuals with Disabilities Education Act, IDEA).
1975	Rehabilitation Act, Section 504, amended to prevent discrimination against persons with disabilities in programs using federal funds.
1984	First national symposium on partnerships in education sponsored by the President's Advisory Council.
1986	Federal Preschool and Early Intervention Program Act, Public Law 99-457, extends PL 94-142, mandating services for preschoolers.
1986	Handicapped Children's Protection Act (PL 99-472) is passed.
Late 1900s	**Parent and Community Involvement in School Policies**
1988	National Association of Partners in Education is formed.
1988	Educational Partnerships Act, Title VI, is passed.
1988	Family Support Act is passed.
1990	American with Disabilities Act extends Section 504 of the Disabilities Act to prohibit discrimination against any person with disabilities in private or public employment.
1992	Head Start Improvement Act passed, extending services to infants and toddlers.
1994	Goals 2000: Educate America Act signed into law.
1996	Personal Responsibility and Work Opportunity Reconciliation Act (Welfare Reform Act) passed.
1997	IDEA reauthorized.
1999	Twenty-First-Century Community Learning Act introduced as part of the Educational Excellence for All Children Act (Title X, *Chapter 1*—a reauthorization of the Elementary and Secondary Act).
Early 2000s	
2001	No Child Left Behind Act (Title I, Section A)—families in Title I schools have a right to select a "preferred" school if their child is in a "chronically underachieving school."
2001	USA Patriot Act.
2002	Education Sciences Reform Act—In Title I schools, the instructional strategies for any new projects are to be based on scientific research.

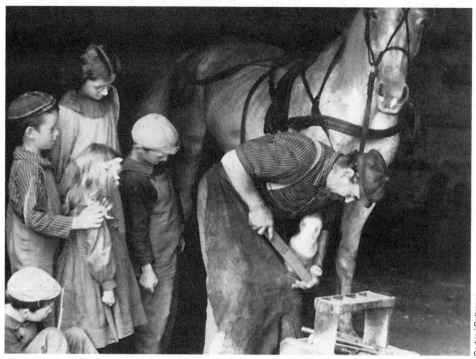

Corbis / Bettmann

The education that children received in colonial times depended on their economic status and needed vocational skills.

Puritans in New England were adamant about the need to learn to read and write and stressed the importance of reading the Bible. Parents assumed this responsibility. In addition, certain women who became more skilled in teaching gathered in their homes children whose parents were unable to teach reading and writing. The practice resulted in the creation of "dame schools," precursors of our current primary schools.

In the southern colonies, wealthy settlers hired tutors to teach their children academic skills, in addition to the behaviors befitting a plantation owner, whereas poor parents were responsible for educating their children as best they could. For the most part, African Americans were forbidden an education, and, because of slavery, Black families were often torn apart, so that even parental teaching of basics was hampered (Berlin, 1998; Travers & Rebore, 2000).

When colonial children needed to learn skills the family was unable to provide, apprenticeships were sought, and boys as young as seven years old were sent to live with a master craftsman. Apprenticeships were the precursors of our later grammar schools, for in many colonies the masters were expected to teach reading and writing as well as the skills of their trade (Webb, Metha, & Jordan, 2007).

In the English colonies, basic formal education was available to established families, but children of slaves and Native Americans were considered unworthy of this basic education (Davis, 2006). There were, however, notable exceptions to this trend. The Church of England in the South and Quakers in the middle colonies provided educational opportunities for a few African Americans, some Native Americans, and some poor European colonists.

COMMUNITY AS A SIGNIFICANT EDUCATIONAL FORCE

As townships in the colonies became more established in the late 1600s and the early 1700s, religious leaders began to dominate the determination of the education of children within the community. Thus began the American heritage, extant today, that a community oversees its schools and determines school policy and curriculum.

The Puritans are credited with establishing the foundation of public education in this country because of their belief that all children, whatever their economic status, need to be educated. They believed that every child in the land should learn the rigid codes of behavior for a religious society and the "meaning of salvation" from Bible reading. As early as 1642, a Massachusetts law required all parents and master craftsmen to teach reading and writing to children in their care to ensure that children attained "religious understanding and civic responsibility" (Pulliam & Van Patten, 2007). There was, however, difficulty in enforcing such a mandate because of widespread illiteracy in the adult population. Consequently, in 1647, the Old Deluder Satan Law was passed; this required townships with 50 or more households to provide a teacher of reading and writing for young children in the community. Townships that had more than 100 households were also to provide a Latin grammar school to prepare boys for university study (Cohen, 1974; Sateran, 2001).

These laws were not easy to enforce, but they were important in establishing a precedent for education as the young nation expanded. First and foremost, the family had primary responsibility for educating a child, but the laws also laid a foundation for community responsibility in assisting families in educating the young. Because communities hired the teachers, they also taxed families on their property so as to have funds to pay them.

In the late 1700s and early 1800s, political and economic factors in the United States again affected the relationship of families and communities in educating children. The advent of the Industrial Revolution meant that families moved from an agrarian-based economy to one increasingly dependent on manufacturing. Now fathers, and sometimes mothers, left home to earn a living, and naturally there was little opportunity to teach children vocational skills or reading and writing in the home. As urban populations began to rise, many families became isolated from their kin. Thus, the changed circumstances demanded a new response to the country's needs.

The republic came into being at the end of the 18th century, and as it unified, the strong influence of religious communities was replaced by the notion of nonsectarian education (Pulliam & Van Patten, 2007). Political leaders such as Benjamin Franklin and Thomas Jefferson believed that the new nation needed a literate populace and that it was not sufficient to educate only the wealthy and the strongly religious. Education, they felt, needed to be available to children from different social and economic classes and should be more functional. Merchants added their voice to that of politicians, for business interests realized that the nation needed workers with more than rudimentary literacy skills and more practical skills than those provided in Latin grammar schools (Sadker & Sadker, 2005).

If wider schooling opportunities were to be available, something needed to be done to help communities establish schools. The new government responded, and significant pieces of legislation, such as the Land Ordinance Act of 1785 and the Northwest Ordinance Act of 1787, were passed by the Continental Congress. These acts encouraged settlers to move to the Midwest and to set aside land to support schools. Such acts indicated the new nation's faith in education, even though in writing the Constitution, the founding fathers left the responsibility for education to the individual states.

The ideas and practices of European philosophers and educators also influenced educational thought in the United States. These new ideas regarding who was to be educated, as well as where and how, did not immediately change American children's education, however (Pulliam & Van Patten, 2007). Community sentiment first had to endorse any practice. Even today, in a general sense, community standards, mores, and expectations are among the strongest determinants of social behavior and participation. We find that community validation continues to be necessary for any substantial change or redirection to take place in children's educational opportunities.

SCHOOL AS A SIGNIFICANT EDUCATIONAL FORCE

The mission of formal schools and support for public education have increased gradually over the more than two centuries the United States has existed as a nation. Our founding fathers expressed a need for universal, free, and secular education, but it has taken a long time to achieve such a goal for all children.

Even in the early 1800s, the prevailing view was that education was a family responsibility; any education beyond a family's immediate capacity to give it was a luxury. Some communities at that time maintained public schools for their children, and some charity schools existed for the poor. In addition, religious sects continued to provide schooling in some areas for all children, and, of course, there were private schools for the wealthy (Cremin, 1982; Fass & Mason, 2000). In the early 1800s, though, universal education was not yet supported in the United States.

It was the mid-1800s before the political and economic climate provided fertile ground for the establishment of free, open, and secular schools in the United States. On one front, new immigrants were voicing dissatisfaction in not being a part of the political process. Trade unions were forming, and unionists believed that the path to success was by educating their children. Also, humanists and educators, such as Horace Mann (1796–1859) and Henry Barnard (1811–1900), wrote and lectured about the benefits of universal and **secular education** (Pulliam & Van Patten, 2007). In addition, the movement of the population from rural to urban areas meant that many families lacked the resources to educate children at home. The time for public education had arrived.

States at this time urged local communities to begin taxing themselves so as to provide public schools for their citizenry. States also started the practice of giving aid to communities needing support. In 1852, Massachusetts began to require compulsory attendance, but it wasn't until 1918 that the last state in the union—Mississippi—enacted legislation requiring children to attend school (Cremin, 1961). With such enactments, parents began to relinquish to schools the responsibilities for educating their children; however, home and community continued to influence many educational trends.

As schools became the major force in educating American children, a professional education establishment emerged that influenced parents as well as local and state government on curriculum. Some collaborations between schools and homes resulted, but often parents and communities were at odds regarding the specifics of children's education.

As compulsory education took hold in the late 1800s, it became apparent that many children in the United States were not being reared in the manner the dominant culture felt necessary. Poor children in urban communities were often viewed as neglected, and new immigrants from southern and eastern Europe, unable to speak English, had different values and views on child rearing (Davis, 2006; Fass & Mason,

2000). It became clear that schools with a prevalent Puritan ethic did not meet the needs of many children. Something needed to be done, and parent organizations with strong female advocates were formed to press for action on more comprehensive schools. Schools were urged to provide hot lunches for needy children, and immigrants were taught English so that they could be assimilated into American society (Fass & Mason, 2000; Kagan, 1993).

Philosophical swings in education, from conservative and academic to more liberal and progressive, have resulted from what the American public has perceived was needed in different periods. For example, with new immigrants and a growing urban, industrialized society, a movement emerged in the 1920s and 1930s for more openness in education, with schooling tailored to the needs, interests, and abilities of children. The methods used reflected the view that if children's innate abilities differed, then the type of teaching should differ, and the materials and time allowed for learning should also differ. Then, in the 1950s, as the space race captured people's imagi-

nations, U.S. citizens became concerned about the lack of an academic focus, and a swing to a more rigorous **academic curriculum** followed. This required that all children learn specific material or face failure.

Following the civil rights movement of the 1960s, social issues were of great concern, and again schools were pressured to change to a more responsive curriculum (Edwards, Derman-Sparks, & Ramsey, 2006; Schuman, 2004). Many recognized that a child's cultural setting had an influence on how he or she learned; therefore it was important to use techniques that accommodated these differences. Then in the 1980s and 1990s, globalization of economy and communications produced pressure from parent groups and communities to again promote greater academic achievements (Eitzen & Zinn, 2005).

As the 21st century begins, there is considerable interest in brain research, which has implications for schools and curricula. Researchers (Bruer, 1999; Dowling, 2004) emphasize the complexities of influences that affect how children grow and develop. Steven Pinker (2002) and

With new immigrants and a growing urban society, a movement emerged in the 1920s and 1930s for more openness in education.

Lewis W. Hine / Getty Images Inc. – Hulton Archive Photos

others have pointed out that environmental, ecological, and contextual factors do make differences: They affect genetic development of the embryo, and then effects extend through the prenatal stage. In spite of beliefs that the nature–nurture controversy would be resolved by now, political and social forces, as well as genetic studies, continue to challenge curriculum and how schools should operate. Families, schools, and communities are challenged to blend in these new perspectives to provide the best learning environment for each child.

Parent Involvement in Schools

At the beginning of the 20th century, as society brought pressure on schools to change the ways in which they operate, similar forces were directed at parents. No longer were parents viewed as the most knowledgeable on how to rear their children. Psychology as a science came into its own at this time, and young children quickly became a focus of study. A number of theories on child development and the best ways to rear children were advanced.

In 1815, the first parent education program was held in Portland, Maine, to instruct parents in proper child-rearing practices. Also, through the efforts of Elizabeth Peabody (1804–1894), a follower of Froebelian programs, kindergartens were established, first by church societies and settlement homes and later as part of public schools. Not only did kindergartens provide moral and religious training and a safe and healthy environment for children, but they also were a subtle and indirect way to reach immigrant families and influence them in rearing children according to beliefs of mainstream society (Fass & Mason, 2000; Weber, 1969).

In the late 1800s and early 1900s, interest in the plight of children in urban settings became a focus for some early childhood educators. Armed with new knowledge of the importance of good nurturing and proper training in the early years, child-care centers and family child-care programs were established as extensions of kindergarten programs. Many of these programs were directed at poor families in which mothers worked outside the home (Seefeldt & Barbour, 1998).

Early parent involvement meant educating parents and encouraging them to support school activities. The National Association of Parents and Teachers, later to become the Parent–Teacher Association (PTA), was established in 1897 for this very purpose. Community involvement in parent education came in the form of women's organizations, such as the Society for the Study of Child Nature (1888), the American Association of University Women (1881), and the National Association of Colored Women (1896). These organizations sponsored lectures and conferences and published magazines promoting parent education and stressing the importance of parents taking an active role in children's education (Sadker & Sadker, 2005; Schlossman, 1976).

Child study in the late 1800s became a focus at colleges and universities as a result of the work of G. Stanley Hall (1844–1924), one of the first psychologists to use a scientific method for studying children. Many universities established laboratory schools for preschool-age children, where educational theories and child-rearing practices could be tested. Supported by federal and private funds, these schools provided courses in child development and parent education, and practice for teachers and researchers, then disseminated information on their research (Gutek, 2005; Schlossman, 1976).

Perhaps the zenith of early parent involvement came with the founding of parent cooperatives at the University of Chicago in 1916. Founded by 12 faculty wives to provide quality care for their children and parent education for themselves, these programs were modeled after the British nursery school program, founded by Margaret McMillan (1860–1931). Although McMillan founded her school for the poor, **nursery schools** and the first **parent cooperatives** were adopted in the United States by middle-class parents, and parent involvement became entrenched.

An open, **play-oriented curriculum** was empha-sized in both nursery schools and parent coopera-tive programs, as they developed. Not all the newer nursery school programs were as commit-ted to total parent involvement as were the parent cooperative programs, however. Parents of chil-dren in cooperative programs were decision mak-ers within the schools. They hired teachers, approved the type of program, served as assistants in classrooms, and planned the parent education programs (Gutek, 2005; Taylor, 1981).

During the first half of the 1900s, parent edu-cation became viewed as vital to the welfare of so-ciety, and professional educators began to feel responsible for providing this service. Parents, even though no longer considered experts in child upbringing, were still viewed as essential compo-nents for children's success in school and later in life. Professionals felt that parents needed help in seeing how they could support their children's learning and thus benefit society (Taylor, 1981). A rather popular belief of the time, at least among the middle-class, was that the mother should stay at home to raise her children, and she should learn how to raise them from the experts. With urban-ization, however, mothers have always worked outside the home, and they have needed child-care services.

During some periods in history more than others, emphasis has been placed on the need for society to help provide child care. In the 1930s, the Works Progress Administration (WPA) offered a program that provided full day care for families in poverty. Then, during World War II, **child-care** centers were set up in factories so that mothers could help in the war effort. Great attention was paid to training teachers in child development and in the creation of curricula. Parents, however, were seen not as collaborators, but rather as need-ing support and education.

Parent involvement in education was given a boost in the 1960s, when President Johnson launched his War on Poverty. The legislation started the Head Start programs that not only provided educational and health services for chil-dren in low-income families, but also mandated

parent involvement in these programs (Lazar, 1977; Withers, 2006).

In the late 1990s, with large numbers of mothers again in the workforce and welfare moth-ers required to return to work, quality child-care services gained importance as a buttress for all par-ents. National child-care organizations such as National Association for the Education of Young Children established guidelines for quality care in the late 1980s, and the Welfare Reform Act of 1996 stressed the need for such care if mothers were to leave the welfare rolls.

During this time, research on early brain de-velopment stressed the importance of home influ-ences on children's cognitive, social, and emotional development. Equally important was the Head Start research that demonstrated posi-tive long-term effects for children in programs with strong parental involvement. The success was not only positive for academic success in later schooling but also for employment later in life (Kamerman, 2005a; Stewart & Kagan, 2005).

REFLECTION

Now would be a good time for you to check with some neighbors who have children in school, to find out what they expect to teach their children themselves and what they expect the school to take care of. As prospective teachers, do you and your classmates feel that the re-sponses reflect current professional viewpoints.?

Federal Involvement

Following the establishment of the U.S. Office of Education in 1867, the federal government took particular interest in families. The first White House Conference on Care of Dependent Chil-dren in 1909 sparked interest in child welfare throughout the nation, and in 1912, as a follow up, the Children's Bureau was established. Fol-lowing that period, educational opportunities abounded through university courses, lectures and conferences, school programs for parents, magazine articles, and books. Later, television programs instructing parents on how to educate their children were developed. A proliferation of publications from various federal agencies has continued into the 21st century, with even more information available through the Internet.

As society has become increasingly urban, decision making regarding children's education has become more complex. The federal government influences educational issues by granting monies for projects or by withholding the same from states not complying with federal mandates. State educational offices, in turn, have also developed curricula and issued mandates regarding what should be taught in schools. The federal government has taken a somewhat different focus in recent years, however, and now requires that the states take more responsibility. Still, by establishing goals and then financially supporting schools by block grants and special funding for specific goals, the federal government continues to play an active role in influencing educational issues (U.S. Department of Education, 2003).

New Federal Directions

The Goals 2000: Educate America Act of 1994, signaled a change for federal involvement in educational practice. Goals 2000 was presented as a new face, in which the federal role was to be one of support and facilitation to improve schools for all children. Provisions in the act established very general goals as incentives and then gave support to states and communities as they worked to meet those standards and objectives (Riley, 1995). The legislation, incorporating eight national education goals, emerged from 1990 legislation by the first Bush administration (U.S.D.O.E., 1993b).

After the establishment of Goals 2000 in 1996, President Bill Clinton added the America Reads Challenge. Recognizing that reading is a skill developed not only in school but also in the home and community, the initiative called for schools to involve community organizations and homes to help ensure that all children would read by the end of third grade (Mitchell & Spencer, 1997).

In January 2002, President George W. Bush signed the No Child Left Behind Act (NCLB) and in November 2002 the Education Sciences Reform Act, as part of Title I, Section A. Under these acts, local, state and federal agencies assume certain responsibilities for ensuring that parents are offered, better and expanded opportunities for their children in **Title I schools**. Institutions must be evaluated on state standards, and failure produces sanctions. For example, if a child is in a chronically underachieving Title I school, a child's parents have the right to select another school and seek supplemental academic help from approved educational providers. Schools, private educational enterprises, and **"faith-based"** organizations are eligible to provide supplemental educational services to low-income students, students with limited English proficiency, and students with disabilities. The approved organizations provide help in language arts, reading, and math before or after school, on weekends, and during the summer. Schools seeking funds to improve their programs must select strategies that have been demonstrated to be effective based on scientific research (Reyna, 2005; U.S. Department of Education, 2003).

FORCES AFFECTING EDUCATION IN THE TWENTY-FIRST CENTURY

As noted previously, practices regarding education in America have changed from one generation to the next. Our perceptions about child development and learning styles change as new studies and findings present evidence to confirm or modify one theory or another. Evolution is natural and ongoing as research and empirical studies continue.

In addition, social changes, political forces, economic pressures, plus beliefs and values continue to develop in our country. These are bound to influence educational practices. Futurists study signals and societal trends and make sobering pronouncements about what will come about in future decades and generations. As writers of this text, we resist any urge to speculate on how new movements will fit into this overview of historical patterns of philosophical outlooks. As observers of current practices and new developments, however, we conclude that the following topics will likely have a significant impact on future school objectives.

Population Diversity

The rapidly expanding mix of culture and ethnicity in America will continue, and the changing demographics will affect U.S. education. Although some legislation and judicial decisions that affect amounts of immigration, employment practices, and educational opportunity in the United States exist, these guidelines will be revisited in the years ahead. American culture has changed rapidly since civil rights legislation was passed in the 1960s, and most agree that minorities, recent English-language learners, and foreign-born residents meet greater acceptance in the majority culture and find more positive responses than before.

Ethnocentrism is less prominent than in previous generations, and most Americans are confident and positive about the "tossed salad" quality of American communities in the 21st century. Multicultural curricula and pointed attempts to foster antibias programs have made a positive impact on American schools and neighborhoods (Derman-Sparks, 1989; Edwards, Derman-Sparks, & Ramsey, 2006). Emphasis will continue, and partnerships formed by families, schools, and communities are the best possible ways to promote the advantages of diversity and demographic change.

Globalization

Interest and concerns about global issues will affect our country's schools and our attitudes toward education for years to come. In a space of two decades, much of American cultural life has been influenced through connections to worldwide products, information on different values and beliefs, and shifting job markets.

Americans have been forced to shed their traditional insular stance and to focus on events taking place on all continents. We rarely think now of a self-sufficient "fortress America" that peers inward for inspiration and services. Each year, new electronic developments tie our U.S. economy and lifestyle to other parts of the world. The end of the Cold War and the beginning of new conflicts brought about a dramatic change in American influence and interest in other regions. A new feeling of "what happens in Africa, Asia, Europe, and South America" engages Americans as never before and is bound to affect all education. Major educational associations in the United States now have an international department, and the increase in international conferences highlights this trend. The achievements of American students have been compared to those of foreign students for more than 50 years, but in the last decade, the intensity has increased and comparisons are now made yearly. All this comes from the question, "Will Americans be able to compete in the **global marketplace?**"

New comparative education procedures are helpful in using global perspectives on education, and this practice provides a logical extension for our need to extend educational partnerships to another level. Already, many schools have established connections with "sister schools" in foreign lands to enhance the notions of worldwide common interests and concerns (Swiniarski & Breitborde, 2003). The Internet and other electronic communication devices make the thousands of miles distance a trivial variable in worldwide communications.

Technology

Technological advances have always been viewed as support and enhancement for schools and other educational projects. During the 20th century, these advances were viewed much like new appliances that would make the home more efficient. Today, however, new technological developments (starting with networked personal computers) influence curriculum decisions, modes of instruction, and communication with families and communities.

Audio–visual devices to enhance curriculum grew rapidly during the last half of the 20th century. In the last decade, however, an explosion of techno-

Changes in the world force Americans to realize educational approaches in other countries will have an effect on American education.

Chandler Barbour

logical equipment to enhance communication, entertainment, and retrieval of information has pushed young children's education and interests in very different directions (Wartella & Gray, 2004).

Media, especially electronic media, has become a preferred vehicle for receiving information and entertainment. This has huge implications for the projects we plan in schools, the nature of the curriculum, the models we use to evaluate our successes, and the equipment used in future classrooms.

The emphasis on ability to use a keyboard at an early age, the skill in flipping from one TV screen or browser window to another, and the location of information in vast databases scattered over the planet all show that education outside a classroom will only increase. Linear paths, chronologies of events, and local schedules have far less importance in a high-tech-mediated environment. The new overarching frame of reference affects our work with children and all that we do with families and communities.

Religious and Spiritual Variables

America, as well as other nations, is witnessing greater interest in spiritual concerns and the expansion of religious practices in local communities and abroad. Most teachers realize that studying about different religious practices can be a beneficial and stimulating project that will enhance a multicultural classroom. In elementary schools, religious dogma must remain outside any curriculum. The science curriculum in American secondary schools, however, has been affected in recent years on the issue of **evolution** vs. **creationism** and **intelligent design**. Statutes in several states and judicial decisions have come about as pressures from special interest groups contested the secular orientation typical in American public schools. As different religious groups become more visible and expand their influence in public education, questions about religious beliefs and principles are likely to receive more study and adjudication.

PARTNERSHIPS AND COLLABORATIONS

Partnerships in education is not a new concept, if we consider the various groups and interests that have worked with schools in this country over the years. As we have pointed out, families and community leaders have great input into the functioning of schools. The question arises as to how these would-be partners for the professional education establishment view their roles and how they assume responsibility and leadership.

In the 1950s and 1960s, the American public, for the most part, viewed all education as the responsibility of schools, and parents were expected to support teachers and their programs. The community school movement also developed at this time, though, and for those subscribing to the movement, the purpose of schools was more comprehensive. Community-school advocates felt that schools, in addition to serving young children, could also serve the larger community by providing various resources for the public within the school facility (Kagan, 1993).

Educators took an active and strong role at this time, often advising parents on their roles and responsibilities. There was prosperity in the United States and a belief that through education the United States could provide equal opportunities for all citizens. In supporting this goal, volunteer programs sprang up in New York City and elsewhere. In the beginning, these volunteers were primarily nonworking mothers, but as the programs expanded and spread to other areas, retirees, college students, and businesspeople also began providing volunteer services.

A new impetus for collaboration came in the 1980s as businesses became concerned with the quality of education in the United States. Some government officials recognized that educational problems could not be solved by the public sector alone. Thus, an Educational Partnerships Program was established under the Educational Partnerships Act of 1988. The purpose of the act was to encourage community organizations, including businesses, to form alliances to encourage excellence in education (Danzberger & Gruskin, 1993; Diffily, 2004).

Partnerships no longer involved just the basics of establishing good relationships with parents and using community resources. Businesses became involved in schools in a variety of ways.

Partnership arrangements grew to include such supports as volunteers for the classroom, internships for teachers, **mentors** and tutors for particular areas of study, visits to business establishments, special projects sponsored by businesses, provision of new technology for classrooms, and assistance in shaping school policy. The businesses for education notion continued to prosper in the 1990s, when the 21st Century Community Learning Centers Act was introduced as a part of Title 20 of the No Child Left Behind Act. Under the act's provisions, communities acquired grants to establish safe places during after-school hours, homework centers, and tutorial services. In addition, special cultural, recreational, and nutritional opportunities were offered. Communities were encouraged to use public schools as a base for uniting the services within a community, to deliver education and human resources for all members of the community.

REFLECTION

Make a brief checklist of parent, volunteer, and community persons involved in a primary classroom with which you have contact. Try to label their contributions and then check with the administrator about the philosophy behind this type of involvement.

CHILDREN WITH SPECIFIC NEEDS

Major social events in each generation result in social policy changes that affect persons with special needs. After World War I, Congress enacted the Rehabilitation Act to assist wounded veterans. The act enabled veterans to receive special training and therapy so they could return to work. In the 1930s, the Great Depression resulted in Franklin Roosevelt's New Deal programs. As education was extended to persons with special needs, it soon became apparent that education alone was insufficient to provide opportunities necessary to use these skills in the workplace. In 1973, the Rehabilitation Act was amended (Section 504). The amendment was intended to prevent discrimination against persons with disabilities; thus, a program receiving federal funding could not refuse employment to individuals solely on the basis of a disability. In 1990, the Americans with Disabilities Act extended these same rights to persons seeking employment in any public or private venue (Turnbull, Turnbull, & Wehmeyer, 2007).

In a similar vein, political movements in the 1960s resulted in sweeping changes for American education and in the corresponding roles of parents, schools, and communities. The civil rights movement resulted in the Civil Rights Act of 1964, which acknowledged that children in segregated schools received an inferior education. Whereas middle-class White parents have always felt themselves a part of their children's educational process, before the landmark legislation of the 1960s, many parents in minority and low-socioeconomic groups felt disenfranchised. Parental involvement for all, regardless of heritage and economics, became highlighted in this era and continues to be an important issue.

Children in Poverty

In the 1930s, social welfare programs were seen as a way to help the poor. Aid to Families with Dependent Children was just such a program. It existed at first primarily to assist unmarried mothers in providing for their children. Even with a rising economy after World War II, large numbers of American children were still living in poverty and entered school with many problems that affected their ability to learn. In 1965, President Johnson launched his War on Poverty, which had a far-reaching impact on children raised in poverty.

The Elementary and Secondary Education Act of 1965 (PL 89-10) was the largest grant ever made by the federal government to aid education.

Educational programs such as Title I/Chapter I, **Head Start**, Home Start, and **Project Follow Through** were designed under this act to compensate for the lack of early education for children living in poverty. In addition to receiving educational experiences, children and families were provided with health, nutritional, and psychological services. Parents also were to play important roles as volunteers, paid aides, and instructors in their children's education. Parents became a part of Head Start advisory boards, thus acquiring decision-making powers both in selecting teachers and in making curriculum decisions (Lazar, 1977). Teachers in these programs were expected to make home visits, and the curriculum used was expected to reflect both the experiences and the cultural heritage of the diverse children. By implementing the federal guidelines, these programs provided an early model for family–school–community involvement.

By the 1990s, Americans believed that although Head Start was deemed successful, the War on Poverty had somehow failed. In spite of many welfare programs, child poverty increased from the early 1970s to the 1990s. In an attempt to change this course of events, the Family Support Act of 1988 stressed education and job training for welfare recipients. Mothers on welfare who returned to work or enrolled in education programs were guaranteed child-care assistance and coverage for health insurance through Medicaid.

After some degree of success, there were new proposals in the 1990s to considerably modify the act. The 1996 welfare reform bill (titled the Personal Responsibility and Work Opportunity Reconciliation Act) replaced child-care entitlement programs with a single federal Child Care and Development Block Grant (CCDBG) and gave states responsibility and authority to administer and fund grants. The bill required all child-care funds to be administered from one lead agency, thus avoiding overlap of programs. Other aspects included the following: (a) A limit was placed on how long a family could receive welfare; (b) persons receiving welfare were required to get a part-time job or receive job training; and (c) mothers with a child under a year old were exempt, but only for one child (Blank, 1997). The funding stressed improving the quality of care for children and providing education for the parents, although child care was not guaranteed (Hagan, 1998).

In 1998 the U.S. Congress reauthorized the Elementary & Secondary Education Act, with provision for appropriations to be made until the fiscal year 2008 (Head Start Bureau, 2006). President Bush's reauthorization of Head Start in 2003 was to ensure that Head Start and other pre-school-prepared children would have higher success rates in school. The reauthorization also stipulated that states receiving Head Start dollars would need to include in their plans certain accountability requirements. The proposal encourages states to develop plans for comprehensive and integrated preschool services within the local school systems (U.S. Department of Education, 2003).

Children with Disabilities

As federally supported programs developed over the years, parent groups realized they had the power to determine educational opportunities for their children. A group of parents in Missouri, concerned about how their children with disabilities were being treated, united with a civil rights organization to focus on rights for children with disabilities. Thus, the Education for All Handicapped Children Act (PL 94-142) emerged in 1975. This legislation ensured a free and appropriate education to all children with disabilities, and in 1986, amendments to that act (PL 99-457) extended rights and services to three-year-olds. In the 1990 amendment, the title of the act was changed to the **Individuals with Disabilities Education Act (IDEA)**, and the term *handicapped* was changed to *disabled*. In keeping with this legislation, the Head Start Act was amended in 1992 by the Head Start Improvement Act, and services were extended to infants and toddlers. In 1997,

the act was reauthorized, with modifications in the delivery systems, requirements in placement of students with discipline problems, and provisions for professional development. IDEA became such a comprehensive law that it was divided into three parts: Part A describes the extent and policies of the law; Part B points to the rights and benefits for 3- to 21-year-olds; and Part C (formerly Part H) addresses infants and toddlers (Turnbull et al., 2007).

Under the preceding acts, parents have the right to be involved in the entire process of their child's evaluation, placement, and educational objectives; and if there are differences of opinion, they have a right to the services of a mediator. Children placed in special education programs now must receive an **individualized education program (IEP)** prepared by a school team, including the parents, and an **individualized family service plan (IFSP)** for families with infants or toddlers with disabilities. Readers will find more specifics on these regulations in Chapter 6.

Since the laws have been enacted, the number of children classified as having disabling conditions has risen steadily (Webb et al., 2007). And in many instances, parents and educators have collaborated successfully in educating children with special needs. They have also used the resources of the community in different ways, including having volunteers work one-on-one with children.

Implications for Minority Populations

The history of parent–community–school involvement has taken a different course for minority families. In the early years of immigration, many families saw their ethnic, cultural, religious, and social traditions blended into a homogenized "American ethic" (Edwards, Derman-Sparks, & Ramsey, 2006). Greater educational opportunities and material benefits were afforded to those immigrants living by the dominant code of values. For many families, however, assimilation was more difficult or less desirable. Poverty and race distinc-

An important aspect of IDEA is that children with disabilities are to be included in the regular classroom setting.

Scott Cunningham / Merrill

tions also caused many families to be denied opportunities for equal access to quality education or job opportunities (Davis, 2006). Today such access continues to be a problem, though in more subtle ways. In spite of antidiscrimination laws all over the United States, many families, though assimilated, still feel the sting of subtle discrimination. Poverty and race distinctions mean that certain persons have to work much harder to gain access to the rights and privileges assumed by White, middle-class Americans.

Marcus, whose Mexican and immigrant father was a struggling tenant farmer in a small midwestern community during the 1960s, confronted poverty and discrimination daily. He was advised to take technical and agricultural courses at his small high school. His adviser pointed out, "After all, your father is a tenant farmer, so hope for college is pretty slim isn't it?" In spite of lack of school support, Marcus persisted in following the college preparatory curriculum and surmounted other challenges—social and financial—as he coped in rural America. Today, he has a doctorate from a prestigious university and is a candidate for a college presidency in the midwest.

Although he achieved his goals, Marcus had to overcome bias toward his ethnic heritage and

prejudice about the abilities of migrant tenant farm families in America. The determination of minority students like Marcus, supportive legislation, and attitude changes in America have produced greater acceptance of other cultures.

The history of the United States is a story of waves of immigration. In the 1600s and 1700s, western Europeans, bringing an Anglo-European culture and a Christian ethic, came to colonize different parts of the United States—crowding out Native Americans and bringing slaves from Africa. In the 1800s, more Roman Catholic groups moved to the United States as a result of the Irish famine and military acquisition of Mexican territories. Then, in the early 1900s, other groups from central and southern Europe and Asia came to the United States seeking new opportunities. In the later part of the 1900s, as other countries sustained internal strife, a large number of immigrants came from Latin America, Asia, the Caribbean, and Middle Eastern countries, seeking refuge from conflict and persecution. By the mid-1900s, three fourths of immigrants each year were from Asia and Latin America (DeVita, 1995). All these immigrant groups have had an impact on American culture, values, and traditions; however, the dominant culture in America has remained

European American, and the dominant religious traditions stem from Judeo-Christian beliefs (Gollnick & Chinn, 2006).

Since the early 1800s, concerns over the impact and challenge to European–American culture and values, from immigrants of non-Western cultures, resulted in a series of immigration acts, several of which were passed in the 1920s (Davis, 2006). The Immigration Act of 1924 was a major step that established a national origins quota system for the United States that narrowed immigration to coming mostly from European countries. The Immigration and Nationality Act of 1965 changed the policy again to one of "first come, first served." Finally, in the late 20th and early 21st centuries, issues of **undocumented immigrants** stirred controversy in political, economic, and educational settings.

In the 21st century, Americans witness national and global events that affect their lives and challenge their lifestyles. A War on Terrorism is being waged worldwide, causing a concern for American borders and making citizens feel more vulnerable to attack. Because of problems in developing countries, an increasing number of immigrants are entering the United States, both legally and illegally. Some Americans feel the need for cheap labor, which new immigrants provide, whereas others argue that schools and social systems are not equipped to accommodate this influx of new residents. The U.S. Congress has debated for several sessions the need for new immigration statutes and procedures. No matter what the resolution, though, in the new century American educational institutions will be challenged to provide an appropriate curriculum to meet the needs of culturally diverse children and to prepare young people to face not only national but also global challenges.

The early minority groups were assimilated in accordance with how much they were able or willing to adapt to the majority culture. Usually working for Europeans but rarely with other ethnically different populations. Today, Native Americans, African Americans, and Hispanics are large ethnic groups in the United States. In spite of civil rights

legislation and affirmative action, however, they have higher poverty rates than Whites (Lichter & Crowley, 2002). Throughout the history of the United States, these particular groups have been denied easy and equal access to quality education, which means their chances of moving out of poverty are less than those of their European–American counterparts (Lichter & Crowley, 2002).

REFLECTION

An educator working in an ethnically diverse classroom with several children with special needs commented, "I do a lot of drill and practice with my students because I'm trying to get them caught up. But, you know, I wish I could do more art and music with them." Which philosophical and societal influences do you think are leading this educator to hold this view?

Minority Populations and Families. During the colonial period, the two major non-White ethnic groups were Native Americans and African Americans. For these two groups, the family, in conjunction with its ethnic community, was the primary means of educating children.

A communal ethic has always prevailed in Native American communities. Historically, community groups helped parents educate children and teach them economic skills, their cultural heritage, and spiritual awareness. The community expected all women to teach necessary homemaking skills, and boys, as they matured, were taught by various elders to hunt, survive, and fight. Through rituals, ceremonies, and oral traditions, the tribal elders passed on the religious beliefs and cultural heritage to young Native Americans (Szasz, 1988).

African Americans have lived in the United States since 1619, when the first individuals appeared as indentured servants at Jamestown. By the 1700s, most African Americans were slaves, and plantation owners exercised complete control over them. Although slaves had few opportunities for formal education, African Americans formed a

Corbis / Bettmann

In the South, despite laws forbidding education for African Americans, some plantation owners did teach the children of slaves to read and write.

distinct culture. It was the family and plantation that taught the children values, community behaviors, and as many of their native customs as possible. In some instances, the children learned to read and write as they played with their owners' children (J. M. Rich, 1997). During these early years, however, the sanctioned education for African American children was limited to the skills necessary for working and living within the plantation community (Davis, 2006).

Minorities and the Community. As the American expansion began, conflicts arose among European American settlers regarding the education of non-Anglo persons. Some colonists believed that Native Americans should be segregated or even annihilated, and that African Americans should be kept from getting an education so as to avoid revolts (Berlin, 1998; Davis, 2006). Others, whether from religious zeal or from practical considerations, maintained it was necessary to

acculturate minority children about European–American culture through education. In different parts of the country, religious groups established schools and missions to educate and convert Native Americans. In the Southwest, priests and nuns taught Native Americans farming practices, vocational skills, and the Spanish language (Kidwell & Swift, 1976). Still, the major emphasis at that time was that all groups should accept the Caucasian conquerors' religious teachings and codes of behavior.

In the South, despite laws forbidding education for African Americans, some plantation owners did teach the children of slaves to read and write so that they could become skilled workers and read the Bible. Owners introduced their own religion to their slaves, and thus a large number of African Americans adopted a form of Protestantism. Later, some African Americans formed their own clandestine schools (Weinberg, 1977). In the early part of the 20th century, a Black

Muslim faith known as the Nation of Islam, emerged to promote different views of Black history and culture (Gollnick & Chinn, 2006).

Despite these modest efforts to provide a better education, the majority community, up through the 1960s, made little effort to work with Native American and African American children and their families. The European American community dictated the rules of conduct, irrespective of the values and culture of other groups. For many minority groups, these early practices were the beginning of problems between schools and families. Such practices of disrespect have resulted in serious alienation problems and further discrimination of minority-group members.

Minorities and the Schools. In the 1800s, as schools became the major force for educating children of the dominant culture, they were also seen as the way of melding the increasing number of immigrants into a common cultural ethic for American society. Mexican Americans and Asian Americans migrated to the United States in increasing numbers during the late 1800s, though, and these groups created more variety in ethnic grouping and therefore more controversy (Davis, 2006). Differences that existed in earlier periods in how society provided schools for minority groups compared to the dominant group reappeared in the 1800s. The controversies continue in some areas today.

Native Americans. To ensure better **acculturation** of Native Americans, boarding schools were established in the late 1800s, and children were removed from their families to attend them. Some schools were established on reservations, but the Bureau of Indian Affairs, not the tribe itself, was in charge of them. European–American–style schools were established to teach Christianity, English, basic skills, and some vocational training to young Native Americans. No sense of partnership on education existed, and each Native American community was expected to submit to the type of education provided by the majority culture (Szasz, 1988).

African Americans. The aftermath of the Civil War offered greater chances for formal education for many African Americans. "Freedman

schools" were established in the South, where former slaves and their children, together with some impoverished White children, were taught the curriculum of the New England common schools. Reading, writing, math, geography, moral development, and industrial education were taught, so that these students would be ready for the labor force (Berlin, 1998; Gutek, 2005). There was, however, so much resistance to literacy for African Americans from southern Whites after Reconstruction that until 1954, African American children were educated in segregated schools. The landmark case of *Brown v. Topeka Board of Education* (1954) precipitated action by African American leaders and many Whites that led to the Civil Rights Act of 1964, forcing school desegregation (Bullock, 1967; Davis, 2006).

Hispanic Americans. For the Hispanic American population, family, school, and community attempts at partnerships have had a history more of alienation than of cooperation. When America gained possession of the northern half of Mexico in 1848, the Spanish–Mexican–Indian population was expected to become American. Attitudes of most Americans at that time were that Mexican Americans were inferior and could be denied their rights (J. M. Rich, 1997). In spite of negative attitudes and unequal treatment throughout the era, however, migration of Mexican Americans to the United States has continued to the present.

Large numbers of other Hispanic groups from Central America and the Caribbean have migrated to the United States, especially since the 1960s. Some new émigrés were affluent and had few economic and educational hardships, but this situation did not exist for the great majority. Presently, over 60% of Hispanic Americans in the United States are Mexican American and, together with Puerto Ricans, experience the most discrimination (Sadker & Sadker, 2005). It is projected that by 2010 Hispanic Americans will number 48 million (U.S. Bureau of the Census, 2004), making them America's largest minority group.

From the beginning, the concept of assimilation in American public schools created conflicts with Mexican American populations. English was the language of instruction, and newly enrolled children were expected to abandon Spanish as well as other aspects of their culture. Although no segregation policies or statutes existed for Hispanic Americans, de facto segregation did, and most Mexican Americans over the years attended separate and inferior schools or were placed in separate classes. Accounts (Sadker & Sadker, 2005) show Hispanic American classrooms over the years reflecting Anglo–American curriculum and traditions, fewer well-prepared teachers, and less money spent on programs.

These circumstances often alienated Hispanic parents, who saw no purpose in education that destroyed their family lifestyles (Weinberg, 1977), even though early political leaders in the Hispanic community urged assimilation to avoid trouble. During the civil rights movement of the 1960s, new leadership appeared for Mexican Americans. Parents and political leaders joined forces in making demands for better schools and more equal treatment. Some gains came in a curriculum more responsive to their cultural heritage, instruction in Spanish, and "culture-free" IQ tests (Weinberg, 1977). The Bilingual Education Act of 1968 and subsequent acts provided non–English-speaking children with instruction in both their native language and English, but much controversy regarding the best way to teach non-English speakers persists. In 1986, then Secretary of Education William Bennett changed the role of the federal government in bilingual education; states were given the responsibility of determining the type of language instruction for their students.

In states with large Hispanic populations, bilingual programs were popular. In these programs, children received at least some academic instruction in their native language. But many believed that the programs delayed Hispanic children's progress in English and denied them academic opportunities. In 1998, California voters replaced their extensive bilingual programs with **Structured English Immersion (SEI)** programs. Children in these programs are immersed in English now—these are labeled **English Language**

Learner (ELL) programs—and get assistance as needed. Shortly after the programs started, achievement scores went up, and opponents of bilingual education used this evidence as a reason to eliminate more programs. This has practically eliminated bilingual education in California. More recent studies (Gandara et al., 1999) challenge these findings, though, and indicate that factors other than SEI programs resulted in higher test scores. Most recent linguistic and sociocultural studies indicate that multilingual and multicultural experiences are very important for both majority and minority students in America (Trawick-Smith, 2006).

Asian Americans. Asian Americans, an extremely varied group, are relatively late arrivals to this country. Chinese workers first came to the western United States in the 19th century to help build railroads. The first Japanese came at the beginning of the 20th century, and Southeast Asians immigrated in the 1970s and 1980s as they fled their war-torn countries. Korean immigrants have steadily moved to American cities over the last half century. As with all immigrants, the cultural and religious beliefs and practices vary, but Buddhism and Hinduism are two strong religious influences for Asians. Asians have been discriminated against and have experienced hardships adjusting to living in the United States. Discrimination was most profoundly felt when Japanese–American families (as well as some other Asians) living on the West Coast were forced into internment camps in 1942 and denied their civil liberties. In spite of the hardships, as a group these immigrants have been more academically and economically successful (Turnbull, Turnbull & Wehmeyer, 2007).

However, like other émigrés, Asian Americans have been expected to put aside their languages, cultural mores, and customs and adjust to European American culture. Because there are many different Asian languages, schools struggle to find the best types of language instruction for Asian children. As with other minority groups, Asian American parents have often been alienated or confused by school expectations and by mainstream American culture. This problem often makes good parent–school–community relations in Asian communities difficult to maintain.

Arab Americans. Immigrants of Middle Eastern and South Asian countries have come to the United States in relatively small numbers throughout American history. Many of them practice Islam, the Muslim faith, and individuals (though Caucasian in ancestry) have become a distinct minority community within the larger American culture. For a large number of Americans, a Muslim presence did not make an impact until the Al Qaeda attack on the World Trade Center in 2001. This tragedy brought the Muslim culture into greater focus in America, and it highlighted the influence of minority religions in our country (Davis, 2006). Religious practices have changed and altered in form in America for generations, and they frequently have an impact on traditional Judaic-Christian practices. In addition to Asian-based religions, we now find a number of European Americans are beginning to seek non-Christian spiritual guidance (Gollnick & Chinn, 2006).

CURRICULUM EMPHASIS ON DIVERSITY

Adjustments in educational opportunity for minority groups have changed dramatically in recent decades. As federal legislation has guaranteed educational opportunities for all children, regardless of race, color, religious beliefs, ethnicity, ableness, class structure, sexual orientation, or intermarriage, a greater voice has been given to minority persons in spite of different orientations. Many authorities believe a multicultural and antibias curriculum is strengthening American educational standards, living conditions, and productivity (Edwards et al., 2006).

Increased migration to America in the 21st century has resulted in a more heterogeneous American society. This heterogeneity, Internet access to the world's different cultures, and globalization of the world's economy require teachers to develop new strategies to respond to children from various language, religious, and cultural backgrounds, and also to respond to the educational needs of the native population. Teachers need to help monocultural children learn how to function in a diverse America and in a world economy where knowledge of other languages and cultures will be a key to success (Stewart & Kagan, 2005). As education for diversity gains dominance, it will be incumbent on teachers to include parents and community members even more in the school curriculum and school staffing and in providing appropriate and authentic materials (Mbugua, Wadas, Casey, & Finnerty, 2004). Education for diversity requires substantial change from the techniques of the **monocultural** curriculum that dominated education in the United States in the 19th and 20th centuries.

Changes in Attitude

At the beginning of the 20th century, the prevailing attitude in the United States held that minority groups and new immigrants should be assimilated. The children from different groups were to learn the behavior codes, values, and cultural expectations of the majority culture. This attitude of assimilation continued into the 1950s and 1960s, with the tacit assumption that "something was wrong with the other culture" that assimilation could fix. **Cultural deprivation** was the term used during the 1960s War on Poverty and in the initial bilingual programs to describe this practice. Officials believed that children needed compensatory programs to make up for this deprivation (Stein, 1986). One healthy dimension in the legislation of this period was that parents became included as decision makers. This important step required teachers and parents to communicate and work together, thus affording all a chance to grow.

As parent–school–community partnerships became established in the 1980s and 1990s, attitudes toward ethnic groups and people of different heritages gradually changed. At first, different racial and ethnic groups were recognized, then steps were taken to incorporate and adjust to these differences. Children from diverse cultural and racial families, as well as those in gay and lesbian

Staff diversity is important in demonstrating positive role models for children from different ethnic groups.

Anne Vega / Merrill

families, contribute important content to others in the classroom and the community when they share with classmates similiar yet different values, religious practices, and family culture. Acceptance of diverse cultural viewpoints and a sense of our pluralistic society are important curriculum goals if the United States is to remain a strong force in a globalized world (Mbugua et al., 2004).

Curriculum and Teaching Materials

Throughout most of the 20th century all curriculum materials were based on a European–American worldview. Caucasian children were the main characters in stories where people lived in pleasant homes surrounded by nice lawns. There were two parents: The father worked hard, and the mother lovingly tended the children. Extended families were rarely depicted. Individuals with different lifestyles were often portrayed as wrong, to be pitied, or quaint (Stein, 1986). Moral lessons, based on Puritan ethics, were often taught along with reading and writing. History and geography were taught from the Anglo-European viewpoint, and the contributions of other cultures to society's development were largely ignored (Sadker & Sadker, 2005).

A curriculum of diversity presents materials from several perspectives. People of all cultures and religious beliefs, and those with differing degrees of disabilities and varied sexual orientations are viewed in a variety of situations, and children study the major contributions of numerous cultural groups (Derman-Sparks, 1989). Customs, rituals, and traditions of different cultures are explored so that students may appreciate both similarities and differences. Teachers can now begin to view minority-group parents as a vital link in communicating aspects of culture to all children.

Problems still exist, though. Textbook companies have, at times, yielded to "political correctness" pressure from ethnic groups and have distorted their presentations of both history and cultures in an effort to "be fair" (Stille, 1998). Alternatively, some school systems have banned textbooks or literary titles that expand on non-mainstream views. Teachers should preview materials to be used with children for their accuracy and currency. When pressure groups exert so much influence that a skewed view of history, different cultural expectations, literary quality, and the makeup of American society hinder children's educational development, teachers must enlist parents and community members to find authentic international, intercultural, and intergenerational materials (Elkind, 1995; Mbugua et al., 2004).

REFLECTION

Consider the different cultures represented in an early childhood classroom with which you are connected. Does the curriculum you have observed relate to or reflect aspects of the cultural backgrounds of the children? Do you find any involvement of parents from the different cultures?

Patterns of Interaction

When minority-group children were first educated in public schools, teachers assumed they learned in the same manner as children from the predomi-

nant culture. If they responded in an unfamiliar way, the teacher assumed they were being impolite or were not very bright (Stein, 1986). Majority-culture America had a "correct" way to rear children, and minority-group parents were expected to learn these ways or doom their children to failure. Competitive, individualistic, and aggressive learning styles have always been rewarded in traditional American schools, and cooperative learning, until recently, was seen as cheating.

In schools where education for diversity is a part of the curriculum, different learning styles are recognized and staff employ different strategies to accommodate all children's learning styles (Banks, 2002). In diverse classrooms, children learn about these different patterns and learn to accept these differences. One can see that the family becomes an important part in providing a bridge from the family's cultural patterns to the more diverse patterns found in a multiethnic and multicultural

APPLYING THESE CONCEPTS TO YOUR WORK WITH CHILDREN AND FAMILIES

Understanding the major issues at different historical periods helps you view current events in a broader light. In studying this chapter, you have seen that home, schools, and communities have always affected how children learn, but recognition or use of this knowledge by educators has varied. In the 21st century, family structure and societal expectations are very different from those at the beginning of the 20th century. Some things haven't changed, though, and how parents, families, and communities were viewed in the past can act as beginning points for how to work with parents today.

1. Interview a senior citizen and determine whether he or she thinks family influence patterns have changed since his or her childhood.

2. Identify a federal law affecting education in the

United States. Interview a teacher, a parent, and a local businessperson to assess their feelings about the law and how it affects them personally. Compare your findings with other classmates. What laws did your associates dislike?

3. Visit a primary-school classroom in your area. Interview the teacher to determine the amount of parental involvement he or she has at present. Ask the teacher whether this level of involvement has changed over his or her career.

4. Examine a primary-grade curriculum guide (or textbook) from the 1950s. Compare the amount of **multicultural** material and the philosophical perspective you find with that found in a current guide (or textbook). Make two columns listing the differences.

society. With proper opportunities, we find that all children can learn to be conversant with more than one culture (Gollnick & Chinn, 2006; Salend, 2001). In a global economy, this is an important goal for our country's schools.

SUMMARY AND REVIEW

Parents, communities, and schools have always assumed significant roles and responsibilities for the education of children in any society. At different times in American history, each of the three social settings assumed greater leadership and responsibility than did the other two. And in most periods, we find some instances of parent–school–community cooperation and collaboration. At other times, conflicts appeared when one institution seemed to dominate the way children were educated.

Parents, communities, and schools have, of course, collaborated from time to time. Not until recently, however, have we seen any significant joining of forces. By the 1980s, it became clear that strong parent–school–community relationships were necessary if schools were to meet the challenge for educating all children. Various partnerships for educating children have been formed since then.

Although free and compulsory education has been a tenet of American educational theory for many years, some communities still have not extended equal opportunity to all cultural groups. From the 1800s to the mid-1900s, most minority-group children attended segregated schools or de facto segregated classrooms with fewer educational opportunities. As desegregation became more prevalent in the 1950s and 1960s, the federal government provided special programs for children living in poverty. Initiators of these programs recognized that to be successful, they must involve parents and the leaders in the community where these children live. As a result, many minority-group parents acquired decision-making powers over their children's education— a situation that had been absent for generations.

In the 1980s, Americans began to realize the importance of multicultural education for all children. Attitudes continue to change, school staffs have become diverse, and curriculum materials now present topics from a multicultural viewpoint. Many educators have started to value differences and, in the process, include parents as valuable partners in the curriculum.

At the beginning of the 21st century, in spite of many federal programs, the number of children in poverty have remained quite constant for a generation. The federal initiatives to address poverty issues have varied but have included welfare reform, the establishment of national goals, and growing support for schools to develop home, school, and community partnerships.

SUGGESTED ACTIVITIES AND QUESTIONS

1. As you review different philosophical beliefs on how children learn, reflect with some classmates on your own experiences in a third-grade classroom. Recognizing that teaching and learning is never linear, speculate on whether you think the teacher followed a more behaviorist perspective or a more developmental view. Justify your decision to the others.

2. Look at the photo on page 35 in which children are observing a process that was a part of their lives— shoeing a horse. Now look at a modern photo— the child at the computer for example, in Chapter 1, p. 12. The boy, too, is observing a process important to his life. Adults in the two pictures realize the important educative process of the physical environment, but how adults handle the learning depends on the times and the culture. In each picture, what do you think were the relationships among parents, teachers, and community members? What effect do you think these events would have had on school expectations for the children in the picture, based on different generational values?

3. As you review the history of major legislation affecting education in this chapter, select laws from different time periods and discuss how even now you may have benefited (or not benefited) from that legislation.

4. As you review a community's involvement or responsibility for children's education, develop a list of ways that you and your classmates have witnessed your own communities' involvement.

RESOURCES

Books

Banks, J. A., & Banks, C. A. (Eds.). (2001). *Handbook of research on multicultural education*. New York: Macmillan.

Delpit, L. (1995) *Other peoples children: Cultural conflict in the classroom.* New York: New Press.

deRamirez. L. L. (2006). *Voices of diversity: Stories, activities, and resources for the multicultural classroom.* Upper Saddle River, NJ: Prentice Hall.

Murphy, M. M. (2006). *The history and philosophy of education. Voices of educational pioneers.* Upper Saddle River, NJ: Merrill/Prentice Hall.

Trawick-Smith, J. (2006). *Early childhood development: A multicultural perspective* (3rd ed.). Upper Saddle River, NJ: Merrill/Prentice Hall.

Zigler, E., & Styfco, S. J. (Eds.). (2004). *The Head Start debates. Are we failing the children most at risk? 53 of America's leading experts weigh in.* Baltimore: Paul H. Brookes.

Films and Videos

Childhood [Video, 40 min]. (2002). Focuses on 20th century developments in childhood education. Companion video for use with publication of same title. Olney, MD: ACEI Publications.

First five years last forever [Video, 29 min]. (2002). Overview of children's early development with insights from T. B. Brazelton and Barbara Bowman. San Luis Obispo, CA: Davidson Films.

Play: A Vygotskian Approach [Video, 26 min]. (1996). Shows how play affects child's development following the Vygotskian philosophy. San Luis Obispo, CA: Davidson Films.

Organizations

American Anthropology Association
2200 Wilson Boulevard
Arlington, VA 22201
http://www.aaanet.org

Children's Defense Fund
25 East Street, NW
Washington, DC 20001
http://www.childrensdefense.org

Web Sites

http://www.nap.edu Site gives information on brain research from neurons to neighborhoods.

http://www.nclb.org U.S. Department of Education—No Child Left Behind Relates to No Child Left Behind legislation—discusses how government is actively involved in education.

http://qouinfo.library.unt.edu/negp/page9-3.htm Gives in formation on the national education goals and progress made in different areas.

http://www.globaled.org Site gives resources for teaching about other cultures and countries.

http://www.headstartinfo.org The federal office for statistics and information on the programs.

http://thomas.loc.gov Site for Library of Congress that tracks the progress of bills in Congress.

Chapter 3

Viewing Family Diversity

A diversity approach requires that we come to terms with the fact that varieties of households exist and that their incidence will almost certainly increase in the new century. Variety is not viewed as a problem to be solved . . . instead it is celebrated as an indicator of freedom.

(Scanzoni, 2004, p. 18)

Families have been an institution since Paleolithic times and are one main reason that humankind has evolved to where it is today. Humans are the only species with a complex code of family relationships stretching through generations. Other mammals form simple family structures for a much more limited time—a few weeks to a few years.

Since the American family is a basic building block in our society, readers need to consider first this primary element in the social setting partnership and the ways these family units work with others and for themselves. The more we understand how families function, endure, and connect, the better we are able to bring them into a positive connection with the schools and communities.

American families vary immensely in makeup, and if you talk with several colleagues, most likely all will have somewhat different descriptions of what "family" means to them. Chapter 3 focuses on the demographics and the diverse nature of families we find in the United States today. After reading this chapter, you will be able to do the following:

1. Identify the many different types of households and family groupings within which American children are being raised today.

2. Discuss the social and economic factors that affect family life.

3. Explain how racial, ethnic, and language differences, as well as marital status of parents, affect the structure and functioning of families.

4. Describe how religious factors, cultural expectations, and conditions of disability have an impact on family life.

5. Appreciate that families are always in a process of change from one stage or condition to another.

The following vignette points out some not so uncommon changes that unfolded in one American family as the members progressed through several years of life:

Five-year-old Jana had just entered Mrs. Thompson' multiage classroom. Mrs. Thompson found her a happy child who came from a "nice family." As did other neighborhood mothers, Jana's mother walked her to school. At noon, her mother met her, and they walked to Gramma's to talk about Jana's day at school. In the evening, Jana bubbled away at the dinner table, telling her father and older brother all about her day. Jana was secure and snug in her world, where love abounded. Jana's world was about to change however.

That winter, Jana's mother became very ill and was often hospitalized. Gramma came to take Jana to school on most days, though the child sometimes was angry with her. Then, Jana became worried that Gramma would not be close by.

Jana's mother died within the year, and the following year, Jana's life was filled with adjustments. Gramma and Grampa came to live at her house and take care of her, and that helped. Jana missed her mother taking her to school, for now she had to go to school with her older brother, who wanted to be with his friends, not with her. Her dad, always involved in his work, just didn't seem to be there every evening, as she would have liked. Jana, however, worked hard in school and enjoyed the consistent routine Mrs. Thompson provided over the three years Jana was in her class.

At age eight, Jana's world shifted again. Her father remarried, and now she had an extra older brother and an older sister. Her own older brother was a "pain" when he looked after her while her father and stepmother were out. Sometimes when that responsibility was shared by her brother and stepbrother, the two boys quarreled and the house got messy. When Jana tried to tell her side of the boys' squabbles, it seemed that her stepmother always became annoyed and then unresponsive. Jana's father tried to comfort her in her room after the quarrels, but he implied that Jana should cooperate more and help become a part of their new life. Gramma and Grandpa had moved away that year, and this seemed to delight Jana's stepmother, who felt they interfered, but Jana missed them.

When Jana was 10, a new baby was born into the family. At times, Jana enjoyed the delightful baby, but she also became jealous when the baby got a lot of attention. Eventually, Jana did begin to develop a more accepting, although shaky, relationship with her stepmother—they especially enjoyed cooking together and taking special packages to neighbors who were ill or in need. ——⟲

What is a family? Family can mean different things at different times. Jana, in this opening vignette, was always part of a family, but the structure changed several times in her growing-up years.

The term *family* describes particular household groupings that occur in all human societies. According to the U.S. Census Bureau definition (2004), a family household has at least two members related by birth, marriage, or adoption. In today's world, however, sociologists argue that "family" also includes clustered adults and children who have formed a unit based on mutual agreement (Casper & Bianchi, 2002). For some families, the cluster remains relatively constant; other families, like Jana's, evolve into different arrangements over the years. Whatever the cluster, the family is a dynamic and ever changing force in a child's life that affects her well-being.

REFLECTION

Think back to your own family and how it has changed over the years. How did these changes affect you during your childhood? As you work with children, remember they need to know you accept their family composition, and they need your support when changes occur within their families.

Though family composition may not have changed a great deal over the years, cultural concepts of what constitutes a "proper" family and the percentages of different family clusters have altered considerably. In the late 19th century, Victorian society in Britain and the United States idealized the family as consisting of two doting and proper parents with several adoring and capable children at their knees. Well into the 20th century, the typical family was considered a father who worked full time and a stay-at-home mother who was raising their children, who were born after their parents' only marriage. Of course, this was far from universal even then (Hernandez, 2005), but through literature and folklore, people accepted this picture of what "ought to be" the situation in their towns, cities, and neighborhoods.

Changes in family arrangement in the latter part of the 20th century certainly were dramatic, and we now find far more diversity in the structural aspects and processes of American families. The idealized family form of a married couple raising children has diminished in contemporary America as other arrangements have grown more commonplace (Allen, Fine, & Demo, 2000; Bianchi & Casper, 2000). Although from 1970 to 2003, the total number of households expanded, the nuclear family (with two parents plus their biological children) decreased from 40% of all household units in 1970 to only 23% in 2003. In the same period, single-parent families increased from 11% of all households to 16%. For families with children, this translates to about 68% of children living with two parents, 26% with a single mother, and 6% with a single father. (U.S. Bureau of the Census, 2004). The number of single-parent families is particularly noteworthy in the African American community, where more than 60% of families are headed by one parent.

There may be distinct advantages for children raised in a nuclear family, but labeling it as the only "good" or "positive" family form is risky. Many other family arrangements have proved coherent and viable (Coontz, 2000; Hetherington & Kelly, 2002). Human service professionals need to be aware of subtle and not-so-subtle prejudices toward families that differ from the nuclear model.

It is all too easy for teachers to value or feel comfortable with only those configurations that approximate their ideal family unit. The important thing to remember is that many arrangements work quite well, and over time many young children will experience changes in their own family structure. As you learn about interacting with families, be sensitive to differences and carefully search out ways to support, value, and work with all the differing types you encounter (Banks & Banks, 2005; Erera, 2002).

The family is the organizational arrangement recognized by almost all societies as foremost in protecting, nurturing, supporting, and mediating for children in their growing years. The term *family* in Western culture frequently connotes heterosexual, married adults. Our definition in this text is broader, as we look beyond marriage and sexual orientation. Many stable and prospering family units involve unmarried adults, and although some partners have been married to others, they have reconstituted a family singly or with a new partner without the formality of marriage.

At the present time, recognized family groups in the United States are very different and vary more from traditional arrangements than ever before (Hanson & Lynch, 2004). It is important to remember, however, that fewer than one third (32%) of all American households have children. Statistics on family makeup cited in this text are based on families with children in the household. See Figure 3–1 for the breakdown of household units and note that our categories include only the first two bars of that graph.

Most families, like Jana's in the chapter's opening vignette, are dynamic. Family structure is never permanent; members may form a particular configuration for only a brief time before change comes about. For example, when Jana was in eighth grade, her teacher asked her to draw and label two pictures: one of her family when she was in kindergarten and another of her family now. Jana's explanation shows her grasp of family changes.

In her kindergarten picture, Jana drew and labeled, "my real mom, my dad, my brother, and me." In her eighth-grade picture, she drew herself

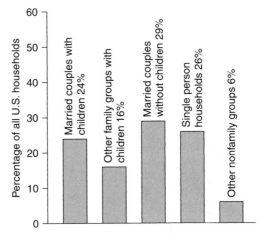

Figure 3–1   Types of American Households in 2000
Source: U.S. Census Bureau, Current Population Report P20-537, 2002.

in the center, with other people in clusters around her. Closest to her were figures labeled "dad and my older brother." On the other side but distanced from her were four people labeled "my stepsister, my stepmom, my stepbrother, and my little sister." In the right corner she had drawn a circle for four people and wrote, "my aunt, my uncle, me, and my cousin." When her teacher asked her to explain her pictures, she said, "This first picture is me and my family before Mom died. Dad remarried, so now I have a stepmom and a brother and sister and a little sister. These people," she added, pointing to the encircled group, "aren't really my family, but I stay with them a lot, so sometimes they feel like my family."

Public schools in the United States must accept all children in a community, with whatever conditions, orientations, and experiences they have. Meaning that any one classroom teacher relates to and interacts with representatives from several different family types. The backgrounds, values, and experiences vary from one child to the next, and teachers and other community workers must accept and value all families as they communicate and work to enhance programs. Sensitive and responsive interactions are the only base for healthy home–school–community relations.

In any description of family lifestyles, it is impossible to include all configurations, but as a prospective teacher or community worker, you will want to ascertain the makeup of homes in your community and assess how they function. Chapter 4 discusses family functioning in depth.

DIFFERENT TYPES OF FAMILIES

Nuclear Families

The term **nuclear family** was coined in the 1940s to distinguish it from the extended family form, a grouping that included parents, children, aunts, uncles, grandparents and others living in one household. The nuclear family originally referred to a family in which the parents are first-time married, the children living with them are their biological children, and no other adults or children live in the home. This form is sometimes referred to as an **intact family**. A minor variation is the home where the children are not biological offspring, but are legally adopted.

From shortly after World War II through the early 1970s, media producers in the United States presented what they considered to be the typical American family. That image of the nuclear family with a father breadwinner and mother homemaker was viewed throughout the United States as the all-American, "Leave It to Beaver" or "The Adventures of Ozzie and Harriet" model family. Both families appeared in film, on television shows such as the two mentioned here, in books and magazines, and in advertisements of all types (Coontz, 2005).

This model, two-parent home with children usually was presented as stable, thrifty, economically secure, and very happy. Of course, individual situations varied with regard to health, social status, and problems encountered for the sake of plot or to meet current marketing needs. The archetype has been part of American and British (and, to a lesser degree, continental European) culture for generations. The nuclear family, and particularly the version with the breadwinner father, however, is much less predominant today, and Coontz

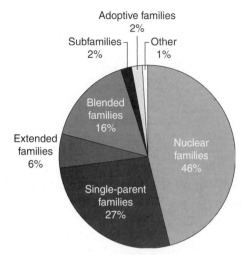

Children in American Families

Figure 3–2   Types of Families Where American Children Lived in 2001
Note: Foster children are included in various categories.
Source: Adapted from 2001 census projections: U.S. Bureau of the Census, Current Population Reports P20-506 & P20-509, 2002.

(2000, 2005) stresses that it was widespread only in the 1940s, 1950s, and early 1960s.

Role redefinitions for men and women, social pressures, changing economics, relaxation of marriage mores, and reconsidered family functions have all affected the nuclear family's dominance, and only 24% of children currently live with both their biological mother and father (U.S. Bureau of the Census, 2002a). Further, the arrangement with breadwinning father and homemaker mother is now true for only 7% of U.S. households, as women have increasingly entered the workforce while raising children (Hansen, 2005). This significant demographic change for the nuclear family household implies concurrent changes for other types. Figure 3–2 shows this demographic distribution as of 2001.

Extended Families

The multigenerational family unit is made up of a nuclear, single-parent, or blended family with additions, usually adult relatives. The identifying

Extended family arrangements provide extra care and nurturing for the young.

feature of an **extended family** is that the reference person, head of household, or wage earner is the adult with young children. Older relatives or other adults are appended to this nucleus. An **extended family** can occur in any of a number of combinations. The following are typical:

1. Mother and father with children, plus one or more grandparents.
2. Mother and father with children, plus one or more unmarried siblings of the parents or other relatives.
3. A divorced or separated mother or father with children, plus grandparents or siblings or other relatives.

The extended family arrangement is typical for agrarian societies, and many farms have had three generations of a family living together. Intergenerational families have advantages over nuclear ones: The "extra" adults can provide care and nurturing for the young, to say nothing of helping with farm chores. The extended family was common in Europe in the 19th century, and immigrants to the United States brought the practice

with them when resettling (Bailyn, Dalleck, Davis, Donald, Thomas, & Wood, 2000).

Extended families survived in urban areas for different reasons than they did in rural areas. The practice fit the need to economize, to bolster the cottage industries, and to stabilize the social situations which newcomers found themselves. Extended families became less common in American culture after industrialization, but the configuration has been retained in many minority-group homes (Webb et al., 2007) and sometimes temporarily in single-parent homes, as in the case of Jana in our vignette. Economics alone can dictate a need for sharing a dwelling when families are pressed. Heritage, a need for security, reverence for elders, and the sharing of materials all combine to make the extended family a logical arrangement for many groups.

Extended families were common throughout the 19th and early 20th century, but the demise of family farms, increased mobility of families, and other social and economic factors have led to a decline in this configuration. Taylor (2000) indicated that only 6% of American children now live in this type of family. However, about 20% of African American children do.

Single-Parent Families

Single-parent families, in which one parent lives with her or his children, have always been a part of society. The death of a spouse was not an uncommon disrupter in the lives of our ancestors. In earlier periods, however, surviving spouses often remarried soon after the death of a partner—creating stepfamilies rather than remaining single parents. In recent years in the United States, divorce and separation, rather than death, have precipitated the increasingly large number of single-parent families, as well as the record number of births occurring outside of marriage. In 2004, nearly 1.5 million babies were born to unmarried women, accounting for 35.7% of all births. Interestingly, the number of single teenage mothers has steadily decreased from 50% in 1970 to about 24% of the total births to unmarried women, and it is women in their 20s, 30s, and 40s who account for the increase.

REFLECTION

Do you use the term *broken family* to refer to a family where the parents have separated or divorced? Be aware that it implies that the resulting single-parent or blended family is wrong in some way. Do you recall hearing educators use gender-neutral, inclusive terms such as *parent*, rather than *mother* or *father*?

For a variety of reasons, the single-parent family is becoming one of the most common family groupings in the United States today. The Kids Count Data Book (Annie E. Casey Foundation, 2005) reported that 22 million children, or approximately 30% of the child population, lived in single-parent homes in 2003, contrasting with 1970, when 11% of children lived with one parent. Projections also show that about 60% of all children born in the last 18 years will spend part of their minor years in a single-parent family

(Annie E. Casey Foundation, 2005). Cohabitation of adults confounds some of these statistics, for some children are born (estimates range up to one third) into the homes of unmarried mothers and fathers. In addition, same-sex couples do rear children, but they are not identified by the Census Bureau as two-parent "families."

Although many single parents achieve noteworthy results, a number of critical issues face the single-parent family, and poverty is foremost. About 42% of children who live with their single mother are poor (Side, 2006), and single-mother families are by far the most common of one-parent families (87%). Father-led families make up a much lower percentage—1.8 million in 2000—but their numbers have doubled since 1990 (U.S. Bureau of the Census, 2002b). The single-parent family has several variations in structure:

1. Single mothers—divorced, widowed, or never married—living alone with their biological children
2. Single fathers—divorced, widowed, or never married—living alone with their biological children
3. Single parents (male or female) divorced, widowed or never married living alone with adopted children
4. Male or female parent living alone with children, and spouse incarcerated, deserted, or moved away.

Blended Families

Most divorced and widowed persons remarry, and **postnuclear family units** emerge from the remarriages. In some cases, a single adult joins an already existing single-parent family to form a stepfamily, and in others, an adult with his or her own children joins a partner with children to form a **blended or reconstituted family**. In any given year, 7% of children live with a legally married parent and stepparent and another 2.5% live with a parent who is cohabitating with a heterosexual partner (Pann & Crosbie-Burnett, 2005). Several studies conducted near the end of the 20th century

(Bianchi & Casper, 2000; Mason, 1998) reported that soon this family form, when we include cohabiting couples with children, will be the most common in America. The following are typical arrangements in blended families:

1. Parent with children remarries a single adult to produce a stepfamily for the new partner.
2. Two parents, each with children, remarry to produce stepchildren for each other and stepsiblings for the children. At least one half of such new marriages produce children who are half siblings for the existing children (Bianchi & Spain, 1996).
3. Cohabiting or common-law couples with children or with children from previous relationships live together but without marrying.

Not all parents seek marriages when realigning their living arrangements. Blended families can easily be formed without marriage; these function exactly as married blends would. The Census Bureau in 2002 revealed that of five million couples sharing a household, more than one third have children under 15 years of age (U.S. Bureau of the Census, 2002b). Figure 3–2 shows only blended families derived from marriages.

Adoptive Families

Most **adoptive families** function as nuclear ones, except that some of the family's children are not biological issue of either parent. Many families include both biological and adopted children, and almost one half of adoptions in the United States are **kinship adoptions** by a stepparent or a biological family member (Geen, 2005). Adoptive families can also be single-parent (divorce occurs in adoptive families, too), and increasingly single adults are choosing to adopt children while foregoing marriage. In addition, single-sex families (gay and lesbian partners) also adopt children. About 3% of American children are adopted, and more than 2% of "couples with children" fall into the adopted family category (Pavao, 1998).

Subfamilies

Though certainly not a new phenomenon, some family groupings, referred to as **subfamilies**, reside in other households for economic or protective reasons. The most common situation is the young single mother who takes up residence with her parents or other family members. The condition is much like the extended family, except that the parent with young children is appended to and is not the central family figure in the household. For tax purposes, these units do qualify for head-of-household status. We also find communal arrangements, in which two or more family groups choose to live together for economic and other support reasons (Gabe, 2003).

Foster Families

Families with **foster children** have been in existence for centuries. Charles Dickens and other novelists have alluded (frequently in poignant terms) to foster home arrangements. The arrangements, both legal and informal, exist today in the United States and are increasing in many urban areas as social welfare agencies try to find suitable living quarters for orphaned, unwanted, abused, and neglected children. Although sources vary on the numbers of foster children, the Child Welfare League of America (2003) recorded 585,000 children, or about 1.3% of our children, in foster care. Two thirds of all foster children are children of color, and whereas one half of the total group are available for adoption, records show that only 18% are actually adopted.

At times, childless couples elect to become foster parents for children, but more frequently it is the nuclear family that extends itself to accommodate additional children. The Child Welfare League of America (2003) advanced the argument that kinship must be considered in any foster care arrangement to preserve a child's culture and family heritage, so **kinship care**, care by close relatives, is often sought first for children needing a home. We also have to remember that children are frequently in foster care because of homelessness, abandonment, abusive situations, or medical involvement situations (AIDS, etc.). This means that challenges are often present for families providing foster care.

Arrangements for foster care are most often financial contracts by which a family agrees with a state agency to accept one or more state wards for a stated remuneration. Time elements vary from several weeks for newborns, who will be placed for adoption, up to 18 years for other children. In the 19th century, foster care often took place without remuneration, and families accepted children for humanitarian reasons as well as economic objectives, such as for securing help for farms or households.

Families Headed by Gays and Lesbians

Gay and lesbian partnerships are becoming more mainstream in America, and this leads to greater acknowledgement of **gay and lesbian** family units. A child becomes part of a gay or lesbian family in several ways: as a product of a previous heterosexual relationship, through **alternative insemination** surrogacy, or via adoption.

Although single-sex partnerships comprise a very small percentage of total family units, they function much like other family configurations, have similar child-care needs, and have comparable numbers of separations. Some employers provide medical and employee benefits to partners of either gender, but few states at present recognize same-sex marriages. Currently, Massachusetts allows such marriages, and seven other states grant status to gay and lesbian couples through civil unions or domestic partnership provisions, although the legal protections fall short of those provided by marriage. Other states, however, are working actively to prevent marriage between same-sex couples and to ban adoption of children by gay men and lesbians. In 2006, only the state of Florida prohibited adoption by gays and lesbians, but at that time six other states were considering such bans.

Because of the current social climate, gay and lesbian families must work through the legal system to assure inheritance and other financial benefits for partners and children. Without the protection of legal marriage, however, gay and lesbian couples and their children are denied rights of hospital visitation, financial security, and other protections established by state and federal government. As the United States continues to debate the issue of gay and lesbian marriage, more than 20 countries around the world, including Canada, Spain, and South Africa, have moved toward legalizing gay and lesbian family relationships through marriage or domestic partnership legislation.

Other Family Groupings

Parental abuse and neglect, substance abuse, HIV/Aids, homicide, mental illness, incarceration, abandonment, death, and other circumstances (Hanson & Lynch, 2004) can cause children to be without parents able or willing to provide care for them. Some of these children, as Figure 3–2 shows, have no organized family, and are living in institutions or boarding facilities that serve as a family substitute, but other runaway and abandoned children, who have escaped social agency notice, find informal living arrangements and temporary homes that provide the basics. These arrangements are always fragile and extralegal. Significant numbers of young children also live with grandparents, aunts, uncles, cousins, and even nonrelated adults. Census Bureau reports show that in 2001, more than 1% of American children were in such arrangements (U.S. Bureau of the Census, 2002a).

Children living with grandparents with no parent present or involved is one of the most common arrangements, and approximately four million children are apart of such families (Hayslip & Patrick, 2006). Taking on the parental role is often an unexpected interruption in their lives, and many grandparents struggle to support their grandchildren and provide adequate housing, nutrition, and care while living on fixed incomes. Despite the difficulties, however, many grandparents find joy in raising their grandchildren and feel the satisfaction of providing a home for children whose lives have been disrupted. Working with this group of caregivers requires teachers and community workers to be sensitive to their needs and alert to social services that might be required.

The family types discussed in this chapter all exist to some degree across the United States, and although the quality of child rearing varies with individuals, all family structures can be viable. It is more than likely that you know people who fit into several of the previously noted patterns, as you do yourself. Economics and social pressures in our country ensure that diversity in family arrangements continues, and transformations from one type of family to another occur daily in thousands of homes, as happened in our opening vignette. One positive result of this continuing transformation is the acceptance by our society of a multiplicity of family forms. This attitude was not present a generation ago.

REFLECTION

Think of ways you can show interest and respect for children's families. How about displaying the family photos on a bulletin board or creating a book about the children's families? Will this encourage children to learn about the different family configurations that exist within the classroom?

Diversity also is a challenge for professionals working with families. As a community worker or an educator, you must come prepared with knowledge, communication, and interaction skills and an ability not to just accept differences but to celebrate families and to help build tolerance, support, and social justice for all kinds of families. Think of how you will work for consensus with the myriad groupings as you help your community care for and educate its children.

SOCIAL FACTORS RELATING TO FAMILIES

Racial, Ethnic, and Cultural Factors

The U.S. Census Bureau has used four "racial" categories (plus "Other"), for a century, but in 1990, when respondents had an additional write-in blank for "race," they indicated nearly 300 different ethnic group labels (O'Hare, 1992). The 2000 census went one step further and provided citizens a place to indicate "more than one race." Although only 1% of the population used the multiple categorization, demographers predict much higher use of the category in another census. **Biracial families** are emerging rapidly, and the public in general attaches less importance to race and ethnicity.

Physical characteristics, language, and cultural factors distinguish some families from mainstream culture in the United States and may give them a different identity. In addition, it is important to remember that race, ethnicity, and culture are terms about human variation that are used constantly in discussions, publications, and research studies. All of this means that students of social action or education must ponder the uses of the terms and appropriateness of their use, because so much information is arbitrary and subjective.

Although racial awareness has a long history in our nation, "race" labels are often unproductive, inaccurate, and meaningless (Mukhopadhyay & Henze, 2003). The American Anthropological Association (AAA), (2002) has labeled race categories as political and social constructions with no basis in human biology. Clearly suggesting that current labels provide inadequate information, but a history of race-based policies in the United States has created social and economic differences that persist to this day (Coles, 2006). With continued reliance on census-based formulas for distributing aid, conducting demographic research, constructing election districts, and tracking racial discrimination, the United States seems destined to use the term for some time yet.

In this text, the authors use the term **ethnic orientation** primarily to refer to the general

Biracial families are emerging rapidly, and the public in general attaches less importance to race and ethnicity.

Marian Fowler

complex of cultural and physical characteristics, and we use the term **cultural background** to refer specifically to that complex of created, linguistic, and societal—but nonphysical—characteristics that distinguish societies and groups. We do use *race* at times, because it is a social reality and communicates generally used demographic data.

Ethnic identification does, however, more accurately represent the wide demographic palette in the United States. Table 3–1 gives statistics for the major racial and ethnic groups in the United States.

Until the 1970s, American schools and communities operated mostly on the basis of assimilating different cultural and ethnic minorities and language groups into the mainstream European American culture (Tiedt & Tiedt, 2001). Since the 1970s, however, the concept of **cultural pluralism** (discussed in Chapter 2) has taken root. A large number of schools and communities currently subscribe to the idea of recognizing the positive contributions and qualities of the numerous ethnic and cultural groups in the United States and use them to build a stronger society.

Most professionals accept the notion that diversity does produce strength (Gonzalez-Mena, 2006; Erickson, 2005).

Applying this notion of acceptance in communities and schools means emphasizing a multicultural curriculum that promotes positive multiethnic relationships among children, school personnel, parents, and community (Banks & McGee-Banks, 2005). As a teacher, you must be prepared to occasionally alter your curriculum to accommodate special cultural characteristics and qualities and to

Table 3–1   U.S. Population by Race and Ethnicity in July 2005

Total U.S.	296,410,000
Non-Hispanic White	199,747,000
African American	37,909,000
Asian/Pacific Islander	13,204,000
Native American and Eskimo	2,863,000
Hispanic	42,687,000

Source: U.S. Bureau of the Census estimates.
http://www.census.gov/population. Retrieved June 26, 2006.

make adjustments in discussions and interactions with parents. Among these are minority versus majority ethnic–cultural status and the presence in your class of children belonging to bilingual and interethnic families.

Majority and Minority Status

The majority and minority denote the percentage of a population, with the former being more than 50% of the total and the latter being less than 50%. Although the majority in the United States remains predominantly of western European, Caucasian (White) derivation, the poplulation has expanded swiftly in the past century to include numerous ethnic and cultural groups. At the beginning of the colonial era, the eastern seaboard colonists were mostly Europeans, with a tiny minority of African Americans. A large group of Native Americans, indigenous to the continent, existed as a separate and parallel cultural complex.

The minority population in the United States reached 20% in 1980; it was 27% in 1995, and in 2003 was about 30% (U.S. Bureau of the Census, 2002a). Projections show that the minority population in 2010 will be one third of the predicted total population of 300 million. Minority families are now common in all but a few of the 50 states. In Figure 3–3 you can see that African American,

Asian, and Hispanic minorities will grow much faster than the Caucasian population in the decades ahead. Minority children currently account for almost 40% of our youth population (18 and under), and 22 of the 25 largest city school systems have more than 50% minority students (U.S. Bureau of the Census, 2002b). Census projections indicate that by 2028, one half of our school-aged children will be minorities. We will soon need a descriptive term to replace *minority*.

Six states have arrived at or are nearing a 50% minority population (U.S. Bureau of the Census, 2002b), which means that European Americans are approaching minority status in some parts of our country. These figures indicate a homogenizing of America, for whereas a few decades ago minorities were concentrated in the West and South, the dispersal of minorities throughout the continental United States has grown rapidly in the last two decades.

Educational orientations, expectations, and learning styles vary within all families, and many minority families have favored and even encouraged different learning strategies (Hrabowski, Maton, & Greif, 1998; Webb et al., 2007). Schools and communities must recognize that people have different ways of "knowing" and acknowledge that many differences can be beneficial. As a teacher, you will be called on to accommo-

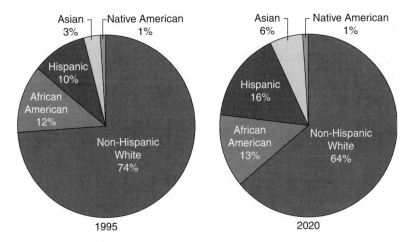

Figure 3–3 Growth of Minority Populations in the United States
Source: U.S. Bureau of the Census, Current Population Report P25-1104 and projections, 1995.

date these different cognitive styles. Chapter 9 includes more information on different learning styles.

English-Language Learners

The number of English-language learners in school is increasing rapidly, and language-minority children are the fastest-growing group in American schools (Ovando, 2005). Although Spanish-speaking households account for the largest percentage of this population and are continuing to increase at the greatest rate, a huge array of other languages are represented in schools and communities around the United States. In fact, more than one fifth of the American population over 5 years of age speaks a language other than English at home, and of these 50 million people, more than 11 million do not speak English well or they speak no English (Population Reference Bureau, 2006). The school-age members of this group may be foreign-born children of voluntary immigrants, **involuntary refugees**, or undocumented immigrants. They may also be U.S.-born children of earlier immigrants or American Indians who have maintained a heritage language in the home. Children may come to school monolingual in the home language, bilingual with that language and English, or with only rudimentary skills in the ancestral language. The diversity of languages and backgrounds is remarkable.

Consequently, about 3.6 million students in the United States show a need for special linguistic assistance in order to participate in a public school curriculum. Less than 10% of that figure are now in such programs (Webb et al., 2007), however. These statistics are significant for communities and schools where concentrations of non–English-speaking families live and work. Particular problems in communication and general acceptance do appear, and because English is the language of instruction in most schools, children with less than full fluency are at a distinct disadvantage. In fact, a disproportionate number of English-language learners do not achieve well in schools (Ovando, 2005).

Despite research supporting the use of bilingual methods with English-language learners in which instruction is provided in the home language and English is gradually introduced, a backlash against bilingual instruction started, and funding for the programs has suffered (Ovando, 2005). For example, in 1998 California approved a referendum that virtually bans bilingual education in that state. Instead, English as a Second Language (ESL) or English for Speakers of Other Languages (ESOL) programs focus on **immersion and submersion** with "all instruction in English." Some programs provide some follow-up work in a child's native language, but the diversity of languages and shortages of teachers who speak them makes this problematic in many locales.

REFLECTION

Learn a few key words in several other languages that you are likely to encounter in your work with children and families. Knowing how to greet, thank, and say good-bye in these languages will help you to establish rapport with families and ease children's transition to school. Remember that using visual cues, repetition, and slower (not louder) speech will help English-language learners to comprehend.

One of your challenges in community and school programs will be to support children and families with different language backgrounds in seeking language instruction. This challenge forms another basis for school–home–community discussion and action. Teachers of English to Speakers of Other Languages (TESOL) provides publications, training, and conferences aimed at ensuring excellence in English language teaching.

Biracial and Interethnic Families

Since **interethnic** and **interracial** marriages are becoming more common, more children with parents of different backgrounds attend American schools today. When given a chance in the 2000 census to indicate more than one race, more than four million (one half were minors) indicated more than one race identity. Demographers predict that this figure will rise dramatically in the next census, because the actual numbers are much higher and sensitivity will be less.

In the popular press, one frequently finds descriptions of the changing racial diversity in the United States, and this indicates a gradual homogenizing of our population. The notion is supported when we find 5% of all births nationally as "mixed race" or having two or more racial heritages (U.S. Bureau of the Census, 2002a). Higher proportions of interracial and interethnic marriages occur in Asian and Hispanic groups. More than anyone else in recent years, Tiger Woods, the professional golfer, drew attention to multiracial backgrounds by labeling himself "Cablinasian." *Interracial Voice*, an independent, information-oriented on-line journal is marketed to this increasing group of Americans with combined heritages.

Because different ethnic groups generally hold differing cultural expectations, interethnic families will have varying perceptions about culture and their child's participation in school and community. There is also the pressure that biracial children feel for acceptance. Although there are advantages of living in two worlds, Coles (2006) noted that some feel rejection by one (or both) parent's cultural group.

Through adoptions, some families are rearing children from a culture or race different from that of the adoptive parents, and many of those parents are interested in preserving features of the adopted child's heritage. In the United States, interracial adoptions are almost always White families adopting children of color (National Adoption Information Clearinghouse, 2004). Over the past decades, in response to various wars and political changes, children from Europe, Japan, Korea, and Vietam have been adopted in America. Currently, the most children are being adopted from China and Russia. The topic of transracial adoption has been debated over the years, but research indicates that

children adopted interracially do as well as other children (Coles, 2006). Still other families have a multiethnic makeup as a result of remarriage or combinations of parent and child ethnicity.

Race has been and continues to be an issue in America, and while great strides have been made in merging the interests, opportunities, and talents of all members on the racial palette, the job of educators, community leaders, and families themselves is to work to celebrate racial differences. Race should not be avoided but instead validated in our community lives.

Annie is an adopted Asian child living in a totally European American small town. She brings no Asian culture to the community, as she would if her biological family resided there, but her race is evident and she constantly brings up the fact of her physical difference. Her fourth-grade teacher works hard in featuring photos of minority persons and particularly Chinese. The objective is to validate the accomplishments, heritage, and history of this particular ethnic group. One new project that has started well, and is exciting for all classmates, is the e-mail writing exchange with children in a Chinese sister-city school.

Wynter (2002) expressed encouraging thoughts on racial acceptance. He indicated that America is moving into a "postracial" period and that multiculturalism will soon be irrelevant. He uses the crossover phenomenon examples in the music, toy, sports, entertainment, and advertising businesses to show how the race of featured persons becomes irrelevant in mainstream America. Madison, a doll in the Barbie line, is typical of the new forms we find in toy manufacture to show ambiguous race. However, this acceptance is still far from total. For the next decade or two, race will undoubtedly be in focus in American schools and neighborhoods.

Culture and ethnicity are family characteristics. As the United States becomes more culturally and ethnically diverse, professionals need a stronger grasp of the range of society's different cultural interests. The history of race relations in the United States has seldom been positive, and most minority-group children have felt the stings of racism and ethnocentrism. If children from our various ethnic groups are to succeed, they need to know and feel that schools and communities want them to succeed. All educators must be sensitive, and a multicultural emphasis is probably required for at least another generation.

SOCIOECONOMIC STATUS OF FAMILIES

During the 1950s and 1960s, American writers, educators, and politicians tried to downplay social class, but class levels have become more obvious in recent decades and greater acknowledgement is now made (Lareau, 2003). One only has to look at the growing polarization of wealth in America to find the vast differences in buying power, access, and vocational opportunity for citizens at different levels of the economic ladder, and this is closely related to socioeconomic status (SES).

Social classes are not easily portrayed because there are overlaps, but in general, class standing is based on the occupation, income, education, and values of the parents in a family. Figure 3–4 diagrams the social classes generally used to show the organization of American society.

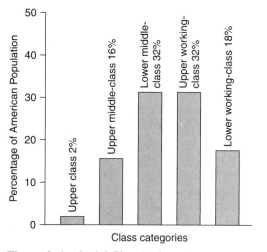

Figure 3–4   Social Class in America
Sources: Adapted from Levine, D. U. & Levine, R. (1995). *Society and education*, 9th ed. Boston: Allyn & Bacon; and Hess, A. (2001). *Concepts of social stratification: European and American models.* New York: Palgrave.

Historic Class Descriptions

The **upper class** in the United States parallels the aristocracy in other societies. These families have inherited wealth and a close-knit circle of friends, family, and colleagues. Children from upper-class families normally attend exclusive private schools and prepare for careers in a family enterprise or in public service, such as in politics or with social help organizations. Family heritage and "proper rearing" are very important in this class, and children are expected to conform to established standards of behavior, etiquette, and education.

Middle-class families are characterized by their pursuit of higher education and occupational productiveness. Upper middle-class American families are generally hardworking and achievement oriented. They are often the community's leaders, physicians, lawyers, and successful businesspersons. A defining quality for these families is the practice of cultivating their children through leisure activities that foster their cognitive and social skills (Lareau, 2003). Middle- and lower middle-class families are much the same as those of the upper middle-class in expectations and desires. Less highly paid professionals are in this category, as are many successful businesspersons. This is "middle America," enjoying many social advantages and high-quality living standards.

Upper working-class families represent skilled tradespersons, factory workers, and other hourly wage earners, many of whom have benefited from membership in unions to bolster their wages and benefits. Members of this class emphasize hard work but hold education to be less important than do members of the middle and upper classes. Working-class children are encouraged to expect a life of wage earning. Economic ups and downs often affect working-class families, who are more likely to suffer in the coming decades with the decline of union jobs.

Lower working-class families are distinguished by their lack of education and skills and their minimum-wage jobs. A majority have not completed high school, and because salaries have declined significantly in the last 30 years for those

Middle-class families enculturate their children through activities that foster their cognitive and social skills.

Laima Druskis / PH College

who have not graduated, they are often at or just above the poverty level, despite working fulltime. Families in this class often live in substandard housing but still spend a significant amount of their income on rent. They often have inadequate benefits, or none at all.

Even though a large part of American wealth, capital, and general services come as a result of working-class labor, 20% of all jobs in the United States pay wages below the poverty level. The minimum wage is not a living wage, and those in the working-class are most at risk for depleting their available resources for unexpected expenses, such as illness. See Figure 3–5 for a graphic portrayal of American incomes. Members of the the upper and lower working-class will face continued economic difficulties in the emerging high-tech global labor market.

Like middle-class parents, working-class parents provide care, food, shelter, and other basic support for their children, but they are unable to provide the enriched leisure time activities that many middle-class parents fund for their children. Instead, working-class children often have more autonomy in their free time, but they are also

expected at an early age to be responsible for taking care of their siblings and doing chores around the house.

The Underclass—A New Dimension

Sociologists and demographers now recognize a subgroup (although not represented in the classic diagram), previously merged with the lower working-class, that occupies the lower margin of our economic and social scales (Rainwater & Smeeding, 2004). The **underclass** comprises individuals and families locked into a debilitating cycle of poverty and despair from which they can find little escape. The combination of **welfare-to-work programs** plus economic boom times in the late 1990s reduced the numbers in this group, but by 2002, with recession and high unemployment figures, the numbers had expanded once again (Urban Institute, 2002).

Underclass families subsist primarily on welfare, other government assistance, and an underground economy. Members live in inferior housing or on the streets, and face lives frequently racked by crime, deprivation, chemical dependency,

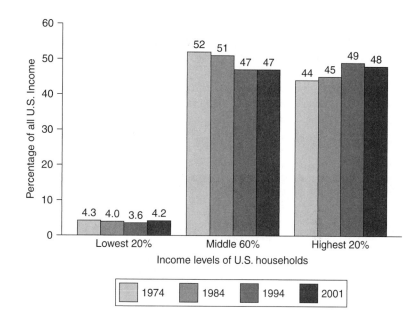

Figure 3–5   Distribution of American Household Income, 1974–2001
Source: U.S. Bureau of the Census, Current Population Report P60-213, 2002.

and abuse. Most individuals in this class possess little education and limited work experience, so the culture of poverty spirals onward. This perpetuation of economic and social dislocation gives individuals and families little chance for working out of the chain of burdens. Renewed concern now appears for children in this group, because many underclass families have exhausted the social benefits of the welfare-to-work programs and must depend again on charitable institutions.

Many children in the underclass are at risk, which means that nutrition and health care are minimal, and illness, disease, and neglect are common. Minority families are also highly represented in this once more expanding group (Goetz, 2003). The dilemma of how to help the underclass is perhaps the greatest challenge we face in our efforts to eradicate poverty (Children's Defense Fund, 2001).

We have considerable evidence that in the past, Americans moved from one socioeconomic or social class group to another via education and successful personal improvement efforts. Indications are mounting, however, that differences in the ways children are raised in their respective classes make it challenging for them to move up to

another class (Lareau, 2003). Although upward movement for middle-class Americans seems assured, future options for the working-class and underclass seem far less promising. Education levels and minimal experiences as well as the neglect by mainstream America represent a fixed ceiling for this group. With welfare reform spreading across America since the mid-1990s, many families suffer even more hardship (Lichter & Crowley, 2002).

Economics and American Families

A family's economic base is extremely important. It determines the family's quality of life, health care, nutrition, and living conditions, as well as the level of self-worth of its members, as well as their ability to function in a community. A majority of U.S. families maintain a high standard of living compared with families in the rest of the world, but we find increasing numbers in poverty. Industrial jobs are rapidly being eliminated in America and are being replaced with lower paying service employment. The effect is that real wages for most families fell 18% between 1973 and 2000 (Lichter & Crowley, 2002), and the buying power of a majority of households was even less throughout the

1990s (Heyman, 2005). Downward rather than upward mobility has become the pattern for more Americans in the present generation. Note in Figure 3–5 that the lowest 20% and the middle 60% of households receive only about one half of the total income distributed in our country. Discouraging as it appears, we seem destined for more bipolar economic situations in most U.S. regions.

REFLECTION

Be sensitive to the economic situation of the families and children with whom you work. Some families live paycheck to paycheck, and others rely on a monthly assistance check. There may be times during the month when families have no money in the house. Can you think of ways families could contribute in nonmonetary ways?

In an attempt to guard against declining living standards, in nuclear families now both parents work. **Dual incomes** may provide families with increased economic support, but child care, home maintainance, and time to participate actively in school and community become real challenges. Economics correlates with risk factors; almost always, the lower the income, the higher the risk. However, we do find "at-risk" children in middle- and upper-income families struggling to balance the needs of home and family, and teachers and other helping professionals must be alert to such situations.

Middle-Income Families. The American dream has been to achieve a middle-class lifestyle. The middle-class are supposed to enjoy full employment and the esteem that society places on the engine that propels the nation. For many, this scenario is true. In 1996, more than 28 million families enjoyed an income above the median, one that permitted them to enjoy a better-than-average lifestyle (U.S. Bureau of the Census, 1998a). We must keep in mind, however, that real earnings slipped badly in the 1970s and 1980s, so to remain

in the middle-class, many of these families have moved to the dual-income plan in order to maintain the features of suburban living, recreational opportunity, and college education for their children (Teachman, 2000). Unfortunately, public policies that would help parents balance their work and family responsibilities have lagged in the United States (Kamerman, 2005a), and middle-income families struggle to manage the challenge of raising a family while working in a demanding career.

Middle-income families tend to follow professional advice with regard to childrearing and have shifted their behaviors as recommendations have changed over the past few decades (Lareau, 2003). Parenting practices tend to feature timeouts, discussion, and reasoning with children in lieu of physical punishment. Communication is valued. Middle-income families are comfortable participating in school and community activities, and the parents' educational level usually makes communication with schools and community agencies easier. Parents' volunteer work can be considerable, and since parents' participation has a long history, minimal instruction or organization is necessary. Members of this group can make valuable contributions to a school program in sharing talents, giving presentations, or managing projects. Time may already be scarce for middle-income parents, though, and new demands—especially with dual-income families—do result in further family time constraints (Almeida & McDonald, 2005).

Working-Class Families. Values in working-class families may differ from those presented in schools. Although there are certainly exceptions, many parents in the working-class tend to favor an authoritarian parenting style (see Chapter 4) and engage in far less discussion and reasoning with their children on behavior issues (Lareau, 2003). These families may also feel constrained in the school setting because of their own negative experiences during their years in school. They may question the value of an education for their children as preparation for the real world of wage earning.

Helping working-class families feel comfortable and welcome in the school is an essential first step in fostering their involvement. Once families feel respected and appreciated, they fit well into school and community programs where tasks are carefully defined and arranged. Family members here consider themselves as "doers" and normally are willing to work avidly on specific projects or use other means to support a school or agency. Comer (1997) pointed out that many schools successfully arrange for participation by up to one half of their working-class family members.

Underclass Families. As discussed, the United States has for generations contained an underclass of families with limited education, limited employment, and a history of subsisting on government and institutional assistance. In addition, financial reversals and economic deterioration in some locations have resulted in poverty for previous working-class American families. In the beginning year of the 21st century, the number of families in the United States at or below the subsistence level was growing again. According to the The National Center for Children in Poverty (2006), the number of children under six who were poor increased by 12% between 2000 and 2004. Currently, 22% of this age group live in low-income homes (an income of less than $40,000 for a family of four) and 21% are members of families that are considered poor (an income of less than $20,000 for a family of four). Minority children under the age of six have the highest rate of poverty, with figures ranging up to 40% (Burtless & Smeeding, 2001). Refer again to Figure 3–5.

Poverty is a risk factor associated with numerous negative outcomes—particularly for children. Poor children tend to have lower attendance in school and may change schools frequently because of the instability of their living situation. In the 1980s and 1990s, poverty became more permanent because of difficulties individuals have in breaking out of menial jobs. The United States appears to now have a permanent underclass (poverty figures have remained almost static for nearly 25 years), and two expanding groups at this level are homeless and itinerant families.

Homeless Families. The main cause of homelessness is a lack of affordable housing for very low-income families (Alexander, 2003). Some families suffering economic hardships must surrender their homes and spend increasing amounts of time in shelters, in automobiles, or on the street. Because poverty is increasing at the present time, more families will undoubtedly be pushed into homelessness in the future (Hanson & Lynch, 2004).

Whereas the typical media image of the homeless person is the unemployed male who abuses substances and wanders the streets, statistics show that more than 25% of the homeless in 2001 were family persons, and 58% of the family members were children (Urban Institute, 2002). The numbers of homeless are difficult to ascertain, and estimates differ sharply. Some estimates indicate that more than a million American children experienced homelessness in 2006 (National Allliance to End Homelessness) and the risk of homelessness is higher the younger the child. The Urban Institute (2002) estimates that 2.3 to more than three million Americans experience homelessness at some point in a given year. This represents about 1% of our population.

Many of the parents in homeless situations are employed but work in low-end jobs that pay insufficiently for housing. A minimum-wage job is insufficient to pay rent on a very modest apartment in any state in the United States. Homelessness is also related to seasons and seasonal work. Winter figures for the homeless (in most states) are almost 50% higher than during summer and early fall.

Children from homeless situations tend to suffer from poor health, anxiety, depression, and developmental delays. Some manage to attend school, but they often have poor attendance, behavior problems, and lower academic achievement than children who are housed. Although shelters can provide a basic refuge from the streets, living in one is often very stressful for families, as parents may be separated from each other and older male children may also have to relocate to another facility. Although housing assistance is available from the U.S. Department of Housing and Urban Development, only 12% of those eligible receive help because of insufficient funding (Ispa, Thornburg, & Fine, 2006).

Tony Freeman / PhotoEdit Inc.

Children from homeless situations tend to suffer from poor health, anxiety, depression, and developmental delays.

Clearly, such circumstances offer a challenge to communities and schools working together to produce basic health and nutrition services for our neediest children (Swick, 1999). One example of success is the U.S. Office of Education's validating the efforts of Sandra McBrayer by naming her 1994 Teacher of the Year for her work with homeless students on the streets of San Diego. Increasingly, school systems such as the Seattle Public Schools provide transportation to children who are homeless and must move to a shelter outside of the district where they have been attending school, so they can continue at that school if they wish. Providing such continuity for children is an important aspect of support.

Migrant and Itinerant Families. Some families are highly mobile because of erratic work availability and the unsettled lifestyles of the parents. These families experience poor living conditions, and their members often suffer from serious health problems (DeVita & Mosher-Williams, 2001; Morse, 1997).

Migrant workers constitute a significant block of both U.S. citizens and resident aliens who move up and down the continent during harvesting seasons. The United States has more than one million migrant workers in any one year (Waller & Crawford, 2001). Many families are without a permanent home—children are in one location for several weeks and then move to another. Life for these children has little security, health care, or stability, and this group has greater likelihood of infant mortality, disabilities, and chronic illness of any other in the nation (Romanowski, 2001; Werts, Culatta & Tompkins, 2007).

Migrant-worker and itinerant families pose a particular challenge for schools and teachers. Children are forced into new situations every few weeks and thus have little continuity in school or community experiences. The progress in cognitive growth for migrant children is often minimal, and such children frequently become socially alienated simply because they cannot feel a part of any school or community (National Commission on Migrant Children, 1992; Tao, Khan, & Arriola, 1997). **Even Start** programs are attempts to bolster educational opportunity for the young children of **at-risk families**, and 5% of Even Start funds are earmarked for migrant families (Dimidijian, 2001; Tao, Khan, & Arriola, 1997).

Low-SES families have been a constant in American society for generations. Large amounts of federal funds have been spent, but positive results come about infrequently. Community action teams, school program developers, and others need to continue to identify realistic educational initiatives that will produce better opportunities for the economically beset. On the positive side, we do have programs that work (see models outlined in Chapter 12). Selected plans across the country show that low-SES children need not follow the spiral of agony and misery so frequently associated with a disadvantaged life.

Ansel's parents are migrant farm workers; they follow employment opportunities from Florida to Maine each year, harvesting crops. Their life is filled with needs for food, clothes, car repairs, and medical treatment. Still, four-year-old Ansel has many happy days exploring farms and playing with pet animals and other migrant children.

The parents work daily in the fields, and the children help with small tasks during the harvest. At one Georgia site, a child-care worker visited the worker's quarters, and in spite of their exhausting day, Ansel's parents learned how to enroll him in the local Even Start program. His experience was a success, and after his first week, Ansel showed off his favorite picture books, an art project, and the three games he had learned. Now, in the few hours at the end of each day, Ansel shares material with his tired but willing parents.

In Maine a farmer's wife gave Ansel a box of paperback picture books, and Ansel enjoys "reading" the pictures to his parents. In another community in early fall, a child-care worker started a portfolio of Ansel's artwork and his writings—from scribbles to forming numbers and letters. She encouraged Ansel and his parents to share these "recordings" at their next several stops on the way to Florida. Gradually, the parents are learning to ask the right questions to find preschool programs in other communities.

Ansel will start kindergarten in the fall and will follow a similar intermittent pattern of schooling. Ansel's parents, however, are beginning to develop skills in reaching out to the community for help and in sharing his portfolio with others. Educating migrant children is never an easy task, but caring parents, interested community workers and receptive schools provide great help for the resilient migrant child. ⟶ ☙

Effects of Economics

The economic foundation of a society governs in large part the socioeconomic status (SES) of individuals within that society. Financial resources for families become the most important variable in determining class status and opportunity—money governs diet, place of residence, access to health care, and chances for the future. Naturally, children's achievement in school is affected tremendously by these factors.

Early studies by Coleman (1966) showed a strong correlation between family SES and children's cognitive development and achievement. More recent studies qualify those findings. Mayer (1997) pointed out the importance of the home

psychological environment for child learning. Hrabowski et al. (1998) and Hrabowski, Maton, Greene, & Greif (2002) found a similar pattern, noting that parental behaviors toward children are more strongly predictive of cognitive growth than are SES variables. We may thus hope to keep alive the chance for upward mobility and improvement for economically disadvantaged populations if we can deliver to these families intervention in the form of educational programs. If parent attitudes and behaviors represent those characteristics that can be affected by education and training (Ramsey, 2004; Walberg, 1984), schools and communities have the best chance for engaging parents in the process of educating their children.

FAMILIES WITH CHILDREN WITH DISABILITIES

The special education of children with disabilities involves a large number of diverse families with children who have learning disabilities, speech and language impairments, autism, mental retardation, emotional disturbance, physical impairments or other conditions. Although all families raising children face challenges, parents raising a child with a disability have additional responsibilities and may vary greatly in their ability to cope with the demands placed upon them.

During the 2003 to 2004 school year, more than 6.3 million children and youth from age three through 21 were served under federal programs for children with disabilities (U.S. Department of Education, 2004). In addition, about 951,294 infants, toddlers, and preschool children received **early intervention services** in that same year (Heward, 2006). This is a significant population (more than 12% of children in that age bracket, according to U.S. Census Bureau statistics) and it places considerable challenge and pressure on available assistive time and resources. When professionals work with schools and communities, they need to understand not only particular disabilities but also those problems and pressures that affect both the family and the child. They must be both sensitive and supportive when working with families of children with disabilities. (See Chapter 6 for more detailed information on children with disabilities and their families.)

Families raising children with special needs are a part of all communities, and since disabilities cut across all socioeconomic groups, affected children will be present in most schools. Diversity is always a challenge for education professionals, but often special-needs families require more school–home–community planning to realize the most positive outcomes. Although major physical disabilities are evenly distributed across SES groups, milder disabilities (called **school-identified disabilities**) occur much more frequently in poor and disadvantaged families (Lichter & Crowley, 2002). Poverty, lack of health care, and particularly lack of prenatal care are responsible in large part (Children's Defense Fund, 2005; Lerner, Lowenthal, & Egan, 2003) for the disproportionate number of disabilities in minority families. Programs for children with special needs are thriving all over the United States. See Turnbull et al. (2007) for a series of life stories that feature youth with special needs prospering in carefully planned programs.

RELIGIOUS ORIENTATION

A family's religious affiliation can be an important aspect of their uniqueness, and teachers and other community professionals need to be knowledgable about different spiritual practices. Yet, in their attempt to follow the requirements of the constitutional indications for "separation of church and state" in the United States, schools often try to ignore or deliberately overlook the religious affiliation of children and their families. It must be realized, however, that religious affiliation and commitment affect how children feel about school activities, rules, and the behavior of others.

Religion helps many persons find purpose and meaning in their lives. Socioeconomic success does not seem to be linked with any particular faith, but some researchers indicate a correlation between religious commitment and moral behavior

(Gorsuch, 1976; Hoge, 1996). This statistic should be comforting, considering that 90% of Americans profess to having a religious attachment. Attendance at religious services rarely exceeds 20% of the population in any one community, however.

Religious practices may affect interaction and participation, holiday observances, foods eaten, and gender roles, so it is important that school and community professionals know and respect the tenets of the different religions represented in community families. A school's ability to accommodate different religious practices directly affects whether the school's work with children, their families, and particular communities will be successful.

REFLECTION

Consider the various religious traditions in the United States and think about ways to present information about different religious holidays. Imagine how you could get different family members to come to share their traditions with your class.

Religious diversity has increased dramatically in the United States since the mid-20th century (Goff, 2004) because of changes in immigration patterns, intermarriage, urbanization, and various other factors. You will find inquiry about America's religious groups highly educational, and the information will be valuable for groups and individuals. For all our ethnic and religious diversity, most American children and adults are ill-informed about Judaism, Buddhism, and Islam, to say nothing of Native American religious practices. References that help in reflecting on religious practice include Melton's (2002) *Encyclopedia of American Religion* and the Gollnick and Chinn (2006) text on multicultural education.

The religious landscape in the United States is in constant flux, as one would expect in a country where religious tolerance abides. New faith traditions emerge frequently, and membership in established congregations moves up and down

Religious affiliations may affect how children feel about school activities, rules, and the behavior of others.

(Lindner, 2003). The major faiths represented in the United States are Christianity, which includes Protestants and Catholics; Judaism; and Islam. Much smaller representations of Hinduism, Buddhism, and other Eastern beliefs are found in major U.S. cities, as well. All major faiths are divided into smaller sects and denominations, which vary considerably. For example, within the Protestant Christian faith are dozens of denominations, ranging socially and politically from liberal to conservative. Catholic subgroups include Roman Catholic and Eastern Orthodox. Jewish groups range from conservative Hasidic sects to liberal Reform synagogues. The rapidly expanding Islamic affiliations in the United States include Black Muslim groups and Near Eastern aggregations, as well as immigrants from East Asia. Mosques are now becoming common in U.S. urban landscapes.

The *Yearbook of American and Canadian Churches, 2002* (Lindner, 2003) catalogs the religious affiliation of approximately 248 million persons in the United States indicating a religious connection. Of that figure, the membership percentage for the predominant groups is as follows: Protestant Christians, 57%; Catholic Christians, 26%; Muslims, 3%; Jews, 3%; no religion, 9%; and other, 1%. These figures affirm a dominant Protestant religious heritage in many areas of the United States that stems from a strong Protestant affiliation during the colonial era of the country.

Religion directly influences how families rear children, as well as how they conduct their affairs and relate to a community (Hoge, 1996). Even though the federal and state court decisions (case law) have traditionally separated church work and state regulations, one finds a great deal in legal codes and the common law of the United States resting firmly on a Protestant ethic (Gollnick & Chinn, 2006; Melton, 2002). The administration of George W. Bush has supported more connections between religious institutions and government programs. Some of the faith-based social support groups and school **voucher plans** that include religious schools do take some new steps to involve federal and state governments in indirect support for religious organizations. Court decisions in 2003 upheld these new connections.

Applications of Religion

All religions deem sacred certain ideas, objects, or aspects of the natural world, and these dictates have implications for observance within those groups. Even though many children are only casually acquainted with the practice of their religion, it is still a background feature in their lives, which their behaviors and reactions will demonstrate. The following are points to consider as you collaborate with parents and community members in educating children and directing programs.

Observance of Holidays. Most religions have selected, faith-specific holidays. Christians celebrate Easter and Christmas; Jews celebrate Passover, Yom Kippur, and other holidays; Muslims observe Ramadan, Bayrami, and other holidays.

Codes. Religious groups have codes relating to sexual behavior as well as to the observance of marriages, births, and deaths. Many religions have dietary laws, and children will seek or avoid specific foods at certain times or during particular occasions.

All religions have a moral code, and when we compare religious practices around the world, many aspects of the different codes resemble one another. Differences are in such features as locus of control. For example, Protestant groups hold that humans are individually responsible for determining their behavior, but other groups teach that it is loyalty to the group that counts and that individuals must adhere to acceptable practices as defined by the religion or its authorities.

Educators and other professional community workers must adhere to the following points regarding instruction about religion or comments and questions about religion (Gollnick & Chinn, 2006; Green & Oldendorf, 2005):

1. Be knowledgeable of the religious affiliations of associates, clients, schoolchildren, and community members.

2. The school should study what all people believe, but should not teach a student what to believe.

3. Learn to value all religious practices and encourage people to share information about their faiths.

4. Learn about the larger community endeavors that focus on religion or feature religious holidays.

5. Learn how to use the various religious links in the school and community to educate children and to help them develop tolerance for others.

REFLECTION

With fellow classmates share the recommendations of Gollnick and Chinn (2006) and Green and Oldendorf (2005) noted earlier. Then, consider what points you feel comfortable with and speculate on how you could share faith information with young children.

The key is for professionals to be knowledgeable and respectful and not underestimate the importance that Americans place on religion.

CHANGES IN CONTEMPORARY FAMILIES

Even though the concept of family has been with humanity since Paleolithic times, we still find gradual changes in form and function of this basic unit. In recent decades, America has seen new family forms and the public acceptance of one-parent households, cohabiting couples, families headed by gay and lesbian parents, as well as multiracial families. The focus of this text is on families in the United States at the beginning of the 21st century, but in this section we consider family evolution over the past two centuries. The comparisons will help explain how we arrived at our present situation.

From its inception to the mid-1800s, the United States had primarily an agrarian economy, and its population was mainly rural. Such circumstances producing a typical farming family structure across the United States. This land-based family was often extended and often included three generations of members. Children were considered valuable assets to families at this time, because farm work involved numerous tasks calling for extra hands.

With the advent of the Industrial Revolution in the late 1700s and early 1800s, the American economy and social structure started to change. Urban centers expanded and whole new classes of jobs in manufacturing and commerce became available. Changes in the economic situation brought changes to families. A large working-class emerged. A whole new ethic was injected into family life. Roles in the home changed. The need for many hands in the home diminished, because children of factory workers did not participate in the work of parents. Homes changed from places where child rearing was linked to acquiring adult skills to environments where only child rearing took place. Education was no longer passed from older to younger family members but became something taught in "schools," as children's need for literacy and calculation skills moved beyond parental expertise.

By the end of the 19th century, the urbanization of the United States was well under way. Industrial and commercial development continued in rapid strides until World War II. Following the Westward expansion in the 1880s and the general availability of railroad transport, relocation became relatively common for American families, especially after the early 1900s. Some families became more isolated from their relatives as they tried to establish roots in other communities and regions (Bailyn et al., 2000). It is during this period that the extended family diminished and the classic model of the nuclear family, typified by the smaller family of children living with their parents in an individual house with mother as homemaker and father as breadwinner became more prominent

(Coontz, 2005). After World War II, mobility intensified as large groups moved to different parts of the country to find better living conditions. Such activity and reorganization increased the prevalence of nuclear family features.

Of course there were many exceptions to these norms in early 20th-century households. Death often left in its wake single-parent families. Single parents clearly had a difficult task, so remarriages and, consequently, stepfamilies occurred frequently. Divorce was rare during this time, but foster care was not.

With World War II, new shifts in economics, a rise in minority populations, and changes in social habits had great impact on families in the United States. These changes included an increasing number of women in the workforce, instability in marriages, a rise in divorce rates, increased mobility for families, and the rise of an influential peer group culture (Bailyn et al., 2000; Gollnick & Chinn, 2006).

Women joining the workforce became more independent, redefined family roles, and changed attitudes for both men and women. Many couples chose separation, remarriage, and different styles of living when they found they now held different expectations of family life. Female heads of households became more common, and there were fewer adults in a family unit. Figure 3–6 shows the dramatic changes in family support in the last part of the 20th century. (Remember that this is not the total work force, but only the workers supporting families.) The traditional breadwinning father and homemaking mother are now below 10%, and the dual-worker family members are now nearly up to 60%. One drawback to this phenomenon is the loss of what Coleman (1991) called "social capital" in families—meaning adults' attention to and involvement with children's learning at home and in community life.

After a decade of legislation and social challenge from the civil rights movement, American social behavior took an even greater turn in the 1960s and 1970s. Younger Americans challenged an older order and experimented with different

Figure 3–6   American Families in the Labor Force, 1940–2000
Source: From "Family Members in the Work Force," by H. V. Hayghe, 1990, *Monthly Labor Review, 113*(3), 16. Reproduced by permission. Extended with information from the following: U.S. Bureau of Labor Statistics, Bulletins 2217, 2340, & 2307; plus U.S. Bureau of Labor Statistics, *News,* USDL97-195, May 1, 2002.

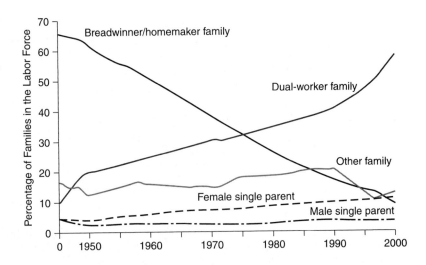

types of living arrangements. The more informal relationships, more flexible marriage and living arrangements, and new lifestyles since the 1980s are outgrowths from this period.

The postindustrial era arising in the United States at the beginning of the 21st century brings new directions and implications for families. The rise of massive service and communications industries shows that the importance of physical labor as it was known to previous generations has lessened considerably. In lieu of high-energy occupations, more U.S. workers now direct their attention to the service of equipment, the service of living conditions, and the transmittal of information and processes. More and more employees work at home and in a variety of locations (Vosler, 1996). Thus, the notion of a constant skill for employment or an established workplace diminishes.

At the same time that the information age and the service industry blossom in the United States, we have a more noticeable differentiation in economic haves and have-nots. Blue-collar workers are finding physical labor less in demand. Automation and robotics increasingly replace manufacturing jobs, and large segments of our skilled labor force is witnessing the end of their vocations.

Younger members of this force find themselves inheriting a decreasing number of available jobs, whereas others are moved to depend on welfare. Although the information age has brought acceptance of different lifestyles, it has produced abrupt economic demands that leave Americans scurrying to find new ways to cope. Sociologists (DeVita & Mosher-Williams, 2001) have recently pointed out the need for recapturing viable communities and family traditions, for our new pace of life and new emphasis on individual work pushes all Americans toward isolation.

All of these changes have immense implications for family and home situations. Our (the authors') recent experience underscores the rising problem of disconnected family members. We sat in a restaurant and observed a party of eight gathered for what appeared to be a Father's Day celebration. Conversation among the participants was intermittent but pleasant; however, it was frequently severed by the cell phone conversations that the senior male and one other male family member attended to. Family members seemingly accepted the interruptions and the disjointed communications taking place.

As we move into the 21st century, new attitudes concerning sexual behavior have also

In recent decades there has been a greater acceptance of different family forms including multiracial and lesbian families.

Patricia A. Scully

emerged, and cohabitation without marriage has become socially acceptable. Interethnic marriages are more common, and out-of-wedlock births appear less controversial. Communal living arrangements are more accepted, as are same-sex partnerships and adoptions. Although flexibility and tolerance are key requirements for new lifestyles, educators must appreciate the need for a far more sophisticated education of all younger people. The demand for literacy, problem solving, and negotiating skills today is higher for youngsters, who as adults will be very mobile and less constrained in living arrangements and will face frequent job changes and must constantly learn new methods for accomplishing things.

SUMMARY AND REVIEW

Family, though undergoing radical change in many communities, is still the primary social unit in the United States. Families vary in cultural, ethnic, religious, economic, and educational features, but all parents contribute in some way to their communities and to the schools where their children seek instruction and guidance.

The diversity of American families is said to be their strength. That fact can be generally interpreted as meaning that different heritages, values, work styles, and habits give a character to the American landscape that is both stimulating and an incentive for production. Members of some of these diverse groups, however, are in dire need of help and special support services.

Families have changed over the history of the United States and will continue to change. Ethnic proportions are constantly shifting, mobility may increase, values will alter, and even socioeconomic status will change. The reality is that children living in nontraditional families now represent a majority of the students in U.S. schools. It means that our schools and communities need a more sensitive and inclusive environment that supports children regardless of their family configuration. In the past, each generation has had its special problems and its particular successes. With this dynamic base, schools and communities must shape programs that can involve all participants fully and productively.

APPLYING THESE CONCEPTS TO YOUR WORK WITH CHILDREN AND FAMILIES

The information in this chapter forms a base of information for the strategies you use in working and interacting with the diverse families with which you will come in contact. The essential element to grapple with is understanding and accepting the wide variety of family groupings in our towns and cities. The following chapters will extend your knowledge of strategies and resources for communicating and for making curriculum decisions.

Think of this as a challenging but interesting time for you to foster healthy change in educational opportunity as you go about school or community work. It means that you must figure out what the children and families in your district have to work with and where they come from. Lerner and Benson (2003), in their ambitious book *Developmental Assets and Asset-Building Communities*, present a fascinating "asset building" vision that helping professionals will want to consider for school and social service careers.

- *Language tolerance*. Think about your attitude toward persons who are English-language learners or use nonstandard forms of English. Develop a tolerant ear for the range of English forms spoken in the area where you work. If possible, identify persons who use the local language and ask them to advise you on improving your communication and understanding of cultural differences.

- *Lifestyles*. Consider your reaction to various lifestyles and how you can increase your acceptance and understanding of families who are different than your family of origin. Can you see quality in these relationships and how they work for the benefit of these families? How will you extend the information you acquired in this chapter about the various ways family can be configured?

- *Diversity*. Stretch yourself to see through different lenses and celebrate the diversity you find by joining the activities in a different community. For example, help plan a craft show for the neighborhood, attend different religious ceremonies, or volunteer in a classroom or on a farm. The main point is to adopt a multicultural ethic as soon as possible.

SUGGESTED ACTIVITIES AND QUESTIONS

1. Discuss the family structure in your own family of origin with several colleagues. Has it changed over time, or has it remained constant during your lifetime?

2. Survey the cultural and ethnic demographics in your school or neighborhood. How do your results compare with the overall U.S. population?

3. Have children in your group draw pictures of their families and then tell you about the persons portrayed. How much information do you receive about the types of families these children have?

4. Find out why children whom you meet in your fieldwork are identified as disabled. Was a school or center involved in referrals? Did diagnosis come through a clinic, a family physician, or another source?

RESOURCES

Books

Banks, J. A., & McGee-Banks, C. A. (Eds.). (2005). *Multicultural education: Issues and perspectives* (5th ed.). New York: Wiley.

Coleman, M., & Ganong, L. H. (Eds.) (2004). *Handbook of contemporary families: Considering the past, contemplating the future*. Thousand Oaks, CA: Sage.

Emery, R. E. (2004). *The truth about divorce: Dealing with the emotion so you and your children can thrive*. New York: Viking.

Hanson, M. J., & Lynch, E. W. (2004). *Understanding families: Approaches to diversity, disability, and risk*. Baltimore: Paul H. Brookes.

Consult Appendix I for a sampling of many useful children's books that focus on family diversity.

Films and Videos

The classroom mosaic: Culture and learning [Video, 30 min]. (2003). This program explains how culturally responsive teaching enables students to create connections, access prior knowledge and experiences, and develop competence. New York: Insight Media.

A family of many nations. [Video or DVD, 54 min]. (2003). Features a school near Seattle where students from 50 countries speak 27 languages and focuses on how a successful diverse school community was formed. New York: Insight Media.

New faces on Main Street [Video, 60 min]. (1998). Presents interviews with community members where new immigrants have settled. Focuses on problems, prejudice, and hopes as integration takes place. Green Bay: University of Wisconsin–Green Bay.

That's a family! [Video, 35 min]. (2001). Presents diverse families—gay, biracial, and grandparent guardian—in a sensitive and educational way. San Francisco: Women's Educational Media.

Working with students from the culture of poverty. [2 DVDs, 116 min total]. (2005). Examines the middle-class values on which schools are based and offers insights on how teachers can increase poor children's acheivement in school and their parents' engagement in the educational process. New York: Insight Media.

Organizations

Family Pride Coalition
P. O. Box 65327
Washington, DC 20035
http://www.familypride.org

National Alliance to End Homelessness
1518 K Street, NW
Suite 410
Washington, DC 20005
http://www.endhomelessness.org

National Council on Family Relations
3989 Central Ave., NE
Minneapolis, MN 55400
http://www.ncfr.org

Stepfamily Foundation
333 West End Ave.
New York, NY 10023
http://www.stepfamily.org

Urban Institute
2100 M Street NW
Washngton, DC 20037
http://www.urban.org

Web Sites

http://www.parenting.adoption.com Comprehensive Web site for general information on adoption, publications, adoption directories, statistics, laws, and other resources.

http://www.colage.org A Web site supporting young people with gay, lesbian, bisexual, and transgender parents.

http://www.prb.org Population Reference Bureau entry Web site for objective demographic statistics and analysis of U.S. and world population studies.

http://www.census.gov The primary Web address for extensive information about your own state, as well as national statistics.

Chapter 4

Understanding Roles
and Experiences of Parents

The single most important factor in an infant's life is the bond formed with a primary caretaker. All other needs begin with this one, the foundation of a primal awareness that needs can be met, comfort can be provided, pain can be alleviated, inner peace can be achieved.

(Levine & Ion, 2002, p. 285)

Although differences in customs, modes of interaction, parenting styles, and outside influences affect the **nurturing practices** in all family situations, the importance of parenting in the lives of children is impossible to overestimate. This chapter discusses how these qualities and conditions affect the parent role and the outcomes of parent practices. After reading this chapter, you will be able to do the following:

1. Explain how parents are key persons in providing the nurturance needs of young children.

2. Describe parental roles in children's upbringing and how these roles have changed in recent years.

3. Compare and contrast commonalities and differences in parenting practices and approaches to child rearing among different ethnic communities in the United States.

4. Identify various parenting styles and how these styles affect children's participation in school and community life.

5. Consider what motivates individuals to become parents, the rewards of parenting, and how new and intensified stressors have had a great impact on parenting in American families.

All families, irrespective of the ways they are constituted, have dreams and aspirations for their children. As their children grow, they participate increasingly in community and school life, and most provide appropriate care for children. Although some household arrangements may be more vulnerable or sensitive, when considered against the dynamics of a particular community, each family can and does make positive contributions to children's development.

When we consider how families function, we find different customs, different priorities, and even somewhat different values. Of course, the differences signal the uniqueness of our diverse society, but at the same time, those very different elements fuse in most families to provide coherence and stability for members in the household.

In spite of the differences, we find some constants in all families with children. The first constant—the nurturance of children—precedes all others. Nurturance is followed by defined family roles, cultural patterns, interaction styles, and family experiences. Additional characteristics, such as child-care arrangements, poverty, and divorce, can emerge as stressors that have an impact on the parenting quality of some family units.

NURTURANCE IN FAMILIES

Generally, nurturance means providing the basic necessities of life for children, but in a wider sense, it denotes general support, love, and cultivation for the growing child. In other words, nurturance is "parenting."

Few adults are actually trained for nurturing roles, but our society expects certain minimums of support and effectiveness from parents as they rear children. The assumption is that nurturance, in its general and wider sense, has been modeled by preceding generations and is refined by an individual's experience and participation in society. The range of nurturing competence in U.S. homes, however, is wide, indeed.

Range of Child Rearing

The nurturer accepts responsibilities not only for giving children basic physiological care, guidance, and love, but also for stimulating a child's investigations of the world and monitoring the child's social relationships with others. The nurturing parent is one who is grounded in humane practice and who has a vision of what children can become.

Traditionally, this role has been filled by mothers and fathers; however, other loving adults, such as grandparents, older siblings, and foster parents can, and do, assume the responsibilities of parenting.

Some aspects of parenting may be instinctual, but the most effective nurturers have certain characteristics in common, such as motivation to be with children and knowledge about how to care for them. Health and a sense of well-being, empathy, predictability, responsiveness, and emotional availability have also been identified as traits that enhance parent effectiveness (Bornstein, 2001). On the other hand, certain traits like self-centeredness, depression, and drug or alcohol abuse can affect parenting adversely and may lead to abuse or neglect of children.

Abusive behavior in families moves parenting toward the antithesis of nurturing. Although few parents are so disordered in outlook as to carry out destructive acts with children, a significant number suffer lapses in judgment and vision that result in psychological and physical abuse or indifferent care practices and neglect. Even families with less desirable child-rearing habits frequently have positive qualities, however, and through education, counseling, and support, they can learn to modify detrimental practices.

In spite of highly publicized accounts of **dysfunctional family situations**, the norm in all communities is that parents are nurturing and concerned for the welfare of their youngsters. Consequently, this text does not focus on the pathologies that accompany abuse and indifference; rather, we have chosen to consider the range of positive nurturance that is featured in the great majority of U.S. families.

REFLECTION

Do you know your responsibilities for reporting abuse and neglect of young children? Reflect with your classmates on the availability of child protective services and obtain materials that will help you recognize signs of abuse and neglect.

Because of the cultural diversity that exists in the United States, communities and schools will serve children who have been reared with various nurturing practices. All families are linked to particular cultural groups, and each group will possess unique values and mores that individual families will follow to a greater or lesser extent. In a community with two or more cultural groups, we find somewhat different viewpoints and probably different practices. Just because a community contains different cultural groups, however, does not mean that antagonism is present. On the contrary, quite different child-raising patterns can easily coexist and interact positively. Cross-cultural exchange might even help families solve child-rearing problems.

Features of Positive Nurturance

Maslow (1970) provided a **paradigm** (Figure 4–1) that shows, in ascending fashion, the scale of human needs. When related to the lives of young children, the levels of the pyramid clearly imply the need for positive nurturance. It is easy to associate the early nurturing practices of parents—and these are almost universal—with the hierarchy developed by Maslow.

Addressing Physiological Needs. Food, warmth, and shelter are bare necessities for survival, and all parents provide them, except in rare cases, when families are caught in physical distress, dislocation, or mental illness. In spite of positive intentions, some financially stressed families find providing these basics difficult. Cold or hungry children cannot respond to any educational program. At the same time, unhealthy living climates can lead to reduced functioning, and improper food choices can lead to obesity and other nutritional problems. Teachers and other service providers must be alert to problems and deficiencies, and arrange referrals for support.

Ensuring Physical Safety. The next level of Maslow's hierarchy involves safety. Ensuring a child's safety is almost instinctive with parents, and we expect this attention to be provided carefully and lovingly. Most parents are alert to dangers

Figure 4–1 Maslow's hierarchy of needs
Source: A. H. Maslow (1968). *Toward a psychology of being.* Princeton, NJ: VonNostrand.

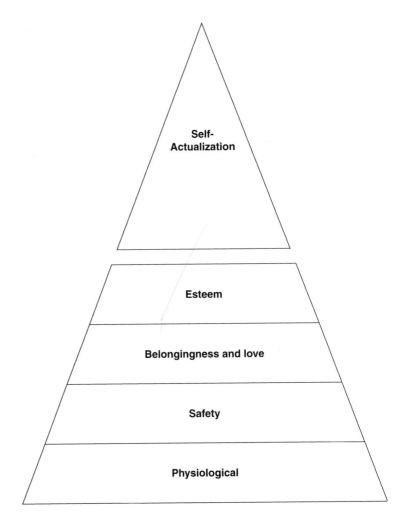

from natural disasters (such as earthquakes and storms), but it is all too easy to overlook hidden dangers, such as lead paint, polluted areas, and unsafe objects and locations.

Providing Love. Giving emotional support and providing love are features of nurturance that occur naturally in typical families. Families express these feelings in different ways. Expressions of love range from nonverbal signals and understated expressions to effusive expressions of affection. Differences in discipline practices are linked to this area of nurturance as well. Some families use physical punishment, whereas others depend on verbal reprimand and discussion or explanation to

rechannel behavior. All practices can be effective under particular circumstances. Occasionally, parents overdo their support role and encourage dependency and immaturity in their child. Overconcern and hovering often have undesirable consequences.

Promoting Esteem, Success, and Achievement. Families vary greatly in how they foster esteem and support the achievements of their children. Some parents campaign vigorously with and for their children, whereas others gently encourage or deliberately withhold praise until the end of an activity or a task. Parents sometimes hold children to adult standards in playing games, conversing, or socializing. These expectations can be problematic if children do not succeed, for their aspirations may be deflated. Adult encouragement and delight in partial success normally provide a foundation for children to lift their levels of aspiration.

Self-actualization. The final level in Maslow's hierarchy is an adult level of competence, but families foster readiness for self-actualization by supporting children's growing independence and sense of responsibility and by encouraging problem solving and decision making at children's appropriate levels of growth.

FAMILY ROLES

The family at the beginning of the 21st century has crucial roles to perform. Because society evolves, these familial roles vary from those of a century ago. Lifestyles are different now, circumstances have changed, and new expectations have emerged. The family, however, continues to serve an essential role in the lives of adults and children who are tied to each other by bonds of love and obligation (Berger, 2002). Certain basics and constants of the parental roles, such as providing economic and emotional support, socialization, and education for their children, remain.

REFLECTION

Think back on your own childhood and the roles the adults who raised you played in your life. Compare this to the families and children with whom you work. Do you note changes in roles?

How these functions are fulfilled varies from family to family, depending on circumstance. When parents are unable to carry out their responsibilities, other persons and agencies may assume parental capacities and duties. In all cases, the family roles are complemented by the efforts of teachers and various community agencies.

Economic Support

We recognized in Chapter 3 that some families in the United States live on a few thousand dollars per year, whereas others enjoy extraordinarily high incomes. This variable determines the differences in the type of shelter and quality of food and clothing families acquire, as well as other family living conditions.

Even though one or more family members are employed, some families are challenged to meet economic minimums and must depend on government assistance and private charities to supplement the basics. Because women in general make only 73% of men's annual earnings, and African American and Hispanic men earn 78% and 63% of White men's salaries (Haddock, Zimmerman, & Lyness, 2003), respectively, the families most likely to struggle economically are single-parent families headed by women and families of color. Although the United States is the wealthiest nation in the world, 17.8% of American children under the age of 18 live in families with incomes below the poverty line (Children's Defense Fund, 2001).

Almost all families do manage their economic responsibility, marginal as it may be at times. Although many U.S. families are subsidized, most do have adequate shelter, food, and clothing. Most families also have reasonable choices in how they allot their finances. Poverty is exacerbated for families struggling to make appropriate choices, though, and those with meager resources may need support and education to learn how to make sound financial decisions. A more desperate circumstance emerges for the underclass, where the basic levels of the Maslow hierarchy are often threatened.

Social agencies are established in communities to guarantee economic basics for all families. The success rate is reasonable, but communities must pursue even more aggressively the task of monitoring and guiding basic economic practices. Although **welfare reform measures** have helped former recipients obtain jobs, adequate resources for housing, healthcare benefits, and child care are often not available (Boyd–Franklin, 2003). Extended training and education are needed to lift people out of poverty for good. Parent education that focuses on the economics of family life as well as parenting skills can be an important step in improving the lives of those living in difficult economic circumstances; it is a focus that integrates well with collaborations among communities, schools, and families.

Emotional Support

Even though most parents have little training or instruction in psychological support roles, emotional nurturance for offspring appears to be a natural response. In addition, although most new parents emulate the parenting skills they observed and experienced in their own childhood (Bornstein, 2001), others make a conscious decision to parent their children differently than how they were raised.

In infancy, parents, who are sensitive to the child's needs, responsive to the child's cues, and both supportive and stimulating, enhance their child's secure attachment to them. The bond between parent and child lays the foundation for children's later loving relationships (Sclafani, 2004).

Physical affection, appreciation of the child as an individual, and acknowledgement of a child's competence all contribute to the development of self-esteem in children, the basis of sound emotional health. Research on "strong families" (Westman, 2001) suggests that emotional development in children benefits from parenting practices that emphasize mutual respect for family members, open communication, and parental authority.

Parenting classes and clinics are available (and needed) for parents who are uncertain about ways to nurture their new children most effectively. A growing problem with our present generation is that smaller families, dual-income families, and, especially, single-parent families provide noticeably less modeling of parenting behavior (Casper & Bianchi, 2002). Again, community policies must ensure availability and use of resources to support parents who need guidance in providing emotional support for their children.

Socialization

Many agents, such as the school, the peer group, the church, and the media, are involved in socializing children, but the family has the primary

Strong social skills, specifically the ability to get along with other children, are the best childhood predictor of adult competence.

Anne Vega / Merrill

responsibility for beginning the process (Bigner, 2006). Socialization of young children involves learning to relate to a variety of people in varying circumstances and modifying behavior in different environments. Strong social skills, specifically the ability to get along with other children, are the best childhood predictors of adult competence (Henniger, 2004). Emotional and social development are closely linked, and children with high self-esteem are better able to face the challenges of social interaction.

As children enter school and community life today, other forces begin to exert increasing influence on their socialization (Berns, 2006). Parental impact on children's socialization was more significant in earlier periods of history. More isolated communities, less mobility, and the virtual dominance of parental figures ensured that values, beliefs, and attitudes were quickly inculcated in children through example and statement. In addition, communities in the early United States were highly idealistic in orientation, and **role expectations** were similar for everyone in the more restricted venues.

Patterns differ today. We have less general agreement in the United States on social mores as a result of the heterogeneous communities in which we live. Schools still have certain expectations for children, however, and those who enter without some of the rudimentary social skills of sharing, taking turns, cooperating, and respecting rules will find themselves at a disadvantage. Families must work harder to prepare their children for the social expectations of the school while maintaining their own values, beliefs, attitudes, family ethnic and religious identity, and gender roles.

Values, Beliefs, and Attitudes. Parents rarely plan to teach about values and beliefs. They do, however, model via their behavior what they value and prize and what they are willing to accept. This practice has both positive and negative implications. If a parent rushes to help a stumbling neighbor, the idea is passed on to children; if a parent models lying, that habit is passed on. Recall that one part of Jana's story in the opening vignette in Chapter 3 was the way Jana's stepmother modeled

"helping neighbors." Today, Jana is raising her own children and responds to neighborhood difficulties by preparing and donating food.

Just as children learn from their parents' examples, they also learn values as they interact with family members. Daily conversations, struggles, and explanations of the world all help to build children's attitudes and beliefs about the world and other people. Spending time as a family playing games, watching a movie, hiking, or just talking conveys to children the priority their parents place on the family.

If we consider that children average nearly 30 hours a week watching TV or playing video games, many beliefs and values accrue to them from participating in these activities (Singer & Singer, 2001; Van Evra, 2004). Of particular concern is the increasing amount and level of violence (DeGaetano, 2005) and sexualized gender roles in media for children (Levin, 2005). The culture of violence and sexualization created by the media teaches children lessons that do not fit into the value systems of most parents. Parents, of course, can monitor and watch programs to discuss actions and make comments, but the problem of media violence and other aspects of media culture is being increasingly viewed as a public health issue, and schools and community agencies are beginning to get involved in protecting children from unhealthy and undesirable images.

Gender Roles. Although both gender and parenting roles in today's society appear quite different from those of earlier generations, and gender-related expectations are less rigid in many U.S. homes, most parents do seek to steer their children toward **gender-appropriate behaviors**.

The process of gender socialization often begins even before a child is born, as parents use information about their coming child's gender in order to choose gender-appropriate names, clothing, and nursery decorations. Parents also tend to give children gender-stereotyped toys and to interact with their children differently, depending on their gender (Haddock et al., 2003). Some gendering in family life is inevitable, but rigid expectations perpetuate the inequities of power between men and women in our society. Many quality children's books, noted in Appendix I, now portray more flexibility in gender roles.

In most U.S. families, fathers are still the primary economic mainstay, but that role is changing. Today, 65% of mothers with children under six are in the labor force (Children Defense Fund, 2001), and 75% of mothers with children between six and 17 are employed (Casper & Bianchi, 2002). In many dual-career homes, mothers and fathers now contribute equally to economic support. In addition, mothers are the breadwinners in most single-parent homes. Thus, the notion of associating economic support with one particular parent does not fit many children's life experiences.

Beyond economic dimensions is the changing character of family duties in the household. Historically, roles determined that the mother was cook and general homemaker, whereas the father was in the field or away at work. In the modern home, duties are not so clearly defined. It is still a small percentage, but some fathers now have major responsibilities for meal preparation and cleaning, in addition to child monitoring. Fathers now attend childbirth and parenting classes together with their wives and take responsibility for infant care. Research also indicates that men born between 1965 and 1979 spend on average an hour or more per workday caring for and doing things with their children than men born between 1946 and 1964 (Piburn, 2006).

The vast majority of married couples, however, still adhere to traditional family roles, and even women who are employed do about 80% of the household chores and child care (Haddock et al., 2003). In addition, although fathers are increasingly assisting with the tasks of raising children and running a household, mothers still have the major responsibility of organizing child care, meal planning, cleaning, and so on (Bookman, 2004).

Attempts to eliminate gender-specific tasks in the family have been slowed by the lack of changes in the workforce. The persisting lag in women's wages compared to men's, traditional full-time work schedules that don't allow flexibility or part-time options, and work that spills over into family life make it very challenging for families to balance the needs of employment and raising children.

Over the course of children's lives, they may live in various family configurations because of separation, divorce, death, remarriage, and other family changes. These reconfigured family structures will expose children to more flexible gender roles. Single-parent households and families led by gay or lesbian parents will also provide a less rigid idea of what roles men and women can play in family life and society (Ramsey, 2004).

REFLECTION

Were there gender-specific tasks that certain family members took on in your own family? Were the expectations different for boys and girls? How do children with whom you work now see their responsibilities for certain tasks? How do you feel about fairness and equity in modern society?

Racial and Ethnic Identity. Defining race and ethnicity in the United States is a complex, and sometimes contested, endeavor. As our society has become more diverse physically (Figure 4–2), it becomes increasingly difficult to categorize by race, as discussed in the previous chapter. In 1998, for example, 5% of Black Americans were foreign born (Banks, 2002). Many of these individuals are far more likely to identify with their ethnic heritage (Jamaican American, for example) than their racial identity. No matter how a family defines itself, however, most are interested in preserving their cultural heritage and teaching their children about their background (Banks, 1996).

Children begin to become aware of racial differences in skin color and other physical characteristics at around age three or four (Katz, 1976; Ramsey, 1987), but their understanding of the social and political implications of race develops much later (Wright, 1998).

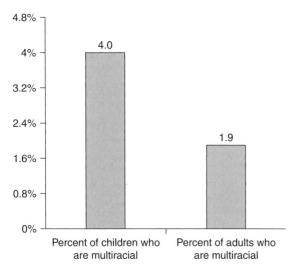

Figure 4–2   Multiracial* children and adults in the 2000 census
*Multiracial refers to people who chose more than one race on the 2000 census.
Source: Population Reference Bureau, analysis of data from U.S. Census Bureau, 2000 redistricting data (Tables PL1 and Pl2), 2003.

⟋— When Catherine, an African American three-year-old adopted by a White family, asked what color her mother was, her mother replied, "Well, I am peach color, but most people would call me White." She went on to say that people would call Catherine Black, to which Catherine replied incredulously, "I'm not Black, I'm silver!" By age five, Catherine was coloring her skin brown in self-portraits and referring to herself as brown. ⟋

Typically, Black children become aware of their race at younger ages than do White children (Wright, 1998), perhaps because of the continued salience of race as an issue for African Americans. Disparagement of a minority heritage typically is initiated by individuals in the dominant culture. Such disparagement leads, as it has in U.S. history, to many minority families' denigrating their own heritage. For example, Butler (1976), in reviewing ethnic preferences in literature, found that up through the 1960s, African American children across social and geographical settings preferred White dolls and White playmates. Since 1970, however, research findings have changed, and in most

studies (Butler, 1976; Cross, 1987; Ramsey, 1987), African American children now show preference for Black characters. Ethnic identity and validation are clearly in the province of the family, and feelings about self depend on accurate information and sensitive guidance (Ramsey, 2004). Some minority homes provide support and foster pride in the family culture and give training on how to overcome derogatory messages. Responsibility for enhancing heritage goes beyond family efforts, though; it must be supported throughout the community.

Multicultural education refers to curricular reforms made in schools and other social institutions to respond to our diverse society (Sleeter & Grant, 2003). A positive outcome of multicultural education efforts is that racial and ethnic heritages are featured in schools, communities, museums, and the mass media. Families celebrate differences now, and few are opposed to sharing stories about their cultural background and traditions in schools or in community programs. Multicultural education has also come to mean a broader school reform effort designed to increase educational equity for various cultural, ethnic, and economic groups (Banks & Banks, 2005).

Much of a family's cultural history comes in the form of stories shared and passed down through generations. In many African American, Latino, Hawaiian, and Southeast Asian families, storytelling is also a way of passing on life lessons and values. Parents who have come to the United States from other countries often seek to preserve their heritage through maintaining their native language in the home and sharing stories of their homeland with their children. Children who maintain and develop a home language while learning English at school and other places outside the home preserve their sense of belonging to their families and become biliterate as well as bicultural, an increasing advantage in our diverse world (Giambo & Szecsi, 2005).

Education

As we noted in Chapter 2, parents in previous centuries assumed a major role in all aspects of educating their children. Even in the 1800s, many families still taught basic lessons for living and vocational preparation to their children. As the 1800s moved into the 1900s, however, schools expanded rapidly in scope and assumed most of the role of educating children in literary skills, calculation, and sciences. They even acquired the job of developing work habits; moral training and health education were added quickly thereafter. Today's school has expanded to include sex education, health and recreation training, vocational training, and other educational aspects that were formerly a family's responsibility. It appears that only the early educative tasks are retained by families in the modern United States.

One regrettable outcome of this transfer of educative roles is that many parents have become much less involved in teaching their children about essential responsibilities. The importance of the parental role in educating the child remains, however, and schools need to help families understand their significance as their children's first and most important teachers. Parents who have high academic expectations, monitor their children's schoolwork, and reward their children's success in school have more successful academic outcomes (Sclafani, 2004). Although demands on today's families are immense, parents are still answerable for 75% of their children's waking hours during the typical school week (Robinson & Godbey, 1999). This amount of parent supervision carries a responsibility for educating, in the broad sense that is too often overlooked.

Families can provide the support, critical demonstrations, and follow-up for a child's learning opportunities if they are mindful of (a) the parents' logical status as guide, (b) their intimate knowledge of the learner, (c) the influence parental status provides, and (d) the many chances for translating text material to everyday life. Most parents do much of their teaching in informal ways; they share their skills, hobbies, and other interests during everyday events and conversations. In fact, the importance of the shared family meal as a socializing and educational factor in children's lives is increasingly recognized, even as the occurrence of such a gathering is decreasing in many

families (Noddings, 2005). Other parents, however, have taken on increased responsibility for educating their children in a more direct and formal way by home schooling. Chapter 8 provides more detail on home learning and on home schooling.

Changes in Functions for the Twenty-First Century

As we have suggested, U.S. families are diverse and will continue to become more diverse in the foreseeable future. Roles for family members in the information age are still evolving, and certainly changes will continue to appear. Although one can only guess how different the typical family roles will be in another few decades, the family has shown itself to be a social form that is strong and adaptable (Berger, 2002).

Some changes in recent decades show increased momentum: (a) fathers are more involved in early education, and this benefits children; (b) mothers are more involved in sports and recreational activities, and this benefits children; and (c) extended families continue to decrease in contact and impact, and this does not benefit children (Bookman, 2004). Single parenting, which can be less advantageous for children, is likely to continue at a similar pace, particularly as single women become mothers by choice. School responsibilities are still increasing, but efforts to share and exchange responsibilities are more in evidence. (See Chapter 11 for particular models of cooperation.)

Children of the 21st century face a very different socializing environment than did children of previous generations. Less constancy is found in family matters, and more adults from outside the family are involved with children's experiences. Peer-group influences have expanded, to say nothing of the explosion in influence of the media and entertainment industries. All human-service personnel must work for more joint efforts among homes, schools, and communities, where well-reasoned decisions about roles will enable families to provide quality experiences and opportunities for their children.

CULTURAL PATTERNS AND FAMILY FUNCTIONS

The United States is a diverse country that encompasses an array of ethnic minority groups, and we thus find differences in the ways groups perform tasks, establish values, and relate to one another (McGoldrick, 2003). Different ethnic groups frequently have varying cultural features, but we also find multiple cultures within the larger groups (Erickson, 2005). Even among the same ethnic groups or culture, individuals vary enormously. Making for an interesting cultural mix in our nation, and one that professionals must study and reflect on.

Ethnic background refers to the shared history and culture, common values, behaviors, and/or other characteristics that encompass a sense of identity among its members (Banks & Banks, 2005). Although some ethnic groups, such as African Americans, can have distinguishing racial characteristics, other ethnic groups, such as Puerto Ricans, include people who belong to several different racial groups. In the case of Jewish Americans, their shared religious and cultural background, rather than their racial identities, creates a common bond.

Culture refers to the attitudes, traditions, beliefs, symbols, and customs held by a group of people. In the United States, there is an overarching core culture shared to a greater or lesser extent by all individuals and groups within the nation. Ideas related to equality, individualism, and opportunity for social mobility are examples of the core ideals of the culture of the United States. Within our country, there are also many smaller subcultures that reflect the components important to particular groups.

Ethnicity and culture frequently overlap; for example, many Native Americans continue to identify themselves by ethnic background and hold cultural beliefs separate from mainstream U.S. culture. We also find groups of people with similar ethnic backgrounds who differ culturally. For example, in English-speaking regions, Appalachian Americans are very different from Oregonian

Table 4–1 Major Ethnic Groups in the United States in 2005

Ethnic Group	Percentage of Population
African American	13
American Indian/ Alaskan Native	1
Asian/Pacific Islanders	5
European Americans	67
Hispanic Americans	14

Note: Persons of Hispanic ancestry may be of any race but are separated from other groups for this table.
Source: U.S. Bureau of the Census, Population Division Estimates, May, 2006.

ranchers or Connecticut commuters, even though they have similar roots. Their traditions, values, and attitudes place them in different cultural groups.

For simplification, we differentiate in this text between the European-American (White), English-speaking majority and non–European-American minorities in the United States, even though each of these delineations contains more than one ethnic group. Table 4–1 presents the proportions of these primary minority groups as of 2005. Although census charts include Hispanic Americans in other totals, our figure divides the population into Hispanic and non-Hispanic, then calculates totals from those two categories, to avoid counting Hispanic Americans twice.

Ethnic and cultural groups may have lifestyles, ways of communicating, and parenting practices that differ from the mainstream beliefs in the United States. Gender roles, social class, socioeconomic status, and parents' occupations are variables that may further impact a group's parenting style in unique ways, depending on the culture. Because of increasing diversity and overlap of cultures, it is essential for professionals to examine their own behavior and increase their awareness of other ways of living and communicating so that discussions with parents are carried out with respect. Professionals must keep in mind that individuals also vary greatly in their identification with their ethnic group, so one must take care not to stereotype people on the basis of their ethnic background.

Despite the differences in parenting practices that families from various cultures may employ, it is important to be aware that most parents do have similar goals for their children. Families want their offspring to live healthy lives, achieve some economic stability, and adhere to certain cultural values (Greenfield & Suzuki, 2001). Parents from different cultures may, however, vary in their expectations about development of competencies at different ages (Bornstein, 2001).

REFLECTION

Consider the different cultural groups you have encountered in your life. Then reflect on the underlying beliefs and values that families in the different groups evidenced. Can you describe how those values were manifested? See if you can set down some similarities and some differences that you note from this experiment.

Families want their offspring to live healthy lives, achieve economic stability, and adhere to certain cultural values.

The values of a culture are transmitted primarily through adult modeling, storytelling, directions and instructions given to children, pressures from the cultural group, and reinforcements for certain serendipitous actions that each child displays. So although the goals for children's development are similar, various cultural groups may rear their children quite differently. You must also bear in mind, however, that values and attitudes for many children are influenced more and more by the media, schools, and peers.

Parenting Features in Various Cultures

Child-raising practices in the United States changed considerably during the 20th century. We now find great variation from one cultural group to another within the society as a whole. The **socioeconomic status (SES)** of different families within one cultural group indicates that other differences exist as well.

For European-American groups, **behaviorism** was valued in the early years of the 20th century, and many parents at that time valued the principles of reinforcement and extinction, popularized by psychologists. A child-centered phase bloomed in the middle years of the century, but in recent decades, the swing has been toward a middle ground. Overall, contemporary European Americans are quite susceptible to current theories and depend less on folklore and tradition than did prior generations. Thus, cultural child-raising practices vary considerably over time. Although most minority cultures in the United States have retained their traditional child-raising practices to a greater extent than have European-American families, the proliferation of ideas in the mass media has altered some of their practices, as well.

Keeping all the complexity about approaches to parenting in mind, certain practices do tend to differ among various ethnic groups. It is essential to remember, however, that these are broad generalizations meant to suggest the range in approaches to caring for children. Although it is possible to find general characteristics of a group, individuals within the group may not conform to the generalizations. Further, socioeconomic level, education, and parental occupation are all important factors in determining an individual's child-rearing practices. The behaviors discussed in the following subsections are adapted from Berns, 2006; Greenfield and Suzuki, 2001; Janosik and Green, 1992; McDermott, 2001; McGoldrick, 2003; and Sadker and Sadker, 2005.

Infant Care. In the European-American tradition, where the development of autonomy and separate individual existence is an important parental goal, babies tend to be held less than they are in many other cultures and to be left to cry after all obvious physical needs have been tended to. In Native American society, however, babies and mothers have traditionally had continuous contact, and other groups, such as African Americans, Hispanic Americans, and various Asian-American cultures, tend to feed on demand and maintain very close physical connections between mothers and infants.

Cosleeping between parents and children is the norm in about two thirds of the world's cultures, and many minority and immigrant groups in the United States still hold onto cosleeping practices. Cosleeping of mother and infant are common in cultures that emphasize interdependence and family bonding above independence. Immigrants from many African countries, as well as Japanese Americans, Korean Americans, and other Asian groups, may cosleep or keep children in the same room with them through early childhood. Babies generally sleep alone in a room separate from their parents in the European-American family.

The European-American way of socializing children has been characterized as geared toward the goal of **technological intelligence**, whereas other groups have a goal of social intelligence (Greenfield & Suzuki, 2001). The emphasis in European-American families is on babies' manipulation and labeling of objects, whereas recent immigrants from Africa and Asian families seem to value positive interactions between babies and other people.

Physical Contact. Different cultural groups vary greatly in the amount and kind of physical contact that takes place between parents and their children. Affection is displayed in different ways, and physical punishment is used to a greater or lesser extent among various groups.

In many Asian-American homes, the physical closeness common between infants and parents becomes more restrained as children grow. In African American families, however, body contact is expected and encouraged throughout childhood. Less physical intimacy is found between parents and children in many European-American homes, although playful interaction is encouraged. Physical punishment is accepted in Hispanic families, but these families also tend to be very physically affectionate with their children. African American families are more likely to use physical punishment than Native American families, who avoid its use.

Family Role. In many cultures, the solidarity and importance of the family is primary; however, in others, children are encouraged to be more independent. In some groups, the nuclear family is paramount, whereas in others the extended family and kinship network are essential aspects of child rearing. **Patriarchal, matriarchal**, and shared leadership can be found in different cultures.

Interaction styles within the family reflect the roles expected of children. In many Hispanic families, for example, children are encouraged and expected to play with siblings rather than peers, whereas European-American families encourage their children to move beyond the family to establish other relationships. Asian-American families expect their children to be family oriented and to work hard for the support of the family. Much value is placed on respect for elders within the family in most Asian cultures. Many African American families also place great emphasis on children being part of an extended family of relatives and other adults who function as part of a large kinship network and all participate in raising the children.

Clearly, differences exist among ethnic groups in parenting practices, although we restate that these are general characteristics only. One can easily find homes displaying few of the practices noted in the preceding sections. As you go forward in your professional preparation, remain open to parenting that may be very different than the way you were raised or intend to raise your children. Parenting practices generally make sense in the context of the culture the parent is trying to preserve. Becoming familiar with different cultural practices by speaking openly and listening respectfully to parents from varying backgrounds will help you to understand how parenting fits in with the larger cultural goals of different groups.

The numerous decisions parents must make regarding the conflicting forces that surround all homes in busy America—media, entertainment, peer culture, and other attractions—can make it very challenging for parents to meet their responsibilities. Parenting is complex, and often factors other than a family's culture or ethnic background can influence child-rearing behaviors. Birth order of children; the child's age, temperament, or gender; parental experiences; and parent temperament will all have an impact on how a parent raises a particular child.

All parents, we find, use a mixture of child-rearing practices, and the impressions and the information from other sources will influence their behavior. Of course, how parents primarily interact with their children will have a significant impact on children's development. In the next section, we explore some of the variations in interaction styles within families that have been studied.

INTERACTION STYLES WITHIN FAMILIES

The child-rearing practices that parents employ influence children's behavior as we observe it in schools and communities, and researchers confirm the effect of parent actions on children's interactions with significant adults. The studies discussed in this section demonstrate connections between parenting and observed child behavior.

Baumrind's Classification

In Baumrind's (1968, 1966) classification, parenting styles were originally placed along a three-part continuum:

1. **Authoritative (democratic).** Controlling, demanding, but warm. Rational and receptive to child's communication.
2. **Permissive (child centered).** Noncontrolling, nondemanding, and relatively warm.
3. **Authoritarian (autocratic).** Detached, controlling, somewhat less warm.

Later work by Baumrind and others (Sclafani, 2004) resulted in a fourth parenting style being added as a refinement of the permissive style.

Table 4–2 illustrates the four parenting types.

In her classic study, Baumrind (1968) found that most children of authoritative parents showed independence and were socially responsible. They were also better able to regulate their emotions and behaviors, and they tended to have good tolerance for frustration as well as the ability to delay gratification. These traits translated into competence and resistance to substance abuse during adolescence, according to a later study (Baumrind,

Table 4–2   Four Parenting Types

	Accepting, Responsive	Rejecting, Unresponsive
Demanding, controlling	AUTHORITATIVE	AUTHORITARIAN
Undemanding, uncontrolling	PERMISSIVE-INDULGENT	PERMISSIVE-NEGLECTFUL

1995). Authoritative parents took into account their child's needs as well as their own before dealing with situations. The parents respected children's need to make their own decisions, yet they exerted control. They reasoned with their children and explained things more often than did other parents.

On the other hand, Baumrind found that those children of permissive parents frequently lacked social responsibility and often were not independent. She concluded that parents who looked at all behavior as natural and refreshing had unrealistic beliefs about young children's growth and socialization.

Baumrind found that children of authoritarian parents also showed little independence and were less socially responsible. Such parents feel that children need restraint and need to develop respect for authority, work, and traditional structure.

The authoritative style requires parents to guide, share activities, and to talk and listen to their children. The following summary illustrates the adult behaviors that produce Baumrind's authoritative style. To foster socially responsible and independent behavior in children, parents

- Serve as responsible and self-assertive models.
- Set standards where responsible behavior is rewarded and unacceptable behavior is punished.
- Are committed to the child in a way that is neither overprotective nor rejecting.
- Have high demands for achievement and conformity but are receptive to the child's rational demands.
- Provide secure but challenging and stimulating environments for creative and rational thinking.

Maccoby and Martin (1983) reviewed literature on parenting styles at a later point and in general supported the findings of Baumrind. Clark (1983) also produced similar findings. His **"sponsored independence" style** is consistent with Baumrind's authoritative style. Later studies measuring the long-term effects of the authoritative style produced more evidence that it engenders positive adolescent behavior (Holmbeck, Paikoff, & Brooks-Gunn, 1995; Steinberg, 1991). Recent research on adolescent development indicates that feeling loved and cared for by parents continues to be of great importance for young people (Steinberg & Silk, 2002).

One caveat is needed concerning this research. Baumrind used White, middle-class parents in her study, whereas later, in their replication studies, Maccoby and Martin (1983) found that Baumrind's conclusions did not always translate directly for poor, minority, and single-parent families. Clark (1983), however, found that the authoritative or sponsored independence behaviors in Mexican American and African American homes often made the difference between success and failure for minority children in schools. As far as parenting in a contemporay society is concerned, the authoritative style of parenting seems to be most effective for preparing children for school expectations as well for later positive outcomes (Noddings, 2005).

Bernstein's Work

Language is a primary avenue through which a child learns to understand and function in the world. Children tend to develop language on a predictable developmental scale, but different parental language styles and interactions affect children's socialization and literacy development. Bernstein's (1972) classic study of family language patterns produced two general linguistic codes used in many homes. He termed these very different patterns *restricted* and *elaborated*. The codes reflect two quite different styles: the **position-oriented family** and the **person-oriented family**.

Position-oriented families use a restricted code, and the family role system is positional, or object oriented and present oriented. In contrast, person-oriented families use an elaborated code, and the family role system is personal, or person oriented and future oriented. The following example illustrates this concept:

Laima Druskis / PH College

The authoritative style of parenting seems to be most effective for preparing children for school expectations.

Members have little choice, and roles are assigned according to family position. According to Bernstein, their communication is object oriented and present oriented. Aspects of **restricted language code** appear, characterized by syntactically simple sentences and concrete meanings. The parents communicate one thing only to the daughter—to obey a single command. There is no explanation, and sentences are simple and direct.

The open quality of the mother and son in the person-oriented family, on the other hand, permits discretion in learner performance. Communication in the open system includes judgments and reasons, and children learn to cope with abstractions and ambiguity. The **elaborated language code** accommodates this type of content. The mother chats with her son about the crosswalk, explaining what is happening. She engages the child in the decision making. Yet, when it appears that he may advance into the crosswalk too soon, she, too, physically restrains the child for his safety.

Teachers must know that children from a closed or position-oriented family must depend on the school and the larger community to help them in acquiring elaborated language. As a teacher, you can become a vital communication model for children from families using restricted codes, as can other children. Older children may often help their teacher communicate with new children not familiar with school language and culture. We find this situation in the following vignette.

In the space of three minutes, two attractive family groups approached a traffic-light-controlled crosswalk at a busy intersection. One mother and her preschool son approached hand in hand, talking freely. Within a few feet of the crosswalk, the mother leaned down toward her son and said, "See the light there? It's red, and we have to stop. See the cars still coming this way? We need to stay right back here, 'til we get the flashing walk light, OK? You watch and tell me when to go." When the boy continued to advance into the crosswalk, his mother tightened her grip on his hand and said more firmly, "Stop here. It's not safe yet."

The second family, a mother, father, and little girl, approached the crosswalk and stopped. Suddenly, the mother noticed the child, who was slightly ahead, start toward the crosswalk and yelled, "Stay here!" The girl continued to advance, and the mother screamed again, "Stay here, I said!" The father leaped and yanked the girl back beside him. "Just stand!" the mother said, and the family waited silently for the signal to change—bodies rigid, the parents holding tightly to the child.

The second family here appears to be more position oriented and has a prescribed role system.

Ms. Dansky, a White teacher, wasn't successful in getting Philip, an African American five-year-old just entering school, to join other children in a circle. She had used a polite invitation to call all the children. When Philip didn't move, she gave a sterner and more specific command to Philip. Then Greg, a seasoned African American eight-year-old, raised his hand and asked quietly, "You want me to get him for you, Ms. D?" Upon receiving a polite "Yes, thank you," he yelled to Philip, "Boy, get yo'r butt over here, yu' hear!" When Philip came immediately to sit beside Greg, Greg leaned to him and continued, "When she say, 'Boys and girls join me,' she mean 'Come here.' And when she say, 'Philip, it's time for circle!' she mean, 'Get yo'r butt here (pats a spot beside himself) NOW!' " (Seefeldt & Barbour, 1998, p. 340)

Greg had learned not only the correct language patterns of the school but also the politeness rules. Then he used language and tonal patterns familiar to Philip, and he skillfully switched between the two patterns to explain what their teacher's words meant. One can appreciate the advantages that elaborated codes have in the broadening requirements of the information age. Research has shown that preschool children who engaged in language with adults that went beyond the here and now to include the past, future, imagined events, and abstract ideas had a larger vocabulary on school entry and performed better on comprehension tests up until sixth grade (Bardige, 2005). Clearly, the languge environment within which a child is brought up will have long-term consequenses.

Hart and Risley Studies

Hart and Risley (1995) also concentrated on language development and demonstrated that quality of parenting and richness of linguistic environment are not necessarily bound with economic status or ethnicity. In their study of homes representing three SES levels, they discussed the linkages between young children's language development and meaningful experiences. The longitudinal study convinces us that the type and amount of interaction between parents and children results in significant differences, irrespective of SES.

According to the study, the quality of interactions in everyday parenting will center on the following five variables:

1. *Amount and richness of vocabulary.* Parents deliberately use various terms, labels, and expressions and model their use when talking. "Yes, these are all clothes—pants, shirts, socks."

2. *Sentence usage.* Parents make a connection between objects and events when responding to children. "Yes, it is a doll, and it's Cindy's, so you need to give it back."

3. *Discourse function.* Quality of utterances used is important when parents give choices or directions to prompt child behavior. "Did you remember to hang your coat?"

4. *Adjacency condition.* This variable centers on the relation between parent and child behavior when the parent listens or initiates for child. Child: "Soup's good!" Parent models by: "Yes, it's delicious, isn't it?"

5. *Valence of communication.* The emotional tone given to interactions is important, whether the parent tries to be pleasant or not. Simply smiling and repeating a child's word: "That's right, juice!" has positive valence.

The positive dimension of this study shows us that parenting behaviors leading to increased child performance can be learned and practiced. Hart and Risley (1995) assert that parents who purposely concentrate on the meaningful differences are being "social partners" with their children.

In a follow-up study, Hart and Risley (1999) suggested that the most important aspect of parent talk to young children is its amount. They learned from their study that parents who talk as they go about their daily activities expose their children to more than 1,000 words per hour. Even more important, however, is the way that conversation between parent and child during the first three years contributes to their relationship and builds a foundation of analytic and symbolic competencies that will serve them for a lifetime. Spending time talking together is the most important way parents can help their child learn to speak and listen, and, of course, speaking and listening are the foundations of literacy.

Summary of Interaction Styles

With parents' busy work schedules and the amount of television viewing by the entire family, substantive conversation—which does not include directions, commands, or reprimands—between parents and children is becoming rare in many homes. Ideally, adults would take time to talk to their young children, focusing on things that the child has done, seen, or heard and using experiences with picture books to move conversation beyond the here and now. Although teachers and community workers alone cannot compensate for the shortage of meaningful parent–child interactions, a quality child-care or school experience can help children develop larger vocabularies and strong functional language (Bardige, 2005).

No two families are exactly alike, and parents have diverse ways of managing. The various features of parenting make family behaviors very complex and difficult to understand. We can examine general patterns of parenting, though, and we can relate these patterns to children's behavior. The investigators previously noted, Baumrind, Clark, Maccoby, and Martin, found that neither extreme of the parenting pattern—referred to respectively as *permissive* and authoritarian—is ideal for children. In his conditional sequence model of disciplinary responses, Larzelere (2001) reaffirmed the need for combining reason and discipline in effective parenting. Clearly, a combination of love and limits appears to be most beneficial.

Always remember that parenting practices are influenced by more than cultural background and interaction styles. As professionals, you must also be alert to the influence of family size, family SES, levels of stress in the home, and different community characteristics surrounding the children with whom you work.

EXPERIENCES OF FAMILIES

The life experiences of children within their families establish a background for their performance and their contributions in their school and community. What children see, hear, smell, taste, and do creates a foundation for their communication patterns, perceptual styles, and modes of thinking. Within the context of learning about life, children begin to comprehend messages and understand their place in the world (Lareau, 2003; Ramsey, 2004). Likewise, children's understanding of encountered images frequently depends on explanations and connections made by nearby adults.

Culture, economic, and experiential background make a significant difference in how a child learns, communicates, and participates. In

addition to basic nurturing, family histories of interactions, experiences, and practices will enhance or detract from children's development potential (Scarf, 1997). When stress or problems arise, some families are **resilient** and display an ability to deal with changes and modify problems; others are ill equipped and cannot cope (McKenry & Price, 2005). Some adults even lean on their own children for support (Garbarino, Dubrow, Kostelny, & Pardo, 1998). Such resilience or its absence derives from many aspects of family experience. The communication styles and parenting practices noted earlier have an effect, but we should also consider the skill levels of parents and the type and degree of family mobility.

Skill Levels and Experience

Most parents and caregivers have extensive knowledge of their world—how to operate within society and how to manage their everyday lives. Passing on wisdom and skills is one of the pleasures of parenting, and some parents impart this knowledge in particularly beneficial ways.

Homemakers know their living quarters and what it takes to live in a particular home. Parents have experiences in food shopping, preparation, and serving, and some have added skills with nutrition and food presentation. Involving children in food management can be realized easily in all homes and contributes a basic foundation for healthy living.

Using tools to build or repair household objects is common in many homes. Some parents have woodworking or metal-finishing skills and perhaps have home workbenches. Almost all parents have interesting experiences involving tools, and many take pleasure in their use. Adults can easily transfer these skills to interested children through demonstration (Voss, 1993), home projects, or children's books, such as *The New How Things Work* (Macaulay, 1998).

Some families invest a great deal of time in gardening for relaxation or for summer vegetable acquisition. The growing of green things fascinates most youngsters, and it is the beginning of a basic science that children encounter during their school years. A child's home is a nice place to learn about gardening, and any growing project provides a healthy venue for discussion and interaction between adult and child. An example of "gardening" learning was demonstrated when our neighbor Melissa involved her three-year-old son, in a very natural way, with her regular gardening, singing, and reading activities.

A child's yard is a nice place to learn about gardening.

Having just received Inch by Inch (Mallett, 1995) from the community's Growing Up Reading Project, Melissa and her son Adam immediately opened the new treasure and looked at the end pages, with pictures of vegetables. Adam saw a picture of a carrot and exclaimed, "That's a carrot." "Yes," said Melissa, "we've just gathered those from our garden, haven't we? See any more vegetables we have?" Adam thumbed through and found a huge beet. "Beet, yum, yum!" He turned to the end pages again and with a scooping motion began to "pick up" the imaginary vegetables, named them, and pretended to stuff them into his mouth. In the next few months, Melissa and Adam often played the "Garden Song" tape that accompanied this new book and sang the song together. It was a delight to see Melissa and Adam in the garden together the next spring, weeding. Adam trotted along the rows singing, "Inch by inch . . . make my garden grow . . . inch by inch, make my garden grow." Then he stopped to pull a "weed" and exclaimed, "A carrot! No, a beet! Yum, yum."

Many games feature family interactions, and by using games as entertainment, parents can provide children with involvement in group activities, experience in strategy development and planning, positive use of aggressiveness, and practice in cooperative activities. Games are fundamentally simulations of life experiences, and children with extensive experience with various games internalize approaches for living and considerable amounts of strategy for facing interactive situations (Jones, 1988). Many families have instituted a family game night, when they gather together to enjoy cards, board games, and time together.

Storytelling plays an important part in children's growth. A large part of language development comes through stories. In families where stories are used for recreating family history, for entertainment, or as examples, listeners grow in appreciation of language, their culture, and their family's experiences and identity. In some cultures, life lessons are passed on through such stories and connect children with their cultural history. One very important manifestation is the story in book form. In a book, the story belongs to someone else, but it gives much the same satisfaction to the young child.

Parents' skill levels in these and other aspects of daily life can and should be passed on to children in the family. All community life and school programs must reinforce these practices. Given the right conditions, home management and repair, gardening projects, game playing, storytelling, and other family-oriented experiences represent important resources and a worthy heritage for parents to relay to their children. Most parents are not skilled instructors but can be very successful in teaching home activities and projects informally. When a caregiver is engaged with a single child on a topic of mutual interest, most classroom "teaching" demands are not present. Instructor and student can go directly to the task of transferring a particular skill to the learner. Most parents are successful at this natural process, and most yearn to pass on their knowledge when an opportunity presents itself.

REFLECTION

Reflect on some of the activities and special skills your parents possessed and that you learned to do. Did they ever visit your school classroom to share their skills? If so, how did you react to that experience

Mobility of Families

Another feature of experience that affects children's emotional and academic progress is the mobility that families have in and around their community and farther afield. Americans move more than people in other countries, and moves frequently place families further from their kin and other members of their social network. On the average, between 16% and 20% of our population moves in a year (McFalls, 1998), but a great deal of that relocating is as young adults move out of the home for work, education, or marriage. We find, however, that 23% of the persons who moved in 2000 were children under five (U.S. Bureau of the Census, 2002a), and this has an impact. Studies of military families who move on the average of every three years indicated that many of the affected children gave up trying to form close friendships (Karpowitz, 2001).

High levels of residential mobility can intensify social problems for both adults and children—if the move is accompanied by significant change in the quality of home life. African Americans and Hispanic Americans move more often than Whites because their residences are often rented (McFalls, 1998). For most relocating families, mobility comes in two forms: forced and voluntary.

Forced mobility for families may be associated with migrant work, homelessness, coping with unemployment, gentrification and resulting higher rents, or escaping hostile actions or trouble. Many children also move after a divorce and go on to experience the difficulty of going back and forth between two homes. Forced mobility (apart from job-related transfers) is always a reaction to undesirable conditions and contributes to erratic lifestyles for parents and their children. Isolation is implied, for forced mobility signifies that a family lacks connections or community linkages that could provide help. Whatever the conditions, a family's forced move to a new environment presents different but rarely positive learning experiences for children. Little pleasure comes with a transfer from one area to another under duress.

On the other hand, voluntary travel and relocation, local or distant, frequently connotes vacation time or an improved socioeconomic situation for the family. Both local travel and long-distance travel involve the positive expectation of new encounters. Arranging for the travel is a learning experience. Getting to a destination involves a certain amount of investigation, map reading, negotiating transportation schedules or checking driving requirements, and anticipating difficulties. Family members learn together, and these social and educational values are important. Transnational or international travel brings a family in touch with other cultures, as travelers need to adapt to new conditions, different foods, and a different sense of space. Such travel is expansive, and families gain psychic income and social capital.

The ways that families exploit surroundings, relationships, agencies, and even challenges show facets of their child-rearing practices and socializing acumen. Some families use their experience with great facility, whereas others do not. Such use of experience may be a function of SES, as economically privileged families have the means to provide the benefits of local and long-distance travel (Coleman,

Illness is a stressor in families.

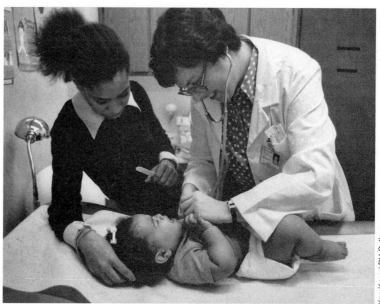

Ken Karp / PH College

1966; Jencks et al., 1972). We also find instances of modestly endowed families enriching their children's lives through carefully developed experiences (Lareau, 2003; Monroe, 1997), however, and some affluent families neglect the need for family interaction and experience and fill their children's lives with sports, cultural, and other activities in a concerted pattern of cultivation (Laureau, 2003).

OTHER INFLUENCES ON PARENTING

Parenting needs to be examined and analyzed in the context of culture and community. As noted earlier, numerous variables affect family life and may be external factors of community and environment as well as internal factors of cultural background, family demographics, and economics. Following is a brief discussion of some of these other dimensions.

Child-Care Arrangements

With extended work schedules for most American families, a huge number of parents now must cope daily with requirements for temporary care of

their children. At one time, when many mothers were homemakers, child care was merged with running the household. Mothers attended their preschool-age children, welcomed their older children home from school, and supervised most at-home activities.

At the present time, however, the situation is far different: Welfare reform has increased the number of parents in the workforce, single-parent and dual-income families grow every year, and fewer extended family members are available to care for children. More than 65% of mothers with children under six are in the workforce (Children's Defense Fund, 2001). This means that a huge number of young children are in some type of child-care arrangement for part of every workday. These arrangements include center-based and family child care as well as less formal situations, such as babysitters or care by slightly older siblings.

Infant, toddler, and preschool child care and after-school care for older children are now facts of life for most communities. As more families, formerly on welfare, enter the workforce, the demands for quality care for children will intensify. Many child-care programs have waiting lists for children who need this service, and added requests will intensify the problem. Although a number of schools now operate their own after-school care programs, the need for care outstrips availability. Furthermore, the quality and costs of care are quite variable—adding another dimension to the problem for parents seeking care for their children.

Good child care, once found, solves many problems for parents. Supportive caregivers become an extension of the family and often develop strong affectional ties to the child and parents. These caregivers know the child well and can offer parents advice and reassurance as issues and concerns arise. This can be especially helpful to single parents. Child care also fosters connections between parents and other families with children, allowing them to develop a larger support network. Knowing their child is well cared for relieves parents of stress and anxiety and allows them to do their jobs. Child care offers benefits to both children and parents. We consider the topic of child care more fully in Chapter 5.

Life-Changing Events as Family Stressors

The circumstances of modern life have led to an increase in stress in children and their parents (McKenry & Price, 2005). Separation, divorce, chronic illness, and death of a parent can negatively affect children's feelings of security and subject them to new patterns of family life. Living within a blended family, a single parent household, or with parents who travel frequently also contributes to the stress level of all involved. These circumstances are difficult for all families, but children and parents who live in poverty or suffer economic setbacks face added challenges that can contribute to additional stress (Bartholomae & Fox, 2005).

Stressors resulting from changes in family life and economic difficulties can be challenging for every family; some families, though, through coping skills and resources, are better able than others to handle problems. Although a few stressors are self-inflicted, many are unavoidable or are developed through conflicts and economic pressures and through racist, elitist, and sexist practices.

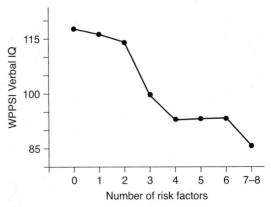

Figure 4–3   Effects of Multiple Risks on Preschool Intelligence
Source: From "Intelligence Quotient on Scores of Four-Year-Old Children: Social-Environmental Risk Factors," by A. Sameroff et al., 1987, *Pediatrics, 79,* 347. Copyright 1987 by the American Academy of Pediatrics. Reproduced by permission from *Pediatrics.*

Accumulated stressors lead to at-risk situations, and policy makers, educators, and others must be mindful of this possibility. The effects of risk on the intelligence measurements of preschool children (Sameroff, Seifer, Barocas, Zax, & Greenspan, 1987) are instructive. As Figure 4–3 shows, most children seem able to cope with low levels of risk, but an accumulation of more than two risk factors jeopardizes their mental development. The message is clear: We must either prevent or compensate for accumulated risk factors (Stanford & Yamamoto, 2001).

Before ending our discussion of family functioning, we review in the following paragraphs the concerns and risk factors that cause stress in families. Bear in mind, however, that strategies exist to deflect or accommodate stress arising from these factors. Helping children and their parents cope with stress is becoming an increasingly important role for teachers and community-service providers (Scully, 2003).

Separation, Divorce, and Reconfigured Families. As noted earlier, divorce has become common for U.S. families in recent decades, and although the divorce rate is no longer increasing, at the present time, first marriages in the United States have a 47% chance of breaking up, and second marriages a 49% chance (Pann & Crosbie-Burnett,

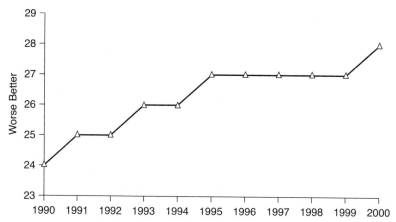

Figure 4–4   Percentage of Families with Children Headed by a Single Parent

Note: Percentage of families with children headed by a single parent is the percentage of all families with their own children under 18 living in the household, headed by a person—men or women—without a spouse present in the home. "Own children" include never-married persons under age 18 who are the sons or daughters of the householder's (head of the household). The householder's stepchildren and adopted children also are counted as "own children."

Source: Kids Count Data Book, The Annie E. Casey Foundation (2003), *www.aecf.org; http://www.kidscount.org*

2005). Consequently, more than 40% of American children will experience the effects of divorce, with nearly 90% placed in the physical custody of their mothers (although increasingly legal custody tends to be shared between parents). Of the children born in the 1990s, more than half will have spent some or all of their childhood in a single-parent household (Anderson, 2003) (see Figure 4–4).

Liberalization of divorce laws in most states permits couples to separate more easily and more amicably, and although parents may adjust reasonably well to a divorce, many children of divorced parents tend to have long-term difficulties (Wallerstein, Lewis, & Blakeslee, 2000). Separation changes all roles in a family and alters the way a family functions. Responsibilities for the custodial parent increase dramatically, particularly with regard to child-care arrangements. There are more household tasks to care for, and financial obligations are heavier than before. Complicating the situation for children is the likelihood of one or more of their parents remarrying (65% of divorced women and 75% of divorced men remarry within four years). Even more likely are the nonmarital

short-lived cohabitations of either parent. Finally, one third of American children today will become part of a stepfamily (Greene, Anderson, Hetherington, Forgatch, & DeGarmo, 2003).

Financial Aspects of Divorce. Mothers are most often given custody of children in a divorce, but this can have dire consequences for the resulting single-parent family (Fine, Ganong, & Demo, 2005). Casper and Bianchi (2002) reported that the poverty rate for single-mother households was 38.7%, compared to a rate of 6.9% in two-parent homes. It is a fact in the United States that women in the workforce earn less than men do, and even though child support judgments are made in divorce cases, fathers frequently do not pay, leaving mothers to assume full financial responsibility for their children. Casper and Bianchi (2002) stressed the financial inequities after divorce: Divorce improves the economic position of men but reduces that of women and children left with their mothers.

Other Consequences of Divorce. Increased work hours for **custodial parents** are typical after divorce, and decreased social interaction with children results (Anderson, 2003). This means less parenting.

Children in the home will face increased responsibilities, less time with either parent, and less emotional support after separation. A serious long-range effect of divorce is the removal of marriage models for children affected.

Behavioral changes for youngsters often result from divorce and separation. A considerable amount of research shows that the negative effects for children of divorce are sadness, anger, fear, aggressiveness, anxiety, and disobedience (Hetherington & Kelly, 2002; Schwartz & Kaslow, 1997; Wallerstein, 2001). Children who have positive, nurturing relationships with both parents, low levels of parental and family conflict, and adequate economic resources, however, seem to adjust better to the diverse forms of family life that occur after a divorce (Fine, Ganong, & Demo, 2005).

For many children, these diverse family forms may include living in a single-parent home, moving between the homes of both parents as part of shared-custody arrangements, or becoming part of a step-family. All of these situations can pose challenges to children, but all can have strengths when compared to a predivorce situation: happier environments, better custodial parent–child relationships, more commitment to a wider community, and better-run households. Hetherington and Kelly (2002), in their review of hundreds of clients, found that most single-parent households do provide the nurturance that children need, despite the challenges. Negative stereotypes continue to affect single parents, step-parents, and their children (Anderson, 2003; Greene et al., 2003), however. For example, teachers have a tendency to assume that problems in school are related to the situation in the home. In the foreseeable future, large numbers of young and school-age children will experience their parents' separation, divorce, and remarriage. Therefore, school personnel and community workers must find ways to accommodate the extra needs these individuals will have.

Support groups are available to help families through the initial period of adjustment after divorce, which is always one or more years. Children's literature, when sensitively read and discussed, can also help children who are caught in a family upheaval. See Appendix 1 for recommended titles.

Dual-Income Families. Management of household life in the dual-income home can produce stress at times (Fraenkel, 2003). As parents try to balance the potentially competing demands of jobs and child rearing, many find the conflict between caring for children and employment physically and psychologically draining. The stress is particularly pronounced for women who despite their increased participation in the work force, still have primary responsibility for children in the majority of families. Research indicates, however, that it is the nature and intensity of the work and family responsibilities, rather than employment or parenthood per se, that determine the impact of parents working outside the home (Fredriksen-Goldsen & Scharlach, 2001).

Although a double income enables a family to enjoy a higher standard of living, it has drawbacks, such as less time for family interaction, tighter schedules, increased dependence on child care, and fewer choices in recreation. Statistics show that 67% of children living with both parents have mothers and fathers in the workforce, and the trend increases each year (U.S. Bureau of the Census, 2001). In addition, more than 7% of American working men and women hold two or more jobs (U.S. Bureau of the Census, 1998b), which could mean a total of four jobs for some dual-income families. Time for family interactions is, of course, minimal in such situations.

Poverty. Poverty restricts many positive experiences for children and their families, because financial resources dictate quality of education, housing, diet, clothing, and amount of health care, to say nothing of entertainment and recreation. Most of all, poverty lays a veil of despair on poor or near-poor families—a group disproportionately composed of single-parent families and families of color—and aspirations and a sense of self-worth become hard to elevate (Dodson & Bravo, 2005). Of all the stressors present in U.S. families, poverty is perhaps the greatest, and it is expanding in the lower-income brackets (refer again to Figure 3–5 in Chapter 3).

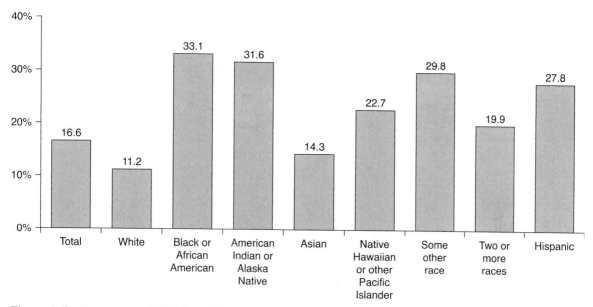

Figure 4–5 Percentage of Children Below Poverty by Race and Hispanic Origin
Source: Population Reference Bureau, analysis of data from the U.S. Census Bureau, 2000 census summary, 2003.

Children's Defense Fund (2005) findings show that in 2004 more than 13 million, or almost 17.8% of U.S. children under 18 were living below the poverty line. In addition, the record demonstrated that poverty in the United States has increased each year since 2000. This is a disturbing reversal of the gains made from 1992 to 2000, when close to four million children were lifted out of poverty. Even more disturbing is the growing number of children who live in extreme poverty, defined as an income of less than $7,610 per year for a family of three. Poverty rates among minority groups are disproportionate to their populations. While the poverty rate for Whites was 14.4%, that for Hispanics was 28.9%, and for African Americans 33.2% (Children's Defense Fund, 2005). Figure 4–5 gives a picture of American children living in poverty.

Poor families are burdened with the challenges of survival, and their lives are punctuated with stress brought on by lack of money. Family members are frequently ill, they sustain injury more often, and they encounter hostility from numerous sources. Lives become saturated with despair, and each new plight adds to family discouragement (Dodson & Bravo, 2005; Laureau, 2003). The buildup of stress in poor families is extensive. Housing that is affordable to families near or below the poverty line tends to be in crime- and drug-ridden areas, where children and many adults lead lives of sheer terror. Cramped living and meager diets result in illnesses that precipitate even more stress. Not surprisingly, children raised in poverty are more likely to become teen parents and as adults will earn less and have more unemployment than those raised with higher incomes. They are also more likely to raise their own children in poverty, continuing the cycle.

Reversing the state of poverty in the United States requires strong community action and large investments in federal, state, and private aid to provide job training, child care, adequate housing, and health facilities to help rebuild families in besieged areas of society. Recommendations outlined in *The State of America's Children* (Children's Defense Fund, 2005) serve as a good starting point. Leach (1994), in *Children First*, reemphasized this challenging prescription, and Schorr (2002) suggested ways in which neighborhoods and communities can help families.

Illness. Illness also is a stressor in families. When a family member becomes injured or ill, numerous interaction patterns must cease or be modified. Family communication can be limited, and attention to those who are not ill is lessened. Realignment of the priorities in family functioning is a consequence of long-term illness. Illness of a wage earner has even greater consequences for the family. Furthermore, if inadequate health care is the cause (which is the situation for one seventh of the nation's population), this particular stress gives rise to others. When a child in the family becomes seriously injured or is chronically ill, parents must develop coping skills to adjust to the needs for medical care and the other issues that arise. (Lee & Guck, 2001).

Children with Disabilities. Caring for a child with a disability presents unique challenges to families and often leads to an increase in the families' stress level (Lancaster, 2001). Although some disabilities are evident from birth or early infancy, others, such as learning disabilities and emotional problems, may not show up until the child attends school. Not only do parents have to struggle with their own acceptance of the disability and the attendant shattered expectations, guilt, anger, and parental conflict, but they must also expend great time and energy on the child. Just getting the child's disability identified can be a long process, and determining treatment, obtaining needed services, and following up on the child's progress are also time consuming. Teachers and community-service personnel play an important support role for families parenting children with disabilities.

Everyday Stress

They are not life-changing events, as the stressors discussed in the previous section, but the hassles of everyday life present another source of stress for families. These day-to-day common annoyances, although relatively minor, are a more frequent and continuous form of stress. Included in this category are the difficulties associated with commut-

ing, balancing work and family life on a daily basis, minor childhood illnesses that require parents to make unexpected schedule changes and arrangements, and the myriad other stressors that occur as a factor of daily life. Research indicates that these everyday hassles can be even more important determinates of family stress than the major life events discussed previously (Helms & Demo, 2005).

As expected, the way parents respond to these everyday stressors determines how much they contribute to the family stress level. Some parents are able to buffer their children from the everyday hassles of life, but others are not. Factors such as socioeconomic status, perceptions of the severity of the hassles, parent temperament, and responses to the ongoing, relentless nature of caring for a family and home all play into the way a family will adapt and cope to the stresses of everyday life.

MEETING THE CHALLENGES OF PARENTING

Despite the well-known stressors associated with parenting, most adults find that caring and providing for children is rewarding and pleasurable. In addition, although families may function in a variety of ways and possess different attributes, most families, given reasonable conditions, develop along healthy lines and rear children who respect a home culture and get ready to meet the world. Though most are independent, others may at times need the help and support of friends, community, and other services.

At times, stresses are too great, and family dysfunction may result. If this occurs, professional aid via the community is the first level of response. It may be possible that school professionals can help by advocating for the family, talking with family members, counseling the family, and listening to family members to show support. Recall the dramatic graph Sameroff et al. (1987) (Figure 4–3) provided. We can demonstrate the likelihood that problems will emerge if risk factors continue unresolved.

Do you ever feel stress? And are you aware of any strategies you use to relieve it? Are these positive strategies for you? Do you know about community resources to help you and others understand and practice stress-reduction techniques such as deep breathing, meditation, and muscle relaxation?

Abuse and Neglect

Abuse and neglect of children can be one outcome of unrelieved stress. Because families in poverty are in dire straits and services are meager, abuse rises in concert with the frustrations and anxieties of needy families (Bigner, 2006; Gersten, 1992; Pipher, 1996). Abuse also occurs at higher SES levels; it is not restricted to the poor. Neglect, and physical and sexual abuse occurs at all levels of society. The Children's Defense Fund (2001) stated that between two million and three million abuse cases are reported each year, with about one third of the cases substantiated. Neglect is the most prevalent form of child abuse, with more than half the children mistreated or suffering from neglect. More than one third of the victims were physically or sexually abused, and one fourth of the children were mistreated in more than one way. Despite these high numbers, caseworkers assert that only a small fraction of abusive situations is ever reported (Osofsky, 1998).

Abuse is insidious and continues in the fabric of families for generations—too many abused children become abusive adults or victims of other abusers later in their lives (Gelles & Cavanaugh, 2005). Abuse is an infection that colors the feelings and attitudes of families, and it destroys normal relationships for the entire family. Research has indicated that parent education can help to break the cycle of abuse and neglect. Interventions that help reduce parents' stress levels, increase their understanding of child development and their social coping skills, and assist them in developing supportive networks are most effective in reducing and preventing child maltreatment (Reppucci, Britner, & Woolard, 1997).

Supporting Families

Children and families all are resilient to some degree. We find situations that appear depressing and even disastrous, but many children survive intact and view the traumatic events in their lives, such as death, divorce, and hardship, with objectivity (Levine & Ion, 2002) and, later, even with humor (Buchwald, 1994). This demonstrates that most children are not so fragile and impressionable that they must succumb to their problems. As a teacher or community service provider, you may be the person who helps a child overcome their difficulties through your support and belief in the child. You must also be mindful that as long as reasonably positive experiences and interventions punctuate the lives of developing children, their outlook and perspective can be ultimately optimistic.

Teachers need to know their students' families as well as their situations, for teachers are in a unique position to explain community to families,

Patricia A. Scully

Children need unconditional love and affection from their parents.

and vice versa. It is imperative for school personnel to take time to learn about family functioning to find out about values, ways of doing things, and methods of care that work for them. When you obtain this information, you may then find ways of integrating schoolwork with the home situation.

What is a competent family? The competent family does not require affluence, extensive education, or a particular setting. It will, however, provide for what Brazelton and Greenspan (2000) described as "the irreducible needs of children." In order to help their children grow and flourish, competent parents meet the following six needs:

1. Ongoing nurturing relationships
2. Physical protection, safety, and regulation
3. Experiences tailored to individual differences
4. Developmentally appropriate experiences
5. Limit setting, structure, and expectations
6. Stable, supportive communities and cultural continuity.

Children need unconditional love and affection from their parents. They also require the security that comes from a safe, familiar environment, a consistent daily routine, and the knowledge that adults expect certain behaviors from them. When planning experiences for their children, parents must consider their children's unique temperaments, learning styles, and interests. Further, parents who understand stages of child development are better able to plan experiences that are compatible with their child's level. Children also need parents who will guide their behavior in ways that will help them make responsible choices, cooperate with others, and develop self-confidence. Both parents and children need the support of the larger community for optimal development.

SUMMARY AND REVIEW

The nurturance of a parent or other loving adult is the most significant factor in a child's healthy growth and development. Despite changes in the role of parents over the years, they continue to provide major eco-

nomic and emotional support for their children, as well as experiences, education, and socialization.

Different styles of interaction exist within families, and various cultural groups may have parenting practices that differ from one another. Research shows that the authoritative parent style, characterized by a warm emotional tone coupled with high expectations and open communication, usually produces better results for most parents and their children than does either a permissive or an authoritarian pattern.

Experience defines a family's quality of life, and all families pass on their culture and attempt to instruct children in profitable ways. Some families have natural gifts for instructing the young about tasks, thereby giving them added command of their lives. Mobility is one avenue for enhancing experience; another is manual work skills.

Economic circumstances, life-changing events, and everyday stressors all impact family functioning. Handling such stressors is a mark of a family's ability to cope with the major and minor stressors that are a part of life. All families encounter stress, but processing and managing it appropriately are hallmarks of stable families. Competent families are those that are able to provide for children's physical and psychological health, promote their growth, and shape their children's behavior to meet socially accepted norms. Poverty can undermine parents' best efforts to provide for their children, and unfortunately the rates of poverty for children are increasing in the new millennia.

SUGGESTED ACTIVITIES AND QUESTIONS

1. Name three ways that families provide nurturance for their children. Speculate about how you see them manifested in one child with whom you work.

2. Consider the home environments of children appearing in the vignettes in the text to this point. Deduce the parenting style of each family and compare to your own upbringing.

3. Select two families represented in your classroom or community setting. What appear to be the social and cultural influences affecting them? Are there differences? What do you infer about the parenting practices in these families?

4. Observe a parent interacting with his or her child in a library. Observe a similar situation in a supermarket. What circumstances do you think account for any differences you see?

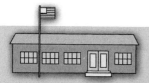

APPLYING THESE CONCEPTS TO YOUR WORK WITH CHILDREN AND FAMILIES

The parenting behaviors you have just read about are, of course, going to have an impact on the children with whom you will work. Because there is a broad spectrum of parenting behavior and competence, you are going to find yourself working with an equally wide range of attitudes, behaviors, and skills coming from these diverse homes:

- Although research indicates that the authoritative style of parenting provides the best outcomes for children, some families will be raising their children using other approaches. Think about how you will help their children adapt to a classroom situation based on authoritative principles. List some specific strategies you can use to help children develop autonomy.

- Remember that many family arrangements are possible and that most can be productive. How

will you seek to understand the positive aspects of different lifestyles and avoid judgmental behavior? Discuss with your classmates any ways that you and they have been recipients of stereotyping and discuss the ensuing feelings.

- As you work with communities and families in any of several social settings, you will come face-to-face with the problems and stressors mentioned in this chapter that confront so many individuals. Think about how you will seek to understand and respond—your responses may be expressions of empathy, guidance to community services, or even reports to authorities about abuse or illness.

- Familiarize yourself with the social agencies, tutoring services, after-school programs, or other services in your community that some children and families may need.

RESOURCES

Books

Bigner, J. J. (2002). *Parent–child relations: An introduction to parenting* (6th ed.). Upper Saddle River, NJ: Merrill/Prentice Hall.

Bornstein, M. H. (2002). *Handbook of parenting: Volume 1, children and parenting* (2nd ed.). Mahwah, NJ: Lawrence Erlbaum.

Westman, J. (Ed.). (2001). *Parenthood in America: Undervalued, underpaid, under siege.* Madison: University of Wisconsin Press.

Consult Appendix I for a sampling of useful children's books related to parenting.

Films & Videos

Developing Minds Video Library includes 22 videotapes with accompanying guides. The library is designed

to help parents and teachers of elementary- and middle-school children explore differences in learning. Examples: *Language, mastering the challenge of reading* (2002) and *Behavioral complications* (2002). WGBH Boston Video in association with All Kinds of Minds.

Learning before school: How adults can help [Video, 19 min]. (2003). This video focuses on how parents can help children in the areas of communication, self-discipline, and curiosity. Crystal Lake, IL: Magna Systems Video (Learning Seed Video).

Shaping youngest minds [Video, 24 min]. (1999). This video is about the day-to-day care of young children's brains and helps parents learn to talk, read, and sign to children and use loving touch. Crystal Lake, IL: Magna Systems Video (Learning Seed Video).

Organizations

American Association for Marriage and Family Therapy
112 S. Alfred Street
Alexandria, VA 22314
http://www.aamft.org

National Parenting Center
22801 Ventura Boulevard, Suite 110
Woodland Hills, CA 91367
http://tnpc.com

Zero to Three: The National Center for Infants, Toddlers, and Families
2000 M Street, NW, Suite 200
Washington, DC 20036
http://zerotothree.org

Web Sites

http://lifematters.com   Life Matters offers a compilation of articles from various authors that promote education, information, and support for those wishing to learn more about democratic styles of parenting.

http://nbcdi.org   Web site of The National Black Child Development Institute.

http://npin.org   The National Parent Information Network (NPIN) offers research-based information about the process of parenting and family involvement in education. It has numerous links to other sites related to education.

Chapter 5

Meeting Child-Care Needs
from Infancy Through School Age

Establishing a network of high quality early learning and parent support programs in a community may not be as glamorous or dramatic as building a sports stadium or convention center but it is likely to have a more immediate and powerful payoff and make a stronger lasting contribution to the public welfare.

(Bardige, 2005, p. 201)

With more than 65% of the mothers of children under six in the labor force and an even greater percentage of mothers of older children working (Children's Defense Fund, 2005), affordable, accessible, quality child care has become an increasingly important issue for families and communities. After reading this chapter you will be able to do the following:

1. Identify the societal changes in family structures and labor force participation that has led to increased need for child care from infancy through the school-age years.
2. List the benefits of quality child care for families and children.
3. Define the following child-care arrangements: **in-home care**, family child care, **center-based care**, and before- and after-school care.
4. Discuss the characteristics of quality child care.
5. Contrast licensing regulations and minimum standards with voluntary accreditation systems.
6. Explain why collaboration between parents, schools, community, and caregivers is needed in order to develop social policies that will enhance the accessibility, affordability, and quality of child care.

In about 3 weeks Renata and her partner Gregg anticipate the birth of their third child. They are excited about the prospect of having another child and have been preparing for the new arrival. Yet, they are feeling anxious, too, because they wonder how they will cope with the additional financial burden. Renata currently works as office manager for a legal firm. When she is working, her 18-month-old daughter is cared for by a grandmotherly neighbor, Mrs. Carlson, at a cost of $75 per week. Their four-year-old son Josh attends a nearby church-affiliated child-care center, at a cost of $80 per week. Neither facility is licensed, but both are in the neighborhood and are supervised by caring personnel.

Renata and Gregg have carefully considered their options. "If we have to pay out another $70 a week for child care," suggests Renata, "it'll hardly be worth my while to keep my job. I'm not sure Mrs. Carlson will want to take both the new baby and Evelyn, and, you know, the center at church won't take Evelyn until she's potty trained," Renata said.

"Yeah, but we need the extra money, and you really like what you do," replied Gregg. Renata is unsure, though. She ponders for a while and thinks to herself. What with paying out more than $200 a week for child care, we're going to have only a little bit left over! I may as well stay at home and look after the children myself. Finally she muses, "Boy, we really do have some tough decisions to make."

Renata and Gregg are part of the growing and changing child-care dilemma that many American families are facing. The number of children needing care outside the home in the United States has increased dramatically over the past 30 years. In 1973, about 30% of children under age six received care, and now about 63% of these children participate in some form of nonparental child care (National Assoociation of Child Care Resource and Referral Agencies, 2006). Currently, about 59% of women with infants younger than one year are employed, compared to 31% in 1976. The percentage of children from ages five to 11 whose mothers work outside the home is even greater than that for younger children. Clearly, the need for child care is a concern, not only for families like Gregg and Renata's, but for many others as well.

In addition to increased dual-earner families, many low-income single mothers have entered the workforce because of welfare reforms. All of this puts more demands on communities and agencies to identify **out-of-home care** facilities. Affordable and accessible child care is increasingly seen as an issue not just for families but for society as a whole. Without child care, families cannot work, and without quality care, children will not succeed.

Child care includes a wide array of arrangements that reflect the age of the child, the setting where care is provided, and the purpose for care, such as infant–toddler centers, family child-care homes, and before- and after-school care. In this chapter, we will focus on the various child-care arrangements made by parents who are working, in training, or unable to care for their children. Remember that although the primary purpose of these arrangements is the provision of substitute care, child care should also positively support children's growth and development.

Increasingly, as parents become more aware of the importance of early learning, they are seeking care arrangements that offer appropriate cognitive stimulation and socialization experiences. For this reason, we find that there are more and more overlaps among the various programs. For example, nursery schools have begun to offer extended-day options, and child-care centers are strengthening their instructional programs. It is difficult to describe these arrangements in neat categories, but early childhood programs defined primarily as educational will be addressed in Chapter 9.

In this chapter we trace the history of child care in the United States and provide an overview of the current state of affairs. A description of each type of child-care arrangement and factors parents should consider when assessing the quality of particular programs will also be included. We will pay particular attention to the costs of care and how this relates to staff quality and turnover. Finally, we will address the effects of child care on children's development and the well-being of families, concluding with some of the policy issues that relate to raising the quantity, affordability, and quality of child-care services.

HISTORY OF CHILD CARE

At earlier times in the United States, **extended family** tended to live with the nuclear family or nearby. When a mother found it necessary to work outside the home or a father lost his wife, the child was usually cared for by a female relative (Scarr, 1998). Since most of these caregivers were assumed to have some commitment to the well-being of their relative's child, quality of care was rarely a concern. Industrialization, which started in the early part of the 19th century, changed these informal family arrangements. As increasing numbers of families moved from rural areas to the cities and as immigrants entered the country, women found work in factories to help support their families. Child-care centers were opened in Boston, New York, and Philadelphia, to provide care for children during the hours their parents worked (Seefeldt & Barbour, 1998). Most of these centers provided custodial care to meet the basic needs of food, shelter, rest, and supervision, but some also provided instruction for both children and families. The care was in large part for reasons of social support, to help needy families (Berns, 2006) in those urban areas.

During World War II, large numbers of women, many with children, went to work in factories to support the war effort by taking the place of men who were fighting. Under the 1944 Lanham Act, the country intensified its mobilization on behalf of the defense industry and increased many services. Under provisions of the act, many communities were able to build excellent child-care centers to serve the children whose mothers were working (Adams, 2001). When the war ended, however, and the men returned to the factories, many of the women lost their jobs, and eventually most of the child-care centers closed. The economic prosperity and sharp increase in births during the postwar years led to an arrangement in many families where the father worked outside the home and the mother cared for the children.

The economic boom of the 1950s, however, increased consumer demands for goods and services, and in turn opened up new opportunities for women to work. Gradually, more women became employed outside the home. As changing attitudes concerning the roles of women that began in the 1960s continued, women increasingly combined motherhood with working, whether from need or preference. Divorce became more common during this era, and often single mothers needed to contribute to their family's income. During the 1960s and 1970s, as more families sought care for their children, there was little support from either the government or the private sector to increase the availability of child care. Concerns about the quality of the child-care centers that did exist began to develop. The concerns focused on health and safety standards, plus the lack of training and the low wages that led to high staff turnover. In the 1980s, additional concerns were raised regarding the consequences of child care on children's development (Casper & Bianchi, 2002).

After-school programs began in the United States in the 19th century, as well (Hirsch, 2005). Programs such as Boys Clubs, YMCAs and YWCAs, Scouts, 4-H, and other youth organizations emerged from programs initially started in storefronts, settlement houses, and churches. Designed to offer places where young people could safely gather to have fun and learn useful skills, some, like the Y, have gone on to become major providers of care for school-age children during the hours before and after school.

CHILD-CARE ISSUES IN THE UNITED STATES TODAY

Although some form of informal, shared child care has always been practiced in the United States, the increased isolation and fragmentation of families, together with other changes in family structure and social expectations, have increased the need for more formal arrangements in recent decades. Nearly 20.5 million children are in nonparental care on a regular basis, according to the

The need for affordable, quality child care is a fact of life in American families because of the dramatic increase in the employment of mothers.

Getty Images Inc.- PhotoDisc

U.S. Department of Labor Bureau of Labor Statistics (2005). In many families today, both parents work outside the home, in order to maintain or increase their standard of living. Other families are headed by a single parent. Welfare reform, which began in the late 20th century, requires many mothers of young children to work. In addition, other women, who have trained for a career, choose to combine work and motherhood in order to maintain their professional opportunities. One of the most dramatic changes in U.S. society over the past 40 years is the great increase in the number of working mothers (Gormick & Meyers, 2005). Consequently, the need for affordable, quality child care is a fact of life for many American families.

Availability of Child Care

For middle-class families, the emergence of a market-based system of child-care services in the late 1980s and 1990s increased the visibility and availability of options for caring for children (Uttal, 2002). During this time, a number of for-profit child-care centers emerged to meet the needs of working families who could afford to pay for it. Resource and referral services made it easier to locate child care, which became more visible as centers sprang up in public places, and family child-care homes become more formally organized as small businesses.

The trend over the past 35 years toward center-based care has been significant. In 1965, only 6% of U.S. preschool children were cared for in centers. By 2003 the percentage was 31. Of the approximately 13 million children under five with employed parents, 11% were in family child care, 48% with parents or in relative care, 10% in babysitter or **nanny care**, and 31% in center-based care (Committee on Family and Work Policies, 2003). Figure 5–1 shows the distribution as of 2003.

The situation for school-age children under 13 is quite different. About 15% are in before- and after-school centers, 7% in family child care, 10% in self care, 4% in nanny sitter/care, 23% in relative care, and 41% in parent and other care. This

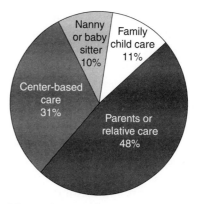

Figure 5–1   Primary Child-Care Arrangements for Children Under 5
Source: Committee on Family and Work Policies. (2003).

last category includes parents who arrange their work schedules to care for their children; it may also include children with parents who may not want to admit that children are in self care (Sonenstein et al., 2002). Figure 5–2 shows the distribution of care arrangements for school-age children as of 2002. In highlighting the needs, one poll in 2000 (Afterschool Alliance, 2002) determined that 60% of voters felt that it was difficult to find afterschool programs in their communities, and 30% of families not currently enrolled in an after-school program would do so if one were available.

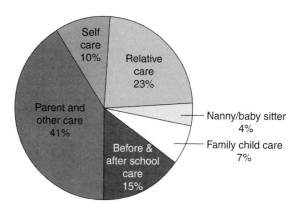

Figure 5–2   Child-Care Arrangements for School-Age Children
Source: Sonenstein et al. (2002).

Low-income families, because of the lack of adequate **subsidized child-care** slots, face significant issues in finding child care and rely increasingly on juggling informal arrangements with relatives and babysitters. Families with two parents and higher incomes have more choice about the kind of child-care arrangements they make and tend to use centers, generally the most expensive option, more than do low-income families. Parents who work nonstandard schedules (Presser, 2003) are also unable to use centers and family child-care homes, which generally provide care only during the day time. Like low-income families, they, too, must piece together care, often using multiple caregivers.

Financing Child Care

Most of the cost for out-of-home care is borne by individual families, and this can be prohibitive for many parents. Low-income families (up to 200% of poverty level) spend approximately 16% and higher earning families only 6% of their incomes (Urban Institute, 2007). As you can imagine, cost in relation to family income is a major factor influencing many families' child-care arrangements. In the past, families on or transitioning off of welfare could receive subsidies for child care. As regulations have changed, these families may no longer receive assistance at the level or for the length of time needed. Middle- and low-income families are generally less able to afford high-quality child care than are high-income families. Consequently, a two-tier child-care system has emerged, in which only certain families have access to the highest quality care (Cryer & Clifford, 2003; Scarr, 1998).

The child-care situation for low-income families varies greatly from state to state. Low-income families can be subsidized for child-care expenses through the Child Care and Development Block Grant provided to states by the federal government, which, in fiscal year 2001, provided $4.5 billion for child-care services for low-income families and other activities related to the provision of child care. The availability of subsidies and the accessibility of programs that accept subsidized children can be major issues in limiting choices. Currently, no state serves all families eligible for child-care assistance under federal regulations, and only 12% of eligible children nationally are receiving help (Children's Defense Fund, 2001). Full-day child care can cost between $4,000 to $10,000 yearly, a significant expense, when one considers that one out of four families with young children earns less than $25,000 a year. In half the states, families with annual incomes above $25,000 are ineligible, and a large number are cutting assistance to families that are just above the poverty line but cannot afford the full cost of child care (Hartman, 2003). Actually, 40 states require copayments from families with incomes below the poverty level. Though Renata and Gregg are above the $25,000 level cut off, they are caught in a situation where their dual income is still not enough to pay for the rising cost of child care. They are ineligible for any government subsidy or assistance.

Although welfare reforms have resulted in dramatic increases in the number of working mothers, the lack of reliable child care and help in paying for it may end up undermining efforts to lift families out of poverty. The rates that states are willing to pay for child care for low-income families reflects the pressure they are under to get as many children into child care at the lowest expenditure. In 2000, only 1.5 million of the 9.9 million eligible were receiving subsidized care. This is a reflection of the limited resources for care (particularly for school-age children), the inability of low-income families to pay the copayments, and their unawareness of eligibility for assistance (Hartman, 2003). Consequently, many families among the working poor are patching together informal child-care arrangements with relatives, friends, or neighbors.

REFLECTION

Think about a young family related to you, and jot down how they are meeting their child-care needs. Then explore with your classmates the different situations you all have identified and compare these to the national norms you have just read about. Do you find that the situations you have found are typical?

Carla, in the following vignette, provides an example of the benefits that subsidized care can offer low-income families. Later, however, she becomes a victim of a system that gives few options and produces a dilemma.

Carla's sons Tommy and Cody both attended Head Start, and Carla became an active program participant. She gained skills and confidence in herself. As a result, two years ago, with Tommy in school and Cody in Head Start, she took a job as a part-time administrative assistant. Her employer was pleased with her work and urged her to continue her education and job training. With her salary added to her husband's part-time work, the family moved off welfare and even obtained medical insurance.

Suddenly things changed. This year, Carla's husband left and provides no financial support. Carla's employer wants to help her and urges her to get more training and become a full-time employee. To continue her training, though, Carla must find partial child care for her boys. Such care is expensive and is hard to find. Carla's salary increment is good, but it no longer covers her insurance payments and child care while still meeting basic needs.

Carla would be eligible for child-care supplements, but when she applies, she is told that all new applicants are placed on a waiting list. As Carla seeks solutions, she is told she could go back on welfare since she hasn't used up all her allotted time. Presently working full-time, she makes too much money to receive any welfare support. If she works only part-time, she can get welfare benefits plus Medicaid, but her employer needs a full-time person. Her job, career training, and future employment are all in jeopardy. Carla is seriously considering going back on welfare until both children are a little older, but she's afraid that by then the skills she has gained plus her employer's goodwill will have vanished.

One can see that those families whose income is above the poverty level but below $25,000 are less likely to be able to afford center-based care, as is the case with Carla in the preceding vignette. In short, these families have fewer options available to them when it comes to selecting appropriate out-of-home care.

The federal government does offer a tax credit to help families with the costs of child care. The Child and Dependent Care (Tax) Credit reduces the income tax liability of families at all income levels with work-related care expenses. Because the credit is nonrefundable, however, its value to low-income families is limited, as the credit amount cannot exceed a family's tax liability. The maximum credit is $3,000 a year for one qualifying individual or $6,000 a year for two or more qualifying individuals. In 2002, it provided $2.7 billion to working families and is considered the second largest source of federal child-care assistance after the Child Care Development Block Grant (CCDBG).

Concerns About Quality

Advocates for children are increasingly concerned about the outcomes for low-income children in the current state of affairs. Substandard care, accidental injury or neglect, and an inadequate developmental environment can have devastating effects on children whose families lack adequate funds for quality child care. Even for families who can afford child care, though, concerns remain about the quality of these settings for young children. The Children's Defense Fund (2001), reporting on various studies on quality in child-care centers, concluded that "much of the child care in the United States is poor to mediocre" (p. 2). In addition, a national study of family child-care programs reported that more than one third of the programs were rated as inadequate. These studies, of course, raise our concerns about children's safety as well as the harm to children's development. Research has confirmed that quality programs are linked to positive outcomes for children (Mardell, 2002). Conversely, children in poor-quality care are at risk when they do not receive the attention, nurturance, and educational enrichment that will help them to succeed. Yet we find considerable variation in the quality of both centers and family child-care homes.

The Cost, Quality, and Child Outcomes in Child Care Centers study conducted by Suzanne Helburn and colleagues examined more than 400 child-care centers and found that only 14% of programs provide high-quality care (Galinsky, Howes, Kontos, & Shinn, 1994; Helburn & Bergmann, 2002). The study also reported that

Federal legislation has stimulated development of services and programs for infants and toddlers and their families.

Anne Vega / Merrill

12% provided poor-quality child care arrangements, and the majority of programs were mediocre. The situation for infants and toddlers is equally disturbing. Some studies suggest that only 9% of the child-care settings were excellent, 30% were good, whereas 53% were of fair quality and 8% of poor quality (Vandell & Pierce, 2003). Research on family child-care programs and relative care is equally troubling. Only 9% of such care was of sufficient quality to positively influence children's development, 56% were considered adequate, and 35% were deemed of such poor quality that children's health and development were endangered (Galinsky et al., 1994; Hofferth, 1991). These are startling statistics for all families and professionals, and it seems that they will not change soon (Greenspan & Salmon, 2001).

The federal government requires states to spend at least 4% of the funds they receive from the CCDBG to improve the quality of care in their jurisdictions. Congress also set aside $173 million of the discretionary funds for additional quality

building activities: $100 million for increasing and improving infant- and toddler-care programs, $10 million for child-care research, and $18.1 million for school-age care and **resource and referral programs** (Children's Defense Fund, 2001). Despite these expeditures, the limited availability of affordable, quality child care remains a serious problem in the United States.

We will now turn to the various types of child-care arrangements and then proceed to a description of the characteristics of quality programs for infants, toddlers, and preschool and school-age children. A discussion of the effects of child care on children's development and the policy issues that will help to ensure available, affordable, quality care for all who need it will conclude the chapter.

CHILD-CARE ARRANGEMENTS

Mr. McGee, Tina's father, is a bit surprised not to see Mrs. Holden in her office as he enters the child care center. The assistant smiles and says that Mrs. Holden is with the infants because an extra lap is needed. On the way to the three-year-old room, Tina urges her father to stop and watch the fish in the tank. A mother watching the fish exclaims, "We've been stopping here lately, too. Just watching seems to help Janda relax before starting the day. Mrs. Holden did tell me what a boon this tank was, and I can see it."

On entering the classroom, Tina notices that Billy is crying loudly. Martha is holding him and saying, "Mama's coming to the phone, and she'll talk with you." Tina goes over to Billy, pats him, and says kindly, "It's okay!" She then puts her coat in her cubbie and hurries over to her friend Claire at the water table. Soon Billy's mother is on the phone, and her voice appears to be quieting Billy. As Mr. McGee waits to talk with Martha, he smiles at Felicity, who is seated on the floor with two other children reading. Several children are working at the table while Miranda pours juice. Martha turns to Mr. McGee, who asks if all is okay. "Oh, yes. Billy does take change hard. His dad brought him today for the first time, and now he seems uncertain about his mama. I got her on the phone, and she's reassuring him."

"Oh, that's good," replies Mr. McGee. "Well, I just need to remind someone that Tina's grandmother will pick her up this afternoon. Tina knows this, and I put it on her chart."

"OK. Just remember to let them know at the office on your way out."

Mr. McGee kisses Tina goodbye, saying, "Remember, Grandma will pick you up this afternoon, 'cause Mommy has to work late."

As Mr. McGee leaves the building, he greets the toddler teacher, who is starting her first outing of the day. Five toddlers are happily seated in their cart for an excursion along the sidewalk to look in the shop windows. Mr. McGee thinks, "I remember how Tina enjoyed those cart rides. Boy, we were lucky to find such a great center so near home." ⎯⎯⟁

Quality child care makes a difference for families, and the McGees reflect the changes now taking place within American families. Tina's parents are both professional and believe it important that Mrs. McGee continue her career. They represent what Elkind (1995) called the **postmodern family**, in which most parenting for very young children is provided by the mother, sometimes with the father's assistance, and by other caregivers. Since Tina's arrival at this center, Tina's family has been

pleased with the program. Though the cost of care is high, this center has provided a consistency of caregivers and a safe environment. Many families use the center even into the school years, since it has extended-day programs.

Parents like the McGees, seeking child care are faced with many issues in determining the appropriate arrangement for their children. Aside from issues of affordability, location, and availability, families also want to ensure that their children receive educational and social enrichment along with nurturing care. Figure 5–3 shows indicators of quality in child-care arrangements. Resource and referral agencies have been established in many communities to support parents in locating child-care centers and family child-care homes, whereas other agencies can assist in locating nannies and au pairs. These various options for child care are described in the following sections.

REFLECTION

Would you feel comfortable leaving your own children in the center described in the McGee vignette? List three features that appeal to you, then note anything that concerns you.

In-Home Child Care

Care that takes place in the child's home is an unregulated arrangement. In the case of a babysitter, the family determines the necessary qualifications, screens applicants, and strikes an agreement with the individual of their choice. The advantage of this type of care for parents with long work days or erratic schedules is its flexibility. The caregiver, who may even live in the child's home, becomes an employee of the family, who then assumes certain financial responsibilities in terms of taxes and Social Security deductions (and some decide not to report the payments or income). Wage levels for these positions are low, and the supply of babysitters is somewhat limited to persons who

- *Supervision:* Children should be supervised at all times, even when sleeping.

- *Discipline:* Children should be guided positively, clearly, consistently, and fairly.

- *Sanitation:* Children and teachers should wash hands frequently. Diapering areas, restrooms, and places where children eat should be cleaned and disinfected regularly.

- *Director qualifications:* Directors should hold at least a bachelor's degree in a related field, have 2 or more years of experience with children.

- *Teacher qualifications:* Teachers should hold a degree in a related field, and assistants should have training about child development and appropriate activities that is ongoing.

- *Child–staff ratio and group size:* The younger the age, the smaller the group size should be and the lower the child–staff ratio.

- *Safety:* Toxic substances and medications should be kept out of reach of children and poison control information posted. Programs should have an emergency plan, first-aid kits, fire drills, and other safety measures in place. Staff should be trained in first aid and know how to administer medications.

- *Child abuse:* All staff should have been subject to a background check and should now how to recognize and report signs of suspected abuse.

Figure 5–3   Indicators of a Safe and Healthy Child-Care Arrangement

may have no training in child care and few options for other work. During the late 1990s, two high-profile cases of candidates for political appointment in the Clinton administration admitted hiring undocumented immigrants to provide child care and household help after experiencing difficulty in finding such assistance (Harrington, 2000).

Families can also hire a nanny to provide in-home care. Generally, nannies are registered with an agency and have had some training in the care of young children. Another option is an au pair, a young foreign-born person who exchanges child care and light housework for room and board and a small salary. The au pair system is organized by the U.S. Information Agency as a cultural exchange program to allow the young and usually well-educated participants to take courses and enjoy living and traveling in the United States. Generally, the au pair has minimum training and experience in child care. Other families make arrangements with a babysitter to provide care in the sitter's own home. This is also unregulated care, that like the options for in-home care can

have considerable variation in quality, depending on the individual caregiver.

Family Child Care

In this arrangement, children are cared for in the home of the provider. Although care is usually limited to six children, regulations now allow providers with assistants to offer care for up to 12 children in what are called group or large-family child-care homes. Care is generally offered all day, five days a week, year-round, and can meet a family's needs for flexibility more easily than a center-based program with fixed hours of operation. Many providers begin this work as an extension of caring for their own children, but some continue it as an intentional career choice and may even become part of the movement to professionalize this type of care (National Association for Family Child Care, 2003). Many caregivers provide enriching educational and social experiences for the children in their care in the context of an appropriate daily schedule and an environment organized to support children's development.

The number of family child-care programs has increased over the past 20 years as the demand for services continues. The 2002 Family Child Care Licensing Study (Children's Foundation, 2003) reported that there were 306,802 regulated family child-care homes in the 50 states, District of Columbia, Puerto Rico, and the Virgin Islands. Of these programs, 44,473 are considered group or large-family child-care centers, serving seven to 12 children. The number of regulated child-care homes has more than doubled since 1984.

Family child care is generally a more affordable option because fees are substantially lower than those charged in child-care centers. Although some caregivers will only accept particular age groups, others care for the same children year after year as they grow older. A family child-care home can mirror a family, serving children from infancy through school age. Many families prefer this type of arrangement, particularly for children under two, because of its convenience, individualized relationships, and homelike environment. In fact, six-year-old Travis expressed surprise upon seeing his mother give money to his child-care provider. "You *pay* Mrs. Black?" he asked in shock. It had never occurred to him that her loving care for him was a job! (Koralek, 2002).

All states have some type of licensing and regulation of family child care, but the requirements and oversight are generally minimal. Unfortunately, with the pressing need for child care for mothers returning to work because of changes in the welfare regulations that began in 1996, regulations may become even less stringent. On the other hand, military family child-care programs, which have high standards for training and requirements for safety, health, nutrition, and developmental care, are increasingly serving as models for states seeking approaches to improve quality.

Child-Care Centers

Center-based child care can serve children from infancy through school age, although some programs limit themselves to a particular age group.

Typically, child-care centers, like the one the McGees selected, are open all day, five days per week, year-round, and close only for major holidays and extreme weather conditions. Many centers provide multiple programs, including half-day nurserylike classes for three-, four-, and even five-year-olds, and many offer extended-day programs for children in kindergarten and up to 12 years old. Child-care centers have long hours of operation and can serve children of various ages, which makes them a particularly convenient and appealing choice for many families.

As noted before, the number of child-care centers increased dramatically between 1977 and the present, with the largest growth area in for-profit programs. For-profit centers include independent programs or those that are part of local or national chains. Child-care centers may also be run as nonprofit operations sponsored by organizations such as the Young Men's Christian Association (YMCA), churches, colleges, social service agencies, or local, state, or federal government agencies. **Employer-sponsored child-care** centers have also opened in recent decades, although their numbers are still quite small. The U.S. Military Child Development Program's extensive system of care centers, like their family child-care programs, are an example of large-scale, employer-sponsored child care and can serve as a model for other organizations (Neugebauer, 2005).

Child-care centers are housed in a variety of locations, including community centers, church basements, former school buildings, storefronts, industrial parks, or in spaces built specifically for the center. Usually, a center will have multiple classrooms, each arranged for a particular age range. Increasingly, centers provide an educational curriculum appropriate for each age group. Although the requirements vary drastically from state to state, there are generally some educational requirements for staff and an expectation that staff participate in continued training activities.

Infant–Toddler Programs. Although infant and toddler care in centers is a relatively recent phenomenon, affluent parents are increasingly turning to this arrangement to meet their family's needs. Center care for children under two can be very expensive in those states that require a high teacher-to-child ratio. This ratio varies from one caregiver for three babies to as high as one to eight, depending on the state.

Infant and toddler programs require particular materials, equipment, and room arrangements. Many centers provide rooms designed for small groups of caregivers and infants in spaces comfortable for both. Rocking chairs, carpeting, mats, and duplicates of popular toys are basics. Ideally, a separate sleeping area is available with a designated crib for each child.

Center care for infants and toddlers should focus on several areas. The first area is the provision of children's basic needs; eating, sleeping, safety, cleanliness, and nurturance. Centers also provide educational support for infants through a developmentally and culturally appropriate curriculum (Bergen, Reid, & Torelli, 2001). Both planned and spontaneous experiences in the context of routine care and play are recognized as essential for optimal growth. As our knowledge of early brain development has increased, infant–toddler programs are recognized to have a great responsibility to contribute to the cognitive and social–emotional growth of the children in their care.

Preschool Programs. Center-based care for three-to five-year-old children is the most popular option for American families. Young children cared for in centers can be there for up to 50 hours a week, so much of their basic needs must be met during that time. Centers make provisions for children to eat up to two meals and two snacks each day. Children also need opportunities to rest, play outdoors and inside, and interact consistently with caring adults.

Providing for children's physical safety and basic needs, however, is only the beginning of what a preschool child-care program should offer young children. Children need opportunities to participate in a program that enriches them emotionally, socially, and intellectually, as well. There are a number of approaches to early education programs for this age group, but it is widely accepted that young children need to make choices

and initiate their own activities for large blocks of time. Although teacher-directed activities, such as stories, songs, and arts and crafts projects, should be part of the daily routine, play and child-initiated experiences should predominate (Copple & Bredekamp, 2005). Table 5–1 illustrates an appropriate schedule for preschool child care.

School-Age Child Care. Although some centers offer school-age care in addition to their services for younger children, other programs limit themselves to this age group. In some cases, centers rent space in the public schools, but increasingly school districts are offering care directly. No matter how they are administered, however, school-age child-care programs provide a number of options for families who need care for the hours before and after school. In many programs, care is also available during weather emergencies, school holidays, and summer vacation.

School-age programs often provide breakfast for children who attend before school and offer a

Table 5–1   Sample Schedule for a Preschool Day

7:30–8:30 A.M.	Arrival, breakfast, table toys, and transition to center
8:30–8:50	Opening circle/meeting
8:50–9:50	Activity period in centers/snack
9:50–10:00	Cleanup time
10:00–10:20	Circle: music, movement, and stories
10:20–10:30	Toileting
10:30–11:30	Outdoor play
11:30–12:00 NOON	Lunch
12:30–2:30 P.M.	Rest and provisions for quiet play starting around 1:15 for nonsleepers
2:30–3:00	Transition from rest, toileting
3:00–3:15	Snack
3:15–4:00	Outdoor play
4:00–4:15	Story and songs
4:15–6:00	Free play, classroom cleanup, and transition to families

Many school-age programs facilitate children's involvement in extra curriculum activities.

Patricia A. Scully

snack as children arrive at the end of the school day. Outdoor play is usually one of the first options for children as they transition from their academic program to the more relaxed setting of child care. Many programs offer time and support for children to do homework, and others facilitate children's involvement in extracurricular school activities such as scouting, sports, and other activities. See Table 5–2 for a sample schedule for before- and after-school child care.

Child Care for Children with Disabilities

Federal laws now prohibit both privale and public child-care programs from discriminating against children with disabilities. Consequently, children with special needs are increasingly participating in child-care programs alongside their typically developing peers. Fortunately, many providers are discovering that including children with disabili-

ties in their programs has advantages for all children. Typically developing children learn to understand and accept differences and serve as role models of age-appropriate communication and social behaviors. Children with disabilities enjoy

Table 5–2   Sample Schedule for Before- and After-School Child Care

7:00–8:00 A.M.	Arrival, breakfast, quiet play, transition from home
8:00–8:30	Outdoor play
8:30–9:00	Quiet play and preparation for regular school
3:00–3:45 P.M.	Choice of indoor or outdoor free play
3:45–4:15	Snack
4:15–4:45	Homework and quiet play
4:45–6:00	Self-selected activities, games, computers, clubs, and transition to home

the activities and materials provided and form friendships with their peers. When needed, reasonable adaptations may be made to allow children of all physical, emotional, and academic abilities to take part in the same learning environment. See Chapter 6 for a fuller treatment of the laws and issues concerning the inclusion of children with special needs.

Other Programs

To meet the needs of families with the kind of informal and infrequent care that used to be provided by family, friends, or neighbors, other programs have emerged.

Mother's-Day-Out Programs. These programs are designed to offer a few hours of child care each week for stay-at-home parents who need time for activities like doctor's appointments, shopping, and respite from their children for a short period of time. Often sponsored by religious organizations or other community groups, **mother's-day-out programs** offer children a chance to play and socialize with other children.

Drop-In Child Care. Some child-care programs provide child-care services for parents with part-time jobs, flexible work schedules, and those who need a place to leave their children for short periods of time on occasion. Increasingly, centers designed only for **drop-in child care** are being offered in shopping centers, gyms, movie theaters, and other conveniently located places. These are casual programs that provide safe supervision in a play environment.

REFLECTION

With a classmate, identify all the child-care services with which you are familiar in your town or community. With your listing, interview parents at the local supermarket to determine if they feel they have acceptable options for child care. What seems to be missing, if anything?

FEATURES OF QUALITY CHILD CARE

Despite the great diversity in child-care arrangements and the wide variations in state regulations governing center-based and family child-care homes, there is much agreement among professionals on the characteristics of quality child care needed to provide the safe, healthy, and nurturing environments that parents want and children deserve.

High-quality care is the result of a combination of a healthy and safe environment together with educational and social stimulation appropriate to the age and development of the children being served (Fraenkel, 2003). These features of quality child care include both structural elements relating to the physical environment and staffing requirement and process elements relating to curricular practices, caregiver qualities, and parental involvement (Wortham, 2006). The McGee vignette suggests that the family has found a center that has both structural and process elements that assure quality.

Structural Elements

The structural elements of a child-care environment establish the foundation for optimal process conditions. Characteristics of the child-care space, for example, are structural elements. The square footage required for each child, the amount and kind of outdoor space, the requirements for furniture, sinks, toilets, windows, flooring material, and myriad other details related to the classroom, kitchen facilities, bathrooms, and diaper-changing areas are included in this category. The adult–child ratio, amount of initial and continuing staff training required, plus the salaries, benefits, and working requirements for staff are all structural elements of child care.

The individual licensing requirements of each state sets minimum expectations for many of the structural elements, and a center or family child-care home can get licensed by meeting these requirements. Unfortunately, these minimum standards do not necessarily lead to a quality program, and professional organizations and individuals have established optimal structural elements that can have a large impact on program quality. For example, although the state may only require one adult for every eight two-year-olds and have no limit on the number in the total group, recommendations from the Center for Career Development in Early Care and Education at Wheelock College recommends a ratio of four children to one adult, with a maximum group size of 12 (Children's Defense Fund, 2001). High adult–child ratios are considered one of the strongest structural elements in supporting the intellectual and social development of children in child care and are important indicators of quality.

Quality programs also set up inviting environments with an abundance of appropriate resources (furniture, equipment, materials, and toys), often far above the minimum requirements. The requirements for staff education and continued training are also above minimum requirements in quality centers.

Process Elements

Process quality refers to the experiences children have in child care and include such aspects as adult–child interactions, children's exposure to and involvement with learning materials, and parent–caregiver relationships. These are critical components that directly affect children's behavior and learning experiences in the child-care setting.

Teachers' Qualities. The most important process element in quality child care is the human relationships between the teaching staff and children and their families (Uttal, 2002). Teachers who interact with children in a nurturing manner help to create attachments between themselves and the children, the foundation for further social development. As they engage children in conversation, ask questions, and respond to them when they speak, they are helping children acquire cognitive and language skills (National Institute for Child Health and Human Development [NICHD] Early Child Care Research Network, 1997). Not only do teachers need to be knowledgeable about the developmental characteristics of the children they serve, understand how to provide enriching experiences for

them, and be able to communicate effectively with the children's parents about their shared concerns, but they must also be warm and nurturing people.

Ideally, those who care for young children will consider themselves professionals and have an educational background in child development and curriculum. Continuing professional education by attending conferences, participating in workshops, reading professional literature, and sharing ideas and information with colleagues are all indications of professional behavior. Partaking in activities like these builds commitment to the field, satisfaction with the work, and a greater sensitivity to the needs of children.

Unfortunately, the low wages associated with working with children in child-care settings has had a very negative effect on the quality of teachers (Harrington, 2000). Nonprofessional entry-level salaries are rarely higher than minimum wage, particularly at national for-profit chains. Starting salaries for child-care center teachers with college degrees was approximately $15,000 to $16,000 in the late 1990s, less than half of what many entry-level public-school teachers receive. Low wages have kept the educational level of caregivers from rising and has spawned an annual turnover rate of about 30%. Programs that manage to retain their caregivers are generally of higher quality than those that have a high turnover.

Curriculum. Given the importance of the early years for children's physical, social, emotional, and cognitive development, another mark of a quality program is the curriculum. Curriculum in child care is generally understood as an approach toward learning that includes both planned and spontaneous educational experiences that occur within a predictable daily routine. Time is designated for outdoor and indoor play. Large group gatherings are used for stories, music, movement, and more, and for routines like eating, toileting, and resting. A well-planned curriculum will meet the needs of the children enrolled by considering their age, developmental levels, interests, special needs, and cultural backgrounds.

A quality curriculum in a program serving infants and toddlers requires that teachers be especially responsive to the rapid growth and change that is occurring during these years. Wortham (2006) summarized characteristics of effective teachers for this age group; they must be able to

- Understand and appreciate children's unique temperaments and developmental stages.
- Meet children's needs for care while encouraging increasing independence.
- Frequently initiate physical, social, and verbal interactions.
- Be responsive to children's physical, social, and verbal behavior as much as possible.
- Be consistent and predictable.
- Plan experiences and interactions appropriate to the children's level of functioning.

Play and routine caregiving activities are the fundamentals of the curriculum with this age group. A quality caregiver follows the lead of the children in determining when they sleep, eat, and need to be changed. Between these times, they interact with the infants and toddlers in an environment that has been set up to enhance their physical, cognitive, social, and emotional development. Children's cultures and families are represented in various ways, highlighting child care as an extension of the home.

As children reach age two and move into the preschool years, the curriculum changes to meet their developing needs. The daily schedule includes opportunities for children to work individually and in small groups most of the time, with some short periods of whole-group gatherings for stories and music. The room is arranged in activity areas, such as blocks, dramatic play, art, science, math, computer, language, and others. Each area is well stocked with interesting materials, which allows the children to make choices about what to do when they are there. Indoor and outdoor play is respected as the best way for children to learn, and teachers facilitate their play to enhance the social, physical, and cognitive benefits for development (Wortham, 2006).

The curriculum in the quality before- and after-school age program tends to be more informal than those for younger children and will vary greatly, depending on the needs and interests of the group.

Centers or family child-care homes of high quality provide many toys and materials appropriate to the children's ages and interests, and lots of free time for children to participate in self-directed activities. In a center, the room is set up in activity areas with space set aside for computer use and homework and other areas devoted to construction, games, music, art, and other interests. The best programs for this age group are seen by the children as clubs where individual interests can be pursued. Generally, the time before school is low-key, with breakfast available and time to participate in individual and small-group projects. After-school usually begins with a period of vigorous outdoor play and is followed by snacks, some time for homework, and individually chosen activities. Allowing children as much choice as possible and providing lots of opportunity for socializing and pursuing interests are hallmarks of the most successful programs for school-age children.

Full days in school-age care that occur during inclement weather, school holidays, and summers are characterized by a camplike atmosphere. School-age children are developing many interests, and the more the program can support the children's choices, the more eagerly the children participate. In the highest quality programs, child-care staff and the children's school teachers confer regularly and communicate issues of mutual concern.

Although quality child care programs may have somewhat different philosophical orientations, all will offer a curriculum that extends the cognitive and socialization processes that have begun in the children's families. For many children, child care is where they first learn to interact with children and adults outside their families, and this marks the beginning of community socialization.

Parent Involvement. Quality child-care programs recognize the importance of parental involvement and the strong need that families feel to be fully informed about their child's progress. In a quality program, parents are asked to share detailed information about their child as they come into care so that teachers can provide continuity with the home. Meeting prior to the child's beginning the program can help to build the rapport between parent and

Play is the best way for children to learn. Teachers facilitate this play and enhance children's development.

Patricia A. Scully

teaching staff, which is essential to the success of the child-care experience. Continuing collaboration facilitates the continuity of experiences for the child and enhances the potential for meeting the child's needs.

Collaboration relies on communication, and it is the teacher's responsibility to establish many ways to keep families informed about their own child. Because most parents actually bring in and pick up their child at the child-care setting, every day presents an opportunity to establish a relationship between the parent and the teaching staff. Once such a relationship is established, information about what is going on with the child can be regularly shared. In infant–toddler programs, parents and teachers often record information about the child in a book that is passed back and forth between the child care setting and the home. Quality programs also schedule formal parent conferences throughout the year.

Parents also welcome opportunities to become involved in the child-care program in ways that don't interfere with their work schedules. Making phone calls to other parents, donating recyclables, sewing smocks, or washing the sheets used at nap time are all tasks parents may be willing to do. By

becoming involved in these ways, parents feel more connected to the program and more committed to supporting it. Potluck dinners, family breakfasts, workshops on parenting, and other events can also build family involvement. Chapter 11 offers additional strategies for establishing positive relationships between schools and families that are applicable to child-care settings, as well.

REFLECTION

On your own or through your campus field office, arrange to visit a nearby child-care center. Try to label the program with one of the types listed in this chapter, then identify at least three "structural elements" that you observe at the center. Also see if you can pick out three "process elements" to discuss with classmates.

Characteristics of Quality Child Care

Exemplary child-care programs do share certain characteristics that can serve as a model for others seeking to improve the quality of care for children. According to Kinch and Schweinhart

(1999), a high-quality program includes the following features:

- *Financial resources.* Uses financial resources beyond fees from parent, such as subsidies for low-income families and donations from individuals and foundations.
- *Creation of alliances.* Forges a variety of alliances with organizations to bring additional resources. For example, a center might collaborate with a community organization on fund-raising efforts.
- *Parent education.* Seeks ways to educate parents about the value of early childhood education. In doing so, parents become better consumers and are more likely to support programs.
- *Staff benefits.* Seeks additional salary and other benefits for their staff. In addition, they secure adequate planning time and arrange opportunities for professional development.
- *Establishment of advisory committees.* Strengthens relationships with the community by establishing a board of directors or a community advisory board.
- *Recognition of needs.* Recognizes family needs and stresses, and works flexibly with families, making a program viable for parents.
- *Institutional structures.* Plans for future existence through structures that promote quality, compensation, and affordability.
- *High standards.* Has established policies and clearly written standards on mission, philosophy, and educational approach.

Child-care quality is essential in terms of children's everyday experiences and their later school achievement and social interactions. When every child receives the highest quality care possible, the beneficial effects of child care will increase dramatically.

Effects of Quality Child Care

Research indicates that although the family remains the major influence on child outcomes, the quality and stability of the child care that young children receive have important effects, as well. The results of three recent longitudinal studies (Vandell & Pierce, 2003) confirm that high-quality child care can have positive effects on children's development in a number of areas. One of these studies, the

NICHD Study of Early Child Care (NICHD Early Child Care Research Network, 2000) reported that the cognitive and language development of children and their social and emotional well-being are positively impacted by high-quality child care. Another of the studies (Burchinal et al., 2000) concluded that higher quality child care was associated with better cognitive development, better receptive and expressive language skills, and better functional communication skills. The third study (Peisner-Feinberg et al., 1999) followed children through two years of child care and the first 3 years of school. Their findings suggest that children from high-quality child care demonstrated better receptive language and math skills. This study and other research indicates that these positive effects on children's development are especially significant for low-income children and those at risk for failure in school (Children's Defense Fund, 2001). Studies have also shown that quality school-age programs play an important role in children's school achievement and long-term success, as well as in their safety and well-being. As we have pointed out in other chapters, those who care for children make an important contribution to their lives.

LICENSING REQUIREMENTS AND VOLUNTARY ACCREDITATION

All 50 states and the District of Columbia have regulations concerning the operation of child-care centers, family child-care homes, and other programs that care for children. In most cases, a child-care center cannot operate unless it is licensed by the state. The regulations for family child care vary from registration to licensing, depending on particular state statutes. Licensing regulations, however, are usually only minimum standards designed to protect the safety and well-being of children. Generally, the procedure for licensing includes regular inspections to ensure that programs are operating according to the guidelines. As you would expect, licensing regulations cover a multitude of issues, such as the ratio of adults to children, health, safety issues, building codes, and

Cognitive development of children and their social and emotional well-being are positively impacted by high-quality care.

staff qualifications. The National Resource Center for Health and Safety in Child Care has a Web site with links to each individual state detailing the family child-care and the center-based licensing regulations. The standards for child care vary greatly from state to state.

Some child-care centers and family child-care providers go beyond state licensing requirements by participating in voluntary accreditation programs. Accreditation is considered an indicator of child care quality and is the result of a process of collaboration between the program and other professionals to determine whether it meets nationally recognized standards of excellence.

National Association of Family Child Care Accreditation

The **National Association for Family Child Care (NAFCC)** is a national membership organization that works with more than 400 state and local family **child-care provider** associations across the United States. It developed its first accreditation system in 1988, and by 1998 there were NAFCC-accredited family child-care providers in 44 states and the District of Columbia. According to a study of accredited providers, accreditation increases providers' professionalism and self-esteem, improves quality of care, and develops leadership skills (Galinsky, Howes, & Kontos, 1995).

In 2005, NAFCC's revised standards went into effect, and the accreditation process includes an observation visit from a representative of NAFCC. The current standards are based on the following five areas:

Part 1: Relationships
Part 2: The Environment
Part 3: Developmental Learning Activities
Part 4: Safety and Health
Part 5: Professional and Business Practices

National Association for the Education of Young Children Accreditation

The National Association for the Education of Young Children's (NAEYC's) Academy for Early Childhood Program Accreditation administers the nation's largest voluntary accreditation system for all types of preschools, kindergartens, child-care centers, and school-age child-care programs. According to NAEYC (1998), a high-quality early childhood program meets the physical, social, emotional, and cognitive needs of children. Such programs also meet the needs of the parents, staff, and administrator who are involved in the program. Their accreditation process includes an extensive self-study by the program directors and a site visit by a team of highly trained assessors who verify the accuracy of the self-study. There are currently about 10,000 NAEYC-accredited programs, which can be located through http://www.naeyc.org. In the fall of 2006, revised standards were established, and, as a result, the following areas are studied in the current accreditation process:

- *Relationships between children and adults:* The program promotes positive relationships among all children and adults, to encourage each child's sense of individual work and belonging as part of a community and to foster each child's ability to contribute as a responsible community member.
- *Curriculum:* The program implements a curriculm that is consistent with its goals for children and promotes learning and development in the social, emotional, physical, language, and cognitive areas.
- *Teaching:* The program uses developmentally, culturally, and linguistically appropriate and effective teaching approaches.
- **Assessment** *of child progress:* The program is informed by ongoing, systematic, formal and informal assessment approaches, sensitive to the culturally contexts in which children develop and in reciprocal communication with families.
- *Health:* The program promotes the nutrition and health of childrern and protects children and staff from illness and injury.
- *Teachers:* The program employs and supports a teaching staff that has the educational qualifica-

tions, knowledge, and professional commitment necessary to promote children's learning and development and to support families' diverse needs and interests.
- *Families:* The program establishes and maintains collaborative relationships with each child's family to foster children's development in all settings. These relationships are sensitive to family composition, language, and culture.
- *Community relationships:* The program establishes relationships with and uses the resources of the children's communities to support the achievement of program goals.
- *Physical environment:* The program has a safe and healthful environment that provides appropriate and well-maintained indoor and outdoor physical environments.
- *Leadership and management:* The program effectively implements policies, procedures, and systems that support stable staff and strong personnel, fiscal, and program management.

The accreditation process represents a professional judgment as to whether a program demonstrates satisfactory performance in meeting the criteria for each standard. NAEYC accreditation is now given for a period of five years, during which time programs submit annual reports and are subject to unannounced visits by the accreditation agency.

Other Types of Accreditation

Although NAEYC sets the accreditation standard, other organizations also offer program accreditation (Surr, 2004). Among these are the National Early Childhood Program Accreditation administered by the National Child Care Association, a group that represents for-profit centers. The National School-Age Care Alliance also offers an accreditation system for programs that serve that age group. A third system is the accreditation program of the National Association of Child Care Providers, which offers an optional faith-based component. Some states, such as Florida, Maryland, and Missouri, also have statewide systems for accrediting child care and other early childhood programs.

MEETING THE CHALLENGES THROUGH COLLABORATION

The greatest concern in the 21st century is no longer that children will be cared for outside the home but that the quality of care they receive will be substandard (Greenspan & Salmon, 2001). Fortunately, numerous groups are working to resolve what has come to be seen as a real crisis for American families—finding affordable quality care for their children so they can work. The National Association of Child Care Resource and Referral Agencies works with communities to improve the supply and quality of child care through its research, ongoing professional development opportunities, parent education component, and support of accreditation. Many other national groups, such as the NAEYC, Children's Defense Fund, National Association for Family Child Care, and the National Child Care Information Center, are committed to working to improve the quality of child care.

It is generally agreed that quality child care is directly related to the adults providing the care (Cohen, 2001). As noted earlier, however, the child-care workforce, which is 98% female and one third women of color, is inadequately compensated. The average center-based teacher earns about $7 per hour, and many receive only minimum wage. Teachers with a college degree and some experience earn on average barely $10 per hour. Family child-care providers are even more poorly paid, and only one third of all child-care staff has health benefits. Many must also contend with poor working conditions. Consequently, approximately one third of those who work in child-care leave the field each year. The shortage of public-school early childhood teachers—because of reductions in class size and increases in prekindergarten programs in elementary schools—has increased the job opportunities for well-trained early childhood teachers. Therefore, many are leaving the child-care field to pursue better paid positions in the public schools. The mission of the Center for the Child Care Workforce, which recently merged with the American Federation of Teachers Educational Foundation, has been to improve the quality of child care services by upgrading the wages, benefits, training opportunities, and working conditions for child-care teachers and family child-care providers.

Providing quality child care for families cannot be based on what parents can afford to pay.

Steven Barbour

School-age child care is receiving increasing attention, and many creative collaborations (Noam & Miller, 2002) are developing to cultivate interesting and worthwhile programs for this age group. Community-based organizations, schools, museums, universities and other groups are also coming together to share resources and ideas for school-age care. Through public–private partnerships, San Diego (Ferri & Amick, 2002), for example, is well on its way to meeting its goal of providing free before and after-school programs for all children.

REFLECTION

As you think and talk about the child-care options available to families in your home community, attempt to assess the following:

- Is there enough affordable child-care service available to all income levels?
- What part of the available service could be called "quality care"?
- Are families satisfied with what they have, or is there a problem in unmet child-care needs?

Although child-care policies in the United States lag behind those of most other modern industrialized countries (Cryer & Clifford, 2003), there are some indications that businesses are beginning to recognize the importance of supporting the family life of their workers. The number of employer-sponsored child-care centers is very small, but a growing number of firms are providing child-care assistance through referral services, partnerships with local child-care programs, and the provision of **backup care** for the children of employees. Changes in benefit packages, including flexible spending accounts that allow employees to pay for child care in pretax dollars, offers some financial support as well.

In the political climate at the beginning of the 21st century, very few federal funds have been allotted to support quality child care (Hartman, 2003). Although welfare reform has successfully introduced many more women into the workforce, the provisions for quality child care have been less forthcoming. Extending tax credits, making parent's expenditures for child care refundable for poorer families, and other federal policies are needed. The reality of quality care is that providing the service can not be based solely on what parents can afford to pay. Families and programs need additional community and government support in order to make quality care available to every child (Lombardi, 2003).

APPLYING THESE CONCEPTS TO YOUR WORK WITH CHILDREN AND FAMILIES

As the need for quality care for infants through school-age children continues to increase, professionals in education and other social services have a responsibility to understand the issues related to child care. Think through and discuss the following issues with your classmates:

- How will you use your knowledge of quality child care to assist and guide parents in finding the best care possible for their children? Make a list of ideas to pass on to parents and care givers.

- Start a file of resources, contacts, and initiatives that will be useful as you collaborate with parents and other advocates to work toward higher standards for child care?

- Find out about initiatives like the Worthy Wage Campaign, which is designed to improve child care through increased compensation and training for child-care teachers.

SUMMARY AND REVIEW

Child care is essential to family life today. National surveys confirm that an increasing number of children are being cared for outside the home so that parents can work. Increasingly, as families recognize the importance of early experiences on children's later development, they are seeking care that goes beyond custodial to that which has an educational component as well.

Child-care arrangements include care that may be offered by a nanny, babysitter, or au pair in the child's home. Family child care occurs in the home of the provider and is offered for small groups of children, often of variable ages. Center-based child care can serve children from infancy through school age, generally in classrooms designed for children of a particular age range.

Considerable variation exists in the quality of child-care services. All states have regulations to govern family child care and center-based programs, but very little oversight is provided for families who use in-home care. State regulations, however, only provide minimum guidelines, and being licensed does not guarantee that a program is of high quality. Nationally accredited centers and family child-care homes, although still a small percentage of the total, serve as models of quality programs. Quality of care includes both process and structural components in the child-care setting.

The most important indicator of quality is the caregiver. The 30% annual turnover rate of those working with children because of poor compensation, lack of benefits, and poor working conditions is a serious issue facing child care. The improvement of the quality, affordability, and accessibility of child care is one of the biggest challenges facing families, schools, and communities today.

SUGGESTED ACTIVITIES AND QUESTIONS

1. Interview several parents who use different kinds of child care arrangements. Determine how they feel about the care their child is receiving and the challenges they face navigating work and parenthood.

2. Obtain a copy of your state's child-care regulations. What are the ratios of adults to children at various ages? What are the qualifications required of caregivers? How do these compare to national recommendations?

3. Visit a child-care center and arrange to observe several of the classes. What elements of a quality curriculum can you see? What changes might you make?

4. In the McGee vignette, pick out the incidents that would indicate to Mr. and Mrs. McGee that the center probably has high structural and process qualities.

RESOURCES

Books

Bender, J., Flatter, C. H., & Sorrentino, J. M. (2000). *Half a childhood: Quality programs for out-of-school hours* (2nd ed.). Nashville, TN: School-Age NOTES.

Bergen, D., Reid, R., & Torelli, L. (2000). *Educating and caring for very young children: The infant/toddler curriculum.* New York: Teachers College Press.

Gonzalez-Mena, J. (2001). *Multicultural issues in child care* (3rd ed.). Mountain View, CA: Mayfield.

Lombardi, J. (2003). *Time to care: Redesigning child care to promote education, support families, and build communities.* Philadelphia: Temple University Press.

Films and Videos

Child care and children with special needs [Video, 52 min]. (2000). This video explains how the Americans with Disabilities Act affects child-care programs. Newark, DE: Video Active Productions.

Early child care and education [Video, 29 min]. (2002). This video portrays different kinds of child care for children from infancy through school age and focuses on issues of quality appropriate for each level. Crystal Lake, IL: Magna Systems Video.

Keys to quality infant and toddler care [Video, 24 min]. (2002). This video helps parents recognize quality child care by focusing on relationships, responsiveness, and individualized care among the children, parents, and staff. Crystal Lake, IL: Magna Systems Video.

Quality child care: Making the right choice for you and your young child. [Video, 30 min]. (2005). Beverly Hills, CA: Parents' Action for Children.

Organizations

National Association for the Education of Young Children
1313 L Street, NW, Suite 500
Washington, DC 20036
http://www.naeyc.org

National Association for Family Child Care
5202 Pinemont Drive
Salt Lake City, UT 84123
http://www.nafcc.org

School-Age NOTES
P.O. Box 40205
Nashville, TN 37204
http://www.schoolagenotes.com

Web Sites

http://www.afterschoolalliance.org   The
Afterschool Alliance provides information for
establishing school-age programs as well as
disseminating research to support after-school care.

http://www.ccw.org   The Center for the Child Care
Workforce is committed to quality early care and
education for all children by promoting policy,
research, and organizing to improve the wages,

benefits, training opportunities, and working
conditions for those who work in child-care settings.

http://www.childcareexchange.com   Child Care
Exchange offers support to child-care directors and
others interested in promoting quality child care
through its journal, Web site, and international
conferences.

http://www.naccrra.net   The National Association
of Child Care Resource and Referral Agencies is a
national network of more than 850 community-based
resource and referral agencies. Resource and referral
centers help families, providers, and the community
find, provide, and plan for affordable, quality child
care.

http://www.nccic.org   The National Child Care
Information Center provides linkages with other
agencies interested in enhancing and promoting child
care.

Including Children
with Disabilities

Continued collaboration and consultation at all levels of the ecological system, including families, teachers, social service agencies, and policymakers, is essential to allow for creative and successful solutions for early childhood inclusion.

(Frankel, 2004, p. 316)

The number of children identified as having special learning needs has increased dramatically over the past 30 years as federal laws mandating appropriate intervention and education have been developed. About 15% of all infants, toddlers, children, and adolescents have been recognized as having disabilities (Turnbull, Turnbull, & Wehmeyer, 2007) and increasingly, such children are being taught in general-education classrooms, an approach referred to as **inclusion**. Other children with more pronounced disabilities need to be educated in special education classrooms and are included with groups of typically developing peers for certain parts of the daily routine, as appropriate. A small percentage of children with severe disabilities attend special schools or receive their education at home or in another kind of facility. No matter the setting, however, ensuring the optimal growth and development of children with disabilities is a responsibility shared by their families, schools, and community agencies. After reading this chapter you will be able to do the following:

1. Discuss the emotional impact that having a child with disabilites can have on a family.

2. Describe why the early identification of disabilities is desirable and how early intervention can help children achieve their maximum potential.

3. Explain the importance of the Individuals with Disabilities Education Act (IDEA) and its six principles governing the education of students with disabilities.

4. Define individualized education plan (IEP), individualized family services plan (IFSP), least restrictive environment (LRE) and how decisions are made about services necessary for a child with disabilities.

5. Make a case for inclusion and its benefits to children with disabilities and children who are typically developing.

6. Assess the importance of community agencies in meeting the needs of persons with disabilities and their families.

As Joan gave the final push and her new baby was born, she was thrilled to hear, "It's a girl!"; Josh, her two-year-old son now had a baby sister. A hush had fallen in the delivery room, however, and Joan, waiting for the baby to be lifted to her, noticed Rob, her husband, staring at the baby in disbelief. "What's wrong?"; she cried. As the baby was gently laid on her breast, Joan's doctor quietly said, "I think the baby has Down syndrome. We'll have to run some tests to be sure." Joan looked at her husband in dismay as tears welled in her eyes, and her newborn was taken from her and rushed to the Neonatal Intensive Care Unit.

Rob and Joan, like many who have a child with severe disabilities, were unprepared for the birth of a child with special needs. As they awaited the test results for the little girl they named Zoe, they clung to the hope that the doctor was wrong and that their child was "normal." Some years later, as they played on the beach with Josh and Zoe, now seven, they couldn't imagine life without their spirited little girl. True, she had had some difficult medical problems early on and now needed accommodations in school, but she had a sunny disposition and brought them all much joy. They didn't think of her as an abnormal child but as a child who in many ways was similar to her typically developing brother.

Zoe was fortunate to have been born during the era of the **Individuals with Disabilities Education Act (IDEA)**. Thanks to increasingly protective laws, she and her family had received early intervention services when she was an infant and toddler (Lewis & Doorlag, 2006). Later, Zoe was able to participate in a community nursery school and was currently attending a second-grade class in a public school, where she also received speech and language services, physical therapy, and counseling.

Children with disabilities are a subgroup of the larger category of children with special needs (Turnbull, Turnbull, & Wehmeyer, 2007). Included in this group are gifted and talented children, children who are linguistically or culturally different from the mainstream, and those children who are at risk for school failure because of poverty or other social conditions. Each of these groups may need special intervention to achieve their maximum potential in school but are not protected by the laws that have been enacted for children with disabilities.

Some children with attention deficit hyperactivity disorder (ADHD), for example, do not qualify for special education services but may require accommodations to function well in general education. These students may need to take a test orally, extra time for tests, a peer note taker, or a behavior plan. A **504 plan**, legally mandated by federal law, is put into place for such children to assure that they receive needed accommodations. When the student does not perform as expected even with the 504 plan, further evaluation may be done to dermine if the child may be eligible for special education services.

Children who are gifted and talented may also benefit from accommodations to the general curriculum in order to achieve their full potential, but such help is not mandated by law at this point. Many school systems do attempt to identify gifted and talented students and provide differentiated instruction for them. Typically, these children are grouped together when possible and the pace of instruction is accelerated and content is enriched with opportunities for creative and critical thinking.

Some parents like Rob and Joan learn about their child's disability at birth or soon after; others find out later. A pediatrician might raise concerns when a child fails to meet developmental milestones

for motor or language development and recommend further screening. Other children are not identified as having a disability until they enter preschool, elementary, or even middle or high school, when their learning differences become apparent.

Although it is impossible to calculate exactly how many children with disabilities are in the United States, the U.S. Department of Education's annual report to Congress on the education of children with disabilities provides the most accurate estimate (See Table 6–1). When all children from birth to age 21 are counted, the total number rises from the 5,655,442 children now served in elementary schools to approximately 6.5 million individuals with disabilities. The majority of school-age children receiving special education services have mild disabilities, with slightly more then two-thirds of these children falling into two categories: specific learning disabilities and speech or language impairments.

This kind of labeling serves to alert you to the kinds of disablties and percentages of children within each category, but it is important to remember that these numbers refer to individual children, who like Zoe, have strengths and weaknesses, like all children. When thinking about children with disabilities, be aware of the person first, and avoid labeling that highlights the disability as an individual's most important characteristic (Turnbull et al., 2007). For example, referring to "the boy who is blind" is preferable to saying "the blind boy." Even better, call children by their names and refer to their disability only when it is relevant.

REFLECTION

You may have had limited experiences with children with disabilities when you were growing up. In the past, children with disabilities were often kept separate from their typically developing peers. Think about how you will educate yourself about disabilities and help children understand the importance of treating all people with respect, regardless of their abilities.

Table 6–1   Number of Students Ages Six Through Twenty-One Served Under IDEA
in the 2003 School Year

Disability	Number	Percentage
Specific learning disabilities	2,866,908	50.6
Speech and language impairments	1,129,260	19.9
Mental retardation	582,663	10.3
Emotional disturbance	417,798	7.3
Multiple disabilities	132,645	2.3
Hearing impairments	72,048	1.3
Orthodpedic impairments	68,234	1.3
Other health impairments	452,442	8.0
Visual impairments	25,879	.45
Autism	141,022	2.5
Deaf-blindness	1,670	.03
Traumatic brain injury	22,534	.39
Developmental delay	305,752	6.3
All Disabilities	5, 655,442	

Source: U.S. Department of Education, Office of Special Education Programs.

After providing an overview of the federal legislation concerning individuals with disabilities, we will look at the issues associated with serving the needs of children with disabilities within the family, school, and community. Collaboration within these social settings is essential for the most successful outcome for children.

OVERVIEW OF FEDERAL SPECIAL EDUCATION LAWS

In Chapter 2 we alerted the reader to the beginnings of federal legislation that ushered in a new era for recognizing and ensuring educational opportunities for children with disabilities. In the subsequent 30 years, America has undergone considerable adjustment (not without difficulty) in providing special education facilities, restructuring buildings, reorganizing staff, and modifying curricula. Perhaps most of all, more educators have a new outlook, appreciation, and interest in accommodating children with special needs in regular classrooms.

Many adults today can remember a time when children with disabilities did not attend school.

Many were cared for at home; some were institutionalized, but the majority of these children were marginalized and lived their lives out of the mainstream of society (Hiatt-Michael, 2004). In some parts of the world, this remains the fate of those who have disabilities. Federal laws enacted over the past 30 years, however, protect children in the United States from being excluded from school based on their disability. These laws also provide early intervention for infants, toddlers, and preschoolers within their families and other natural settings to provide the services that will help them achieve their full potential.

As Table 2–2 in Chapter 2 indicates, several legislative endeavors since 1975 have expanded and clarified the provisions for special education. In 1986, legislation expanded school programs to cover preschoolers (ages three to five) with disabilities. The notion driving this move was that early identification of disabilities meant that additional time and instruction would enhance the child's later schooling. It was only a matter of time until the first three years of a child's life were also considered for special services, when needed. Therefore, in 1997, legislation brought services (though

George Dodson / PH College

A child who is physically handicapped is receiving the services of a physical therapist in a home setting.

not through schools) to infants and toddlers. Specialists meet with parents of children in this group to help establish a better foundation for their later schooling.

Now known as the Individuals with Disabilities Education Act (IDEA), this legislation has been immensely important in making certain that children, adolescents, and young adults to age 21 have access to and benefit from special education services. The law is very specific about who is eligible for special education and how this education is individualized to meet the unique needs of the individual. Consequently, special education is seen as a service and not a place. Instruction may take place at home, in a hospital, or in a regular classroom and be supplemented with speech therapy, physical therapy, occupational therapy, and other services necessary for the child to benefit from special education.

Readers anticipating a career in early-childhood education or related human services professions must be cognizant of several provisions in the legislation designed to protect the rights of children with disabilities. The following six principles undergirding special education reform (summarized from Turnbull et al., 2007) have become the specialized language of special education.

1. *Zero rejection.* A provision against excluding any student from school because of behavior that violates school rules but is a manifestation of the student's disability.

2. *Nondiscriminatory and multidisciplinary evaluations.* A rule that requires a nondiscriminatory evaluation to determine, if indeed, the student has a disability and to determine the kind of services the student should receive. This rule requires schools to assess children in their own language using a team of evaluators who avoid procedures that may be culturally or racially discriminatory.

3. *Appropriate education.* A rule requiring educators to plan individually tailored education and related services for each student with a disability.

4. *Least restructed environment.* A rule requiring schools to merge children with disabilities with typically developing peers in regular education classrooms, to the maximum extent appropriate for the child.

5. *Procedural due process.* A rule that establishes the safeguards that make the school and parents accountable to each other for carrying out the student's IDEA rights, safeguards all students' rights for privacy, and establishes procedures for legal redress.

6. *Parent and student participation.* A rule requiring schools to collaborate with parents and adolescent students in designing and carrying out special education programs.

Parents and special education leaders have been at the forefront of the movement to establish laws that guarantee children with disabilities an equal opportunity for education (Hiatt-Michael, 2004). It was because of the commitment and **advocacy** of these families and educators that legal actions in the courts and in the federal legislature have evolved to the present inclusion of children with disabilities in mainstream education. In some cases, parents continue to struggle for the appropriate educational services for their children within the courts. Ideally, of course, families, schools, and communities work together, sharing their expertise, support, and resources to provide the best outcome for all children.

REFLECTION

Arrange to interview the parents of a child with disabilities. Ask them about their experiences receiving services for their child in the schools. Think about how you would work with their child in your classroom.

FAMILIES RAISING CHILDREN WITH DISABILITIES

Trish had been dreading the conference with Katie's preschool teacher at Grove Nursery School. Ms. Criner had been calling almost every day with concerns about three-year-old Katie. "She wouldn't stay in circle, she grabbed things from other children, she hit and kicked them when they grabbed back, then she ran away from the teachers." As soon as Trish sat down, Ms. Criner smiled kindly but wasted no time getting to the point of the conference stating, "I'm afraid we are not going to be able to continue *Katie here at Grove. We don't feel we can keep the other children safe from her aggressive behavior. We don't think this is the right place for her." Blinded by her tears, Trish rushed from the room and out to her car.*

Emotional Impact

Having a child with special needs presents unique challenges to parents, and for some, the initial discovery can be an intense and traumatic event. Studies reported by Heward (2006) indicated that parents of children with disabilities go through an adjustment process similar to grieving in working through their feelings. Initially, parents may experience shock, denial, and disbelief. These feelings may be followed by periods of anger, guilt, depression, shame, rejection, or overprotection of their child. Eventually, most parents move on to accept their child's disability and some grow to appreciate the positive impact their child has had on their lives (Hanson & Lynch, 2004).

Although research indicates that some parents move through a grief cycle of confronting, adjusting, and adapting, it is inappropriate to believe that all families will react in similar ways. Parents are unique and should be supported sensitively in their adjustment process. Depending on the nature of the disability, parents and siblings may need to make many changes as they learn how to provide the appropriate care and accommodations for the child. Often the family routines, resources, and activities will need to be modified, and this can cause resentment and stress. Families raising children with disabilities need teachers and community-service personnel who are sensitive, tolerant, and helpful.

Early Identification and Intervention

When Katie, in the vignette above, was dismissed from Grove Nursery School, her mother was devastated. For several years, Trish had been ignoring the warning signs that Katie was developing differently than others. She walked and talked very late and seemed to have more difficulty getting along with others. Now that the nursery school had confirmed her fears that something was

Merrill

Very young children diagnosed with developmental delays, such as Down syndrome, are eligible for preschool programs that provide natural settings, such as a playground.

wrong, Trish finally decided to have some testing done. Through the **child-find** process in her local school district, Trish was able to have her daughter evaluated. When Katie was identified as having a language processing disability, she became eligible to attend a prekindergarten program in a local elementary school that served children with developmental delays and other learning problems. By the time Katie was in first grade, she was progressing well in a general education class with support from the resource teacher of special education. Katie's success in school was largely the result of the **early identification** of her disability and the intervention services she received.

The benefits of early identification and intervention are well documented (Lerner, Lowenthal, & Egan, 2003). When children's learning problems are recognized early, behavior problems and school failure can be prevented or reduced. Early intervention is generally a family-centered approach, so the

parents of children with disabilities also benefit as they learn ways to support their child's development at home. Society also profits from the early identification of children with disabilities because these children, like Katie, are often ready to participate in a general education classroom at significantly less cost than that of extensive special education services (Schweinhart & Weikart, 1997).

Early Intervention Program for Infants and Toddlers with Disabilities

The Early Intervention Program for Infants and Toddlers with Disabilities was established in 1997 as Part C of the IDEA—1997. To be eligible for services, children must be experiencing developmental delays in cognitive, physical, communication, social or emotional, or adaptive development, as measured by appropriate diagnostic instruments. Children whose diagnosed medical condition has a high probability of developmental delay (Lerner, Lowenthal, & Egan, 2003) are also eligible for services.

The evaluation of infants and toddlers requires a comprehensive, multidisciplinary approach, which often results in a variety of needed services, such as family training and counseling, home visits, speech or language pathology and audiology, occupational and physical therapy, and health services. By law, these intervention services need to be provided at the child's home, in a child-care facility, or in another setting natural for children of this age group. The law also requires that a service coordinator be provided to help guide the family and manage the efforts of the various agencies that provide services to the infant or toddler.

REFLECTION

Do you feel you know enough about the early identification of children with disabilities? If not, contact your state department of education and begin collecting materials related to services for children with special needs and compile them in a resource notebook.

Section I:	**Enrollment Information** (name, contact information for parents and caregivers)
Section II-A:	**Family Considerations for the IFSP** (parents' perception of child and family strengths and needs, including a checklist of concerns)
Section II-B:	**All About Our Family** (narrative of family members, what they do, neighborhood information, and other people important to the family)
Section II-C:	**All About My Child** (checklist of things child likes to do or parent would like child to do as well as a narrative section on who the child spends time with)
Section III:	**Summary of Child's Present Levels of Performance** (completed by the IFSP team as a summary of their observations and evaluations of the child's physical, communication, and social and emotional development, cognition, and motor and adaptive skills)
Section IV:	**Natural Settings/Environment** (includes a checklist of settings that could be considered as options, as well as those that have been selected and why they reflect the most natural settings for the child)
Section V:	**Major Outcomes** (a listing of the major goals, current status, needed changes, and what will be done to accomplish these changes)
Section VI:	**Transition Planning Checklist** (information about transition to community programs)
Section VII:	**Early Intervention Services** (a summary of the kinds, duration, and outcomes of the related services the child has received, including service coordination and assistive technology)
Section VIII:	**Other Services** (medical and other services that the child needs but are not funded by the infant–toddler program and the funding source)
Section IX:	**IFSP Implementation and Distribution Authorization**
Section X:	**IFSP Team** (names, titles and roles, agencies, and signatures of all involved in the interdisciplinary team)
Section XI:	Progress Summary/Modifications/Revisions to Outcomes in the IFSP

Figure 6–1   Components of the Individualized Family Service Plan (IFSP)

Zoe, identified with Down syndrome soon after birth, began to receive services as an infant guided by the **individualized family service plan (IFSP)**, required for children ages birth to three years. This plan, which is developed once a child has been deemed eligible for service is based on the results of comprehensive assessments and is reviewed at least every six months. Parent participation in the development of the IFSP is essential and parent input is sought for decisions related to evaluation, identification, possible placements, and services. Although a detailed discussion of the IFSP is beyond the scope of this text (see Appendix D in Lerner, Lowenthal, & Egan, 2003, for a complete example of an IFSP), Figure 6–1 provides an overview of the categories addressed in this important document.

Multicultural Issues

A growing concern among educators and child advocates is the disproportionate number of minority children who receive special education services. Both African American and Hispanic students are more likely to be referred to special education than are European Americans. Although multiple factors may account for the overrepresentation of children of color in special education (Gorman, 2004), one possible explanation is the fact that children from diverse backgrounds are also disproportionally from families with low incomes. There are strong connections between low income and exposure to toxins, poor nutrition, lower birth rate, and less stimulating home and child-care environments. Others (Heward, Cavanaugh, & Ernsbarger, 2005) suggest that there is some evidence that some children's placement in special education is a result of culture, class, or gender influences. A study by The National Research Council (2002) addressed this issue and noted that the referral process for special education is subjective, and bias could be a factor in diagnosing more minority children as having disabilities than their percentage of the population seems to justify.

When working with families from minority ethnic or language groups, it is essential that professionals display respect for the parents' culture and provide the legally mandated translations of important documents and a translator during meetings about the child. Some families will have great difficulty acknowledging that their child has a disability. They may not agree with the diagnosis or not wish their child to participate in the services that are being suggested. These disagreements can occur with any family, but professionals working with families from diverse cultures must be especially sensitive to misunderstandings and miscommunications. The collaborative nature of developing an individualized plan for children with disabilities requires a high level of trust between professionals and parents, which may need time to develop.

As an educator or community-service professional, you will be part of the stronger efforts that are being made to provide early intervention for children at risk for educational failure because of poverty or lack of English language in the home. There is long-standing evidence that early intervention and quality early childhood experiences can significantly lower children's need for special education services later (Schweinhart & Weikart, 1997). To reach those children most in need of these services, professionals need to work hard at communicating well with families who may be struggling with anger and denial with regard to their child's possible disabilities and who may be distrustful of the educational system.

Medication

The decision to give medication to a child with disabilities can be a difficult one for parents. Since this is a medical decision, they must work closely with their child's physician to determine if the use of drugs will be beneficial for them. Medication is most often recommended for children diagnosed with attention deficit hyperactivity disorder (ADHD), who usually take a stimulant. The use of stimulant drugs is controversial to some extent. Although there are known side effects, such as loss of appetite, stomach pains, headaches, irritability, sleep problems, and mood changes, the long-term impact is not well researched. Children who have been diagnosed with anxiety or mood disorders such as depression or bipolar disorder, may also benefit from medication therapy.

Parents are cautious about having their children take a medication and worry about their growth, health, and the long-term effects of drug therapy. On the other hand, many teachers are strong supporters of the use of medication. Research indicates that children correctly diagnosed and appropriately medicated do demonstrate improved classroom performance (Anstine-Templeton & Johnson 2004). Children who are medicated should have full-treatment plans that include behavior interventions and therapy, as needed. When medication is given, parents and educators need to monitor the child closely to ensure that the right dosage is being given. Finally, teachers must respect and support the decisions of those parents who oppose medication for their children and disallow its use.

Respite and Support

Parenting a child with a disability can be demanding, and the more severe the child's disability, the more challenges the family faces. Programs, trainings, and support groups for families raising children with disabilities can sustain parents and provide much needed information. These supports can also help families find others who are dealing with similar issues. Research indicates that families who participate in support groups are more likely to be involved in their children's schooling (Newman, 2004), and this involvement leads to higher acheivement.

Respite care, which provides temporary releif from the caretaking responsibilities associated with parenting, is especially needed for families whose children have problem behaviors and severe disabilities. Parents of children with challenging behaviors may be harshly judged by strangers or family members, who may perceive the child's behavior as the result of poor parenting rather than a reflection of a disability (Lee & Ostrowsky, 2004). Parenting such children can be very stressful, and if the family does not have a network of extended family and friends to assist them, they can become burned out from trying to meet the demands of their responsibilities. Professionals such as teachers, social workers, and psychologists need to be able to help families locate support groups, therapy, print and on-line resources, and sources for respite care.

REFLECTION

What do you think about the increased use of medication for behavioral and emotional issues in children? Make a list of the pros and cons of medication therapy in order to understand the various perspectives on this issue.

CHILDREN WITH DISABILITIES IN SCHOOL

Although parent involvement and input remain essential as the child enters preschool, families who have been part of the infant–toddler program do experience a transition at this juncture. Children who are diagnosed with disabilities as infants and toddlers transition to the preschool program when they turn three and shift from the IFSP to an individual education program (IEP). This can be a significant passage for the child, as services at the preschool level are generally provided away from the home. For some families, this can be a traumatic adjustment because they may be separated from their child for the first time. Other children are newly diagnosed as preschoolers and still others may not be identified as having a disability until later in elementary school. The following sections address the services provided by the preschool program of IDEA and the aspects of the law that apply to children during the elementary school years.

Preschool Program

One aspect of IDEA mandates school districts to locate, identify and evaluate preschool children with disabilities within their communities through the **child-find** process. The goal of child find is to locate children who may need early intervention. As you work with parents of young children, you can help them determine if their child may need such screening. Working with the family to answer the following questions might be helpful (Lerner, Lowenthal, & Egan, 2003):

- Is the child developing typically and achieving developmental milestones?
- Does the child exhibit appropriate behaviors for his or her age level?
- Are there any factors in the child's developmental history that cause concern?
- Are there any situations in the home that might influence the cognitive, physical, linguistic, and emotional development of the child?
- Does the child require more stimulation and nurturance than the typical child?

Child-find efforts are enhanced by the work of pediatricians, early-childhood educators from Head Start, child care and nursery schools, personnel from community agencies such as public

Special educators, such as a speech therapist, are to be provided for a child with a hearing impairment who is in a nursery school and involved with a group of peers.

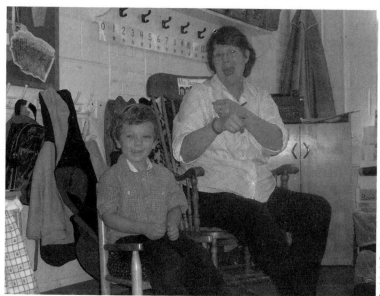

Patricia A. Scully

health and social services, and others who come in contact with preschool children. These professionals can alert parents to the child-find process and can even refer the child if the parent is reluctant.

After an initial screening, the child-find team will arrange for a full evaluation of the child's strengths and weaknesses for those children who require it. If the child is diagnosed with a disability, the next step is to develop an individualized educational program (IEP) for intervention, which will focus on the instruction goals for the child.

Another section of IDEA devoted to preschool mandates that three- to five-year-old children with a diagnosed disability receive a **free appropriate public education (FAPE)** and the related services they require. Zoe, who had been receiving services under the early intervention program for infants and toddlers with disabilities, made a smooth transition to the preschool program. Because she had been helped in developing self-care skills and had had many opportunities to interact and play cooperatively with other young children, Zoe had the **adaptive behaviors** needed for social acceptance in a general education setting. Thus, when she turned three, Zoe's parents

decide to enroll her in the same neighborhood nursery school her older brother had attended, because they wanted her to have the same opportunities that he had.

This nursery school had never had a child with an IEP before, but the staff was willing to work with Zoe's family and the related professionals who would help to meet her IEP goals. The early childhood special educator, speech pathologist, and occupational therapist came to the nursery school to work with Zoe and a small group of peers when appropriate. They also collaborated with the nursery school teachers and staff to make sure Zoe was progressing. See McCormick, Wong, and Yogi (2003) for a full description of how a nursery school planned for the successful inclusion of a child with Down syndrome.

Attending school with typically functioning children allowed Zoe to be in the **least restrictive environment (LRE)** based on her educational needs another facet of the law, which requires children with disabilities to be in the most normalized settings possible. Zoe's strong social skills were a plus in her success at nursery school. She established friendships with some of her peers, which led to play dates and birthday invitations.

Although she continued to need extra services and assistance with certain tasks, she was a well-liked child who was fully included in the school's program.

Katie, the child with a language disability who had been excluded from Grove Nursery School, was later placed in the preschool classroom at a nearby public elementary school. In this preschool program for children with developmental delays and diagnosed disabilities, typically developing peers are invited to participate in the program, allowing all children to benefit from the experience of learning together.

General Educators and Children with Disabilities

Children with disabilities receive a continuum of services provided by both general and special educators, as well as other specialists. Hence, there are a number of ways that general educators have responsibilities related to children with disabilities. Children with a diagnosed disability may be placed in their classroom full time, in what is often termed **full inclusion.** These children will also receive services from a special educator and other specialists but will spend the majority of their in-school time in a general education classroom. Other children may be placed in a self-contained special education classroom but be included in a general education class for lunch, recess, and specials like art and music, so they can benefit from social interaction with typically developing peers. The individual child's IEP will determine the extent of their participation in a general education classroom based on their needs and the least restrictive environment.

It is beyond the scope of this text to detail information about each kind of exceptionality and the ways that teachers can work with students with particular disabilities most effectively. Teachers who appreciate individual differences and are prepared to differentiate instruction based on these differences, however, will have the most success integrating children with disabilities into their classroom. With some disabilities, of course, the issues go beyond differentiation, and general educators will need guidance on how best to include specific children in their classrooms. It is essential that general education teachers and other professionals who work with children with disabilities recognize the importance of working as a team with parents, special education teachers, and other specialists. The most successful outcomes result from the collaborative efforts of a team working together for the child's optimum education. See Heward (2006), Turnbull et al., (2007), and Wood (2002) for a fuller treatment of specific disabilities and how general educators can adapt instruction to accommodate students in inclusive classrooms.

Referral Process. As mentioned earlier in the chapter, some disabilities are diagnosed at birth, others during the preschool years and still others during elementary school. General educators may be the first to suspect that a child has special learning needs and may require special education. General educators do not have the responsibility or training to diagnose disabilities, but they are often in a position to recognize learning and behavior difficulties that suggest a child may need further evaluation. Well-developed observation skills and a strong knowledge of child development and typical patterns of behavior and learning at various developmental stages are essential for teachers and others working professionally with children. Their observations will assist the team in making a diagnosis of a disability.

Educators, together with doctors, nurses, other school personnel, or parents, can make a referral to determine if a child needs special education. Typically, a referral must be a written document sent to the school principal, special education director, or chair of the committee that oversees special education placements. The referral must include the date the request is being made, as well as the child's full name, date of birth, home school, and why the sender believes the child might need special education. The referral should specify what the child is currently not doing that peers are able to do. School personnel must then evaluate the child and, if it is determined

Figure 6–2 Processing a Referral for Special Education
School personnel follow a sequence of events and meetings after receiving a referral. The sequence may be repeated annually or modified.

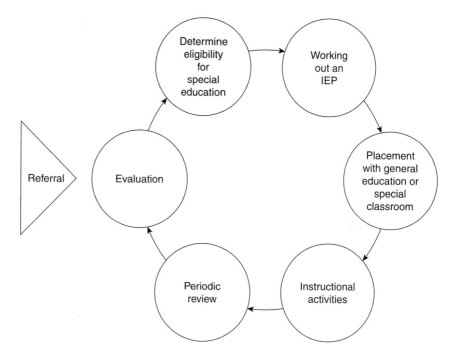

that the child qualifies for special education, they will write an IEP for the child and determine where the child will go to school. All this must be done within 90 calendar days.

REFLECTION

Think about what you need to know about different disabilities. Then, plan how you will educate yourself about how to work effectively with children who have various disabilities.

The IEP Process. Once a child has been referred for special education, an evaluation team will begin the assessment process. The evaluation team is made up of certain core members, such as the resource teachers, speech and language specialists, school psychologist, and school administrators. They will gather information from the child's parents and from former and present teachers who have worked with the child. They will

determine the kinds of testing that need to be done and may call on the school psychologist, speech and language specialist, or resource teacher to evaluate the child using various assessment instruments. Parents, teachers, and other concerned individuals become equal partners with the core members on the IEP Team when they are discussing the referral and the results of the evaluation for a specific child. See Figure 6–2 for a summary of the referral and placement process.

Ideally, parents will take the opportunity to become active partners in the evaluation and placement process and attend all meetings concerning their child. As the experts on their child, parents have much to contribute to the evaluation team, but it can be intimidating to them to sit at a table with professionals who use terminology and abbreviations that may be unfamiliar to a layperson. It is essential that the core members of the team work hard to make certain parents feel welcome and understand everything said about their child. If the parents do not speak English, a translator must be made available and important written materials must be translated into the native language, if at all feasible.

Once the child has been evaluated, the evaluation team will meet to share the findings of the various professionals who have tested the child. Each professional will supply a written report that summarizes the results of their testing, together with the observations and insights of the child's parents and teachers. At this point, the team will determine if the child has one or more of the impairments that are considered disabilities and will decide if the child is eligible for speical education services.

Once eligiblity has been established, the team writes the individualized education plan and determines where the child will go to school and what specific services the child needs. Parents will receive copies of the IEP; they will also receive reports on their child's progress in meeting IEP goals several times during the school year. If the child is not making adequate progress, the team will meet to revise the IEP. Parents may also request changes to the IEP based on their perceptions of their child's growth.

The protections of due process of the IDEA legislation determine the timing of the course of action on the referral and admission to special education procedures, as well as the written notices to parents that are required. Once the evaluation of the child is completed and it has been determined that the child is eligible for special education, the evaluation team has 30 days to write the IEP. Parents must be notified in writing before the team evaluates the child, before the school provides special education services to the child, and before the school changes the IEP. Parents must give their permission for the child to be evaluated and to receive special education services. Schools are also required to inform parents of their educational rights and to let them know how they can request a hearing if they disagree with the school's findings with regard to their child.

The IEP. An **individualized education program (IEP)** contracts for carrying out instruction for a special-needs student ages three to 21. The term has been in education practice for the past 30 years, and it means basically what the phrase implies, that is, a plan worked out by the team of general education teachers, specialists, parents, and sometimes the learner, as well, to serve the learner's needs. (See Figure 6–3 for the general components of the IEP.) At least once a year, an IEP will be written for the child. Every three years, children who have an IEP will be reevaluated to ascertain if they still require special education services.

Assistive Technology. Under IDEA, **assistive technology** is defined as "any item, piece of equipment, or product system, whether acquired commercially off the shelf, modified, or customized, that is used to increase, maintain, or improve functional capabilities of individuals with disabilities" (Individuals with Disabilities Education Act, 1997, p. 20). The term *technology* may conjure up images of computers and other hardware, but it actually refers to both high-tech and low-tech devices that help children with disabilities accomplish practical tasks.

The use of assistive technology, although not an actual IEP goal, can help children accomplish their goals by increasing their independence and allowing them to participate more fully in classroom activities. For children unable to move freely from place to place, motorized scooter boards, wheeled go-carts, and wheelchairs are a necessary assitive device. Taped books, devices that read printed books aloud, and talking computer programs are all available for children who have problems reading and writing.

The IEP team should carefully consider any assistive devices that may be necessary to help a child move, communicate, and learn most effectively. Choosing and modifying these technologies can be challenging, but the increasingly sophisticated computer and other assistive devices available are bringing individuals with disabilities into the mainstream.

One controversial aspect of technology is the cochlear implant device, which can restore hearing for people who are deaf. The implant bypasses the damaged part of the ear and transmits digitally processed sound directly into the cochlea, and the surgery is best performed on very young children.

Part 1:	**Identifying Information** (child's name, birthdate, grade, current placement)
Part II:	**Meeting Information** (type of meeting, particpants, and notice and permission information)
Part III:	**Current Assessment Information** (data source, scores, strengths, indicated areas of need)
Part IV:	**Eligibility** (educational impact of the disability, disability codes)
Part V:	**Parent Information**
Part VI:	**Progress on IEP Goals and Objectives on Benchmarks**
Part VII:	**Instructional Areas** (annual goals and short-term objectives for each instructional area)
Part VIII:	**Supplementary Aids and Services** (needed accommodations, modifications, and adaptations)
Part IX:	**Nonparticipation with Nondisabled Peers** (percentage of time the student will not participate with nondisabled peers in general education environment)
Part X:	**Primary Special Education Services**
Part XI:	**Related Services to Support Instruction** (speech/language, occupational or physical therapy, counseling, or others)
Part XII:	**Least Restrictive Environment** (placement and rationale for the decision)
Part XIII:	**Placement Decision**
Part XIV:	**Referral for Consideration of Alternative Placement**
Part XV:	**Specialized Transportation**
Part XVI:	**Summary**

Figure 6–3   Components of the Individualized Education Program (IEP)

Many members of the deaf community, however, feel it threatens the deaf way of life, which is based on American Sign Language. The debate continues on this issue, but other uses of technology are less controversial, and children with disabilities benefit from the advances being made in many areas of assistive technology.

Inclusion

⟳— *As the IEP meeting came to an end, Pat and Joan, parents of third-grader Devin, said, "So the bottom line is, Devin has been diagnosed with a language impairment. And, instead of going to the school in our neighborhood, he'll be attending Page Elementary School, where they have a special class for children with learning dsabilitiess. Because he will be in special education, he'll*

receive bus transportation from our home to the school, right?" One of the team members quickly assured them that this was the case and reminded them that Devin would be participating in lots of activities with one of the "regular" third-grade classes, at Page Elementary based on his IEP goals. "Remember," said Mr. Robey, his current teacher, "he'll still have recess, specials, and lunch with the kids who are in general education." Pat and Joan sighed and signed the IEP, hoping that this was the best course of action for their struggling child. Now they had to tell him that he'd be changing schools and convince him that this was going to be a new adventure. —⟲

Although Pat and Joan reluctantly accepted the advice of the evaluation team that the best placement for Devin was in a self-contained special education classroom, other parents would push

Assistive technology includes devices that help children with special needs, such as a child with hearing and speech impairments, to be more independent and more fully involved in classroom activities.

Patricia A. Scully

for full-inclusion. In the full inclusion model, children with disabilities are educated in the general education classroom all day. In this model, children have a home base in a general education classroom, and any different instructional approaches or services that they require are offered within its parameters. Proponents of this approach argue that placing children in as typical a setting as possible is essential for three reasons:

1. Separation in inherently stigmatizing to students with a disability.
2. Children with disabilities benefit from peer interaction with nondisabled peers.
3. Children placed in separate classrooms function at a lower level and with lowered expectations and become a self-fulfilling prophecy (Simmons, 2004).

Others argue that not all children with disabilities benefit from full inclusion, and the environment should be appropriate for the child. Some children really need the small group size, close monitoring, and individualized interactions that a separate classroom provides. Other children may require instruction in a special school or may need to be educated at home for a period of time. See Figure 6–4 for the continuum of possible place-

ments meeting the criteria for the least restrictive environment.

Critics of full inclusion also consider the needs of nondisabled students, whose learning may be interrupted by the socially inappropriate or disruptive behavior of some children with disabilities. Although the issue of full vs. partial inclusion continues to be debated in the professional literature and in the courts, general educators can expect to have children with disabilities in their classrooms on a full- and part-time basis for the foreseeable future. The principle of the least restrictive environment always makes the general education classroom a desirable option or goal for the majority of children with disabilities.

Welcoming a Child with Disabilities into the General Education Classroom

Teacher attitude is the single most important influence on the success of a child with disabilities placed in a general education classroom. Fortunately, research indicates (Wood, 2002) that teachers' attitudes about inclusion are becoming more positive. In addition to this positive attitude, however, teachers do need training and support in

---

Most Restrictive to Least Restrictive

Home or hospital placement

Full-time placement in residential facility

Full-day placement in special education school (public or private)

Full-day placement in special education class

Full-day placement in special education class with social integration with general school population

Part-day general class placement and part-day special education class placement

Part-day general class placement and part-day resource or itinerant services

Full-day general class placement with instruction delivered in regular class by specialist

Full-day general class placement with consultation services for the teacher

---

Figure 6–4   Continuum of Possible Placements for Children with Disabilities
Source: U.S. Department of Education (2002). Twenty-fourth annual report to Congress on the implementation of the Individuals with Disabilities Education Act. Washington, DC: Author.

order to best meet the needs of the children with disabilities assigned to their classrooms. They also must learn how to work collaboratively with special educators and other specialists who will be part of the child's team.

Once assigned a child with a disability, general education teachers will need to find out as much information about the child as possible and may want to become educated about the specific disability. They may also want to prepare typically developing children for the presence of a child with disabilities in their classroom. Helping the children recognize that everyone has strengths and weaknesses will be an appropriate starting point to ensure that all learners will be welcomed. Through their positive attitude and warmth, teachers will model acceptance of all individuals and set a respectful tone. Some teachers find that children's literature is helpful in introducing different kinds of disabilities and opening up discussion. Others follow up this discussion with a conversation involving the child and his or her parents, as appropriate. For example, children who use a wheelchair or other assistive devices can demonstrate how the devices operate and how they help them to move and learn.

Although Georgie was over six years old when he entered Ms. William's kindergarten class for the first time, he was very small for his age and very busy. Within minutes, he was running around the classroom, shrieking and laughing. As the days went by, it was clear that Georgie would be having difficulties participating in the kindergarten curriculum. Ms. Williams began to have him sit on her lap during circle time, which calmed him down and helped him focus. When other children wanted to sit on her lap as well, Ms. Williams gently reminded them that they didn't need this assistance. Soon the other children were helping Georgie through the daily routines, and he began to sit in the circle with a friend on either side holding his hands and reminding him about the rules. Later in the year, Georgie was diagnosed with a disability and began receiving services from the special education teacher, Ms. Britt. She was delighted to see that Georgie was a fully accepted member of the kindergarten. What pleased her, too, was the empathy the other children showed for Georgie and how proud they were of his accomplishments.

Although the debate continues about the merits of full and partial inclusion, it is certain that all children benefit when children with and without disabilities attend school together. Special educators who work carefully with general educators in preparing for inclusion and offer support during its implementation can help to promote the positive attitudes essential for a successful experience. Together, the general educator and special educator will determine how to help the child understand and follow class rules and routines and to fit in socially with the other children. Depending on the nature of the disability, accommodations and modifications may need to be made in the physical environment and in academic expectations. A well-functioning team of skilled professionals can make all the difference in making certain that the inclusion of children with disabilities is a positive one for all concerned.

Working with Parents of Children with Disabilities

Chapter 11 offers many general strategies for collaboration between schools, families, and communities. Professionals working with parents raising children with disabilites, however, have some unique challenges in establishing and maintaining positive relationships with these families. The importance of a trusting relationship between educators and parents in these situations can hardly be overstated. Families are an integral part of the educational process, from referral through the evaluation, placement, and reevaluation process. Parents are equal partners in decision making for their children.

Research conducted with parents of children with disabilites (Gorman, 2004) reports that families regard the following behaviors from school professionals as especially important in establishing collaborative relationships:

- Friendliness
- Optimism
- Patience
- Sincerity and honesty
- Tact
- Responsiveness
- Openness to suggestions

Other researchers (Hanson & Lynch, 2004) suggest that professionals need to have a family-centered approach in order to work successfully with children with disabilities. This includes acknowledgement and respect for each family's strengths, culture, language, and ability to make decisions for their child, even if these decisions differ from what the professionals would choose. The starting point for establishing a relationship with parents is to get to know them and to allow them to get to know you. Before attempting to communicate about sensitive topics, make a sincere attempt to establish rapport with the family through positive phone calls and general meetings. Remember, just as children with disabilities are much like their typically developing peers, so are their parents like all parents. The strategies you will read about in Chapter 11 will also be effective for parents of children with disabilities. In addition, Gorman (2004) offers an extensive list of ways to work well with parents of children with disabilities.

COMMUNITY SUPPORT FOR CHILDREN WITH DISABILITIES

Although schools play an important role in educating children with disabilities and supporting their parents, the larger community also offers resources for these children and their families. Teachers and other professionals can be instrumental in helping to link families with needed services available in the community and also with on-line organizations and resources.

As Laverne and Reggie sat in the stands watching their nine-year-old daughter, Latisha, dribble the ball down the court and successfully sink a basket, they grabbed each others' hands and lept to their feet, cheering. The idea of Latisha, diagnosed with autism during her second year of life, competing in a basketball tournament was something that they had never even considered a few years ago. Special Olympics had made it possible.

Fortunately for Latisha and her family, her special education teacher had informed them about the opportunity for Latisha to participate in Special Olympics. With 30 Olympic-like summer and winter sports available in more than 200 programs around the United States, Special Olympics has given individuals with intellectual disabilities the chance to be part of a team and to compete with others of similar ability. Besides this national organization, many local communities also provide sports and recreational activities geared toward children with disabilities. These children may also need before- and after-school child care, occasional evening babysitting, and chances to participate in community events and activities with typically developing peers.

Teachers and other school personnel who are knowledgable about their community can help parents and children access these out-of-school opportunities. They can also help families connect with other parents raising children with the same disability in the local or on-line community. Finally, community agencies have a responsibility to reach out to families raising children with disabilities, to alert them to the resources available for them and their children.

Support for Parents

As a warm and sympathetic person who genuinely cares about children with disabilities and their families, you may find yourself in an uncomfortable position when a parent shares personal information about family issues that are beyond the scope of their child's education. In these cases, it is particularly important for you to have resources for support to suggest to the parent. The school psychologist, social worker, or counselor can be a great help in generating a list of community services that can be accessed by families. Helping parents learn how to obtain needed help for themselves and their children will enable them to meet their ongoing needs.

REFLECTION

It is natural to be nervous about teaching or working with children with disabilities if you have not had very much experience or preparation for doing so. Arrange to visit some of the settings along the continuum of most-to-least-restrictive educational settings for children with disabilities mentioned in Table 6–4 and talk to the teachers about their experiences.

You may want to suggest resources and support to those parents who seem stressed and over-burdened with the responsibilities of caring for their child with a disability. Other parents may seem to need guidance in providing the best parenting. Disability rights organizations, respite programs, parent networks, and family resource centers are found in many communities. Although you may have many ideas to share with families about parent-to-parent support groups and on-line communities that address issues related to parenting children with disabilities, remember that it is the family's decision about whether or not they wish to participate in such organizations and activities. The role of the professional is to provide the information to the parents and to respect their decisions about how they choose to utilize it.

It is important to remember that families find support in many ways. Some will chose to participate in formal networks of parents, professionals, and helping agencies, but others will rely on informal networks of extended family, friends, neighbors, and members of their spiritual congregation. Many families will utilize available support from both the formal and informal networks that they establish. Over time, their needs may change, and they will establish new connections and discontinue participation in some groups.

Darcie smiled at the group of nervous-looking women gathered in the meeting room of the family support center. When Becki, the social worker, arrived, she greeted Darcie warmly and then introduced herself to the other women. All were mothers of boys with complex social and behavioral disabilities, but Darcie was the only one who had been participating in such groups for many years. As the weeks went by, she realized that she was practically coleading the group with the social worker, as she shared her experiences with her son, Abe. While she was gratified to recognize how far she had come in meeting Abe's needs and was happy to help the others, she also recognized that her need for this kind of support group had diminished, and she began to make plans to leave the group. Before she left, however, Becki invited Darcie to formally colead the group, and Darcie accepted this new challenge.

As Darcie's story indicates, parents raising children with disabilities often develop great expertise

Children with disabilities need
to be included in community
activities such as clubs, before- and
after-school care programs, and
scout programs.

David Mager / Pearson Learning Photo Studio

in successfully working with their child and with others with the same disability. Their input and perspectives are helpful both to other parents coping with the same issues and also to professionals. So, although it is important to provide parents with resources for support, also remember that many parents can be a support person, as well.

Children with Disabilities in the Community

As the earlier vignette about Latisha and the Special Olympics basketball team relates, children with disabilities can participate in community activities that are planned just for them. Various community organizations, spiritual groups, and family support networks often plan activities, field trips, recreational classes, dances, and other gatherings geared toward children with particular disabilities. Some day and residential camps also offer summer programs that meet the needs of children with various physical, behavioral, and cognitive disabilities. All these activities help children with disabilities make friends and increase their social network.

As important as these opportunities are, however, it is also essential that children with disabilities are included in the general community activities

provided for all children. Consequently, we are increasingly seeing children with disabilities participating in clubs, scout troops, before- and after-school child-care programs, sports teams, performing arts groups, and other activities alongside their typically developing peers. Building community connections foster children's sense of belonging, which helps them to develop friendships, social skills, and the support system necessary to fully partake on community life (Falvey, 2005).

Throughout their childhood years, children with disabilities will transition from one setting to another. Those who are diagnosed early in life transition from preschool and early intervention services to the elementary school. Later, they transition to the middle and high school, and finally they must make the transition to adult lives. For those children who have actively participated in the community, these transitions are less traumatic, because the child has other relationships and activities that continue even when their school setting changes.

Early intervention, inclusion, and the general change in society's attitude toward persons with disabilities that has occurred over the past 35 years has made a huge difference in the opportunities that children with disabilities have to participate in

APPLYING THESE CONCEPTS TO YOUR WORK WITH CHILDREN AND FAMILIES

As a future teacher or community-service professional, your attitude toward children with disabilities will have a powerful effect on the children with whom you work. Take a few minutes to reflect on the following children and write a few words that come to mind when describing each of them: the girl who is blind and deaf, the blind man, the ADHD teenager. Put your list aside for a moment and then do a similar activity using adjectives to describe the following people: Helen Keller, Stevie Wonder, Cher. If your lists of descriptive words differ from list to list, you may want to think about some of your attitudes toward disabilities. Begin to educate yourself about the person-first approach mentioned in this chapter and why individuals with disabilities prefer not to be termed handicapped or have their disability described as their primary characteristic.

Special educators and general educators who team up to provide the best possible education for all children suggest the following strategies for working with children with disabilities:

- Simplify the environment.
- Slow down the pace of instruction for those need it.
- Provide choices of activities and appropriate alternatives.
- Use cooperative learning strategies, paired learning experiences, and "buddies" to support children with disabilities.
- Create a community of learners who care about and support each other.

the mainstream life of childhood, both in and out of school. With advances in technology and increased awareness of the benefit of inclusion for all children, we can only expect that children with disabilities will have even greater chances of developing to their full potential within their families, schools, and communities.

SUMMARY AND REVIEW

Federal legislation over the past 35 years has had a profound effect on children with disabilities and their opportunities for education. Early identification of disabilities and developmental delays and the provision of intervention services for infants, toddlers, preschoolers, and their families have helped many young children acquire the skills and behaviors that allow them to participate in the activities typical for their age group.

One of the most important aspects of the Individuals with Disabilities Education Act (IDEA) is the principle that regards parent collaboration as essential in the process of determining the best educational setting for

the child. Parents have expert knowledge of their children, and their perceptions of their child's strengths and needs are important to the process of evaluating and placing their child. Effective collaboration requires mutual trust and respect. Professionals must be especially sensitive in helping parents negotiate the complexity of the process of identifying children with special needs and the legal procedures involved in making a placement. For parents, school meetings can be an alphabet soup of acronyms that they may not understand (e.g., IFSP, IEP, FAPE, LRE). The law requires a translator for those families who do not speak English, but the sensitive teacher will find ways of making the complex process understandable for all parents.

Most children with disabilities benefit from being included with their typically developing peers for as much of the school day as possible, and their peers will also gain from their presence. Children with disabilities also profit from participation in community activities designed for all children, and teachers can play an important role in helping to connect families and children to resources and supports available both in school, in the community, and on-line.

SUGGESTED ACTIVITIES AND QUESTIONS

1. Make arrangements to visit an inclusion classroom, self-contained special education classroom, or a school for children with disabilities. Prior to your visit, develop a list of questions you wish to answer through your observation and conversations with school personnel. Get together with peers who have visited other settings and compare what you have learned.

2. In an effort to understand the various perspectives on inclusion of children with disabilities in general education classrooms, arrange to interview a general education teacher, a special educator, and a parent of a child with a disability. What do you learn about the issues and challenges of this approach? What more do you need to learn?

3. In order to learn about specific disabilities, select one that you wish to learn more about and do an Internet search. Develop a 1-to-2 page fact sheet to share with your peers, detailing some of the characteristics of children with this disability and ways that the general educator can work successfully with such children.

4. Do a search for articles about inclusion in the general education journals available in your chosen field. Write a brief review of one of the articles that you feel is most helpful to you.

RESOURCES

Books

Cumine, V., Leach, J., & Stevenson, G. (2000). *Autism in the early years: A practical guide.* London: National Autism Society.

Falvey, M. A. (2005). *Believe in my child with special needs: Helping children achieve their potential in school.* Baltimore: Paul H. Brookes.

Gorman, J. C. (2004). *Working with challenging parents of students with special needs.* Thousand Oaks, CA: Corwin Press.

Killoran, L., & Brown, M. (Eds.). (2006). *There's room for everyone: Accommodations, supports, and transitions—Infancy to postsecondary.* Olney, MD: Association for Childhood Education International.

Widerstrom, Anne H. (2004). *Achieving learning goals through play: Teaching young children with special needs* (2nd ed.) St. Paul: Redleaf Press.

Films and Videos

Living with ADHD [DVD or Video, 50 min]. (2004). Demonstrates clincial advances enabling children to learn constructive behavior, build relationships, and experience success in school. Princeton, NJ: Films for the Humanities & Sciences.

ADHD & LD: Teaching strategies and accommodations. [DVD or Video, 52 min]. (2004). Offers a full range of teaching strategies to engage children's attention, manage behavior, and support children with ADHD, learning disabilites, and related disorders in the inclusion classroom. Lake Zurich, IL: Magna Systems Video.

Differentiating instruction to meet the needs of all students: Elementary edition [2 Videotapes, 77 min]. (2002). A practical approach to differentiating instruction to meet the needs of all learners in the inclusion classroom. Port Chester, NY: National Professional Resources.

Assistive technology: A way to differentiate instruction for students with disabilities [DVD or Video, 43 min]. (2005). Demonstrates high- and low-tech solutions that enable students to function at their highest potential.

Organizations

American Speech-Language-Hearing Association
10801 Rockville Pike
Rockville, MD 20852
800-638-8255
http://www.asha.org

Autism Society of America
7910 Woodmont Avenue
Suite 300
Bethesda, MD 20814-3067
http://www.autism-society.org

Council for Exceptional Children
1110 N. Glebe Road, Suite 300
Arlington, VA 22201
http://www.cec.sped.org

National Center for Learning Disabilities
381 Park Avenue South, Suite 1401
New York, NY 10016
http://www.ncld.org

Web Sites

http://www.familyvillage.wisc.edu   Provides resources for persons with disabilities, their families, and professionals.

http://www.nichcy.org   The U.S. Office of Special Education Programs sponsors this site, which provides information on IDEA and NCLB, as well as research-based information on effective educational practices.

http://www.ldonline.org   A wide-ranging source of information about learning disabiliites and ADHD, offered as a community service of WETA, a public broadcasting system in Washington, DC.

http://www.thearc.org   Offers information on mental retardation and related areas, and discussion boards and access links to related sites.

http://www.irsc.org   Internet Resources for Special Children.

Chapter 7

Responsibility for Educating and Protecting Children

Families, neighbors, community members, and educators together create a web of support that contributes to the healthy and meaningful growth of children.

(Arce, 1999, p. 136)

Before discussing in the following chapters the particulars of curriculum and experiences that produce the healthy settings for learning, we will focus on the division of responsibility that society anticipates for acculturating youth in America. The general public expects a division of educational effort among the three settings, but this does not deny the great benefits of collaboration and partnerships. In this chapter, we consider the obligations for educating and protecting American children and the people and agencies that bear the responsibility for meeting these obligations.

After studying this chapter, you will be able to do the following:

1. Discuss the societal traditions that convey responsibilities to families, schools, and communities for educating and protecting our young children.

2. Outline the legal requirements that exist and hold families, schools, and communities accountable for providing different aspects of education and protection of children.

3. Describe the informal or nonacademic curriculum that society anticipates to be fulfilled by homes and communities.

4. Discuss the formal academic curriculum, although overseen by the community, that is largely the responsibility of school personnel.

5. Identify the overlaps and disagreements that occur regarding responsibilities and obligations for some aspects of children's experiences.

6. Describe how partnerships among homes, schools, and communities produce the best and most meaningful experiences for children.

Maria had been annoyed with her son's school for more than a month. Tony had been bringing home from his second-grade class paper after paper with instructions for Maria to go over and practice lessons with him. Maria felt the teacher couldn't be doing her job, because Tony never seemed to understand what the assignments were all about. One day when Tony brought home a math sheet, a reading paper, and a social studies assignment, Maria had had enough. She stopped working on the meal she was preparing for her five children and gathered up a basket of sweatshirts that needed mending. With the pile of clothing and Tony, she marched the three blocks to school. Maria entered Ms. Srichan's classroom and plunked the laundry basket on the teacher's table. "You expect me to do your work? I think you should help me with mine," she remarked angrily, then marched off, with Tony in tow.

Whose responsibility is it to see that Tony learns his math, reading, and social studies concepts? In our opening vignette, the teacher and parent seem to have little contact. Both have expectations about what Tony should be doing, yet there is a gulf in communication.

In Chapter 1, we assert that young children become what their world provides and that they learn concepts and skills to the degree that surroundings guide, entice, or motivate them. The influences and forces affecting children at the beginning of the 21st century are numerous and constant, and children encounter them in all three of our fundamental social settings: family, school, and community. As you prepare for a career in teaching or community work, it is important for you to identify and understand where and how adults in each setting assume responsibility for children's learning and protection. You also need to understand that each institution can work in tandem or in conflict with the other two, as seems to be happening in Tony's case.

EDUCATIONAL OPPORTUNITY

An academic curriculum is provided for children enrolled in different types of school environments: private and public schools, preschool, and child care. A school's formal academic curriculum is constantly affirmed by school professionals, as well as by laypersons, and its general purpose, as readers realize, is to help children accumulate appropriate knowledge and skill. Much of what children learn in their formative years, however, actually comes from the experiences, associations, and interactions they have outside and beyond scheduled school activities. This is the unplanned, covert, or hidden curriculum that teachers and parents often don't recognize or overlook. This associated curriculum is a dominant part of any child's life, and it should be related to the formal curriculum as prepared and implemented by schools whenever possible (Apple, 1995; Giroux, 1978).

We often hear adults discussing their career choices, avocations, or other major interests that have come from their childhood experiences. If we examine the seminal experience, we often find it had little to do with schooling but emanated from some family ritual or experience, some childhood encounter, or a community project.

Two mothers and a grandmother waited for their children to come from the gym after practice and pondered their own interests (professional pursuits) in elementary school and in later life. "You know," said the first mother, "I love seeing these shell collections that group three has displayed here in the hall. Goes way back for me. I still recall our visits to the Cape, where my brothers and I collected tons of shells. I've continued that line right along with my work in advertising and illustrating." "I know what you mean," the grandmother allowed, "but it was quilting that grabbed me. Learned all about it from my own grandma in Georgia when she and Aunt Essie would work for hours piecing a top before stitching. And I've still got the bug—make a few every year even now."

Children's interests and stage of development determine what is meaningful for them, and the stimuli and experiences that result in learning come from many forces within each child's life (Bronfenbrenner & Weiss, 1983). When we consider who is responsible for children's education, we must ascertain who has the most substantial and direct access to children's time, minds, and interests at various times of the day, week, or year. In addition, we have to take into account all the forces bombarding children with information and experience. For example, a definite curriculum of the home exists, although we do not label it as such. It starts at birth and continues to be dominated by primary caregivers during children's earliest years (note Fig. 1–1). The community begins to affect children by the time they are toddlers, and children identified with special needs may begin receiving intervention services from community agencies and school programs soon after birth.

Many families do not go to extremes, but they recognize that quality conversations, regular book-sharing sessions, and lots of hands-on experiences around home help to "prepare" their children for formal schooling. On the other hand, some families have been unable to adequately prepare their children for school. Although low-income families and those linguistically and culturally different than the mainstream want their children to succeed in school just as much as their middle-class counterparts do, they sometimes lack the necessary skills to prepare their children for typical schooling. Programs like Head Start and other publicly funded preschool and **family literacy programs** (Paratore, 2001) have been established to help minimize that problem by working with parents on routines and basic skills that help children make a more successful transition from home to formal schooling. In addition, the larger community creates an impression on all citizens, one that children feel and internalize. Communities do affect children's learning by (1) providing (or disallowing) opportunities in sports facilities, recreation arenas, libraries, museums and arts areas, and clinics and other health facilities, and (2) supporting or challenging particular attitudes, lifestyles, and mobility patterns. The "way of doing things here" is the community ethos and therefore part of children's informal curriculum. Children of color, for example, are still very young when they encounter the attitudes and mores, whether positive or negative, of the dominant racial group (Lightfoot, 1978).

REFLECTION

Reflect on your growing up years and the "way you did things" in your own family. For example, what was the Monday morning ritual for your family, and for school, and for the community? Now compare that to what you do now and what your friends do now. Have things changed for you and are these rituals different from those practiced by your classmates?

HOME RESPONSIBILITY

Parents and caregivers bear great responsibility for children's early learning and for the genesis of and support for the curriculum that children will use for their entire lives. Parents also have a significant role in nurturing the academic work children experience after entering school. In Chapter 8, we discuss the many opportunities for learning in the home, but the following provides an overview. No formal or legal demands exist that require parents to instruct their children. At the same time, common cultural assumptions regarding child rearing imply that parents will guide and prepare children for life in a community. Also, statutes concerning abuse and neglect have emerged over the years, and parents parsimonious in nurturing and guiding their children risk citations of maltreatment and its consequences (Lazzara & Poland, 2001). Parents must also be vigilant in protecting their child from abuse from others entrusted with their care.

Most societies do little to formally prepare parents for rearing children, and the United States is no exception. When extended families were more common, child raising was probably more coherent. Informal advice from other parents and extended family was more available, community standards were more constant, and families were far less mobile (Walsh, F., 2002). In today's society, with its matrix of ever-increasing forces producing stress, mobility, and differing home styles, child-raising practice has become less consistent and more pressured (Elkind, 2001, 1994). Daily

lives now are more frenetic, and some families come close to abandoning responsibilities for home guidance, and by default the media assumes a larger role. Unfortunately considerable amounts of information on television, films, video games, CDs, and the Internet tend to offer role models that "emphasize commercialism, sexuality, substance abuse, and violence" (Bronfenbrenner, 2001, p. 199). Readers may wish to see Chapter 8 for more detail on mass media effects.

Nonetheless, expectations for parents do exist, and persons in other social settings anticipate that families will provide these beginning experiences as children grow and move into the conventional school environment and the neighborhood. We describe some representative areas in the following subsections. As you read through the following sections describing home and family practices, think about how these situations will affect a primary teacher who works with children from these homes.

Providing Consistent Social and Emotional Environments

Effective homes develop environments that nurture children's social and emotional well-being, and the overriding dimension is one of care and interest. All of this translates into positive self-concepts for children, plus a good foundation for children's self esteem. In addition, the child's **locus of control** is directly related to the parenting that a child receives (refer to Chapter 8). Whether children see themselves or others in control determines the way they look toward the future.

How can we encourage parents in guiding and nurturing their children and at the same time to establish contacts outside the home? Workshops, information distribution, and discussions that parents attend are only part of the answer. Supporting families through family–school–community collaborations and involving parents in extended networks will do the most to enhance social and emotional health in homes. Benson (1997), Hammer and Turner (2000), and Gonzales-Mena (2006) all have nicely developed collaboration schemes.

Many parents recognize the importance of providing their children with educational toys and experiences with other children.

Marian Fowler

Parents' workplaces affect their perceptions of life and the way they interact with children and other family members (Bronfenbrenner & Crouter, 1982; Wohl, 1997). In turn, these perceptions foster parenting styles that conform to parents' experiences and how they see themselves in the world. On the positive side, we have the effective-family investigations (Clark, 1983; Noddings, 2002; Scarf, 1997), showing that the functioning family views itself as a problem-solving unit with a mutual support system and a spiritual life that is valued.

Child-rearing patterns certainly affect children's level of moral development. Children's attitudes form early, and parents and peers have a significant impact through instruction, modeling, rewards, and punishments (Bronfenbrenner, Moen, & Garbarino, 1984). Children's values tend to reflect those of their family, but other experiences also affect this development. Individuals exposed to many socializing agents (e.g., clergy members, family network friends, peers, and teachers) are more likely to achieve a higher level of moral reasoning than those exposed to only a few (Coles, 1997; Damon, 1988).

Developing Interactive Skills. Imparting basic wisdom about human relationships must begin in the home. It is the family's responsibility to develop children's initial interaction and negotiating skills, even though these are extended considerably in other groupings (i.e., peer group, child care, and school situations). Teaching about sensitivity to others, the logic of cooperative action and taking turns, and the need to respect others and to share materials has its place in the social life of growing children (Black & Puckett, 2005).

Competent families demonstrate interactive skills that permit children to interact with the world with their values and moral notions in place. Modeling and discussions in the home will help, and when the family is an active part of the larger community, this extends children's social contacts so that they use more than one interactive style (Salzstein, 1976; Walker & Taylor, 1991). Children's growth will reflect their participation and experience.

Except in cases of severe neglect, parents and other family members automatically instill in children the basics of socialization. Children early and naturally learn to greet and respond to others, recognize acquaintances, play games with siblings, and mimic and follow one another. In addition, many parents recognize the importance of providing their children with educational toys and experiences with other children as part of the socialization process (Kieff & Casbergue, 2000). As noted in Chapter 5, more than 65% of American preschool children are in some form of child care, and this means that socialization skills are affected considerably by events and people outside the home.

Negative Social Behaviors. In concert with expanded violence and aggression in the media, American schools and neighborhoods are experiencing an intensity of negative social behaviors, such as hazing and bullying. **Bullying** is unprovoked verbal or physical aggression toward others and is traced to aggressive behaviors in homes and in media, to attachment problems, to child abuse, and even to genetics (Okagaki & Luster, 2005). Often linked with men in previous generations, bullying has become common among girls today (Prothrow-Stith & Spivak, 2003). Both the socialization practices in the United States and the entertainment media condone and excuse more aggressive and often violent behavior. Families as well as schools and communities are justly concerned about the increase, and plans need to be made to modify this dangerous behavior. Socialization processes for youth need ongoing evaluation, and all families need to work with their schools to develop skills in anticipating **harassment** and bullying acts and also to put in place strategies to teach negotiation, compromise, and **conflict resolution**. See Siris (2001) and Center for Mental Health Services (2003) for a listing of basic strategies.

Producing a Literacy Atmosphere

Babies are immersed in language from birth and begin to develop communication skills during the earliest months of life. Their skills expand rapidly because of planned and unplanned family interactions and experiences (Sparling, 2004). Parents echo their infant's vocalizations, name things, and direct the baby's attention to the objects, people, and events around them. Parents, other family members, and caregivers often explain to the baby what they and the baby are doing, demonstrating

with real objects accompanied by language. Families often introduce babies to books during their first year: Talking about the pictures, turning the pages, and sharing the pleasure of snuggling together with a book will become the foundation for later reading development. Writing emerges in much the same way. Toddlers, given paper and crayons, will scribble, draw, and make lists in imitation of their parents' writing. All young children find it necessary to communicate with different adults and with their peers, and this develops language, which is the base for literacy.

Later literacy development in the home includes listening to, discussing, and making up stories; practicing reading and writing; and modeling more elaborate speech (Beaty, 2006; Jacobs, K., 2004). Research with children involved in a family literacy project (Paratore, 2001) indicates that "children who have parents who read to them, help with homework, monitor their performance in school by asking questions of them or their teacher, and who urged them to be on time and to behave courteously achieved success in school." Readers will find more information on home language development in Chapter 8.

Providing for Wellness

Health implies attention to complete personal well-being, not just the absence of disease or infirmities. Instruction in and attention to healthy practices is considered part of normal child raising, and most parents readily accept the responsibility for promoting the health of their young. Most health and safety concepts that parents focus on do grow out of situations associated with everyday living. Effective families attend to medical checkups and immunizations, and they ensure that their children live and play in smoke-free buildings that are well ventilated and well lighted. They are attuned to mental health evaluations in cases that show symptoms.

On the other hand, marginalized families frequently suffer from chronic health problems, accidents, and inadequate nutrition. Smoke pollution, high population densities, poor sanitation, bad food choices and poor habits in managing resources engender unhealthy homes. Some problems stem from ignorance about basic home maintenance, some come from inadequate planning and substance abuse, and many come from the inability of persons to secure and follow through on available care and help from social agencies. Illness and health problems become all too often a function of income.

Physical Education. Provision for physical activity, exercise, and movement skills is almost a given in most American homes. Parents readily encourage all types of informal as well as structured games and practice for their children. This can include everything from encouraging the toddler to take more steps to urging the primary-aged child to sign up for Little League. In addition, healthy homes stress proper bathing, keeping rubbish cleared, and avoiding toxic substances. Guided activity and more concentrated practice can be found in homes where disabilities are present.

In spite of expectations, in recent decades educators and medical practitioners have registered concerns about diminishing physical activity in many children's lives. Busy family lifestyles and overly attractive media outlets are often blamed. Ensuring adequate exposure-to physical activity and arranging programs is another area that should become a common focus for homes, schools, and communities, to promote the use of playgrounds, gyms, and parks.

Providing Good Nutrition. Competent families know about healthy food preparation and use, the basics of nutrition, and how to deal with allergies. They are alert to regular meal times, good sanitation, and making mealtimes pleasant experiences. When health and nutrition standards are preserved, we in healthy homes eat meals with food from the major food groups, plus the following:

- Reduced use of packaged, treated foods containing high levels of fat, salt, and chemical additives
- Reduced use of sweets and soft drinks
- Regular eating habits and sensible snacks

Lifelong eating habits are formed during the early years (Aronson, 2002), and families and child-care providers play an important role in introducing new foods and establishing a relaxed eating environment. Hand washing, teeth brushing, and caring for bodily functions are other expected home responsibilities. These are also practiced in child-care settings, where many young children spend a large part of the regular workweek. Alarming statistics in recent years point to the need for families, with help from schools and communities to address problems of overeating and poor food choices. Obesity is recognized as a problem for America's youth and has implications for the emotional health, and the later physical health issues for children (Institute of Medicine, 2006). Liverman, Kraak, and Koplan (2005) state that 22% of American children ages six and up are now **obese** or **overweight**, and this figure has doubled in fewer than 20 years. These statistics concern many citizens and call for pointed action to inform families of later dangers.

Paul was restacking shelves in the small rural grocery, when he was approached by two huffing and excited young boys with large bags of potato chips under their arms. "Hey, mister," said the eight-year-old, "there's no big bottles of cola on the shelf over there. Mum's lettin' us pick out our lunch, and we want cola."

Paul smiled at the overweight youngsters and said, "Sure, I'll get some," and he went to the storeroom to get liter bottles of Coca Cola. Upon returning, Paul noticed that an overweight mother has arrived with a grocery cart heavy with more soft drinks, stacks of bread, frozen dinners, and cold cuts. He handed bottles to the two boys, saying, "Is this what you needed?"

"Yep," replied the seven-year-old. "Okay, Mum, we got our lunch. Let's go!" Then the boys and their mum moved slowly along the aisle to the checkout counter.

At that moment Paul noticed the large sign showing healthy lunches that the Healthy Community Project volunteers had posted near the potato chip shelf. Neither potato chips nor cola is pictured on the poster.

The vignette illustrates a weight problem already evidenced in the young children, and we surmise it comes from a family that struggles to implement good nutrition practices. This problem could continue for years and will be costly not only for the family but for the community, as well. Good food choices and nutrition make excellent topics for family, school, and community collaborations. Units on nutrition carry little controversy and when initiated by a school can easily extend to families and community agencies for support. Figure 7–1, which shows the USDA Food Guide Pyramid, provides a good starting point.

REFLECTION

Recall scenes in your family life that indicate your family's involvement in your learning to read, to make nutritionally wise decisions, and to get along with others. Have you moved away from these "teachings," or do you still retain these habits?

Providing for Sex Education. Health education is always a part of a quality child-care experience, but sex education can be a controversial topic. Families have the initial responsibility for children's sex education, and at the minimum, families should focus on attention to gender differences, names for body parts, words for toileting, attention to privacy, and knowledge of "good touching" and "bad touching." Chrisman and Couchenour (2002) suggested that although there are different approaches to sex education among families, families who support healthy sexual development "include respectful interactions with one another, appropriate expressions of affection among family members, and a sensitive awareness of both expected behaviors and unacceptable behaviors" (p. 5).

Because sex education outside the home, can be controversial, child-care centers and schools must be very clear on their procedures and maintain good communication with homes on the content of their curriculum. Although some child-care programs have a planned curriculum for sexual education, most take a more informal approach. For example, when children ask questions or behave in

certain ways, the adult provides accurate information and positive guidance. Child-care programs can also serve as a resource for families and support their role in children's sexual development. Readers may wish to consult Essa and Murray (1999) for a brief but helpful background on the sexual behavior of young children and how parents and teachers can cope with their concerns over identifying normal and deviant sexual play.

Providing Organization and Management in the Home

As we discussed in Chapter 3, the United States contains numerous cultures, each of which represents a somewhat different pattern of child rearing. Across cultures, however, we find strands undergirding the proficient home and differentiating it from less effective ones. All homes are responsible for a basic organization of routines and procedures that acculturate youth.

Since the Bernstein (1972) and Baumrind (1966) studies, social scientists have continued to recognize the several general management styles found in U.S. homes. The styles overlap and combinations exist, but most families seem to tend toward one style or another. Baumrind (1966, 1968) labeled three basic parenting styles: authoritarian, authoritative, and permissive. Family members managing according to the authoritative style are democratic and controlling but warm and receptive. These attributes contrast with the authoritarian's detached control and the noncontrolling and nondemanding approach of the permissive style. Readers may wish to review Chapter 4 for more discussion on parenting styles. In the present context, readers should know that all home management styles can be successful, but the wealth of anecdotal evidence points to the success of the authoritative management style.

Inadequate Home Nurturance

Some families provide minimal support for their children's education, either through lack of experience or uncertainty about how to help. Although

Figure 7–1 Food Guide Pyramid
Source: USDA Center for Nutrition Policy and Promotion (2006).

173

they provide the basics of primary care—food, shelter, clothing, and safety—parents in impoverished homes may not fully appreciate the notion of educational practice, how learning comes about, or their effects on a child's life. **Parent education** (Moriarty & Fine, 2001) and family literacy programs (Paratore, 2001) can make a difference for minimally supportive families. Such programs help parents understand how to become more involved in their children's schooling and community life.

Marginalized families have few financial and emotional resources to use in supporting children's growth. This special class of family has extensive need for social intervention, and we know some rehabilitation efforts have been successful. When school programs are able to include marginalized family members into planning sessions and management teams, there is substantial evidence that these families' self-concept and levels of achievement, and the motivations of their at-risk children, are raised (Haberman, 1992; Maeroff, 1998).

Peggy left the homeless shelter for the day with her two children, walking to the Head Start community center. She hoped the teachers there will keep her two children while she inquires about a job she'd heard about. She doesn't make it to the center, though, as the distance is far and the children start crying and are too heavy to carry. Dejectedly, she sits on the curb, then spends the rest of the day wandering in the open-air market looking for handouts.

Peggy has no immediate family and just moved to the shelter to get away from her abusive boyfriend. She has a history of moving in and out with her boyfriend, then living for short times with a friend and then her aunt—only to lose these places because of financial problems that lead to quarrels. Peggy has a brief work history, but she lacks the sense of well-being that would give her confidence in her abilities. She does not feel connected to the larger community, and she has little understanding of how her condition might change. The social worker at the shelter enrolled her three-year-old son in the community Head Start program. Head Start personnel and the social worker are trying to connect Peggy with the community's educational and outreach projects, but Peggy's absenteeism from the project sessions she starts and the periodic appearance of her belligerent boyfriend make any progress difficult.

Peggy's situation demonstrates the crying needs of marginalized families in America. The lack of skills, lack of options, and being locked into undesirable situations make progress difficult. Peggy has few connections to a social network for support and has difficulty keeping any commitment she makes and little knowledge of how to get help. Aspiration is lacking—only the basics appear to be a concern, and those, at times, seem difficult to manage. What will her children become? The nurturance here must be considered minimal and will not change until intensive social reconstruction is arranged.

In some instances, parents are so remote and out of touch that the best teachers can do is to give constant support, believe in children, and hope that some success unfolds in the classroom. Some hard-to-reach parents can be included through persistent communication and emphasis on their strengths and their successes with their children. Effective parent education means seeking ways to support parents to gradually accept responsibilities in their children's overall education—and at the parents' level of ability. It means trying out different approaches, such as listening to parent responses, and building on what works.

REFLECTION

Think of young children you have worked with and reflect on the needs that their families support well. Also reflect on situations where support seems to be missing. Could you use this information if you were the assigned community worker or the child's teacher?

Protecting Children at Home

Danger has invaded America from many sides, and the impressions we get from classic plays and stories about the past conflict with our anxiety about living conditions now. Although society at large expects parents to be the primary advocate, protector, and supervisor of children in the family unit, most families regularly depend on others—to alert them to danger, to tell when problems are near, and notify them when toxic substances or dangerous individuals are in the neighborhood.

Society expects **family units** to discuss societal dangers, traffic hazards, toxic substances, plus environmental problems, such as polluted streams. Families are expected to instruct children about hazards and then monitor streets and children's play areas for dangerous conditions and individuals. The National Center for Missing & Exploited Children (2006) reported that 58,200 children were abducted in one recent year by non–family members. Many community agencies work with their schools and neighborhoods to monitor dangerous local conditions, make plans to educate children on those problems, and publicize strategies for avoiding the pitfalls.

Home accidents are common in our country. Thousands befall children each year in the typical home, and these increase dramatically when adult supervision is lacking. Injuries from falls, fires, ingesting toxic materials, explosions, and toy malfunctioning occur frequently and call for careful home safety instructions, cautions and guidance. Family planning, discussion, and instruction about common hazards are critical in avoiding accidents and other dangers.

Some children need protection from themselves. Although uncommon, some children have disabilities that require special parental effort to ensure a safe home. Children with personality disorders, impaired mental functioning, and physical impairments require more supervision and monitoring by caregivers to ensure the child's safety.

EVALUATING FAMILY EFFECTIVENESS

Irrespective of culture, economic situation, and different modes of parenting, almost all family units can be effective. Observers will find that most of the features noted in Figure 7–2 are present in competent families.

SCHOOL RESPONSIBILITY

A formal curriculum starts with "schooling," no matter how young the child. Schooling, whether at nursery school, child care, or public or private school, will begin where the informal home curriculum has paused or proven inadequate in preparing children for their next educational step. For example, Head Start and Early Start are comprehensive child-development programs that serve children from birth to age five in getting ready for school.

So, we expect in all parts of the country that schools of all types will consume a large amount of children's time and be responsible for delivering many services to nurture children's education. These schools are, on the whole, very helpful and effective in what they do. Numerous publications discuss the programs and character of "effective schools," and we frequently see such items as student achievement, inclusive programs, or values and beliefs highlighted in the media. On the other hand, some school programs and policies can have a negative effect on children's success (Evans, 2004; Fried, 2005).

Educating Children in Schools

The word *curriculum*, used constantly in most schools, serves as an organizer for all school programs. Different conceptions of curriculum do exist, and the philosophical orientation of a particular school's staff members will determine the how and what of children's learning. In some schools, curriculum will be an outline of content and skills presented in a tightly scripted sequence of lessons, whereas in others it will be a constantly changing set of experiences that children and teachers decide to pursue in satisfying their interests (Doll, 1995; Pinar, 2004). All gradations between these are found in schools in the United States. As a beginning professional, you should anticipate the definition of *curriculum* to be "the formal and informal content and processes used by and for learners in gaining skills, knowledge, and appreciation" (McNeil & Darby, 2005) and accept this major responsibility for guiding children in productive school activities. We discuss school

In evaluating effective families, assessors will answer yes for most of the following questions:

1. Is a consistent parenting style evident?

2. Is there consistency in home management, family routines (bedtime, meals, and relaxation), and household regulations?

3. Are rules and codes of conduct understood and consistently enforced?

4. Are discussions, conversations, and interactions noticeable and frequent?

5. Do children have responsibilities in the home?

6. Are expectations of children in keeping with the children's stages of development?

7. Do parents have high hopes for their children's success?

8. Do family members evince a sense of success and pride?

9. Are good nutrition practices observed?

10. Are sanitary practices in evidence?

11. Do family members know where others work, play, and socialize?

12. Is there warmth in the home—do members accept others?

13. Do family members encourage and praise each other?

14. Does the family have a social network of friends?.

15. Are values and moral codes apparent in the family?

16. Are literary and other intellectual stimuli present in the home?

17. Do members read to each other?

18. Does the family show skill in using the social and welfare services available to them?

19. Are health checkups done regularly and immunizations scheduled?

20. Can parents verbally and kinesthetically lead children through tasks and problems with appropriate questions, comments, and demonstrations?

Figure 7–2 Evaluating Family Effectiveness
Source: Adopted from Berger, 2000; Berns, 2006; Galinsky, 1987; Rich, 1992.

curriculum more fully in Chapter 9, but for now, think of preschool and primary-school teachers as responsible for extending the skills started in the home and the child-care center. The following are competencies that would normally comprise a typical teacher's objectives for a year:

1. *Language and literacy skills:* reading, writing, speaking, and listening competencies

2. *Math competencies:* numeration skills, calculating, measuring, spatial relations, and problem solving

3. *Physical and natural science competencies:* observing phenomena, representing observations, drawing conclusions, experimenting with plant growth, animal care, and everyday chemical combinations

4. *Social studies skills:* those related to a variety of people in different circumstances—making friends, cooperating, respecting rules, the study of human relationships. These increase and intensify as children grow

5. *Health education, nutrition, sex education, recreation skills:* extension of skills and habits begun in the home that address emerging concerns on obesity and inactivity

6. *Aesthetic education:* participation in and appreciation of music, dance, graphic arts, crafts, and other fine arts

7. *Negotiating skills:* procedures for planning activities, arranging teams, cooperative learning, and developing **assessments** (mostly in the informal curriculum)

8. *Attitudes and values:* social, ethical, and moral judgment; respect for and cooperation with others

Recognizing Student Achievement

Often we assume that standardized achievement test results are proof of what happens in schools. When related to aptitude scores, program resources, or support, these tests may indicate statistically whether particular school programs have realized expected gains. The federal NCLB requirements started in 2001 have intensified the urge for schools to measure learning results more vigorously. Caution is needed, however, because results from norm-referenced tests cannot be used in guiding individual children. Teachers must use observation based diagnostic tools and inventories to guide selected children. If overall success rates are high, educators and citizens alike often assume that all is right at their school and that programs must be appropriate. Group tests often hide areas of deficiency, though, and they often fail to assess specific children's skills (Stiggins, 2005). Frequently, a test may be inappropriate for a particular subgroup in the school. For example, gifted children, although performing adequately in school, sometimes receive lower than anticipated scores on tests.

When problems appear in effective schools (for example, if scores are well below an area norm), educators, parents, and other community citizens demand explanations. Are community problems or area demographics confounding parts of the program and school curriculum? Are scores lower because schools are reserving time for nonacademic areas, such as developing esteem and readiness or expanding cultural background, before returning to achievement-tested basic skills? Again, standardized tests measure particular academic skill levels and do not assess achievements in all the curriculum areas in which schools work today (refer to Chapter 9). Schools can, however, determine children's achievement using tools other than batteries of norm-referenced tests. In effective schools, teachers incorporate other assessment forms, such as diagnostic instruments, portfolios of children's work, or observation devices to diagnose needs for remediation or program changes. (For a thorough discussion of the relative strengths and weaknesses of the different types of assessment available to teachers, see Stiggins, 2005.)

REFLECTION

The next time you visit a classroom, take note of the way the teacher evaluates children, then consider how you were evaluated in your earlier years. Are the methods similar? Can you recall how these evaluations made you feel? What ways were most effective for you?

Fostering Values and Beliefs

Anna Freud once observed that the early elementary years are "times when a child's character and conscience is built—or isn't!" With school comes the beginning of a child's community participation, and of course there is much to wonder and to learn about regarding the rights and wrongs of life.

Just as parents model values and beliefs, so do teachers and other school personnel (Coles, 1997). Getting along with others, sharing possessions, and helping others are areas that successful

Anne Vega / Merrill

Children and teachers pursue a changing set of experiences to satisfy children's interests.

schools expand on after these basics (Evans, 1996) are started at home or child care centers. It is one thing to post rules for courtesies or sharing, but another to inculcate these valuable features in an effective school. First, teachers, like parents, must model these behaviors. In effective schools, primary teachers develop units on social communication and ways of getting along with others. Challenges can be taken from everyday life or even from newspapers, and the students have an opportunity to analyze and discuss ways to work through the problems.

Many teachers find that some of the best ways to address values is to use a story narrative. (The children's book section in Appendix I includes many suitable titles.) Others have used film or video clips focusing on a challenging social situation, considering diverse cultures, or making positive connections with persons with special needs.

Provision for Individual Differences and Inclusion

Many American schools at the beginning of the 21st century are administered under the principles of diversity, or inclusion. We have used a generation to move to this place, but at present, all schools are obligated to provide educational experiences for children at all learning levels and in the "least restrictive environment." We discussed inclusion from a historical perspective in Chapter 2, and we present a curriculum viewpoint in Chapter 6.

More than restructured buildings and more specialized personnel, what you will notice most in a school practicing inclusion is the attitude and demeanor toward the abilities of all children. Remember that typically developing children of a generation back rarely encountered diversity in their classrooms. Most schools up through the 1960s were monolingual and monoracial and showed little evidence of special needs (Turnbull et al., 2007). In effective schools today, the mix is truly comprehensive, and most educators agree that living and learning with diversity makes all individuals more tolerant, accepting, and eager to use the skills and talents of persons they previously did not come to know or value.

Confronting Bias and Prejudice

Our society still struggles to shed the problems associated with racism, ethnocentrism, elitism, **sexism, homophobia**, and discrimination against certain disabilities; these qualities regrettably still affect some schools. Perpetuating stereotypes in monocultural schools is a problem; stereotyping restricts everyone's social competence. When hints of bias and careless use of ethnocentric language appear in ethnically integrated schools, the problem has immediacy. When demeaning language and actions surface, minority persons are affronted, their aspirations suffer, and children's growth in social competence is diminished (Comer, 1988; Sadker & Sadker, 2005). For all persons involved, bias is costly.

All school personnel have a responsibility to confront bias and prejudice and help young children move beyond it. Bullying and other types of school violence, which is often associated with prejudice, have appeared with greater frequency, and concerns are registered often. All schools must assume a leadership role in organizing resources from homes and communities to work toward resolution of bias, prejudice, and bullying. A multicultural currriculum that involves significant help from parents and community members is the appropriate way to address this issue.

Coping with Lobbyists and Policy Advocates

Volunteer groups often come together to be advocates and sources of support for schools. For example, a group formed to lobby for school building improvements can be positive in impact. However, some lobbying groups are formed, as in the following vignette, to counteract educational projects or to prevent curricula from being implemented.

A group of parents and two clergymen in one Texas community organized themselves as a self-appointed school review committee. When they reviewed the reproduction-of-creatures unit for the second-grade classrooms, the books and charts used became a highly charged topic. The group's complaints about the material became intense, and the committee visits to the school caused confrontations and wild charges. One teacher resigned because of accusations, and negative publicity dragged on for weeks before the administration abandoned the unit. Even though the unit had been developed in previous years and had been accepted by the health education committee, a militant anti-sex-education group spread dissension and won their case in this community. Community and school working relations were set back considerably for several years.

Censorship of books is still a common occurrence in school districts throughout the United States (American Library Association, 2005). Too often, schools acquiesce to pressure from lobbying groups to abandon certain publications and other resources. Then, programs can suffer in scope and purpose. All challenges are accommodated better when schools have well-planned school objectives and an educational process that involves homes and communities in handling curriculum.

Planning for Changes in Schools

Schools in the United States are always evolving. New building plans, new procedures, new equipment, and curriculum innovations appear in school districts on a regular basis. Adjustments appear that seem serious or far-reaching at times, but in fact schools change very slowly in philosophy, procedures, and practices (Demarris & LeCompte, 1998; Webb et al., 2007).

It takes time for a school's staff to adopt a new method of teaching: New materials are needed, inservice education must be arranged, and teachers need to be convinced of the method's efficacy. Even though a few teachers implement a new plan, the school as a whole often lags behind. Consider the phased-in **"writing to read"** program discussed in the following vignette.

⸺ In the fall of 1994, a New Jersey school system set up a "writing to read" workshop. Two second-grade teachers from Elwood Elementary were interested in trying the new plan immediately, and their experiment encouraged them. The two gave glowing reports at faculty meetings the following spring, but only one third-grade and one first-grade teacher agreed to try the plan the next year. Halfway through the year, the first-grade teacher supplemented her program with basal readers, and she evaluated the experiment as mediocre. With heavy urging, two more teachers agreed to experiment later that year. At the end of three years, only half of the primary-school teachers in the building were involved. Although most evaluations were positive, the principal still wondered how she could increase participation. It took five years and repeated reports of success before most of Elwood's primary-school teachers made a serious commitment to the program. ⸺

Schools change faster socially than they do academically. Neighborhoods can change quickly in urban and suburban areas, and the cultural and socioeconomic mix can alter demographics in a school within a few years. Many U.S. schools have experienced this phenomenon in recent years (refer to the demographic changes discussed in Chapter 3). For many reasons, many schools are less successful today than they were in previous decades. Achievement results, SAT scores, school attendance, the rising number of school-identified disabilities, plus crime and other social problems have alarmed many. The result has been a host of studies and evaluations to assess what is happening in U.S. education, and most studies have recommendations. This means educators must select rational recommendations and supporting evidence to present to communities for decisions.

Educational Assessments. A number of task forces representing various interests have conducted national studies to identify problems in U.S. education. Some offer recommendations to correct the problems they find. Some results concern school practices and curriculum, but many

have implications for vast changes in society at large, in areas such as health care, the prevention of substance abuse, correcting violence, and changing U.S. attitudes. Some studies also include new plans for teacher preparation. The warning *A Nation at Risk* (National Commission on Excellence in Education [NCEE], 1983) was published in 1983 and *A Nation Prepared* (Carnegie Forum on Education and the Economy, 1986) following a few years later. These reports identified lessened achievements in U.S. schools and energized dicussion. Minimal improvement has been found so far, however, and the most positive outcome has been to stimulte more government interest.

Government Action. The accumulation of education reports has prompted the last three administrations to address issues and concerns identified in U.S. schools. The first Bush administration in 1990 advanced *America 2000: An Education Strategy* (U.S. Department of Education, 1991), a formula for addressing the large problems in the country's education. The Clinton administration followed with Goals 2000: Educate America Act, in 1993. Although the administrations emphasized social reconstruction and implementation of the principles, most states remained in the beginning stages. The new Bush administration has started a vigorous set of proposals to support education and increase the federal role in schoolwork. The No Child Left Behind statute in 2001 has received considerable press attention and professional scrutiny but remains controversial in many areas. Negotiations for adjustments to the requirements are being worked on at the time of this writing. The awareness of difficulties and educational needs in poor and minority groups in the United States has reached high levels. At the same time, continuing problems with instituting higher standards, student achievement, and approving voucher plans continue to worry many (Goertz, 2001; Webb et al., 2007). On a positive note, some communities have started experimental programs, which do provide models for use. See Chapter 12 for several examples.

Protecting Children in Schools

Protecting Children from Bias and Prejudice.
Bias and prejudice appear with regularity in all social situations. These behaviors are based on fears, insecurities, and ignorance, and school personnel must plan carefully in addressing all forms of racism, elitism, sexism and other forms of prejudice that appear. Using multicultural materials in as many school projects as possible is a good start. And planning regular units on diverse cultures and observing a variety of ethnic and religious holidays point students in positive directions. The researchers deRamirez (2006) and Banks and McGee-Banks (2005) contain excellent sources for materials and strategies in addressing this topic.

Protecting Children from Bullying. Bullying is mentioned as a growing concern in many schools today (Siris & Osterman, 2004). Though dominative and aggressive behavior has always been a feature of many social groups, some authorities feel that the proliferation of violent games and videos extends and enhances a youth culture that prizes domination and stimulates more violent behaviors (Prothrow-Stith & Spivak, 2003). Most of this behavior appears at recreation venues and in after-school activities. Teachers must anticipate occasions by preparing careful guidelines for group participation, and then follow through with examples of helpful behavior in social situations. Siris and Osterman (2004) indicate the key lies in preventing exclusion in classrooms and working hard on nurturing child-to-child relationships.

Protecting Children from Dangerous Adults.
Community violence can spill over into schools. Weapons are carried to school too often by children who seek to protect themselves, prey on others, or maintain status in a peer group (Garbarino, 1999; Jenkins & Bell, 1997). In addition, whereas some schools have been considered safe havens from distressful conditions in a neighborhood, too often this protected space is savaged by intrusions, bullets, and intimidation from gang activities. Any talk about use of weapons has an unsettling effect on any school climate, of course, but in the hands of secure teachers, the trauma resulting from witnessing violence can become a part of the school curriculum. One teacher, trying to resolve fears in a Baltimore neighborhood experiencing periodic violence, used story writing and sharing to deal with children's anxieties and to help the children understand precautions and safety measures (Notar, 1992).

In addition to hostile and aggressive outside groups, school personnel must be aware of predatory adults that focus on schools. Without causing alarm, educators must inculcate in children the basic defenses about being alert to possible dangers, how to move to safe places when they are concerned, and how to report suspicious adult behavior.

Protecting Children from Home Neglect. In addition to tending to children's educational needs, school personnel must be aware of children who may be mistreated by their families or other adults and step in to assist them. Many factors contribute to the maltreatment of children, and a discussion of this complex topic is beyond the scope of this text. It is essential, however, that educators and other community workers understand the types of abuse and neglect, and recognize the signs and symptoms of children who may be mistreated (Aronson, 2002). They must also be clear on the procedures for reporting their suspicions. Although the Child Abuse Prevention and Treatment Act of 1974 required all states to establish some mandatory reporting of suspected abuse or neglect, the agencies involved, definitions of abuse, and reporting procedures vary from state to state. School professionals are obligated to know the regulations in their state. Figure 7–3 offers a summary of commonly accepted definitions, symptoms, and signs of child maltreatment, which include intentional physical injury, neglect, sexual molestation, and emotional abuse. The Resources section at the end of this chapter also provides additional sources of information.

REFLECTION

This may be a good time to think back to your own primary-school years and reflect on how people at your school protected you. Can you identify some of their actions? Now, do you think those practices exist in the schools you see today?

Maltreatment	Definition	Signs and Symptoms
Physical abuse	An intentional act affecting a child that produces tangible physical harm and can include shaking, beating, striking, or burning	Suspect physical abuse when a child has bruises, welts, burns, cuts, tears, scrapes or head injuries. The child may have repeated, unexplained injuries, complain of pain, report harsh treatment, show fear of adults, wear clothes to hide injuries, be frequently late or absent, or display withdrawn, anxious behavior or act out, especially if either is a change from usual behavior.
Emotional abuse	Psychologically damaging acts, such as verbal abuse, rejection, ignoring, terrorizing, isolating, or corrupting by parent or caregiver	Suspect emotional abuse when a child is generally unhappy, seldom smiles or laughs, is aggressive or disruptive or unusually shy and withdrawn, reacts without emotion to unpleasant situations, displays behaviors that are unusually adult or childish, exhibits delayed growth or delayed emotional and intellectual development, has low self-esteem, receives belittling or degrading comments from parents or guardians, or fears adults.
Sexual abuse	Any sexual act, such as rape, incest, fondling of the genitals, exhibitionism, or voyeurism, performed with a child by an adult who exerts control over the victim	Suspect sexual abuse when a child has physical indicators, such as difficulty walking or sitting; complaints of pain, itching, or swelling of genitals; pain when urinating; vaginal discharge; bruises or bleeding in external genitalia, vagina, anal areas, mouth, or throat. The child may also have behavioral indicators, such as unwillingness to have clothes changed or assistance with toileting, holding self, unwilling to participate in physical activities, withdrawn or infantile behaviors, unusual interest in or knowledge of sexual matters, or extremely aggressive or disruptive behavior.
Physical and emotional neglect	The failure to provide a child with the common necessities of food, shelter, a safe environment, education, and health care	Suspect when a child is unwashed and wears dirty clothes inadequate for the weather, is left unattended at a young age or left in the care of other children, lacks dental and medical care, is chronically absent, complains of hunger or rummages for food, or lacks safe housing.

Figure 7–3   Definitions, Signs, and Symptoms of Child Maltreatment
Source: Adapted from Aronson, S. S. (2002), (pp. 172–174).

By expanding and building on the protective strategies started in the home, partnerships between school and home assure protection for children and continuity of their learning. Whenever one enhances the objectives of the other, the result is enriched experience for children.

EVALUATING SCHOOLS

We do have measures to assess the effectiveness of particular school programs, and school effectiveness researchers have identified several characteristics that are observed consistently in schools

For effective schools, assessors will answer yes to most of the following questions:

1. Is consonance of philosophy found among board of education members, administrators, and teaching staff members, as well as aides and volunteers?

2. Are school facilities adequate and is space used efficiently?

3. Is the school facility safe and serviced well?

4. Does continuity of content and concepts exist between grade levels and from home experiences?

5. Are collaborations between home and school evident?

6. Do children evidence achievement in social and academic skills through their practices and activities?

7. Do teachers show a command of various teaching strategies and techniques?

8. Are teaching techniques varied for different children?

9. Are children constructively engaged in projects, follow-up activities, or the application of ideas? Or are they nonfocused, disruptive, glancing about, or wandering from place to place?

10. Is time off task kept to a minimum?

11. Do children evince various levels of thinking as they work and investigate?

12. Is a pleasant climate for learning and enthusiasm noticeable?

13. Are children allowed opportunities to interact with others and grow in social relationships?

14. Are teaching approaches sensible and realistic for the particular classrooms?

15. Do teachers praise and encourage learners and value different contributions to classwork?

16. Do all children succeed from time to time?

Figure 7–4   Assessing Schools for Effectiveness
Source: Adapted from Good and Brophy, 2002; Joyce and Weil, 1996; Rich, 1992.

demonstrating good achievement gains (Cruickshank, Jenkins, & Metcalf, 2002; Good & Brophy, 2002). Figure 7–4 presents questions that professionals will wish to use when evaluating the effectiveness of a particular school. The questions will reveal much about a school's adequacy and chances for success. An effective school will display positives for most features indicated.

The quality future school will emerge from secure connections among homes, schools, and communities as they become complementary and supplement all school objectives. Educational change and enhancement affect more than academic achievement, however. Also linked to school success are changes in health care, improved living conditions, improved interethnic relations, and diminished crime in neighborhoods. Liston and Zeichner (1996) remind us that "what goes on inside schools is greatly influenced by what occurs outside of schools" (p. xi).

COMMUNITY RESPONSIBILITY

Communities, large and small, are made up of individuals and what those people bring to their surroundings. The combination of persons and activities produces a community in which the ventures, endeavors, projects, and programs form a unique social setting. All communities have multiple facets, and the impact of different agencies and

Patricia A. Scully

Communities provide special events, and parents communicate pride in participating rather than winning.

Creating Cognitive Impact

Each community supplies news and information through publishing, television, radio, and **signage** that provide children with specific bits of knowledge. Religious centers have definite goals for developing understanding and practice. Recreation areas promote physical skills, exercise, and knowledge about sports and other activities. Libraries support literacy for even the youngest members of the community. Parks, zoos, museums, and theaters all provide information and aesthetic appreciation that benefit the growing child. Community-service offices all have informational outlets to promote health, safety, and good parenting practices. These social organizations, religious institutions, and educational outlets interrelate with and expand the home and school curricula to promote skills, knowledge, and attitudes on various subjects. Figure 7–5 illustrates how the social settings interrelate to develop and reinforce one cognitive area—mathematic ability.

Recognizing Affective Impact

In the affective domain, communities and neighborhoods provide children with a sense of security, well-being, and identity. The kinds of protective services available and the attitudes and values modeled by citizens and leaders send children clear messages about community values and concerns. For example, citizens can demonstrate and support fair play in games and sports. By playing fairly and rewarding all players, rather than emphasizing and rewarding only winners, sports directors and spectators communicate pride in striving and participating instead of in winning at any cost.

Community services and functions do not, of course, fall easily into categories of formal and informal learning, but in differing ways they do show children the range of human responses—from sensitive and reasonable to greedy and malicious. Lessons emerge as children sense their community at work and at play, when celebrating, and when struggling economically and politically or with natural disasters.

enterprises is pervasive in the lives of children. Although it is true that the youngest children have limited contacts beyond their home or child-care situation, primary-school children will experience, at some level, almost as much community conditioning, pressure, and influence as do adults.

The community as an institution is responsible for supporting its citizens, families, and schools and for furnishing a "curriculum" of experiences and opportunities. No laws or mandates require this involvement, and few would enumerate the particular services of a community as features of a curriculum. In formal and informal ways, though, each community provides a way of life, bits of knowledge, chances for skill development, values and moral education, aesthetic validations, and an array of opportunities that will affect children's perceptions and promote particular attitudes (Haberman, 1992; Heath, 1983).

	HOME	SCHOOL	COMMUNITY
Age 1	Exploring nearby space		
Age 2	Rote counting, comparing objects for size		Sensing larger spaces
Age 3	Contrasting sizes More counting	Nursery rhymes of counting	Rote counting experiences
Age 4	Seriation, placing objects in sequence, acquiring number sense Grasp of time	Distinguishing geometric shapes Determining more and less, basics of addition and subtraction	Applying number sense to the larger world Counting games
Age 5	Ordering objects, grasp of money Sense of measurement in cooking and home projects	Making one-to-one correspondence Grasp of rational numbers Starting to understand time	Noting sizes of larger and less; noting geometric shapes
Age 6	Using knowledge of time; using concept of number in home to calculate	Addition algorithm, subtraction algorithm Measurement study Geometric study	Applying knowledge of money for purchases
Age 7	Application of measurement to projects and hobbies Estimating quantities, distances, etc.	Continuing practice of number facts Estimation problems	Figuring how far to throw a ball Sensing how long to walk to friends' homes
Age 8		Multiplication algorithm	Using math concepts to solve problems in play, etc.

Figure 7–5   Children's Math Development Interrelated in Three Social Settings
Source: Adapted from Seefeldt & Barbour, 1998.

Communities and Nurturance

In many communities, pride and care for schools are evident to visitors and newcomers. A groundswell of support for promoting education does not just happen, however; such support indicates that committees, groups, and leaders have been active in establishing goals and lobbying for better conditions. We find that the electorate and the community decision makers are almost always motivated to strive hard to support increased educational opportunities—particularly for young children.

Regrettably, some communities do not facilitate and nurture children's education. Some references in this text portray conditions of despair and social crisis in too many U.S. communities (Coles, 2006; Garbarino, Dubrow, Kostelny, & Pardo 1998). Extensive social remediation is needed in all those locations. The community context affects and controls family and school settings to a large extent, and when economic, social, and political crises arise, community problems always detract from school programs and other educational objectives. Controversy often minimizes nurturing, and too often it prevents the community from making changes that have been initiated in schools and the community at large.

Effective Communities

Because communities are made up of sets of subsystems, research on competent communities is problematic. It is difficult to determine cause-and-effect relationships within a community, especially those that affect children. The following items, however, are closely related to effectiveness.

Health Services. Children must remain healthy to develop properly, yet access to a healthcare system depends on the community in which children live and on the economic status of the family. It is well documented that poor families have greater health problems, including chronic health conditions, more infectious diseases, higher incidence of low-birth-weight babies, and higher infant mortality rates (Children's Defense Fund, 2000).

The effective community will have comprehensive care systems that strive to serve citizens impartially. Many communities have both neighborhood health centers (such as those funded through the Office of Economic Opportunity) and a private healthcare system. By uniting family-care offices in one setting, officials diminish the expense, frustration, and transportation problems that poor families experience when seeking services.

In addition to offering health care, all medical facilities have an educational function. Health services also fulfill the important function of distributing materials about disease prevention and offering counseling by personnel who are positively oriented to their clients.

Welfare and Social Services. Employment offices, legal aid offices, and counseling centers cut across socioeconomic levels and are needed to address concerns for most U.S. communities. Regrettably, welfare services in the United States have always carried a stigma, and only in recent years have programs such as Head Start led to changed attitudes and the welcome involvement of middle-class citizens.

Religious Institutions. Churches, synagogues, and mosques are central facets of many communities. Although less so in recent decades, religious associations have dominated large portions of community life in the United States. In fact, they represented the largest part of the out-of-home activity for pre-20th-century Americans.

National surveys reveal a drop in religious participation in recent years (Lindner, 2003), but still, more individuals belong to church-related groups than to any other voluntary grouping. Religious institutions continue to influence many segments of U.S. communities, promoting ethnic as well as theological identity. With outreach programs and social action objectives, many places of worship now provide social, cultural, and other support for their communities, as well as spiritual nurturance for their membership groups. Food pantries, soup kitchens, and drug abuse and family counseling services are all operated by or through religious organizations in thousands of communities. Many care programs are not-for-profit arrangements developed and maintained by local religious organizations, even in the smallest communities. This service has received more attention since the Bush proposals of 2002 and 2004 for **"faith-based" group** funding for community welfare. It is controversial in political as well as educational circles.

Civic Services. All communities require fire departments, sanitation programs, and public safety offices. Supported by tax revenues, these services provide for the general stability and safety of the community.

Community services provide an educational function for children. What goes on in those departments, how the jobs are done, and the problems workers encounter are of interest to all children. Most offices publish materials and have personnel who head information programs for schools and other local groups. Elementary school children, when directed by their teachers, learn to understand the meaning of organized communities and the interdependence of community residents. They learn how community services affect their lives and perform for them as individuals.

Businesses. Most communities include private commercial enterprises linked to daily life in those areas, such as the filling stations, newsstands, and grocery stores found in nonindustrialized suburbs. Other communities contain factories, wharves and piers, large merchandise outlets, plus financial and information-processing establishments that employ residents and give flavor to a community. As children become acquainted with local businesses, they become knowledgeable about the economics of their town—where people work, what they produce, and where products go. They also learn of the need for many specialties as they become attuned to the world of work and the effects each institution has on community life and interaction.

In effective communities, commercial establishments cooperate with schools and families. Such cooperation demonstrates commitment to the interdependence of community settings and the need for mutual support. (Refer to Chapters 11 and 12 for discussions of techniques and models for such collaboration.)

Media Outlets. With the explosion and transmission of knowledge in the information age, communities are engulfed by media of all kinds. From standard newspapers to television programs to the Internet, visual and aural messages descend on citizens across the United States in increasing levels. Whether in an isolated prairie town or an urban neighborhood, the impact of the media is all encompassing.

Media affect all other institutions of a community. The type, quality, and amount of information an area receives produce responses from individuals, families, and schools. Effects can be positive or negative, but they are rarely neutral. Since most media are protected under First Amendment provisions, media outlets are largely self-policing, and public acceptance of the products determines the boundaries for individual distributors. Appropriateness of media products is a significant issue when we consider children's education. Many publications and recordings are adult oriented in topic, format, and relevance, but children are nonetheless exposed to large quantities of them. The V-chip for television, and Internet filters such as KidWatch, will block only a fraction of adult material (Winn, 2002). Media products that fall outside a community's standard invite thoughts of censorship, and problems always surface when that issue is raised. It is there-

fore desirable for communities, through public forums, to reach consensus on acceptable quality and then to work for that standard through educational programs and lobbying efforts when required.

Special-Interest Groups. In the late 20th century, the United States witnessed the formation of numerous special-interest groups, from the small group of citizens seeking to pressure schools to include or exclude something to the highly organized lobbying groups seeking changes in legislation. As we noted in Chapter 1, a special-interest group has a particular cause and stance (e.g., antinuclear energy, save the whales, antipornography, prochoice or antiabortion regarding abortion). Many groups disappear after accomplishing a mission; others become entrenched because their cause is ongoing.

Special-interest groups are grassroots associations that are very American in concept. Taking as their basis the constitutional amendment protecting association and assembly, citizens come together to work for or against some cause. In this way, altruistic groups have formed to gain privileges for disenfranchised persons (they achieved passage of an education bill for persons with disabilities in the 1970s) or to highlight a public problem (such as cleaning up the Nashua River, in Groton, MA; Cherry, 1982). Other groups form to oppose regulations or practices. A nonsmoking lobby is one example; a group censoring local library materials is another.

How do communities respond to special interest groups? If partnerships are in good working order, we normally find that special-interest-group pressure can be accommodated and processed in a healthy fashion. All too often this is not the case, and a part of the community bows to the pressure of the campaigning group. For example, one Pennsylvania library contained several volumes on cults and pagan rituals. When a member of a PTA subgroup saw these volumes, the group started a search through the library to identify and condemn all volumes containing information about the occult—even children's fantasy books featuring ghosts and goblins. Having no agency and

Informal contacts with neighbors and friends provide social networks that help children gain new understandings.

little organization to counter the arguments of the group, library staff quickly acquiesced to the demands and removed all offending materials. This established a dangerous precedent for handling library materials in this community.

Social Networks

The informal, everyday contacts of relatives, neighbors, friends, and colleagues produce social networks for adults and children in almost all neighborhoods. These groupings, which can cross gender, age, and socioeconomic status lines, provide enormous support for individuals. Werner (1999) showed in *Through the Eyes of Innocents* the strong impact of healthy behavior in a community on children caught up in war.

Positive Adult Groups. Social science research shows the importance of friends and relatives in providing exchanges of goods and services as well as psychological support (Berns, 2006;

Coleman, 1991). Werner and Smith (1992) and Cochran and Davila (1992) indicated that support groups are especially important for at-risk families when kin and colleagues provide emotional support for child raising, on confronting adversity, or even on integration into the community—the targeted family benefits. Healthier adult groups mean healthier environments for children. Information about social services, work opportunities, or new resources in a community is often delivered through the social networks of adults, and this benefits children.

Children's Peer Groups. As we noted in Chapter 1, peer groups exert a strong influence in any community. **Peer groups** are social in nature and inculcate a curriculum of experience in those involved. Constructively, peer groups provide children's all-important coming-of-age experiences, where children encounter folklore and rituals, experience a sense of belonging, and begin to develop competitive skills (Ladd & Pettit, 2002).

Peer groups also provide early experience in social interaction and cooperation. Destructively, peer groups may evolve into alienated gangs that commit acts of violence and hostility.

Victoria and her mother walked next door to welcome to their southern California community the new family that had just arrived from Hawaii. The two new girls, Terry and Adrianne, came the next day to Victoria's yard to play. They taught Victoria a new version of hopscotch. But while the girls were playing, the neighborhood "gang" appeared and told Terry and Adrianne they had to leave because "we don't play with Chinese kids." Victoria's mother, witnessing the scene, hurried out to the yard and asked the new neighbors to stay. "All children are welcome in this yard, as long as you play well together. Now, I saw the fun you two had showing Victoria that new hopscotch. Perhaps you'll teach these other children how to play it, too?" The mother tended her shrubs and observed for a while, but as all the children got involved in play, she left them to negotiate on their own.

Victoria's mother warded off hostility toward the new children in the neighborhood by suggesting and guiding a constructive experience. Both teachers in schools and family members have a responsibility to monitor and guide children's peer interactions when conflict seems imminent.

REFLECTION

Consider children's interactions you have witnessed recently or observe a small group of children at play in your neighborhood. Now, reflect on the social and educational value of that group's activities. Can you tie any of their planning, compromising, or maneuvering into the greater educational picture for the children's future skills?

Entertainment Facilities and Media

The entertainment industry is a part of the greater community and is probably the most pervasive force in children's lives today (Strasburger & Wilson, 2002). From earliest times, societies have recognized a need for activities that lift spirits and entertain, and a thriving community sanctions and supports entertainment for its citizens.

Communities have planned occasions and established recreational facilities that provide for entertainment—sports areas, natural areas, and parks. Also, parades, community fairs, and other celebrations are typical. In addition, an entire private industry has grown up in most communities for the purpose of entertainment on command, day or night. The following are typical entertainment formats that children and young people now possess or have ready access to from family members:

- Radios, CD players, cell phones, play stations, iPods
- Cable and broadcast television
- Theaters, cinemas, malls, coffeehouses, arcades and theme parks
- VCRs and DVD players for film viewing
- Computer games and Internet linkages

Although much of the entertainment industry's offerings are consonant with typical community endeavors, the time and expense allotted to them can intrude on families' and children's schedules, personal objectives, creativity, schoolwork, and socializing (Gunter, Harrison & Wykes, 2003; Singer & Singer, 2001). The challenge that parents and schools are faced with is that entertainment may be over utilized in proportion to other aspects of the home and school curriculum.

When is the community responsibility for expanding or limiting its entertainment opportunities? Communities have legal responsibility to protect children from inappropriate situations but assume little responsibility for children's overexposure to sanctioned entertainment forms (Van Evra, 2004). The American Academy of Pediatrics officially recommended in 1999 that children under age two watch no television at all, but responsibility in guiding television viewing at all ages rests primarily with families and primary caregivers; some cannot manage this well. Technology, including filters for Internet surfing and the V-chip for TV programs, has been developed to help parents control what comes in and out of the home, and other devices can actually control the time when the television is on and off.

Assessors will find most of the following characteristics in effective communities:

1. A workable healthcare system available to people of all income levels

2. Social programs, health facilities, and health offices clustered to maximize usage and cut logistics

3. Community programs designed to educate children as well as serve families

4. Religious institutions participating in community life and demonstrating concern through social-action programs

5. Religious associations that nurture children's ethnic and spiritual identities

6. Municipal service departments that are stable, well maintained, and available for educational visits

7. Commercial enterprises that welcome visits and conduct information sessions

8. Commercial establishments that see adopt-a-school plans as an enhancement to the business

9. Media producers who realize the effects of mass communication and who responsibly produce material appropriate for young children

10. Communication between media outlets, schools, and community agencies regarding available media

11. Special-interest groups responsive to community questions about their objectives and policies

12. Positive social networks in evidence (social gatherings, block parties, community clubs)

13. Social clubs for children (sports programs, scout programs, 4-H clubs, seasonal recreational facilities)

14. Citizens showing interest in community schools, neighborhoods, and individual children

Figure 7–6   Assessing the Competent Community

Some schools, communities, and families have successfully run programs in which children and their parents pledge to watch no television for a week. At the end of the week, sessions are planned to help the participants discuss the experience. The nonprofit organization TV-Turnoff Network provides an array of information and resources to encourage children and adults to watch less television, in order to promote healthier lives and communities. See the Resources section of this chapter for further information.

EVALUATING COMMUNITIES

Communities vary in makeup and quality, but all have some features that enhance educational opportunity. Observers will find most of the elements specified in Figure 7–6 in an educationally productive community.

LINKING RESPONSIBILITIES

All communities have established schools within their boundaries to develop children's cognitive and affective skills. In recent years, however, increasingly heavy burdens have been placed on schools. In addition to normal monitoring activities, many present-day schools provide two meals per day and pair with nonprofit (or for-profit) organizations for before- and after-school care. Schools are assuming a larger part of the parenting role, and this increase requires good communication, more understanding, and cooperation from families if the overload taking place in some schools is to be successfully managed.

Some skills and attitudes are best enhanced through projects and activities under community sponsorship. We as educators must be alert for collaborations between community agencies and schools that promote children's education and welfare. The following vignette illustrates this point.

Life in the small coastal community was quiet, but Josh and his friends were restless after a month of summer vacation. Returning from the ball field one day, they pedaled their bikes toward home, throwing rubbish from their lunches at poles and fences. They seemed intent on marring their community's quiet roadside beauty. At one lovely spot near the ocean however, they noticed a painter setting up his easel and stopped to watch. The painter paused, then asked the boys if they would help him clean up debris near the shoreline so that he could paint without distractions. The boys did, and then stayed to watch the man work. The boys became fascinated with the artist's rendering, and the painter became aware of how little experience these youngsters had in developing a sense of their surroundings.

A few days later, the artist and a colleague invited Josh, his friends, and their parents to their studio to talk about their art and its relationship to the world around them. This worked so well that the artists, with the help of a small group of parents, persuaded town officials to budget space and funds to open a modest gallery in the community. Classes in painting and art appreciation are now offered in the gallery, and the artists are helping teachers at the local elementary school integrate art into its curriculum.

No single agency—home, school, or community—felt a need or responsibility for developing the aesthetic senses of Josh and his friends, but an interested citizen was able to establish a link with this responsibility and provide a needed aspect of curriculum for the youth in that community.

GOVERNANCE OF EDUCATION

Governance for educational opportunity is, like nurturance and curriculum, a shared responsibility for the institutions involved with children's welfare. Governance involves the management, coordination, and evaluation of children's educational opportunities, and frequently the factors are summed up by the word *administration*. Both legal requirements and traditions relate to these responsibilities. Although governance in education would seem in today's world to be a basic function of schools, some features of governance devolve to homes and the community setting.

The community at large must be the general overseer for educational practice, opportunity, and development. Direct administration and supervision are assumed by the local community school board.

Legal Requirements

Tradition, to some extent, and the large volume of local, state, and national statutes and regulations, to a major extent, are the means by which the several institutions focus on educational opportunity. All school officials and administrators are aware of these requirements.

Our federal government, using some provisions of the U.S. Constitution as authority, has developed a number of significant education-related programs and laws over the years. Head Start, for example, was established in the late 1960s as a federally funded educational program for young children at risk for school failure. Public Law 94–142, the Education for All Handicapped Children Act of 1975, and its three later amendments established fundamental education rights for children with disabilities and their parents. The No Child Left Behind Act of 2001 is another recent example of educational reform initiated at the national level.

The federal government was conceived as a minimal force in education, because the Tenth Amendment to the Constitution relegates education (and many other responsibilities) to the individual states. Consequently, federal law is based on selected parts of the Constitution—those that invoke the government's role as protector of individual rights. The U.S. Supreme Court has done likewise in settling educational disputes referred to it. Most education court cases are heard and settled at the state level, but the disputes over desegregation of schools in the 1950s are an important example of Supreme Court involvement in education law.

Legally, then, the bulk of education governance comes from state constitutions, statutes, and regulations although statutes and regulations change on occasion when political processes shift (Fuller & Olsen, 1998). States are responsible to provide free public education to all children, to compel students to attend school, to maintain the separation of church and state, and to implement federal mandates such as those required by the No Child Left Behind Act. Each state has established a department of education to oversee matters within that state. One appendage of each state education department is the **local education authority (LEA)**, often called the local school board which serves to operate the state-required schools.

Local-Level Decisions. At the local level, the school board (LEA) operates as an agent for the state but makes its own rules, regulations, and policies, which in turn serve the community involved. LEAs develop budgets, determine policies and oversee the schools in their jurisdiction, and hire administrators and teachers to carry out the day-to-day operation of the schools.

Court Decisions. One other agency is involved is the judiciary—the courts. When adjudicating differences of opinion, courts may have much to say about education. Even though courts interpret rather than make laws, it is fair to say they became extensively involved in education matters in the late 20th century (Fuller & Olsen, 1998; Shoop & Dunklee, 1992). Some court decisions have pushed educational requirements in very different directions (Valente & Valente, 2005). Examples involve civil rights and free-speech issues, religious group connections to schools, and definitions of unreasonable search and seizure. In addition, claims of sexual and racial harassment connected to schools and communities have increased in recent years as growing awareness and diversity have brought these issues forward.

Home Governance

Various state laws specify parent or guardian responsibilities toward children in their care. These regulations reside in the general welfare statutes and are minimal. The laws are invoked when neglect is an issue and when local authorities or agencies find that families are not providing general safety and support for children in their care (Webb et al., 2007). In addition, all states have laws requiring home responsibility for supervising children and making sure they attend school (Valente & Valente, 2005). The general requirements for home support have come down through the culture and are responsibilities that most families accept without question. Child maltreatment becomes an issue when families are in trouble. If social welfare agencies are alerted by other parents, schools, or public safety officials, they may initiate legal proceedings to remove children. Although child maltreatment is the exception to the rule in most families, abuse and neglect of children is a significant social problem in the United States. Neglect continues to be the predominant type of maltreatment, and about 80% of the perpetrators of child maltreatment are parents (Reppucci et al., 1997). As children mature, home governance practices become more indirect, but laws and traditions still require basic support, parental guidance, and family monitoring through young adulthood.

Other Family Governance. All families informally evaluate their schools, teachers, and communities. Without objective criteria for making these highly subjective and personal assessments, families use whatever they have at hand—their own experiences in school; what they have read, seen, or heard; and their own perceptions of what is right for education. Most schools do not have a process installed whereby outsiders may evaluate personnel, programs, or other school undertakings. As a result, feedback from families regrettably is often overlooked or neglected (De Carvalho, 2001).

Although rare, some school districts have provisions for direct family involvement in public school management and governance. We do find family involvement most often in early childhood programs, such as Head Start child care-center boards, and in **parent cooperative nursery schools**. One well-known international program that actively pursues parental involvement at the primary level is the Reggio Emilia plan in Italy (Gandini, Hill, Cadwell, & Schwall, 2005). A number of schools in the United States are now modeling their programs on this

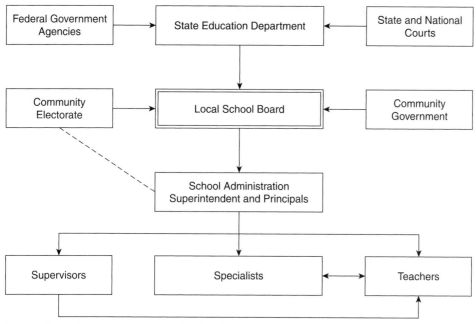

Figure 7–7   Governance of Local Schools

plan, in which parents and others are elected to hold advisory and even directory roles for school programs. (See Chapter 12 for a full description of the Reggio Emilia programs.)

Families are normally disenfranchised in governance of school curriculum, except in the role of follow up for schoolwork (De Carvalho, 2001) and minor supporting roles as school helpers (Cutler, 2000). Actually, most families are quite willing for the school hierarchy—school board, administration, teachers, staff, and specialists—to continue with governance of the academic curriculum. The regrettable dimension here is that the close working relations with parents that could come about do not, and a potent resource is underused. Schools lose chances to unite community members and develop better programs when they do not seek to involve parents.

School Governance

Schools are a highly visible feature of any society's structure. Although a few citizens in the United States contest the school's viability and purpose, most accept schools as necessary for the proper development of educational opportunity for young children. The Phi Delta Kappa/Gallup survey (Rose & Gallup, 2006) finds year after year that Americans rate their own local schools highly.

Schools are established for the management, sequencing, and coordination of formal curriculum, as we noted earlier, as well as to provide other educational services. In some cases, this responsibility has resulted in bureaucracies with all the trappings of large, multifaceted agencies (see Figure 7–7). Because of the structure and rigidity in many large school systems, in recent years, some communities have argued for decentralization and **site-based management** for individual schools. Responsive school situations often result when decentralization is done carefully and with community involvement. The charter school movement (discussed in Chapter 12) is one recent example of decentralizing.

The preceding notwithstanding, we probably have no alternative to the school bureaucracy for supporting general education for the large numbers of school-age children in our highly technical and work-oriented society. The demands for literacy, scientific understanding, math and social science training, to say nothing of the socializing, recreational, and health needs of children are immense in the United States today. To accomplish this basic formal curriculum, our society needs carefully organized schools for the majority of the population. One has only to note situations in which communities experience extended school strikes to see the confusion and exasperation that come with trying to fill in the gaps left by school closings.

As agents for the community school board (the LEA), administrators and teachers exert the greatest influence and authority over what happens in a community's schools in several areas: management and coordination of curriculum, time commitments, and assessments. This underscores the vast responsibilities that devolve to school personnel in all communities.

REFLECTION

In the school you are visiting, ask the classroom teacher who decides what is to be taught to the children this week and how that content will be handled. Is it the teacher herself, is it a team, is it the administration, or someone else? Did your classmates find similar decision makers in their schools?

Community Governance

In theory, all educational governance starts with the community. All states delegate most responsibility to the local community for oversight of public safety, child welfare, and the development and operation of schools. That community may be a small municipality of a few hundred persons in Vermont or a huge metropolitan district like New York City or Dade County, Florida.

Deriving from state mandates, all initiatives in local school governance begin with the community school board (LEA) elected or appointed to oversee schools. As noted, the LEA delegates

authority for administration and implementation. Monies are raised from community taxes to support school programs the LEA has proposed. The school board's central office hires personnel to carry out these programs, and the board sets general directions for the curriculum and considers program evaluations. To a large extent, board members depend on their superintendent and principals to give counsel for board actions and to carry out the day-to-day operation of schools. This means that most of the responsibility for operating or managing schools, interpreting curriculum, and conducting assessments is in the hands of school administrators and teachers.

Curriculum content for schools is also supposedly determined by the community served, but only in a general way does a community decide what is to be developed in its school programs. Community citizens most often surrender governance to the school board (whom they have elected) and its administrators. They become involved in school matters only when a crisis surfaces in the curriculum or in response to political repercussions from nonaccomplishment, such as falling SAT scores.

A community's citizens do evaluate their schools, however. We find that most persons judge school performance by happiness of the children, tangible outcomes such as report cards, the later success of students, and how school is like or unlike what they experienced in their generation. These are valuable criteria and should be held as general guides. With the increased reliance on outcomes of standardized tests mandated by the No Child Left Behind Act, however, schools are being assessed by measures that may not connect with community aspirations for its schools.

Considering the anxiety about school programs in the United States and the burgeoning problems in many school districts, it may well be time for more direct community involvement in school life and governance. Shared decision making, more extensive exchange of information between school and community, and alliance among community representatives would produce more thoroughly understood programs, more successful outcomes, and a more supportive constituency.

APPLYING THESE CONCEPTS TO YOUR WORK WITH CHILDREN AND FAMILIES

Children are the weakest, most dependent, and most vulnerable persons in our society; yet, we do not have assigned advocates for them. Governing agencies assume that persons working with them—family members, school professionals, and members of the community—will do the best job of protecting and educating the nation's children. This means that you, as a developing professional, have an obligation to find the best opportunities for the children you encounter. In order to do this, you must be knowledgeable about the delegation of power, authority, and responsibility for children's lives and know how to initiate action, if necessary.

So, think of yourself filling a new niche in the home–school–community matrix, and speculate about how it would unfold when you teach. As you approach the classroom, think of yourself as a type of "peace corps" worker who will analyze the classroom situation and then figure out how to best serve the population of young people in front of you.

Ask yourself, "What should be happening for these children in language arts development, in science and math understanding, and in social and physical development.

- Speculate on how other responsible adults can be helpful as you produce a curriculum.

- Meet the home caregivers to confer about reasonable objectives for the children and steps to take in meeting them.
- Consider how you can use community resources to enhance or illuminate a subject area or project. See the next paragraph for an example.

The following scenario serves as an example of one simple collaboration on a social science project: Your local chamber of commerce has invited your class to visit the local water treatment plant to learn about its operation and effect on the community. Your small group of parent helpers will help plan the trip and study the site as a place for learning. After the visit, you can use in-class cooperative learning activities as well as coaching skills and resource persons to help students list the particular benefits of the treatment plant for their city. Finally, you can guide children to use their literacy skills in describing the treatment plant in reports, drawings, and letters for their parents, other students, and community members who have worked with them.

Now, try to identify one other community event that will lend itself to this type of partnership work. How will community adults participate, and how will the children's caregivers be involved in processing the learning and follow-up work?

SUMMARY AND REVIEW

It is important to see the overall responsibility of who speaks and acts for children in our society. The three social settings have a shared responsibility for making certain that optimal conditions and arrangements are in place for protecting children and enhancing educational opportunities. A curriculum of experience accrues to every child, and this differs depending on the circumstances in the three social settings. Each child's curriculum is divided into two interactive parts: formal, or

academic, and informal, or hidden. Tradition and law impose requirements on homes, schools, and communities to do their share in presenting the curriculum, but overlap, disagreements, and redundancies are not unusual as children move from one setting to another. Education is most productive where strong cooperation and alliances exist among homes, schools, and communities.

The objective observer can see the unique and vital position of the school in any cooperative endeavor. Parents and communities, of course, have a vested interest

Direct community involvement in school governance produces better-understood programs, successful outcomes, and a supportive constituency.

Larry Hamill / Merrill

in the education of their children. Public schools are delegated the responsibility of accepting all entrants, organizing a curriculum, executing that curriculum, and generally steering children through the educational process. Because educators are trained professionals with daily contact with children, they are in a unique position to monitor them for possible maltreatment. Educators can also see the places where involvement from parents and the larger community will help. If the school as an institution neglects to engender cooperative action among all social institutions, though, the interests and hopes of parents and communities are difficult to realize.

SUGGESTED ACTIVITIES AND QUESTIONS

1. Because of your role as a child development services specialist, you must plan how to build support for two children whose families recently arrived in the United States. You know that the families are struggling economically, and they are also trying to learn a new language and culture. Even though all three social settings bear responsibility, how can you best enhance educational opportunity for these youngsters?

2. Find a copy of your state's statutes regarding child maltreatment. Itemize the steps you are to take in reporting suspected abuse, then discuss with a teaching colleague your responsibility and its implications.

3. Construct a chart showing the areas of sex education you think children normally encounter between ages three and eight. Indicate home, school, and community responsibilities at each age level.

4. Imagine you are designated as the leader of a new home–school–community collaboration effort based at your school. Outline for participants at the first meeting six particular ways that the three settings can support one another.

5. As a teacher, you are invited to a church preschool program to talk about "literacy atmospheres." Outline the several points you wish to communicate to your mothers and fathers for making a meaningful literary focus in their homes.

RESOURCES

Books

Conley, D. T. (2003). *Who governs our schools? Changing roles and responsibilities.* New York: Teachers College Press.

Diffily, D. (2004). *Teachers and families working together.* Boston: Allyn & Bacon.

Epstein, J. L. (2001). *School, family, and community partnerships: Preparing educators and improving schools.* Boulder, CO: Westview.

Kyle, D. W., McIntyre, E., Miller, K. B., & Moore, G. (2006). *Bridging school and home through family nights.* Thousand Oaks, CA: Corwin Press.

McNary, S. J., Glasgow, N. A., & Hicks, C. (2005). *What successful teachers do in inclusive classrooms.* Thousand Oaks, CA: Corwin Press.

Films and Videos

Make a difference: Report child abuse and neglect [Video, 28 min]. (1999). Discusses the indicators of abuse/neglect, what to do if maltreatment is suspected, and the impact on society. Washington, DC: National Association for the Education of Young Children.

Nutrition for infants and children under six [Video, 30 min]. 1994. A program on nutritional needs for three specific stages of development. Cambridge, MA: Cambridge Educational.

Raising healthy kids: Families talk about sexual health. [Video, 30 min]. (1997). For parents of young children. Shows importance of parent-child communication and deals with the issue of parent as the child's primary sexuality educator. New York: Media Works.

The role of parents and teachers [Video, 29 min]. (2001). Examines how parents and teachers help children develop literacy. Crystal Lake, IL: Magna Systems Video.

Organizations

Child Welfare League
440 First Street NW
Washington DC 20001
http://www.cwla.org

Child Welfare Information Gateway
Children's Bureau/ACYF
1250 Maryland Avenne, SW
Washington, DC 20024
http://www.childwelfare.gov

National Network of Partnership Schools
Johns Hopkins University
3003 N. Charles Street, Suite 200
Baltimore, MD 21218
http://www.csos.jhu.edu/p2000/

TV-Turnoff Network
200 29th Street, NW,
Washington, DC 20007
http://www.tvturnoff.org

Web Sites

http://www.childtrendsdatabank.org   The Child Trends Data Bank provides an extensive amount of information on children's well-being.

http://www.futureofchildren.org   The Future of Children promotes effective policies and programs for children by providing policy makers and service providers with timely, objective information based on best available research.

http://www.nea.org   The National Education Association presents an overview of the major U.S. teacher association plus links to publication, reports and statistics on U.S. schools.

Chapter 8

Curriculum of the Home

They gave him afterward everyday . . . they and of them became part of him.

The family usages, the language, the company, the furniture . . . the yearning and swelling heart.

Affection that will not be gainsayed.

(Walt Whitman, 1855, p. 91)

A broad definition of *curriculum* signifies "all the experiences children have from the moment of waking to the moment of falling asleep" (Doll, 1995, p. 5). Because most of a child's waking hours are connected to family, this implies the home must provide a great deal of children's learning experiences.

No single **home curriculum** is like any other, because America is one of the most diverse nations in the world, with a mix of "cultures, races, old and new immigrants, exceptionalities and talents" (Futrell, Gomez, & Bedden, 2003, p. 381). This cascade effect of influence from the external cultural factors, plus the internal or home factors, becomes the home curriculum and leads children in their perceptions and interpretations of the world.

In this chapter, the authors give examples of the many experiences children have at home and with family members, the implications of these experiences, and the resulting potential for expanded learning. After reading this chapter, you will be able to do the following:

1. Explain what families do that undergirds children's language and literacy development and relate how this impacts cognitive development.

2. Define **code switching** and tell why adults' involvement is important when children learn multiple languages and dialects.

3. Point out what parents do to instill their own belief systems as children form values and habits and develop a sense of purpose for their lives.

4. Give examples of how parents provide an environment in the home that supports children's learning.

5. Demonstrate how children's academic learning is enhanced by: (a) daily routines in the home, (b) amount and use of space, (c) family traditions, and (d) religious practices.

6. Compare and contrast your own experiences to those of the children in the vignettes.

7. Point out uses parents make of technology to lay a foundation in a globalized society for their children's emerging world view.

8. Explain ways in which extended family members—particularly grandparents—affect features of the home curriculum.

9. Discuss the pros and cons of home schooling and explain why some families embrace this trend.

The educative processes of all homes are important ingredients for society in the United States, because, as social–cultural–context theorists indicate, how each person develops affects all who relate to that individual. In Chapters 3 and 4, we discussed the diversity and functions of U.S. families and defined a family unit as any two or more persons living together and sharing common goals, resources, and commitment to each other. Children in any family household will have at least one adult (referred to in this text as a parent) who is responsible for them. Siblings, who play an important role in any child's learning, also may be present.

Because of the diversity in U.S. families, we find not one single home curriculum but many variations. Too often, professional educators underestimate the power of the home curriculum and miscalculate the learning that children have acquired outside of school. When there is disparity between children's home learning and the expectations of the school curriculum, children can be judged to be deficient rather than having different skills that may assist them in attaining skills of a higher level.

Research, over time, indicates that regardless of the ethnic or socioeconomic makeup of the family, a warm and responsive parenting style, a structured environment, and stimulating activities that include a variety of materials, plus parents involvement as children use these materials, support children's growth toward a productive lifestyle (Bronfenbrenner, 2005; McGroder, 2000; Wade, 2004.) Conversely, in some family situations, parenting styles and habits mitigate against children's natural pursuit of knowledge and positive development.

All families have an organizational structure that defines family members and their roles. Many households have kinship networks of extended family members who may or may not be living in the home but who give added support and nurturance. The kinship influences on the family organizational structure is also augmented by personal social networks that parents develop (Cochran & Walker, 2005). This structure provides physical and emotional support as the child moves into the school and community, where all are expected to adapt to the prevailing structure of obligations, rights, and labor divisions. The rewards system in the child's outside environment (Bronfenbrenner [1995] labeled it the *mesosystem*) is determined primarily by the predominant culture and may shift as the needs of the culture shift (Coontz, 1999). In the 21st century, the rapid growth of technology is revolutionizing our society and presents us with new and altered perspectives. Just as young parents rely on technology and media for their outlook on child rearing, so, too, do the different cultural values bombard families. The resulting world view may therefore come in conflict with many traditional family values and perspectives (Long, 2004).

Still, whatever their environment, children first learn valuable information and life skills from their families. They learn who they are, how to communicate with others, what their role is in society, how to function in their environment, and the kind of world they live. No matter their family structure, this learning will be a consequence of family interactions *and stimulations*. The greater the variety of these influences, the richer will be the learning.

Early learning of appropriate or inappropriate communication behaviors, developing language, and acquiring literacy skills are the underpinnings of children's later cognitive development. Besides child–parent interactions, home learning is further supported by a family's use of time and space, the household routines, the sharing of interests and skills, the family rituals and religious practices, plus family outreach to others. In all situations, children's learning depends on their readiness for the tasks and experiences they encounter. Figure 8–1 shows the range of children's learning at home and the involvement of particular family members.

NURTURING COMMUNICATION, PRELITERACY, AND COGNITIVE SKILLS

Language, literacy, communication skills, and cognitive development begin at birth. Parents and significant others talk to the baby, intrepret the baby's responses, and establish communication patterns. They interpret the baby's movements, coos, laughs, cries, and other nonverbal behaviors. They enjoy interpreting, to babies and to the "world at large," what these behaviors mean, as illustrated in the following vignette.

During a family get together, Christine was cuddling her six-week-old niece, Lorelei, against her shoulder and neck. Murmers and coos between the two seemed to indicate contentment on both their parts. Suddenly Lorelei begins sucking on Christine's neck.

"Oops, honey", Christine exclaims, "I guess you need your mommy!" Christine calls across the room, "Jenny, you're needed. Lorelei is hungry, and I sure can't provide for her." She passes Lorelei to Jenny, who snuggles Lorelei as she offers her her breast, saying "There! You're happy now." Gentle murmuring sounds can be heard from other family members in the room as they acknowledge that the important role of feeding the youngest in this extended family is appropriately met.

Although crying is one of earliest forms of infant communication, other nonverbal behaviors work (Trawick-Smith, 2006), as we just witnessed.

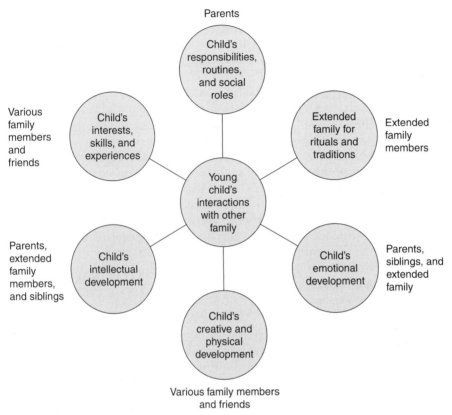

Parents

Various family members and friends

Extended family members

Parents, extended family members, and siblings

Parents, siblings, and extended family

Various family members and friends

Figure 8–1   Different Family Members Nurture the Home Curriculum
Note: Foundational skills, concepts, attitudes, and experiences are developed in the child's home environment. Some areas are influenced more strongly by particular family members and the child's peers.

Even though some of the interpretations may be incorrect, the fact that parents are responding provides the basis of child language development. Babies sense that their needs can be met, if they in some way initiate the action. When certain actions get no response, the action is likely to be stopped. The baby's skills expand rapidly because of planned and unplanned family interactions and experiences. Parents echo their infant's vocalizations, name things, and direct their attention to the objects, people, and events around them. Parents, other family members, and caregivers explain to the baby what they and the baby are doing, demonstrating with real objects accompanied by language.

Families extend the communication process as children grow. In the first year, they will introduce babies to books. Adults read and reread the books; they talk about and ask questions about the pictures, such as "where is the dog?" As they turn the pages, they ask "Oh, what do you think is going to happen?" or they may point out where they are reading. They read books in a variety of settings, often snuggling with the child in a warm and pleasurable manner. The progressively more sophisticated manner of reading provides a foundation for later reading development as well as cognitive development. Writing emerges in a similar fashion. Children observe parents writing lists, notes, and letters, and drawing pictures. Parents give paper and crayons to children, who then scribble, draw, and write sounds for letters or words, imitating their parents' writing.

Parents assist children's later literacy development as they listen to, discuss, and make up new stories. As children develop new skills, parents expand this development by using more elaborate speech, by reading with their children in a variety of ways (for example, by taking turns reading familiar passages), or by children reading the dialogue (Beaty, 2006). Literacy expands as extended family, friends, and neighbors become a part of the communication process: engaging children in more and more extensive conversations, writing notes or letters, sharing pictures and scribbles, providing materials and books. Children get the message that reading and writing is important to the entire family and communication patterns vary from one to another (Christie, Vukelich, & Enz, 2006). This added stimulation and variety accelerates the child's language, literacy, and cognitive development (Wade, 2004).

Children first learn vocabulary and grammatical patterns as important adults model language in the course of family interactions (Heath, 1983; Sigel, Dreyer, & McGillicuddy-DeLisi, 1984). In a rich home curriculum, important adults engage children in conversations beyond giving directions and correcting behavior, for example, teaching **active listening skills**, and involving them in "give and take" discussions. As parents extend children's social contacts to the extended family, in the neighborhood, and in the larger community, children observe more than one one way of communicating. It is in these different settings that children develop and expand their **interactive skills** (Salzetein, 1976; Walker and Taylor, 1991).

In homes where multiple languages or dialects are used, children learn *code switching* to deal with different social venues (Tabors & Snow, 2001) as children observe adults using different language codes. Language expands and develops for all children as they are exposed through connections with extended family, family friends, neighbors, and playmates to various dialects or culture patterns. Hearing the language patterns of stories from different cultures, discussing these stories, and then dramatizing them, so the patterns become familiar, is also important to children's expanding understanding of how language works (Fried, 2001; Pinnell, 1996).

REFLECTION

Who in your family read to you in your early years? Do you remember any special words or expressions from that early book sharing that you liked? Can you see how these preliteracy events connected with later schooling?

Parent Knowledge of Child Development

In the homes of interested parents, instruction and expectations are adapted to account for their children's development. These adults rely on different sources to obtain this information, even though this appears in nonsequential ways and in an almost "hit-or-miss" fashion.

Over the years, young parents often looked to extended families and social networking established in their neighborhood, schools, and commumities for sources of information. They read books and articles published by authorities such as Dr. Spock or T. Berry Brazelton as guides for raising children. Many depended on neighboorhood knowledge and interactions. Some attended parent education programs, developed by such organizations as **Women, Infants, & Children (WIC)**, well-baby clinics, Head Start, and other social service programs. Some high schools provided basic courses on home management and child development for students even before they become parents.

Now, in addition to the sources just listed, technology is expanding to give parents access to information far beyond what was available in the past regarding the upbringing of their children. In the past, television offered entertainment programs, like "Leave it to Beaver," that modeled positive middle-class White family interactions. Today's "sit coms" portray culturally different family structures and unique parent functioning. Parents, linked to computer and Internet resources, have unlimited access to information from experts with whom they can link and get their questions answered. These parents have the capacity to interact with other young parents as they visit **Web logs** and exchange emails. In this manner, they can form close personal relationships and sense of community without leaving their homes (Long, 2004). A positive aspect of such availability is a sense of unity with a larger group and a feeling of being in the mainstream. A negative aspect is that all available information is not necessarily based on sound practices or good research (Long, 2004), and suffers from the lack of a moderating environment provided by personal encounters. All linkage, of course, depends on a parent's interest and the time to investigate good sources of information. Often, these are hurdles not addressed in a busy world.

LEARNING VALUES, ROLES, AND RESPONSIBILITIES

An important part of the home curriculum is for children to learn family values and changing role expectations for themselves toward other members of the family or neighbors and friends. Children also learn the role expectations of family members toward each other and the extended family.

Parents Foster Beliefs and Value Structures

All families have commitments, values, and priorities. Some of these sentiments are explicit and well defined, but often many are only implied, and this is especially true for **marginalized families** (Garbarino & Abramowitz, 1992). Some family values and goals are more immediate and are often expressed as wishes or "as what we are trying to do." Some families have both long-range goals and those planned for a limited period of time, whereas other families are able only to plan from one day to the next.

A number of writers point out that children's attitudes, beliefs, and values resemble those of their parents (Coles, 1997; Goleman, 1995; Scarf, 1999), but all allow that schools and communities extend these considerably. Educating

about stealing, lying, and disorderly conduct is normal for most families, although the instruction can take different forms. Some parents teach morals and values through intimidation and punishment, whereas others approach the challenge by explaining children's problems and the impact of one's actions on others. The latter approach results in stronger development of conscience and internal control (Sadker & Sadker, 2005). Families who focus on values, morals, and attitudes characterized by modeling behaviors, reasoning through solutions, and labeling the behavior when seen in public (see Figure 8–2) give children a much-needed sense of purpose and direction in their lives.

Whatever the organizational structure of the family, children absorb these values and goals and their role in accomplishing them. As children grow older and other events happen to families, such as the birth of a child with exceptionalities, what children learn about themselves can be vastly different and can be quite contrary to school or the societal expectations of families. The following vignette shows one family's approach—a strongly goal-oriented one by societal expectations. The second vignette demonstrates how this family adapted its expectations after the birth of a child with Down syndrome.

Every morning before her children left for school, Mrs. Martinez wished each child a good day in Spanish. She would remind each of strongly held family principles. She then asked each child to make a small commitment for the day. Studying hard, practicing the piano, or improving at shooting baskets were acceptable goals. At dinner one evening when the family shared accomplishments and worries, José told his family he wasn't going to read with Louie (a child with a learning disability in his class) anymore because Louie was "just too hard to deal with." The older brothers and sisters sympathized with José, but they also reminded him of the ways they had read to him when he was little. Mrs. Martinez hugged José hard a few days later when he told her, "I'm going to read with Louie. I found out yesterday he can read lots of words if you start them out and whisper the real hard ones."

In the Martinez family, the mother was a strong and dominant influence. She believed in

1. Allow children to accept consequences for their actions; for example, they can manage cleanup after some water play.

2. Avoid performing tasks children can do for themselves. Caregivers encourage effort and experiments so children learn to do for themselves.

3. Give children responsibilities that fit their age and skill levels.

4. Praise children when they perform well; be encouraging and supportive when they make mistakes or fall short of expectations.

5. Model behaviors and attitudes that show you are proactive; for example, communicate to children that persons can make things happen.

6. Encourage and support children's particular interests and show respect for their accomplishments.

7. Be consistent in expectations by establishing reasonable standards of behavior.

8. Explain the reasons for needed rules and limits, as well as any deviations from normal expectations.

9. Allow children to make age-appropriate decisions (including rules and guidelines) as often as possible. Start with minor choices and graduate to consequence-bearing actions.

Figure 8–2   Helping Children Develop Internal Locus of Control
Source: Adapted from Berns, 2006; Sadker & Sadker, 2005.

goal setting and certain family values and made them clear and explicit for her children.

Whether values and goals are stated each day, written, or merely implied, notions of having purpose and direction in one's life are modeled and communicated to children. Such strong purposes can help a family adjust and adapt to an unexpected event as the Martinez family experienced.

At the end of José's third-grade year, Manuela, a child with Down syndrome, was born to the Martinez family. José was thankful for his earlier school experiences with Louie, for they helped him and his family as they weathered the many and dramatic effects of this event. The strong sense of unity in the family allowed them to adjust their lives so that all shared in the responsibilities for this child. José always came home on Tuesdays to help his mother. He was faithful to his task and enjoyed watching Manuela develop. The following vignette demonstrates how one strong family helped the school to change its policies and also helped their child cope with conflicting expectations.

One Tuesday, José's teacher informed the class they would all have to stay after school because of their rowdiness. José, greatly dismayed, tried to explain to her why he couldn't, then walked out of school and went home. His mother was both pleased and dismayed, for she had received a phone call from the office, telling her about the event. When José explained that he hadn't been rowdy and he couldn't let his mother down, the two of them began to work out plans for communicating their needs to the school personnel. Mrs. Martinez then called the school to make an early-morning appointment with the teacher and principal. At this meeting, many important changes between home and this family began to take shape. Besides being a step that enabled the teacher and principal to reevaluate how they worked with families' changing needs, Mrs. Martinez showed José how, by being proactive, she could make things happen.

Most families have expectations for their children to undertake responsibilities within the home. Some responsibilities may be explicit, and others implicit. In some families, the responsibilities are fairly consistent with changes being negotiated, but in others they may be haphazard and even confusing to children. They may be communicated in dictatorial fashion, explained reasonably, or expected to be learned through observation. As with José in the vignettes just described, changing family circumstances and expectations can affect children's behavior in schools.

At times, home expectations can be in conflict with school expectations. Children can't always express or explain conflicting values. When this happens, children become caught in the middle. In the preceding vignette, parents were able to handle the situation and seek school support. In other families, negative attitudes can result in poor school and family relationships, with which both parents and schools must struggle. If you are to support the growth of all children in your community center or classroom, you must recognize that children and their families come with different skills, values, and circumstances.

Extended Family Fosters Roles and Rituals

In many families, parents garner emotional support from the extended family, and in some cases, they receive economic support as well. Extended family members may live close by, or they may live at some distance but still have strong ties. In addition to teaching about role expectations and hierarchical structures, the extended family helps children absorb the traditions and rituals of the larger group. An interesting example of such learning is told by Oladele (1999) as she explains how her mother, during the daily routines, taught her academics and spirituality and also about her African heritage. Her grandparents also influenced and reinforced this learning, beginning with a ritual of listening to her Bible verse recitations.

Celebrations are often a time when children learn about who they are, as extended members share the rituals and customs of their particular culture. Children in bicultural homes often have very different experiences, especially when both sets of the extended family share holidays with the nuclear family. Sila, in the vignette that follows, is the child of a European-American father, Dan, and a Turkish mother, Nara, whose own family members are practicing Muslims. Nara no longer observes religious practice, but Sila is introduced to the Muslim faith through visits from extended family members.

Seven-year-old Sila is excited about the upcoming holidays, because both Easter and Kurban Bayram are being celebrated close together. Greg, her father's brother, will be joining them for Easter week, and as he does every year, will help her dye Easter eggs, take her shopping, and on Easter Sunday will help her hunt for Easter eggs on the church lawn. Sila is only beginning to understand that Easter week is about Christ's crucifixion and has begun to ask questions such as "Why was Jesus killed? Did bad people kill him?" Though her father tries to explain, Sila is anxious for Uncle Greg's answer.

Then, at the end of the month, her mother's sister, Bilge, will join them to celebrate Kurban Bayram. Sila will not wear her new Easter hat or dress during this time, but instead will wear a special head scarf. The family will then go to the Muslim market to buy a lamb and have it killed in some special way, Sila believes, although she isn't quite sure how. Last year, her aunt explained that they kept only a small part of the lamb for cooking. She will need to ask about the lamb again this year. Though they have no relatives in the Muslim community in the city, Aunt Bilge and her mother will take her to visit the mosque. She does remember Aunt Bilge telling her that Mohammad was the great prophet in the Muslim faith, as Jesus was in the Christian faith. She wondered if they were friends. She would certainly ask her Aunt Bilge this time.

In some families, both sets of extended family members have equal access to the nuclear family, then the customs and habits children learn from these members are of equal importance. Because family structures differ however, what children learn from the extended family depends on the influence these relatives have on the nuclear family (Berns, 2006). The extended family expands the home curriculum by sharing its own values and interaction patterns. When extended family members work out the cultural differences and values of the others, children like Sila will learn how to solve the problems or confusions that arise because of these differences.

Anne Vega / Merrill

Extended family expands the home curriculum by sharing values and interaction patterns.

Siblings Aid in Role and Gender Identification

When children grow up with other children, they experience changing role patterns not dependent on age. A new baby in a home will alter the roles that family members have. A child with special needs, as in José's family, can affect children's school behavior. When parents see behavior change, they need to communicate with teachers and work to resolve the situation. Hopefully these parents will also be open to teacher concerns and observations. José's mother contacted the school and received support in resolving the conflict. When a new baby is born or when older siblings start school or leave home, circumstances within the family change for all members, and a different "curriculum" emerges. An older sibling who has been a playmate may suddenly become bossy after starting school, and younger children must learn new ways of interacting. Older children teach younger siblings "the

ways of the world," but what is learned will depend on the younger children's interactions and emotional relationships with the older ones.

The siblings in the following vignette react differently to their older sister, and this difference could partially explain their different rate of learning certain concepts.

Much to her mother's surprise, Caitlin learned to spell some words when she was but three years old. Her older sister Jennifer, returning from second grade, often made Caitlin "her pupil" and insisted she "write her letters," giving her words and letters to do. Brad, closer in age to Jennifer, didn't know letter names until he entered first grade, even though Jennifer at times tried to be his teacher as well. As a baby, Caitlin often called Jennifer her "other" mama and thus apparently was more receptive to her teaching, whereas Brad and Jennifer were closer in age, and Brad resented Jennifer's bossiness.

Academic learning is only part of the curriculum children learn from siblings. For example, children may learn physical skills faster and at an earlier age by competing with a more skilled family member. Children learn strategies for convincing others of one's point of view as siblings squabble and solve their differences within the family unit. Even learning how to unite in family loyalty against the outside world gives children important social skills—although not always desirable ones.

Children tend to overcome adversity and adapt best to changing circumstances in environments of positive sibling relationships, low conflict, and supportive extended families (Hetherington & Stanley-Hagan, 2002). Harris (1998) maintained that this learning from siblings and peers is even more potent than that from parents.

REFLECTION

Make a brief listing of things that you feel you have learned from your siblings, and then compare this with a few classmates' lists. There will be differences among you. Can you speculate as to why these differences exist?

LEARNING FROM PHYSICAL ENVIRONMENTS OF THE HOME

Children's learning is greatly influenced by environmental factors. The amount of space, the kinds of materials in the space, and the ways in which families allow children to use the space all affect what children learn in the home. Children living in crowded conditions can be successful when family is nurturing and supportive; if children are restricted in movements or ignored in their environment, no matter the amount of space, learning is lessened. Clark (1983) found in his study of high and low achievers from poor families that, among other nurturing qualities, high achievers' parents appropriately supervised their children's use of time and space.

Space Influences Emotional Growth

Great differences occur in the amount and kind of space that children have in their growing years, and space can be a factor in the family's ability to support children's physical and mental health. Of course, as family situations change, so can the amount of available space. Galle, Gove, and McPherson (1972) reported, from an early study on the amount of space families had per room, that the greater the density, the more the family was subjected to unhealthy conditions and stresses affecting children's development.

Children learn different things about themselves, depending on the amount and quality of space and how the adults respond to these conditions and their children. Hill (1967), in *Evan's Corner,* created a poignant story of a child's desire for private space.

— Evan lives with his family in a one-room flat. There is little sense of privacy; even the bathroom is shared with other families in the building. Evan longs for a little bit of space he can call his own. With the help of his mother, he clears a corner of the room, which he barricades and furnishes with things he cherishes. Evan's sense of well-being is clearly portrayed, as he has the nurturing support of his mother for his own space. In the crowded space, however, Evan also has another lesson to learn. His younger brother wants to come into his space, and it is not without a struggle that Evan learns the joy of choosing to share. —

Though not stated explicitly, Evan did learn his family's value of sharing what they had with others, even though theirs was a home with limited privacy.

Space Influences Intellectual Development

When rooms have different functions, children learn categorization skills for where household items belong and where people do different jobs. When families are crowded, rooms may have more than one function, and children learn that the same space is used differently. For example, in one crowded one-room apartment, an investigator (Barbour, N., 1989) found two people sleeping, another cooking, and two children playing on the floor most of the day. There appeared to be limited adult–child interaction. Across the hall, the same limited space for another family had distinct functions at different times of the day; the room was a living room during the daytime hours, a kitchen and dining room during early morning and evening, and a bedroom at night. During each part of the day, the second family appeared to use the space cooperatively; that is, helping to prepare meals, making beds, and listening to TV together. With the support of the entire family, household furniture was rearranged to fit the family needs, although a lot of discussion (even argument) ensued about what belonged where. The processing skills of children in these families appeared to be affected by these situations.

In their classroom, two children, one from each of the preceding homes, were asked to put household items into categories and place them in appropriate spaces. The child whose home space was haphazard did a random assignment for the items and had no explanation of why he organized the items that way. In fact, when asked to explain his strategies, he began to rearrange the items. The other child had a definite pattern to his selection of items for each category and a clear reason for putting each item where he did.

Space Influences Problem-Solving Skills

Homes foster problem-solving skills through encouraging observation, exploration, and experimentation. When parents both wittingly and unwittingly allow children to explore their indoor and outdoor environments, children's problem-solving skills expand. In the early years, the sandbox or the dirt in the backyard offer countless experiences for curious children. One preschooler spent almost an hour observing an ant carry a large crumb to its nest in the sidewalk and try to poke it between the cracks. The boy ran to his mother for help, but she encouraged her son to watch and see what the ant might do to solve his problem. Later, after the ant had broken the crumb into small bits, he excitedly explained the ending process to his mother .

Three-year-old Jack discovered that the cookie jar could be reached by shoving a chair next to the cupboard and then climbing up. When his mother put the cookie jar onto the refrigerator, farther from his reach, he had a new problem to solve. He began some experimentation, first with a chair and then with different-sized boxes. Finally, he discovered that if he piled the boxes one on top of another, he could reach the forbidden cookies.

Such learnings are usually not planned by parents. In the first instance, the mother was delighted with the child's interest and absorption. Jack's mother was none too pleased, however, with the child's cleverness at the moment she discovered him teetering on the piled-up boxes. Still, when homes are organized so that items for children's use are within easy grasp and other items are stored out of reach for various reasons, curious and determined children will try out their ideas if allowed enough freedom to explore safely.

By modeling problem-solving skills and exploring problems and solutions with children, parents steer their children toward competence (Leach, 1997). Homes where highly directive and punitive behaviors are the norm actually discourage interest and skill for analyzing tasks, and some even produce a sense of helplessness (Bronfenbrenner, 2005).

Space Influences Physical and Creative Development

Family space isn't necessarily limited to the indoor space. Outdoor space and the freedom to explore it safely will assist children in developing physical skills and creative endeavors.

Kenisha shared a bedroom with her sisters wherever they lived, and as the family moved from farm to farm, they usually shared their meals in a crowded space. Kenisha's outdoor space, however, provided greater opportunities for physical and creative development. Many of the farms had large barns and fields where Kenisha and her siblings could play. There were trees nearby and beams in a barn where she and the others could climb when not expected in the fields. Cardboard boxes, old blankets, boards, nails, and hammers enabled them to create their own fantasy worlds. Kenisha and her siblings made creative use of the strong ropes that the family used to tie up their goods. They often tied the ropes to the barn beams or to strong tree limbs and then developed skill in climbing and swinging on ropes.

Children thrive in whatever space they live in when adults provide consistent care, nurturing, and support while guiding their behavior and prizing their creations. Children learn important self-concepts when they are supported in their endeavors when family members praise them for successes and help them overcome frustrations at times of failure. When children do not experience such nurturance, the home curriculum is more limited (Hymowitz, 2002).

FAMILY PRACTICES AND HOME LEARNING

In Chapter 7, we defined the following areas of home responsibility for children's learning: early socialization skills; language learning; beginning experiments with natural phenomena; interaction and negotiation skills; values and attitudes, including aesthetic appreciation; and health and sex education. It should be clear that the home's responsibility is to develop basic skills—many taught through daily rountines—that prepare children to function successfully in society, and parents fulfill these responsibilities to differing degrees.

Daily Routines

Although modern family lifestyles appear to be hurried because of job requirements, child care, children's sports, and other recreational activities, all families establish some sort of routine. It is during the routine events that children learn to assume certain roles and responsibilities within changing family structures.

When events happen in the home in a timed sequence, children develop a better sense of society's meaning of time. First is the process of getting up and getting ready for school or work. When mealtimes are regular, the second routine involves preparation and a specified mealtime. A further set of routines revolves around bathing and other toileting procedures. The family reuniting at the end of the day is often another routine event. Bedtime is the final routine, as family members prepare for the night. During these daily

events, parents support and encourage or negate and suppress children's physical, emotional, social, and intellectual development.

Preparing for the Day. Children who arise, dress, eat breakfast, and then brush their teeth as a routine morning activity establish a pattern whereby they learn through habit about a sequence of events. Parent–child discussion about these events reinforces parental values and attitudes toward the activities, assists in children's language development, assists in children learning a sense of time, and supports children's memory and recall. When parents can give explanations or answer children's questions when varying routines, they often lessen the stress and help children learn to reason, question, and adapt to new situations. Children develop a sense of well-being and security when limits are clear and deviations to routines are dealt with in a caring and supportive environment.

Even in **homeless families**, the risk factors diminish for children when the parents are able to maintain some daily routines and rituals and are able to strengthen their positive interaction patterns by playing with their children and caring for their emotional needs (Letiecq, Anderson, & Koblinsky, 1998).

Mealtimes. Mealtime in families offers many educational opportunities. How events are handled determines the amount and types of learning that take place. Two examples will serve to support the idea and suggest the degree of variation in family habits.

In Bonita's family, mealtimes had established routines and consistent hours. There were expectations for shared responsibilities and behaviors. On one particular day, Bonita retuned from ballet lessons at 5:30 to find her father and brother starting dinner. They asked her to set the table and not to watch TV, since Mum was late and Joe needed to leave for tae kwon do at 7:00 p.m. When mother arrived at 6:00, the family sat down and after a blessing began to eat. When Bonita started to protest that she didn't like peas, her father quietly said, "Don't eat them then, but don't fuss." Joe was going for his red belt that evening, so the family discussed how he was progressing. Then Bonita wanted to choose a word for her word bank. When her father said that the dinner was scrumptious, she wanted to use that word but didn't know how to spell it. Her mother suggested that she get the dictionary and the family would help her find the word and then practice it on the way to Joe's red-belt test. The entire family cleared the table and put the dishes in the sink for later washing. ⟿

Although Casey's family was equally supportive, their mealtimes reflected a different ambiance.

⟿ *Casey's father picked her up at the child-care center, then had to get ready for an evening meeting. On his way home, he had picked up pizzas. He then engaged Casey in getting plates and helped her count the silverware for everyone. Casey read the instructions on the pizza package with her father as they warmed enough for each of them. Casey then went to the den to watch TV while she ate. Her father watched the news on the small kitchen TV. Her two older brothers arrived home, and greeted their father and Casey. They got themselves pizza, milk, and ice cream, and sat at the kitchen bar, discussing their soccer practice. Ready for his meeting, the children's father indicated that their mother would be home soon, so the boys were to help Casey if she needed something. When their mother arrived, she, too, had some pizza, watched some TV with Casey, and reminded the boys about homework.*

When it was Casey's bedtime, the mother asked the boys to clean up the counter and then do their homework. Casey, with her mother supervising, followed her routine of getting undressed, brushing her teeth, kissing her brothers goodnight, reading a story with her mother, and then climbing into bed. The mother then went downstairs and supervised her sons' homework while preparing some materials for her own job. The father arrived home from his meeting just in time to share the day's events with them before bedtime. ⟿

In both families, mealtime is an end-of-the-day event with all family members sharing a meal. However, the purpose of the meal is very different in each family. In Bonita's family, mealtime is not only a time for feeding the family, but also one of sharing responsibilities and learning about each person's day. A special effort is made to keep the family a single unit during that time. Evening events are often shared by the entire family. There is not much freedom of choice, as adults make most of the decisions.

In Casey's home, mealtime is not that significant. The members eat as they come in. All members are united in greeting each other and

assuming responsibilities, though, which are usually dictated by one of the adults. No attempt is made to keep the family as a unit. Although adults are definitely in charge, there are more choices and freedom allowed.

REFLECTION

After reading two vignettes about mealtime, do you see any home teaching that comes about in the two families other than that mentioned. Do you think mealtime is a good time for teaching children, or can you think of other times that may be better?

The entire process of food preparation and mealtime provides children with many learning opportunities, no matter the circumstances and whenever families share in the process:

- Fine-motor skills are developed as children help in food preparation, such as cutting vegetables.
- Quantity measurement is learned as children help to bake cookies or a cake.
- Following along as the adult reads the recipe or the packaged directions develops sequencing skills and other prereading skills.
- Helping make a grocery list supports writing and spelling skills and language development.
- Observing the change that takes place as liquid gelatin becomes solid in the refrigerator or as runny cake batter becomes solid in the oven provides basic scientific understanding of a change process.
- The kinds and varieties of foods children eat during mealtime communicate the family's values regarding nutrition or the family's concern with obesity.
- Preparing or securing meals in a variety of settings extends children's knowledge of how foods are prepared (e.g., in the kitchen, with a microwave oven, while camping, or when ordering in a deli and watching how the order is processed).

Food preparation provides
children with many learning
opportunities.

David Young-Wolff / PhotoEdit Inc.

Different parental or sibling involvement in preparation and cleanup after meals teaches children the family attitude toward gender-role responsibilities. In some families, the mother is expected to get meals and clean up afterward, especially if she stays at home to care for the children. In other families, we find a sense of shared responsibility, particularly in homes where the mother works outside the home. A growing sense of maturity and responsibility develops as children assume some of the tasks in the mealtime process.

Family Reuniting at the End of the Day. When the family's routine is such that each member goes off to work or to school, there is often a homecoming routine. The end of the day can be a stressful time, and both positive and negative lessons are learned.

Members of the family are usually tired, hungry, and anxious at day's end, particularly when both parents are wage earners or if a single parent must do more in meal preparation or if sleeping arrangements change frequently. Often this will be a time when children begin to learn how to cope in difficult situations. When partners argue and disagree, children are often frightened of the anger, and their sense of security is threatened. Nurturing

partners resolve their differences and provide models of negotiating behaviors. Partners who lash out, demean each other, or even strike each other are modeling ways to diminish another's self-concept. When parents or partners are able to resolve differences through discussion, apologizing, and coming to agreement, they provide lessons in how to negotiate a peaceful settlement.

Many end-of-the-day routines are pleasant experiences. In some families, children and adults at home share what happened to them during their absence from each other. In homeless situations, some parents are better able to cope and share their daily experiences with their children (Lindsey, 1998; Swick, 2004). In such sharing, children learn important **socialization skills**, such as how to listen, how to take turns talking, and how to explain so that someone else can understand, and, in some instances, they learn the skills of sticking to the topic being discussed. How much understanding and skill children develop in the routine situations of the home depends on a combination of factors, such as the age and genders of the children, **socioeconomic factors**, the children's interest, the level of previous understanding, and adult–children interactions (Fine, 1993).

Bedtime. As children prepare for bed, one finds many procedures that assist children's development. As in all routines, regularity and consistency help children develop a sense of time and order of events and a sense of security.

Four-year-old Kevin's parents went out for the evening, and Kevin had a new babysitter, whom he appeared to like very much. The sitter played games with him and read him his very favorite stories. At his regular bedtime, she helped him get undressed and brush his teeth. After one last story, she tucked him in, turned out the light, and went downstairs. A little later, she heard Kevin crying and went up to see what was the matter. As she calmed Kevin down, she finally heard him whimper, "I want Mommy. She says my prayers, and you didn't."

Kevin derived a great deal of security from a series of routine bedtime activities. Though he apparently forgot a part of the routine, he sensed something was wrong, and when he remembered, he became upset. In addition to satisfying Kevin's sense of security, the episode also demonstrates activities whereby Kevin's parents (or babysitter in their absence) fulfill their educational responsibilities. As Kevin washes and brushes his teeth before retiring, he is learning good health habits. Saying prayers at night or at mealtime can be the beginning of religious training.

Rituals and Traditions

The established definition of family ritual is the formal procedure for defining routine patterns of behavior (Bossard & Boll, 1949). These rituals and traditions are important to any society, for it is by such behaviors that individuals show respect for the value system within a family or clan (Goffman, 1967). Certainly, children learn many social, cognitive, and affective skills that are also learned in other families. Perhaps the most important learnings children gain from rituals are the importance of family structure and the commitment that an individual makes to the solidarity of the group (Evans, R., 2004). In rituals and traditions, behavior patterns are neither questioned nor examined; the behavior is continued because it is important to the family. As children learn the expected

behaviors of the rituals, they learn a sense of identity and self-concept. In addition, religious ceremonies involve rituals where children extend their understanding about the world and their connection to family (American Family Traditions, 2006).

Customs and folklore are often part of family traditions. Bettelheim (1976) stressed the importance of folklore to children's psychological and emotional development. He maintained that as children hear the old tales, they sense deeper meanings and thus find emotional security and comfort. Such stories serve as moral lessons, as well. Oladele (1999) related how the rituals in her family of memorizing Bible verses, singing spirituals, and reading created a sense of connection to her heritage.

In addition to providing emotional or moral support, rituals provide an intellectual stimulus. Traditional rhymes, chants, and incantations have a language pattern and a story structure that support literacy development. In many families, adults chant or read the rhymes they learned as children, often in the course of playing with children. "This Is the Way the Lady Rides," "One, Two, Buckle My Shoe," or "Shoe the Old Horse" provides rhythms and language patterns that form the foundation of children's developing language. Opie and Opie (1969) pointed out how older children teach younger ones the special games, rituals, and chants of childhood that parents do not attend to. Whether singing traditional songs, writing a letter to Santa Claus, helping count candles on the cake, or learning to read their part for the seder, parents and older siblings are engaging children in literacy events.

Sharing Interests and Skills

The amount of knowledge that parents transmit to their children varies widely from family to family. The greatest differences in children's special knowledge occur between families who explore their interests together and those who ignore each other. For example, when computer enthusiasts involve their young children in learning rudimentary computer skills, their children often enter

When computer enthusiasts involve their children in learning rudimentary skills, the kids become adept at using the computer.

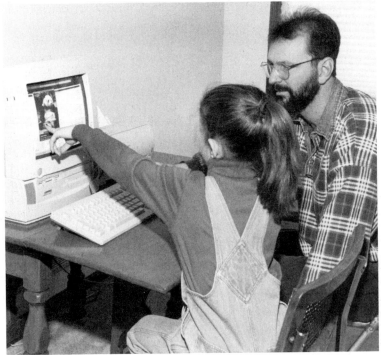

Anthony Magnacca / Merrill

kindergarten very adept at using computers. Saul and Newman (1986) pointed out how important parents are in stimulating children's interest in science, and when researchers asked winners of Westinghouse's Science Talent Search how they became interested in science, most claimed it was their parents who sparked their interest.

Families may also share an interest in the arts, as the following vignette shows.

When Mrs. Jacobs placed a Seurat print in her third-grade classroom, Roberto explained to the class that Seurat used a special technique called pointillism. He and his artist father had experimented with the technique after a visit to their nearby museum. Roberto had been fascinated with the Seurat paintings, and his dad had extended that interest as the two explored the technique together through art books and in the studio.

Children's curiosity leads them to ask many questions. Parents respond differently, depending on their own interests, knowledge, and style of interaction. Children's learning and continued interest depend greatly on the response they elicit.

Eager adults can turn off children's interest as well as expand it. For example, children may learn different things from the simple question, "Where does the wind come from?" One parent may reply, "Gee, I don't know!" Given that answer too many times, children learn that their questions are not important or that they shouldn't bother trying to find answers. Another parent may respond, "From the east," and point in the direction the wind is now blowing from. If that is the end of the conversation, children may learn where east is, that the wind's origin is east, and that adults know things and you can get information from them. Another parent may expand on this answer by pointing and then adding, "See, you can tell by how the trees are swaying." Children's knowledge is expanded to finding out something about how one determines the direction of the wind. Another parent, whose own knowledge about wind and directionality is limited, may answer, "I'm not sure exactly. Let's see if we can find out." When parents and children pursue an answer together, children learn about the importance of questioning and new ways of knowing.

Gardner (1983, 1999) discussed various intelligences that result because of children's different learning styles. These styles may be innate, but parents also support, reinforce, or even squelch their children's natural learning style by the way they respond. Linguistically oriented parents tend to teach their children through explanations and expressive use of language. Parents with strong logical–mathematical orientations enjoy math and strategy games and encourage orderly and logical thinking in arriving at solutions. Spatially and kinesthetically oriented parents help their children move through space and use their bodies as they figure out how the world functions. Artistic parents expand their children's knowledge through imagining and creating. Naturalist-oriented parents discriminate among living things and are very sensitive to features of the natural world, such as cloud, rock, and land formations and configurations. These responses do not only reflect the parents' orientations, but they also communicate different ways of knowing.

Children whose parents reinforce their ways of knowing have better success in school, but when learning styles of home and school are too disparate, children are at a disadvantage. Teachers who try to understand what and how children have learned at home, however, can create classroom opportunities for supporting and expanding children's skills and knowledge. Parents can help teachers understand how their children learn by initiating contact with the teachers and by following up when their children experience problems (Fried, 2001).

REFLECTION

Do you know of a child who seems to learn things differently than do others in his class? If so, watch him or her for a while, then try to relate the learning style to the notion of multiple intelligences.

As a teacher-researcher, Voss (1993) pointed out how she discovered a student's learning style by visiting his home and watching as his father taught him how to build. Eric could never explain in class how he did something other than by using his hands and saying, "I first did this and then this and then this." No amount of questioning and attempts at expanding his language worked. Expressing himself orally and in reading was painful for Eric. Eric enjoyed school only when the class worked on projects, and he spent hours figuring out how something went together. Upon visiting the home and getting to know the parents, Voss discovered that Eric had a special relationship with his father and was allowed to work on the projects his father did as a business or around the house. Eric's father rarely explained what he was doing, but when asked by the child how he was doing something, he would slow down his activity to demonstrate. Realizing how kinesthetically oriented the child was, the teacher was able to adjust the classroom learning to accommodate Eric's way of knowing and to expand his ability in other areas.

Other Family Activities that Educate

The home curriculum is enriched or limited in the ways families engage in various activities in and out of the home. The amount of learning varies as a result of many factors, including economics and personal preferences. Even though parents living on a limited income can provide their children with many and varied learning opportunities, poverty does have a debilitating effect and reduces family choices and energies for learning opportunities. Extreme poverty limits families' ability and energy to interact with their children even more, often communicating a sense of hopelessness and cynicism (Sugrue, 1999).

Affluent parents have the means to provide an array of toys and reading materials in the home, and their children often have their own television sets and computers. These parents arrange trips for their children as well as a variety of entertainment events, cultural activities, and recreational opportunities. Other families can't afford as many opportunities, but the children learn important coping skills as their parents try to overcome economic deprivation. They learn to develop kinship relations with family and neighbors as they all share material goods, share responsibility for children's safety, and help each other cope in a sometimes hostile environment (Sugrue, 1999). Although poverty is limiting, it does not mean that poor families are not committed to their children's education. We find that many do make wise choices, enriching their children's experiences with appropriate toys, books, family outings, and even scheduled home lessons.

Learning opportunities for children vary not only with parental involvement but also with the way that parents interact with their children during these activities. The vignette in Chapter 1 about Steven's riding lessons demonstrated that curriculum provided by structured lessons is not limited to the skills being taught. In that example, Steven, encouraged by suggestions from his mother, was also learning important skills regarding social interaction with adults. Four other examples of the family outreach curriculum are recreational pursuits, toys and games, family use of technology, and travel.

Recreational Pursuits. Recreation, gaming sessions, and play with family members have great emotional, physical, social, and intellectual value for children, and few activities bond families better than recreational pursuits. Children normally select their own levels of participation in play, sports, and creative work, but parents and other family members can always encourage and support their interest. Children require time, space, and equipment to pursue recreation, and effective parents will plan for this, support it, and even participate. Children derive the following benefits from recreation and play (Seefeldt & Barbour, 1998):

- Working with others
- Small and large muscle exercise
- Establishing an interest in fitness
- Lifelong interests and attitudes about recreation

- Guided exploration of challenges and new ventures
- Sensible and accurate use of equipment
- Release from tension
- Experiencing pleasure, gratification, and satisfaction.

Toys and Games. The types of toys parents provide reflect the parents' value structure and extend development in different ways.

On the birth of her daughter Delaney, Mrs. Babbitt bought a complete set of unit blocks. When Delaney was old enough to sit and stack things, Mrs. Babbitt would take out a few blocks for the child to play with. The blocks were always stored according to their unit size, and gradually Delaney became involved in restoring them to their correct place on the shelf as she expanded her use of the blocks. Over time, other materials were added, such as play animals, toy trucks and cars, pieces of cloth, and paper and crayons for signs. At times, Delaney's father would join her in playing with the blocks, building towers or complicated structures.

Ashley's father, delighting in his new daughter, bought her a huge toy panda. He would sit on the floor beside the panda holding his infant as he fed her or played with her. As Ashley grew older, the panda became an important source of comfort and a wonderful companion to sit with while hearing a story or watching television. Ashley had many small toys that entertained her, and she punched them, turned them over, and examined them when playing.

Zena, a staff member at the community-subsidized child-care center, often took home toys discarded by the center. One day she brought several sets of playing cards that were discarded because there were cards missing. At home, using the numbers and pictures, she and her children made up several games of naming, sorting, matching, and trading, and these were shared by children in the apartment complex.

All children experience a curriculum provided through the toys they receive, and all three sets of parents described play with their children as they use various types of materials. By selecting blocks as the most important toy for her daughter, Mrs. Babbitt established a highly cognitive curriculum that expanded with Delaney's growth and development. Ashley's father's first gift reflected his wish to provide a warm, cozy support system to be supplemented with random selections of fun toys. Zena provided her children with what she could find but recognized that these toys gave both nurturance and some academic support. All the children are prized and cherished, and their caretakers are teaching important self-concept and academic skills that will help them as they enter school.

Family Use of Technology. Although this is not the case with published materials, almost every home in the United States has one or more television sets, and children from six months to six years spend as much time watching TV as they do playing (Rideout, Vandewater & Wartella, 2003). How each family uses television is, of course, the salient factor. Sitcoms, game shows, and soap operas provide some stimulation, but unless parents and children both watch and discuss them, the shows appear to have little cognitive benefit (Singer & Singer, 2001; Van Evra, 2004).

Television watching and its association with aggression and violence has been a concern for decades. Readers may recall the startling statistics on the number of violent acts viewed every hour by elementary-school children (McChesney, 1999). These are sobering and seem not to be diminished in spite of the V-chip for controlling access to particular programs and the increase in children's programming. For example, wars around the globe are covered daily in the news media, and children of all ages view ethnic conflicts, terrorism, and the destructive effects of these wars on "ordinary" people (Strohmaier, 2004).

Positive links to achievement have been found when children viewed television programs such as *Sesame Street and Blue's Clues.* These programs traditionally have focused on American values and cultures, however, and in our era of globalization, there is great need for American children to expand their understanding of different world cultures. The Sesame Street Workshop is already having an impact, as their Global Grover travels around the world encountering children of many different cultures (Wartella & Gray, 2004) and showing cultural interactions. What is true for American children's TV is also true for children around the world (Strasburger & Wilson, 2002).

Researchers have found greater benefits from TV viewing when parents watch television with their children, then discuss the programs (Alexander, 2001; Gunter et al., 2003). Community and school programs can have a similar positive effect with "education via media" for at-risk children if advocates can influence home behaviors through parent education. As we noted, Sesame Street Workshop works in other countries, and its creators are producing locally specific and socially relevant versions of Sesame Street. They also bring to the United States their international programs for parts of the K through eight curriculum (Wartella & Gray, 2004). Guidelines for management of family TV and strategies for effective TV use are listed in Figure 8–3.

Like TV, because Internet access is available in virtually all schools in America (U.S. Bureau of the Census, 2005) and a growing number of homes, it is now a part of young children's lives. In 2003, statistics showed that 50% of five to seven year olds used computers at home and 68% at school.

Recommendations similar to those concerning TV go with children's use and parents' supervision of the Internet. Parents can seek to control children's access to Web sites through Internet filters such as Content Protect or CyberSitter (more information on filters can be obtained through http://www.internet-filter-review.toptenreviews.com). Family agreements and sharing about positive Web sites is a far better method of control, however. Nationally, more concern about distasteful on-line material has appeared, and media manufacturers now distribute software to limit children's on-line experiments (Thornburgh & Lin, 2002).

The Web site FreeZone.com, shows the latest in a protected virtual community for youngsters (Hafner, 2002). Its **chat rooms** are constantly monitored by "**chat jockeys**," who can even provide homework help. It is not free, though, and this limits participation in a quality venue. Other quality sites that have subscription fees are http://www.juniornet.com and http://www.iknowthat.com. Lin (2002), however, a longtime researcher in child use of the Internet, is not encouraging

Pediatricians, media specialists, and teachers advocate TV controls, as well as "media literacy," for children. Parents, however, are in the best position to shape any media effects into positive influences for their children.

1. Keep children under two away from TV programs. Avoid using TV as an emergency babysitter.

2. Ration children two years and older to two hours of screen time daily (e.g., TV, computers, iPods, etc.).

3. Monitor what children watch, and coview the programs with your youngsters.

4. Encourage children to watch international programs such as Sesame Street's Global Grover that foster understanding of other cultures.

5. Encourage child interaction with beneficial TV shows, then talk about the program after the set is off.

6. Place the TV set apart from family living areas so it doesn't intrude on meals and other family times together.

7. Keep TV out of children's bedrooms. This leads to TV overdose.

8. Exploit the TV and book connection. Children's programming for shows such as *Arthur* and *Book of Pooh* comes from well-known books. After watching, children are often enthused about reading the "real story."

9. Parents must watch their own TV behavior. Predetermine programs for everyone to watch, watch those, and then turn the set off. Surfing through programs encourages children to do the same.

Figure 8–3   Sensible Television Use: Controlling TV Use at Home
Source: Adapted from Andreason (2001); Singer & Singer (2005); Van Evra (2004).

when he states that presently there is little stimulating and compelling material designed for children.

REFLECTION

Most likely you are a well-experienced user of the Internet and have profited from its existence. Now, how would you communicate to a group of parents the advantages of the Net for classroom learning?

In addition to monitoring children's use of Internet, parents can use the Internet to connect their children and themselves to educational endeavors (Dowd, Singer, & Wilson, 2005). For example, parents can seek help or information about child development that enables them to more appropriately respond to their children at

their appropriate level of development. Internet access means parents can communicate easier with their children's teachers and schools especially when parents live in areas where it is more difficult to get to their children's school programs. Parents can make use of Internet to connect their children with school programs, pen pals, and, if monitored, childrens **Web logs** (Ray & Shelton, 2004). Figure 8–4 lists some general rules for families to follow when allowing children to use the Internet.

Travel. Most families take trips together, some to the grocery store or to visit local relatives, others on lengthy vacations traveling throughout the United States or abroad. Local trips provide rich learning experiences when parents extend the experience with observations about the scenery and what has changed in the familiar environment or with discussions about what is to be bought, why, and where to find it. Such involvement helps children learn about their natural environment

1. Adults must be familiar with the Children's Online Privacy Protection Act of 2002.

2. Adults must have a procedure for monitoring, and blocking if necessary, young children's use of the Internet. Software programs that perform this function are available from AOL and Microsoft Network.

3. Caregivers should know their children's on-line visits and the amount of time spent on-line.

4. Adults must know the safe Web sites and how to steer children toward them. Parents should discuss with the child the Web site content and their chat room participation.

5. All learners agree there will be no rudeness on-line and that they will not impersonate another person.

6. Adults and children should agree that learners need to be as wary of persons met on-line as they are of those met off-line.

7. All learners should agree with their parents and instructors about not posting any personal data (including names, addresses, and phone numbers) to on-line diaries, to Web logs, or in chat rooms.

8. Parents and instructors should know that on-line accounts, diaries, and chat rooms all can be "password protected."

Figure 8–4   Internet Safety for Children
Source: Adapted from Hafner (2002); Singer & Singer (2005); Thornburgh & Lin (2002).

and become keen observers of change. Among other things, they learn the give-and-take of discussion, reasons for doing things, and classification skills. Parents provide valuable emotional support and express values as they demonstrate pleasure in sharing these times with their children.

Ricardo, living in a subsidized housing unit in a small community was a town rubbish collector with responsibility for retrieving collectible bottles and cans. He was caregiver for his two children and often took them on his rounds. The children counted the collectibles, and sorted materials according to the amount of refund they would produce. Ricardo, a naturalist by interest and with some training, also enjoyed pointing out to his children features along the route, such as birds, new flowers in bloom and interesting rock formations.

The following vignette illustrates some values coming from a camping trip.

Camping across the country, the Hi family discovered that temperatures varied considerably when they awoke in the morning. Mai Lin never seemed to dress right for the travel days. She was either too hot or too cold as they hiked or drove. Without saying anything to anyone, *she began to solve her problem by sticking her hand out of the tent each morning to "test" the weather. As the trip progressed, she began to get better at sensing what the day's weather would be like and became a much happier traveler. She also learned how to dress by observing her parents and hearing their discussions on what they were going to wear that day. She discovered how to adapt to the abrupt changes in temperatures that sometimes occurred within a few hours as the family traveled through snow in the mountains to a hot desert valley below. In addition to learning about geography and its effect on changes in climate, Mai Lin learned during the trip to figure out how to make herself more comfortable.*

All families educate their children to some level of functioning in society. Although we have dysfunctional families, where children's learning is hampered or even distorted, most families provide varied educational opportunities for their children through daily routines and ongoing family activities. The best outcomes occur when families assume their share of responsibility for the education of their children and work with schools and communities to assist in the process. In Chapter 7, we discuss more aspects of family functioning and

Local trips, even to a nearby playground, can provide rich learning experiences for children.

Steven Barbour

delineate the characteristics of competent families where positive learning takes place.

GRANDPARENTS PROVIDE A CURRICULUM

In this section, the authors present some features of grandparent influence on home curriculum. The selections and examples are chosen from the authors' experiences working with grandparents from varying cultures and from several qualitative research studies (Barbour, Barbour, & Hildebrand, 2001).

Grandparents Influence Children's Development

Like other providers of home curriculum, grandparents' influence on children is diverse. Although research on this question has existed for 50 years, the results of each study depends so much on ecological, historical, and cultural variabilities that it is difficult to filter out generalizable results (Tomlin, 1998). Age of grandparents, age of grandchildren,

geographical differences, relationships of grandparents with the nuclear family, plus factors of family structure and processes have an impact that ranges from minimum to substantial (Berns, 2006). Studies indicate four different categories of grandparenthood: the custodial grandparent, the nearby grandparent, the distant grandparent, and the emotionally remote grandparent.

The custodial grandparent influences the child's development in a manner much the same as a parent, so there is significant influence. The emotionally remote grandparent has little contact with the child, so there is probably little influence. Caring and supporting grandparents, living nearby or in a distant area, who keep close contact with their families, will have considerable influence on the home curriculum.

Directly or indirectly, grandparents express to their grandchildren a value system and philosophy of how children are to be instructed, whether morally, religiously, culturally, or intellectually. Elizabeth, in the following vignette, is learning two ways of writing and expressing herself because of her grandmothers. Because both grandparents live at some distance, they keep contact with her through letters, e-mail, and telephone calls.

Elizabeth was an active six-year-old who had discovered the rhythms of language early. Her grandmother Dailey, a former English teacher, firmly believed that children should learn to speak correctly and not use "silly phrases" or "special invented terms." Her grandmother Denato, howerver, delighted in the "discovered" terms Elizabeth used and would often repeat the terms, thus reinforcing that language can be created. At Christmas, Elizabeth received a collection of rocks from Grandmother Denato and books from Grandmother Dailey. Her thank you letters to both grandmothers consisted of a drawing of the gift plus a statement. Before sending the letter to Grandmother Dailey, Elizabeth asked her mother about Babar, one of the book characters, and with her mother's help carefully copied on her drawing the words "I liked the elephant book best." On the picture she sent to Grandmother Denato, she wrote by herself, "Rnd redrks spkls lgblk rks wjshin ilvu Dne" ("Round red rocks with sparkles long black rocks which shine. I love you, Donny"—her pet name for her grandmother).

At age six, Elizabeth has already learned what each grandmother valued. In wanting to please each grandmother, she is learning valuable things. For the grandmother who is precise, she learns about story characters, and she has learned to copy a few short words with her mother's help. With her other grandmother, she has learned the fun of playing with words and sounds and is willing to experiment and try out her knowledge of letters and sounds. Elizabeth's mother supports the values of both grandparents by supporting Elizabeth's efforts without judgment.

In some situations, children receive mixed messages concerning their competence, their sense of safety, or the importance of taking risks. David, in the following vignette, receives two different messages about the same situation from his grandparents. Of course, other cultural and sociological factors will determine how he interprets these messages, especially because he sees his grandmother Hu, who lives nearby, more often. Visits to grandmother Williams are each summer for three or four weeks, plus other holidays.

David Hu, now four years old, was born with a partly developed left hand. He has only stubs for fingers, though his thumb appears to be well developed. His father is Chinese and his mother is European American. David, his mother, father, and grandmother Hu are visiting at the summer home of his maternal grandmother in a small seashore community. The grandmothers are supervising David at a summer playgroup program, and he has gone outside to play on the slide. Grandmother Hu immediately goes with him. His grandmother Williams finishes her reading with a group of four-year-olds and follows later. When she arrives, David has begun climbing up the front of the slide with his thumb firmly grasping the side of the slide. Occasionally he slips but catches himself. Grandmother Hu is trying to stop him from climbing, but David ignores her. Grandmother Williams speaks to Mrs. Hu rather sharply. "Oh, leave him alone, he's doing a great job."

Mrs. Hu pleads in a worried voice, "But he might get hurt" and then points to his left hand.

Mrs. Williams replies, "We don't know that. Let's just watch and see how he handles it."

David continues to climb two or three times, sliding gleefully down the slide. On his last slide, he jerks back, loses his grip, hits his head on the slide, and begins to howl. Both grandmothers rush to him and try to comfort him. Suddenly, he breaks away from them both and begins climbing and sliding again. While the two grandmothers argue over his "safety," he happily continues his activity until one of the helpers calls to him that the rest of the class is doing an art project. David rushes inside with the other children.

The two grandmothers have different views of how David should be treated. Mrs. Hu feels great responsibility and anxiety about his safety, but according to Mrs. Williams, she is overprotective. Mrs. Hu even hovers over him while he is doing his artwork. She is always ready to help him do the project "correctly." Mrs. Williams is satisfied with a cavalier approach, feeling the art project is uniquely "his."

David is developing his physical skills in a "mixed message" environment. He already knows that he can "do" more around Mrs. Williams and less around Mrs. Hu. He knows Mrs. Hu will protect him more and make sure he doesn't overextend himself. Mrs. Williams will allow him to experiment more, but he is likely to hurt himself more.

Perhaps David will learn a middle course, where he is willing to take risks, but experiment more to test out his skill level before plunging in.

Both "nearby" grandparents and "distant" grandparents can have a great influence on children. In general, the nearby grandparent has shorter but more frequent contacts, but the distant grandparent's visit involves contacts that are sustained longer but are fewer in number. Grandparents tend to have more fun with their grandchildren than they had time for with their own children, and they tend not to feel as responsible for the well-being of their grandchildren. Cultural differences become blurred when living in the United States, but we often find differences in how families view their kin relationships (Tomlin, 1998). European Americans, although often close geographically, believe in developing independence in their children and grandchildren. They encourage their children to move away, especially for college and work, and to become financially and socially independent. Grown children attend "family gatherings," but one's social network in European American families tends to include one's own age group. In other cultures, family relationships normally extend into their children's lives. In the families shown in the chapter vignettes, the children experienced connections to their grandparents through the rituals of their heritage—Christmas giving and other holiday observations. Figure 8–5 gives cues on the different influence patterns found in extended families.

REFLECTION

Think back to the things you learned from your grandparents. What activities would you consider important enough to add to the list in Table 8–1?

Advantages of a Grandparent Curriculum

Although they have neither curriculum goals nor activities to achieve them, grandparents do realize that to establish a relationship with a grandchild they need to make an effort to know them as they

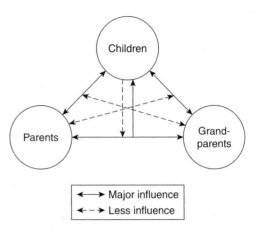

Figure 8–5   Grandparent Connection to Nuclear Family Members
Note: For most families, there is substantial engagement between child and parents, parents and grandparents, and also between child and grandparents. The extent of engagement is related to living arrangements, marital situation and condition, and family history. The diagram assumes a typical nuclear family with grandparents living nearby and no estrangement. Note the lessened influence of grandparents on the parent-child connection and a similar lessened influence of parents on the grandparent-child interaction. Child influence on parent-grandparent interaction is different still.
Source: Barbour, Barbour, and Hildebrand (2001); Tomlin (1998).

mature and change. An important aspect of grandparenthood is "having fun with them" or finding satisfaction in their encounters, whether one visits a zoo, reads a story, plays games, listens to them, or attends their activities (Cherlin & Furstenberg, 1992). Some advantages of grandparent influence are shown in Table 8–1.

HOMESCHOOLING

Families that assume total responsibility for their children's education often opt to educate their children at home, at least for part of their schooling years. The term *homeschooling* is used to define academic learning that occurs as a result of activities provided in the home (or extensions of the home), with the parents acting as teacher–facilitators.

Homeschooling is not a new concept, but it has gained popularity in recent years, and we find enrollment figures ranging from 850,000 (U.S.

Table 8–1   Advantages of a Grandparent Curriculm

Goals	Activities
Sharing values and adapting to different value systems	Elizabeth's adaptation to cultural influences was on her developing literacy skills, whereas David's focus was developing physical skills.
Child gaining knowledge from grandparents	The Williamses are sailors, and at age four, David was allowed to help steer the boat. Later he learned to sail by himself.
Grandparents learning from grandchildren	Elizabeth's grandmother Denato learned many computer skills from six-year-old Elizabeth, including how to use e-mail. David's Grandmother Hu was timid when climbing, and four-year-old David showed her where to put her feet and where to hold on as they climbed ledges together.
Learning the skills of interaction with older people and grandparents of different cultures	David learned to speak directly to his grandfather Williams (a bit deaf) by looking him in the eye and "speaking up." With Grandpa Hu he spoke softly and was deferent. As he learned expressions of greeting, politeness, and questioning in both languages, he learned different inflections and different body language for each grandparent.
Understanding the geography and history of family members	Elizabeth's Grandmother Denato frequently traveled and sent post cards to Elizabeth. Later, Elizabeth and her grandmother played games; they found these places on maps, and recalled who lived there.
Understanding the different household tasks and responsibilities	At one grandmother's house, Elizabeth learned that she was to make her bed, take her dishes off the table, and help with the sweeping before playing or watching TV. At Grandmother Denato's, her responsibility was to get her grandmother up, and then the two would figure out the day and who would do each task.
Building healthy self-esteem	Elizabeth and David's grandparents both helped build self-esteem, because they praised them, expressed their love, attended their grandchildren's sporting events and reward ceremonies, and expressed pride in their grandchild's art, music, and school papers. These grandparents listened to their grandchildren's successes and empathized with their struggles. Self-confidence was supported as the grandparents accepted help from the grandchildren, respected their opinions, and reinforced the parents' child-rearing practices.

Source: Adapted from Strom & Strom (1997); Cherin & Furstenberg (1992); Barbour et al. (2001).

Bureau of the Census, 2002a) to two million (Kochenderfer, Kanna, & Kiyosaki, 2002). Home schooling is a flexible and diverse system of teaching and learning with a variety of practices. Just as various philosophies guide curriculum in schools, parents also approach teaching and learning using a traditional approach as well as constructive approaches. Because of the tutorlike environment, the homeschool curriculum activities are more likely to be geared to children's interests (Kochenderfer et al., 2002; Ray, 2002). The definition is made more clear by Kerman's (1990) description

of a typical day of homeschooling, summarized as follows:

Their day starts with the family eating breakfast. Afterward, the nine-year-old daughter leaves with her father for the library, where she will do preplanned library study, then will carry out some errands for the family. At home, the mother provides unscheduled activities for the two preschoolers that relate to the children's interests, to household needs, and to events that happen in the neighborhood. They read several stories, wash dishes, make play dough, do "dress-up" and dramatic play, and then walk down the road to watch a fire truck putting out a fire.

Grandparents tend to have more fun with their grandchildren then they did with their own children. They can be more relaxed and enjoy the pleasure at hand.

Valerie Mekras

History of Homeschooling

Homeschooling was the norm for most families during the early years of the republic. In the late 19th and early 20th centuries, with the advent of compulsory education however, the practice of homeschooling diminished. In the late 1970s, John Holt became an advocate of homeschooling. Some parents, disenchanted with their local schools, found support for their efforts in his writings, and especially from his newsletter *Growing Without Schooling* (Gorder, 1996). Since the 1980s, interest in homeschooling, driven by differing motivations, has increased dramatically. We now find specialized publishing houses, advocacy groups with legal departments, and national conferences supporting homeschooling programs.

Increased networking among homeschoolers and Internet access have provided parents with organizational support, publications, workshops, and legal support for those who have difficulty meeting state mandates. One prominent support agency,

the Home School Legal Defense Association (HSLDA; http://www.hslda.org), maintains a large database of litigated cases on homeschooling.

The demand for information about homeschooling has become a sizeable industry. Walsh (2002) estimated that Americans spend $700 million per year, or from $400 to $1,200 per student, for materials. Consolidation of support systems, plus easy access to a variety of resources, is now accompanied by greater public acceptance of homeschooling as a viable alternative to public education.

In some school districts, educators join parents in a team effort and allow homeschooled children dual enrollment—they attend some classes, participate in extracurricular activities, and use schools' special services (Eley, 2002). In the past 10 years, some school systems have organized education centers, and other districts share their resources and allow homeschooled students to take special classes (Deckard, 1996; Duffey, 1998).

Motives for Homeschooling. Parents home-school their children for a variety of reasons, but most parents fall into two distinct groups—the **ideologues** and the pedagogues. Both groups disagree with educators about what is happening in schools today (Kochenderfer et al., 2002). Ideologues disagree with the values presented by teachers or their children's peers; therefore, these parents choose to homeschool so the family's religious values are what their children internalize (Lines, 2001; Reich, 2002).

The growing group of pedagogues, troubled by their perceptions of school curricula, feel their children can receive a more personalized and better education if taught at home. Some parents choose to homeschool because they fear their children's exposure to problems such as violence, drugs, and disruptive behavior in the public school system. Others disagree with the instructional and managerial styles of teachers and school administrators. Some are concerned with the inability of teachers to meet all the individual needs, interests, and learning styles of their children and are concerned that school will turn their children off to learning (Ray, 2000a; Stevens, 2001). Some had unpleasant experiences in their own schooling and wish to prevent that for their children. Still other parents decide to homeschool because their children experience difficulty in school, and they feel school personnel are inadequate or punitive when addressing problems (Gorder, 1996; Ray, 2000b).

Who Homeschools? If the reasons for homeschooling are varied, the largest number of homeschoolers is amazingly alike demographically. The typical homeschooling family has two parents, has an income near the U.S. median, and is Caucasian and Protestant. Parents tend to have some college education, are professional or skilled workers, and come mostly from rural areas, although some are suburban. Homeschoolers appear to be conservative and law abiding but also individualistic and very child centered (Lines, 2001; Stevens, 2001). Most authorities now agree that homeschooling has become a forceful social movement, with effective lobbies in state and national government circles (Carper, 2000; Reich, 2002).

Teaching Methods in Homeschooling

Curriculum and methods for homeschooling depend on the home, but most methods fall into three categories: **fixed curriculum**, **units of study**, and **unstructured learning events** (Rupp, 1998; Wade, 2004). The fixed curriculum consists of published guides with specific lessons, suggestions on how to teach, and evaluation techniques. This curriculum satisfies parents who are unsure of what to teach and who find comfort in a fixed schedule and prescribed curriculum. Some parents, especially those who view homeschooling as a temporary solution to their children's educational needs, use the same texts used in the local schools. Correspondence schools, in which some parents enroll their children, meet this need and provide a structure and routine for homeschooling. More and more homeschooling parents are using Internet resources to provide learning opportunities for their children.

Homeschool organizations, such as Oak Meadows (Brattleboro, VT; http://www.oakmeadow.com), as well as regular publishing companies, have curriculum guides and suggestions for units of study. In these materials, the teaching and learning is more flexible and children move through specific units at their own pace and as their interests dictate. Homeschoolers themselves encourage others to use various teaching strategies that customize learning for a particular child (The Teaching Home, 2002).

The unstructured learning method deals with subjects in which the children are interested, and development of skills takes place as children experience various events in their family life. Each child's curriculum will be very different when parents follow this outlook. Parents using this method often write about the many ways they enable their children to be successfully schooled. Some read to their children a great deal and provide a range of quality materials. For these families, books of all sorts, including reference materials, are always available. In addition, computers provide these knowledgeable homeschooling families with many more learning opportunities: access to the

Steven Barbour

Children schooled at home are included in all family work activities, such as cooking.

Internet for searches on current events or other topics, use of e-mail for communicating with friends or relatives in distant places, and a multitude of computer games.

Children schooled at home are normally included in all family work activities, such as cooking, doing laundry, or construction projects. Family recreational and educational activities, such as visiting libraries and museums, are also done together. Some families write plays and poems together, and some share their musical talents. Math skills are developed as parents involve children in building, using money, and calculating out family finances. Many children and parents explore their environment together, learning science concepts as they follow their interests.

Even within a single family, the routine and methods followed by homeschoolers will vary from year to year as children develop skills, new interests, and the ability to pursue their own learning. The common element is that children's

interests are always paramount, and drill or practice is done at the pace the children set. Home-schooled children are less likely to become bored with learning tasks because they have greater access to their mentors. Also, parents are more likely to respond to a child's complaints about the material being too easy or too difficult (Fried, 2005).

Legal Aspects of Homeschooling

Laws concerning homeschooling vary, and as homeschooling has gained momentum, many states are changing statutes. All 50 states have compulsory attendance laws, and homeschoolers can encounter legal problems, depending on how state offices interpret these laws. Court and state offices use the following issues in deciding the legality of homeschooling:

1. Parental rights of choice regarding their children's welfare
2. Equivalency of education
3. Home schools defined as a viable way to educate children
4. Home schools considered as private, religious, or charter schools
5. Need for qualified teachers

Specific state laws range from a most rigorous approach to parent-friendly support for homeschooling. The National Home Education Network and the National Challenged Homeschoolers Associated Network (an international association that helps in educating children with special needs) are both excellent sources for information on laws and regulations regarding homeschooling.

REFLECTION

Try to contact a parent who has homeschooled children, and list the advantages that person perceives. Then check with various school personnel to see if they share those views. Do any negatives appear in your discussion with all parties?

Criticisms and Successes of Home Schools

As the homeschooling movement has grown, some states and school districts have registered concerns about truancy issues, appropriate curriculum, student achievement, and loss of matching funds.

Few data have been collected to support or to refute criticisms of homeschooling, but in those states requiring standardized tests, homeschoolers score an average of 15% higher than their public school peers (Ray, 2000a). Studies also indicate that no significant relationship exists between homeschoolers' achievements and their parents' education level (Ray, 1997; Stevens, 2001). This appears to counter the argument that parents lack the skills to teach a variety of subjects.

Examining the individual success stories of homeschooled children, we find evidence that many homeschoolers do well academically and socially when they return to public school, find jobs in the community, or gain acceptance to college (Barfield,

2002; Colfax & Colfax, 1992). Communities and authorities do have an obligation to all children under their jurisdiction, however, and educators recognize that homeschooling is not for all parents or for all children. The reported successes are probably attributable to parents who wish to be an integral part of their children's learning and are willing to devote the hard work and commitment it requires. Certainly not all parents have the time, inclination, patience, or ability to sustain such nourishment on a long-term basis. We must keep in mind that teachers are key personnel in many phases of children's education, including those children being homeschooled. Therefore, communication with homes where children are homeschooled is vital. As a teacher, you need to give support and keep communication lines open. The situation must be analogous to the home–school–community partnership.

APPLYING THESE CONCEPTS TO YOUR WORK WITH CHILDREN AND FAMILIES

By understanding how rich the home curriculum can be—whether through regular routines, family events, or the total homeschooling process—you will recognize the many events that affect your students' development and thus enable you to provide a school curriculum better geared to each child's needs. This knowledge and understanding comes from careful observation, interested listening, and learning about children's home and community environments. You can of course glean a greater appreciation of diverse lifestyles by comparing your experiences with others. The following are a few specific experiments to relate the chapter content to your professional growth:

- As you read about the foundations of literacy and the vignette about Christine, Lorelei, and Jennifer, consider the teaching or learning events that take place. Who is doing the teaching? What is being taught? What is being reinforced?

- Compare with a classmate the physical environments of your childhoods, and discuss the amounts of restriction and freedom to explore what you each had. Speculate on how this may have affected your development.

- Review the vignette about Elizabeth and her grandparents' differing values on learning to write. As a teacher, reflect on how you might engage a child in writing (to be taken home) when you know different family's perspectives on "valuing right answers" vs "creative responses," as in this vignette. State your opinion on how the parent handles the situation.

- Discuss with your classmates or friends the different trips they have taken this week. Devise ways to include the various family members' responses to their trips in your curriculum.

SUMMARY AND REVIEW

Children receive a great deal of education outside the classroom walls, and whether intentionally or accidentally, parents provide a rich and varied curriculum in the home. Although great differences appear in quantity and quality of home curricula, all parents, as well as other family members, provide emotional, social, physical, and intellectual stimuli for children's development.

Parents begin the process of educating their young as they respond to the infant's vocalizations. These interactions nurture preliteracy and communication skills. Children learn role expectations and responsibilities as the family carries out routines and rituals. Parental interaction styles, the type of environment, and the space in which children are raised also affect children's learning.

Children's home curriculum is an accumulation of all the experiences they have in their home. Thus, each child's curriculum is different, but similarities occur as a result of daily routines that exist for most families. Both skills and knowledge about the world are acquired as children participate in preparing for the day, meal preparation, and bedtime rituals. From family traditions and rituals, children gain an understanding of their ethnic and cultural identity and of their place in the world. As parents share their own special interests and talents, children expand their concepts of the world around them. The expanding world of technology provides an extended curriculum, and how parents monitor and interact with their children regarding new media determines the benefits or pitfalls of their use.

Extended family members will also provide stimulus for children's development. There is a "grandparent curriculum" that reinforces and supplements—or differs from—the nuclear family practices. The amount of influence depends a great deal on the relationships between the nuclear and extended families and the caring and involvement of grandparents.

Although a small group has always believed in education at home, the homeschooling movement has grown rapidly since the 1960s. Numerous reasons are given for this increase, but most parents choose this route for religious reasons or because of philosophical differences with schools regarding education. Homeschooling is not for everybody, and all agree that this process requires a lot of hard work and a strong commitment to sustain positive outcomes.

SUGGESTED ACTIVITIES AND QUESTIONS

1. Visit a suburban home and a city apartment and compare the amount of living space. What are some of the things you think children living in each space would learn about themselves?

2. Ask a child to share a story or event about home activities. Plan how you can extend the child's retelling or get additional information from him. What skills do you need to listen well?

3. List the kinds of trips you took with your family when you were growing up. Include events such as shopping, visiting relatives, and recreational outings, as well as vacation trips. From your memory of the experiences, what do you think you learned (physically, emotionally, socially, and intellectually) from these trips?

4. Watch a news report that a child might watch with a parent and discuss with colleagues the violence that children would witness. Make a list of comments and questions you believe will help a child process any violence they might have viewed.

5. Check with your state's department of education to find out about the regulations for homeschooling in your state. Discuss with classmates your feelings about the success of parents who choose this route for their children.

6. Make a list of some childhood things you did with your grandparents, then share with classmates some valued learning that came from those interactions.

RESOURCES

Books

Applebee, A. N. (1996). *Curriculum as conversation.* Chicago: University of Chicago Press.

Bigner, J. J. (2006). *Parent–child relations: An introduction to parenting* (7th ed). Upper Saddle River, NJ: Merrill/Prentice Hall.

Edwards, P. (2004). *Children's literacy development. Making it happen through school, family, and community involvement.* Boston: Allyn & Bacon.

Fuller, C. (2004). *School starts at home*. Colorado Springs, CO: Pinon Press.

Hargrove, A. (2003). *How children interpret screen violence*. London: British Broadcasting Company.

Wasserman, S. (2001). *The long distance grandmother* (4th ed.). Point Roberts, WA: Hartley & Marks.

Films, DVDs, and Videos

Growing minds: Cognitive development in early childhood. (1996). San Luis Obispo, CA: Davidson Films.

Infant curriculum: Great explorations; Toddler curriculum: Making connections. [Videos, 20 min each]. (1997). South Carolina Educational Television with National Association for the Education of Young Children.

Nourishing language development in early childhood [Video, 31 min]. (1998). San Luis Obispo, CA: Davidson Films, with National Association for the Education of Young Children.

Organizations

Family Service Association of America
44 East 23rd Street
New York, NY 10010

Holt Associates/Growing Without Schooling
2380 Massachusetts Ave.
Cambridge, MA 02140
http://www.holtgws.com

National Homeschool Association
P. O. Box 157290
Cincinnati, OH 45215
http://www.N-H-A.org

Web Sites

http://www.amazon.com   Lists the 100 top picks for home school curricula.

http://www.edexcellence.net   Thomas B. Fordham Foundation sponsors the Education Excellence Network site to promote voucher programs, charter schools, and privatization.

http://www.ehow.com   Thousands of files offering step-by-step instructions for all sorts of home tasks and projects.

http://www.homeschoolreviews.com   Contains curriculum materials related to different philosophical views of curriculum, such as a Waldorf approach, an eclectic approach, a classical approach, or unit studies.

http://www.inspiration.com/   Inspiration K through 12 supports visual and thinking techniques to help children brainstorm, plan, organize, and create.

http://www.zerotothree.org   An excellent resource for parents and professionals working with infants and toddlers.

Chapter 9

Curriculum of the School

Or, could I dare propose that the overarching purpose of our schools is to awaken and nurture young minds to a love of learning that lasts a lifetime, and help young people take that learning wherever it might lead them in a free and open society?

(Sacks, 2005, p. 186)

Following the first several years of life with their families and other caregivers, young children enter school, and a different world emerges for children as well as for parents. The school curriculum will determine to a large extent the interests, schedules, practices, and many of the cognitive skills developed during these years. In addition, we find that school curricula will vary considerably among educational institutions because the type of program and practices reflect underlying philosophical beliefs. After reading this chapter, you will be able to do the following:

1. Explain how the curriculum of schools and other educational programs, such as Head Start, child care, and public and private prekindergartens, enhance the cognitive and socialization processes that begin in the home and expand into the community.

2. Compare and contrast the three major curriculum orientations: traditional, constructivist, and personal relevance.

3. Discuss the ways that school administration, teachers, and other personnel, as well as the location and organization of the school, affect the curriculum.

4. Identify common elements that indicate a quality educational program.

5. Consider how school programs are enhanced when homes, schools, and communities collaborate and have common and complementary goals for youth.

Because schooling extends the cognitive and socialization processes children have begun with their families, the relationships between home and school are of major importance for children's growth. In addition to providing skills and content, the school affects children's self-concept, molds aspirations, lays the foundation for community participation and future employment, and provides a good deal of preteen socialization. Schools that provide an atmosphere that is warm and accepting of all children are particularly important for integrating and including minority and immigrant at-risk children, as well as children with special needs.

The success of children in school depends heavily on the relations that exist between home and school. Conflicts over skills and values, differing views about content, or confusion about roles erode the effectiveness of schoolwork, confuse the objectives that both homes and schools subscribe to, and detract from children's functioning (Patrikakou, et al., 2005). Cooperation and compatibility between home and school enable both institutions to provide stability for children and engender progress toward healthy development.

Schools are more impersonal than homes, but children are required to function in a different way when they are at school. Most schools have a distinct chain of command, various authority figures, and specific rules and regulations. Children are expected to act in specific ways, which may vary considerably from the expectations at home. The following vignette dramatizes the situation of a seven-year-old entering a conventional school after being home schooled.

"Jessica, please return to your seat. You shouldn't be wandering out to the hall."

The second-grader turned and blurted, "I . . . saw my brother, and he needed some help."

"I understand Jessica, but there is a school rule—no leaving the classroom without permission," Ms. Strong said firmly.

When Jessica was seven, she entered school for the first time. Her mother had rejoined the family lumber business after homeschooling Jessica and her five-year-old brother.

Now in second grade, Jessica was just getting used to things that her neighborhood friends had been doing for the past two years. "We get lots of books," Margo had said, and that was true, but they were a lot different from the library books and magazines Jessica's mom had used in teaching Jessica. "I really liked the number blocks we used last year," Cicely had mentioned. "I hope we get 'em again." Jessica enjoyed most school activities, but she yearned for the casual pace with her mother. She was reprimanded twice in one day for chatting with two boys in her cluster and then for reading a book from home instead of doing her math assignment. Ms. Strong didn't like to have social conversations going on, and visiting anyone else in class was forbidden. She expected all children to do the task assigned. "Mom, she gives us directions all the time. I can't keep track of the things she says. It's a good thing Harry showed me where to put the date on my spelling paper."

Curriculum for any child involves what happens to the child each day from the time he or she wakes until he or she goes to sleep. For children five years old and older, the school will have a significant impact on that total life curriculum. For an increasing number of preschool children (more than 60% now), Head Start, prekindergarten, and child-care experiences affect that life curriculum as well.

Schooling involves a **formal curriculum** of skills and content, an **informal curriculum** (which starts at home) of habits, practices, and attitudes that all school personnel seek to implement, and a **hidden curriculum** that unfolds in an unintended way but nonetheless permeates children's consciousness. Each curriculum will be affected by educators' philosophical orientations, which in turn influence the organizational arrangements and patterns we find in individual school buildings and classrooms. The following sections discuss the typical school curriculum and its impact on children.

OVERALL PROGRAM OF THE SCHOOL

In general, schools are seen as places where 'kids grow up," learn to interact more skillfully with other children and adults, and assume new responsibilities.

Although still nurturers, early childhood and elementary educators play a role different from that of parents; their attitudes, goals, and procedures also are usually quite different. Everyone knows that a teacher's association with a group of students will be short lived (usually less than a year), and most parents and teachers thus feel that more formality in relationships is normal. Children, of course, must adjust as they move between home and school, from one teacher to another, and from one group of children to others.

In most schools, children find themselves in a rule- and ritual-bound environment. Teachers frequently compare children to one another and regularly evaluate their performance. Jessica, in the preceding vignette, was accustomed to more independence, and it was hard for her to learn the school culture and to operate in a particular manner when rules and time constraints did not always make sense to her.

Consideration of what happened prior to a particular grade are no longer relevant in most school situations. It is what you know now and how you score on the standardized tests mandated by federal regulations that have become important for the agenda of most schools. Children in elementary school are expected to be more conforming and less assertive, to accept responsibility for behaviors and achievements, and to be part of a group that they know little about. Increasingly, however, children have experiences prior to school that help them adapt. Nursery schools, Head Start, child care, and public prekindergarten programs are now part of the lives of large numbers of young children.

During the 20th century, school represented one major link to adulthood, and in recent years school experiences seem even more necessary for children to adjust to a postmodern, technological, and multicultural society. Success is sometimes limited, but school aims and objectives are still focused on preparing children for later roles in a bureaucratic, industrialized, high-tech society. The advantages or disadvantages that children bring to school and the school's ability to adapt to these features will naturally influence their progress in the formal learning environment. In addition, experiences in nursery school, child care, religious programs, summer camp, or libraries will help children make adjustments and transitions more easily.

What of children in the danger zone, though—the child in poverty and the child whose home and culture is very different from the middle-class patterns seen in the schools? It is especially imperative for these at-risk children to have healthy school experiences. Schools that find the necessary resources to assist at-risk children are frequently the only safe, stable, or consistent environments in these children's lives. Numerous accounts show that endangered children linger at their schools as long as possible to avoid neighborhood conflicts and abuse (Garbarino, Dubrow, Kostelny, & Pardo, 1998; Werner & Smith, 2001). The rise in numbers of at-risk children in the United States is sobering—one fifth of our young are exposed to endangerment (Garbarino, Dubrow, Kostelny, & Pardo, 1998; Urban Institute, 2002).

The case is clear for dramatically increased collaboration by all human-services institutions to produce more inclusive environments and provide better transition experiences between home and school. Educators, communities, and health-care providers also need to incorporate services and programs for even the youngest children (birth to age three) in plans for 21st-century schools. These plans must recognize the strengths and advantages that all families can contribute to society. At the same time, we must find ways to help children succeed despite the disadvantages of poverty, an inability to speak English, and cultural backgrounds that vary considerably from the norms of school.

PRESCHOOL, HEAD START, AND PREKINDERGARTEN

Before moving to components of elementary school programs, which have traditionally begun for five-year-olds entering kindergarten, we should point out how various programs for younger children fit into the overall curriculum picture. As noted in Chapters 4 and 5, more than 60% of American preschool-age children are in some type of care facility for at least part of each week. Situations include child care in homes or centers as discussed in Chapter 5, Montessori and other private preschools, prekindergarten programs in elementary schools, and Head Start and **Early Head Start**.

Head Start was developed in the 1960s to provide for the educational, nutritional, and social needs of poor children at risk for educational failure. Head Start can be associated with public school systems or other community agencies and can be a half- or a full-day program serving children beginning at three or four years of age. Early Head Start was established in 1994 as an extension of the traditional Head Start program. It provides child development and family support services during the prenatal period through the child's first three years of life. Focusing on prenatal health and infant and toddler physical, social, emotional, and cognitive development, Early Head Start also has a primary long-term goal of helping children be ready for school (Ipsa et al., 2006).

Although Head Start was developed by the federal government to help children living in poverty achieve success in school, state governments are beginning to fund prekindergarten programs for all four year olds, regardless of income. **Universal pre-K**, as this movement is termed, was first implemented in Georgia in 1995 (Raden, 2003) and is slowly being implemented in other states, most recently New York and Florida. The goal of these programs is to provide all preschool children with the opportunity to participate in a high-quality, literacy-rich early childhood experience. At this point, enrollment is voluntary, unlike kindergarten, where enrollment is mandated, and the pre-k may be in a public, private, or faith-based school.

Like the curricular approaches you will read about in the following sections, programs for young children vary from play-oriented, child-centered experiences to direct instruction models.

Some will have a structured scope and sequence chart of particular objectives and others will be more home-like and informal. In most programs for three- and four-year-olds, you will find definite planned activities with expectations identified for the enrolled children. Early literacy experiences designed to help children learn to read successfully are increasingly part of the preschool curriculum in most programs (Wortham, 2006). Preschool teaching personnel who are considerate of young children's developmental levels and have means for adjusting expectations to the learning styles and backgrounds of individual children (Bredekamp & Rosegrant, 1995; Trawick-Smith, 2006) are the most likely to provide appropriate experiences for this age group.

REFLECTION

Formal schooling for most children is now beginning at younger ages. Compare your early school experiences with your friends' and consider if those of you who started school earlier seemed to have an advantage. Does anyone think of disadvantages?

CURRICULUM ORIENTATIONS

As an educator, you will develop expectations for children's conduct and accomplishments, and these expectations will reflect your philosophical orientation. Because one character or disposition normally dominates in a particular school building, we usually find the educators there similar in orientation and outlook. Of course, teachers and administrators attempt to accomplish school expectations using different teaching styles, and frequently it is with varying degrees of success.

We find a number of learning theorists with varying philosophical orientations, and the different perspectives lead them to recommend specific but different school practices (Marsh & Willis, 2003). For this text, the continuum discussed ranges from a traditionalist, teacher-dominated

stance at one end to a progressive, child-centered stance at the other. All curriculum orientations focus on developing children's potential, but how to best do that and with what tools define the different perspectives. As shown in Table 9–1, we can section the continuum into several parts and ascribe to each a philosophical base, authorities, significant features, and teacher roles.

Five categories or positions that appear consistently in the literature and are supported by curriculum authorities (Eisner, 2002; McNeil, & Darby 2005; Pinar, 2004) are academic, **technologist**, **cognitive process**, **social reconstructionist**, and personal relevance. Webb, Metha, and Jordan (2007) noted that all these positions have evolved historically as a protest against some of the prevailing ideas and practices of the times. Table 9–1 provides a summary of these orientations. You will note that borderlines are ambiguous, categories overlap, and authorities use different terms to describe each perspective. Other texts have somewhat different names for these general categories.

In the last decade, scientists have examined vigorously how genetics influences human development. Several studies explain in great detail how genes and environment interact from the moment of conception (Pinker, 2002; Ridley, 2003a). This research advances the notion that learning is not a result of either genetic endowment or environmental experiences, but a combination of factors that affect and produce changes in each other. It also suggests that individuals are unique in their development. We must acknowledge that learning is so person specific that no one set of outcomes can be dictated for a given time period. If American schools are to keep abreast of the changes in the 21st century, then how teachers, parents, and community members (including politicians) interpret high-stakes testing as the means to improve schools is very important (Wagner, 2003).

We describe here a three-section continuum of curriculum orientations condensed from the perspectives in Table 9–1. These three areas represent

Table 9–1   Typical Curriculum Orientations

Labels	Academic rationalism; humanism	Technologist	Cognitive process; constructivist	Social meliorist; reconstructionist	Personal relevance; individual fulfillment
Philosophical Bases	Idealism	Realism	Pragmatism, experimentalism	Experimentalism	Existentialism
Proponents	Adler, Hirsch, Hutchins, Bennett	Bobbitt, Tyler, Hunter, Bloom	Bruner, Piaget, Vygotsky, Dewey	Counts, Apple, Freire	Rousseau, Neill, Holt
Features	Classic studies; wisdom of the ages; focus on arts	High order and discipline; back to basics; mastery of here and now	Learning to learn; experiencing world and accepting changes; problem solving	Study of world and improving one's surroundings; social experiences	Freedom to choose; student assisted in exploring personal learning journey
Teacher Role	Teacher mastery and enthusiasm required; models the ideal; lectures and discusses	Well-planned and detailed objectives; lectures and demonstrates; interprets and informs	Develops projects, stimulates study; directs attention to levels of analysis and progress	Suggests explorations supporting learners; resource person	Assists learners in explorations; minimal teacher agenda

situations observed in many early-childhood classes today:

1. *Traditional:* combines aspects of **academic rationalism** and the **technologist curriculum**.
2. *Constructivist:* combines aspects of **cognitive process** and **social reconstructionist curriculum**.
3. *Personal relevance:* follows the **personal relevance curriculum**, or orientation for individual exploration.

We find the first two orientations in most U.S. schools today. Though aspects of the third orientation may occur within the first two, curricula based solely on this perspective are found only in a few private or experimental schools and in some homeschooling environments.

Traditional

Traditional academic and teacher-dominated programs expect children to be conforming, respectful of authority, and anxious to learn and to look to their teachers for guidance and stimulation. Intellectual growth in "worthy subjects" is the agenda, and programs of this kind will be as structured and efficiently organized as the teacher is capable of making them. Classrooms are replete with **behavioral objectives**, and standardized tests are most often used for assessing because the goal is to develop a particular core of knowledge that all children are expected to attain at a given age.

This orientation is known as a **traditional curriculum**, and it has held sway for generations. It has become the preferred disposition, witnessed by legislation (No Child Left Behind, for example) recently enacted by congress that takes the traditional position on how children learn. Schools are now held accountable and are ranked as to quality; rankings are based on the results of standardized tests. All of this assumes that states can agree on specific standards and can develop fair tests for all children (Meier, 2002a).

Traditional programs are replete with behavioral objectives and standardized tests.

Given the right circumstances—well-focused and humane teachers working with interested and organized children—this traditional didactic curriculum can be extremely successful in promoting basic skills and **cultural literacy**. The following vignette illustrates a well-functioning traditional classroom.

Ms. Washington is noticeable and vibrant in her second-grade classroom. The room purrs with efficiency, and Ms. Washington covers every part of the room dozens of times each day in maintaining control and helping children. The class has won the PTA banner for five months running now, and the seven-year-olds eagerly inform visitors that theirs is the best room.

The class is arranged into three reading and two math groups, using textbooks that Ms. Washington occasionally supplements with her own material. Assignments are neatly and clearly presented on a side chalkboard, which children consult periodically. Every student is busy at 9:15 A.M.—two groups work quietly on skill sheets while Ms. Washington conducts a directed reading activity with the third group. As she works with the group, she beckons two children from the seated groups to check their progress. She gives frequent signals to class members in response to their raised hands; her eyes sweep across the class like a lighthouse beam on a recurring pattern.

A change in groups is handled like clockwork. In less than two minutes, groups have rotated and are at work

once more. Ms. Washington's pleasant voice distributes accolades: "Wonderful work in Jawon's group!" "All papers are completed here, too. Super!"

Ms. W. carefully plans all activities and is ready to go at 9:00 every morning. Even such activities as science projects, which the curriculum guide called for children to do at home, have been scheduled for school, where Ms. Washington can monitor and supervise. Her movements are quick and energetic, and the class emulates her.

Ms. Washington is the classic traditional teacher; she has everything down pat. She does all the planning, demonstrating, and guided practice and anticipates almost every problem. "I work hard at what I do, and I get good results," she noted, and this is demonstrated in her students' yearly achievement test scores.

Teachers in traditionally oriented schools think of themselves as in a means-to-an-end situation, as Ms. Washington does. They see themselves working diligently to overcome obstacles—whether ignorance, missing skills, or lack of interest—and devise strategies that will entice learners and build skills to support later education. The curriculum is didactic and teacher centered in nature, focused on structure; such teachers are businesslike, and their can-do aura permeates the traditional classroom.

In keeping with the **industrial model**, contract learning, programmed learning, and mastery learning all fit with this design. Time-on-task studies, goal-analysis plans, scope and sequence charts, critical paths for learning, and management by objectives all fit here very well, too. Because accountability is foremost, **norm-referenced testing** is appropriate. The expectation is development of literacy, as well as computational, scientific, and social skills. The traditional orientation makes for a socially efficient, skills-outcome-based educational system, which is easy to rationalize. A clear goal is in sight, and teachers look for ways to get there.

No Child Left Behind (NCLB) legislation adheres to this type of curriculum. Standardized tests mark the success or failure of a student's education. In order to graduate from high school, a child must pass selected exams. Because selected skills and knowledge are required for everyone, it is relatively easy to give report cards to the nation regarding the standing of each state's schools.

Traditionalists accept new objectives as they become relevant for contemporary living. Personal living skills, health education, and computer literacy all make sense for primary-school-age children in today's world, so schools with the traditionalist orientation assume responsibility for these areas to produce students tuned to today's needs.

The traditional program has a long line of advocates. Franklin Bobbitt was an early proponent when, in the early 20th century, he made the case for a curriculum responsive to the time. Since then, advocates such as Benjamin Bloom, Hilda Taba, Ralph Tyler, and Madeline Hunter have propounded the idea. William Bennett, a one-time secretary of education, supports the bases of traditional education, as does John Silber (1989) in his best-selling book *Straight Shooting: What's Wrong with America and How to Fix It.*

A school with traditional outlook and academic goals does not always have a successful program. Some schools have evolved this way because that is the heritage for the community. Even when a program has questionable objectives for the population served and garners unenthusiastic responses, school boards often perpetuate it. Many low-achieving schools are of this type; they cling to inappropriate goals and teaching methods seen by their communities as irrelevant. Critics of this type of teaching and testing suggest that teaching practices will become subservient to the tests (Meier, 2002b; Meier & Wood, 2004). Teachers are encouraged to find out about the content of tests and then teach to the test. It disallows that the material might be developmentally or culturally inappropriate (Wagner, 2003).

The ongoing popularity of the traditional curriculum (Fried, 2005) assures its continued existence, but the lockstep approach seems deadly for some learners. In addition, teacher-centered programs in preschools seem to hold some risk for increasing the later antisocial behavior of disadvantaged children (Schweinhart & Weikart, 1997).

Certainly, the traditionalist plan does not accommodate different learning levels in the flexible way that constructivist and personal relevance orientations do. Traditional education appeals to many educators working with **marginalized learners**, however. Because the programs are carefully structured and are developed in steps, dedicated teachers can provide consistency, predictability, and stability for children who would otherwise not find this pattern in their lives.

REFLECTION

In your own experiences with schools, did you have mostly "traditional" teachers? If so, how did you progress in this type of classroom? Did you enjoy learning in that environment, and if so, why? Or why not?

Constructivist

Constructivist curricula have social efficiency goals similar to those of the traditional orientation, but they employ quite different strategies, permitting individualized instruction and varied content. Instead of employing the traditionalist emphasis on skill sequence, the constructivist works to develop children's thinking skills. Valuing the process rather than the product, the constructivist's objective is

A constructionist teaching style encourages free pupil participation while the teacher serves as a helper and guide.

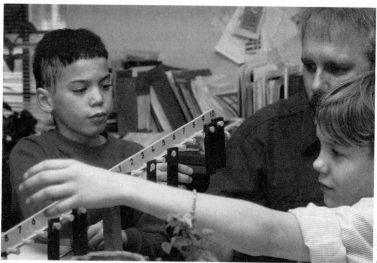

David Napravnik / Merrill

for children to learn how to learn, so they can adapt knowledge and skill to new situations. Teacher behaviors differ from those of the manager–director stance of the traditionalist, but constructivists maintain a strong teacher presence in their classrooms to arbitrate when needed, direct projects, anticipate next steps, and coordinate activities with a general school curriculum.

Rather than use carefully designed **skills ladders, scope and sequence charts**, and behavioral objectives, constructivists favor problem-centered work. **Theme-focused programs**, units of study, project approaches, and similar programs belong in this camp. Because content is often serendipitous and subject to change, teachers with a constructivist orientation must be very secure in knowledge of content and perspectives on child development. They must keep programs relevant to the age levels of students and move the students in the direction of social and cognitive competence.

The constructivist orientation stems from educational theorist Dewey's (1913–1975) writing, and the progressive education movement of the 1930s and 1940s was based here. It is supported by Piagetian and Vygotskian theories of development and more recently in Howard Gardner's theory of multiple intelligences. Gardner (1983 & 1993) proposes eight different intelligences that reflect children's abilities and capabilities. See the Table 6–1 in McDevitt & Ormond (2002, p. 202) for a good summary. In the late 20th century, we found team-teaching, cooperative learning, and **whole-language program** strategies based on constructivism, and in some ways 21st-century findings in brain function research correlates with this orientation (Bruer, 2002; Ridley, 2003b).

Constructivist teacher styles encourage free pupil participation. The school program will be heavily project centered, and teachers think of themselves not as founts of knowledge but as helpers and guides. We do not find a predetermined knowledge base or a set of learnings such as those found in traditional schools; teachers and students enter into investigations and develop or refine skills as they proceed. Curriculum content often focuses on what is interesting and important to children and allows children to approach their learning in different ways. For example, because social consciousness begins in the primary grades, a focus on environment and care for the earth may be appealing to second- or third-grade children. Constructivist teachers would move in that direction, allowing some children to do a great deal of reading and writing about the topic or others to construct projects and experiments. Finally, some children might spend time observing nature and others develop a music or dance to explain their understanding.

Some teachers will retreat to specific tasks at times, and some do have drills and lectures, but group work dominates, and teachers easily move from whole-class to small-group to individual instruction. As in traditional rooms, children in constructivist classrooms are expected to be cooperative, good helpers, willing to share, and anxious to learn. In the following vignette, Mr. Perez conducts his primary program in a way quite different from what we would find in a traditional classroom.

Mr. Perez's third grade is relaxed. Two large rugs cover most of the floor, and well-worn sofas occupy the center of the room. Mr. P. has no desk at all and spends almost the entire day conferencing with small groups and individuals. Children are at different stages in their writings about people living in their neighborhoods. Mr. P. suggested the activity more than a week ago, and students approached it in different ways—interviewing people, observing folks at home, and just recalling recent events. Youngsters are working this morning all over the room trying to get their final drafts ready for presenting to one of the response groups. Two children are sitting with Mr. P. on one sofa discussing their impressions of the custodian. They read each other's papers and nod. One asks about the word codruy.

"Maybe it's corduroy?" Mr. P. wonders. "That right, Jason?"

"Yup," comes the answer.

"Do you want the dictionary spelling, Tyrone?" Mr. P. smiles. Both say, "Yeah, OK," and Mr. P. spells it for them. "These papers both make good sense to me," he states several minutes later. "Where do you want to go from here?"

Mr. Perez teaches from a constructivist philosophy. He is casual and relaxed and corrects indirectly. All children seem happy with the slightly noisy room, and students seldom interfere with each other's projects. One of Mr. P.'s few rules is that everyone sit on the rug near the end of the day to listen to those who have decided to share their projects. Today, Andrea does not wish any reactions to or comments on the model neighborhood street she is building; she just wants to talk about it. The other presenter, Shana, does

ask for comments on her description of the school principal.

Mr. Perez says, "It's easy to get this group to plow ahead on things like this. I think we're keeping up with reading skills, and I know we're way ahead on writing skills. We'll do fine at the end of the year." Kyle, McIntyre, Miller, and Moore (2007) presented a detailed description of how this type of curriculum works.

Evaluation or testing in constructivist programs is more likely to be **criterion referenced** and to involve teacher-developed instruments. Teachers following a **constructivist curriculam** favor **holistic evaluation** to determine group progress, and assessment is frequently based on presentations or portfolios. (For a thorough discussion of this type of assessment, see Rinaldi, 1998; Stiggins, 2005). Under current requirements of the No Child Left Behind Act, however, public school children are required to take standardized tests, regardless of the curricular orientation.

Generally, constructivist teaching is not undertaken unless personnel are confident about their background, committed to flexibility, and earnest in developing an experimental design. Curricular models such as the High/Scope Curriculum (Weikart & Hohmann, 2002) and the Project Approach (Katz & Chard, 2000) are examples of programs that follow a constructivist philosophy. In its true form, it exists in fewer than 10% of all classrooms in the United States, with the large majority of these in early childhood programs and in private schools. Some elementary schools, however, use a constructivist approach for science teaching and for some special projects during the year (Wortham, 2006).

Personal Relevance

In the personal relevance, or completely child-centered, program, teachers assume a counseling or resource role. Some would say that the child-centered orientation is rooted in Rousseauian philosophy, but it is more than that. The orientation's basic premise is that children possess natural motivations for learning, and adults help best by making things available, interacting to guide and stimulate, and being supportive. The Summerhill program (Cassebaum, 2003; Neill, 1960) is the prototype for the totally child-centered program. Presently, this orientation is found in a few laboratory schools, some **alternative schools** (the Pathfinder Learning Center in Amherst, Massachusetts, is an example), and a number of preschool programs. Many homeschooling situations also are very much of this order.

Responsibility for all educational progress and work is shifted to the student in these liberal programs, and learners must be proactive to make progress. Children must be interested in exploring, setting their own agendas, and working individually. Students are likely to challenge authority and abandon their projects on occasion, and often they come up with very different results. These behaviors can be disconcerting for parents and teachers who have firm ideas about what children should learn.

Since motivation and incentive are expected to rise from within, students with teacher guidance in personal relevance programs determine where, when, and how to go. These learners are often aggressive and highly individualistic, often going on "work binges." Because no published curriculum exists, teachers are responsible for displaying a smorgasbord of materials, ideas, and projects to encourage interests. Children make choices and follow their interests with all they can muster. Typically, children work by themselves for several weeks exclusively on one study, perhaps of insects, airplanes, or computers.

Some stunning examples of success for the personal relevance orientation are evident when we view programs such as the Sudbury Valley School and other schools modeled on this approach (Greenberg, Sadofsky, & Lempka, 2005) and those at other alternative schools. Many aspects of the Italian Reggio Emilia programs (see Chapter 12) might be considered personal relevance–type curriculum, too. At the same time, we can find situations that proved disastrous because students were not oriented to the programs or because teachers lacked commitment to this pattern.

Completely child-centered programs represent a tiny proportion of all school plans because they depend on highly committed staff members with dispositions for guiding and nurturing and require a community favoring this type of education. These conditions are quite foreign to the general American public.

We find combinations and variations for these three curriculum orientations, and different degrees of "purity" exist for all types. How do these orientations relate to marginalized children, inner-city programs, and multiethnic situations? The traditional schooling orientation is based on European American, middle-class values, which do not always make sense to poor and disadvantaged populations. Still, some (O'Shea, 2005) would argue that the most structured plan allows marginalized children to learn basic skills, which some maintain must be attained before further learning can occur.

On the other hand, the project focus of the constructivist orientation, especially when its programs include social investigation and social relevance aspects, seems logical for improving understanding among culturally and ethnically diverse groups. We find, however, that such plans are rare in schools for children from such communities. The constructivist orientation requires children to acquire patterns of self-control and to assume responsibility for classroom learning. When children are raised with little or no structure or security in their lives, many teachers find their classroom exploration difficult to manage.

Programs with minimal structure, such as the **personal relevance program**, which depend on individual incentive, also may be difficult to manage with some at-risk populations. If children lack experiences in work and study habits and if their world is a confusing one, programs based on personal relevance will likely render minimal value even though they are based on the premise that children's needs are foremost. On the other hand, a personal relevance program may work to an advantage in an ethnically diverse community. A positive aspect could develop when children are motivated to learn about **cross-cultural** experiences in order to operate in different cultures. New immigrants might also find such a program comfortable, because these programs are not so time or goal oriented. When schools provide after-school activities and summer programs for at-risk children, conducting a program using a personal relevance curriculum could extend children's enthusiasm for learning.

REFLECTION

Have you or any classmates been taught in a "constructivist" or a "personal relevance" program? Share your experiences and reactions to school under those programs. If no one has had these experiences, speculate on what life in these schools might be like. Would it have been better for you, worse, or not much different?

SCHOOL ORGANIZATION

Funding for U.S. public schools comes from a combination of federal and state funds and local taxes. Consequently, spending varies widely from state to state and among communities within a state. Although the average expediture per year per child in the United States was $8,287 during 2002 to 2003, New Jersey spent $12,560 and Utah spent $5,008 during the same time period. Such economic disparity as well as other differences contribute significantly to a school's culture and characteristics. In this section, we will examine the organization of the school in terms of the adults who staff programs and the school's physical arrangement, two of the most important and costly aspects of educating children.

Staffing Plans

Staffing involves administrators, teaching personnel of all types (classroom teachers, specialists, aides, and volunteers), and the service personnel (secretaries, nurses, custodians, foodservice employees, bus drivers, social workers, school psychologists, and others) associated with the school. All individuals affect the school program, and the character a school possesses comes largely from the personalities, attitudes, and styles of the people who work there.

Administration. Principals and, to a lesser extent, supervisors set the programmatic, social, and emotional tone for the schools with which they are associated. We find several administrative styles commonly observed in U.S. schools.

Businesslike administrators who place a premium on efficiency, organization, and discipline inject those qualities into a school building's life. This style fits well for the school with a technologist or academic orientation. Managed with skill and tenacity, these schools show a no-nonsense air of business and urgency. Although not always the most friendly or open communities, they are predictable, clean, and usually efficient. Rules and regulations are in evidence, things happen on time, all people know what is expected, and most feel secure. There are no surprises. It is the industrial model brought to school. Opinions vary on the appropriateness of the business or bureaucratic model. Many teachers, parents, and students enjoy the comfort of the school's organization, discipline, and high expectations. Others do not enjoy it, labeling the program as patronizing, stifling of creativity, and not conducive to teachers exercising professional judgment or to students learning decision-making skills (Pinar, 2004).

Inner-city schools with the right mix of personnel have often followed the businesslike style profitably. The combination of rigorous discipline and personal power and charismatic enthusiasm has produced highly touted success stories, such as those of Joe Clark at Eastside High in Patterson, New Jersey, in the late 1980s, and more recently Thaddeus Lott's work at Wesley School in Texas (Brouillette, 2002).

Other schools are run on a more democratic, less stringent, basis. Democracy is the objective in many schools, and one finds a partnership tone and an agenda for cooperative action. Principals in these buildings are normally exuberant and accepting, and people thrive in their own way. Naturally, the characteristics of these schools are considerable movement, activities that are encouraged (and that can bring about a high noise level), lots of experimentation, and even friction. The school is the playground energy and spirit brought indoors.

Many people find the less directive stance and the accepting tone of the democratic administrative position to be conducive to working at one's own pace and to one's own agenda. Teachers with charisma, dramatic flair, and outgoing personalities find this climate suitable; they can do what they enjoy doing, and incursions on their turf are not demands but collaborations. On the other hand, low-key persons often will not respond to this type of school atmosphere. They feel lost in the busy shuffle and cannot tolerate the high energy levels, noise, or distractions. A democratic principal, who should be a quiet consensus builder, however, will take time to nurture, listen, and build support for programs and policies. These consensus-seeking persons are highly valued in many American communities. For example, Mr. Rider made all persons entering School 6 in Baltimore feel welcomed and valued. He arrived early in the morning and spent the hour before classes complimenting custodians, welcoming faculty, and asking children how their day was starting. This value produced an emotional environment that supported the esteem of all persons associated with the school.

Another good example is Mr. Irons, who has been at Farragut Elementary School in St. Louis for 30 years and has helped teachers and community members form strong intergenerational bonds. He built on the historically stabilizing effect of the segregated schools, in which African American communities claimed ownership of the Black schools. He belongs to the community and is a part of the culture. His caring manner serves as a model for his staff and for community members. Students in the school have one of the highest attendance rates in St. Louis and consistently outperform other city students on standardized tests (Morris, 2002).

Children always sense the administrative tenor in buildings and adapt to it. They know what they can expect of principals and how far they can go in approaching them. This is all part of the informal curriculum discussed later in this chapter.

In the final analysis, it is the public served that determines the patterns and style for a school. A community gradually asserts its wishes for an organizational plan and a climate that fit it best. Administrators must accommodate the community served if programs are to go forward.

Teachers. In keeping with administrative styles, teachers bring a presence to schools. Much of the teacher's style is a function of his or her philosophical orientation or belief about how children learn and how schools should work. Just as there are parenting styles (refer to Chapter 4), we find comparable teaching styles. These are merged with personal outlooks and methods of presentation. In general, they form a four-part grid on two axes (Table 9–2): warmth (responsive vs. nonresponsive) and control (demanding vs. undemanding). Note that categories in Table 9–2 are similar to Baumrind's (1968) categories for parenting. In the following vignette, the teacher's style works well in her school, where teachers collaborate in a team spirit to ensure inclusion of students with disabilities.

Mrs. Larkin is seated in her multiage primary classroom with children who are sharing their morning work before heading for their gym activity. Eric, a child with special needs and an abusive family background,

Table 9–2   Matrix of Different Teaching Styles

	Responsive	Nonresponsive
Demanding manner	Businesslike teacher: demanding but responsive	Autocratic teacher: demanding and nonresponsive
Undemanding manner	Permissive teacher: undemanding but responsive	Indifferent teacher: undemanding and nonresponsive

Source: Adapted from Cruickshank (1990); Good and Brophy (1986); Joyce and Weil (1996).

enters the room accompanied by Mrs. Stanford, his counselor, who nods to Mrs. Larkin and then leaves. "Good morning, Eric. We're ready for gym. You're just in time," says Mrs. Larkin. Eric doesn't respond, but walks behind the circle to the class folders and picks up his folder. Then he bops the child nearest him on the head with it. Mrs. Larkin says quietly but firmly, "Eric, that is not acceptable. Sit at your table there and work on your folder. I'm sorry, but you'll need to miss part of gym class." Eric responds by sitting and opening his folder. From time to time he looks at Mrs. Larkin, who sort of smiles but gently shakes her head.

After five minutes, the class lines up to wait for the gym instructor. As the instructor appears at the door, he looks questioningly at Mrs. Larkin and at a seated Eric. "Yes, Eric will be a bit late for class. I'll bring him shortly." As the class leaves, Eric's counselor returns and says she'll take Eric to gym. "He did so well with me this morning." Yesterday had been a difficult day, and the two had struck a deal about Eric's behavior and rewards for the next day. Mrs. Larkin explains the new situation to Mrs. Stanford, then says to Eric, "I was so pleased to see you come in and go right to your folder, but I'm sorry you weren't able to do the next step. Because your day has been so good otherwise, though, and you have worked well for these past five minutes, I think Mrs. Stanford will agree that you may go to gym." Eric's face lights up, and he hurries to put his folder back.

Eric is a child with attention deficit hyperactivity disorder, and his individualized education plan provides for an increasing length of time in the regular classroom. His teachers dislike keeping children from needed physical activity, but it is the one thing they have found that Eric considers worth "behaving" for. Other strategies are used, and although Eric's teachers all have somewhat different styles, they all agree on certain rules and procedures that Eric is expected to follow. With warmth but firmness, they consistently maintain this emotional environment. The other children in the classroom are friendly with one another and with Eric.

Eric has some difficult days, improvement is growing in how he manages his behavior. At the beginning of the year, Eric spent most of his time with the counselor and a special-needs instructor. He now receives more than half of his instruction in the regular classroom setting with other students and participates in special activities with his classmates.

The demanding but responsive teacher, similar to the authoritative parent, is normally popular because this person pursues plans aggressively but in a humane and friendly fashion. Mrs. Larkin, in the preceding vignette, exemplifies this style. The style coordinates well with all curriculum orientations except personal relevance, in which an undemanding but responsive teacher is more likely valued. The demanding and nonresponsive, or authoritarian, style can exist in traditional programs but seems out of place in constructivist programs, where human dynamics play such an important part. The undemanding and nonresponsive profile produces an indifferent demeanor, which has little chance of succeeding in any program.

Teaching styles relate to all levels of teaching, because volunteers, aides, and specialists all project a teaching style. Various styles can be successful in different venues, and teachers are aware of this; however, all must be able to match children's learning modalities with different circumstances and different materials (Dunn & Dunn, 1999; Dunn & Frazier, 1990). Good and Brophy (1986) stated that "different situations and goals call for different methods [and] a given method may have different effects on different students" (p. 375).

Service Personnel. Although teaching and administrative staff dominate the adult interaction time with schoolchildren, other members of the school community also project social and emotional qualities. Custodians, nurses, lunchroom workers, and secretaries all play a part in a school atmosphere. Teaching style is not an issue with these adults, but the responsiveness they show toward children and the manner in which they cooperate with teachers add to or detract from the overall school environment.

Service personnel are important in communicating and maintaining the climate of the school. A kind custodian who keeps the building clean and yet welcomes a confused parent creates a positive effect on the parent. A secretary who ignores parents entering the office can terrify newly arrived, inexperienced, or culturally different parents. A confused or fearful parent will leave with a distaste for schools and may well become one of the "difficult to reach" parents.

Volunteers. Partnership for education means that parents and interested community members will be in schools in various capacities. See Chapter 12 for Epstein's six levels of parent involvement.

Many members of a school community project a social and emotional atmosphere that supports positive learning.

Dan Floss / Merrill

They, too, are important in helping create a caring and positive learning atmosphere for children.

These volunteers will also have different styles and ways of interacting, just as teachers do. Volunteers may be less aware of how their behavior affects children, however. As children become more comfortable interacting with different adults, they grow in their ability to communicate in different ways. Volunteers offer a wide range of talents and resources to teachers as they develop and carry out the curriculum. Adults attending school events hopefully model the desired behavior at these events, reaching out and praising different student efforts. These interactions often help to increase children's self-concept and pride of accomplishment.

When adult volunteers and teachers work together amicably, children discover how teamwork results in greater opportunities for learning. It is important for teachers to reinforce this adult involvement. At the end of a very successful unit of study, one teacher invited the aides, the volunteers, and the children to share their learning. She listed the activities done and what they had accomplished. The teacher exclaimed at the end, "Wow, look at all that has been done! I couldn't

have done it alone." Some teachers, at meetings or elsewhere, when they meet the volunteers, take a moment to share with them individual anecdotes of ways the children have responded to their help.

A series of meetings or workshops help teachers and adults to find mutual satisfaction. When teachers can match parents' skills with children's needs, and when adults are able to blend into classroom routines and respond positively to the style of teacher interactions, all projects are more successful. Calfee, Wittwer, and Meredith (1998) have many suggestions for volunteers, teachers, and other staff working together.

REFLECTION

Visit an early childhood or elementary classroom and find out who, other than the classroom teacher, is working with children. Then compare the "teaching staff" of this classroom with your own schooling. Would you have succeeded better with more volunteer help, or do you think your regular classroom teacher was better equipped to work with you on all things?

Physical Organization

The physical aspects and space associated with schools differ with age and location, but these elements always suggest what can happen in particular educational environments. The majority of U.S. children of primary-school age attend schools in classrooms containing 20 to 25 students and one teacher per group. The physical plant for most school programs is still the **"egg-box" construction**, with a central hallway and branching individual classrooms. Variations exist for the basic plan and also may exist within the egg box, including learning stations and highly flexible constructions and equipment.

One can see that physical organization of schools and classrooms relates to the program (Figure 9–1). A traditionally organized room is likely to have a traditional orientation. This message communicates itself quickly to children and others who enter a school. Some older schools built for traditional programs have been reorganized into settings that contain open spaces, workstations, and resource areas. Space, including hallways and out-of-doors areas, can be used in an entirely different way to support a program where teachers want experiments and freedom in movement. Ironically, some **open-space buildings** built for more innovative programming have been reorganized in a traditional way. Teachers who push to reorganize their space give new life to the adage "form follows function."

Open-space schools were developed in the 1970s in many U.S. communities. In general, they were large buildings planned around pods, or divisions, that housed various grade levels or "families." The large spaces, or pods, were generally allotted to specific grade levels, and the teachers for each space developed the area as they saw fit. This often meant that one group of 25 second-graders was within sight and hearing of two or more other groups.

With this plan, many activities in open-space schools are total-group events, and subgroups move between the designated sections in the pod. Noise levels tend to be higher in open-space schools, but with carefully scheduled activities, study, and transition time, the interruptions are minimized. The open space permits the flexibility to move to other groups within or outside the pod for specific activities or for partnerships, and then to move back when the home group is called to session. The plan fits well with the cognitive process (constructivist) orientation and other, more individualized orientations. It does not jibe with academic or traditionalist patterns and has for this reason lost popularity in many school districts.

CURRICULUM FORMS

Schools were established originally to teach areas of skill and knowledge more efficiently and with better results than could be achieved at home. Even though the nature of this task has changed and expanded over the years, the need for skills and knowledge is still the basis for school curricula. In the 19th century, the overarching objectives were to ensure reasonable competence in the ability to read, compose written work, and master computation skills and general problem solving. Schools were arranged exclusively on the traditional or teacher-dominated plan. Schools assumed an extensive role in providing more and new content for children as time went by. At present, U.S. schools have curricula that include not only language arts and mathematics but also social studies, science, health and recreation, and fine arts. As noted at the beginning of this chapter, the school curriculum has three distinct forms or zones—formal, informal, and hidden. All are evident each day that children attend school.

The formal, or explicit, curriculum includes the established content, concepts, and skills found in curriculum guides and teacher plan books. It is the material included in textbooks or in the projects that teachers and students decide to pursue.

The informal curriculum zone includes the social learnings, work and study habits, and protocols that learners must master to fit into school life. Students learn these through modeling by school adults, by persuasion and advisement, and sometimes simply by having a buddy to associate

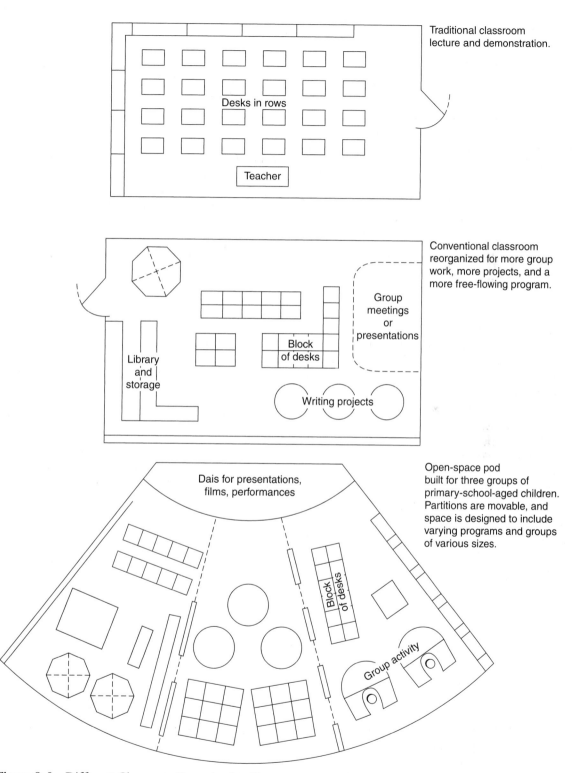

Traditional classroom lecture and demonstration.

Desks in rows

Teacher

Conventional classroom reorganized for more group work, more projects, and a more free-flowing program.

Group meetings or presentations

Library and storage

Block of desks

Writing projects

Open-space pod built for three groups of primary-school-aged children. Partitions are movable, and space is designed to include varying programs and groups of various sizes.

Dais for presentations, films, performances

Block of desks

Group activity

Figure 9–1   Different Classroom Organization Patterns

with and thereby to "learn the rules" from. This process can be compared to the etiquette practices of homes and the social organization rules found in any subculture.

The hidden, or covert, curriculum consists of unintentional learnings accruing to children from their school experiences. Informants in this case are frequently peers; children also absorb messages from adults by observation. Through the hidden curriculum, children learn such things as whether it is a good time to make a request, which teachers get the things they want from the school office, or that third-grade boys "do not play" with girls. They also learn how school personnel and peers view their habits, dress, and home-life experiences.

Formal Curriculum

The formal, explicit, or intended curriculum of a school is the plan of action or experiences delivered to attending children. Curricula are promoted in different ways and, as noted, can differ considerably from one school to another, depending on staff, district philosophy, materials and equipment involved, type of community, and acceptance level of teachers.

Often the curriculum is a detailed, written document produced through the work of teacher study groups and disseminated from a central office. The content fits neatly into a scope-and-sequence chart, and material often correlates closely with published textbooks. Many state offices of education publish curriculum guides for particular grade levels or subject matter guides for all grade levels, developing them in a manner similar to that of local school districts.

In each of the curriculum orientations discussed in this chapter, educators have different preferred ways to organize and schedule curriculum content. The following sections present examples of how a formal curriculum is developed for each orientation in contemporary schools.

Formal Curriculum in Traditional Schools. Predetermined curricula fit academic or traditionally oriented schools because the philosophy of such schools holds that a common core of knowledge

exists. Then the facts, concepts, and skills of that core can be written down, turned into objectives, which are developed with children, and children's learning is evaluated by standardized or teacher-made tests.

Schedule and Structure. Grade levels for elementary schools established in the early 19th century have remained much the same to the present day. Although somewhat arbitrary and contributing to many lockstep curriculum designs, the practice arranges a considerable amount of content into grade-specific levels. Teachers in traditionally oriented classrooms organize a day primarily through various routines, then schedule lessons and practice, followed by evaluation of some type. A typical day in a traditional school is shown in Figure 9–2. This is a minimal plan, showing only the highlights, but it suggests the extent of schoolwork for six- to eight-year-olds in a traditional program.

Organization. An exception to the self-contained classroom with children of specific ages is the **departmentalized program**, where children move from room to room for instruction in particular subjects. Departmentalized plans, normally associated with upper-elementary grades, also

9:00–9:15 A.M.	Opening activities
9:15–11:15	Reading and other language arts
11:15–12:00 noon	Mathematics
12:00–12:45 P.M.	Lunch/recess
12:45–1:15	"Specials": art, music, or physical education
1:15–1:45	Science or social studies
1:45–2:15	Computer or media work
2:15–3:00	Language arts
3:15	Closing

Figure 9–2   Traditional Classroom Day for Grade 2

have been developed in primary areas. Teachers specialize in one or more areas; for example, one teacher develops reading, writing, and spelling (language arts) and handles those areas for two or more classrooms. Team teaching is another model that combines departmentalized features with group planning, support, and evaluation.

Cooperative learning models replace many individual assignments with a small-group focus and responsibility. Teachers may combine this strategy with most staffing arrangements and classroom organization patterns. The strategy blends most successfully with constructivist classrooms, however.

Formal Curriculum in Constructivist Classrooms. A **constructivist curriculum** is carefully thought out. The teacher's plans are developed in conjunction with school and community expectations; children's developmental stages and individual patterns of growth are accounted for. A constructivist teacher may use a curriculum guide but will freely interpret it as needed. Content covers all disciplines—reading, writing, math, social studies, science, fine arts, and physical education. Rather than following a sequenced listing of content and concepts, classes pursue investigations of differing topics, projects, or themes. The curriculum is integrated and involves children in active learning. Through involvement with different issues in the units studied, children develop the same set of basic skills encountered in a traditional school plan. Teachers are responsible for content and for providing continuity of experience and opportunities for learners. Classroom social interactions, which are important to curriculum development, are provided through shared experiences, flexible groupings, interactions with the teacher, and opportunities for children to reflect on their learning.

A constructivist at work is presented in the following vignette, as one teacher tells visitors about her Grade 3 unit on trees (adapted from Scully, Seefeldt, & Barbour, 2003).

I operate my third grade by establishing a flexible schedule, so I can reorganize if interests and projects require more time. I have a framework of the subject-area skills that children should acquire that I pulled, along with themes and unit suggestions, from the curriculum guides. Beyond that, I try to be flexible enough to respond to children's interests and needs.

Planning for our tree unit went something like this: Children were just finishing explorations on different birds when one child brought in an apple tree branch about to blossom. Children had all sorts of questions, so I suggested that our next unit could be on trees. I encouraged children to bring some books about trees, and I gathered several, as well. The next day, I read Parnall's Apple Tree, and we discussed some of the things in the book that interested the students. Some of the concepts were that trees provide food for us and for other animals, trees change during the seasons, trees provide joy and delight, and trees provide shelter for some creatures.

Then I thought of some activities we could do that connected to our reading, social studies, and science curricula. In reading, we're looking at settings for stories; in social studies, we're doing mapping skills; and in science, we're studying the environment. I began to devise some projects that would engage the class in learning more about trees and their importance to the environment but that would still be linked to subject-area skills.

In reading, children are studying story settings, and from reading Apple Tree and other books, they'll examine settings and thus learn about the environments that trees need.

In social studies, children are studying mapping skills. On global maps, children will locate places where our "tree stories" take place. Children will then make topographical maps and place models of their trees appropriately. In art, they'll portray different houses that animals develop in trees.

In writing, children will reflect in journals what they're learning about trees and what is of particular interest to them. Because children are always encouraged to list new and interesting words, as they attempt creative writing, they'll have a list of new words to use.

In science, we'll examine the different foods that trees provide. We will collect some of these foods for snacks on different days.

Some of the presentations or projects will involve the whole class, and others will require children to work in groups or individually. As a total group, we'll discuss the findings and plan out the different projects: topography, reading discussion groups, snack preparations, creative stories or reports, and house-building projects. Four basic work areas will be prepared: maps, house-building, food-preparation, and arts and creative writing. Depending on children's discoveries and their interests, they can elect to be part of two, three, or all four activities. There will be a formal independent reading time, when children read

Curriculum covers all disciplines, including physical education.

Dan Floss / Merrill

from their selected books, and then the children will meet in a discussion group to share information from the stories. Discussions during snack time and after reading time, children's journals, their creative stories, and their art projects will provide me with information on what students have learned. At the end of all our units, I will ask children to reflect on what new information or skills they've acquired. You see, I'm trying to get them to become aware of their own learning.

The typical day in a constructivist class is organized through various routines, projects, meetings, and skill sessions. Activities are usually followed by evaluations, sharing, and exhibiting. A typical schedule for a constructivist school day is shown in Figure 9–3.

REFLECTION

Share with your classmates any experiences you have had so far in a constructivist classroom. If no one has had such experiences, then think of what you have read, then comment on your feelings about the teacher's tree unit in the vignette just related.

9:00 A.M.	Meeting time, greeting friends, checking and discussing day's schedule
9:30	Reading and writing workshop
10:30	Class meeting
10:45	Recess
11:00	Skill session on subtraction
12:00 noon	Lunch
12:45 P.M.	Class meeting
1:00	Independent work time for projects
2:00	Art and music sessions
2:30	Presentations, publishing, and wrap-up
3:15	Closing time

Figure 9–3   Constructivist Classroom Day—Grade 2

The advantage of doing projects in the cognitive process and constructivist programs is that such work is more informal and lends itself to experimentation and collaboration. Assignments tend to hold children's interest longer, especially when they get to help choose the topics and how to extend their study. Some sessions will seem disorganized, with children searching for materials or collaborating with others, but the advantage is that the approach to mastering material is self-selected. In these programs, children feel empowered for much of their own learning and grasp concepts and skills far beyond traditional grade expectations.

A major disadvantage to constructivist plans is that projects can become trivial or repetitive. In addition, some teachers have difficulty incorporating or inserting reasonable skill development sessions in the investigations that classes propose.

Formal Curriculum in Personal Relevance Programs. A truly child-centered program is difficult to describe, because all content emerges from the interests of the children involved. As an illustration, however, imagine that a small group of children has elected to consider frogs for a week, whereas other groups or individuals are focused on different topics. The classroom teacher and aides would provide as much help, guidance, and support as possible for their study, and a scenario such as the following might develop:

- Teachers accompany children on a visit to a nearby wetland after they decide to observe frog habitats.
- Discussions about materials collected follow the visit, and children ponder ways they wish to continue.
- Teachers, children, and helpers assemble books, magazines, films, and other resources, while students explore whatever they wish.
- The group shares with the entire class, and children brainstorm, or at least discuss, how they could learn more. They consider books, museum exhibits, presentations by persons in ecology departments, and interactions with local specialists and other classrooms or

nearby schools. New members might join the group at this point.

- Students incorporate writing and mathematics into their study by keeping journals on experiences and planning experiments, such as hatching frog eggs in different media. Teachers help and provide information or instruction when needed.
- The project evolves into a larger study of swamp ecology as it serves the interests of students and continues to be a stimulating topic.
- Evaluation is through documentation: children's journals and other writing, art and music compositions, skill mastery list, and other expressions of children's work. See *The Hundred Languages of Children* (Edwards, Gandini, & Forman, 1998) for an extensive listing of assessment modes.

Certain homeschooling programs are conducted along this line, and evidence shows that children's interest blooms when they are given chances to investigate their surroundings. One fascinating example is the plan the Colfax family used with their four sons (Colfax & Colfax, 1992).

The content examples presented here are all explicit or intended curriculum activities of a school program. This means that teachers feel a responsibility to plan for and to steer children toward some substance or experience. As we have stated, other forms of curricula also are associated with all schools. The informal curriculum is acknowledged by most educators and parents as part of what we come to school for. The hidden curriculum is rarely apparent to teachers and parents, but its effects often outlast those of the explicit curriculum. These curricula are discussed in the following sections.

Informal Curriculum

Much of the informal curriculum is implied and unplanned; it consists of those learnings teachers and parents expect to come about but rarely bother to state, plan for, or present to children. The informal curriculum has to do with socialization into school and community life, and it is similar to the etiquette of other institutions in children's lives.

This curriculum includes events such as teachers' expecting their new students to discover procedures for lining up, passing in papers, getting recognition in class, or responding. No one plans the activities, but all are expected to follow the rules. Recall the vignette in Chapter 4, where Greg helped Philip understand their teacher's request. Informal curriculum was at work when Greg instructed the younger child. The teacher expected Philip to know the practices, but because he did not, the older child interpreted.

All teachers expect children to internalize a number of general school procedures and protocols. Some teachers, particularly those in primary schools, are more cognizant of this area of informal curriculum than are others. For instance, they are aware of the need to remind children of appropriate responses and helpful communication. They often discuss possibilities for team efforts and list things to consider. We find the following items of informal curriculum in typical U.S. schools:

- School activities are organized and differ from spontaneous situations at home. Children are expected to differentiate, adapt, and fit in without any focused instruction.
- Competition is a fact of life in U.S. schools. Teachers employ notions of being first, being best, and achieving more in all areas of classwork and sports. Children are expected to absorb this value.
- Time and schedules are paramount in school life. Children are expected to work on command, change quickly to new ventures, and meet deadlines many times per day.
- Group activities are common in all schools. Children are expected to learn group roles and participate in groups cooperatively and smoothly.

The home curriculum is basically an informal curriculum (refer to Chapter 8), and learning accrues there in a haphazard but reasonable way. Few formal or organized experiences are associated with the home—exceptions are music lessons, homework, and the like—unless parents have developed a homeschooling program. Language skill is a good example of the informal home curriculum. Families have no planned times for language instruction. By the time children enter kindergarten, however, they have almost complete control of their native language, and this has all come through interaction with family, caregivers, and peers.

Language development begins early and, though subject to direct instruction in school, is mainly the result of the informal curriculum. The results from family to family can be tremendous. For example, Hart and Risley (2003) pointed out the wide gap between different children's vocabulary development by age three. The differences relate to the vocabulary, quality of language, and amount of "encouraging words," as opposed to "prohibitions" in the child's parental and community social class. Simply put, children in welfare-dependent homes hear one half as many words as children in the average working-class family and fewer than one third of those heard in a professional family. The differences are found to exist as late as ages nine and ten. Language development is only one part of the informal curriculum, but it certainly affects many other areas of learning.

Hidden Curriculum in Homes, Schools, and Communities

We have defined *curriculum* as those experiences that make up children's waking hours, and when you consider carefully, you can see that the thousands of impressions, interactions, and experiences children have each day do amount to a curriculum. Children constantly receive stimuli that contribute to learning. Some stimuli are intentional; adults plan things that children are "supposed" to learn through school, home, or community instruction. Some learning is unintended, however; it comes about in accidental ways as children observe phenomena, experience situations, and associate with others. This is often called the hidden,

Children constantly receive stimuli that contribute to learning, and they often receive it in accidental ways, as children observe phenomena, experience situations, and associate with others.

Bangor Daily News

or covert, curriculum and makes a considerable impression on the growing child.

Unintended learning relates to a child's gender, social class, race, and ethnicity, although its extent and effects are frequently ignored. Examples include the nonverbal language features of tone, facial expressions, and gestures, as well as the patterns found in the family's **social network**. Recall Jana's drawings from the vignette in Chapter 3 about her family configurations at different periods in her life. These drawings indicate Jana's evolving hidden curriculum.

Children continue to encounter the hidden curriculum after entering school. When we examine it closely, we find that the hidden curriculum occupies a large part of the school day. For example, first-grade teachers plan about five hours of in-class time per day, but when calculating the time actually spent on planned activities, we often find that less than one half is spent on task work. In fact, some **time-on-task** studies reveal that primary classrooms in some cases were on task less than one hour of the total day (Good & Brophy, 1986). This leaves a large amount of in-class and out-of-class time, in addition to time spent going

to and from school, given over to the hidden curriculum. Whether beneficial or negative, the hidden curriculum is a potent force in any child's learning.

Ryan only shrugged when, during dinner, his father asked him about his school day, but later when they were reading the comics in the newspaper, some things came up about a new child in Ryan's class.

"I think Charlie takes money," Ryan said.

"Oh, really," said his dad.

"Yeah, he had three quarters that he spent on candy at Ed's Variety today ... said he found 'em."

"Maybe he did," his dad replied.

"Yeah, but he didn't know where. . . . I think he stole 'em."

"Has Charlie been here visiting?" Ryan's father asked.

"Nope. I asked him over last week, but his dad don't let him go places. It's funny, 'cause he knows a lot."

"Oh, that so?"

Ryan nodded and volunteered, "He told me all those dirty words on the fence back of the variety store."

"Hmmm, well . . . when . . .," his dad began.

Ryan continued as he picked up the comics again, "There's those funny red marks on Charlie's arms. I'm gonna ask him tomorrow if we walk home from school."

Ryan is a seven-year-old doing well in his traditional second-grade class, but you will note a host of items he is learning that are unrelated to school objectives. In his walk home with the new boy, Ryan is encountering a hidden curriculum. Its features are unrelated to his formal school curriculum, but the stimuli: scatological language, questions about theft, and hints of abuse all have an impact on Ryan.

The covert or hidden curriculum for at-risk children can, of course, have a negative impact and may have heartrending consequences. Aspects of these experiences surface in media reports describing particularly poignant family situations. The distressing accounts of children's lives given in Chapter 4 present all too graphically a savage curriculum that cries out for redress.

Gender, social class, race, and ethnicity, plus previous learnings, determine what children learn about themselves. For example, children may be encouraged by the words "You can be anything you want to be." The negative effects of a bombardment of statements such as "Girls can't climb trees, but boys can," "Mommies can't be doctors," or "Blacks aren't allowed," however, influence a child's perception about life.

Children are always learning about others, and this kind of learning can affect their treatment of other children. For example, a White middle-class man can get an exaggerated message about his superiority in a physical accomplishment. Girls may feel less qualified than boys because of remarks or assignments, and a Black child feels chastened when she senses intolerance. As the following vignette shows, teachers often, if unwittingly, reinforce these notions.

A poorly dressed Pauline sat down at a first-grade table to work with two other children on a learning center. She is told by Andrea and another well-dressed child that she can't sit there because she smells. Feisty Pauline began to battle for her rights, but her teacher intervened and said, "Pauline, you'll have to sit elsewhere today. Andrea was here first and doesn't want to work with you now."

When a number of events such as this occur, Andrea acquires the feeling that she has more

rights, while Pauline will take away from the experience negative feelings about herself and her ability to participate.

Adult attitudes, values, and interests are communicated not only through language but through the organization of the classroom, structure of the day, and the choice of children called on most often (Webb et al., 2007). Some features of the **covert curriculum** for at-risk children can have a very negative impact, and too often we find a savage curriculum unfolding for children in America's underclass.

REFLECTION

Brainstorm about the things you learned via the hidden curriculum in your own elementary-school days. Do some of your classmates' experiences surprise you?

Multicultural Education

Multicultural education emerged in response to the concerns about educational equity in the United States. The term is used in various ways to describe programs and practices that schools have developed to ensure that all students—regardless of their gender, social class, abilities, or ethnic, racial, or cultural characteristics—have equal opportunities to learn in school (Banks & McGee-Banks, 2005). Because schools are social systems with many interrelated parts and variables, multicultural education aims to help change the culture of the school. This may take the form of integrating content in the formal curriculum and including a variety of cultures and groups, to illustrate key concepts. It may also include acknowledgment of negative attitudes toward different groups that children bring with them from home and become part of the hidden curriculum. Through prejudice reduction activities, students are guided in devloping positive attitudes toward various racial, ethnic, ability, and cultural groups.

Although curricular inclusion and prejudice reduction are important parts of multicultural education, the larger culture of the school must also be examined and restructured by teachers and other school staff to ensure that equity is being promoted for all. Teachers may need to modify their teaching to facilitate the learning of various groups, adminstrators may need to investigate interactions among groups and the differences in achievement and participation by different groups. School personnel and families will need to come together to explore these issues and make the school a place that is welcoming to all. A large body of literature exists about multicultural education that can help guide you in understanding how to be more inclusive and fair to all children (Derman-Sparks, 1989; Ramsey, 2004; Sleeter & Grant, 2006)

Special Education and Curriculum

Like members of minority groups, children with disabilities have been excluded from school and discriminated against in the past. Over the last three decades, legislation has been enacted that provides all children with a free and appropriate education and great strides have been made to remove barriers for an equal education to those who differ in their abilities.

As we noted earlier, 12% of American schoolchildren have special needs, and you will encounter some children in almost all schools who do require special services or some adaptation of instruction. If you work in urban areas where poverty and minority representation is considerable, you will find even larger proportions of children diagnosed with special needs. As we have noted before, poverty is linked to more problems in health, social situation, and learning difficulties. Some scholars question the underrepresentation of children of color in programs for gifted and talented, though, and their overrepresentation in special education (Heward et al., 2005). Some have raised the issue of the influence of a child's culture, class, or gender on their being labeled disabled.

Initially, **mainstreaming** brought children with disabilities into regular schools and classrooms in limited ways, such as for art, music, and other "specials" but usually not for instruction in academic areas. **Inclusion** emerged in the 1990s, and many students with special needs became part of a regular class and participated fully in that class for almost the entire day. Inclusion practice has generated more controversy among regular and special-education teachers, but in its true sense, it calls for teachers (regular or special) to modify content, adjust material, secure more support services, and take other measures to enable the learner with special needs to enjoy the full life of a classroom. The most practical way to accommodate these children in the regular classroom is by using a team approach in planning for all children in the classroom. Such an approach would require more small group and individualized instruction. This requires a huge leap for the typical traditional educator and would move instruction toward a constructivist approach. See Chapter 6 for a more detailed description of programs and approaches on working with children with special needs.

Almost all educators subscribe to the principle of including a large majority of children with special needs in regular schools and regular classrooms. Over a period of a generation (and numerous defining court cases), this adjustment has come to pass. A debate continues on how best to accommodate students with severe disabilities. Full inclusion for this last group involves restructuring classrooms, and adding extra services and more personnel, as well as seriously modifying curriculum content and delivery of that content. You will meet educators and specialists with differing opinions about whether full inclusion is workable.

RESULTS OF SCHOOL EDUCATIVE PROCESSES

A growing body of research (Kostelnik, Soderman, & Whiren, 2004) indicates that the presence of certain structural components are necessary for optimum results of the school educative process. A stable staff, including well-trained teachers with knowledge of child development and content who are able to establish warm and attentive relationships with children is foundational. Safe, stimulating environments with appropriate materials and a well-rounded program that focuses on physical, social, and cognitive learning are also essential. Finally, quality schools support parents, encourage their involvement, and link community services to families.

Millions of children attend schools in the United States each year. Also each year, more than four million young Americans (this includes dropouts) move beyond school to the workforce, college, homemaking, or unemployment (U.S. Bureau of the Census, 2002b). It is common knowledge that outcomes for differing educational environments, vary greatly, and this variance ranges from the sublime to the pathetic.

Some schools have an easy time. Schools accepting highly motivated, advantaged students with few deficits in background and experience frequently produce quality results. With skilled administrators and energetic and focused staff members, students from these schools measure up

against all community expectations. Selective private schools and well-endowed suburban schools in affluent areas show these results.

Other schools are far different and need extraordinary energy from all sources to produce even modest gains. This problem escapes the attention of many of America's middle-class community agencies. Schools in disadvantaged areas frequently enroll children with problems in nutrition, health, and socialization, and even emotional stability. The background of deprivation has taken a toll on interest and outlook and all things of an educational nature, for day-to-day survival is the paramount consideration in the American underclass (Bradley, 2002; Ipsa et al., 2006). The comprehensive nurturing from community families needed to engender children's self-esteem and a positive self-concept or readiness is often lacking. These schools need outstanding teachers and skilled administrators, but they often get neither, as staff assignments are often determined by length of tenure. How can

APPLYING THESE CONCEPTS TO YOUR WORK WITH CHILDREN AND FAMILIES

Schools differ in structure, view of curriculum, equipment, and space. School leadership varies, as does the skill of staff members in charge of day-to-day activities. The background, support, and preparation that enrolled children possess will differ. Differing curriculum orientations and various teaching strategies and techniques will all fit into the teaching equation. Keep in mind that all can be successful.

- Think about your own elementary education and the curricular orientation that was in evidence. Discuss your recollections with others who may have had different school experiences.
- Consider your own philosophy of education and what you believe about how children learn and your role as a teacher. Compare your beliefs

with the Typical Curriculum Orientations listed on Table 9–1.

- Design a template of a classroom that would be in keeping with your philosophy. Then share the sketch with colleagues and ask if they can detect your perspective.

In the final analysis, teachers must know who they are, where they are going, and the best ways to get there. If you plan to teach, this means that you must have a clear grasp of your skills and your preferred work style and then be able to see how that style matches children's interests and work habits. Teachers who are not self-aware in this way must depend on circumstances to place them in comfortable situations with eager students.

schools like this compete? The answer is that they cannot. Most will continue to struggle unless or until they receive massive investments of support and supplements from outside and well-organized cooperative action with the community served. (In Chapter 12, we identify productive models for school–community partnerships.)

SUMMARY AND REVIEW

In this chapter, we have discussed the dimensions of school curricula, the philosophical orientations associated with curricula, and the variation in practices and structure found in U.S. schools. Philosophical orientations differ from school to school and from teacher to teacher, and orientation greatly affects the content teachers consider for classrooms as well as how teachers approach instruction. The physical organization of a school also reflects the school's philosophical orientation.

Formal, informal, and hidden curricula exist in all types of schools. The results of school educative processes can be positive or negative, and all results have implications for the school program, the surrounding community, and the families involved.

Schools are taken for granted in U.S. society, and parents send their children to schools expecting them to partake in productive activities. The public expects schools to provide care and safety for children, the stimulation of minds and bodies, and the skills and knowledge necessary for participation in adult life.

In productive schools, irrespective of curriculum orientation, children will master basic literacy skills, interactive and social skills, general study habits, computational skills, social and natural science concepts, and the ability to experiment and learn through investigation. All schools have a duty to meet these basic features of curriculum, although each may approach this duty differently. Schools showing minimal or incomplete results for these basic expectations cannot survive in the 21st century.

SUGGESTED ACTIVITIES AND QUESTIONS

1. Observe the classroom behaviors of the teacher in your field assignment and determine from things said, assignments given, and general demeanor which of the philosophical orientations that teacher holds.

2. Take the matrix presented in Table 9–2 and use it to assess teaching styles of your college instructors, high-school teachers, other teachers you recall, and classroom teachers you are in contact with now. Which quadrant contains the most?

3. Develop a profile of interests, habits, and skills on one child you are working with now or one you know well. Determine which curriculum orientation would suit the child best. Defend your choice.

4. Interview several children to identify the informal curriculum they experience at school. You will have to start them off with suggestions about lining up or taking breaks, and so on. Try to determine yourself, or get them to tell you, where the expectations originated. Were these rules stated, picked up from others, inferred, or carried over from other years?

5. Select two vignettes from this text and identify examples of the hidden curriculum contained in the stories.

6. Do a 15-minute observation of a classroom and list the features of the informal curriculum you find there. Discuss and compare your observations with others observing in the same room.

RESOURCES

Books

Bowman, B. (2003). *Love to read: Essays in developing and enhancing early literacy of African American children*. Washington, DC: National Child Development Institute.

Gay, G. (Ed.). (2003). *Becoming multicultural educators: Personal journey toward professional agency*. San Francisco: Jossey-Bass.

Noguera, P. A. (2003). *City schools and the American dream: Reclaiming the promise of public education*. New York: Teachers College Press.

Ramsey, P. G. (2004). *Teaching and learning in a diverse world: Multicultural education for young children*. New York: Teachers College Press.

Films and Videos

Cooperative Learning [Video, 33 min]. (2002). Establishes the rationale, benefits, and step-by-step process for using cooperative learning in the elementary classroom. New York: Insight Media.

Leading for Diversity [Video, 45 min]. (2004). Demonstrates four key principles for improving ethnic relations in K–12 schools. New York: Insight Media.

Planning Instruction [Video or DVD, 29 min]. (2006). One in a series of four selections in the "Succeeding as a Teacher" series, which also includes *Instruction for All Students, Managing the Learning Environment,* and *Communication and Professional Growth.* Crystal Lake, IL: Magna Systems Video.

Organizations

Association for Childhood Education
  International (ACEI)
17904 Georgia Avenue
Olney, MD 20832
http://www.acei.org

Association for Supervision and Curriculum
  Development (ASCD)
1250 N. Pitt Street
Alexandria, VA 22300
http://www.ascd.org

National Education Association
1201 16th Street, NW
Washington, DC 20036
http://www.nea.org

Web Sites

http://www.highscope.org   This Web site provides complete information about the High/Scope Curriculum.

http://www.ncss.org   This is the Web site of the National Council for the Social Studies.

http://www.nsta.org   This is the Web site of the National Science Teachers Association.

http://www.projectapproach.com.   This Web site contains information about this approach and includes background on the philosophy of the program and practical ideas for implementing projects in the preschool or elementary classroom.

http://www.reading.org   This is the Web site of the International Reading Association.

Chapter 10

Curriculum of the Community

The child is an ever-attentive witness of grown-up morality—or lack thereof; the child looks for cues as to how one ought to behave, and finds them galore as we parents and teachers go about our lives, making choices, addressing people, showing in action our rock-bottom assumptions, desires, values, and thereby telling those young observers much more than we may realize.

(Coles, 1997, p. 5)

The purpose of this chapter is to examine the rich but often overlooked features of the community for children's learning. Just as we have a curriculum of the school and of the home, we also have a curriculum of the community. After reading this chapter, you will be able to do the following:

1. Describe how organizations and agencies within a community provide many and varied learning opportunities for children.

2. Compare community education that is purposeful and planned by members of community organizations and agencies with **incidental learning** that occurs informally.

3. Specify how children's learning within the community is a result of their observations of how things work and how people interact with materials and other people.

4. Discuss how the physical, emotional, and moral attributes of a community support and extend or hinder children's opportunities.

5. Explain how social networks, involving both adults and peers, affect the amount and quality of learning children derive from their community.

Although the family and school are important influences on children's development, the community also contributes to their knowledge and understanding. Most commonly associated with our dwelling places in neighborhoods and towns, the concept of community also includes the kinship community of extended family and close friends and communities of the mind, such as religious organizations and interest groups (Noddings, 2005). As is the case with the family and school curricula examined in Chapters 8 and 9, the community curriculum is affected by the type,

location, cultural aspects, and physical makeup of the region, plus the social networks established by its inhabitants.

In the 21st century, the gap between the rich and poor grows wider, and many adults and communities try new strategies to overcome the social, economics, and physical environment that hinder some children's positive learning. Most investigators agree that children growing up in affluent communities or with strong parental support have a greater chance of school success than those in poor communities with high crime rates, transient family life, and poverty where parents have trouble just providing shelter and food (Adelman & Taylor, 2002). Under poor and depressed conditions, the school is the social setting typically stretched to assure that all students succeed. All of society, however, needs to examine the structures that produce inequality for learning and develop integrated approaches to support children's development. Community social agencies, entertainment outlets, and business organizations have an obligation to work with schools to find new solutions. We have some evidence that this effort works.

Chapter 1 presented the many influences on children's learning, and we found that all curricula are affected by these influences. Although we find great differences among communities, we also find many commonalities that suggest similar educational experiences.

Every community is composed of interconnected social systems, and how the people of these systems relate to one another greatly affects children's learning and development (Bradley, 2002; Bronfenbrenner, 1979). Various organizations within the community offer different aspects of curriculum, and children learn just by being exposed to these organizations. In addition, the physical, moral, and emotional environments children encounter in their immediate neighborhoods enhance or hinder intellectual development. Whereas some communities deliberately plan additional opportunities for children's growth, others seem oblivious to how their organizational structure affects children's learning and make no attempt to remove barriers.

In this chapter, we consider the context of the wider community and its potential for helping children grow. We examine community organizational structure and suggest how some of the diverse agencies "educate" children. The physical and social–emotional environments in a community together constitute a basic support system for all families, one that enables parents and child-care staff to stimulate children in different ways. In some communities, however, the physical and social–emotional environment is so destructive that children are placed at great developmental and educational risk (Small & Newman, 2001). There, the supportive interaction of community agencies with families and schools is key. The level of children's positive participation in the community and the social networks that they establish depend on that interaction.

COMMUNITY STRUCTURE AFFECTS CURRICULUM

Although every community varies in structure and the kinds of services available to its citizens, we find similar human, natural, and material resources. Figure 10–1 presents a partial listing of these resources. A child's neighborhood may be in a city, small town, suburb, or rural area. The resources available in each of these settings will vary, but all provide the bases for a community curriculum. Whether in a rural area or in a city, children observe different aspects of nature. Trees, birds, animals, and stars at night are more available to rural children, but city children also witness the warmth of the sun, wetness of rain, scrubby grass and small plants pushing up between concrete slabs, and ants carrying away crumbs. Southern children know palm trees; northern children,

deciduous or fir trees; and southwestern children, juniper and cacti. Weather provides learning experiences, as well. Some children experience tornado conditions and the haphazardness of destruction. Others may enjoy long spells of soothing hot weather but then learn the distress of drought.

Children constantly learn from persons in their neighborhoods. How much learning children gain from others besides kin in the home depends on how much association they have, how safe their neighborhood is, and how many community services and agencies their parents use. In safe neighborhoods, children have more freedom to move beyond their homes and to observe and interact with people involved in various activities and occupations. How people dress, what distinguishes young people from old, how adults treat each other and children in passing, and many other qualities and interactions teach children about life. In violent neighborhoods, children also learn important lessons from observation of community activities, but too often, out of fear, parents must confine their children or closely supervise them. This limits children's opportunities for physical exploration and thus limits their intellectual and social experimentation in favor of simple survival skills (Magnuson & Duncan, 2002).

Children learn from various materials generated by people in society. Some materials, such as a brochure about good eating habits for primary-school-age children, are prepared with educational intentions. Toy companies induce adults to buy various items for children, and often advertisements will suggest a device's educational value. Children also learn from many other materials, including those that adults consider junk. From observing, touching, smelling, and manipulating wood scraps, earth and sand, Styrofoam, bottles, shells, cans, and the like, children learn variations in texture, size, shape, and smell. Without adult support, the learning may be minimal, or the result could put children in harm's way. Even so, children left on their own do gain considerable knowledge about materials around them.

NATURAL RESOURCES

Plants, animals, insects, fish, minerals, bodies of water, beaches, parks, nature preserves, farmland

SERVICES

Education: Zoos, museums, libraries, schools, parks

Communication: Telephones, radio and TV stations, post offices, newspaper offices, computer networks

Entertainment: Theaters, music halls, movies, fairs, festivals, circuses, restaurants, TV and radio stations

Recreation: Playgrounds, church or community clubs, athletic facilities, ballparks, tennis courts, parks

Transportation: Airports, train and bus stations, taxis, gas stations, car rental agencies

Commercial: Department stores, grocery stores, pharmacies, different types of farms (orchards, fish farms, dairy farms), special shops (toy stores, ice cream shops, salons, pet stores, craft shops), factories, other business enterprises

Professional: Offices of physicians, dentists, lawyers, and other professionals, fire and police departments, funeral homes, courts, clinics and hospitals, political offices, university campuses, school department headquarters

Service agencies: Employment offices, social services and public assistance offices, counseling centers, food co-ops, mayor's office

Living environments: Children's and teachers' homes, apartment complexes, mobile homes, new home sites, real estate offices, retirement communities, **assisted living facilities**, and nursing homes

MATERIALS AND MEDIA

Print: Books, pamphlets, brochures, magazines and newspapers, advertisements

Audiovisual: Films, TV, radio, audio and video cassettes, compact discs, DVDs, computer programs, Internet sites, exhibits

Recyclables: Scraps of fabric or wood or carpet samples, buttons, ribbon, wallpaper samples, bottles, cans, boxes, wire, spools, cartons, used paper

SOCIAL NETWORKS

Adult: Friends, neighbors, colleagues and coworkers, social clubs, religious groups, sports groups, family members, community theater groups

Peer: Young relatives, school and neighborhood friends, club and team partners

ETHNIC ASSOCIATIONS

Contacts: Various languages, cultural festivals, religious activities, artistic expressions

Figure 10–1 Community Resources that Educate Children

Every community has **service agencies**, political establishments, **social–agencies**, and business enterprises. Just as schools and homes provide a curriculum, so do community establishments and agencies. The efforts, products, and resources of each agency will provide formal, informal, and hidden curricula, similar to the school environment.

Children learn variations in texture, size, shape, and smell from touching and manipulating earth, sand, rocks, and shells.

Belle Kuhn

Children acquire knowledge, values, and social skills (positive as well as negative) from their experiences within their communities and interactions with community workers. We will find, of course, no single established curriculum for a community, any more than we find a common curriculum for all families. Resources vary, and how these resources are made available, plus the family's and children's ability to make use of them, determine learning potential.

Service Agencies

Service agencies provide families with health, transportation, protection, communication, and professional services. These agencies provide experiences from which children gain knowledge, both through the formal presentation of materials and in informal ways. Formal educational experiences from most agencies have been carefully thought through, and prepared materials are directed toward parents or teachers to assist in instruction. Other materials or experiences are directed toward children. A child's first experience with the family

dentist is one example of a community professional "educating" young clients.

Since Rodrigo was three years old, he accompanied his mother to the dentist for her semiannual checkup. While his mother was in the chair, he would sit nearby with a few toys. One day, Dr. Garcelon asked him if he wouldn't like to sit up in the big chair where his mother had sat. As Rodrigo climbed up, the dentist allowed him to touch the instruments and told him what they were for. He encouraged him to press the water tap and to rinse his mouth from the paper cup nearby. Gradually, over two or three visits, he introduced all the cleaning instruments and even turned on the polishing brush so Rodrigo could see how it vibrated. At first Rodrigo refused to have the brush in his mouth, but gradually he became so intrigued with the instruments that he wanted to see what would happen. One day a small squirrel came to the dentist's window and chattered away. Dr. Garcelon and the young child took a moment to feed the squirrel before the dentist gave Rodrigo a toothbrush and toothpaste with verbal and written "picture" instructions on how to use the brush at home.

This dentist had a planned program for introducing dental hygiene to young patients. At first, children observed parents' experiences—a rather informal learning experience. Parental comfort and the dentist's reassuring ways provided a safe and secure environment for the next phase. The formal instruction on what happens in a dentist's chair was designed to build children's trust as well as to start children on the road to good dental hygiene. The pamphlet Rodrigo received had simple instructions, with pictures, so that even at age four, he could see how to brush his teeth. The squirrel's appearance was an accidental event, during which Rodrigo observed an animal close-up, discovered something about feeding animals, and experienced an adult's gentle treatment of a particular animal.

Just as teachers and homes vary in how they instruct children, so do people in various agencies and professions. Some dentists are not as thorough as Dr. Garcelon in giving information to parents, whom they expect to instruct children. Many medical professionals work with schools, childcare centers, and health fairs to provide free initial health checkups. In some communities, free health clinics (many as mobile units) are regularly available for needy families. It is through these avenues that materials and curricula on health care are provided by medical professionals.

Most community agencies provide materials that schools and parents can use to feature the functions of the agencies. Police and fire departments, for example, normally provide speakers for schools or encourage field trips to their stations. Some police officers and firefighters get special training in how to work with young children, and children who visit are allowed to climb, under supervision, onto fire trucks or into police cars. Department representatives wear their uniforms and explain the equipment they carry and use. They also explain what children are to do when a police officer or firefighter is trying to assist them.

Transportation Services

In a mobile society, transportation is often necessary for children to participate in community events. Children who live in cities may experience various forms of public transportation, whereas those in suburbs may travel primarily in cars.

Transportation in rural areas can be a limiting factor, as large distances may exist between homes and other facilities. Travel can also provide children with many enriching, as well as hostile, experiences, depending on the political, societal, or physical environment. An airport depot can be explored freely in a small airport, but at large terminals, children must be under close supervision.

In times of tight national security, young children's needs are often disregarded because of the nervousness of officials. After 9/11, the authors witnessed a three-year-old child being pulled from her father's protective arms and made to walk through the metal detector while in hysterics. Yet, at a less tense time, the official invited a child to watch what others did and then politely asked the child to remove her shoes and together they watched them go through the scanner. She then skipped happily through the machine, smiled at the guard, and retrieved her shoes. The few adults around her smiled as they observed the interactions.

Transportation agencies provide many formal learning experiences for children, as they collaborate with schools in planning trips to airports, train stations, or bus stops. Much of the learning about modes of travel comes from schools studying such a unit or from parents as children accompany them, or from materials (maps, brochures, schedules) that adults collect. Informal learning as children use different modes of travel is enormous. One six year-old's explanation of how she got from her home in Minnesota to visit her grandmother in Russia is a small example of the range of learning.

— In answer to her grandmother's question about her trip, an eager Galina replied in one breath. "It took a l-o-o-ng time, grandma, and I slept on the plane and I watched a movie. It was dark when Daddy put our luggage in the car and we drove to the airport. Daddy had to park our car, right Daddy, and Mommy and I took our luggage inside the station. I remember going through this machine and the man asked me to take off my shoes. We were in lots of lines and there were sooo many people. There was a man with a gun, and I sat close to mommy until he went, but mommy said he was just making sure we were safe. On the plane I fell asleep after we got some food on a little tray. Here in Moscow, we took a long escalator, and

then I think some kind of train. Anyway, after we got our luggage, we had to wait in a long line until someone looked at the little book with our pictures in it. I think it's a passport. Right, Mommy? I am so glad to see you, grandma! Just look at my red suitcase!! Uncle Vanya sent it to me—see, it has wheels, and it sure helped, 'cause mommy said I had to carry my own luggage. ⟶

Galina's parents capitalized on her experiences and discovered that she was aware of many other aspects of transportation. Her cards to her friends, her journal writing, her drawings, and her conversations with her relatives not only revealed what she had assimilated, but also reinforced her understanding of a new environment.

REFLECTION

After you review Figure 10-1 on Community Resources, consider each area and recall some things you have learned as a result of these resources. Share with classmates any memories of your own experiences the vignettes evoke.

Political Agencies

All communities have government agencies, school boards, and task forces or committees empowered by the community government to provide different types of community curricula. The management decisions these agencies make will affect—directly and indirectly—the social, intellectual, and physical development of children in that community. As with social agencies, political agencies often provide written materials, films, or audiotapes designed to educate the public about their functions or the community. Such agencies make use of newspapers, magazines, radio, television, and the Internet to carry their message to the public, and the assumption is that families and schools will then "educate" children.

In some communities, the formal curriculum on political organizations usually handled through the schools, is more apparent, especially during election years. Mock elections are held in some schools, using local political campaign materials.

Students sometimes visit local and state political offices, where teachers and political workers attempt to explain the functions and responsibilities of the resident officials. Children whose parents are active politically may begin to comprehend the functions, hierarchies and decisions of an area's political agencies. The political implications of messages are usually beyond the comprehension of primary-school-age children, however. Children whose parents use social services managed by political officials can acquire confusing notions, especially when their parents have difficulty obtaining services. The political knowledge that children gain from such experiences tends to be serendipitous.

In the United States, national policies for children and their families have only begun to be formulated in the past 30 years (Bogenschneider & Corbett, 2004). Unlike other wealthy nations, the United States lacks supports for family life in areas such as adequate parental leave and child sick leave, universal healthcare coverage for children, a living minimum wage, and affordable, quality child care (Olfman, 2005a). Consequently, available resources vary significantly from community to community.

Social policies established by community leaders affect the options and determine the resources of any family to establish networks and make use of available resources (Cochran & Niegro, 2002). For instance, people living in wealthier communities often are able to negotiate with political figures for funding of well-equipped and well-maintained parks or recreational areas. They also see that libraries and museums have appropriate materials and outreach programs. Citizens in affluent areas have better access to child-care support services, community-based activities, and protective and health services. They tend to be better educated and so have developed better **networking** skills, which enable them to access these services (Cochran & Niegro, 2002). Children reared in poor communities, on the other hand, are often discriminated against and have fewer opportunities for learning. Parents in these neighborhoods appear to have less clout with governmental and management agencies, and with less education thus have fewer skills that enable them to access fully the benefits of community learning. The following vignette illustrates different potentials for social, intellectual, and physical learning as a result of two different policies for park maintenance.

In Wexton, the recreation department provided a park with grassy areas and paths. There are two swings, one piece of climbing equipment, and a basketball court. Maintenance of the park is poor. Swings are always in disrepair; garbage and debris litter the ground. Parents who bring children to the area will briefly exchange a smile or a word with the homeless man who frequents the park and occasionally with adults rushing through it on their way to work or with those bringing dogs for an outing. Parents appear to allow their children to use the park for play, but they display little sense of coming here to meet other people. Parents are likely to discourage their children from interacting with others in the park.

In Overton, situated near a small shopping area, the community provided a small park with lots of climbing equipment, paths for tricycles, a basketball court, bicycle paths leading off into an open grove area, and benches where parents sit and supervise their children's play. The park is well maintained, with little debris. Paths are well cared for, as is all equipment. Park maintenance people are seen frequently cleaning up the area and have been known to remind the older, unsupervised children to watch out for others as they play. In this park, parents chat with each other, watch their children interact with one another, and often begin to develop friendships. There is a sense that children are brought for outings, but also that parental contacts with others in the neighborhood are expanded.

Children in these situations will learn many things in both parks, but the park in Overton, where more people, materials, and natural resources exist, has greater potential for positive learning opportunities. In both parks, one observes children gaining physical skills as they climb on equipment or play ball. Children use various strategies to engage other children in their play, and some appear to be skilled in interacting with other adults, such as when they crouch to pet a visitor's dog. There are differences, however.

In Wexton, there are fewer chances for personal interaction, because most parents discourage such interchanges, especially with "disreputable-looking characters." Park maintenance is poor, so children receive different messages about the value of a clean environment. Some adults passing through the park are seen picking up trash and throwing it in available receptacles, but children witness others carelessly dropping litter. More potentially dangerous spots exist in Wexton, and children learn to be wary of their environment and aware of the danger signals.

In Overton, a different learning potential exists. Safe paths for children riding bicycles and tricycles from their homes to the park provide more opportunities for expanded physical development. Adults feel more comfortable with each other. The ambiance is welcoming, and the sense of trust among adults provides a stronger sense of trust in children. The park is kept free of debris, and maintenance personnel do not hesitate to remind children about respect for their environment. On the other hand, opportunities for learning danger signals may be more limited.

The community policy of providing and maintaining a park varies in these two communities. These policies are management choices, which in turn are influenced by the residents' pressure (or lack of such pressure) for maintaining a safe environment. Certainly, adults' abilities to use the resources available in the parks either enhance or limit what is learned in both situations.

It is not just with parks that communities provide options for adults to develop the social networks that enable them to use their community more advantageously. Governmental policy is inextricably interwoven with a community's social fabric. In some communities, policies regarding social service agencies make it much easier for adults to get the services they need (Cochran & Niegro, 2002).

Darlene, a shy mother, had moved to a new community with her new baby and four-year-old son. She needed help but dreaded applying for food stamps at the Women, Infants, and Children (WIC) program because of unpleasant experiences she had had before. When in desperation she finally went, however, she was pleasantly surprised at the quality of support. A community health

organization had pressured the mayor's office into allow-
*ing food stamps to be distributed at their **well-baby clinic**.*
Also, a group of volunteers had begun a program of read-
ing with the babies and older children at the clinic while
the parents waited for appointments or discussed their
children's health and nutritional needs. Darlene and the
nurse discussed ways to entice children into good eating
habits, and during her first visit, one of the volunteers in-
vited Darlene to attend a parent support group for moth-
ers with new babies. At these meetings, Darlene gained
new confidence in herself, new skills in raising her chil-
dren, and new friends. ⟶ ↺

Political decisions can affect the community
curriculum presented to children. Not only is Darlene gaining help in feeding her children, but she
is also learning how to educate them about good
eating habits and learning to make social contacts
with others. Now she joins a group of mothers
where children play together while the adults visit
and exchange ideas of child rearing. In a more
subtle way, parents at the WIC office and in the
parent support group are exposed to models of
adults reading to and interacting with children,
and thus they may in turn provide expanded language experiences and positive social interactions
for their own offspring.

Social and Cultural Agencies

The more skilled parents become at securing community services, the more opportunities they have
to use other community resources, as illustrated in
the following vignette.

↺ ⟶ *Louisa's husband abandoned her and their two*
small children after they moved to a new state. Louisa was
left with little money and no extended family support. After
a few weeks, she swallowed her pride and went to a church
soup kitchen so that she and her children could have one nu-
tritious meal a day. A series of contacts with people at the
center led her to the social agencies in her community, where
she learned how to tap into resources for herself and her chil-
dren. It wasn't always easy, for some of the policies seemed to
hinder Louisa's progress. The support systems she began to es-
tablish for herself, however, enabled her to continue. Louisa
eventually was able to finish high school and find a part-
time job, and she now has a federally funded scholarship to
college. In the process, she expanded her network of friends

in the service areas so that she could use community pro-
grams to enrich her children's experiences, of which library
and museum programs and a two-week summer recre-
ational program were recent highlights. ⟶ ↺

Churches, libraries, theaters, and recreational
facilities are community agencies that supplement
children's education. As with all situations, some
children experience a richer curriculum than others.
How well families are able to use available resources
and how well agencies are able to reach all families
in the community account for some of the disparity.
These social and cultural agencies do not exist apart
from one another, as the vignette illustrates. A
church agency providing physical and social nurturance helped Louisa work through the governmental policies, which in turn helped her find other
community resources for her children.

Governmental policies, concerned with separation of church and state, can limit the resources
that a church receiving government funds can provide a community. Church leaders, concerned with
developing memberships, often wish to provide
religious activities for young people within schools,
but community policies normally exclude such
events. However, under the recent "No Child Left
Behind" legislation, such restrictions are beginning to change, so that "faith-based" organizations,
as well as nonprofit organizations, can receive
funding to provide supplemental educational services, such as after-school programs and summer
programs for economically deprived children
(Community Update, 2002).

Librarians, theater personnel, and museum
directors often try to develop programs with
schools whereby children are invited to cultural
offerings at their centers. Too often, though,
communities will not financially support such
programs, or they believe that children are missing "schoolwork" and so must not be permitted
to go. Those children whose parents have financial and social capital are able to profit by such
community curriculum offerings, whereas other
children are left out. Some cultural agencies
locate financial resources other than political agencies to help community programs expand their
curriculum to include more children and families.

Science museums, aquariums, and zoos have hands-on and formal presentations for young children.

Greg Mekras

In one New Hampshire community, when schools eliminated art programs because of cutbacks in funding, the local artists' association extended art lessons to all children in the community with help from a local community foundation.

Many social and cultural agencies provide a rich formal curriculum to children. Such settings have a strong impact on children's information-processing skills, as well as on their physical, emotional, and moral development, but unless all families have equal access to these opportunities, a gap will remain between those who can afford to participate and those who cannot. The Walters Art Gallery in Baltimore, for example, has obtained grant funding to rescind their entry fee, so everyone in the community can visit the museum, regardless of ability to pay.

Art museums like the Walters offer both art instruction and art appreciation, as do other arts organizations, such as orchestras, opera companies, and theaters. Often, theaters provide acting lessons, summer camp experiences, children's performances, and lectures about plays and playwrights. Not only do these groups want to enhance children's learning about the arts, but they also want to develop future audiences. Science museums and zoos often offer hands-on experiences and formal presentations for young children. National and state parks give various educational programs that emphasize education relating both to the park theme and to conservation and environmental protection (Johnson & Mappin, 2005). These groups hope to build future stewards of the environment (Orr, 2004).

Most libraries also seek to enhance children's appreciation of literature and learning through educational lectures, storytelling events, and book talks. Wilson (Wilson & Leslie, 2001) described a library program in which she uses guest speakers, media, Web sites, books, and hands-on experiences to enhance children's knowledge of the culture of Japan. The theme expands as children use reference books to find facts about Japanese food, celebrations, and cultural beliefs and storybooks that describe everyday life in Japan. Children who participate in these **literacy events** expand their language, reading, writing, and computer skills, as well as personal interaction skills and knowledge about where to find information.

Churches offer summer day camp and religious education classes, and many of which integrate art, drama, and music as a part of the instruction. Recreational facilities offer a wide array of courses in sports, such as gymnastics, basketball, golf, or archery, as well as health-related classes, such as aerobics, nutrition, and physical fitness.

As with curriculum in any context, children acquire a great deal of knowledge through the informal and hidden curricula of these social and cultural agencies. For example, posters announcing coming events and programs inform adults, but in indirect ways, they inform children as well.

In a local theater while awaiting a performance, a five-year-old observed an adult pointing to an announcement of the next production and commenting, "Oh, look, Bill Braunhof will be playing in Cats! I wonder what the dates are?" Running her finger under the date, she exclaimed, "Oh, too bad. It's Wednesday the 22nd, and we won't be here."

With no intention of teaching young children, theater personnel have provided materials that can and do instruct. The adult, in seeking information for herself, unwittingly demonstrated to the child that such a poster offers information and that pieces of that information are found in different places on the poster. The child may even have discovered that "C-a-t-s" spells *cats*, and recognized it when seeing it again, or that "22" can mean 22nd.

Sometimes such informal teaching is intentional. In Overton, the community librarian discovered that children would pick up, look at, and often take home books that were displayed attractively. He began to more carefully select for display outstanding books that had heretofore sat unused on the shelves. The quality of books selected by young readers took a quantum leap. The librarian then began to coordinate his efforts with units of study done by local teachers. The teachers were pleased to find children bringing into class these extra resources from the local library for current topics.

Community clubs are another means of educating children. Scout organizations, trail clubs, outing clubs, ski and skimobile clubs, and others often sponsor projects in which students participate with adults. Some take trips into the community and surrounding areas, where children cook outdoors, practice trail maintenance, clean up lit-

ter on roadsides, observe different natural phenomena, and learn lessons in getting along with others. Some lessons are intentional, and some are unexpected. On one such trip, three eight-year-old boys came upon a family of skunks in a meadow. Wondering what the skunks would do if startled, the children gently tossed some pebbles toward the nest. To their and the other campers' dismay, the boys learned how startled skunks respond.

REFLECTION

Examine the picture on page 268 and speculate about what the child may be learning. Is it an intentional curriculum of the museum staff, or is it accidental and informal learning? Consider one other community service that was meaningful in your life. How were you connected to that through your family or through your school?

As Lareau (2003) pointed out in her book *Unequal Childhoods* that a family's social class determines how much children will participate in community opportunites, some of which are fee-based. Low-income and working-class families may not have the money, transportation, or time to avail themselves of these extras or may not be aware of the many free programs presented by the local library. Organizations that reach out to this underserved group will help all children benefit from these experiences.

Business and Commercial Enterprises

All communities have business and commercial enterprises, many of which are located in large malls or along highways, although in some communities they still exist along main streets and are neighborhood shops. Wherever they are, these establishments have identifying marks to advertise what they sell or what service they perform. Intentionally and unintentionally, adults and older children help younger ones sort out information regarding such businesses. Drive or walk through any of these commercial areas and observe carefully what the buildings or shops look like, the signs advertising them around the community, the types of vehicles in the parking areas, and the displays in the windows to get a feeling for what information children learning about their world must sort through.

Children hear comments from adults, note certain identifying characteristics of buildings, and learn without specific instruction where to buy ice cream, get stamps, find interesting books, or buy a desired toy. Children begin to recognize similar and different shapes. The stop sign is always red and octagonal. Children may question why their parents are stopping or may even figure out from adult conversations what *stop* means. They learn to recognize their own car and eventually are able to find it in a large parking area.

Business enterprises distribute advertising circulars and put signs in shop windows. Such materials provide information about prices and the kinds of items a store sells. Window signs, especially in smaller communities, may also present information about events in the community. Children who become adept at using such resources acquire many skills about how to get information. They may also become skilled in using adults as resources for achieving certain ends. As with other curricula, how and what children learn depend on many factors, including the kind of community in which they live, their developmental stage, and how significant adults share such information with them.

Parents, of course, are major influences, and how much parents talk and interact with their children as they are involved in the community also influences children's learning. Sometimes an important community person compensates for parental neglect or disinterest. Comer (1988) told about a shopkeeper in his community who taught a child, whom everyone believed couldn't speak, to talk. The shop was a candy store, and the child would only point to candy when he entered the shop. By refusing to acknowledge the child pointing out candy, the owner gradually got the child to tell her what he wanted and then eventually to talk to her. In large and impersonal malls, the lessons learned may not always be so positive, but many clerks will take the time to answer children's questions and assist parents as they support children's learning. Many business enterprises have special programs or relationships that support children's learning. Chapter 11 discusses several examples.

Media

Media, in the form of educational and commercial television, Internet sites, electronic and computer games, and print material, expose children to a world beyond their immediate communities and contribute to their learning. Some of this learning takes place serendipitously, but adults who extend and enhance children's media experiences through activities, conversation, and reflection help to maximize the learning potential.

Clearly, media provide education for children, but concerns about the amount of time children spend immersed in media are on the rise. Of particular concern is the sexual content (Levin, 2005) and violence (DeGaetano, 2005) that appear on television, Web sites, and video games and the marketing to children that occur through these media. Some altruistic advertisements are aimed at drug or nutrition education, but most advertisements are directed at enticing children to be lifelong consumers (Horgen, 2005; Meier, 2003). A study of programs will show that the media have their informal and hidden curricula. Much of television, radio programming, and Internet sources are for adult consumption, but many children are exposed to programs that confuse, frighten, or misinform them when there is little or no adult guidance. The vast number of programs and information that children can connect to makes it difficult, even with adult supervision, to be assured that children will not be exposed to inappropriate materials.

Television. The Public Broadcasting System has for years provided appropriate educational programs for young children. These include *Sesame Street, Mr. Rogers' Neighborhood, Barney,* and *Teletubbies,* which in spirited ways introduce children to the alphabet, new words and concepts, and interesting stories and facts about everyday events. Extensive research on *Sesame Street* over the past 30 years (Fisch & Truglio, 2001) indicated that children watching the program were learning the alphabet, numbers, and vocabulary faster than children not exposed. Subsequent analysis of *Sesame Street* indicated, however, that rather than being a boon to disadvantaged children, the show was more likely to be watched by middle-class children, and the gains children maintained were dependent on adult reinforcement of concepts. Other research on educational television (Fisch, 2004) confirmed the importance of adult co-viewing shows with their children and using the content of the programs for further learning and enriched experiences.

On both educational and commercial television stations, science and social studies programs, story reading, and reenactments of children's literature offer rich educational opportunities. In addition, network educational offices often provide teacher or parent guides for assisting children in gaining more from these programs. Some learning from these programs may have an unintentional and perhaps undesirable effect, however. Children become accustomed to fast-paced materials and do not develop longer attention spans or the ability to sustain interest in events that aren't moving rapidly. Gutrel (2003) discussed the vast changes to children's use of new media and highlighted new concerns about attention span and brain processing that were noted 30 years earlier.

The average American child or adolescent watches approximately 3.5 hours of television a day (Gentile & Walsh, 2002). This amount of time takes away from other pursuits, such as reading, indoor and outdoor play, and socialization with other children. Studies have also indicated that other negative effects, such as an increase in aggressive and sexual behavior, obesity, and substance use, are associated with excessive television viewing of shows with violent and sexual content. Although parents are ultimately responsible for monitoring and limiting their children's television time, they can also use the television rating system and V-chip to block out inappropriate shows. The American Academy of Pediatrics also recommends that televisions be removed from children's bedrooms and that viewing be limited to one to two hours a day.

Internet. The Internet is now a part of many young children's learning environments. With access to the Internet, a child's world expands tremendously. Children have access to Web sites, chat groups, bulletin boards, and connections to individuals through e-mail, instant messaging, and home pages. In some ways, this larger networking is very positive, but the openness of the World Wide Web and its lack of regulation presents dangers to children. Adult-oriented material that a parent might find too sexual, violent, racist, or offensive is easily accessed and downloaded by young children (Lin, 2002). In addition, children may become the target of unwanted attention from adults, adolescents, other children, or advertisers. Some children become so involved with their cyber journeys that they become addicted and have difficulty reconnecting to their off-line peers.

Parents can take steps to protect their children from dangers posed by the Internet by using blocking or filtering software. They also need to educate their children about Internet safety and establish rules about the kinds of family information that a child can divulge. With safeguards in place, the Internet can support children's school work and enhance their interests, hobbies, and play. See Chapter 8 for guidelines on internet use.

Video Games. The United States video game market of nearly $10 billion in sales in 2004 (National Institute on Media and the Family, 2006) indicates the popularity and pervasiveness of this media in American homes. Children are being introduced to these games at younger ages and are spending increasing time playing them (Gentile and Walsh, 2002). These games appeal to some children because the children perceive them as fun ways to feel in control. They also give them opportunities to follow directions, learn computer technology, and achieve a sense of mastery as they move through the various levels of the game. Unlike television and the Internet, however, it is difficult to make a case for these games as being educational. Their purpose is largely entertainment, and many children and adults use gaming for relaxation and enjoyment.

With parental guidance, children can use the Internet to support their schoolwork and enhance their interests, hobbies, and play.

Vic Bider / Photo Edit Inc.

The amount of time that children spend playing video games can be problematic, however, because the games are often played alone and restrict children's interactions with others. The content of many games is also an issue as they have been cited as violent and sexist. Fortunately for parents, video games are rated with a logo showing age recommendations. Games are marketed to children as young as three years with an "EC" rating for early childhood, an "E" for children over six, and an "E10+" for children ages 10 and over. Although theses guidelines are helpful for parents, monitoring the content, limiting time spent playing games, and explaining why content is objectionable will further protect children from the ill effects of excessive game playing.

REFLECTION

Think for a moment about the media's impact on today's children and how this has changed during your lifetime. Are there positive and negative implications for the current situation?

Print Media. In nearly all families, we find printed materials in the form of books, pamphlets, magazines, and newspapers. Unlike with electronic media, parents have much more control when it comes to the kinds of print media that enters their home. Children observe parents and older children looking at and reading these materials and early on begin to imitate these literate behaviors. Many parents also begin reading to their children at a young age, and the youngsters learn to associate reading with pleasure and warm interactions with others.

Printed materials educate children through pictures and printed words. Children learn early that pictures relate to real objects and have names. As stories are shared, children learn more about their world. For example, when children read Parnell's *Apple Tree*, their knowledge and concepts expand as they view the artist's interpretation and hear language describing the different ways the familiar features of apple trees are used. Children have experienced apples, if not apple trees, but may never have realized that ants and other insects feed from the trees, as do birds, who feed on the insects.

Children grow emotionally and intellectually when they can find, through books, security in loving and being loved, even while learning academic content. In Bang's *Ten, Nine, Eight,* a loving father hugs and tucks in his child as the two count objects in the room. Such a book conveys, besides the knowledge of rational counting, many different messages to children. One child may have his understanding of a caring parent reaffirmed, whereas another child may realize that men as well as women can be nurturing. An Anglo child sees that African American children do things just like she does.

Children feel secure when they see that book characters like themselves can be angry, frightened, frustrated, hateful, sad, or lonely. They see models for resolving conflict and learn valuable lessons. In Zolotow's *The Hating Book,* children learn how misunderstandings come about when one listens to gossip and doesn't trust a friend.

Most newspapers have a special children's section, and some offer guidance on how to use the newspaper with children. Comics have always been a way of nudging children toward reading. Comer (1988) told how his mother always read the comics from three different newspapers to him and his siblings each Sunday. This undereducated mother instinctively realized the importance of rereading the parts that especially interested each child and how this would assist her children in learning to read.

The influence printed materials have on children is not necessarily positive, however. Many comic strips portray stereotyped characters and advocate violence as a way to solve problems. The excitement of Max chasing his dog with a fork in Sendak's *Where the Wild Things Are* may be so attractive to a four-year-old that a mother finds her child imitating the action with another child. Stories and other printed materials, as with television programs, also can reinforce prejudice and bias when characters of a different ethnic origin are interpreted as having the stereotyped characteristics of a certain cultural group. Fairy tales have been cited as reinforcing men and women stereotypes. It is possible to interpret such female characters as Cinderella, Snow White, and Rapunzel as passive women in need of rescue by active and handsome Prince Charmings.

Cornell (1993) maintained that stereotyping may be especially true for children coming from particular cultural heritages. For example, many European tales present witches as old, ugly, mean, and to be feared, but in Asian cultures, the old are wise, kind, and to be revered. The clash of cultures may be confusing, especially to new immigrants. In the 21st century, the globalization of technology is subsuming cultural and ethnic interests, priorities, and expectations across the planet (Dickey, 2003) in a way earlier media did not.

Further, not all books and printed materials are well written, and the language in some is stilted and uninteresting. Children acquire language and richness of expression from books. Hackneyed, mundane expressions do nothing to enrich a child's vocabulary or imagination. A rich curriculum can be provided through printed materials when adults are sensitive to children's acceptance or confusion about these materials and help them interpret printed matter in light of their own experiences.

When stories, other printed materials, television, computer programs, and Internet information are not comprehensible or within children's range of experience, then, without support from an adult, the influence may be harmful to a child's self-concept and to the child's emotional, social, or intellectual development. In order for children and thus society to benefit from this huge amount of community curriculum, parents, schools, and community members must work together to teach children how to make wise choices as they use the media tools and to learn important Internet behaviors as they use e-mail, chat rooms, **blogs**, and other means of communication. Community members have a responsibility to engage schools and parents in forming healthy policies regarding media.

REFLECTION

Reflect for a minute about your own family's use of broadcast programs and relate that to the use of print media in your home. How much is selected for young children?

PHYSICAL, SOCIAL, AND EMOTIONAL ENVIRONMENTS IN A COMMUNITY

The physical and social–emotional environments in a community provide a curriculum that both positively and negatively affects children's development. Children look to adults in the larger community and model their behavior on these adults. Usually, children look to parents as role models and will identify with their positive qualities, such as caring, loving, and protecting. Depending on their age, children often find attractive models in their peer group, among adults they know, and among media personalities (Anderson & Cavallaro, 2002).

Children's chances of becoming healthy, confident, and competent adults are greater when they have both a safe home environment and a safe neighborhood, in which they are able to play, explore, and form relationships (Swisher & Whitlock, 2004). Regrettably, today many children are exposed to dangers within their family situations, in their communities, and from unhealthy media programs. When too many risk factors exist (see Chapter 4), children's total development is affected. Emergent intellectual capacity, motor development, coping strategies, social–emotional development of trust, autonomy, a sense of self-worth, and the ability to benefit from the environmental curriculum can be hampered (Hamilton, Hamilton, & Pittman, 2004).

Social Networks

Children's ability to benefit from their neighborhood is influenced extensively by the social networks their parents have established. As children mature, they develop additional social networks within their peer groups. In earlier generations, family structures tended to be stable, and community members formed bonds that enabled them to look after each other's children and to some degree control children's peer groups. Nowadays, however, children and their families need community support more than ever because parental supervision is far less in **dual-income** and single-

parent homes (Adelman & Taylor, 2002; Bookman, 2004).

Adult Connections and Support. In today's society, adults are likely to move often during children's growing years, and children's development is affected by adults' ability to adapt to change (Lichter & Crowley, 2002). Some parents establish new relationships easily, thus helping their children profit by participating in neighborhood activities, but in general high mobility is a risk factor.

The ambiance of a particular neighborhood may be welcoming or threatening, making it easier or riskier to initiate social contact. For example, in one part of Eastern City, homes, streets, and sidewalks are well maintained. One residential street is a dead-end street with little traffic, so residents sit outside on doorsteps and watch their children play close to the street. Families moving into this community feel secure in reaching out to others. Children come to know the adults in the neighborhood easily and are able to interact with them.

In another part of Eastern City, broken bottles litter sidewalks, poorly maintained buildings restrict families from venturing out, and illicit activities are common. Adults and neighborhood gangs are in such conflict with each other that children feel unsafe, even in their own homes. The street violence causes such trauma for families that children have difficulty learning anything positive from any community source.

Rural and suburban neighborhoods also vary in providing physical and mental safety for inhabitants, which influences learning. Poverty is perhaps the greatest deficit, as it limits families in making the diverse social ties that enable children to participate in a neighborhood's growth opportunities (Cochran & Niegro, 2002; Lichter & Crowley, 2002). When children are able to move comfortably throughout their neighborhoods, socialization becomes more available, and children benefit.

Janice and Peter lived on the same street in look-alike houses in a large suburban neighborhood. Although the yards were all fenced, children felt free to visit from one house to the other, stopping to watch and ask endless questions of kindly neighbors. One day, Janice and Peter roamed and stopped to watch while one neighbor trimmed roses in her front yard and another washed his car. They even got to spray some water on the soapy car, getting a bit wet themselves. After a while they wandered onto a muddy area in another neighbor's backyard. Making a few mud balls, they proceeded to toss the balls at the neighbor's garage. When Janice's mother caught up with them, she obtained buckets and water from the neighbors and insisted that the children clean up the mess they had made. With help from some of the older neighbor children, Janice and Peter managed to get the garage quite clean.

That day, among other lessons, Janice and Peter learned a bit about the why and how of gardening, how cars are cleaned, and what makes water spray. They also discovered they would be held accountable for any mess they created. They learned about helping others when they received help from the older children. Of course, children's everyday lessons from the neighborhood are not always the ones for which adults might wish. Still, Cochran and Niegro (2002) pointed out that when children have more adults and older children with whom they do a variety of activities, they tend to do better in school. Children who have caring adults beyond family members to assist them in mastering skills and attitudes in a gradual way have greater **metacognitive** and problem-solving strategies. Children learn how to cope with their environment differently, depending on their circumstances.

Not all children have extended support, and many can have regrettable experiences that create serious barriers to their cognitive accomplishments. Kumove (1966) found that when children under age seven were able to move freely in their immediate environment, they became more independent than children whose parents found it necessary to keep them homebound. Children unable to move about in their community because of pervasive community violence often are unable to develop coping skills and thus are more likely to become aggressive or violent themselves (Swisher & Whitlock, 2004). If reforms are to take place in neighborhoods that are unsafe, these require help and support from schools. Some authorities contend that community-type schools are needed in

this case. Neighborhood schools would be places "where people from the neighborhood come to learn and play together; share experiences and wisdom; nurture each other; and strengthen young people, families, and the fabric of community life. . . . It becomes a home away from home" (Adelman & Taylor, 2002).

Peer Group Settings. Peers become strong socializing agents (Karcher, Brown, & Elliot, 2004). Both in school and in the community, children learn more about who they are and how to behave in society from their peers. When the cultural milieu is diverse and inclusive, children can learn different interactions and expand their repertoire of social and language skills (Trawick-Smith, 2006). Parents teach children moral and ethical values, but the peer group is powerful in setting the social tone and imposing behavioral patterns.

Even as young as 18 months, children learn how their actions affect others and thus begin the process of learning behavioral codes (Hartup, 1983). A toddler who tries to take a desired toy away from another child soon learns the consequences of the behavior. It may be an indignant yell; it may be a slap; it may be acquiescence and subsequent loss of a playmate. As children begin to form peer groups and play with one other, they begin to form rules of conduct so that they can continue to operate as a group. It is in peer groups that children learn to negotiate, problem solve, and compromise, to continue to play and work together. Some children will be more dominant than others and will learn the rules for domination and acquiescence. Children are often rewarded by **significant others** in the group for conforming, or they are ostracized (Elkin & Handel, 1989).

Children experiment with various roles (leader, compromiser, follower, negotiator, etc.) and discover from their peers how to act to fulfill roles. They also see how their peers respond to them. Children learn about their own abilities from their peers. They learn that they can run faster, jump higher, or read better as they compare their skills with others. The group also dictates what skills are prized, however.

Peers become socializing agents as children learn about who they are and how to behave in society from them.

Anne Vega / Merrill

Although parents teach children about gender roles, by preschool, peers begin to segregate into boy and girl groups that dictate what roles each group is permitted to play. A physician's daughter, after beginning preschool, insisted that her doctor mother was really a nurse. At school, she had learned in her play group that doctors are boys and nurses are girls, even though her teacher and parents insisted differently. In addition, children learn cultural and social differences as they interact with their peers. They compare notes about their own family's customs, values, and ways of doing things. Peer group acceptance or rejection can influence how individual children change their own behaviors (Bigner, 2006).

Sexual understandings and misunderstandings are learned from family, extensive media exposure, and peers. Many young children learn the physical difference between boys and girls by examining each other. They often learn about birth, when some "wiser" child informs them of their knowledge or misunderstanding. It is through such discussions, along with other teachings, that children figure out for themselves the confusing information they receive (Sadker & Sadker, 2005b).

Cognitive information and development of numerous skills come from children's interactions with peers. Children have rituals and routines, just as adults do. Older peers teach younger ones the chants and rhymes of childhood. Memory skills and counting, as well as physical endurance, are enhanced as children jump rope to such rhymes as "One Potato, Two Potato" or "First Comes Love, Then Comes Marriage." As they play together, children learn from more skilled peers how to climb higher, catch a ball, read a story, or add up their money for ice cream. Learning may result from a desire to compete with a peer or because the peer has more information and passes it on. Learning may also come because a new idea has been introduced and children need to test out the new concept.

REFLECTION

What games did you play in your neighborhood when you were growing up? Think about positive things you learned as a result of these interactions. Were there some aspects that may not have been so healthy? Did adults supervise any of the activity?

Billy was watching Ahmed copy words from a book he was reading. "Whatcha doing?" asked Billy.

"I'm making an "r" for red," replied Ahmed.

"Nunh, nunh, that's not an R. I'll show you how to make an R." Billy wrote a capital R.

Ahmed retorted, "Oh! That's a big R, and I'm making a little r!" After much discussion, Ahmed in disgust turned to his book. "Look," he pointed, "that says 'Red' and that says 'red.' See, that's a big R and that's a little r."

Ahmed has challenged Billy's thinking, so now Billy will examine writing in a new way. New learning has been opened up to him by a friend. Ahmed's scorn for his not knowing seemed to spur Billy on, for later he got a book and paper and came to sit beside Ahmed and tried to make the little *r*, asking his friend for help.

Not all learning from peer groups is positive. Gangs can be a destructive force in any society, as children seek approval and find that they must develop antisocial codes of behavior to be accepted. Some children can be targets for peer victimization, but when these at-risk children have a "best friend," this friendship acts as a strong buffer against such attacks (Orpinas & Horne, 2006). When a community provides opportunities for children to develop social networks among different adult and peer groups, children have more options. When this happens, the lure of destructive peer groups is lessened, and children are helped to find more positive peer associations.

Ethnic Community Contributions

As we noted in Chapter 3, most American communities are becoming ethnically diverse. In recent decades, immigration to the United States (both sanctioned and illegal) has intensified to such a degree that immigration can represent up to 50% of population growth in selected counties each year since 2000 (United States Census Bureau News, 2006). In addition, ethnic minority groups are dispersing throughout the United States. When observing the *American Demographics* minority population maps, we find only a handful of the neutral areas showing no increases in integration in 2005.

All of this means that our country is rapidly becoming a highly multiethnic nation, and schools need to take advantage of the dynamic aspects linked to ethnic differences in their communities. In almost all communities today, there is a rich mixture of culture and races from which children learn about differences and how to accept and learn about each other. Often, however, children do not understand their own culture, and in order to be enriched by another culture, it is important that children first understand their own culture and its variations. This understanding should be the start of multicultural education.

Schools can profit from the various ethnic cultures in learning about the richness of community life, and students learn to be analytical thinkers as they discover the cultural orientations of other persons in their school and community. In the past, schools have focused more on the outward manifestations of culture—clothing and celebrations—not recognizing variations of behavior. It is important to get beyond the stereotypic images that schools often have used in the past to present different cultures—Japanese women appearing with kimono, obi, and parasol, or a Hawaiian appearing barefoot with a grass skirt and leis.

Attainment in the arts, the special festivals and entertainment performances, plus business and commercial successes of ethnically different individuals in a community are highly visible areas for enhancing a multicultural curriculum. Comparing similarities and differences in the daily events of children in one community offers insights to another culture as well as variations within a culture. Becoming knowledgable about the history of a group of people is another way of learning about them and civil rights organizations like the Urban League, Anti-Defamation League, and the National Association for the Advancement of Colored People (NAACP) can provide some of this information. Individual ethnic groups may also have organizations and societies that can be useful in obtaining information about their culture.

We have to remember that the unique behaviors, language, learning patterns, and values of different ethnic groups are acquired for a reason. The fact that they differ from mainstream society means that these have a particular purpose in another cultural milieu, and when we seek to learn about and from the differences, we come closer to an appreciation of the rich cultural history we all have around us. If we have different cultures in our community, we should want to understand and appreciate their talents and traditions. Everyone is proud of his or her culture and background, and if given a chance to share it, will do something that enriches our knowledge. Some teachers have used the following objectives in seeking to acknowledge a community's various cultural groups:

1. Research the stories behind the food choices that different ethnic groups prize.

2. Uncover the history of the dances and music that each ethnic group possesses.

3. Compare different family schedules, approaches to rearing children, and ways different families praise individual successes.

4. Find out and record the stories behind the immigration journeys individuals in the community undertook to reach where they are now.

In one ethnically diverse classroom, a teacher extended the "homework" project designed for parent–child reading to promote different viewpoints. While reading In Monet's Garden to her class, Mrs. McCloud introduced a doll of Linnea, the story's main character, and talked about Linnea's interest in Monet's house and garden. From there, the children became intrigued with taking the Linnea doll home and introducing her to their families. With their parents' help, each child pretended to be Linnea and wrote in her journal the food they were eating that day, what games they played, the TV they watched, and stories they read. At school they developed charts to list experiences Linnea had in each of their homes. The journal always went with Linnea, so the parents could read about the different adventures in other homes. Parents and children started to see commonalities they all shared, and they noted differences. This led to curiosity about the different ethnicities represented in their community and opened up an appreciation of the differences and the challenges of other's lives.

In literature class, the teacher introduced stories with different ethnic protagonists, and the children took these books home to share with parents. The librarian noticed that children started to select more books on different cultures, so she began displaying different aspects of life in a single ethnic culture. Children's artwork and projects brought out diverse cultural elements. PTA meetings became quite lively, and Mrs. McCloud even introduced to parents Mary Pipher's (2002). The Middle of Everywhere: The World's Refugees Come to Our Town. Parents discussed the book and then began to share stories of their own family's arrival in the United States and how they adapted. Mrs. McCloud had each child develop a personal book of "Who am I and where did I come from?" This meant that all children began to research their own family's history and arrival in this country.

During this unit, the teachers, students, and families all witnessed the many cultural variations represented in the classroom. Thanks to the student's projects, parents and community members could appreciate differences in diets, clothing, living conditions, communication styles, celebrations, choice of music, literary interests, and skills in crafts, as well as everyday vocations.

The changing demographics in our society means that our children must be learning about and accepting differences. No longer are schools a "melting pot" for immigrants in this country, but places where a **mosaic** of cultures exist and where we learn from each other's experiences (Futrell, Gomez, & Bedden, 2003). Many now refer to this cultural pluralism as a tapestry, where individual cultures add their uniqueness to the continually expanding American fabric (Ramsey, 2004).

Natural Environments

As children move about their neighborhood, the outdoor environment offers a rich curriculum from which they gain understanding about their world. This curriculum is, of course, all of nature. Learning differs depending on the combination of children's ability, social interactions regarding the environment, and children's freedom of movement to explore. Louv (2005) discovered that many U.S. children spend very little time outdoors. Although they do learn about nature in various ways, their understanding and appreciation of nature are limited.

Children may learn about snow and ice from books, but their knowledge is limited without experiencing the snow and ice of a northern milieu.

Stephen M. Katz / Bangor Daily News

Studies on children's play activity indicate that the quality of children's outdoor and indoor play differs, and thus different learning opportunities emerge. Children engage in more dramatic and **constructive play** outdoors and in more **exploratory play** (Steglin, 2005) when they feel, touch, examine, crunch, and test materials, such as when learning the sounds different rocks make when dropped into the water. Balancing while walking on uneven rocks in a dry riverbed develops different skills than balancing on the smooth surface of a gymnasium balance beam. Children may climb indoors, but viewing the world from a tree branch gives them broader perspectives. With increasing concerns about childhood obesity, the need for active play environments both indoors and out can hardly be overstated (Pica, 2006).

Good children's books capture the many wonders of nature and can extend children's appreciation of what they experience, but without experiencing the reality of the world, a child's knowledge is limited. In the following vignette, Davon has book knowledge about snow, but it is the real experience that enriches his understanding.

Davon lived all of his five years in Florida. He had heard lots about snow and was especially fond of Ezra

Jack Keats's The Snowy Day, *but he had never seen real snow. While visiting his cousin in Boston that winter, he awoke to white flakes floating down from the sky outside his window. He had never imagined snow to look like that. As the week wore on and more snow fell, Davon learned much more about the feel of snow on his face and the taste of snow as he and his cousin held out their tongues to catch it. He learned how snow could limit and enhance activity and how it felt to walk through drifts.*

Of course, not all of nature's lessons are pleasant. The first snow can be an exciting and beautiful time, but a blizzard followed by power outages and snarled traffic teaches a different lesson. Learning to observe the outdoor environment enhances children's cognitive learning as well as their social and emotional understanding. Joshua learned many things about his surroundings one late-winter day while watching the waterfront.

Joshua lived near the St. Lawrence River and with his mother loved to watch the seals bob up and down in the harbor. One winter day, a small, and undoubtedly ill, seal crawled out on the ice floe and collapsed. While watching and wondering about the seal, Joshua noted two eagles swoop down on the seal and begin tearing at the carcass. Alarmed, Joshua ran to get his mother, who tried to explain about the natural process of creatures in the wild. Then she remembered Cherie Mason's book, Everybody's Somebody's Lunch. *Together they read how a young girl whose cat was devoured by a fox discovers that there are predators and prey in our world and that all are part of nature's food chain. Joshua then became quite fascinated with the eagles and their three-day venture of cleaning up the dead seal. He watched as several crows tried to claim their share but were chased away. A neighbor farther along the shore telephoned and asked Joshua's mother whether she knew what was agitating the crows. An excited Joshua took the phone to explain to the neighbor about the eagles.* ⟋⟋

Joshua's nature lessons didn't all happen in one day, but he gradually became a more interested and astute student of the world around him, discovering other fascinating avenues for learning.

INTERACTIONS AMONG COMMUNITY AGENCIES, FAMILIES, AND SCHOOLS

The learning that took place in the vignettes in this chapter did not happen in isolation within these communities, for the community curriculum was affected by how the families and schools linked children to community resources and agencies (see Figure 10–2). Stronger links heighten the potential for children's learning.

Many community agencies welcome children's visits, either with their families or with schools. Some agencies actively attempt to reach families of differing cultural and economic backgrounds. Other agencies limit their support to those families who can afford their services, or to those families who reach out. Teachers and other community-service personnel can help families become aware of community organizations, events, and experiences that will enrich their children's lives. Louisa, in the earlier vignette, was able to use more community resources because church members aggressively presented programs to assist her in her dilemma. As she became more confident of her ability to help her children, she more actively sought those recreational programs that provided richer learning experiences.

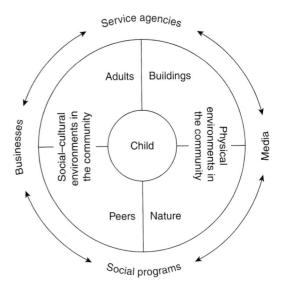

Figure 10–2   Community Impact on Children Through the Environment, Social Networks, Cultural Events, and from Interactions Among Agencies

REFLECTION

The next time you go shopping, observe the children in the store to see what is happening to them, their parents, and store personnel. Then speculate about what the children might be learning—emotionally, physically, and cognitively.

All families use the business enterprises of a community, at some time although many are increasingly using on-line resources to shop, pay bills, and obtain information. In today's society, many families also patronize large, impersonal organizations for purchases, banking, and communicating, and the education that children receive is more limited than what happens in a small neighborhood, such as Joshua's, with supportive parents and neighbors.

Some community agencies that offer programs to children depend on family or Big Brother and Big Sister types of support. A Scout-sponsored camping trip, for example, may include one or both parents or another adult accompanying children.

APPLYING THESE CONCEPTS TO YOUR WORK WITH CHILDREN AND FAMILIES

As you think about community as a source of learning for children, remember that the concept of community includes the extended family and close friends; a particular place, such as a village, town, or neighborhood; and larger entities, such as the media, church congregations; plus cultural, ethnic, and civil rights organizations. Being part of a community means that one is recognized and can take part in the various opportunities for learning that it provides. As a future teacher or community service professional, you will be in a unique position to expand and enrich children's connections with the various communities with which they are connected.

- From the list of community resources in this chapter, identify those with which your family was connected as you grew up. Reflect on the things you think you learned from involvement with these resources and think about how you could help the families with whom you will work become knowledgeable about such opportunities for their children.

- Consider your own experiences with media as you were growing up and compare these to the media that are available now. What do you recollect about the ways your experiences with media was monitored by adults in your family? How have the issues changed since you were a child?

- Become familiar with the various ethnic and cultural organizations in your community and try to participate in some of the activities they sponsor in order to increase your knowledge of the diversity of the people in your area.

Trailblazing and fire-building lessons may be a planned part of the trip, but how the learning is extended depends on parental involvement with the organization. Some churches sponsor family nights, where leaders invite entire families to be involved in extended learning situations.

Communities and schools can collaborate to provide concrete experiences to extend children's learning, but this is not done as much as is possible. Trips into the community are enriched when the agencies have materials, people, and specific events appropriate for the learning level of the children visiting. When teachers make visits and discuss the trip with community agencies beforehand, learning is more likely to be enhanced. Some school trips within a community are not done collaboratively, however, and children's learning is thus limited and may even be negative.

One child-care center decided to make a trip to McDonald's without checking first with the establishment.

It was noon when they arrived, and the restaurant was crowded. When the children were let off the bus, they ran to the play area and began to play noisily. Teachers' attempts to find a place for the children to eat together and to give them experience in selecting and ordering food were disastrous. The bus driver had left, and the harassed teachers had to keep track of the children as they rushed to the playground, roamed the restaurant, and visited other children waiting for lunch. Another distraction was a family watching a miniature TV while eating their lunch, which attracted children from the child-care center. The teachers struggled to get children to order their food. While in line, however, the children pushed and jostled the adults waiting to order. Some children finally received their food, but then the bus returned, and the teachers hurried everyone onto it. Some carried uneaten food, while others protested they hadn't gotten anything. The children, the teachers, and the McDonald's personnel were all unhappy with the experience.

Many restaurants welcome children's visits and provide opportunities for children to visit the kitchen and to experience ordering and eating food in a relaxed manner. In the preceding episode, lack of planning resulted in an unpleasant experience for both adults and children. It would be wrong to assume that no learning took place during this trip; however, with more care, the trip could have been more valuable and pleasant for everyone.

REFLECTION

Consider with your classmates what the children on the trip, described in the above vignette, might have been learning about nutrition. About themselves? About adults? Do you see any positive aspects of this questionable trip?

In community programs, where children interact with materials, observe events, or see animals acting in a natural situation, youngsters usually learn more than they do in those programs where adults lecture, expecting children to be enraptured with what they say. The community, through natural phenomena and by the nature of the community's organization, offers a rich curriculum for all children. Children learn from this curriculum in direct relationship to the social networks available to them.

SUMMARY AND REVIEW

Most community curricula can be made rich and varied, depending on how adults in society structure the environment and how they develop supportive educational policies in various service agencies. Political, social, cultural, and business agencies offer, both intentionally and unintentionally, a learning environment and materials aimed at educating the public about their services. What children learn from these environments depends largely on the use parents and teachers make of them.

The natural and manufactured resources found within communities provide learning experiences even when there is little adult intervention. Children see signs, notice buildings, observe nature, note adult actions, and learn something from all their encounters. Increasingly, children also interact with the larger world through their experiences with media. Print materials,

television, video games, and the Internet expose children to ideas, concepts, and images in ways both positive and negative. The ways that important adults guide children's media encounters and use community resources by choosing wisely, explaining things, and interacting with them all enhance children's learning.

Lacking a national policy of family support, political decisions in different communities can result in vastly different learning experiences. Children who live in communities providing safe physical, emotional, and moral environments have more educational opportunities, for in these areas families are better able to establish social networks that enable them to tap community resources. For children outside such safe environments, schools, parents, and other agencies must work especially hard to compensate and must strive to build a solid curriculum so that these children, too, will thrive in tomorrow's world.

SUGGESTED ACTIVITIES AND QUESTIONS

1. Explore the area around a school neighborhood. List all the natural resources, human resources, and materials that you observe. Rate the learning potential linked to them for children living here and start a resource file from information gathered. Compare your list to others in your group.

2. Expand your **resource file** using the categories in Table 10–1 to organize the information you find that will support your work with children and families. Share your resources with others in the group.

3. Visit a business establishment in your community. Interview the owner or manager to learn whether they have materials aimed at educating children and how they distribute such materials. While there, ask yourself what children might learn just from being in the building.

4. Select a children's television program, watch it, and note positive and negative examples of learning opportunities for children. Review the program to determine if you would recommend that children of various ages be encouraged or allowed to watch it.

5. Explore the Internet to locate five or more Web sites you would recommend for children under six.

RESOURCES

Books

Carroll, K. (2007). *A guide to great field trips.* Tucson, AZ: Zephyr Press.

Carroll, K. (2002). *Family matters: Understanding self, others, community.* Tucson, AZ: Zephyr Press.

Kelly, D. (2006). *Web hunts and virtual field trips: Grade 1–3.* Westminster, CA: Teacher Created Resources.

Louv, R. (2005). *Last child in the woods: Saving our children from nature-deficit disorder.* Chapel Hill, NC: Algonquin Books of Chapel Hill.

Steyer, J. P., & Clinton, C. (2002). *The other parent: The inside story of the media's effect on our children.* NY: Atria Books.

Films and Videos

Community and literacy [Video or DVD, 30 min]. (2003). Features successful city and community-wide literacy programs. New York: Insight Media.

In and Out of School [Video, 30 min]. (2002). Highlights a community-wide math carnival and a hands-on science trip. New York: Insight Media.

The roots of violence, addiction, and neglect [Video or DVD, 33 min]. (2005). Crystal Lake, IL: Magna Systems Video.

Organizations

The National Institute on Media and the Family
606 24th Ave. S.
Suite 606
Minneapolis, MI 55454
http://www.mediafamily.org

National Association for the Advancement of Colored People
4805 Mt. Hope Dr.
Baltimore, MD 21215
http://www.naacp.org

Web Sites

http://www.aap.org   Web site for the American Academy of Pediatrics.

http://www.childrenssoftware.com   Web site for Children's Technology Review, a searchable, on-line database and print publication helping teachers and parents select appropriate interactive media for children.

http://www.fieldtripfactory.com   Web site that links teachers and community members with free field trips in their communities.

http://www.kidsnet.org   Web site that helps children, parents, and educators access the educational opportunities afforded by television, radio, and multimedia sources.

http://www.wilderdom.com   Web site of the Outdoor Education Research and Evaluation Center.

Chapter 11

Strategies for Working Together

In partnerships, educators, families and community members work together to share information, guide students, solve problems, and celebrate successes. Partnerships recognize the shared responsibilities of home, school, and community for children's learning and development.

(Epstein, 2001, p. 4)

Someone must start collaborations, and the beginning steps may be small ones. If partnerships are to flourish, teachers need a wide range of approaches for building relationships and establishing communication with parents and community agencies as the first steps toward increased involvement in children's learning. This chapter examines various practices for collaborative action and discusses things to consider when using these strategies. After reading this chapter, you will be able to do the following:

1. Explain why it is essential to involve parents and community members in children's schooling.

2. Describe a range of practices to develop rapport with parents, communicate with them about their children's progress, and encourage their involvement in the classroom and school.

3. Design options for parent involvement along a continuum that moves from basic to **participatory levels** to advocacy levels.

4. Consider appropriate strategies for working with parents who are difficult to reach.

5. Identify effective strategies to facilitate community involvement in schools.

Our changing society, even with the advantages of mass communication systems, has evolved to a point where at the beginning of the 21st century, school programs alone are not sufficient for the task of formally educating children. The collaboration of parents and community agencies is essential if schools are to succeed in educating young children for a rapidly evolving society. More than 30 years ago, Evans (1975) pointed out that the ultimate goal of active parent involvement is "enhancing the family's ability to respond to its children" (p. 11). This goal is as vital today as it was then.

Parental and community involvement have always been a part of U.S. education. As we discussed earlier, historically, most parents were in charge of their children's education, but beginning in the 1800s, schools accepted more responsibility for academic learning. Later, professional educators began to educate parents about children's growth and development, instructing them on ways to prepare their children for school and advising them on how to support their children's education once they began formal schooling.

By and large, parental cooperation in educational matters during the 20th century meant parental acquiescence to school suggestions, but this has begun to change. Parental and community involvement in some districts has moved gradually from teacher-dominated procedures to collaborations with parents and community agencies (Chadwick, 2004; Wohlstetter & Smith, 2006). We contend that to cope with increasing challenges in the educative process, successful schools need to become **embedded partners** with parents and community members. In this chapter, we discuss a wide array of strategies that schools and teachers use for building partnerships with parents and community agencies.

To establish such parternships, teachers need to consider ways of interacting with parents and community members that respect diverse communication and work styles. If children are to benefit, teachers must provide the impetus to break down communication barriers resulting from different cultural expectations and habits of interacting. For example see Figure 11–1 for ways to understand and involve African American parents. Of course, to be successful, both teachers and parents need to adapt and respond to each other's interests, concerns, and needs. Keep in mind though, that it is the school's responsibility

---

Understanding and Involving African American Parents

Alvin F. Poussaint

IT IS IMPORANT FOR TEACHERS to make African American children and their parents feel welcome in school. Teachers cannot be passive in this regard. African Americans often feel that public places aren't welcoming to them and might avoid school involvement because they don't feel comfortable.

African American parents sometimes think that teachers dismiss them too easily in tense situations. They may perceive a situation to be racist when it is not necessarily so. It is extremely important for teachers to take time to listen to families and acknowledge their concerns. For example—and this is quite common in preschool settings—a White child may ask a Black child about his or her skin color in this way: "Can't you wash the color off? Is it dirt?" If the Black child relates the comment to his parents, they may not know what to do. We know that a comment like this from a preschooler is not racist; it is merely an expression of curiosity. African American adults may make negative associations when their child is told that his skin is dirty, however. Teachers should address such topics directly and with sensitivity: "No, the color can not be washed off—that's the color of his skin." They can follow up by talking positively with the children about differences.

Here's another example. An African American preschooler comes home upset because some other children keep touching her hair. What may be an issue of personal space can be perceived by the parents as a racist issue, even though it is not. To prevent misunderstanding, teachers should remind the children, "We don't touch people's hair if we don't have their permission."

When these issues come up, administrators and teachers should consider forming a committee to address multiculturalism and diversity within the school. What should a teacher or a principal do if a parent says that there are not enough books or materials that represent African Americans? When families come to school, will they see pictures of diverse people—such as African American scientists or Latino artists—that might help everyone feel welcome? A committee can raise awareness of these issues and help teachers, administrators, and parents address them as they arise.

Alvin F. Poussaint, MD, is director of the Media Center of the Judge Baker Children's Center in Boston. He is also a professor of psychiatry and faculty associate dean for student affairs at Harvard Medical School. He is coauthor, with James P. Comer, MD, of *Raising Black Children*.

Figure 11-1   Relating to Parents
Source: Poussaint, A. F. (2006). Understanding and involving African American parents. *Young Children* 61 (1), 48. Used with permission of the National Association for the Education of Young Children.

to lead, and teachers should be prepared to go more than halfway in reaching out to parents and community.

Schools that develop more welcoming strategies help parents and other community members feel comfortable in visiting classrooms, becoming aides or volunteers, and contributing special expertise to children's learning. These individuals learn about the schools and about school culture, which enables them to help their children and to communicate their sense of the

importance of school programs to others in their community.

The larger community is also an important educating force. Schools and families have always made excursions into their communities for educational purposes or have invited community members into the classroom. This involvement becomes even more important as schools include community and local social and environmental issues as part of the curriculum and as community agencies become partners with their neighborhood schools.

ESTABLISHING RELATIONSHIPS WITH FAMILIES

Establishing good relationships with children's families early in the school year is important. Many teachers have found that reaching out to children even before school begins can be a useful way to get to know families.

Tools for Early Contacts

Home visits, telephone calls, letters, post cards, or invitations to school for brief, informal meetings are all tools teachers use to set a welcoming tone and lay the foundation for an effective working relationship.

Letters, Post-Cards, and E-mail. During the summer, some teachers send children a short note or post card to introduce themselves and to welcome the child to the class. The following vignette demonstrates how one kindergarten teacher created enthusiasm and excitement for a child and established a sense of security and trust with the parents even before school began.

Jack's eyes shone as he tore open the envelope that had come for him in the mail. As he reached into the letter, he found a small plastic dinosaur that he clutched eagerly, as he handed the letter to his mother to read.

Dear Jack,

Welcome to the Dinosaur Kindergarten Class! We are so excited about your coming to our class. You can bring a favorite toy or book from home for your first day of school. We have lots of places ready for you to keep your things and each place will have your name and special sticker. Your sticker looks like this:

We sent you something special from the Dinosaur teachers. You can bring it to school, too. We will see you at school on Tuesday, August, 26th!

Your teachers,
Ms. Howell and Ms. Moll

Jack's excitement over receiving mail and the family's satisfaction in this individual welcome to their child created an immediate bond between them and his new teachers. Carrying his dinosaur to school on the first day and knowing that there was a place waiting for him marked with some hearts eased Jack's transition into school.

REFLECTION

Consider the grade level you wish to teach and ways to welcome children of that age to your classroom. Now think about some ways you could communicate over the summer with children who will be placed in your class in the fall.

Telephone Contact. In the past, parents and teachers telephoned each other only when concerned about a child's progress. Today, the telephone is a tool for collaborating on all aspects of a child's education. Teachers can begin this process with a brief telephone conversation before or soon after school begins for the year. In this first call, introduce yourself to the family and express pleasure in having their child in your class (Olsen & Fuller, 2003). Inform parents that unless they wish otherwise, you would like to call or e-mail them on a regular (once a week or month) basis just to keep in contact, inform them of their child's progress and school events, and answer any questions or address any concerns they might have (Powers, 2005). Establishing positive communication early in the school year enables parents and teachers to be comfortable about contacting each other when later confusion or misunderstanding arises, as the following vignette demonstrates.

Melissa Jacobs was entering third grade in a new school. She knew no one and was terrified, especially since she "didn't read so good." Mrs. Jacobs was relieved when Ms. Thomas called to welcome Melissa to school and to invite the mother to visit. As the year wore on, Mrs. Jacobs was delighted in Melissa's successful adaptation to school. So she called Ms. Thomas one November morning to see how Melissa's reading was going.

The next day, Melissa came home very angry, not wanting to go to school. "I don't see why I have to go to that dumb teacher and do **phonics**. *I hate phonics!"*

Distressed, Mrs. Jacobs immediately called the teacher to ask what was happening. Before Mrs. Jacobs could say much more than hello, Ms. Thomas said, "I am so glad you called. I was about to call you. You know, I really don't think it's a good idea for Melissa to go to the reading teacher. I know you are concerned about her reading, but she was just miserable today. Her reading is coming along well, and she doesn't need this extra pressure."

In the course of the conversation, it became clear that there had been a misunderstanding during the last telephone conversation. Mrs. Jacobs had intended to just maintain contact, and Ms. Thomas had interpreted it as concern. Since good communication had been established early, both teacher and parent could resolve the misunderstanding in good faith and do what was best for Melissa. ⌒

Formal and Informal Classroom Visits

In the past, parents were invited to children's classrooms only on special occasions, such as during National Education Week, or as audiences for special events. Increasingly, however, schools are establishing an open-door policy and welcome parents at any time. To initiate this approach, many schools invite parents and children to drop in during one of the days before school begins in the fall to meet the teacher and see the classroom. These short, 10- to 15-minute visits are especially helpful for younger children or children transferring into the school and can help ease some of the anxiety parents and children feel about entering a new classroom. As the following vignette illustrates, having a simple activity for parent and child to participate in can set a welcoming tone.

⌒ *After brief introductions, Ms. Bender gave Avi and his mom a pencil and a "Treasure Map" to locate various places in the classroom. As they explored the room, checking off the locations of the coat hooks, bathroom, and learning centers, and locating Avi's name on a bulletin board and on his desk, Ms. Bender chats with other arriving families. Avi and his mother leave the classroom, talking excitedly about the start of the new school year.* ⌒

A school in Baltimore County, Maryland, makes a point of inviting all parents to come to the first day of school each year. A celebratory atmosphere is created as families accompany their child to the classroom and stay for a while. The level of parent involvement has increased dramatically in this school since this policy was established several years ago.

Back-to-School Night gives parents a more formal introduction to their children's classroom. This event, held on an evening early in the school year and generally for adult family members only, gives teachers the opportunity to meet children's parents or caregivers. This is also a time for teachers to introduce themselves and help parents get to know them and why they became a teacher. Families meet other parents at Back-to-School Night and learn about the curriculum, classroom procedures, discipline policies, and ways the teacher plans to communicate with parents.

The following vignette demonstrates an innovative twist that one classroom teacher instigated, in the way that invited parents were to participate in some of the classroom activities on Back-to-School Night. While people participated, the teacher gave information about the value of the different activities and an overview of their child's day.

⌒ *During the day before Back-to-School Night, Jack's teacher asked each child to tell what area of the classroom they thought their parent might want to explore. As a result, when Jack's mother arrived for the Open House, she was instructed to start her evening at the snack table. Later she had a chance to make something for him in the art area that he would find in his cubby when he arrived at school the next day.* ⌒

Recognizing the needs of families, some schools are also offering child care during the Back-to-School Night so that single parents or both parents can attend. Many schools use this event to introduce the many ways that families can contribute to the success of the classroom and to assist parents in getting to know one another. Since much important information is communicated at Back-to-School night, teachers should prepare a written summary of key ideas; this will benefit the families who were able to attend as well as those who were not.

Home Visits

Visiting the homes of preschool-age children prior to the start of school has been common practice in some programs for many years. This is

Home visits provide teachers with new insights into the social, cultural, and cognitive functioning of children and their parents.

Scott Cunningham / Merrill

particularly true for Head Start, where such visits are required several times a year. Many public school prekindergarten classes, child-care programs, and private nursery schools also require or encourage teachers to visit children in their homes. Although these visits can be aimed at assisting parents in providing better health care, obtaining needed social services, and supporting their children's academic progress, they also serve to help teachers become more knowledgeable about individual children and to get to know the child's family.

Such home visiting programs are designed to establish family–school relationships early by helping children become acquainted with the teacher and helping the teacher to understand the home situation (Morrison, 2006). The responsibility for such visits always rests with the classroom teacher, but most will have an assistant teacher or other adult accompany them on the home visit. This practice meets needs for safety and also allows one visitor to talk to the parent while the other plays with the child.

Successful home visits depend on a teacher's ability to develop a trusting relationship with parents. Home visits can provide teachers with new insights into the social, cultural, and cognitive functioning of children and their parents. By

working cooperatively, parents and teachers can more easily support children's development and learning. Keep in mind, however, that some parents may decline a home visit for various reasons, and their refusal must be respected and an alternate plan for meeting arranged (Hanhan, 2003).

Accepted practices for making the home visit comfortable for both teachers and parents abound in early childhood literature. Recommendations include the following:

1. Clarify the purpose of the visit with an initial telephone call.

2. Arrange a convenient time so that children will be part of the process.

3. Set a specific time for the visit. Arrive and depart on time and leave earlier if events warrant it.

4. As a guest in the home, respect the cultural and ethnic values the family exhibits.

5. If other family members are present, include them in your conversation.

6. Be an attentive listener, but don't oversocialize or get drawn into family controversies.

7. Be prepared to suggest agencies and types of services that parents might pursue in getting help if the family asks.

8. Invite the parents to become active participants in the school program, suggesting several levels of involvement.
9. Follow up the visit with a thank you note and indicate action for what was agreed on during the visit.

Teachers have resources and information to share with parents, especially to help them understand how they can support their children's education, they also seek to make home visits collaborative efforts. The teacher acknowledges the parent as the expert on that particular child and seeks to get to know the child better through the visit. Parents can also initiate visits, plan an agenda, and discuss educational aspirations for their children. When teachers work to establish positive relationships with parents, the outcome can be a more equal partnership in developing good educational programs for children (Ball, 2006).

REFLECTION

Think about some of the reasons families might be hesitant to have a teacher make a home visit. What alternatives could you offer these parents that would still allow you to get to know the child's family life better?

ESTABLISHING ONGOING COMMUNICATION WITH PARENTS

Almost all parents are keenly interested in their children and what happens to them at school. Teachers, knowing of this concern, have developed various ways to communicate to parents about their children's school experiences. Parent–teacher conferences, newsletters, telephone contacts, e-mail, Web sites, and written notes inform parents about children's progress, school programs and curricula, and ways parents can help their children. Most techniques have proved very successful, and teachers have developed a number of ideas that are variations on these basic strategies.

Informal Contacts

Parents with children in preschool normally accompany their children to school, which gives both parents and teachers a chance to talk informally. Teachers can allow time at the beginning and end of the day for brief conversations with parents. Parents like to hear what their children have been doing, and a brief statement, such as "Phil climbed to the top of the jungle gym for the first time today; he'll be excited to tell you about it," communicates to parents that you are aware of what is happening with each child.

Parents also must share in the communication process. Parents who comment about how their child is at home or note their child's enjoyment of a school activity communicate their involvement in their child's learning. Teachers who post daily digital photos and a short synopsis of the day on the parent bulletin board labled "Ask your child or me about . . ." help to foster communication between parent and child. By asking questions and being attentive, you can help parents feel more comfortable when talking with you.

Lengthy conversations, however, are a problem at the beginning or end of the day. Busy parents are anxious to get to work or home, and busy teachers need to prepare for the day or clean up after a long one. Brief statements at this time are important, and if a parent needs more time, you should suggest either a scheduled conference or telephone call. When parents linger in the classroom at the beginning of the day, skilled teachers suggest that they observe something special or help their children in some constructive way.

Parents usually do not accompany their older children to school but are often present in welcoming schools where partnerships have been formed with parents and communities. These parents still anticipate brief words of welcome or an exchange about what is going on with their children. Such exchanges communicate to all parties, including children, that responsibility for educating the young is shared by the entire community.

All school personnel can assist or hinder parents' reactions to schools. School custodians, secretaries, and classroom aides are especially important members of the school team. They often live in the neighborhood and, when they are friendly and open, can offer a bridge to the school community. Principals and teachers who look up from their work and smile at, greet, or offer assistance to persons entering give parents the feeling that the school community cares about them.

Written Communication

Although face-to-face contact is ideal for establishing relationships between families and schools, by necessity, much communication must also occur in written form. School and classroom handbooks, newsletters, bulletin boards, Web pages, and informal notes are all used by teachers to communicate with families about their children's school involvement.

Handbooks. Every school and early childhood program should have a family handbook that communicates policies and procedures. Handbooks can include such information as the school's philosophy; operating procedures, including the yearly calendar, daily schedule, and emergency plans; as well as parent involvement opportunities (Berger, 2004). Specialized classroom handbooks can supplement the general handbook and provide more detailed information on the curriculum of the particular age or grade level.

Homework. Research indicates the importance of parents' involvement in their children's education, so schools increasingly look for ways to reach parents at home. Traditionally, teachers have given homework with the hope that parents would oversee the assignments and help their children as needed. Homework provides children with practice on skills and concepts taught at school, and parents who review the work with their children get information about what they are expected to learn. Homework assignments are often seen by teachers as a parent's obligation and by parents as a great nuisance (Kralovec & Buell, 2000).

All too often, traditional homework consists of worksheets to complete or drill work on specific skills. Changing the emphasis of homework,

however, can help parents see that they are indeed a contributing member of their child's classroom success. Assignments can be given that develop certain skills but are also part of the family's life (Hong & Milgram, 2000). For example, children and parents might cook something together to share in the classroom. One teacher had children and parents look at the moon each night and mark the time of observation and the spot on the horizon where it was seen. Another teacher devised a Love Note Project, whereby children selected a book to read with a parent or special person each evening. The parent wrote a simple love note about the interaction, and the child (or teacher) read it to the class next morning. In all the preceding examples, the teacher created a follow-up system that informed parents of the success of their work with their children.

Parents also appreciate having advance notice of upcoming homework projects and adequate time to complete them during the busy school week. Some teachers now provide a calendar for upcoming projects and a weekly homework packet that children and parents can work on at their own pace. Some schools have also established a homework hot line to help parents help their children. Community libraries are increasingly partnering with schools to support children and parents with homework (Mediavilla, 2001).

Bulletin Boards. All classrooms have bulletin boards, and most schools have boards in the halls. Teachers place children's work, information about special events, and material for a particular unit on these boards to inform parents of ongoing classroom activities. They also see their children's artwork, their written or retold stories, reports on books they have read, and information on units they have studied. They read the teacher's explanation of the work and what it shows about the children's learning. Photos with captions are especially appealing to parents, as they show children's involvement in classroom activities. The increasing use of digital cameras (Good, 2005/06) allows teachers to easily share such photos with parents through e-mail as well. Some teachers also include family photos in the classroom, so that children stay connected to their loved ones during the day and visiting parents are reminded of their importance in their children's lives.

Many schools also provide bulletin boards just for parents, and the interests of parents dictate what is posted. Parent volunteers often arrange the board or assist teachers in highlighting information, such as bibliographies of children's books, educational toy suggestions for birthdays or holidays, and recipes for nutritional snacks. Sometimes teachers photocopy materials and put them in a wall pocket for parents to take home. Information about school and community events, social services, and health and nutritional assistance may be provided, and if postings are changed regularly, parents will learn to look to the board for information. Parents are also invited to post materials of interest for other parents, and one school even added a wipe board for parents to write notes to other parents.

Newsletters and Web Sites. Classroom and school newsletters, while varying in purpose, are useful ways for schools to communicate with parents. Most newsletters convey school news, including notices of school events, parent–teacher conferences, and other important meetings. Many newsletters also include tips for helping children at home and resources for parents. All information can go on a school Web site, too, with paper copies sent home to those families without a computer.

Increasingly, teachers are finding extended purposes for classroom newsletters or Web sites, supplementing them with a calendar of upcoming events and using them to recap what has been going on in the classroom. One teacher gives out the first newsletter at Back-to-School Night and uses it to communicate much of the information she shares verbally. Another teacher includes in her newsletters artwork by children, photos of classroom activities, thank-you notes for parental and community support, examples of how children use materials that parents contribute, and extracts of classroom discussions children had because of parental support. Such a complete newsletter provides parents with many examples of what and how children learn from various resources.

Informal Notes and E-mail. Traditionally, teachers have used informal notes to alert parents to their concerns regarding students' work. Now, more teachers recognize the value of notes that reflect students' special accomplishments in developing social, cognitive, or physical skills, thus giving both parents and children a sense of well-being. Of course, all notes can go to parents via e-mail in homes so equipped. Most notes don't require a response, but you may occasionally wish to query how parents see their child's skill development at home. You also want to invite two-way communication through notes for parents who find this a helpful way to keep in touch. Some teachers provide a composition book, which is passed back and forth via the child's backpack, for both parent and teacher to write notes to each other.

Like the first telephone call home, the first note should be a positive communication designed to build a collaborative relationship. Some teachers like to send home some kind of weekly report for all children (see Figure 11–2) and ask parents to sign and return the report. Informal notes or weekly reports can also express concern about a change in a child's behavior.

When notes are positive in tone, even if you have some concern, parents come to understand the importance of working cooperatively to provide the best for their children. Most teachers believe it is wise to let children know about communications with their parents and, in general, what the notes contain. Children's involvement is essential, for children need to know that parents and teachers are working together to help them learn. Electronic mail and telephone answering machines are other ways that teachers provide more information to parents. Some teachers update a Web site or an answering machine to record brief messages for parents concerning children's home assignments, events of the day, upcoming meetings, or things that children are asked to bring to school. Teachers have elicited the aid of bilingual parents in translating notes sent home to families who speak a language other than English.

WEEKLY REPORT

Dear Parent/Guardian,

We will be sending home weekly reports this term for all children. These will keep you aware of your child's progress in social skills.

NAME: _____ DATE: _____

In general, your child's behavior this week was:

(G) GOOD   (F) FAIR   (N) IN NEED OF IMPROVEMENT

_____ Listening skills   _____ Behaves in specials

_____ Works quietly   _____ Behaves in hallways

_____ Stays on task   _____ Shows respect

_____ Completes class work   _____ Completes homework

_____ Interacts appropriately with peers

TEACHER COMMENTS

Figure 11–2   Weekly Progress Report

Web sites that translate notes into other languages are also available.

Interactive Portfolios. In many classrooms, teachers now have children assemble their work in a portfolio. Over time, the work accumulated here provides materials for children, teachers, and parents to assess the child's learning. Technology expands possibilities for communicating with parents via these portfolios. For example, digital cameras allow teachers to record classroom events and share these photos with parents on a regular basis. Some teachers print the photos and include some in individual, **interactive portfolio** notebooks that are shared between the home and school (Gronlund & Engel, 2001). Periodically, the teacher will write a short entry about a special event, accomplishment, or issue in each child's portfolio and send it home with the child to share. The family is invited to write a response or to share information, photos, and news from home and add to the portfolio.

REFLECTION

In your field-experience classroom, check to see how the teacher keeps in contact with parents. Has he or she used any of the suggested techniques discussed in this section? Does he or she view these ideas as realistic for a busy teacher?

Parent–Teacher Conferences

Conferences are one of the most frequently used methods of parent–teacher communication and have been a successful way to discuss a child's progress. As schools begin to develop a sense of partnership, conferences, although not different on the surface, become forums for mutual exchange. Partnership conferences mean that both partners share examples of children's development, show respect for each other's responsibility, and propose ideas for continuing a program or changing direction. In successful conferences, parents and teachers are able to communicate the child's strengths, progress, and possible areas for improvement in more detail than in any other format (Henniger, 2004).

Although initiating conferences has traditionally been the teacher's responsibility, schools are increasingly encouraging parents or other involved adults to suggest meetings and to come to conferences prepared to share their perspectives. Current strategies reflect changes in attitudes of teachers and parents as they see conferences as a joint venture that may even involve the participation of the student. Figure 11–3 presents a general scheme that you as a teacher may use to ensure that your parent–teacher conferences result in effective collaboration.

Parental Involvement. To enhance participation and involvement in conferences, teachers need to communicate the significant impact these meetings can have on children's learning. By anticipating the needs of individual families and sharing the following information in the classroom newsletter or in a note or email home, teachers can help parents prepare for the conference more effectively.

- If children have more than one adult responsible for them, both adults should plan to attend, if possible. Other significant adults in the child's life are also welcome.
- Early morning, late afternoon, and evening appointments will be available for parents who need them. Since the conference is an important part of the child's education and evaluation, adults should make the appointment a priority and get it on the calendar early.
- Children's understanding of the purpose of the conference is important, and parents or surrogates should talk with children about the conference and ask for their input about school and how they view their progress.
- Parents should bring any materials that they or their children want to share with the teacher to the conference.

- Adults attending the conference should make note of any questions or concerns that either they or their children wish to share with the teachers.
- Afterward, parents need to talk about the conference as positively as possible to help the children see the relationship of the home environment to school life.
- A follow-up letter or e-mail to the school clarifies for the teacher the parents' or surrogate's view of the conference.

Student Involvement. Traditionally, students have had little say or involvement in parent–teacher conferences. As parents assume more responsibilities for conferences, both teachers and parents may seek input from children on questions they would like the adults to discuss. Another facet of innovative conferences is including students themselves. When students are included in the conferences, the following steps need to be taken to prepare them:

- Determine the reason for including the children; for example, the students' work has been collected in a portfolio and evaluation of the work will be enhanced with their input.
- Review with the class the purpose of the conference, and help the children as a class to develop some possible questions and ideas to discuss in upcoming conferences. Students may want to consider their strengths as learners, how they have changed during this time period, any difficulties they may be having, and how they might improve (Weldin & Tumarkin, 1999).
- Help students gather materials they wish to bring, to demonstrate their strengths and progress.
- During the conference, have students describe their materials and how they see their progress. Have them ask questions of both teachers and parents.
- Have parents discuss their observations, and then discuss yours. Make sure that the children's are addressed, too.

PREPARATION FOR THE CONFERENCE

1. Develop mutual respect by scheduling conferences at convenient times for both teachers and parents.

2. Establish a sense of equality with seating arrangements. Avoid physical barriers by sitting beside parents at a table where everyone can view all materials.

3. Prepare an agenda and send it to the parents. Include a statement of purpose and allow times for parent input, your input, and questions from both you and parents.

4. Assemble materials from areas of the curriculum that demonstrate children's classroom work over time.

5. To demonstrate the value placed on parent teaching, invite parents to bring items their children have produced at home, such as charts of children's home responsibilities, craft projects children have made, food they have prepared, letters they have written, any collections, or sets of favorite books.

THE CONFERENCE

1. Begin the conference on a positive note by sharing children's accomplishments at school with parents.

2. Invite parents to share their children's meaningful achievements at home.

3. Share your mutual academic and personal concerns.

4. Discuss ideas for resolving these concerns.

5. Allow time for parental questions. If parents appear reluctant to ask questions, assist them by suggesting what other parents often ask: codes of behavior for the classroom, academic questions not attended to in this particular conference, parent involvement in schools or in children's learning.

6. Keep the conference to the allotted time. If you need more time, schedule a new conference.

ENDING THE CONFERENCE

1. End the conference on a positive note; be complimentary to the children involved.

2. Review conference highlights.

3. Restate your understanding of any decisions mutually made.

4. Indicate how information or material parents have shared has helped you understand their children better.

5. Thank the parents for coming and inform them of the next conference period, next school event for parents, or next PTA meeting.

6. Indicate your anticipation at seeing the parents again.

CONFERENCE FOLLOW-UP

1. Write a brief summary for your records. Include any and all parental suggestions or questions.

2. Follow through on your promises and inform the parents of your efforts.

Figure 11–3   Making Parent–Teacher Conferences Work
Source: Adapted from Seefeldt & Barbour, 1998.

It is important that conferences be planned to meet the needs of individual families. It may mean including the children in the conference.

Linda Coan O'Kresik / Bangor Daily News

- Review the conference highlights and recommendations made.
- Understand the importance for all parties to follow up conferences with notes to one another.

Although there are advantages to including children in a parent–teacher conference, there are drawbacks, as well. Some information that the adults wish to share may not always be appropriate for the child to hear. In nearly all classrooms, teachers and children often have individual conferences without the parents. If children are included, it is important that they understand that parents and teachers will also have some conferences without them.

Keys to Effective Communication

Whether communication is verbal, written, or electronic, there are certain key elements to consider for effective communication and for avoiding misunderstandings:

- Work at understanding the other's point of view. It is important to listen carefully to parents without interrupting. When responding to parent messages, try to consider their perspective without becoming defensive. Repeat what you think you are hearing, seek clarification, and try to be empathetic in responding to concerns.
- Language differences can cause misunderstandings when care is not taken. Avoid appearing to model or correct another's speech pattern. When terms are used that either party is unfamiliar with, ask for or give an explanation in a nonjudgmental way.
- Traditionally, the teacher has been seen as the expert. Good collaboration requires a partnership in which teachers and parents acknowledge the contributions each makes to the child's development. Body language, such as pursed lips, folded arms, and hands on hips, can undermine positive communication by conveying a different message than the words expressed. Try to be aware of your own body language and respect the communication styles of various families.
- Voice pitch and tonal qualities are used to convey different meanings. Cultural and family differences exist, and they can cause

Table 11–1   Parent and Teacher Communication Strategies that Foster Collaboration

Conferences	
Traditional	**Collaborative**
Conferences are scheduled only during the school day and children are not permitted to attend.	Early morning, evening, and lunch-hour appointments are available, and child care is provided.
Teacher prepares materials, provides input, and directs conference.	Parents, as well as teachers, prepare for conferences.
	Child contributes ideas to the conference or attends.

Home Visits	
Traditional	**Collaborative**
Teacher, in the role of expert, attempts to understand the home, establish positive relations, and explain parental responsibility with regard to children's education.	Teacher assumes the role of facilitator and seeks to build a partnership with family.
	Parents are encouraged to plan visits and share ideas.
	Parent empowerment is sought.

Telephone Contact	
Traditional	**Collaborative**
Teacher initiates calls only when concerned.	Teacher establishes relationship by initiating a friendly call early in the year.
Teacher uses phone as substitute for conference.	Both parents and teachers call occasionally to communicate about the child.
	Leaving messages about schedules, homework, and other issues on answering machines permits exchange of information.

Informal Contact	
Traditional	**Collaborative**
Beginning and ending of the school day are times for brief exchanges between parent and teacher.	Schools establish open-door policies and welcome parental visits during the school day.
Demonstrating interest is the goal.	Parents are encouraged to communicate regularly.

(Continued)

Table 11–1   (*Continued*)

Written Communication	
Traditional	**Collaborative**
Teachers develop bulletin boards. Newsletters include school news, dates to remember, and tips for helping children at home. Informal notes are ways to keep in contact with and inform parents of difficulties.	Parent information bulletin boards are provided, and both school personnel and families provide materials. Bulletin boards include family photos, photos of children in action, artwork, notes on parents' contributions, and what children have learned. Web sites highlight school news: Notes, emails, and program Web sites reflect children's special accomplishments and are designed to give both parents and children a sense of well-being. Program chat rooms encourage communication among families as well as between teachers and parents.

misunderstandings. Learning about these differences in a reciprocal exchange can ease potential conflicts. In Chapter 4, Greg helps Philip learn "the school way." In the same way, it is incumbent on the teacher to lessen the gap by recognizing that parents may not know "the school way." Being honest in how you have been affected by differences will open communication and will help parents recognize and even accept differences.

Thoughtful, ongoing communication with parents is an important component of parent–teacher cooperation. It involves parents at a basic level in their children's education. Table 11–1 summarizes the shift from a traditional teacher-centered approach to the collaborative communication strategies discussed in this section of the chapter.

As you consider the strategies presented here for building collaborative relationships with families and community members, think about how you would use what you have learned to foster involvement in your classroom. Remember not all families or agencies can participate fully, nor is it even desirable for them to do so. What are some ways you will initiate communication with parents?

How will you help them feel welcome in your classroom and understand their importance in their child's education? How will you use technology and other modes of communication to reach out to parents?

REFLECTION

Ask a fellow student to role-play a parent conference with you and another student to observe or videotape the role play. Then review your observer's comments, and think about how you "come across" in working with parents.

PARENTS IN THE SCHOOLS

Many teachers invite parents to special events throughout the year, knowing that getting families in the classroom can be the first step toward further involvement. When parents are in classrooms, they see firsthand how their children respond to the school learning environment. Although we find exceptions, involved parents usually become strong supporters of their children's schools. They come

When parents volunteer in classrooms, they come to appreciate what is involved in educating their children.

Barbara Schwartz / Merrill

to appreciate what teachers are doing and what is involved in educating their children. In addition to basic participation as visitors or observers, some parents make a commitment as volunteers, classroom resource persons, or even paid aides. Teachers need to help parents understand that there are different levels of involvement (see Chapter 12, Figure 12–1) and encourage them to contribute where they can on the continuum.

School Visitation

As schools welcome parents with open-door policies that invite them to drop in on their child's classroom at any time, certain guidelines must be developed so the visits are productive. Back-to-School Night and the follow-up newsletter provide two ways of introducing parents to routines of the day and how children are involved. Parents will know that when they visit, the teacher may suggest where they should sit to get the most from their observation. If there is activity that parents can observe better by moving about the room, the teacher suggests the best time to do so.

In some classrooms, children are accustomed to adults and are comfortable asking them for help. In such cases, parents are advised that children will approach them. If parents are visiting to observe general classroom activities and how children interact with one another, the teacher provides a list of things parents can watch for. If a parent is visiting for a particular reason, the parent and the teacher confer regarding what to look for and how.

In some families, grandparents, uncles, and aunts are closely involved in a child's life. Teachers should make it clear that these other important people are welcome in the school. At the Kensington/Forest Glen Children's Center, one of the classes has an "I Love You" dinner each February. The children cook and serve a simple meal to all their loved ones, including siblings, parents, extended family, and other important people in their lives.

Most classrooms have special events to which teachers invite parents. (Some interesting examples are noted in Figure 11–4.) Such occasions give children experiences in writing invitations, planning for the event, demonstrating some skill or talent, and even preparing special snacks. Increasingly, teachers are planning family breakfasts once a month or several times a year. Parents all bring some simple breakfast foods to share and join with their children, the teachers, and other families in an informal gathering that can fit easily into the

1. **Stone Soup Day.** As part of their folktale study, a third-grade class invited their families to celebrate the end of the unit. Children performed their version of "Stone Soup" and then had their families join them in eating a nutritious meal of "stone" soup and corn muffins, which they had prepared the day before.

2. **Royal Reader.** Once or twice a month, a kindergarten teacher invited a member of the community to come in and read to the children. The special reader wore a cape and crown as regal music played. After the reading, the guest would tell children a little bit about their job and join the group for a snack.

3. **Coffee Hour.** At one school, the principal, staff members, and teachers, on a rotating basis were freed from responsibilities each Friday morning. Families were invited in to have coffee and chat with them about school in general and to get to know one another. As the year progressed, sharing "things that were working well" and "things that could work better" became part of the agenda. Gradually, the evolving good fellowship and trust led to both parents and school personnel taking responsibility for seeking solutions for expressed concerns.

4. **Literacy Night.** Parents were invited to bring their children to school one evening dressed in their pajamas. As children participated in storytelling sessions led by education students from the nearby college, parents had short, interactive workshops about how to encourage reading at home. The local library sent the bookmobile, and staff assisted parents in obtaining library cards. The evening ended with a bedtime snack and a story told to parents and children by a master storyteller.

5. **Heritage Night.** One school with a large international population invited families to come to school on a spring Friday evening dressed in native clothing and with a special dish to share. Some families brought music to share and other items that were important in their culture. An informal fashion show was staged. The evening was so successful that the school decided to hold the event earlier in the year so that the involvement that was sparked could begin in the fall.

Figure 11–4   Special Events for the Classroom

daily routine. The list of events for such visits is almost endless but when planning, teachers need to consider any family-related barriers that might inhibit involvement (Kieff & Wellhousen, 2000). See Figure 11–5.

Children need to be prepared for adults visiting their classroom. Teachers usually have explained to their classes that parents and other adults enjoy coming in to see what they are doing. Traditionally, teachers introduce visitors, explaining to children the purpose of the visit. An innovative approach to these visits is to help children take responsibility for welcoming visitors.

Mrs. Horton has many visitors to her class at school near Atlanta, and she established the role of greeter to be filled as one of the weekly classroom duties. Children practice the role so they will feel comfortable with adults. When adults come into the room, the greeter quietly welcomes them, takes their coat, and suggests where to sit. The child points out the daily schedule, which is always posted, and tells the visitors what is currently happening.

Parents and Community Members as Volunteers

Most teachers realize that having parents to regularly assist children in the classroom pays off in a richer curriculum for students. Schools are also turning to grandparents, active retirees, high school students, and other community members as volunteers. While some schools have money

Barriers	Modifications
Time	☐ Breakfast meetings
	☐ Weekend events
	☐ One event scheduled over a number of days
	☐ Open invitations
Transportation	☐ School bus or van
	☐ Car pool arranged by teacher or parent volunteer
	☐ Buddy system among families
Child care	☐ School-provided child care
	☐ Child care provided by parent organization
	☐ Buddy system among families
Decorations/celebrations	☐ Artwork created by children in the art center
	☐ Artwork generated during a theme/project study
Curriculum	☐ Opportunities for children to make multiple gifts and cards and to pick their recipients
	☐ Family members share expertise and culture
	☐ Bias-free curriculum
Food	☐ Multiple menus available
	☐ Buffets
	☐ Picnics
Printed material	☐ Translate copies
	☐ Make audiotapes
	☐ Make telephone calls
	☐ Use voice mail or e-mail
Special guest	☐ Guest not specified by role
	☐ A pal or friend
	☐ Open invitations to extended family members or a noncustodial parent
Expense	☐ Support provided by community businesses underwriting the event or materials needed
Misunderstanding the role as parent volunteer in the classroom	☐ Volunteer training sessions
	☐ Specific routines created
	☐ Recorded or printed instructions
Misunderstanding the parental role in home-extension learning activities	☐ Specific routines created for home-extension learning activities
	☐ Parent workshops to explain activities
	☐ Demonstration tapes
	☐ Demonstrations during home visits
Discomfort in school situations	☐ Alternative home visits or neighborhood meetings
	☐ Buddy systems among families
	☐ Small-group meetings

Figure 11–5 Common Barriers and Possible Modifications Checklist

Source: Kieff, J., Wellhousen, K. (2000). Planning family involvement in early childhood programs. *Young Children* 55 (3), 23.

allotted to hire one or more parents to work as aides in classrooms, volunteers are increasingly needed to serve a variety of roles in schools.

To be most effective, classroom volunteers need orientation and training in order to participate in ongoing classroom activities. Teachers are legally responsible for the children in their classroom, and if volunteers don't understand the rules and procedures, conflicts can arise. Misunderstandings can result, and neither children, parents, nor teachers are well served. Back-to-School Night can provide a forum for teachers to acquaint parents with the volunteer opportunities in the classroom. At this point, some parents may be able to commit to a regular schedule of classroom participation, whereas others may only be able to contribute occasionally. A later meeting, sometimes led by the reading specialist or guidance counselor together with the classroom teacher, introduces parents to the classroom routines and provides guidelines for their participation.

Regularly Scheduled Volunteers. Schedules for regular classroom volunteers work more smoothly if teachers make a monthly calendar and send parents reminders of the volunteer days. Each morning before the children arrive, the teacher and volunteers spend a few minutes discussing the events of the day. At the end of the day, they meet again briefly to discuss how the day went. For the experience to be successful, both teachers and volunteers need to recognize that the teacher is the major decision maker and authority figure in the classroom. Teachers must respect the skills volunteers bring, but they must establish and communicate the classroom rules to volunteers, so children do not receive mixed messages.

Occasional Volunteers. Since many parents and community members are employed, teachers have become more flexible in their expectations of volunteers. Schools must also consider ways to involve parents who are home, caring for younger children. Facilitating a babysitting exchange or providing child care would allow such parents to volunteer.

To involve those who can only participate occasionally, one creative teacher has an open policy on volunteers and invites working parents to observe and help whenever they have time off. He keeps a list of special activities that need extra classroom help. When parent volunteers arrive, the teacher is then ready to use them productively to assist children. This policy has been especially helpful in securing more male volunteers.

When parents do not have time for regular classroom volunteer work, they can also help with special activities, such as planning, organizing, or accompanying the class on field trips. Classrooms use materials that can be prepared or repaired at home. Parents can help by making play dough, sewing smocks, or cutting out items, and many parents are happy to participate in this way. Schools also hold functions in which parents can render support services; these include helping organize for National Education Week, participating in fund-raising activities, or supporting the Read-a-Book Club.

Parents as Tutors. Many programs use volunteers to help children with reading and provide special training sessions to help them to develop skills for literacy tutoring (Lilly & Green, 2004). Volunteers commit to come regularly, take children to a quiet area, and read with and to them. The volunteers also help individual children with projects and assist them in practicing certain skills. This individual attention is especially helpful for children whose parents are unable to read to them at home or otherwise lack the time or ability to assist them with their developing reading skills.

Parents Sharing Expertise. Some educators have devised plans whereby volunteers offer an enriched program for children in their school. In one Maryland program, on Wednesday afternoons, community members present a variety of programs that reflect particular volunteers' skills and interests. An expert quilter provided quilting lessons for six weeks. A bird carver introduced the beginning steps of carving. There were flower-growing and -arranging classes, bird and rock identification classes, and discussions on topics from Caldecott and Newbery Award–winning children's books. At the beginning, volunteers wrote a brief description of their "course," indicating the number of lessons and appropriate age range. Children then signed up, but as the program developed, some adults began to join their children in taking the classes. Both children and adults found that they enjoyed learning in such multiage groupings.

Expressions of Appreciation. Volunteers receive rewards for their efforts in different ways. Seeing children's progress is very satisfying, and children have their unique ways of showing delight in having someone read to them or help them with a project. Reaching to take the adult's hand, offering a hug, expressing, "I read this entire book to my mom after you helped me yesterday," or making a special drawing of "us reading together" expresses better than anything how much children benefit. Letters of appreciation can come from children, teachers, the parent coordinator, or the school principal. Many schools have special dinners or events to formally thank volunteers.

REFLECTION

Consider honestly your feelings about having classroom volunteers. Would you be apprehensive about inviting parents and others into your classroom when you are a beginning teacher? If so, resolve to talk with practicing teachers about how they coped with their anxieties about parent volunteers.

Parents and community members regularly involved in classrooms or school events find themselves at a committed level of involvement from which they gain knowledge about their schools. Children's education is further enhanced when the entire community recognizes the importance of this level of cooperation and participation.

Parents and Community Members as Advocates

In general, teachers expect parents to be involved with their children's education at the basic or **minimum level**. This means communicating with the school about the child's progress and participating in major events, such as conferences and special occasions. Some parents and community members become involved as more committed participants in the classroom by tutoring or volunteering in other ways. Teachers encourage this increased level of involvement because they find that it produces better results for their students (Berger, 2004). A third level of involvement involves individuals who take on additional responsibilites at the school by assuming the role of advocates.

When parents or community members become advocates for children, they seek to influence school policy. Some parents in this role work within the framework of committees and the administrative structure. Parents who feel that the school policy is adversely affecting their children may initiate action. In such cases, they meet with teachers, principals, school-board members, and even local and state legislators to advocate a change in policy. Recall that it was a single parent, and then a group of parents on a grassroots level, who eventually succeeded in securing appropriate education for children with disabilities through PL 94-142, the Individuals with Disabilities Education Act (IDEA).

Other parents become strong advocates for change within an entire school system. Parents may seek election to school-board positions because they wish to see change and feel that this is a way for their voices to be heard. Federal legislation also has resulted in some parents having a policy-making role. Head Start Chapter I programs, and programs under IDEA are required to have parents on their policy-level councils. These parents then have a voice in program development, hiring teachers, the kinds of training offered to teachers, and other policies that affect the programs.

Not all school systems or teachers embrace parent advocacy enthusiastically, nor can all parents operate at an oversight level of involvement. Such advocacy and involvement work well only when both parties—parents and teachers—have a voice in the decisions and work cooperatively together. Some parents have served on curriculum committees, steering committees, or school improvement teams and have advocated or demanded change, only to find that nothing changes. This means frustration. Only when parents, teachers, and school administrators are able to recognize each other's expertise and are willing to assume responsibility for pulling together can change occur. Building coalitions of parents and teachers working for the best interests of their children is the most powerful advocacy role any person can undertake (Bloom, 1992).

Parent Education

Chapter 2 discussed the trends of parent education over the past century. As noted, in the early history of the United States, parents learned about educating their children from their own parents or relatives. Then, as psychology moved to the fore, professionals became the experts, and parent education regarding child development and wise parenting practices became a part of the school's responsibility.

Presently, we again find recognition of parents' skills and expertise. In some innovative programs, parent education means that teachers are learning new skills for interacting with parents. Teachers value parents' ideas, help parents understand their own skills, and more effectively integrate home and community knowledge with classroom learning. In addition, innovative practices in parent education reflect efforts to include parents from all economic and ethnic groups within a community (Fine & Lee, 2001).

Some schools attempt to involve their parent group in those education programs that parents themselves see as particularly needed. Seefeldt and Barbour (1998) described a program of outreach in which a principal succeeded in getting parents involved by allowing parents to choose and plan their own topics. Many hard-to-reach parents became intrigued and began coming to these informal but educational sessions.

Some schools find that developing a **parent center** within the school gives parents a sense of belonging. Sessions in parent centers run the gamut from reviewing general child-rearing practices to dealing with behavioral problems and drugs in the community, to providing language instruction for non-English speakers. The meetings often are unstructured, led by laypersons, and involve a great deal of discussion and idea exchange among the participants. Some schools provide a collection of materials, including books, videos, and articles related to child development, health and safety, managing behavior, and other topics of interest, in their parent centers and encourage parents to check them out. The center may also have listings of local resources and social services for parents.

Several specially designed programs exist for helping parents develop skills in working with their children. Three popular program models used during the past 25 years include Gordon's (2000) Parent Effectiveness Training; Popin's (1990) Active Parenting Discussion Group; and the Dinkmeyer, McKay, and Dinkmeyer (1997) Systemic Training for Effective Parenting.

Children's Resources International (Daniels, 2002) in partnership with Montgomery County, Maryland, Early Childhood Services, developed a unique series of workshops designed to assist parents in helping their children develop the skills needed to learn to read and write. Each literacy-learning party, as these workshops are called, introduces a specific literacy component and offers parents practical and useful activity suggestions for home use. Like most effective parent education, these workshops include lecture and discussion, practical suggestions, and lots of opportunities for interaction among the participants. The Home Connections to Learning strategy (Mass & Cohan, 2006) incorporated videotaped classroom lessons that demonstrated how teachers were guiding and instructing children in literacy and math. Parents were encouraged to borrow the videos and use

Michael Newman / PhotoEdit Inc.

A learning-literacy party workshop assists parents in learning about and discussing ways to help their children develop literacy skills.

the suggested follow-up activities provided in a packet that accompanied the videos.

Education Through Materials. Learning packets and family theme bags are two practices that teachers have devised for helping parents of at-risk children. In these, parents receive a packet of information and ideas for how to interact in a way that increases children's early literacy development (Spewock, 1991). This idea has been taken a step further with videotapes (Mass & Cohan, 2006) and on-line (Narvaez, Feldman, & Theriot, 2006) modeling of strategies for teaching children at home with follow-up materials for parents to use.

In one Maine program, learning packets are sent to parents of newborns and each succeeding year until age five. The packet contains information about child development, ideas for fostering growth, and tips on good parenting. Ideas include ways to use books, simple games to play at each age level, and artworks or crafts to create using inexpensive materials.

Family theme bags are cloth bags sent home with preschoolers that contain a stuffed animal, a journal, a file-folder game, "What if . . .?" cards,

songs–finger plays, a storybook, and art supplies. An introductory letter outlines the purpose of the bag and the value of the activities suggested. The stuffed animal or puppet provides a theme, and games, songs, and activities relate to that theme. For example, the zoo bag contains ideas for making zoo sandwiches, a song about an elephant, and a simple board game with a zoo pattern. The journal is provided so that parents can write their comments on how children respond to the materials and games. When children return the bags, the teacher reads the journals to the class (Helm, 1994).

WORKING WITH SELECTED FAMILIES

The strategies used for collaborating with parents of all children in your classroom can be effective, no matter what the circumstances are. However, some groups need special consideration, especially when traditional methods are not working.

Members of ethnic minorities, **homeless** and migrant families, gay and lesbian parents, and certain individual families may be hard to reach. Yet, it is imperative that schools find ways to connect with all families. The first step is for teachers to examine their own feelings toward parents who are outside the mainstream and with whom it may be more difficult to establish contact. It is natural for teachers to feel angry, guilty, frustrated, exhausted, and even disapproving when no communication seems to work or when others exhibit different priorities or a different lifestyle from ones own. Being honest about your feelings and discussing them with others will help you to avoid using terms or making statements that hurt or anger parents who may have been rejected in other situations (Olsen & Fuller, 2003).

Culturally Diverse Families

When working with culturally diverse families, teachers must understand the differences that exist between the language of the school and that of the home (Neito, 2002). Keep in mind that more than 13 million residents of the United States do not speak English well, and another four million have almost no English language facility. If parents speak limited English, it is essential to find someone who can translate written documents as well as oral communications during conferences and other face-to-face interactions. When teachers work with different linguistic groups, learning some words and expressions in the other language communicates to parents that the teacher values their language and accepts the two-way responsibility for communicating. Even when working with families whose native language is English, teachers must refrain from using educational jargon or other language patterns that may inhibit communication.

Teachers must also recognize that different cultural groups may have differing understandings about the roles of families and schools and may need to adjust to the heightened expectations of parents in American schools. In some cultures, it is considered the sole responsibility of the teacher to educate, and parents would

hesitate to intrude on the teacher's job (Joshi, 2005).

Maria, a recent immigrant from El Salvador, noted, "Once I put my kids on the bus for school in the morning, I felt like my parenting job was complete for the school day. I felt like they (the school) didn't want me there; only white people go in to help. It wasn't for me." Taking advantage of a parent-training program sponsored by a nonprofit community organization, Impact Silver Spring, Maria learned how to read a report card, press for the right class placements, and become more involved in her children's education. She went on to become a regular classroom volunteer and eventually was hired as an outreach coordinator for Hispanic parents.

Minority families who see pictures of diverse people represented on classroom walls, books and materials representing various racial and ethnic groups, and signs in their native language will feel recognized and welcomed at the school. Educational activities designed to respect all cultures in the classroom also enhance communication between home and school. By making a special effort to involve families from ethnic minority groups, teachers can strengthen understanding. Most parents have special knowledge of their heritage and culture that they will share with a class when approached in a positive way.

In one California school, parents of different ethnic backgrounds contributed in several ways. A Mexican American parent helped children prepare traditional foods for a holiday celebration, and a Japanese American mother showed children how to make origami birds. A Native American father invited a second-grade class to his workshop and demonstrated basic skills in silver work. A recent German immigrant brought her collection of dolls to the school and explained the regional costumes the dolls wore. Inviting parents to add special items to the classroom, such as food containers and clothing to dramatic play area, is another way to help the classroom environment reflect the lives and cultures of the children. Home-activity bags that include books from various minority groups and related information and activity ideas is another way to promote understanding across cultures

(Pattnaik, 2003). Children's literature is particularly useful in presenting abstract concepts about cultures in a simple yet meaningful way.

REFLECTION

Visit your local library to find children's literature about cultural groups you may encounter in your work with children and families. Consider how you can use these books to help families feel at home in your classroom, and add the titles to the collection in Appendix I.

Homeless and Migrant Families

Working with homeless and migrant families is one of the most challenging tasks a teacher faces. In spite of the McKinney Homeless Assistance Act of 1987 (PL 100-77) and subsequent amendments, which require states to guarantee access to education for homeless children, many homeless children are not in school. The requirements for registration, such as proof of residency, age, immunizations, and health records, are too much for many homeless families to cope with, and often these families find it easier to keep their children out of school (Ames & Farrell, 2005; Eddowes & Hranitz, 1989). Parents may also avoid putting their children in school because they are shamed and embarrassed about their living situations. When children do have access to schooling, they often are not in the school for long before parents are forced to move again.

Often homeless families are struggling with other problems, such as illness, spouse abuse, depression, and poverty. Migrant farmwork is a dangerous occupation, and children are exposed to hazardous materials, motorized machinery, and a lack of sanitation. Many migrant workers do not receive prenatal care, dental care, or other basic health care. Consequently, children are at higher risk for disease and chronic illness than is the general population (Duarte & Rafanello, 2001). These families need assistance in securing health

and social services, and if asked to help a school educate their children, the request may be beyond the skill of many homeless and migrant parents. It is important to remember, however, that the lack of a permanent home and financial resources doesn't mean that parents don't love their children and want them to succeed. When homeless and migrant children are in a school, personnel need to unite their efforts to find services that will enable parents to support their children's education. The following list contains several suggestions for teachers to assist parents in homeless situations (Quint, 1994; Rafanello, 2004; Yamaguchi, Strawser, & Higgins, 1997):

1. Provide information about the availability of various services and funding options and how to qualify for mental health services, child care, after-school care, and transportation arrangements.

2. Suggest options for parent involvement in the school. Although regular commitment to volunteering in classrooms impossible for most homeless parents, it is wrong to assume that the parents are unable or unwilling to help. They may be able to spend a day tutoring or supervising recess. When they give comfort to another child, they receive the joy of assisting someone else.

3. Be sensitive to parents' ability to provide baked goods, pay for special class events, or have children bring materials for classroom projects. Children whose families cannot provide such materials are often discriminated against by other children and even by teachers. Consider asking homeless parents to assist in the classroom as their way of contributing.

4. Keep in mind that homeless parents, too, need parent workshops and opportunities to share their concerns and "stories." It often takes special handling to get these parents to trust enough to be a part of such sessions.

5. Coordinate efforts with local shelters. Some school programs or workshops can be started at shelters. If parents develop confidence in shelter personnel, those parents often are willing to participate in school programs with support for transportation and even child care for younger children. We must

try not to segregate the homeless, denying children and parents opportunities for interaction with diverse groups.

Gay and Lesbian Parents

Most teachers today are sensitive to different family structures and are trained to support children when families are in the process of change because of death, divorce, remarriage, or adoption. Less attention has been given to working with gay and lesbian parents or with families who have relatives who are gay or lesbian. Although relatively small in number, this group is increasingly visible, and these parents need to be supported as partners in their children's education. Teachers may need workshops (Gelnaw, 2005) to enable them to deal with their feelings about this family configuration and to find ways to support children whose parents or other important family members are gay or lesbian.

In a diverse society, parents expect that their family structure will be treated with dignity and respect in the classroom. Some educators, however, may fear being accused of promoting homosexuality when they are sensitive to the needs of children from gay and lesbian households. It may be helpful to recognize that this is not an issue of sexuality but of relationships. Children whose parents are gay or lesbian feel the same sense of belonging and being taken care of by their parents as all children. Using children's literature that includes various family configurations will reinforce this similarity and promote understanding of diverse families.

When children of gay and lesbian parents experience school difficulty related to their parents' sexual orientation, teachers must approach the parents to discuss their problems. By developing a zero tolerance policy toward bullying and harassment, administrators, teachers, and parents can work together to promote respect and tolerance. In classrooms where some parents oppose books or discussions related to this topic, special handling is required. Janosik and Green (1992) have substantial recommendations for working with families that include gay members. Also, some communities have gay and lesbian groups specially trained to work with adults whose strong beliefs reject this lifestyle. Inviting parents to join you in one of these sessions can open the door for discussion and for better understanding of this controversial topic.

REFLECTION

Think back on your own childhood and the family configurations you encountered then. Compare that to the families you are reading about in this text and consider how you will welcome all kinds of families into your classroom.

Other Family Situations

Parents raising children with disabilities may need to be treated with sensitivity as well. It is also essential that educators and community workers be knowledgeable about disabilities and their implications for families. Some families may be working through the grief that can accompany the realization that a child is going to require special care and services (Lerner, Lowenthal, & Egan, 2003). Others have developed extensive knowledge about their child and have much information that will be helpful to the teaching staff (Hiatt-Michael, 2004). Effective communication between teachers and parents of children with special needs is key as is the importance of clarity and precision about procedures and objectives. See Chapter 6 for an in-depth exploration of ways parents and teachers can work together to share information, deal with everyday situations, and ensure the best outcome for children with disabilities.

Both typically developing children and those with special needs are being raised in foster families, by grandparents, by parents sharing custody, and by other adults in various family configurations. These parental figures may be difficult to reach, yet their participation in school is especially important to children who may have experienced

Figure 11–6   Inclusive Definition
of Family
Source: Adapted from an exhibit of the
Boston Children's Museum as quoted by
Gelnaw, 2005.

Families

We may be related by birth or adoption or invitation.

We may belong to the same race or we may be of different races.

We may look like each other or different from each other.

The important thing is we belong to each other.

We care for each other.

We agree, disagree, love, fight, work together.

We belong to each other.

much disruption in their short lives. Teachers need to reach out to these families with an especially inclusive and welcoming manner. Learning the name by which children call the adults who care for them is especially important. Many teachers are careful to avoid saying gender-specific parental labels and instead will urge children to bring important papers home to their grown-up. Further, using inclusive language when defining family (see Figure 11–6) will feel welcoming to gay and lesbian parents as well as to others whose family configuration is different than the one mother and one father model.

HANDLING COLLABORATIVE RELATIONSHIPS

As noted in earlier chapters, we have a long history of parental involvement in U.S. schools. Some relationships have been very positive for particular parents, teachers, and community members. Good relationships do not just happen, however. Both internal and external conditions and factors help establish better relationships.

Conditions for Positive Relationships

One important human factor for developing positive collaborations is mutual respect. Each party in

a collaborative effort needs the concern of the others as well as the expertise, viewpoints, and experiences others possess.

Recognizing and supporting the expertise of others is not always easy. Comer (1980), in developing his collaboration model, maintains that the project nearly failed several times. It took three years to develop the trust and respect necessary for the school to begin a change process that would offer equal access and opportunity for all students. Commenting on this, Comer stated, "In order to provide good learning experiences for students, trust and respect must exist so that behavior, teaching and learning issues can be addressed. Such a climate cannot be imposed: it must grow out of governance and management arrangements and ways of working based on knowledge of social conditions and human and system behaviors" (p. 230).

Developing such respect requires compassion, a willingness to listen to others' points of view, and a willingness to compromise. Often it is school personnel who must take the initiative in establishing a sense of respect. For the relationship between teachers and parents to develop its fullest potential, however, both must consider each other as equals and share a commitment to open, two-way communication (Hanhan, 2003). No one right way exists to accomplish this, but concerned teachers and administrators devise ways that establish relationships with their students' parents through face-to-face, electronic, and written communication.

There are two very simple and immediate techniques that teachers can use to improve communication with parents. One is to *ask* instead of *tell*. The other is to *listen* instead of *talk*. A key component in establishing good partnerships is people's ability to really listen to each other. Regrettably, although professional adults are involved in communication activities about 70% of the time, less than half of that is spent listening, and even at that, the listening is not done well (Studer, 1993/1994). When teachers listen well, they do not interrupt to move on to their own agenda. When they reply to parents, they reflect back what they have heard and seek to validate, empathize, and problem solve with the parent. When both teachers and parents are willing to learn about and practice communication skills, student success increases (Gonzalez-Mena, 2006).

Beyond the willingness to establish respect and develop good communication, external factors help collaborative efforts to function. It is important to establish support systems such as workshops to assist people in developing better communication skills. Time must be provided for meetings to discuss needs and objectives. To meet parent, teacher, and community members' time constraints, schedules must remain as flexible as possible. Teachers may need to be released from classes or compensated for evening meetings. Businesses need to examine the possibility of flexible hours of operation or flexible working hours for their parent employees. Having options for parent and community member involvement establishes a good basis for collaborative efforts, allowing all who are or wish to be involved to select a comfortable participation level.

A welcoming physical and social environment is an essential first step in creating a school climate that encourages parent and community involvement (Lim, 2003). Schools must place a priority on image. Sometimes a simple change in what visitors see when they enter a building makes a great difference. Student artwork and other projects brighten up an entrance. A welcome sign directing visitors to the school office is more effective when it is in English and other langues spoken in the community. A smile and positive attitude from the office staff once a visitor arrives is essential. Space where parents can comfortably wait, perhaps with a coffee pot and some interesting literature about schools, makes visitors feel welcome.

The process of collaboration is one of identifying, establishing, and cultivating positive factors to support interactions. Many ideas make sense for cooperative arrangements—the strategies of most any helping profession can be adapted appropriately. If schools are to become engaged in true partnerships, everyone concerned must expand and refine their communication, negotiation, and cooperation skills.

Barriers to Good Relationships

No matter how well intentioned people are, some barriers surface that will result in breakdowns of communication and good relationships. One basic hurdle revolves around the different philosophical positions and perspectives people have regarding how children learn and what they should be taught. For example, if a school attempts a constructivist approach to learning and parents do not understand how their children are being taught to read, write, and learn number facts, a barrier can develop. Parents could well become angry and accuse the school of ignoring discipline and not teaching the basics.

Different beliefs about how and who should teach sex education can create misunderstandings. Or, parents may consider discipline measures as either too harsh or too lenient, and these different perceptions will cause friction between home, school, and community. Issues such as these can spark problems, and they will fester and add to existing subsurface distrust if no mechanism is present to address them.

Attitudes can also present barriers to good relationships. Parents and community members

Scott Cunningham / Merrill

A welcoming physical environment always helps to establish good relationships.

have feelings and attitudes about school that date back to their own childhoods. Parents who had unpleasant school experiences are often reluctant to become involved with their children's schools. A diminished self-concept is often present in such cases, and the isolation breeds more fear. Such parents resist contact with schools out of fear of criticism of themselves and their children. This circumstance helps no one, least of all the children. Schools need to work gently but with determination to overcome negativism and encourage positive contact.

Nonverbal interactions often cause barriers to good relationships. Teachers or parents may state one thing, but their nonverbal stance communicates another. For example, during a conference, one parent crossed her arms, saying, in what seemed an annoyed tone, "I thought Janey did well on that project." The teacher interpreted this to mean, "I don't agree with what you said." The teacher then paused, moved slightly away, and murmured, "Well, it was an interesting project." When both moved on to another topic, the real significance of Janey's effort was lost. Both left the situation feeling defensive because the

nonverbal behavior of both parties cut off further communication.

Fear affects teachers as well as parents, and teachers may do little to encourage parental or community involvement. When teachers are uncertain or insecure about their own teaching skills, they fear criticism of how they do their job and discourage parent participation in their classrooms. When we have local criticism of schools, teachers become tired of being scapegoats for all the wrongs of society, and they often express a desire to be left alone to teach. When such attitudes permeate the school, parents are made to feel unwelcome in many different ways.

When wide socioeconomic and cultural differences exist between school personnel and local families, misunderstandings can cause friction and often anger. Barriers are created when value systems differ and neither party is willing or able to examine differences and find common ground.

External features may also become barriers. Entering a school for the first time can be daunting even for the experienced. In some instances, doors are locked for safety reasons, and one must ring to enter. Sometimes the first thing one sees on entering a school is the notice, "All Visitors Must Report to the Principal's Office." Parents who were often sent to the principal's office during their school years will not feel very welcome. When the office is difficult to find and no one is around to assist, schools again communicate that visitors are unwelcome. Office personnel are sometimes too busy to assist or may appear annoyed at the interruption, or they may ask in an intimidating way, "Do you have an appointment?" Unwelcoming signals are easily discerned and too often found.

REFLECTION

Visit several schools to find out what is it like going into a new school? Try to visit a library and a gym, as well as a classroom. Then, imagine yourself as a parent and speculate about how would you feel in these schools.

Teachers and administrators are busy people struggling to maintain a productive environment for student learning. That is their most important task, and many think the time and energy needed to add parental and community involvement to their workloads just isn't available. Such school personnel communicate the unimportance of parental involvement.

COMMUNITY INVOLVEMENT

Like family involvement in schools, community involvement occurs at various levels ranging from minimal contact through advocacy. Again, teachers and administrators have the greater responsibility for reaching out to the community to develop partnerships, but parents often play a role in getting individuals, agencies, and business engaged with the local schools. Such involvement may entail a one-time contribution of goods and services, an on-going site for field trips, or a continuing volunteer relationship.

Good ideas for collaboration aren't always between school and community agencies. The Chicago Public Library and the Chicago Police Department teamed up to provide a number of interactive programs. One program was a Mystery Beat Book Club, where students read mysteries and met various police officers who explained how mysteries are solved in real life. Another was a Get Hooked on Fishing, Not on Drugs program. Police personnel spent time with youngsters, both in the library and at special fishing spots, examining the art of fishing. All agreed that the programs helped the police reach youngsters in positive ways, the library maximized its resources, and children had fun, associated with good role models, and became involved in interactive activities that enhanced their reading skills (Burnette, 1998).

Trips into the Community

All children have experience with their community and have learned many different concepts from these encounters. Building on this familiarity, preschool and primary schools take field trips that focus on specific aspects of community life and provide children with new and extended insights. Carefully planned field trips enhance and make more meaningful the objectives of a unit of study. Students studying economics, for example, can set up a bank and a store in their classroom and practice using the bank and store in ways they learned from their parents or from books they have read. A trip to an actual bank and store, where they can ask specific questions, though, allows them to view how adults behave in such places. It gives students behind-the-scenes experience.

When children have particular questions to ask or things to see or do, they gain skills in observing, collecting information, making inferences, comparing information with others, and drawing conclusions. Also, trips produce new ideas, which children transfer to their dramatic play, reading, writing, and other classroom instruction. A trip provides motivation for further

Field trips enhance and make
meaningful objectives of a unit of
study.

Kevin Bennett / Bangor Daily News

interests and learning, as it did for the first-graders in the following vignette.

Nigel's class, accompanied by several parents, took a walking trip to the pet store to get food for the lizard they had found in the play yard and were now studying in class. While at the store, they were fascinated by a hermit crab and convinced their teacher to buy one for further study. Nigel became so interested that with his parents he visited the local aquarium. A naturalist at the aquarium told him more about hermit crabs and where they lived. With this information, the family took a trip to the seashore, and all were able to observe hermit crabs in their natural habitat. Nigel's stepfather videotaped the family's excursion, and Nigel showed the tape to the class and described his experience to his classmates.

Trips into the community are not restricted to gaining understanding of the neighborhood. Children can make trips intended to contribute in some way to the community, such as enhancing the local environment. Trips around the school can focus on cleaning up the area or planting flowers or shrubs. Some organizations "adopt" a highway, assuming the responsibility to clean up litter along a specific section of the road. Classrooms can adopt a neighborhood park, a playground, or a street and keep it attractive.

A visit to a nursing home or hospital presents opportunities for children to show older or ill people their artwork, sing or play some special songs, or present a dramatic presentation. When child-care centers are located in adult day-care centers or nursing homes, older persons often regularly read to children or engage in activities, such as cooking or making collages, with the children.

A related idea became a project for older children, who followed the Foxfire concept of visiting and interviewing older residents to hear their stories of the past. The class collected and published the stories in book form and sold them at school functions. In this case, the intent was not to help other people but was rather to help children interact, appreciate, and be involved with an older generation.

Bringing the Community into the School

Children can travel in their community for educational purposes, but it is also possible to include community members in the classroom. Traditionally, teachers have invited doctors, firefighters, or police officers to share their services with children, but imaginative teachers have found other ways to involve community members. One kindergarten teacher instituted a "Royal Reader" program and each week invited a person from the community to read aloud to the class. Using some regal music as background, the teacher introduced the reader, who entered the room wearing a crown and cape. Over the course of the year, employees of the power plant, water company, community college, retail stores, and various other local business and services came to the classroom to read and tell a little bit about their work.

REFLECTION

Think about the resources available in your community and the kinds of activities that community members might be able to provide to the children in your class. What value do you see in such activities? How will you build such experiences into your curriculum?

Teachers also invite specific community members to the classroom to extend or enhance a unit. One biology professor enjoyed taking part of his collection of rare butterflies to a second-grade classroom each year during their "butterfly unit." In the spring, he walked in nearby fields with children hunting out cocoons or newly hatched butterflies.

Increasingly, community agencies such as libraries and museums, are offering "reverse field trips" by sending a member of their staff to schools with selected materials to present to children. At one nursery school, naturalists from a nonprofit foundation brought several rehabilitating owls to the school for the children to observe and then led an evening "owl prowl" in the woods surrounding the school. A twist on this evening was that fathers and other special adult males were invited on the owl prowl, offering them an opportunity to participate in a unique and appealing manner. Artists, musicians, and other performers can also be invited to schools to provide children with arts-based experiences.

As in planning for field trips, teachers need to plan for special guests. They tell children about the guest, encourage them to think of things they want to know, and help them understand how they are expected to act during the visit. It is important that teachers remind visitors of children's interest level, attention span, and need for hands-on experience.

Some resources from the outdoor environment can be brought into the classroom for closer examination, but teachers must carefully choose these resources. Endangered plants must not be disturbed, and certain animals are unsafe to bring into classrooms. But colorful leaves, nuts, fruit, twigs fallen from trees, rocks and seashells, minerals embedded in bits of rock, insects in aerated jars, and pond creatures for classroom aquariums are specimens that children can examine and study in the classroom. See Figure 10–1 for a listing of community resources.

Involving the Business Community

Businesses have provided support for schools in various ways for many years, most often in the form of contributions of goods or funds. Restaurants have contributed gift certificates but may also contribute a percentage of their profits on a particular night that has been designated a school fund-raiser. Parents are encouraged to patronize the restaurant on that evening. Other restaurants have established a "Dine Out for Charity" month and will donate a percentage of each order to the local school or agency. Still other businesses will contribute funds for some particular project or materials. Band uniforms or costumes for a school production are items that local businesspeople take pride in providing for community junior and senior high schools.

Other businesses have contributed classroom equipment, such as calculators and computers. Some businesses will sponsor special programs such as "Read to a Parent and Get a Pizza." A school-supplies store agreed to provide one enterprising kindergarten teacher with a year's supply of fingerpaints when her classroom budget was

Some businesses will provide
funds for sports uniforms.

Pearson Learning Photo Studio

APPLYING THESE CONCEPTS TO YOUR WORK
WITH CHILDREN AND FAMILIES

As you consider the strategies presented here for
building collaborative relationships with families and
community members, think about how you could
use what you have learned.

- Once you have established a relationship with
  parents, consider how you will communicate
  with them about their child's progress. What systems will you use to communicate expectations
  for homework? Will you have weekly progress reports, a newsletter, or a classroom Web site? How
  will you prepare for parent conferences?

- Classroom volunteers will help you provide
  more individualized attention to the children in
  your classroom. How will you establish a volunteer program? How will you ensure that working parents have opportunities to make
  contributions to the class?

- Also think about how you will reach out to the
  community. Brainstorm about the kinds of field
  trips that can be taken in the neighborhood to
  enhance children's learning and give them opportunities to contribute to the good of the
  community.

- Think about how you will use technology and
  other electronic modes of communication to
  reach out to parents and community.

- Do an on-line search for ideas on welcoming
  children, parents, and community members to
  a classroom. Select the ones that appeal to you
  and add them to your resource notebook.

reduced. In return, children's work, demonstrating the creative potential of finger paint, was exhibited in the store.

Businesses also cooperate with schools by providing release time for employees to volunteer in the schools. In some instances, it is parents and employees who wish to be a part of their children's classroom, but in other instances, time is allowed for unrelated employees to become volunteer readers or mentors or to relate their special expertise with children.

Collaborating with business for better schools requires a spirit of mutual respect and reciprocity of benefit. For partnerships to be effective, teachers must visit the business establishment to determine its educational possibilities, and business personnel should visit the schools to become acquainted with their function, goals, and daily operation. Each partner needs to know the other's resources, ideas, and commitments. Committees for each organization need to make decisions affecting the support and purpose of the collaboration. Teachers must be represented on the appropriate business committee, and involved business personnel should be a part of the school planning committee. Through such collaborations, teachers, parents, and community members gain new understanding of the importance of good schools to a community and of how the community can contribute to the school's excellence.

SUMMARY AND REVIEW

Forming special relationships with parents and communities to enhance the education of children is not a new concept in the United States. As educators have gained more responsibility and authority over children's education, they have realized that increasing family and community involvement enriches the experience for all. Although educators have normally considered themselves experts in teaching children, they acknowledge that without parental and community support, their job is more difficult.

Frequent communication between home and school is important. Parent–teacher conferences, newsletters, phone calls, home visits, e-mail, and Web sites as well as parents' participation in classroom and school

activities are more effective when teachers experiment with different strategies so that each family is reached at some level.

Many educators now recognize that when teachers, parents, and community members form a relationship of equality and shared responsibility, schools become strong and children acquire greater cognitive and social skills.

SUGGESTED ACTIVITIES AND QUESTIONS

1. Ask your parents (or someone you know well) about parent–teacher conferences or home visits in which they were involved when you were a child. Determine how useful they felt such activity was. If you know a parent of a primary-school-aged child, ask the same questions and compare strategies and parental reactions then and now.

2. Interview parents who volunteer in their children's classroom. Solicit their opinion of this involvement, asking how often they volunteer, how they became involved, why they think it is important, and what they are learning from the experience.

3. Locate a commercial establishment that displays children's work and ask how the school became involved. Compare notes with classmates who have interviewed other establishments to determine what kinds of involvement your community appears to have with schools.

4. Obtain from a school administrator (or parents of a school-age child) copies of newsletters sent home to parents. In your class, compare the kinds of information they contain. Discuss whether some are more "parent friendly" than others, and why.

5. Locate a Web site designed for parents of children with special needs, to determine some of the issues that are important to them. Develop a list of strategies that would help teachers build relationships with parents of children with disabilities.

RESOURCES

Books

Epstein, J. L., Sanders, M., Salinas, K. C., Jansorn, N. R., & Van Voorhis, F. (2002). *School, family, and community partnerships: Your handbook for action* (2nd ed.). Thousand Oaks, CA: Corwin.

Patrikakou, E. N., Weisberg, R. P., Redding, S., & Walberg, J. (Eds.). (2005). *School–family partnerships for children's success.* New York: Teachers College Press.

Powers, J. (2005). *Parent-friendly early learning tips and strategies for working well with families.* St. Paul, MN: Redleaf.

Films and Videos

Building bridges between teachers and families [Video, 21 min]. (2003). Seattle, WA: Harvest Resources.

A children's journey: Investigating the fire truck [Video, 45 min]. (2000). New York: Teachers College Press.

Conducting effective conferences with parents [Video, 22 min]. (1998). New York: Insight Media.

Partnerships with parents [Video, 28 min]. (1996). Columbia: South Carolina Educational Television with the National Association for Education of Young Children.

Organizations

Community Action for Public Schools
Center for Law and Education
1875 Connecticut Avenue, NW
Suite 510
Washington, DC 20009
http://www.cleweb.org/caps.htm

Learning First Alliance
1001 Connecticut Avenue, NW, Suite 335
Washington, DC 20016
(http://www.learningfirst.org)

National Coalition for Parent Involvement in Education
3029 Old Lee Highway
Suite 91-A
Fairfax, VA 22030
http://www.ncpie.org

Web Sites

www.cec.sped.org   The Council for Exceptional Children is an organization for professionals and parents and provides multiple resources, such as training opportunities and legislation updates.

www.csos.jhu.edu/   Center on School, Family, and Community Partnerships, a component of Center for Social Organization of Schools, helps families, educators, and community members work together to improve schools.

http://www.naeyc.org/ece/eyly   Early Years Are Learning Years from the National Association for the Education of Young Children offers short articles for teachers, parents, and community members that are suitable for newsletters.

www.ncela.gwu.edu/library/parent.htm   The on-line library of the National Clearinghouse for English Language Acquisition provides materials on different ways schools can encourage parents and the community to take an active role in the education of linguistically and culturally diverse students.

Models for Parent–School–Community Partnerships

We are all the crew of Spaceship Earth. Like Apollo, the crew must work and learn together and manage the resources of this world with new imagination.

(Jim Lovell, Apollo 13 Commander, in *Lost Moon* [1994])

Much is right with U.S. educational experiences in spite of some well-publicized problems. Education planners and policy makers in most communities have a suitable base to build on, and they can draw from numerous models to bring about improvements and viable partnerships. This final chapter presents the issues to be considered when working together, and it highlights several worthy collaborations found in American school districts today. After reading this chapter, you will be able to do the following:

1. Discuss the levels of involvement by community adults in a true collaborative program.

2. Identify the conditions that enhance the growth of partnerships as well as factors that serve as barriers.

3. State the criteria that demonstrate the status of partnerships.

4. Discuss how thoughtful planning, careful implementation, straightforward accountability, and honest communication produce healthy partnerships.

5. Explain the commonalities found in partnership models and how these remain constant in differing programs.

Although they seldom use the term *collaboration*, residents in rural and urban communities have always exercised ways of influencing the upbringing of their youngest citizens. In the following vignette, a now-retired teacher recalls her childhood years in a poor rural community in the 1930s and indicates some ideas that can serve us well in the 21st century.

A minister, the school principal, and our town fathers frequently discussed school problems in our little town and recommended solutions. Their efforts were supported by local parents, and our party-line telephone system, where most families could listen in, aided communication. For example, one child, returning late from school on a spring day was easily found, reprimanded by a passerby, and sent on his way with knowledge that his parents would follow through on the reprimand. Children who needed clothes were identified at school, and with the support of "town fathers," teachers and sometimes others visited the homes. Food, clothing, and other resources were found and delivered, and at times, negligent parents were counseled informally by other parents and by teachers. Our teachers taught formal lessons in the schoolrooms, but they often walked home with us, continuing our education as they discussed the natural world all around us. The community was our playground, and adults who were present supervised everyone's children. Older children educated younger ones in many skills and safety rules. One could feel that this was a cohesive community and one marked by caring. It was, of course, not an ideal system: A few children didn't reach their potential. An overarching support system enhanced our opportunities, though, and all 13 children in my first-grade class completed high school, and seven went on to college in the 1940s.

The narrator of the preceeding vignette demonstrates how parents, schools, and community members all assumed responsibility for children's development. Times were simpler then, and many communities were closely knit, but the aura of communal caring and the need for shared expectations are still valid today. Author James Comer lived in a close-knit urban community during his childhood, and he tells of a similar collaboration of the social institutions that cared for him. In *Maggie's American Dream: The Life and Times of a Black Family*, Comer (1988) recalled his parents, neighbors, and teachers reinforcing each other's goals for children's engagement in learning. The process in Comer's case was also informal, but individuals in each social setting seemed to understand each other's roles. In both stories, these neighborhood children whose parents were sympathetic to the school's and community's goals were more successful than were children whose parents were out of touch.

Society at the beginning of the 21st century is different from that of several decades earlier. It is more difficult to establish common objectives where social institutions can work effectively together. Families have new pressures and heavier burdens, and children have fewer advocates. In many locations, schools have assumed more of the educative, counseling, and social oversight for children (Good & Early, 2000; Olsen & Fuller, 2003), but from many accounts, it is apparent that schools cannot effectively do the job alone (Meier, 2002a).

In this chapter, we detail seven particular program models that have shown success in improving schools and children's education through family, school, and community collaborations. We examine the components that have led to the success of these models and remark on some of the changes made as a result of implementing them on a larger scale. First, though, we discuss some basic principles and distinctive features that one sees with collaborative efforts.

LEVELS OF INVOLVEMENT IN COLLABORATIONS

Good collaborative efforts mean that the individuals in an evolving group endeavor will recognize that different levels or a hierarchy of involvement exist in a partnership (Epstein et al., 2002; Rubin 2002). Some community participants will participate at a minimum level, others at an **associative level**, and still others at a **decision-making level**. Though educators are in the best position for encouraging and establishing partnerships in an area, we find that parents and community members will also assume stronger leadership roles in a collaborative effort.

Understanding Involvement

Laypeople interpret parental and community involvement in school affairs in different ways. Some citizens are proactive and feel naturally connected

to their schools. A larger group views teachers as having total control of children's education, and they either do not seek involvement or feel shut out of the process. This latter group tends to view schools from afar, but its members are often critical when their children don't progress well. Therefore, all educators and involved community workers have a duty to work on attracting this part of the constituency.

So, how much involvement is productive? Different programs will call for differing amounts of involvement by parents and community members, and generally, participatory intensity varies with level. The key to successful collaboration is for almost all community citizens to be involved at one level or another, with a few individuals contributing at all levels.

Minimum Level. For generations, school personnel have reached out to parents and community members in seeking basic support for school programs. For example, children have homework, which teachers request parents to supervise. Or a principal may request help from citizens to advertise some school events. Educators expect parents and other community members to respond to these requests and help with the projects.

The community at large is normally invited to school-sponsored events, and teachers often seek assistance. For example, parents and community members help make costumes for school plays or props for exhibits. Schools have various fund-raising events, such as bake sales and fairs. Again, school personnel seek cooperation from parents and others to attend, contribute items to, and help with the events. Calls go out for such items as egg cartons, juice cans, or carpet samples to use in school projects.

The preceding are all examples of minimal involvement, and most readers will recognize and recall similar events from their own childhood. Such minimal involvement is commonplace; it serves a definite purpose, and it is a good foundation from which to start working for more complete community participation.

Associative Level. Many teachers request parents and community members to become classroom volunteers on a regular basis. These volunteers assist teachers in various ways—from copying materials to reading with children and assisting them in activities. Still others become room mothers (or fathers), organizing other community members, helping to supervise children on school trips, or making calls to solicit classroom support. Some volunteers become involved in enrichment programs, where they offer their special expertise with children in a classroom. Another example is the advocacy work of parents of children with disabilities. These parents frequently become knowledgeable about their child's special needs and also about school processes, so they can go on to become local leaders and advocates for teachers working with children with disabilities. These are examples of associative level participation.

At the associative level, community members also participate in local organizations that support schools. Parent–Teacher Association (PTA) chapters have traditionally supported schools, and through them, parents and teachers cooperate in school improvement ventures. At times, PTAs center on fundraising events; at other times, they may become a political force in the community to improve conditions for children.

Children benefit from adult involvement at the associative level; because of their school experience and intensified role, school expectations are much clearer to these parents, and all communication is facilitated. Stronger ties mean stronger programs, and divisiveness is far less likely when schools and communities enjoy this level of interaction. At any point in time, fewer parents will be involved at the associative level than at the minimal level. Comer (1980) noted that if 5% to 10% of parents become actively involved at this associative level, that number makes up an adequate group, as long as it represents a cross-section of the community.

Decision-Making Level. The third level of parent and community involvement in schools is the **decision-making level**. At this level, individual parents, businesspersons, professionals, and community leaders participate actively in decision making for the education of children.

Parent participation produces little controversy at the minimum and associative levels of involvement. Teachers and school administrators are still in charge of all educational decision making, and parents and community members assist and support the decisions. When parents and others become involved in decision making, however, friction can result (Rubin, 2002). Controversy that paralyzes is, of course, not in the best interests of children. Therefore, successful collaboration of parents, teachers, administrators, and community members at this level requires mutual respect and a new definition of shared responsibility and accountability (Comer, Ben-Avie, Haynes, & Joyner, 1999; Sanders, 2006). Acting at this tier of involvement requires hard work.

Parents at the decision-making level move beyond being committed advocates for their children into sharing responsibility for providing quality (school) education for their own and other children. They serve on curriculum committees, identifying goals and objectives and deciding how to achieve them. At this level, parents are expected to serve on committees that hire school staff. They also might assist in forming advocacy groups to secure necessary local, state, or federal funding. Again, the parents of children with special needs are often able to take leadership roles because of their prior experience working with school personnel, making decisions for appropriate placement of their children, and developing their children's individualized education programs (IEPs).

Usually, parent and community involvement at this level requires only a small percentage of parents, but these representatives must represent the different constituencies within the community. Such involvement dictates changes within the school hierarchy, and such changes can be detrimental unless teachers, administrators, parents, and community members work carefully and with genuine mutual respect to bring gradual change (Comer, Haynes, & Joyner, 1996). Figure 12–1 illustrates the collaborative relations of each level of involvement.

Thus, having community adults functioning at the decision-making level marks a true collaborative

Figure 12–1   Three Levels of Involvement

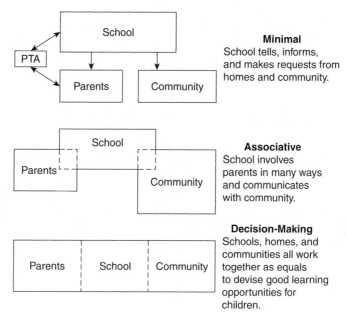

Minimal
School tells, informs, and makes requests from homes and community.

Associative
School involves parents in many ways and communicates with community.

Decision-Making
Schools, homes, and communities all work together as equals to devise good learning opportunities for children.

venture—and that is the goal. To get there, let's follow the ideas in the following section, then look at some examplary programs in the United States today.

REFLECTION

Think about your childhood and consider how your parents were involved with your schools. Try to recall the level of their involvement when you were in grades 2, 3, or 4. How did you as a student feel about this?

COMPONENTS OF SUCCESSFUL CHANGE

Research (Epstein, 1999; U.S. Department of Education, 2006) shows that children improve academically when schools work for better family and community involvement Because of this finding, and because of extensive federal interest in partnerships, a number of school districts are now caught up in the rhetoric of "collaboration." Some have taken serious steps to establish links with other agencies to become full-service schools, where municipal services and social agency support are available at the school site. Others have struggled and had little success beyond goal statements and committee assignments (Sanders, 2006).

As more businesses and community agencies become involved with schools, there always exists a danger that leaders in these agencies start to usurp the rights and responsibilities that classroom teachers owe to their students. In any collaboration, parents and teachers must assume the ethical responsibility for ensuring that everyone involved understands children's developmental levels and vulnerability. Most school personnel want parents and community members to share in the responsibility of educating children, and they seek outside support for resolving nonacademic problems. In academic matters, however, educators are more hesitant to involve parents and community members. Nonetheless, successful partnerships mean shared responsibilities, and successful schools mean that parents, school personnel, and community groups share responsibilities for educational decision making.

Children improve academically
when schools include family and
community members in establishing full-service schools.

Lori Whitley / Merrill

We find that successful partnerships have different strategies for achieving collaboration, but
all have certain elements in common, which Gardner (1993) called "the hooks and glue of joint
ventures" (p. 15). Collaboration will include three
common elements: a planning process, an implementation process, and an accountability process.
Equally important is that in each process, all involved pay constant attention to establishing good
communication and nurturing trust (Sheldon &
Epstein, 2005).

Planning Process

Collaboration requires a communitywide team.
Members of social agencies, businesses, and government agencies, plus teachers, administrators, and
parents, come together, and all make a commitment
to work for the benefit of the community's children.
The community team needs a strong leader, and key
people in the community are crucial for the project
All participants must be willing to work out differences when necessary, and trust and respect for
other viewpoints are even more vital.

During planning, the team determines the
needs of children in the community, develops goals,
and designs procedures for accomplishing these

goals. The team identifies children's particular
needs within the various community contexts, then
assesses the community to identify resources to
meet these needs. Communication, collaboration,
and cooperation among the various team members mean that all agencies will surrender some autonomy in seeking solutions, but in so doing, all
recognize their mutual benefits.

Implementation Process

As the collaboration team develops procedures for
implementing strategies, members ascertain which
agencies can provide personnel and financial resources. Implementation is guaranteed greater success when a team provides orientation and training
sessions, ensuring that parents, teachers, and community people have some basic collaborative skills.

A major step in beginning collaboration is providing workshops that reduce the social distance
among participants and that also improve relationships among parents, community workers, school
staff, and students. Another involves understanding
the interests and expertise of teachers, parents, and
other volunteers, so that all can contribute their best.
Ideally, all participants gain an understanding of how
their service contributes to the goals and objectives.

After the team sets the priorities for the community's needs, it begins to plan and collaborate on such activities as providing families with needed services, improving school and home discipline, adapting curriculum to particular community needs, establishing appropriate social activities, and developing program evaluation strategies.

Assessment Process

People working with collaborative programs must have ways to determine how well their goals are being met. Most projects will review students' classroom work, and many programs develop questionnaires to get feedback from the community about the success of their activities. Data are collected and interpreted regularly, then strategies used in the school programs are altered or continued, accordingly. At least once a year, parents, school staff, and community members will be informed about progress and the changes being made to improve conditions.

Communication

The success of all collaborative programs depends on good communication and careful monitoring of activities. Parents must feel welcome to visit schools and to participate, and teachers must feel they are able to visit homes as needs arise. Community persons must also be part of the communication loop. All must feel welcome in schools and free to offer suggestions.

Good partnership teams will provide many avenues for parents and community members to get information about school activities and the status of the collaboration. Routine notices, telephone messages, personal notes, newsletters, articles in local papers, a Web site, and the direct visiting approach, which volunteers employ in contacting hard-to-reach parents, are all used. Parents are encouraged to write notes, use e-mail, or call teachers when concerns arise and are also encouraged to express appreciation. See Chapter 11 for a larger listing of communication ideas.

PROGRAM MODELS

In this section, we examine the characteristics and the arrangements exhibited by seven program models. Although changes have been made in each, the underlying concepts remain the same as when they started. As you read about and compare these models, you should get a feeling for how the partnership process unfolds.

Head Start

Head Start is one of the best-known educational programs in the United States. It enrolls approximately one million four- and five-year-olds each year (National Head Start Association, 2006). It precedes our current focus on family, school, and community collaborations by many years, yet it fits the "conditions" of a true partnership.

When Project Head Start was conceived in 1965, authorities acknowledged that children were not only family members but were also community members. Thus, if Head Start was to succeed in improving the lives of poor children, parental involvement and community commitment to the program's goals were paramount. Through this involvement and commitment, Head Start began to provide, in holistic rather than fragmented ways, comprehensive services in health, nutrition, and economic counseling for individuals, as well as school readiness for children and their families. Today, Project Head Start is referred to as an integrated service program for low-income families. A caseworker is assigned each child, and that person monitors the health, education, and social services provided for the child and his or her family (Hurd, Lerner, & Barton, 1999).

Objectives and Goals. Communities were involved in Head Start to make the community aware of the importance of providing adequate health, educational, and nutritional services for children's development. Further, if skills developed in the Head Start programs were to be sustained, the developers knew parents and community had to reinforce the learning. Parent involvement reached even further, because the programs created avenues for parents to gain skills for participating in different social contexts and thereby gain greater confidence and self-esteem.

Structural Features. Parents assist at Head Start centers and classrooms in a variety of ways. The Head Start Manual of Policies and Instruction, still used today, outlines the types of parental involvement available.

Parents as Partners. Parents are partners with professionals in the decision-making process, and we find two levels open to parents of Head Start children. At the informal level, parents work with center staff in determining program content and how their children will participate. At a more formal level, parents serve on a parent policy committee or council. Fifty percent of council membership must be parents of Head Start children and be elected by other parents. Council parents are involved in program improvements, parent activities, recruiting volunteers, and planning and developing a budget for the parent activity fund. They are also involved in decisions about program goals, criteria for the selection of children, hiring of Head Start staff, and major changes in budget and work programs.

Parents as Observers. Parents participate in Head Start classrooms as visitors, volunteers, and paid aides, to see different ways they can work with their children. They gain a better understanding of what their children are learning and what they can do to assist them at home. Children seeing their parents in the classroom know that their parents are interested in their learning and witness the cooperation and support between parents and teachers. When parents become more involved as volunteers or as paid aides, they gain skills and confidence, which in turn help them qualify for employment elsewhere.

Parents as Learners. Head Start parents enhance their own learning by planning and identifying opportunities that correspond to their own interests and aspirations. Workshops and other learning experiences for a center are often requested and designed by parents, who in this fashion increase their own education. Career ladders have been developed, where parents are able to progress through workshops to obtain their high-school general equivalency diploma (GED), and some parents in Head Start have continued their education at technical schools and colleges.

Supporting Children's Learning. Parents work at home with their children to support and reinforce children's Head Start experiences. Center personnel create and distribute ideas and suggestions for home activities and often visit homes to observe and suggest ways family members can support children's education. As parents become aware of their impact on children's learning, they become confident about helping their children grow and develop (Greenberg, 1990; Zigler & Styfco, 2004).

REFLECTION

In any of your field placements or observations have there been any former Head Start children? If so, how does the teacher describe the parent's support for those children? Do these statements reflect what you have read here about Head Start?

Research and Assessment. Since the inception of Project Head Start, the effects of early intervention on children's development have been a subject of much research and public concern. Initial studies by Westinghouse Learning Corporation–Ohio University (1969) indicated cognitive gains for Head Start children after the first year, but by the third year, these gains had nearly disappeared.

Critics pointed to limitations of that first study, for example, viewing all Head Start programs as if they were of equal quality, and ignoring the questionable validity of some evaluation instruments (Evans, 1975). The study did alert the public that a basic assumption of the War on Poverty was unrealistic, however: A single summer or one-year program could not produce a rapid turn around for economically disadvantaged children. This led to federally supported extensions and outgrowths of Head Start, for example, *Even Start* and *Follow Through*. Private foundations also began to support compensatory programs for young children at that time.

Long-term studies of the initial Head Start programs (Schweinhart & Weikart, 1997) reveal that the programs have been both cost effective and beneficial to society. Although initial achievement gains tended to disappear and Head Start children never "caught up" cognitively with their middle-class peers by high school, these children demonstrated significant differences from those disadvantaged children who had not attended Head Start. The Head Start children did better in school, repeated fewer grades, had fewer emotional problems, and were less often placed in remedial classes. As adults, they were less likely to end up in jail, more likely to attend college, became more active volunteers in their communities, and were more likely to marry than peers who had not attended Head Start (Schweinhart & Weikart, 1997).

Studies (Administration for Children and Families, 2000) also revealed that Head Start children's social development improved to equal their middle-class peers. Children became more task oriented, sustained attention to task longer, and developed curiosity about learning. Children with disabilities appeared to benefit the most after involvement in Head Start programs. Collins's (1984) synthesis of more than 1,500 Head Start studies confirmed the positive impacts on children's cognitive, social, and health development, as well as improvements in parenting.

Many Head Start programs successfully coordinated health and social services for children, so a large percentage of participants received immunizations as well as physical and dental exams. As a result of this medical attention and the positive nutritional programs, today, Head Start participants are healthier than all other disadvantaged children. This feature has been emulated by other programs as they attempt to include medical and social services within the school program.

As noted, parental involvement is a requirement of Head Start programs, which marked first large-scale involvement of parents in children's formal education. Parents have served as policy makers, teachers, aides, and volunteers, and two of every three students in Head Start have parents involved in one of these capacities. An additional payoff exists for that connection: Studies indicate that children of involved Head Start parents had higher academic achievement in later grades, were more likely to graduate from high school, and were more apt to have full-time employment.

Communities that established and maintained Head Start programs have benefited, as well. A number of poor and minority parents in these communities have moved into the workforce, and area public schools have changed programs because of the models that Head Start provided. Advantages include providing strategies for parental participation, implementing developmentally appropriate curricula, mainstreaming children with special needs, modifying health services, and implementing practices accommodating the needs of poor children and minorities. Readers searching for current information on Head Start will want to check the Head Start Web site: http://www.headstartinfo.org and also Zigler & Styfco (2004) for good critiques.

Certainly, Head Start has not succeeded in fulfilling the dream of diminishing poverty in the United States or in eliminating all learning gaps, but its impact has been positive, and its benefits for helping poor and minority families become partners in their children's education outweigh the costs. In addition, more recent collaborative efforts have profited from the procedures and experiences of this model program.

Outgrowths of Head Start. Head Start evaluations in the late 1960s showed that poor children from birth to age 4 needed help earlier if they were to overcome the debilitating effects of poverty. This information led to ideas for developing home-based programs (e.g., the Ira Gordon and David Weikart models) in the late 1960s and 1970s that would serve as precursors of Head Start extensions.

Even Start. Funded in 1988 and administered since 1992 by individual states, Even Start continues on a modest level as a pre-Head Start program centered in the child's home. A primary focus of Even Start is promoting family literacy with help from an educational social worker.

Early Head Start. Several offshoots of Head Start programs are now grouped under the Early

Early Head Start Programs enhance children's total development while helping parents become better caregivers.

Robert Brenner / PhotoEdit Inc.

Head Start label, which was organized in 1994 when Head Start was reauthorized by Congress. The focus is to insert early intervention to enhance a child's physical, social, and cognitive development while helping parents become better caregivers and teachers.

Even Start and Early Head Start programs use the home as a beginning point in children's education, and the emphasis since the early 1990s has been on family literacy. The concept recognizes that parents are children's first teachers and that it is important to help parents become more effective teachers. The program was to provide all-encompassing support to enlist parents as partners in their children's education, with the hope that they could then help their children reach their full potential as learners (Even Start, 1999). The parent educator, with help from local Head Start teachers, works directly with parents in the home. This person, a sort of educational social worker, plans home activities and arranges other social services needed by the family. Figure 12–2 presents the relationship of federally funded early education programs to typical elementary school programs.

Success in all the pre–Head Start programs depends on the quality of the individual venues.

We find that research on the programs, often encouraging on the basis of a single program, is also difficult to reconcile because of variations in programs and the difficulty in maintaining consistency of participation. Still, we have some very encouraging results: When participation is high and many services are offered, children gain significantly in tests of school readiness and language development (Weikart, 2004).

Comer's School Development Program

In 1968, James Comer and his colleagues at the Yale Child Study Center began the School Development Program, a collaboration with two New Haven elementary schools to increase parental involvement in children's education. Both schools were located in low-income areas, all children were African American, and parent participation in school activities had been very low. When the Comer team examined parent interest, however, they discovered three patterns that revealed potential home–school linkages.

1. Most parents expressed interest in the activities in which their children participated at school.

2. Some parents were interested in volunteering for particular activities in the school.

Figure 12–2 Relationship of Federally Funded Compensatory Programs to the Typical Elementary School (Ages may vary at each level.)

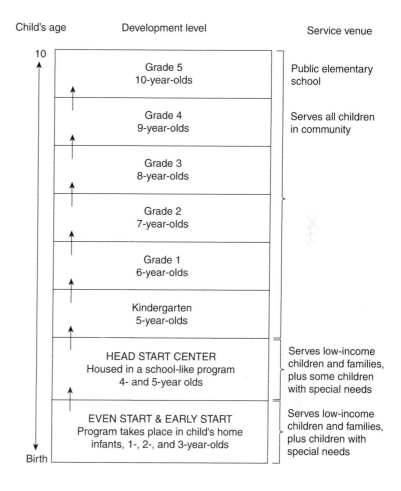

Child's age

Development level

Service venue

10

Grade 5
10-year-olds

Public elementary school

Grade 4
9-year-olds

Serves all children in community

Grade 3
8-year-olds

Grade 2
7-year-olds

Grade 1
6-year-olds

Kindergarten
5-year-olds

HEAD START CENTER
Housed in a school-like program
4- and 5-year olds

Serves low-income children and families, plus some children with special needs

EVEN START & EARLY START
Program takes place in child's home
infants, 1-, 2-, and 3-year-olds

Serves low-income children and families, plus children with special needs

Birth

3. A few parents were interested in curriculum and how teachers instructed their children (Comer & Haynes, 1991).

With this knowledge, Comer and his team began a series of experiments and adjustments that used parents' interests to bring about collaboration. Now, more than two decades after the conclusion of the project, the experiment has become a highly touted model for involving parents.

Goals and Objectives. The initial School Development Program evolved over a five-year period, and participants adjusted the structure as programs evolved and needs changed. A steering committee, formed of administrators, teachers, parents, aides, professional and nonprofessional support staff, and the Yale Child Center mental health team,

established the following major goals for the project (Comer, 1980):

- Modify the social and psychological climate of the school to facilitate greater student learning.
- Improve students' basic skills.
- Raise students' motivation for learning and their academic and occupational aspiration level.
- Create a sense of shared responsibility and decision making among parents and staff.
- Connect child development and clinical services to the educational program of the schools.

Structural Features. The program consisted of three teams: the school planning and management team (SPMT), a Yale Child Study Center mental health team, and the pupil personnel team, plus four major features: a parent program, a focus program, workshops, and an extended-day program.

School Planning and Management Team. The School Planning and Management Team (SPMT), composed of **stakeholders** in the school, developed and implemented academic and social programs, designed staff development, evaluated the program, and made necessary adjustments. After various experiments, three important guidelines evolved for the SPMT: (1) solving problems with a no-fault approach, (2) using principles of child development for decision making, and (3) ensuring that collaborative management did not paralyze the school principal (Comer & Haynes, 1991).

Mental Health Team. The mental health team consisted of a child psychiatrist, two social workers, an educator with early childhood education training, an educator involved in teacher training, and a psychologist–program evaluator. Its main purpose was to assist school staff in understanding and applying principles of social and behavioral science to school problems and opportunities.

Pupil Personnel Team. A pupil personnel team cooperated with the principal, community social-services personnel, and special teachers by giving services directly to students who needed such support. As conditions in the school changed and behavioral problems lessened, this service then became more educational and less behavioral in nature.

Parent Program. A parent program started, with a small group of parents receiving a stipend for assisting teachers. This core group formed the nucleus of the parent group and served on governance bodies and subcommittees that helped plan social and educational programs. Their function was to "bring the attitudes, values, and needs of the community to these committees and their activities" (Comer, 1980, p. 65). As the program changed to meet school and community needs, the parent program evolved to include parent involvement at three different levels.

At the first level, five or six parents were elected to serve on the school planning and management team, where decisions about programs and operations were made. These parents enlisted other community residents for other levels of participation

and helped overcome the barriers inhibiting hard-to-reach parents.

At the second level, parents were involved in helping in classrooms or in sponsoring and supporting school programs. The strength of this involvement was that parents and teachers worked together to motivate students to achieve academically and socially.

At the modest third level, parents became involved in activities in which their children were engaged. They attended student performances and other teacher–parent activities, where "good news" was shared, and generally supported the program from a distance.

Focus Program. At the start of the project, a focus program was established to help children one or more years behind in reading and math skills. Three times a week, these children were taught in small groups to supplement classroom teaching of reading and mathematics. The focus groups changed as children's learning needs were identified.

Workshops for Adults. From the onset, 2-week summer workshops allowed parents and teachers to get to know one another and share their perspective on the academic and social experiences they felt children needed. Workshops became ongoing and were offered when teachers or parents indicated a need.

Extended-Day Programs. This program included workshops for teachers to learn more about child development and behavior, teaching and curriculum development, and the use of arts in promoting academic skills. In addition, teachers developed skills in meeting with parents and planning parent participation projects.

Social Skills Curriculum. In establishing community involvement, Comer's team found that many distinctions between low-income and middle-income children involved differences in social skills. As a result, the team devised a social skills curriculum for inner-city children consisting of four units: politics and government, business and economics, health and nutrition, and spiritual and leisure time. Field trips, visits by community members, and lots of hands-on activities—related to banking,

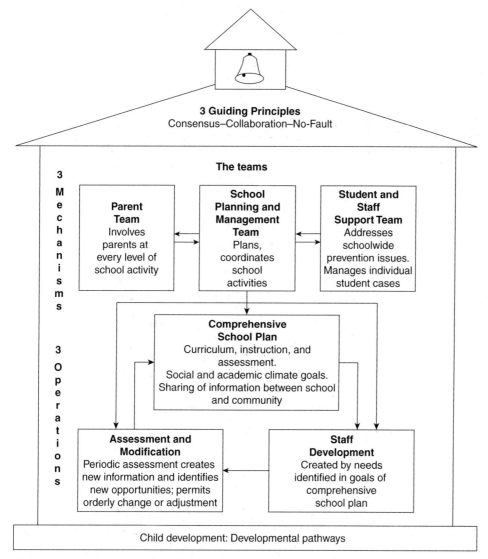

Figure 12–3 Comer's School Development Program
Source: From *Rallying the Whole Village: The Comer Process for Reforming Education* (p. 10), J. P. Comer et al. (Eds.), 1996. New York: Teachers College Press. Reprinted with permission.

musical productions, and local government organizations—enabled low-income children to enhance their interpersonal skills, writing skills, and ability to interact with adults.

School Development Program. Many aspects of the original implementation serve as guidance for schools associated with Comer's School Development Program. Figure 12–3 illustrates the current "Comer process." To implement a model that offers respect to all and sustains learning, Comer et al. (1996) maintained that there are three guiding principles, three teams, and three operations:

- *Three principles: consensus* (planning requires that all parties come to agreement on the plans), *collaboration* (all work in tandem with each other), and no-fault (no one party is at fault for any lack of success, but all share in the responsibility to improve).

- *Three teams:* the *school planning and management team,* which plans and coordinates all school activities; the *student and staff support team (SSST),* which addresses student and staff problems and manages individual situations; and the *parent team (PT),* which involves parents at all levels.

- *Three operations: comprehensive school plan,* developed to meet academic and social goals; *assessment and modification,* for periodic assessments and provision for change when necessary; and *staff development,* as needed to achieve goals.

Comer, Haynes, and Joyner (1996) believed that this model permits communities to transform and change their programs by involving school personnel and families in a participatory approach. To sustain change, they emphasized that all adults must feel respected and all children must feel valued and be motivated to learn and achieve.

REFLECTION

The Comer model is a comprehensive model of partnership. Has this been mentioned as a partnership model in schools with which you are acquainted? Reflect for a moment on how teachers you know might perceive this much involvement.

Research and Assessment. After five years of working through problems and modifying procedures, rules, teaching strategies, and programs, the School Development Program showed remarkable success. The two participating schools progressed from having the worst attendance records in New Haven to having the best. Overall academic achievement went from third from the bottom to among the top schools in the city. Behavior problems were greatly reduced, and parent–teacher misunderstandings lessened as parental participation in school activities increased. The consensus is that home, school, and community links growing from the School Development Program in New Haven have provided essential ingredients for children's healthy development (Comer & Haynes, 1991).

Outgrowths of the Model. The Comer model has been replicated in more than 650 schools across the nation. In Washington, DC, several neighborhoods have successfully changed their schools from places where violence, drugs, and crime were paramount to schools with "high expectations and where everyone working together . . . has become an attitude, a way of learning and an education for life" (Ramirez-Smith, 1995, p. 19). Further success of the Comer process is explicated in the publication by Comer, Ben-Avie, Haynes, and Joyner (1999), in which readers find firsthand accounts of communities working through the model. Comer's 1996 book, *Rallying the Whole Village,* is the publication that best describes the Comer process.

Reggio Emilia

The Reggio Emilia program was developed in northern Italy by a group of parents soon after World War II. The first school, built with revenues from sales of scrap materials in the war-torn countryside, was staffed by parents and community members who held to a profound belief and respect for children's natural learning. Under the leadership of Loris Malaguzzi and the community's strong commitment to be decision makers for their children's education, the Reggio Emilia approach to education was born.

The curriculum in these municipal preprimary schools has evolved as teachers, children, and parents worked together, learned about each other, and valued each others' ways of processing information. The Reggio Emilia philosophical and educational precepts have also matured over the years, though never straying from the basic premises: Children are active participants in their own learning, and schooling should reflect community values, beliefs, and a wealth of materials (Edwards et al., 1998). In the past decade, American educators have attempted to emulate the practices of the Reggio Emilia approach, as it epitomizes a significant success for parent–school–community collaborations.

Goals and Objectives. The purpose of Reggio Emilia is to develop a school where children are at the center of the curriculum, where they develop a sense of belonging by participating in the school community. Leaders find that children's self-concepts are strengthened over their three years of belonging to the same group of children and adults (Gandini, 1993). From the beginning, the founders recognized that parents, teachers, and community members were partners in planning and executing any curriculum, and they felt that a curriculum should be reflective of the community's values and distinct qualities, including all of nature. Young children in Reggio programs are viewed as informants to adults on their current interests, unique learning styles, and prior knowledge. Therefore, the children are active participants and decision makers in what, when, and how to study. It is up to adults to follow and plan accordingly.

Philosophical Perspective. One basic principle of Reggio Emilia is that a program for children must be dynamic, vibrant, and evolving (Gandini, 1997). As new theories of children's development emerge, new political orders occur, and new social events unfold, the directors expect that the program's philosophical and psychological underpinnings will change and programs will reflect these changes. New (1998) pointed out that fidelity to a single theory is really unnecessary in Reggio Emilia, and that as theory informs practice, so practice and documentation of children's learning will inform theory.

The ever-evolving philosophical views found in Reggio schools have reflected for some time the perspectives of Dewey, Piaget, Vygotsky, and other developmentalists. In recent years, New (2003) found substantial incorporation of Comer's partnership ideas and Gardner's views on multiple intelligences. Quite logically, decision makers in these schools also subscribe to Bronfenbrenner's social–cultural perspective. The expectation is that teachers, children, and other adults learn from each other and are both facilitators and constructors of new knowledge.

Structural Features. We do not find a set of procedures in Reggio schools, as we can in Montessori or Waldorf schools, because situation and context is considered first. We do find, however, common practices and modes that help describe the everyday school endeavors.

Organization. A beginning objective for a Reggio school is to provide an amicable environment for children, families, and teachers. The classrooms are organized so that projects or themes are pursued according to children's and adults' interests. When people make arrangements, they need to consider that collaborative problem solving among children and children with adults is important. Spaces for individual study (*ateliers*, "àtt'l yáy"), as well as small group and total group activities, are provided. Teachers and other adults are considered guides for children in exploring and investigating.

Children demonstrate their growth through many different "languages," or modes of communication: words, movement, artistic expression, play, music, and the like. Analysis of these communication activities by adults is the documentation of what is being learned (Gandini, 1997). Because learning is viewed as spiral rather than linear, children continually examine their own development through this documentation. They observe what they have accomplished, consider what else they might learn, then reconsider their objectives (Gandini, 1997). Space for displays, documentation of children's individual and communal projects, and analyses are accommodated in the *ateliers.*

Scheduling. Because the philosophy of Reggio is that children learn by continual active involvement in their environment and by doing projects, the daily routine is related more to scheduling the staff time rather than children's. Teachers spend most of their 36 hours per week observing children's activities, talking with them about what they are doing, and planning for children's additional study. Each week, staff spend 4.5 hours in meetings, planning, and in-service training, plus 1.5 hours in documenting and analyzing children's work. They keep records (*diarios*) of the children's work, communications, and their own analyses for parental and administrator preview (Giovanni, 2001).

Implementation is Evolving. Society in Italy has changed since 1946, and the idea of schooling and who is responsible for schools has also changed.

Children demonstrate their growth
through many different languages
or modes of communication:
words, movement, artistic expression, play, and music.

Greg Mekras

For example, in the 1960s, national and regional policies dictated guidelines and new goals for all of Italy. Reggio Emilia programs, however, maintained their credibility by insisting on local decision making—a process approach by all participants to have a say in what was to be studied. Learning, they maintain, is not dictated from "above," but "negotiated" with those who will benefit. Content and sequence in any project is determined by the particular group, which takes responsibility for maintaining connections among all the parties (Terzi & Cantorelli, 2001). Validation for the process culminated in the 1970s, as national laws in Italy were passed to formalize community-based management for schools similar to that advocated at Reggio Emilia We find this is similar to many **charter school** programs in the United States today.

Parents and community members are also a very important part of the network. They serve on the community advisory councils, attend various school meetings for planning, and work in classrooms on specific tasks and projects. Teachers do not assign tasks to these other adults, but because they are part of the planning, they become part of the execution (Gandini, 1997). In a dinosaur project, for example, a parent typed up the conversations of children discussing and arguing about what they knew. Later, when the children seemed to lose interest, the parent was part of the discussion on whether the project should be dropped. The parent helped in reviewing children's discussions and found areas that everyone continued to be excited about. So, the group decided to go on with the project, but because of new interests, it decided on a different direction (Rankin, 1998).

The network of educational services has evolved over the years (see Figure 12–4). The line of authority proceeds upward, from the Community Advisory Council (parents, all school staff, and townspeople) planning, making decisions, and supporting the educational process. Every two years, the community elects representatives to the Municipal Advisory Council Board. With members experienced in communicating and planning, this board forms strong subcommittees, each with specific objectives that take on different concerns related to children. Because of such involvement, families have learned that fully educating a child requires solidarity and support. Not only do children gain from such programs, but so do the families and municipalities (Spaggiari, 1998).

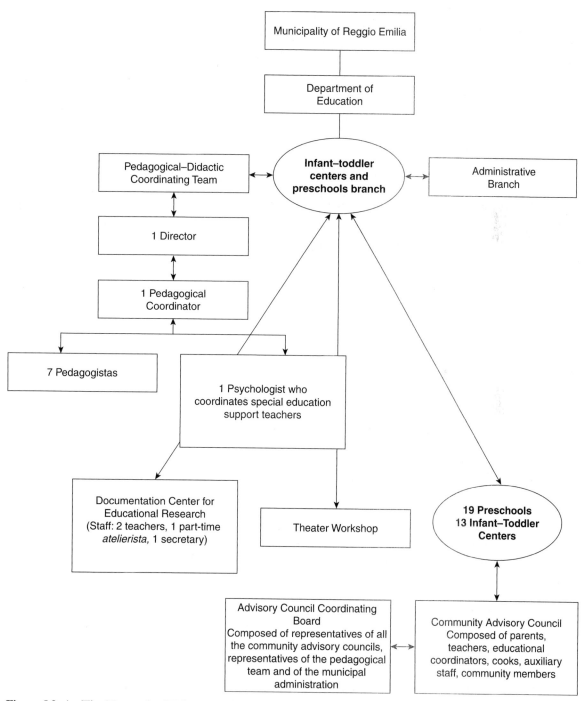

Figure 12–4   The Network of Educational Services of the Reggio Emilia Municipal Administration
Source: From *First Steps Toward Teaching the Reggio Way* (p. 12), J. Hendrick (Ed.), 1997. Upper Saddle River, NJ: Merrill/Prentice Hall. Reprinted by permission.

Research and Evaluation. Unlike our American penchant for assessment, there has been no attempt in Italy to validate by empirical research the practices of Reggio Emilia, nor has children's learning been measured by tests that compare children's learning to predetermined scales. Children's learning is viewed as spiral and the mode of evaluation used in Reggio programs is similar to qualitative research in the United States.

The components of evaluation in Reggio schools are the same both for the children and for a program. The "researchers" are the teachers and other adults who record children's dialogues or monologues and reflect on children's other modes of expression. Children's work is collected, stored, and filed in spaces (*ateliers*) to which everyone has access.

Adults working in the school record anecdotes and reflections on children's activity in a notebook for "two voices" (the child's and the adult's). When children first enter school, they receive a personal calendar that contains a record of each child's particular activities. From these materials, a diary reflecting the child's development from beginning to end is developed.

These two sets of materials form the basis of information for any qualitative research. In 1996 and again in 1998, the Spencer Foundation supported Rebecca New as principal investigator in examining the role of culture on adult beliefs and decision making regarding the quality of children's care and education in Reggio Emilia. New (2001) concluded that a society that has a commitment to high standards with multiple interpretations of quality, and a sense of shared responsibility for children's well-being, does foster healthy child development, enhances adult lives, and contributes to a vital community.

REFLECTION

Reggio Emilia is a grassroots model of partnership Think for a moment about how this model compares to Head Start and the Comer Model. Does one have more appeal for your own work right now? Could Reggio Emilia happen in the United States?

Outgrowths of Reggio Emilia. The exchange of ideas and the traveling Hundred Languages Exhibit by Malaguzzi has created a burgeoning interest in the **child-centered**, developmentally appropriate early childhood curricula of Reggio Emilia. Many Americans see Reggio Emilia as an "idyllic place in which all members of society support each other and where children never throw tantrums." To implement a Reggio Emilia program, however, Americans must first come to grips with significant differences in American and Italian culture.

A number of American teachers presently experiment with aspects of the Reggio Emilia philosophy by using projects that are suggested by children. Teachers then listen and document how children learn to read, write, count, and increase language skills while they are learning science concepts.

The Grant Early Childhood Center in Cedar Rapids, Iowa (Edmiaston & Fitzgerald, 2000), with 350 children, is a designated site for inclusion of children with disabilities. Ten percent of the children attending the program have special needs, and the directors have combined the local and national requirements for special education with Reggio Emilia's approach of collaborative relationships. Children learn to develop a project working with a typically developing peer or a friend with disabilities who is also interested. Project groups learn how to be inclusive as they work with children with particular talents as well as children with disabilities. They also use a Reggio Emilia–style documentation: a process that examines student growth in a variety of ways and facilitates successful inclusion.

Readers will find *The Hundred Languages of Children* (Edwards et al., 1998) the most useful reference on all aspects of Reggio Emilia. In addition, several volumes discussing American experiments with Reggio are valuable: *Bringing Reggio Emilia Home* (Cadwell, 1997) and *Next Steps Toward Teaching the Reggio Way* (Hendrick, 2004) give helpful examples of teachers working in American classrooms with this philosophy.

National Network of Partnership Schools

Joyce Epstein, with colleagues at Johns Hopkins University, has worked for more than 20 years conducting studies and establishing programs to enhance educational opportunity for children and to demonstrate values of partnerships. In 1995, Epstein established the National Network of Partnership Schools at Johns Hopkins to demonstrate the important intersections of research, policy, and practice for school improvement. To date, more than 1,700 schools in 150 school districts across the United States have been involved to some degree in this network, which features partnerships.

As in other partnership models, the framework of Epstein's program is centered in the idea of the shared responsibilities of home, school, and community for children's learning and development. She referred to this as the "overlapping spheres of influence" in a student's schooling (see Figure 12–5), and she articulates this in her writings (Epstein, 2001; Epstein et al., 2002), which present the important structures and processes needed to develop effective partnership programs. We should note that Epstein places the school in the center of her paradigm and promotes the idea of school as a broker for starting and facilitating the partnership.

Epstein firmly believes that the concept of a community school is reemerging in American society. She noted that we now find it in more schools,

programs, and services for students and parents, and also in before-school, during-school, and after the regular school-day activities everywhere. She feels confident that the education enterprise can work toward creating more "familylike" schools and more "school-like" families when the full power of partnership is employed. A familylike school makes each child feel special and included; a school-like family reinforces the importance of schooling and provides activities that build student skills and a feeling of success. Communities also create familylike settings, services, and events to enable families to better support their children.

Goals and Objectives. The underpinnings and necessary ingredients, attitudes, and work ways that maximize the endeavors of National Network programs are as follows:

1. "Caring for the children we share." Epstein feels that if this condition is present, then schools, parents, and communities recognize their shared interests in and their responsibilities for children.

2. Help children succeed in school and in life. She points to the "overlapping spheres of influences" of the three social contexts as the key for harnessing their united power.

3. Students are central to a successful partnership and must be part of decision making. She shows several items and qualities that we often overlook when planning programs: The student

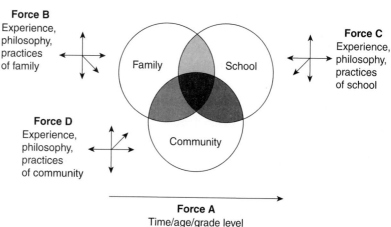

Figure 12–5 Overlapping Spheres of Influence of Family, School, and Community on Children's Learning
Source: From *School, Family and Community Partnerships: Your Handbook for Action* (2nd ed., p. 163) by J. L. Epstein et al., 2002. Thousand Oaks, CA: Corwin. Reprinted by permission.

Force B
Experience, philosophy, practices of family

Force C
Experience, philosophy, practices of school

Force D
Experience, philosophy, practices of community

Family   School   Community

Force A
Time/age/grade level

determines learning, and we should not think of him or her as something to do things for or to; and the student interprets school activities to parents, interprets home activities to schools, and interprets the community for both teachers and parents.

4. The student is the stakeholder and has the most to gain or lose in schoolwork.

5. Effective partnerships have an accumulation of support. Whether our team is "raising a barn, playing tug of war, or building materials for learning units," the enthusiasm and commitment from the group effort is far more than what individuals can accomplish singly.

6. Healthy partnerships tolerate changes, challenges, and disagreements because there is a base of trust and respect. Basic ground rules on communication and expression will develop the base of trust required for any cooperative endeavor. This validates the reason to aim for a multiyear cycle of long-term improvement rather than a "fix-it" blitz of action for one year.

7. Partnerships will differ in size, particular focus, and arrangement but will have many common elements (see Figure 12–5).

8. Establishing an action team is key. All collaborations require some type of steering group if the program is to involve more than a handful of workers.

9. Collaboration focuses on curriculum areas. Participants must keep in mind that their work and energy is directed to enhanced educational opportunity. Public relations, community celebrations, and the like all have a cohesive quality but mean less if the student is not gaining in schooling.

Considerable research supports the need for these underlying qualities in programs using National Networks designs.

Structural Features. In the Network programs, six levels of involvement have evolved. These provide a basic structure for the National Network designs, and they help educators and other leaders develop a comprehensive schedule for any particular partnership. Each level of involvement (see Figure 12–6) will have many different practices from which schools can select to help them achieve a goal they have identified. Thus, any partnership will make a commitment for the six types of involvement as a framework; then, each venue

---

Keys to Successful School, Family and Community Partnerships

- **Focus on Parenting.** Work with families on child-rearing skills and understanding child development. Assist schools to understand families.

- **Focus on Communicating.** Devise strategies for school-to-home and home-to-school communication about school programs and student progress.

- **Focus on Volunteering.** Strengthen the recruitment and training of family members as volunteers and audiences at school and other locations.

- **Focus on Home Learning.** Produce helpful and interesting tactics to involve families in learning activities at home and in the community.

- **Focus on Decision Making.** Include families in school decisions, governance, and advocacy through action teams and parent organizations.

- **Focus on Community Collaboration.** Work with businesses and other groups to coordinate community resources and services to benefit students, families, schools and the community itself.

Figure 12–6 Epstein's Six Types of Involvement
Source: Adapted from Epstein et al., 2002 and Sanders, 2006.

will select practices that will produce results for their particular area of involvement. For example, if a partnership selects "Parenting" to focus on, they might select practices such as (a) set up parent education courses, (b) develop support groups on child rearing, or (c) develop home visiting teams to help needy families. All challenges must be addressed, and in many cases a "redefinition" made for the goal or practice that seemed promising. Epstein teams have provided a listing of protocols that groups work through in settling their differences (Epstein et al., 2002).

Action Team. The most essential component of the programs will be decision making. For this, Epstein advised the establishment of an action team, or general steering committee to guide the partnership effort and to act as the direction-setting team. The group membership is important and includes a reasonable arrangement of delegates from the following constituencies:

1. A few teachers from different grade levels
2. A few parents
3. The school principal
4. At least one community delegate
5. A student delegate if at junior-high level or above

The job of the action team is to assess the partnership practices, arrange for the implementation of the agreed-on activities, and to improve and coordinate all practices for the types of involvement. The action team leads in these responsibilities but is assisted by other teachers, parents, students, administrators, and community members.

Each year, the team updates its three-year outline and develops a detailed one-year action plan. In other words, the team continues to find out how it can improve its structure and practices to increase the families as partners.

Research and Assessment. Research on the success rate of programs in the National Network is ongoing. Each year, an annual survey is returned to the Headquarters from the numerous participating schools. These are helpful in giving data about the successes, problems, and changes in the various programs. Research on individual experiments is also proceeding. These findings all result in new recommendations to practitioners who are in the Network programs.

Most of the current recommendations on levels of involvement, practices, and recommendations have come about from the 20 years of research on particular parts of the Network's activities. In addition, considerable research efforts continue at the headquarters for the Network. For instance, the Teachers Involve Parents in School work (TIPS) program has carried out research on the efficacy of homework and developed criteria for home activities as a result of its study on family practices. Research on discipline and student behavior is another area currently investigated. (See Sheldon & Epstein, 2002, for a description of improved student behaviors in programs with family and community involvement.)

Outgrowths of the Network. As noted previously, the National Network has expanded over the years and is now located in 20 different states. Formal links with the League of Schools Reaching Out was accomplished more than 10 years ago, and a number of partnership plans and collaborative efforts across the country have adopted parts of Epstein's recommendations for National Network programs. Readers wishing to examine detailed examples for the National Network programs will find Joyce Epstein and her colleagues (2002) most helpful.

REFLECTION

Compare the features of the National Network of Schools with the other programs identified in this section. Again consider how you would feel as a part of the team working with a National Network School, either as a parent or as a teacher.

Community Schools

The community school concept has a history dating back to the early 20th century, when Marie Turner Harvey, with help from John Dewey, established the

Community schools tap
community resources to enhance
school projects.

Anthony Magnacca / Merrill

Porter Rural School in Kirkville, Missouri in 1912. Harvey's focus was a school curriculum that both drew from the community and also worked to improve living conditions in the district served (Dewey, 1919). Newer examples of community schools (often called "full-service schools") have a mission similar to that of the Porter School. This concept relates to the writers' beliefs that children's education is best advanced when families, schools, and communities are involved in the day-to-day decisions concerning curriculum and instructional practice.

Community schools are public schools serving as sites that provide a range of services to children and their families. These all come because the schools partner with community agencies and organizations. The school building becomes a central site for a community, and typically the school facilities stay open after school hours and on weekends. The school offers afterschool activities, adult education, health classes, recreation, and family support services of various types. Although the central aim is to improve education, this is achieved by improving the community around the children and using all resources fully. So, energy directed at parents and other community facilities is a way to make a community rich in educational experiences.

Goals and Objectives. A community school differs from other public schools in several ways. It offers a full schedule of school curriculum, but it also seeks to offer an array of health and social services typically handled by a city health department, welfare agencies, and adult education offices, as well as child care and after-school programs (Dryfoos, 2003). By sharing facilities and overlapping and intergrating the concerns of educators and community case workers, the objective of improving the whole community is served. Typical objectives include the following:

1. To have programs operating day and evening to serve the total community. This means that in addition to regular school hours, the community school will have before- and after-school programs, plus evening programs for parents and other community members.

2. To enrich life in the immediate community by using the community as a laboratory and a focus of study and to tap resources for school projects.

3. To eliminate logistical problems for families needing health and social services while they are involved with the school activities (a one-stop

shopping feature that minimizes transportation problems).

4. To facilitate the delivery of appropriate services to children and their families.

5. To focus on educational improvement by bringing additional services to the school, while building connections to the outside world for work opportunities and career planning.

6. To improve the life chances for a community's children by mobilizing community resources to head off social problems of delinquency, teenage pregnancy, and substance abuse.

Structural Features. Community schools are built on the premise that "educators can't improve schools without paying attention to the children, their families, and the community around them" (Warren, 2005, p. 135). This basically sets the agenda for forming a "full-service" community school that blends and integrates a large number of services that young children (particularly in low-income areas) need to thrive as learners and as developing youth. It means thinking of a school as a campus holding, not just regular and special classrooms but also health clinics, sports and recreation clubs, social support facilities, adult education facilities, and care programs that become the domain of community people and organizations in addition to teachers. All services under one roof minimimizes communication problems and travel problems. The school becomes a hub for the community and in many ways strengthens all aspects of a community mission and pride in itself (Dryfoos, 1998). We have strong evidence (Warren, 2005) that community schools have turned communities around and enhanced the education of youngsters and the aspiration of parents and community adults, as well.

The following is an outline of offerings found in a typical community school.

Extended School Day. The community school will be open all the time, that is, day hours, evening hours, plus weekend hours and summer programs, too. Before-school hours and after-school hours are arranged for child-care service, and these are linked to homework help, academic enrichment, and other school-related projects. Sports and adult education programs are features associated with the extended school day.

School-Based Health Clinic. One valuable feature of community schools is an on-site clinic that works closely with teachers in assessing health needs of children. The clinic would provide state-mandated health screening and immunizations, as well as referrals for more complicated problems. School nurses, social workers, plus part-time pediatricians, dentists, and mental health workers would work with the clinic. The clinic is available to adults on the campus also and for community members when large-scale screening and immunizations are needed.

Community Focus. Community schools develop a large and potent work force. Community projects such as development of parks, securing additional facilities for the campus, cleaning up the neighborhood, and improving transportation around the area, are all projects that one of these schools has tried. Field trips into the larger community, so that children and adults can experience museums, nature preserves, and musical and dramatic productions, are frequent and common. The number of parents and community agencies involved makes a compelling force for securing facilities and enhancements that stimulate community pride. With community schools comes an interest in all community services and cultural experiences.

Parent Involvement. A community school only becomes successful when it brings in a large number of parents to work and advocate for the total school campus. Some parents will work as classroom, cafeteria, or recreational aides. Others will volunteer to mentor children or do clerical work. Many will link the volunteer work with their own education enhancement through the day and evening classes in adult education opportunities. The intense involvement of numbers of parents stimulates school pride and spirit to bring about total neighborhood improvement. This means that all programs work together for everyone's benefit. The idea of separating out special services for this and that does not work in the espirit de corps of a community school. Also, in this fashion, children see that the community works as a unit— they see the relationship between community services and what they do as students.

Research and Assessment. Test results show that academic achievement is improved in community schools (Dryfoos, 1998). In addition, improvements in behavior and socialization, as well as fewer problems in delinquency and truancy, are shown. Surveys of parents, teachers, and community workers show significant positive changes in families and school staff members.

The success of programs does depend on several key factors: strong leaders (including school personnel), open communication, a full-time services coordinator, true integration of educational and support components, plus some initial funding to support planning and incentives to take the initial steps in cooperative work (Dryfoos, Quinn, & Barkin, 2005). Additional money is needed to support programs that have a longer school day and school year than traditional programs. The health- and social-services funding can be transferred from other municipal budgets, of course, but accessing these programs and getting started requires an additional investment of time and energy.

Outgrowths of the Program. Community schools are growing in many areas in the United States and abroad. Their function in combining services makes for a very practical procedure in cutting down on logistical requirements. The integration of school and community services also solves many difficulties that seem to increase in some areas each year. For example, community schools have helped by doing the following:

- Cutting back on youth alienation by providing helpful recreation.
- Supplying child-care services that fit better with dual parent work schedules.
- Giving all personnel a better idea of what is available for social, welfare, and educational services in the community, making for more knowledgeable communities.

Note: Community schools will mesh with the objectives of all other models presented in this chapter. The notions of parent education, parent involvement in a child's work, and enhanced communication show all personnel that they are partners in efforts to help youth succeed. Readers will find a good description on the basics of community school arrangements in Joy Dryfoos's (1998) book, *Full-Service Schools: A Revolution in Health and Social Services for Children, Youth, and Families.*

Freedom Schools

The Childrens Defense Fund Freedom Schools program is a new endeavor by CDF to connect children and families to their cultural heritage and to their communities. It is primarily a summer program echoing the thrust of the 1964 Freedom Schools organized in the South to support civil rights initiatives. Although open to all applicants, the summer programs are aimed at African American children, to focus on literacy enhancement, cultural heritage, parent involvment, and neighborhood social action. In 2006, 90 summer school programs were operated throughout the United States; they enrolled 7,500 children.

The Childrens Defense Fund, a leading advocate for poor and minority children, has been for 30 years one of America's strongest voices in educating our nation about the needs of children. CDF established Freedom Schools in 1993 and has set a course of objectives and schedules that individual sites in various states carry out with local leadership and sponsorship (Childrens Defense Fund, 2006).

Goals and Objectives. The overall aim of a Freedom School summer session is to enhance the educational and social capabilities of young children, while nurturing a group of **"Servant–Leader" interns** to advocate on behalf of children. The following particular objectives can be found in the five- and six-week summer programs:

1. Focus on high-quality educational enrichment for children and the promotion of cultural awareness.

2. Parent and caregiver involvement in children's daily activities and participation in workshops on child development, child advocacy, and child welfare.

3. Community adults volunteer time and experience with children and serve as role models. This reunites generations and taps into the community traditions of self-help and mutual support.

4. Children focus on and learn about community problem solving.

5. Student interns focus on civic engagement with children, parents, and community partners to assess community needs, and then address these through rallies, town meetings, letter writing, voter registration, health projects, and other activities.

6. Servant–leader development: The college-age interns staffing the summer activities receive training on leadership and community-building skills.

Structural Features. The summer session Freedom Schools are generally a five- or six-week program set up to develop literacy skills, conflict resolution skills, and critical thinking skills, plus artistic and athletic competence (Childrens Defense Fund, 2006). The central academic curriculum is enclosed in the Integrated Reading Curriculum (IRC). In addition to literacy development, however, the program focuses on cooperative learning, critical thinking, social action, and conflict resolution. Thus the IRC becomes an activity-oriented phase, intended to motivate, expose, inspire, and rejuvenate young participants each day. The program uses a core of selected books, which interns and volunteers work with in creative ways to stimulate reading, presentation, discussion, and interpretion by all participants.

Most of the recommended books have lesson plans that guide the use of these titles and serve as anchors for the work of the site coordinator and the interns. Field trips, presentations on the book themes, and social activities are also worked into the daily schedule (see Figure 12–7).

Individual sites for the program are under local sponsorship and leadership. The national CDF office acts as coordinator and supplies materials and trainers to work with persons who wish to sponsor a program. The responsibility for operating

8:00–8:30 A.M.	Breakfast with children and staff
8:30–9:00	*Harambee* (Swahili for "pulling together," informal sharing and celebration)
9:00–10:30	Integrated Reading Curriculum, conflict resolution and social action
10:30–10:45	Morning break
10:45–11:45	Integrated Reading Curriculum, continued
11:45–Noon	Drop Everything and Read (DEAR) time
Noon–1:00 P.M.	Lunch with children and staff
1:00–3:00	Afternoon activities: arts and crafts, dance, music, sports, computer lab, field trips, social action projects, and finale rehearsal
3:00	Dismissal
3:30	Daily staff debriefing

Figure 12–7　Sample Daily Schedule for a Freedom School Group
Source: CDF Freedom Schools program description. http://www.freedomschools.org/program

a program is in the hands of a local sponsoring agency and its project director.

Sponsor. The sponsoring agency can be a school district, college, community agency or a church. This agency has legal and fiscal responsibility for operating the particular Freedom School site, and sponsors ensure that the program is in compliance with local, state, and federal regulations, including fire, health, safety and civil rights. In addition, sponsors do the following:

1. Secure funds and space for a program.
2. Select a local advisory committe to promote community support.
3. Recruit a Project Director and a Site Coordinator to oversee and manage the program.
4. In conjunction with the Director and Coordinator recruit and manage a staff of interns and volunteers.

Project Director. This key person maintains communication with the national office, does staff recruitment, and supervises the program staff. Directors are trained at the CDF national training site.

Site Coordinator. The site coordinator is in charge of day-to-day activities and ensures that the program and curriculum are implemented. He or she is key for maintaining spirit and good communication among staff, parents, and community helpers. Coordinators are also trained at the national training site.

Servant–Leader Interns. The servant–leader interns are college-age staff members responsible for the front-line care and nurture of children in the program. They facilitate in the classrooms and lead the community outreach activities. The interns, who receive a stipend for their work, come from the local community and are selected for potential as future leaders in child advocacy. Maturity and ability to handle responsibility are required.

Volunteers. Other adults contribute to the program by demonstrating skills, sharing expertise, mentoring individuals, and helping with routine jobs. These are usually parents, extended family members, and community agents.

Skjold Photographs / PhotoEdit Inc.

Servant–Leader Interns in the Freedom Schools are responsible for care and nurture of the children.

REFLECTION

Try to get information on a Freedom School in your area. Would this program benefit young children that you know? What would attract you to that program? Would you consider being a "Servant-Leader"?

Research and Assessment. End-of-program evaluations for summer Freedom Schools are collected by site directors, but these are informal and focus on local priorities. The evaluations show enthusiam for and satisfaction in the individual programs, with notations about increased literacy skills for children, plus positive changes in social adjustment and the increased involvement of parents and community agents in the program. Only one area (Kansas City) has developed a statistical study of a Freedom School summer program. This study focused on the scholastic and social achievements of 1,338 students in 2005. The results showed significant improvement in reading ability when measured against a comparison group. Data from parent surveys showed positive changes in children's attitudes toward learning, cultural appreciation, community involvement, and conflict resolution (Childrens Defense Fund, 2006).

The Kansas City corps of 14 Freedom Schools has obtained a substantial Kauffman Foundation grant for evaluating the long term effects of the Freedom School programs in that area. The evaluation started in 2004.

Outgrowths of the Program. Freedom Schools have been in operation for 13 consecutive years and have expanded from two sites to 90 sites (in 2006) in 24 states. The main extension of the program is the weekend and after school programs that are now sponsored in a similar fashion as the summer programs.

Readers can obtain information on the Freedom School programs from the Childrens Defense Fund offices (telephone: 202-628-8787) and can download materials and examples from their Web site: http://www.freedomschools.org.

Charter Schools

Featuring Charter Schools as a positive model, for family–school–community cooperation is risky, because in the 16 years of their existence, the philosphical direction of these school programs has moved in many directions. For example, we find charter schools with traditional and highly directive programs that come nowhere close to the cooperative models espoused by the writers. At the same time, there are others with a structure so relaxed that they resemble an alternative school of the 1970s. In the mix, however, there are some charter schools that truly reflect the best practices of the partnerships highlighted in this text. At the end of this section, we refer to several exemplary charter schools functioning in a collaborative model. Readers are provided with references and for Web sites with descriptions of those particular examples.

The charter school movement began in the early 1990s and grew rapidly. In 2006 we found more than 3,000 charter schools scattered over 37 states and serving almost one million students (Center for Education Reform, 2006). As noted before, though, the expectations for charter schools at present falls all along the education continuum, and the proponents make strange bedfellows. For example, current legislation proposed in several states is supported by traditionalists seeking a return to classic study, by parents' rights advocates annoyed by school bureaucracy, and also by progressives seeking a **project-oriented curriculum**.

Goals and Objectives. The basic concept of the charter school movement is to free individual public schools from large-district bureaucracy and grant them autonomy to make decisions regarding structure, personnel, curriculum, and educational emphasis while holding them accountable for academic achievement. This stems from the idea of "decentralization," in which parents, teachers, and local citizens are the decision makers, as opposed to centralization and use of "best practices," as determined at the state or district levels (Wang & Walberg, 2001).

Research and Assessment. Vast differences exist in the effectiveness of charter schools, and there is minimal evidence that charter schools, especially in urban systems, produce better academic results than does the larger system as a whole (Center for Educational Reform, 2006; Fuller, 2003). Yet, other studies have found that, especially after the second and third years of operation, parents and children are better satisfied with their new school experiences and support the new policies (Bulkley & Wohlstetter, 2004; Vanourek, 2005).

Findings show that almost all charter schools are smaller, friendlier, and more open. Students get more personal attention, and although in many instances the teachers are less experienced and have minimal credentials, they show students they care, are knowledgeable in content areas, and are excited about teaching. Most of these schools are places where parents have some decision-making power and develop a sense of community. Thus, teachers and students feel more comfortable in examining values, long-term goals, and a sense of morality (Naisknov, 2002; Schorr, 2002).

The charters are also effective in bringing changes to the professional cultures, where new ideas in teaching are integrated with other ideas and result in a more cohesive program (Murphy & Shiffman, 2002; U.S. Department of Education, 2004). In districts where there are enough charters to affect the traditional schools financially, investigators find that some regular school personnel have started to make changes in their public schools. In addition, mainstream school administrators appear to reach out more to the particular communities, make schools more attractive, expect more of students, and offer more challenging courses (Center for Education Reform, 2003; Vanourek, 2005). These observations are satisfying to those proponents who expect the competitive effect of charters to enhance all education.

The following are examples of successful charter schools that operate with a true collaborative system:

1. KIPP Academy, Houston. http://www. kippschools.org or http://www.kipphouston. org
2. Fenton Avenue Charter School, Los Angeles. http://www.fentoncharter.net
3. Community of Peace Academy, St. Paul. http:// en.wikipedia.org/wiki/Community_of_Peace_ Academy
4. Oglethorpe Charter School, Savannah. http:// www.oglethorpecharter.org
5. King Center Charter School, Buffalo. http:// www.kingcentercharterschool.org

Outgrowths of Charter Schools. As we noted earlier, charter schools have proliferated in unprecedented fashion during the last decade, as most states have granted authority. Although significant amounts of literature exist to guide new groups, some have borrowed models from existing pilot schools in the Comer model, a National Network school, and even the Reggio Emilia plan. Comer has sage advice on the degree of success found in school reform and experimental programs. He states that his experiences have shown that about one third of our experimental projects maintain the changes made, one third achieve limited change until the initiators depart, and one third do not have any success at all (Comer, 1997).

FEATURES OF SUCCESSFUL COLLABORATIONS

New partnerships are emerging across the United States. The stimulus varies, but projects often begin in response to educational problems at the local and state levels. Irrespective of the motivation, we find that collaborative efforts do result in greater opportunities for students when the "whole child, whole community" concept is adopted. Frequently, each successful partnership is unique, but they all seem to include the following features (Comer et al., 1996; Rubin, 2002):

- Programs integrate educational and social services for all children, and especially for needy families.
- Parents, school personnel, and community members are empowered to make decisions about, to plan for, and to implement changes for their community's children.
- School bureaucracy is reduced, and involvement of families and community members in school management increases.
- Schools become family centers to promote better interactions among teachers, children, parents, and community members.
- Programs include strong volunteer programs, with parents, grandparents, and community members contributing expertise to support children's learning and to assist in school operations.
- Community and home are viewed as important child learning environments and are integrated into school learning.
- Programs have strong leadership and committed partners able to gain the support of **power brokers** in their setting.
- School faculty and staff develop skills needed to build and maintain relationships of trust and respect with children and families.
- Researchers, teachers, and parents work together in assessing the successes of school programs.

Researchers, teachers, and parents work together for the success of school programs.

Getty Images, Inc. – PhotoDisc

REFLECTION

Think back over the models described in this chapter and reassess your reactions to being a part of a team in partnership with homes and communities. Could you see yourself as a contributing member and promoting the features of successful partnerships in one or more of these models? List some items that you feel confident about now.

ACHIEVING PARTNERSHIPS

As we have discussed program models, we have demonstrated that true collaboration does emerge when properly nurtured. These model collaborations take time to build, and as each continues, even more time is required to monitor and fine-tune it, for it to stay healthy. Successful models may be found in systems with schools of choice, such as charter schools, or in systems where there is centralized control for education but where teachers form a succesfull collaboration with parents and the community.

As such models show, the effort is worthwhile, and the reported educational benefits to children and communities are often inspirational.

Anyone interested in achieving partnerships for their schools should carefully examine the literature on established programs. Information about the sustainability of these programs is helpful for beginners developing their own particular plans.

Individual Responsibility

Realizing the dream of partnerships requires more than the effort exhibited in most U.S. school districts today. A spirit for undertaking change has germinated in many areas but seems slow to blossom fully. We all know that change takes time. The recent surge of interest at state and federal levels for partnerships must be viewed positively, and publications, funding, and legislation all provide a fertile base for more collaboration.

When reading about model programs, we can certify that those programs that included a research and assessment dimension have shown great strides in reaching a new level of participation. We also find from those model programs that exciting things happen when new ideas are introduced, nurtured carefully, and built as change mechanisms. The results certainly reinforce the desirability of bringing more collaborative work to our nation's schools.

APPLYING THESE CONCEPTS TO YOUR WORK WITH CHILDREN AND FAMILIES

Partnerships can begin with a single teacher and a parent collaborating in a classroom, although possibilities exist for enthusiastic colleagues and parents to expand all sorts of desirable educational programs in any school. When you affiliate with a program that is launching a collaborative venture, you will want to consider the following important steps.

When your team considers collaboration, first define your objectives and agree on what changes are necessary. It's also wise to find out how collaboration has worked for others. Your team will need to locate resources and decide how to assess the progress it makes. Bringing in new helpers and involving them in collaborative ventures always requires finesse. Communication is often a problem as more people become involved in collaborations. You and your teammates must be alert to how you are communicating and how your messages are being interpreted. Finally, you will want to first try out ideas on a small scale and then expand the experiment.

As you continue planning to move a large school unit toward collaboration, other requirements appear.

You'll want to keep the following essentials in mind when planning and implementing any large-scale home–school–community partnership:

1. Community spirit for welcoming new ideas is primary. Success comes naturally when dedicated and committed people are working together to make a difference.

2. Proactive planners, leaders, and researchers must initiate, guide, and polish emerging plans for collaboration.

3. Financial resources, such as grants, must be available to subsidize pilot programs.

4. Interested citizens and community officials must commit to enacting and supporting partnerships.

5. Educators must appreciate public input and want better communication with homes and community agencies.

6. Training and development programs must be available to nourish beginners and provide a background for new leaders. Too many programs erode when a strong leader leaves.

SUMMARY AND REVIEW

When schools are brokers for new learning communities and invest time and energy in forming links with homes and communities, exciting and productive results materialize. Much evidence proves that this is true. The work of James Comer in New Haven, Connecticut, and the expansion of Epstein's National Network of Schools, to name two successes, show that we have both reason and compelling need for communities to reach out further to achieve better functioning school operations.

This chapter presents the levels of involvement that parents and community members can have in a collaboration with a school and the conditions that enhance partnerships. We have also seen the steps taken by people moving into collaborative ventures. The seven examples of existing collaborations show how those programs started and the reasons for their success. New collaborations demonstrate that similar goals and objectives can be reached by different routes and at different rates. Even implementing the principles of partnerships in part of a school district eventually enriches the experiences of all district students.

Schools are still the catalysts in most new educational endeavors. No other social institution in the United States has the oversight or the trained personnel to serve in this capacity. Partnership programs can start with a few small projects or may grow from a well-conceived and well-directed program. However it grows, a plan must call for teachers and administrators to be committed to the new practice. Being committed, gaining knowledge about other programs, devising a plan, establishing means for communicating the plan, and involving others are necessary to the success of any project.

SUGGESTED ACTIVITIES AND QUESTIONS

1. Talk with three teachers about parent involvement in their programs. Have them describe the things parents do when they come to school. To determine the stage of collaboration, relate their statements to the three levels of involvement discussed in this chapter.

2. Interview three parents to learn how they have participated in their children's school programs within the past year. What levels of involvement do you find?

3. Examine a school district with which you are acquainted, to ascertain its stage of evolution in collaborative efforts. How does your district compare to one or more of the programs featured in Chapter 12?

4. Select a school and start at the front door for a virtual tour of the facility. Make notes on the following as you walk; (1) your initial impressions, (2) classroom activities, (3) hallway activity, and (4) central office atmosphere. Now stop and reflect about what changes you would see in four years if this facility had joined a collaborative program for that length of time.

RESOURCES

Books

Bulkley, K. E., & Wohlstetter, P. (Eds.). 2004. *Taking account of charter schools: What's happened and what's next?* New York: Teachers College Press.

Cadwell, L. B. (2003). *Bringing learning to life: The Reggio approach to early childhood education.* New York: Teachers College Press.

Joyner, E. T., Ben-Avie, M., & Comer, J. P. (Eds.). 2004. *Dynamic instructional leadership to support student learning and development: The field guide to Comer schools in action.* Thousand Oaks, CA: Corwin Press.

Lerner, R. M., & Benson, P. L. (Eds.). 2003. *Developmental assest and asset-building communities: Implications for research, policy and practice.* New York: Kluwer Academic/Plenum Publishers.

Sanders, M. G. (2006). *Building school–community partnerships: Collaboration for student success.* Thousand Oaks, CA: Corwin Press.

Films, Audio Cassettes, and Videos

Cultivating Roots—Home/school/partnerships (1997). [Video, 30 min]. Washington, DC: National Association for the Education of Young Children.

Not just any place—Reggio Emilia: An education experience as told by the protagonists [Video, 72 min]. (2003). The video highlights the uniqueness of the program. Burlington, VT: Learning Materials Workshop.

Promoting family collaboration [Video, 24 min]. (1998). Video demonstrates relationships between families and healthcare providers. Princeton, NJ: Films for the Humanities & Sciences.

Rethinking school organization [3 audiocassettes, 1 hr. each]. (1996). Six authorities on schooling processes, parent involvement, and other educational developments. Bloomington, IN: Agency for Instructional Technology.

Organizations

Council of the Great City Schools
1301 Pennsylvania Avenue, NW
Washington, DC 20004
http://www.cgcs.org

Phi Delta Kappa
408 N. Union Street
Bloomington, IN 47402
http://www.pdkintl.org

Web Sites

http://www.cgcs.org   Council of Great City Schools Online. Presents information on the nation's large public school systems and their interschool projects.

http://www.classroom.net   Classroom Connect has an on-line magazine for all levels of teachers and features on-line educational programs.

http://www.dac.neu.edu/ire   Institute for Responsive Education (now connected to Cambridge College) Web site. Contains extensive reports and publications on partnerships and collaborations.

http://www.eric.ed.gov   The ERIC (Education Resources Information Center) Web site for information on Reggio Emilia.

http://www.ncpie.org   The National Coalition for Parent Involvement in Education Web site features a database for partnerships for family involvement in education and gives examples of successful collaborations.

APPENDIX I

Bibliography of Children's Books

The following selected bibliography of children's books portrays a variety of American family structures where individuals are learning together in the home, the school, and the community. Codes used are as follows:

H Indicates that the book reveals children learning through the home environment.

S Indicates that children from different family structures are learning together at school.

C Indicates that different family members are sharing and learning from their community environment.

Different Cultures

Anacona, G. (1998). *El barrio, Jose's neighborhood*. New York: Harcourt. **C**

Ashley, B. (1991). *Cleversticks* (D. Brazell, Illus.). New York: Crown. **S**

Banks, L. R. (1992). *One more river*. New York: Morrow. **S, C**

Bartoletti, S. (1999). *Polish dancing with Dziadziu*. (A. Nelson, Illus.). New York: Harcourt. **H**

Breckler, R. K. (1992). *Hoang breaks the lucky teapot*. (A. Frankel, Illus.). Boston: Houghton Mifflin. **H**

Bunting, E. (1996). *Going home* (D. Diaz, Illus.). New York: HarperCollins. **H, C**

Bunting, E. (1997). *Moonstick, the seasons of the Sioux*. (J. Sanford, Paintings.). New York: HarperCollins. **C**

Calhoun, M. (1996). *Tonio's cat* (D. Stanley, Illus.). New York: Morrow Junior. **C**

Carling, A. L. (1998). *Mama and papa have a store*. New York: Dial. **H, C**

Cohen, M. (1989). *See you in second grade*. New York: Greenwillow. **S**

Crowley, J. (1998). *Big moon tortilla* (D. Strongbow, Illus.). Honesdale, PA: Boyd's Mills. **H**

Cummings, P. (1991). *Clean your room, Harvey Moon!* New York: Macmillan. **H**

Curtis, J. L. (2006). *Is there really a human race?* New York: HarperCollins. **S, C**

Diouf, S. (2001). *Bintou's braids* (S. W. Evans, Illus.). San Francisco: Chronicle. **H, C**

Dooley, N. (1991). *Everybody cooks rice* (P. J. Thornton, Illus.). Minneapolis, MN: Carolrhoda. **H, C**

Fazio, B. L. (1996). *Grandfather's story*. Seattle, WA: Sasquatch. **H**

Franklin, K. L. (1994). *The shepherd boy* (J. Kastner, Illus.). New York: Atheneum. **C**

Germein, K. (2000). *Big rain coming*. (B. Brancoft, Illus.). New York: Clarion. **H, S**

Good, M. (1993). *Reuben and the fire* (P. B. Moss, Illus.). Intercourse, PA: Good Books. **C**

Greenfield, L. (2003). *Honey, I love*. (J. Gilchrist, Illus.). New York: Amistad. **H, S**

Hamilton, V. (2004). *The people could fly*. (L. & D. Dillon, Illus.). New York: Knopf. **S, C**

Hartman, W. (1993). *All the magic in the world* (N. Daly, Illus.). New York: Dutton. **C**

Heide, F. P., & Gilliland, J. H. (1990). *The day of Ahmed's secret* (T. Lewin, Illus.). New York: Mulberry. **H, C**

Hooks, B. (1999). *Happy to be nappy* (C. Raschka, Illus.). New York: Jump at the Sun/Hyperion for Children. **H**

Hoyt-Goldsmith, D (1990). *Totem pole* (L. Migdale, Photographs). New York: Holiday House. **H**

Katz, K. (1999). *The color of us*. New York: Holt. **H, C**

Kendall, R. (1992). *Eskimo boy: Life in an Inupiaq Eskimo village*. New York: Scholastic. **C**

Knight, M. (1995). *Talking walls*. (A. O'Brien, Illus.). Gardiner, ME: Tilbury House. **S, C**

Kroll, V. (1994). *Masai and I* (N. Carpenter, Illus.). New York: Four Winds. **C**

Kurtz, J. (1998). *The storyteller's beads*. New York: Gulliver. **S**

London, J. (1997). *Ali, child of the desert* (T. Lewin, Illus.). Shepard, NY: Lothrop, Lee & Shepard. **C**

MacDonald, S. (1995). *Nanta's lion: A search-and-find adventure*. New York: Morrow. **C**

Markhun, P. M. (1993). *The little painter of Sabana Grande* (R. Casilla, Illus.). New York: Bradbury. **C**

McCloskey, R. (1952). *One morning in Maine*. New York: Viking. **H, C**

Mora, P. (2003). *The rainbow tulip*. New York: Puffin. **S**

Onyefulu, I. (1995). *E Meka's gift: An African counting book*. New York: Cobblehill. **C**

Partridge, E. (2003). *Oranges on Golden Mountain*. New York: Puffin. **H, C**

Pinkney, A. (2001). *Mim's Christmas jam* (B. Pinkney, Illus.). New York: Harcourt. **H, C**

Pinkney, B. (1994). *Max found two sticks*. New York: Simon & Schuster. **C**

Polacco, P. (1990). *Just plain fancy*. New York: Simon & Schuster. **C**

Pomerana, M. (1998). *The American Wei* (A. Di Salvo-Ryan, Illus.). Morton Grove, IL: Whitman. **C**

Pryor, B. (1996). *The dream jar* (M. Graham, Illus.). New York: Morrow. **H**

St. James, S. (1996). *Sunday*. New York: Whitman. **H**

Say, A. (1991). *Tree of cranes*. New York: Scholastic. **H**

Smalls, I. (1994). *Dawn and the round to-it* (T. Geter, Illus.). New York: Simon & Schuster. **H**

Smith, D. J. (2002). *If the world were a village*. (S. Armstrong, Illus.). Toronto: Kids Can Press. **S**

Soto, G. (1993). *Too many tamales* (E. Martinez, Illus.). New York: Putnam's. **H**

Steptoe, J. (1997). *Munfaro's beautiful daughters*. New York: Lothrop. **H, C**

Stroud, V. A. (1994). *Doesn't fall off his horse*. New York: Dial. **C**

Surat, M. M. (1993). *Angel child, dragon child* (V.-D. Mai, Illus.). New York: Carnival. **S**

Villanueva, M. (1993). *Nene and the horrible math monster* (R. Unson, Illus.). Chicago: Polychrome. **S**

Waboose, J. (2000). *Sky sisters*. (B. Deines, Illus.). Niagara Falls, NY: Kids Can Press. **C**

Watkins, S. (1994). *White bead ceremony* (K. Doner, Illus.). Tulsa, OK: Council Oak. **C**

White Deer of Autumn. (1992). *The great change* (C. Grigg, Illus.). Hillsboro, OR: Beyond Words. **C**

Williams, K. L. (1998). *Painted dreams* (C. Stock, Illus.). New York: Lothrop, Lee & Shepard. **H, C**

Woodson, J. (2001). *The other side*. New York: Putnam's Sons. **C**

Wright, C. C. (1994). *Jumping the broom* (G. Griffith, Illus.). New York: Holiday. **C**

Yamate, S. (1991). *Char Siu Bao boy*. Chicago: Polychrome. **S**

Divorced Families

Abercrombie, B. (1995, 1990). *Charlie Anderson*. Upper Saddle River, NJ: Simon & Schuster. **H**

Bernhard, D. (2001). *To & Fro, Fast & Slow*. London, Walker. **H**

Binch, C. (1998). *Since dad left*. Brookfield, CT: Millbrook. **H**

Brown, M. & Brown, L. K. (1988). *Dinosaurs divorce*. New York: Little Brown. **H, S**

Bunting, E. (2001). *The days of summer* (W. Low, Illus.). New York: Harcourt. **H**

Girard, L. W. (1987). *At Daddy's on Saturdays* (J. Friedman, Illus.). Morton Grove, IL: Whitman. **H**

Mayle, P. (1988). *Why are we getting a divorce?* (A. Robins, Illus.). New York: Harmony. **H**

Rodgers, F. (1998). *Let's talk about it: Divorce*. New York: Putnam. **H**

Rotner, S., & Sheila, K. (2002). *Something's different*. Brookfield, CT: Millbrook. **H**

Rush, K. (1994). *Friday's journey*. New York: Orchard. **C**

Schotter, R. (2003). *Room for rabbit* (C. Moore, Illus.). New York: Clarion. **H**

Watson, J. W., Switzer, R. E., & Hirschberg, J. C. (1988). *Sometimes a family has to split up* (C. B. Smith, Illus.). New York: Crown. **H**

Weinger, B. (1995). *Good-bye, Daddy* (A. Mark, Illus.). New York: North–South. **H**

Blended Families

Boyd, L. (1990). *Sam is my half-brother*. New York: Viking Penguin. **H**

Brooks, B. (1992). *What hearts*. New York: Dutton. **H, C**

Gibbons, F. (1996). *Mountain wedding* (T. Rand, Illus.). New York: Morrow Junior. **H, C**

Hines, A. G. (1996). *When we married Gary*. New York: Greenwillow. **H**

Hoffman, M. (1995). *Boundless grace* (C. Binch, Illus.). New York: Scholastic. **H, C**

MacLachlan, P. (1985). *Sarah, plain and tall*. New York: Harper & Row. **H, C**

Ransom, C. F. (1993). *We're growing together* (V. W. Frierson, Illus.). New York: Bradbury. **H, C**

Rodgers, F. (2001). *Let's talk about it: Stepfamilies*. New York: Putnam. **H**

Vigna, J. (1980). *She's not my real mother*. Chicago: Whitman. **H, C**

Willner-Pardo, G. (1994). *What I'll remember when I am a grownup* (W. L. Krudop, Illus.). New York: Clarion. **H**

Single-Parent Household and Special Relationship with One Parent or with Grandparents

Ackerman, K. (1988). *Song and dance man* (S. Gammell, Illus.). New York: Scholastic. **H**

Ackerman, K. (1994). *By the dawn's early light* (C. Stock, Illus.). New York: Atheneum. **H**

Atwell, D. (2003). *The Thanksgiving door*. Boston: Houghton Mifflin. **C**

Bunting, E. (1994). *Smoky night* (D. Diaz, Illus.). San Diego, CA: Harcourt Brace Jovanovich. **C**

Chaconas, D. (2003). *On a wintry morning* (S. T. Johnson, Illus.). New York: Puffin. **H, C**

Cleary, B. (2000). *Dear Mr. Henshaw*. New York: Morrow. **H, S**

Clifton, L. (2001). *One of the problems of Everett Anderson* (A. Grifalconi, Illus.). New York: Holt. **H, S**

Cohen, C. Lee. (2003). *Everything is different at Nonna's house* (H. Nakata, Illus.). New York: Clarion. **H**

Cooper, S. (1993). *Danny and the kings* (J. A. Smith, Illus.). New York: McElderry. **C**

Eager, E. (1999). *Half magic*. (N. Bodecker, Illus.). New York: Harcourt. **H, C**

Greenfield, E. (1988). *Nathaniel talking* (J. S. Gilchrist, Illus.). New York: Black Butterfly. **H, S, C**

Haggerty, M. E. (1993). *A crack in the wall* (R. de Anda, Illus.). New York: Lee & Low. **H**

Harrison, T. (1994). *The long weekend*. New York: Harcourt Brace. **C**

Joosse, B. M. (1991). *Mama, do you love me?* (B. Lavallee, Illus.). New York: Scholastic. **H**

Lindsay, J. W. (1982, 1991). *Do I have a daddy? A story about a single-parent child* (2nd ed.; C. Boeller, Illus.). Buena Park, CA: Morning Glory. **H**

McKissack, P. (2000). *Ma dear's aprons*. (F. Cooper, Illus.). New York: Atheneum. **H**

Moon, N. (1994). *Lucy's picture* (A. Ayliffe, Illus.). New York: Scholastic. **S**

Parr, T. (2002). *The daddy book*. Boston: Little, Brown. **H**

Peterson, J. W. (1994). *My mama sings* (S. Speidel, Illus.). New York: HarperCollins. **H**

Plourde, L. (2003). *Thank you, Grandpa* (J. Cockcroft, Illus.). New York: Dutton. **H, C**

Rosenberg, L. (1997). *Monster Mama*. (S. Gammell, Illus.). New York: Putnam. **H**

Sharp, N. L. (1993). *Today I'm going fishing with my dad* (C. Demarest, Illus.). Honesdale, PA: Boyd's Mill. **C**

Sisulu, E. B. (1996). *The day Gogo went to vote* (S. Wilson, Illus.). Boston: Little, Brown. **H, C**

Smalls, I. (1992). *Jonathan and his mommy* (M. Hays, Illus.). Boston: Little, Brown. **C**

Smalls, I. (1999). *Kevin and his dad* (M. Hays, Illus.). Boston: Little, Brown. **H, C**

Testa, M. (1996). *Nine candles* (A. Schaffer, Illus.). Minneapolis, MN: Carolrhoda. **C**

Tran, K.-L. (1994). *Tet: The new year* (M. Vo-Dinh, Illus.). New York: Simon & Schuster. **C**

Vigna, J. (1987). *Mommy and me by ourselves again*. Morton Grove, IL: Whitman. **H**

Waddell, M. (1994). *The big, big Sea* (J. Eachus, Illus.). Cambridge, MA: Candlewick. **C**

Woodson. J. (2002). *Visiting day*. New York: Scholastic. **H, S**

Ziefert, H. (2003). *Home for Navidad* (S. Cohen, Illus.). Boston: Houghton Mifflin. **H**

Ziefert, H. (2003). *31 Uses for a mom* (R. Doughty, Illus.). New York: Putnam. **C**

Adoptive Families

Bloom, S. (1991). *A family for Jamie: An adoption story*. New York: Potter. **H**

Brodzinsky, A. B. (1996). *The mulberry bird: An adoption story* (D. Stanley, Illus.). Indianapolis: Perspective. **H**

Cais, S. (1998). *Why so sad, Brown Rabbit?* New York: Dutton. **H**

Cole, J. (1995). *How I was adopted: Samantha's story* (M. Chambliss, Illus.). New York: Morrow. **H**

Curtis, J. L. (1996). *Tell me again about the night I was born* (L. Cornell, Illus.). New York: HarperCollins. **H, C**

D'Antonio, N. (1997). *Our baby from China: An adoption story*. Morton Grove, IL: Whitman. **H, C**

Girard, L. W. (1989). *We adopted you, Benjamin Koo* (L. Shute, Illus.). Morton Grove, IL: Whitman. **H, S**

Kasza, K. (1992). *A mother for Choco*. New York: Putnam. **H**

Katz, K. (1997). *Over the moon: An adoption tale*. New York: Holt. **H, C**

Koehler, P. (1990, 1997). *The day we met you*. Old Tappen, NJ: Simon & Schuster. **H**

Lamperti, N. (1999). *Brown like me*. Johnstown, NY: New Victoria. **H, C**

McCully, E. A. (1994). *My real family*. San Diego, CA: Harcourt. **H, C**

Miller, K. A. (1994). *Did my first mother love me? A story for an adopted child* (J. Moffett, Illus.). Buena Park, CA: Morning Glory. **H**

Okimoto, J. D., & Aoki, E. M. (2002). *White swan express* (M. So, Illus.). New York: Clarion. **C**

Rogers, F. (1995, 1998). *Let's talk about it: Adoption* (J. Judkins, Illus.). New York: Putnam. **H**

Say, A. (2004). *Allison*. Boston: Houghton Mifflin. **H**

Turner, A. (1990). *Through moon and stars and night skies* (J. Graham Hale, Illus.). New York: Harper & Row. **H, C**

Foster Care, Orphanages, and Shelters

Blomquist, G., & Blomquist, P. (1993, 1990). *Zachary's new home: A story for foster and adoptive children*. Milwaukee, WI: Stevens. **H**

Bunting, E. (1996). *Train to somewhere* (R. Himler, Illus.). New York: Clarion. **C**

Cannon, J. (1994). *Stellaluna*. San Diego, CA: Harcourt. **H, C**

Chalofsky, M., Finland, G., Wallace, J. (1992). *Changing places. A kid's view of shelter living*. Mt. Rainier, MD: Gryphon. **H, C**

Jarrell, R. (1996). *The animal family*. New York: HarperCollins. **H, C**

Herbert, S. (1991). *I miss my foster parents*. Washington, DC: Child Welfare League of America. **H, C**

MacLachlan, P. (1995). *Baby*. New York: Delacorte. **H**

Nixon, J. L. (2000). *The orphan train adventures*. New York: Bantam. **H, C**

Steptoe, J. (1969). *Stevie*. New York: Harper. **H**

Multigenerational Households and Extended Families

Bauer, M. D. (1995). *When I go camping with gramma* (A. Garns, Illus.). New York: Bridgewater. **C**

Burden–Patman, D., with Jones, K. D. (1992). *Carnival* (R. Ruffins, Illus.). New York: Simon & Schuster. **H, C**

Chiemruom, S. (1994). *Dara's Cambodian new year* (D. N. Pin, Illus.). New York: Simon & Schuster. **H**

Choi, S. N. (1993). *Halmoni and the picnic* (K. M. Dugan, Illus.). Boston: Houghton Mifflin. **S**

Coleman, E. (1996). *White socks only* (T. Geter, Illus.). Morton Grove, IL: Whitman. **H, C**

Crews, D. (1991). *Bigmama's*. New York: Greenwillow. **H, C**

Dorros, A. (1991). *Abuela* (E. Kleven, Illus.). New York: Dutton. **C**

Falwell, C. (1995). *Feast for 10*. New York: Clarion. **H, C**

Fox, M. (1989, 1994). *Sophie* (A. Robinson, Illus.). New York: Harcourt. **H**

Guback, G. (1994). *Luka's quilt*. New York: Greenwillow. **H**

Heide, F. P., & Pierce, R. H. (1998). *Tio Armolo*. New York: Lothrop & Shepard. **H**

Hoffman, M. (1991). *Amazing grace* (C. Binch, Illus.). New York: Dial. **H, S**

Howard, E. F. (1991). *Aunt Flossie's hats (and) crab cakes later*. New York: Clarion. **H, C**

Jones, R. (1995). *Great Aunt Martha*. New York: Dutton. **H**

Levine, A. (1995). *Bono and Nonno* (J. Lanfredi, Illus.). New York: Tambourine. **C**

Lewin, T. (1998). *The story tellers*. New York: Lothrop, Lee & Shepard. **C**

MacLachlan, P. (1993). *Journey*. New York: Delacorte. **H, C**

Mathis, S. B. (1975). *The hundred penny box* (L. Dillon & D. Dillon, Illus.). New York: Viking. **H**

Matthews, M. (2000). *Magid fasts for Ramadan* (E. B. Lewis, Illus.). Boston: Houghton Mifflin. **H**

McCully, E. A. (1993). *Grandmas at bat*. New York: HarperCollins. **C**

McFarlane, S. (1991, 1993). *Waiting for the whales* (R. Lightburn, Illus.). New York: Philomel. **H, C**

Miles, M. (1971). *Annie and the old one* (P. Parnall, Illus.). Boston: Little, Brown. **H**

Mills, C. (1999). *Gus and grandpa.* (C. Stock, Illus.). New York: Farrar Strauss & Giroux. **H, C**

Moore, E. (1995). *Grandma's smile* (D. Andreasen, Illus.). New York: Lothrop, Lee & Shepard. **H**

Parr, T. (2006). *The grandpa book*. New York: Little Brown. **H**

Polacco, P. (1990). *Thunder cake*. New York: Philomel. **H**

Polacco, P. (1992). *Mrs. Katz and Tush*. New York: Bantam (Little Rooster). **C**

Poydar, N. (1994). *Busy Bea*. New York: Macmillan. **H**

Reiser, L. (1998). *Cherry pies and lullabies*. New York: Greenwillow. **H**

Say, A. (1993). *Grandfather's journey*. Boston: Houghton Mifflin. **H, C**

Simon, F. (1998). *Where are you?* (D. Melling, Illus.). Atlanta, GA: Peachtree. **C**

Swartz, L. (1992, 1994). *A first Passover* (J. Chwast, Illus.). New York: Simon & Schuster. **H**

Swentzell, R. (1992). *Children of clay: A family of pueblo potters* (B. Steen, Photographs). Minneapolis, MN: Lerner. **C**

Wells, R. (1996). *The language of doves* (G. Shed, Illus.). New York: Dial. **H**

Wild, M. (1994). *Our granny* (J. Vivas, Illus.). New York: Ticknor & Fields. **H**

Wild, M. (1996). *Old pig.* New York: Ticknor & Fields. **H, C**

Williams, V. (1997). *Lucky song.* New York: Greenwillow. **H**

Woodruff, E. (1998). *Can you guess where we're going?* (C. Fisher, Illus.). New York: Holiday House. **C**

Zalben, J. B. (1996). *Papa's latkes.* New York: Holt. **H**

Zamorano, A. (1997). *Let's eat* (J. Vivas, Illus.). New York: Scholastic. **H**

Religious Traditions

Demi. (1997). *Buddha stories.* New York: Henry Holt. **H, S**

dePaola, T. (1989). *The clown of God.* Orlando, FL: Harcourt. **H**

Graham, R. B. (1995). *One wintry night.* (R. Watson, Illus.). New York: Baker Books. **H**

Johnson, J. W. (1994). *The creation.* (J. Ransome, Illus.). New York: Holiday House. **H, S**

Johnston, T. (2000). *Day of the dead.* (J. Winter, Illus.). Orlando, FL: Harcourt. **H, C**

Macaulay, D. (1981). *Cathedral: The story of its construction.* Boston: Houghton Mifflin. **S**

Macaulay, D. (2003). *Mosque.* Boston: Houghton Mifflin. **S**

Oberman, S. (1994). *The always prayer shawl.* New York: Puffin. **H, S**

Osborne, M. P. (1996). *One world, many religions: The ways we worship.* New York: Knopf. **H, C**

Palacco. P. (1998). *Chicken Sunday.* New York: Philomel. **C**

Pinkney. A. (1993). *Seven candles for Kwanza.* (B. Pinkney, Illus.). Cambridge, MA: Candlewick. **H, C**

Shazi, S. H. (1996) *Ramadan.* (O. Rayyan, Illus.). New York: Holiday House. **H, C**

Wildsmith, B. (1996). *Saint Francis.* Grand Rapids, MI: W. B. Eerdmans. **C, S**

Yolen, J. (1996). *Sacred places.* Fort Worth: Harcourt. **S, C**

Homeless Families

Barbour, K. (1991). *Mr. Bowtie.* San Diego, CA: Harcourt. **C**

Bunting, E. (1991). *Fly away home* (R. Himler, Illus.). New York: Clarion. **C**

Bunting, E. (1999). *December* (D. Diaz, Illus.). New York: Harcourt. **H, C**

DiSalvo-Ryan, D. (1991). *Uncle Willie and the soup kitchen.* New York: Morrow Junior. **C**

Guthrie, D. (2000, 1988). *A rose for Abby.* Nashville, TN: Abington Press. **C**

Hathorn, L. (1994). *Way home* (G. Rogers, Illus.). New York: Crown. **C**

Park, L. S. (2003). *A single shard.* New York: Yearling. **H, S**

Paulsen, G. (2006). *The crossing.* New York: Scholastic. **H, S**

Sendak, M. (1993). *We are all down in the dumps with Jack and Guy.* New York: HarperCollins. **C**

Snyder, Z. (1996). *Cat running.* New York: Delacorte. **S, C**

Voight, C. (2003). *Homecoming.* New York: Aladdin. **H, S**

Weninger, B. (1997). *Lumina* (A. Bell, Trans; J. Wintz-Litty, Illus.). New York: North–South. **C**

Wolf, B. (1995). *Homeless.* New York: Orchard. **H, C**

Migrant Workers and Immigrants

Bunting, E. (1988). *How many days to America? A Thanksgiving story* (B. Peck, Illus.). New York: Clarion. **C**

Bunting, E. (1994). *A day's work.* New York: Clarion. **H, C**

Garland, S. (1997). *Lotus seed.* (T. Kiuchi, Illus.). New York: Harcourt. **S, C**

Herrera, J. (2001). *Calling the doves.* (E. Simmons, Illus.). New York: Children's Book Press. **H, S**

Holm, J. L. (2001). *Our only May Amelia.* New York: HarperCollins. **H, C**

Krall, K. (2003). *Harvesting hope* (Y. Morales, Illus.). New York: Harcourt. **H, C, S**

Levine, E. (1994). *If your name was changed at Ellis Island.* Berkeley, CA: Tricycle Press. **H, S**

Rosenberg, M. (1986). *Making a new home in America* (G. Ancona, Photographs). New York: Lothrop. **H**

Williams, S. A. (1992). *Working cotton* (C. Byard, Illus.). San Diego, CA: Harcourt. **C**

Gay and Lesbian Families

Bosche, S. (1983). *Jenny lives with Eric and Martin.* London: Gay Men's Press. **H**

Brown, F. (1991). *Generous Jefferson Bartleby* (L. Trawin, Illus.). Boston: Alyson Wonderland. **H, C**

DeHaan, L., & Nigland, S. (2002). *King and king.* Berkeley, CA: Tricycle Press. **H, S**

Elwin, R., & Paulie, M. (1990). *Asha's mums* (D. Lee, Illus.). Toronto, Ontario, Canada: Women's Press. **S**

Greenberg, K. E. (1996). *Zack's story.* Minneapolis MN: Lerner. **H, S, C**

Heron, A., & Maran, M. (1991). *How would you feel if your dad was gay?* (K. Kovick, Illus.). Boston: Alyson Wonderland. **H**

Newman, L. (1991). *Belinda's bouquet* (M. Willhoite, Illus.). Boston: Alyson Wonderland. **H, C**

Newman, L. (1991). *Gloria goes to gay pride* (R. Crocker, Illus.). Boston: Alyson Wonderland. **H, C**

Newman, L. (1993). *Saturday is pattyday* (A. Hegel, Illus.). Norwich, CT: New Victoria. **C**

Newman, L. (2000). *Heather has two mommies, 10th anniversary* (D. Souza, Illus.). Boston: Alyson Wonderland. **H, S**

Quinlan, P. (1994). *Tiger flowers* (J. Wilson, Illus.). New York: Dial. **H**

Vigna, J. (1995). *My two uncles.* Morton Grove, IL: Whitman. **H**

Willhoite, M. (1990). *Daddy's roommate.* Boston: Alyson Wonderland. **H**

Willhoite, M. (1993). *Uncle what-is-it is coming to visit!* Boston: Alyson Wonderland. **H**

Children, Family Members, and Friends with Special Needs

Cohen, M. (1997). *See you tomorrow, Charles.* New York: Yearling. **S**

Cowen-Fletcher, J. (1993). *Mama zooms.* New York: Scholastic. **H**

Day, S. (1995). *Luna and the big blur: A story for children who wear glasses* (D. Morris, Illus.). New York: Brunner/Mazel. **H**

Dugan, B. (1992). *Loop the loop* (J. Stevenson, Illus.). New York: Greenwillow. **C**

Dwight, L. (1998). *We can do it.* New York: Starbright. **C**

Fleming, V. (1993). *Be good to Eddie Lee.* (F. Cooper, Illus.). New York: Putnam. **S**

Gantos, J. (2000). *Joey Pigza swallowed the key.* New York: Farrar Strauss & Giroux. **S**

Hines, A. G. (1993). *Gramma's walk.* New York: Greenwillow. **C**

Karim, R. (1994). *Mandy Sue day.* New York: Clarion. **H, S**

Konigsburg, E. L. (1998). *A view from Saturday.* New York: Atheneum. **S, C**

Kroll, V. (1993). *Naomi knows it's springtime* (J. Kastner, Illus.). Honesdale, PA: Boyd's Mill. **C**

Lakin, P. (1994). *Dad and me in the morning* (R. O. Steele, Illus.). Morton Grove, IL: Whitman. **C**

Miller, M. B., & Ancona, G. (1991). *Handtalk school.* (G. Ancona, Illus.). New York: Four Winds. **S**

Mohr, N. (1995). *Old Lativia and the Mountain of Sorrows* (R. Gutierrez, Illus.). New York: Greenwillow. **H, C**

Osofsky, A. (1992). *My buddy* (T. Rand, Illus.). New York: Holt. **H, C**

Rabe, B. (1988). *Where's Chimpy?* (D. Schmidt, Photographs). Morton Grove, IL: A. Whitman. **H**

Stuve-Bodeen, S. (1998). *We'll paint the octopus red* (P. DeVito, Illus.). Bethesda, MD: Woodbine. **H**

Thompson, M. (1992). *My brother Matthew.* Rockville, MD: Woodbine House. **H**

Waddell, M. (1990). *My great grandpa* (D. Mansell, Illus.). New York: Putnam. **C**

Defining Families

Abramchik, L. (1993). *Is your family like mine?* (A. Bradshaw, Illus.). New York: Open Heart, Open Mind. **H, S**

Adoff, A. (2002). *Black is brown is tan* (E. A. McCully, Illus.). New York: HarperCollins. **H**

Jenness, A. (1990). *Families: A celebration of diversity, commitment, and love.* Boston: Houghton Mifflin. **H**

Kroll, V. (1994). *Beginnings: How families come to be.* Morton Grove, IL: Whitman. **H**

Leedy, L. F. (1995, 1999). *Who's who in my family?* New York: Holiday House. **H**

Littlefield, G. (1993). *This land is my land.* Chicago: Children's Book Press. **S, C**

Morris, A. (1990). *Loving* (K. Heyman, Photographs). New York: Mulberry. **H, C**

Skutch, R. (1995). *Who's in a family* (L. Nienhaus, Illus.). Berkeley, CA: Tricycle. **H, C**

Strickland, D. S., & Strickland, M. S. (Eds.). (1994). *Families: Poems celebrating the African American experience* (J. Ward, Illus.). Honesdale, PA: Boyd's Mill. **H**

Valentine, J. (1994). *One dad, two dads, brown dad, blue dads* (M. Sarecky, Illus.). Boston: Alyson Wonderland. **H**

APPENDIX II

NAEYC Code of Ethical Conduct and Statement of Commitment

A position statement of the National Association for the Education of Young Children, Revised April 2005

Endorsed by the Association for Childhood Education International
Adopted by the National Association for Family Child Care

Preamble

NAEYC recognizes that those who work with young children face many daily decisions that have moral and ethical implications. The **NAEYC Code of Ethical Conduct** offers guidelines for responsible behavior and sets forth a common basis for resolving the principal ethical dilemmas encountered in early childhood care and education. The **Statement of Commitment** is not part of the Code but is a personal acknowledgement of an individual's willingness to embrace the distinctive values and moral obligations of the field of early childhood care and education.

The primary focus of the Code is on daily practice with children and their families in programs for children from birth through eight years of age, such as infant/toddler programs, preschool and prekindergarten programs, childcare centers, hospital and child life settings, family childcare homes, kindergartens, and primary classrooms. When the issues involve young children, then these provisions also apply to specialists who do not work directly with children, including program administrators, parent educators, early childhood adult educators, and officials with responsibility for program monitoring and licensing. (*Note:* See also the "Code of Ethical Conduct: Supplement for Early Childhood Adult Educators," on-line at http://www.naeyc.org/about/positions/pdf/ethics04.pdf.)

Core Values

Standards of ethical behavior in early childhood care and education are based on commitment to the following core values that are deeply rooted in the history of the field of early childhood care and education. We have made a commitment to

- Appreciate childhood as a unique and valuable stage of the human life cycle
- Base our work on knowledge of how children develop and learn
- Appreciate and support the bond between the child and family
- Recognize the children are best understood and supported in the context of family, culture,*community, and society
- Respect the dignity, worth, and uniqueness of each individual (child, family member, and colleague)
- Respect diversity in children, families, and colleagues
- Recognize that children and adults achieve their full potential in the context of relationships that are based on trust and respect

Conceptual framework

The Code sets forth a framework of professional responsibilities in four sections. Each section addresses an area of professional relationship: (1) with children, (2) with families, (3) among colleagues, and (4) with the

*The term *culture* includes ethnicity, racial identity, economic level, family structure, language, and religious and political beliefs, which profoundly influence each child's development and relationship to the world.

community and society. Each section includes an introduction to the primary responsibilities of the early childhood practitioner in that context. The introduction is followed by a set of ideals (I) that reflect exemplary professional practice and by a set of principles (P) describing practices that are required, prohibited, or permitted.

The **ideals** reflect the aspirations of practitioners. The **principles** guide conduct and assist practitioners in resolving ethical dilemmas.* Both ideals and principles are intended to direct practitioners to those questions which, when responsibly answered, can provide the basis for conscientious decision making. While the Code provides specific direction for addressing some ethical dilemmas, many others will require the practitioner to combine the guidance of the Code with professional judgment.

The ideals and principles in this Code present a shared framework of professional responsibility that affirms our commitment to the core values of our field. The Code publicly acknowledges the responsibilities that we in the field have assumed, and in so doing supports ethical behavior in our work. Practitioners who face situations with ethical dimensions are urged to seek guidance in the applicable parts of this Code and in the spirit that informs the whole.

Often "the right answer"—the best ethical course of action to take—is not obvious. There may be no readily apparent, positive way to handle a situation. When one important value contradicts another, we face an ethical dilemma. When we face a dilemma, it is our professional responsibility to consult the Code and all relevant parties to find the most ethical resolution.

Section I

Ethical responsibilities of children

Childhood is a unique and valuable stage in the human life cycle. Our paramount responsibility is to provide care and education in settings that are safe, healthy, nurturing, and responsive for each child. We are committed to supporting children's development and learning: respecting individual differences: and helping children learn to live, play, and work cooperatively. We are also committed to promoting children's self-awareness, competence, self-worth, resiliency, and physical well-being.

Ideals

I-1.1—To be familiar with the knowledge base of early childhood care and education and to stay informed through continuing education and training.

*There is not necessarily a corresponding principle for each ideal.

I-1.2—To base program practices upon current knowledge and research in the field of early childhood education, child development, and related disciplines, as well as on particular knowledge of each child.

I-1.3—To recognize and respect the unique qualities, abilities, and potential of each child.

I-1.4—To appreciate the vulnerability of children and their dependence on adults.

I-1.5—To create and maintain safe and healthy settings that foster children's social, emotional, cognitive, and physical development and that respect their dignity and their contributions.

I-1.6—To use assessment instruments and strategies that are appropriate for the children to be assessed, that are used only for the purposes for which they were designed, and that have the potential to benefit children.

I-1.7—To use assessment information to understand and support children's development and learning, to support instruction, and to identify children who may need additional services.

I-1.8—To support the right of each child to play and learn in an inclusive environment that meets the needs of children with and without disabilities.

I-1.9—To advocate for and ensure that all children, including those with special needs, have access to the support services needed to be successful.

I-1.10—To ensure that each child's culture, language, ethnicity, and family structure are recognized and valued in the program.

I-1.11—To provide all children with experiences in a language that they know, as well as support children in maintaining the use of their home language and in learning English.

I-1.12—To work with families to provide a safe and smooth transition as children and families move from one program to the next.

Principles

P-1.1—**Above all, we shall not harm children. We shall not participate in practices that are emotionally damaging, physically harmful, disrespectful, degrading, dangerous, exploitative, or intimidating to children.** *This principle has precedence over all others in this Code.*

P-1.2—We shall care for and educate children in positive emotional and social environments that are cognitively stimulating and that support each child's culture, language, ethnicity, and family structure.

P-1.3 —We shall not participate in practices that discriminate against children by denying benefits, giving special advantages, or excluding them from programs or activities on the basis of their sex, race, national origin, religious beliefs, medical condition, disability, or the marital status/family structure, sexual orientation, or religious beliefs or other affiliations of their families. (Aspects of this principle do not apply in programs that have lawful mandate to provide services to a particular population of children.)

P-1.4—We shall involve all those with relevant knowledge (including families and staff) in decisions concerning a child, as appropriate, ensuring confidentiality of sensitive information.

P-1.5—We shall use appropriate assessment systems, which include multiple sources of information, to provide information on children's learning and development.

P-1.6—We shall strive to ensure that decisions such as those related to enrollment, retention, or assignment to special education services, will be based on multiple sources of information and will never be based on a single assessment, such as a test score or a single observation.

P-1.7—We shall strive to build individual relationships with each child; make individualized adaptations in teaching strategies, environments, and curricula; and consult with the family so that each child benefits from the program. If after such efforts have been exhausted, the current placement does not meet a child's needs, or the child is seriously jeopardizing the ability of other children to benefit from the program, we shall collaborate with the child's family and appropriate specialists to determine the additional services needed and/or the placement option(s) most likely to ensure the child's success. (Aspects of this principle may not apply in programs that have a lawful mandate to provide services to particular population of children.)

P-1.8—We shall be familiar with the risk factors for and symptoms of child abuse and neglect, including physical, sexual, verbal, and emotional abuse, and physical, emotional, educational, and medical neglect. We shall know and follow state laws and community procedures that protect children against abuse and neglect.

P-1.9—When we have reasonable cause to suspect child abuse or neglect, we shall report it to the appropriate community agency and follow up to ensure that appropriate action has been taken. When appropriate, parents or guardians will be informed that the referral will be or has been made.

P-1.10—When another person tells us of his or her suspicion that a child is being abused or neglected, we shall assist that person in taking appropriate action in order to protect the child.

P-1.11—When we become aware of a practice or situation that endangers the health, safety, or well-being of children, we have an ethical responsibility to protect children or inform parents and/or others who can.

Section II

Ethical responsibilities to families

Families* are of primary importance in children's development. Because the family and the early childhood practitioner have a common interest in the child's well-being, we acknowledge a primary responsibility to bring about communication, cooperation, and collaboration between the home and early childhood program in ways that enhance the child's development.

Ideals

I-2.1—To be familiar with the knowledge base related to working effectively with families and to stay informed through continuing education and training.

I-2.2—To develop relationships of mutual trust and create partnerships with the families we serve.

I-2.3—To welcome all family members and encourage them to participate in the program.

I-2.4—To listen to families, acknowledge and build upon their strengths and competencies, and learn from families as we support them in their task of nurturing children.

I-2.5—To respect the dignity and preferences of each family and to make an effort to learn about its structure, culture, language, customs, and beliefs.

I-2.6—To acknowledge families' childrearing values and their right to make decisions for their children.

I-2.7—To share information about each child's education and development with families and to help them understand and appreciate the current knowledge base of the early childhood profession.

I-2.8—To help family members enhance their understanding of their children and support the continuing development of their skills as parents.

*The term *family* may include those adults, besides parents, with the responsibility of being involved in educating, nurturing, and advocating for the child.

I-2.9—To participate in building support networks for families by providing them with opportunities to interact with program staff, other families, community resources, and professional services.

Principles

P-2.1—We shall not deny family members access to their child's classroom or program setting unless access is denied by court order or other legal restriction.

P-2.2—We shall inform families of program philosophy, policies, curriculum, assessment system, and personnel qualifications, and explain why we teach as we do—which should be in accordance with our ethical responsibilities to children (see Section I).

P-2.3—We shall inform families of and, when appropriate, involve them in policy decisions.

P-2.4—We shall involve the family in significant decisions affecting their child.

P-2.5—We shall make every effort to communicate effectively with all families in a language that they understand. We shall use community resources for translation and interpretation when we do not have sufficient resources in our own programs.

P-2.6—As families share information with us about their children and families, we shall consider this information to plan and implement the program.

P-2.7—We shall inform families about the nature and purpose of the program's child assessments and how data about their child will be used.

P-2.8—We shall treat child assessment information confidentially and share this information only when there is a legitimate need for it.

P-2.9—We shall inform the family of injuries and incidents involving their child, of risks such as exposures to communicable diseases that might result in infection, and of occurrences that might result in emotional stress.

P-2.10—Families shall be fully informed on any proposed research projects involving their children and shall have the opportunity to give or withhold consent without penalty. We shall not permit or participate in research that could in any way hinder the education, development, or well-being of children.

P-2.11—We shall not engage in or support exploitation of families. We shall not use our relationship with a family for private advantage or personal gain, or enter into relationships with family members that might impair our effectiveness working with their children.

P-2.12—We shall develop written policies for the protection of confidentiality and the disclosure of children's records. These policy documents shall be made available to all program personnel and families. Disclosure of children's records beyond family members, program personnel, and consultants having an obligation of confidentiality shall require familial consent (except in cases of abuse or neglect).

P-2.13—We shall maintain confidentiality and shall respect the family's right to privacy, refraining from disclosure of confidential information and intrusion into family life. However, when we have reason to believe that a child's welfare is at risk, it is permissible to share confidential information with agencies, as well as with individuals who have legal responsibility for intervening in the child's interest.

P-2.14—In cases where family members are in conflict with one another, we shall work openly, sharing our observations of the child, to help all parties involved make informed decisions. We shall refrain from becoming an advocate for one party.

P-2.15—We shall be familiar with and appropriately refer families to community resources and professional support services. After a referral has been made, we shall follow up to ensure that services have been appropriately provided.

Section III

Ethical responsibilities to colleagues

In a caring, cooperative workplace, human dignity is respected, professional satisfaction is promoted, and positive relationship are developed and sustained. Based upon our core values, our primary responsibility to colleagues is to establish and maintain settings and relationships that support productive work and meet professional needs. The same ideals that apply to children also apply as we interact with adults in the workplace.

A–Responsibilities to co-workers

Ideals

I-3A.1—To establish and maintain relationships of respect, trust, confidentiality, collaboration, and cooperation with co-workers.

I-3A.2—To share resources with co-workers, collaborating to ensure that the best possible early childhood care and education program is provided.

I-3A.3—To support co-workers in meeting their professional needs and in their professional development.

I-3A.4—To accord co-workers due recognition of professional achievement.

Principles

P-3A.1—We shall recognize the contributions of colleagues to our program and not participate in practices that diminish their reputations or impair their effectiveness in working with children and families.

P-3A.2—When we have concerns about the professional behavior of a co-worker, we shall first let that person know of our concern in a way that shows respect for personal dignity and for the diversity to be found among staff members, and then attempt to resolve the matter collegially and in a confidential manner.

P-3A.3—We shall exercise care in expressing views regarding the personal attributes or professional conduct of co-workers. Statements should be based on firsthand knowledge, not hearsay, and relevant to the interests of children and programs.

P-3A.4—We shall not participate in practices that discriminate against a co-worker because of sex, race national origin, religious beliefs, or other affiliations, age, marital status/family structure, disability, or sexual orientation.

B—Responsibilities to employers

Ideals

I-3B.1—To assist the program in providing the highest quality of service.

I-3B.2—To do nothing that diminishes the reputation of the program in which we work unless it is violating laws and regulations designed to protect children or is violating the provisions of this Code.

Principles

P-3B.1—We shall follow all program policies. When we do not agree with program policies, we shall attempt to effect change through constructive action within the organization.

P-3B.2—We shall speak or act on behalf of a organization only when authorized. We shall take care to acknowledge when we are speaking for the organization and when we are expressing a personal judgment.

P-3B.3—We shall not violate laws or regulations designed to protect children and shall take appropriate action consistent with this Code when aware of such violations.

P-3B.4—If we have concerns about a colleague's behavior, and children's well-being is not at risk, we may address the concern with that individual. If children are at risk or the situation does not improve after it has been brought to the colleague's attention, we shall report the colleague's unethical or incompetent behavior to an appropriate authority.

P-3B.5—When we have a concern about circumstances or conditions that impact the quality of care and education within the program, we shall inform the program's administration, or when necessary, other appropriate authorities.

C—Responsibilities to employees

Ideals

I-3C.1—To promote safe and healthy working conditions and policies that foster mutual respect, cooperation, collaboration, competence, well-being, confidentiality, and self-esteem in staff members.

I-3C.2—To create and maintain a climate of trust and candor that will enable staff to speak and act in the best interests of children, families, and the field of early childhood care and education.

I-3C.3—To strive to secure adequate and equitable compensation (salary and benefits) for those who work with or on behalf of young children.

I-3C.4—To encourage and support continual development of employees in becoming more skilled and knowledgeable practitioners.

Principles

P-3C.1—In decisions concerning children and programs, we shall draw upon the education, training, experience, and expertise of staff members.

P-3C.2—We shall provide staff members with safe and supportive working conditions that honor confidences and permit them to carry out their responsibilities through fair performance evaluation, written grievance procedures, constructive feedback, and opportunities for continuing professional development and advancement.

P-3C.3—We shall develop and maintain comprehensive written personnel policies that define program standards. These policies shall be given to new staff members and shall be available and easily accessible for review by all staff members.

P-3C.4—We shall inform employees whose performance does not meet program expectations of areas of concern and, when possible, assist in improving their performance.

P-3C.5—We shall conduct employee dismissals for just cause, in accordance with all applicable laws and regulations. We shall inform employees who are dismissed of the reasons for their termination. When a dismissal is for cause, justification must be based on evidence of inadequate or inappropriate behavior that is accurately documented, current, and available for the employee to review.

P-3C.6—In making evaluations and recommendations, we shall make judgments based on fact and relevant to the interests of children and programs.

P-3C.7—We shall make hiring, retention, termination, and promotion decisions based solely on a person's competence, record of accomplishment, ability to carry out the responsibilities of the position, and professional preparation specific to the developmental levels of children in his/her care.

P-3C.8—We shall not make hiring, retention, termination, and promotion decisions based on an individual's sex, race, national origin, religious beliefs or other affiliations, age, marital status/family structure, disability, or sexual orientation. We shall be familiar with and observe laws and regulations that pertain to employment discrimination. (Aspects of this principle do not apply to programs that have a lawful mandate to determine eligibility based on one or more of the criteria identified above.)

P-3C.9—We shall maintain confidentiality in dealing with issues related to an employee's job performance and shall respect an employee's right to privacy regarding personal issues.

Section IV

Ethical responsibilities to community and society

Early childhood programs operate within the context of their immediate community made up of families and other institutions concerned with children's welfare. Our responsibilities to the community are to provide programs that meet the diverse needs of families, to cooperate with agencies and professions that share responsibility for children, to assist families in gaining access to those agencies and allied professionals, and to assist in the development of community programs that are needed but not currently available.

As individuals, we acknowledge our responsibility to provide the best possible programs of care and education for children and to conduct ourselves with honesty and integrity. Because or our specialized expertise in early childhood development and education and because the larger society shares responsibility for the welfare and protection of young children, we acknowledge a collective obligation to advocate for the best interests of children within early childhood programs and in the larger community and to serve as a voice for young children everywhere.

The ideals and principles in this section are presented to distinguish between those that pertain to the work of an individual early childhood educator and those that more typically are engaged collectively on behalf of the best interests of children—with the understanding that individual early childhood educators have a shared responsibility for addressing the ideals and principles that are identified as "collective."

Ideal (Individual)

I-4.1—To provide the community with high-quality early childhood care and education programs and services.

Ideals (Collective)

I-4.2—To promote cooperation among professionals and agencies and interdisciplinary collaboration among professions concerned with addressing issues in the health, education, and well-being of young children, their families, and early childhood educators.

I-4.3—To work through education, research, and advocacy toward an environmentally safe world in which all children receive health care, food, and shelter; are nurtured; and live free from violence in their home and their communities.

I-4.4—To work through education, research, and advocacy toward a society in which all young children have access to high-quality early care and education programs.

I-4.5—To work to ensure that appropriate assessment systems, which include multiple sources of information, are used for purposes that benefit children.

I 4.6—To promote knowledge and understanding of young children and their needs. To work toward greater societal acknowledgment of children's rights and greater social acceptance of responsibility for the well-being of all children.

I-4.7—To support policies and laws that promote the well-being of children and families, and to work to change those that impair their well-being. To participate in developing policies and laws that are needed, and to cooperate with other individuals and groups in these efforts.

I-4.8—To further the professional development of the field of early childhood care and education and to strengthen its commitment to realizing its core values as reflected in this Code.

Principles (Individual)

P-4.1—We shall communicate openly and truthfully about the nature and extent of services that we provide.

P-4.2—We shall apply for, accept, and work in positions for which we are personally well-suited and professionally qualified. We shall not offer services that we do not have the competence, qualifications, or resources to provide.

P-4.3—We shall carefully check references and shall not hire or recommend for employment any person whose competence, qualifications, or character makes him or her unsuited for the position.

P-4.4—We shall be objective and accurate in reporting the knowledge upon which we base our program practices.

P-4.5—We shall be knowledgeable about the appropriate use of assessment strategies and instruments and interpret results accurately to families.

P-4.6—We shall be familiar with laws and regulations that serve to protect the children in our programs and be vigilant in ensuring that these laws and regulations are followed.

P-4.7—When we become aware of a practice or situation that endangers the health, safety, or well-being of children, we have an ethical responsibility to protect children or inform parents and/or others who can.

P-4.8—We shall not participate in practices that are in violation of law and regulations that protect the children in our programs.

P-4.9—When we have evidence that an early childhood program is violating laws or regulations protecting children, we shall report the violation to appropriate authorities who can be expected to remedy the situation.

P-4.10—When a program violates or requires its employees to violate this Code; it is permissible, after fair assessment of the evidence, to disclose the identity of the program.

Principles (Collective)

P-4.11—When policies are enacted for purposes that do not benefit children, we have a collective responsibility to work to change these practices.

P-4.12—When we have evidence that an agency that provides services intended to ensure children's well-being is failing to meet its obligations, we acknowledge a collective ethical responsibility to report the problem to appropriate authorities or to the public. We shall be vigilant in our follow-up until the situation is resolved.

P-4.13—When a child protection agency fails to provide adequate protection for abused or neglected children, we acknowledge a collective ethical responsibility to work toward the improvement of these services.

Glossary of Terms Related to Ethics

Code of Ethics. Defines the core values of the field and provides guidance for what professionals should do when they encounter conflicting obligations or responsibilities in their work.

Values. Qualities or principles that individuals believe to be desirable or worthwhile and that they prize for themselves, for others, and for the world in which they live.

Core Values. Commitments held by a profession that are consciously and knowingly embraced by its practitioners because they make a contribution to society. There is a difference between personal values and the core values of a profession.

Morality. People's views of what is good, right, and proper; their beliefs about their obligations; and their ideas about how they should behave.

Ethics. The study of right and wrong, or duty and obligation, that involves critical reflection on morality and the ability to make choices between values and the examination of the moral dimensions of relationships.

Professional Ethics. The moral commitments of a profession that involve moral reflection that extends and enhances the personal morality practitioners bring

to their work, that concern actions of right and wrong in the workplace, and that help individuals resolve moral dilemmas they encounter in their work.

Ethical Responsibilities. Behaviors that one must or must not engage in. Ethical responsibilities are clear cut and are spelled out in the Code of Ethical Conduct (for example, early childhood educators should never share confidential information about a child or family with a person who has no legitimate need for knowing).

Ethical Dilemma. A moral conflict that involves determining appropriate conduct when an individual faces conflicting professional values and responsibilities.

Sources for glossary terms and definitions

Feeney, S., & Freeman, N. 1999. *Ethics and the early childhood educator, Using the NAEYC code.* Washington, DC: NAEYC.

Kidder, R. M. 1995. *How good people make tough choices: Resolving the dilemmas of ethical living.* New York: Fireside.

Kipnis, K. 1987. How to discuss professional ethics. *Young children* 42 (4): 26–30.

Statement of Commitment*

As an individual who works with young children, I commit myself to furthering the values of early childhood education as they are reflected in the ideals and principles of the NAEYC Code of Ethical Conduct. To the best of my ability I will

- Never harm children.
- Ensure that programs for young children are based on current knowledge and research of child development and early childhood education.
- Respect and support families in their task of nurturing children.
- Respect colleagues in early childhood care and education and support them in maintaining the NAEYC Code of Ethical Conduct.
- Serve as an advocate for children, their families, and their teachers in community and society.
- Stay informed of and maintain high standards of professional conduct.
- Engage in an ongoing process of self-reflection, realizing that personal characteristics, biases, and beliefs have an impact on children and families.
- Be open to new ideas and be willing to learn from the suggestions of others.
- Continue to learn, grow, and contribute as a professional.
- Honor the ideals and principles of the NAEYC Code of Ethical Conduct.

*This Statement of Commitment is not part of the Code but is a personal acknowledgement of the individual's willingness to embrace the distinctive values and moral obligations of the field of early childhood care and education. It is recognition of the moral obligations that lead to an individual becoming part of the profession.

GLOSSARY

academic curriculum The objectives, procedures, and materials schools use to ensure children's acquisition of the knowledge and skills affirmed by the community.

academic learning The acquisition of knowledge and skills relating to subject-matter disciplines and organized fields of study.

academic rationalism Curriculum focused on education as the pursuit of knowledge in specified study fields and subject-matter disciplines to develop the rational mind.

acculturation Modification of an individual's cultural behavior patterns by another cultural group (usually the dominant group).

active listening skills Ability to perceive and process what another person communicates (both verbally and nonverbally).

adaptive behaviors Ability to change one's behavior as the situation requires.

adoptive family A family unit with at least one legally adopted child.

advocacy The process of publicly supporting a group, person, or cause.

after-school care Care provided for working parents' children (usually 5–10 years of age) during after-school hours.

age-appropriate curriculum A course of study based on helping children develop and learn according to their age level. (See age- and gender-appropriate behavior.)

alternative insemination A method of conception by inserting gathered sperm into a woman's uterus to fertilize an egg. Also known as artificial or donor insemination.

alternative schools Schools organized with curricula different from and usually in reaction to conventional public school curricula.

assessment Evaluation or determination of the extent of learning or change in behavior.

assisted living facilities Residences for older adults who need some help in daily routines but do not need nursing home care.

assistive technology Both high-tech and low-tech devices that children with disabilities may need to accomplish practical tasks.

associative level When parents and community members accept some responsibility for helping in a school program. (See **participatory level**.)

at-risk children (families) Children or families in danger of experiencing developmental gaps and other problems because of poverty, abuse, illness, or social disturbance.

authoritarian parenting style Baumrind's term for an autocratic, controlling, and somewhat detached method of raising children.

authoritative parenting style Baumrind's term for a receptive and somewhat democratic, although firm and in control, manner of raising children.

autonomy The ability of persons to regulate and determine their own behavior.

backup care Child care provided on an occasional basis when regular arrangements are not available (e.g., school is closed) or inappropriate (e.g., child is ill).

behavioral objectives Intentions of education stated in terms of observable actions.

behaviorism The belief that learning occurs because of a system of rewards, punishments, and reinforcements.

bidirectional process Process whereby the influence of genetics and environmental factors have equal importance for development.

bilingual education Teaching practices designed to encourage fluency in two languages.

bioecological theory Theory of development espoused by Bronfenbrenner that recognizes both biological (genetic) and ecological (environmental) factors as important aspects of explaining development.

biracial family Family in which the racial makeup of the parents is different. Some U.S families claim multiracial makeup because of past generations' biracial marriages.

blended family Two basic family units with children that join together to form a single family unit; often a remarriage, although some partners choose to forego wedlock.

blogs Abbreviation of Weblogs—an interactive Web site.

bullying Intimidating another.

center-based care (See **child-care center**.)

charter school An authorized school designed to improve educational opportunities and supported but not regulated by a local or state authority.

chat jockeys A monitoring and screening system of Internet exchanges.

chat rooms Internet sites where people can exchange communications on a particular topic.

child care Programs provided for children whose parents work outside the home.

child-care center A facility providing care and educational programs for children from infancy to five years old.

child-care providers Adults who care for a group of children in family child care or a child-care center.

child-centered curriculum Teaching practices and materials focusing on children's interests, needs, and desires. Teachers respond to these interests by providing materials and guidance.

child find Process of locating children who are in need of special services. The term derives from a federally funded program called Child Find Project.

code switching The ability to move easily from one language or dialect to another.

cognitive process A series of actions producing changes in learners' methods of thinking, organization of perceptions, and problem solving.

collaboration Two or more persons or groups working together on joint endeavors for mutually determined objectives.

conflict resolution Using peaceful discussions and interactions to reach agreement on differences in attitudes, feelings, and beliefs that have caused disharmony.

constructive play Stage of play whereby children begin to build and create things.

constructivist curriculum Curriculum based on the premise that the goal of education is for children to learn how to learn; when the individual is active in the learning process and is internally responding to outer stimuli.

cooperative learning Group work and projects in which all members of the group share responsibility and rewards for the group's effort.

covert curriculum The curriculum parents and teachers are unaware of. (See **hidden curriculum**.)

creationism A belief that the earth and all life was developed according to God's plan as described in Genesis.

criterion-referenced test Test designed to examine how well students have mastered a set of materials based on specified instructional goals and predetermined criteria.

critical periods of development Erikson's label for periods of human development when positive aspects of behavior need to be satisfied if development is to proceed in a positive manner.

cross-cultural Involving features and objectives of more than one cultural group.

cultural deprivation Formerly used to describe the problems of certain families and groups. The notion that individuals lacked certain skills for productive school learning as a result of gaps in cultural background.

cultural literacy The body of knowledge of major historical and literary events that all literate persons should know to be considered "educated" in their culture by society.

cultural pluralism The concept that all cultures have value and contribute to society.

custodial parent The parent to whom a court assigns the primary responsibility of a child's care and upbringing.

decision-making level Parents, community members, and educators sharing equally in making decisions regarding school policy.

departmentalized program School practices in which students are taught different academic subjects by specialists in these academic fields.

dialoguing with students Passing on information and concepts through informal and unstructured conversations with students.

drop-in child care A place where parents may find child-care services for brief periods of time and with flexible schedules.

dual-income family A family where both parents or resident adults earn an income.

dysfunctional family situation Abnormal, impaired, or incomplete functioning of the family unit.

Early Head Start A component of the federal Head Start program that focuses on children younger than three and assists parents in improving their nurturing skills.

early-intervention service Service provided in natural environments to infants and toddlers at risk for developmental delays.

egg-box construction A popular school design of the 1950s and 1960s. The building resembled an egg box, with a central corridor and classrooms on either side.

elaborated language code Syntactically complex speech that requires the persons with whom one communicates to use judgment, imagination, and reason to interpret ambiguities and abstractions.

embedded partners Parents, teachers, and community persons who are an integral part of the education process for children in the community.

employer-sponsored child care Child care provided for children of employees, generally at or nearby their workplace.

enculturation The process by which one learns the mores and habits of a particular cultural group.

English Language Learner (ELL) (See Structured English Immersion [SEI].)

ethnic orientation Relating to the complex set of characteristics and values, including national origin and linguistic, physical, and religious traits, by which a social group identifies itself.

ethnocentrism The process by which one concentrates and specializes in the values of one's own cultural milieu.

Even Start Federally funded home-based family literacy program requiring established links to the Head Start program.

evolution A belief based on Darwinian theory that the earth and living organisms developed by a gradual process of mutation and adaptation so that living creatures evolve to more complex forms.

exploratory play A type of play where children begin to expand their horizons and experiment.

extended family The kin of the basic family unit who are economically dependent on or emotionally attached to the household.

faith-based Institutions and organizations affiliated and normally supported by religious groups.

family child care Care provided to children in a home setting but outside the child's own home.

family literacy program Approach to helping children learn to read and write by assisting parents in improving their skills so that they can help their children and improve their own prospects.

504 Plan A legal document under provisions of the 1973 Rehabilitation Act providing a program of services for students identified with special needs but placed in a regular education setting.

family Two or more persons living together and linked for emotional and economic support.

fixed curriculum The curriculum, often perceived to be mandated by local, state, and national education boards, that has been determined for a particular grade level.

formal community structure The organizations and agencies within a community that support services for that community.

formal curriculum The curriculum authorized by state and local education boards that is public, usually printed, and indicates the objectives, procedures, and materials for student learning.

foster children Children in the legal custody of a state office placed in an arranged living situation for a period of time.

foster family A family unit wherein adults offer support to children who are not related by blood or adoption.

free appropriate education (FAPE) A legal term used to indicate that a community must provide appropriate education, without cost to the family, for a three- to five-year-old diagnosed with a disability.

full inclusion Term used to indicate that children with disabilities are to be educated in a regular classroom full time but also are to receive from the trained specialist special services required as a result of their disability.

gay and lesbian Persons with a sexual preference for a person of their own sex. *Gay* is a generic term; *lesbian* refers specifically to women.

gender-appropriate behavior Qualities and behaviors a community or culture considers appropriate for female and male roles and actions.

general equivalency diploma (GED) Certification equal to a high-school diploma but not granted by an accredited high school.

global market place An economy based on events and interactions that happen around the world.

group norm   Way in which most people in a group respond.

harassment   Incessant badgering or troubling of another person.

Head Start   Comprehensive federally funded program for poor preschool children and their families. It is designed to provide health, nutritional, social, and educational experiences to compensate for the negative effects of poverty.

hidden curriculum   Instructive events in a child's life that influence learning and attitude, often seen as hindering the stated goals of the school.

holistic evaluation   Assessment based on examination of a child's total accomplishments, then synthesizing the judgments.

home care   Care of children by someone other than the parents but provided in the child's home setting.

home curriculum   Learning that children acquire while under the influence of family members.

homeschooling   The education of children undertaken completely by parents and done in the home environment.

homeless family   A family that regularly has no permanent place of residence and thus constantly moves from one place to another.

homophobia   Fear and rejection of same-sex partners and their lifestyles.

hyperactivity   Behavior characterized by excessive or abnormal body movements and high expenditure of energy.

ideologues   Advocates of ideas reflecting the social needs and beliefs of a particular group.

incidental learning   Learning as result of an event but happening without any adult planning .

inclusion   Instruction for each child provided, preferably in a regular classroom, with support services from personnel most appropriate at that moment in the child's schedule.

individualized education program (IEP)   A program, mandated by law, developed by those responsible for the education of a child with special needs.

individualized family service plan (IFSP)   A written plan, mandated by law, that provides appropriate services for at-risk infants and toddlers and their families.

individualized teaching   Teaching that requires the teacher to adjust materials and concepts to be learned and the type of instruction for each individual in the class.

Individuals with Disabilities Education Act (IDEA)   Reauthorization and amendment of the 1975 Education for All Handicapped Students Act, which governs how students with disabilities are to be educated in today's schools.

industrial model   A model for educational practice based on the manner in which industry operates.

infant–toddler program   Program that offers a combination of play activities for infants and toddlers and parent education for the adults.

informal community structure   The personal relationships that families establish with members outside the home or extended family.

informal curriculum   The events, stimuli, and activities that children undertake outside classrooms and from which learning occurs.

in-home care   (See **home care**.)

intact family   A married couple living with their biological, adopted, or foster children

intelligent design   A belief that the earth and living organisms developed according to a plan by a Superior Being.

interactionist–constructivist theory   Theory of learning (development) that maintains that through interacting with their environment, children begin to acquire a body of knowledge and understanding.

interactive portfolio   A student's work and materials collected in a folder or portfolio, shared with and commented on by parents and teachers.

interactive skills   Ability to exchange thoughts, ideas, and actions both verbally and nonverbally.

interethnic family   A family unit that has more than one ethnic group represented in the unit. Blood parents may be of different groups, but children of different groups may be adopted by parents of a single group.

internal control   Self-determination guided by one's own behavior and actions. (See **locus of control**.)

interracial   A relationship where racial groups are combined; for example, interracial marriages.

involuntary refugees   Persons who have been forced to leave their homes and seek safety and sanctuary elsewhere.

itinerant family   A family unit that moves regularly, often following crop harvests, or is engaged in other temporary work.

kinship adoption   Child adopted into a family related by blood or marriage.

kinship care   Care of children provided by close relatives.

least restrictive environment (LRE)   Environment that suits the particular learning needs of children without constraining them.

literacy development   The process of acquiring meaning from signs and symbols and of transferring meaning to signs and symbols.

literacy event   Activity related to reading and writing that supports literacy development.

local educational authority (LEA)   The agency with the obligation and right to oversee the education of children in its jurisdiction.

locus of control   The perception one has of where responsibility for one's actions lies. May be internal or external.

lower working-class   That part of the population, usually consisting of unskilled laborers, which is less secure financially, at risk of unemployment, and at times receiving government assistance with basic living needs.

mainstreaming   Integration of special-needs children into the regular classroom. (See **inclusion**.)

marginalized family (children)   Persons responsible for the welfare of families and children who are unable or unwilling to provide for basic needs and nurturance. Also those not having needs met.

marginalized learner   Child denied educational benefits because of environmental difficulties or problems in school, home, or community.

matriarchal   A form of family organization in which the mother or eldest female is recognized as head of the family.

mentor   Person serving as guide or teacher to others on a one-to-one basis.

mesosystem   Bronfenbrenner's label for the area of secondary importance in a child's life space—usually home and neighborhood.

metacognitive   The process used in understanding how one gains knowledge.

microsystem   Bronfenbrenner's label for the area of primary importance in a child's life space, such as the nuclear and extended family.

middle class   That part of the population whose income falls within the median range for the whole. Professionals and businesspersons are often in this class.

migrant worker   (See **itinerant family**.)

minimum level   The minimal participation of parents and community members in school programs, for example, contributing cakes to a bake sale.

monocultural   Reflecting the beliefs, behavior patterns, and characteristics of a single cultural group.

mores   Those rituals, traditions, customs, and behavior patterns seen as essential for a social group's survival and well-being.

mosaic   A design made by laying small bits of colored stone, paper, or other material side by side. In educational terms, it means a variety of racial, cultural, and ethnic people that make up a society.

mother's-day-out programs   Programs that offer children a few hours of supervised care so that their mothers may take time for themselves.

multicultural   Association with and appreciation of the practices of different cultures, religions, and ethnic groups.

multicultural education   Curriculum based on the inclusion and appreciation of the practices of different cultures, religions, and ethnic groups.

NAEYC   Acronym for **National Association for the Education of Young Children**.

NAFCC   Acronym for **National Association of Family Child Care**.

nanny care   Care provided by a specially trained person to care for children in their homes. Au pair care is similar but refers to foreign students who care for young children in exchange for room and board.

National Council for the Accreditation of Teacher Education (NCATE)   National organization that sets standards for and evaluates teacher education programs.

nature–nurture controversy   The polarization of two opposing views of child growth and development—an innate plan of development vs. development as a result of stimuli from the environment.

networking   A system of making connections with individuals and groups that allows communication and involvement as a unit.

No Child Left Behind (NCLB) Act   Congressional legislation adopted in 2001 to stimulate school performance.

norm-referenced testing   Assessment whereby evaluation is based on comparison to a predetermined control group, often peers of the individual being tested.

nuclear family   A family unit consisting of two parents and their biological and/or adopted children.

nursery school   A program, usually private, designed for two- to five-year-olds. Often a half-day program, but may have a full-day schedule.

nurturance   (See **nurturing practice.**)

nurturing practice   The process of raising and promoting the development of children.

obese   Clinical definition—extremely overweight.

open-space buildings   School buildings with large open spaces, or "pods," in which several teachers organize the space to fit the needs of their particular students.

out-of-home care   Regular care provided to young children outside the home setting.

overweight   Having more body weight than is normal or healthy.

paradigm   A pattern, example, or model.

parent center   A specific location, usually within a school, where parents can work, socialize, and feel they are a part of the school.

parent cooperative   Private nursery school or preschool program where parents share both the teaching and administrative decision making.

parent cooperative nursery school   (See **parent cooperative.**)

parent education   Courses, workshops, and reading materials designed to assist parents in improving their nurturing skills.

parent empowerment   A process whereby parents become decision makers, often in collaboration with school personnel, for the education of their children.

participatory level   The second level of involvement for parents in school partnerships whereby they cooperate and work as volunteers and helpers. (See **associative level.**)

partnerships   Relationship among different groups in which each group has equal influence on decision making.

patriarchal   A form of family organization in which the father or eldest male is recognized as head of the family.

peer group   People of similar race, ethnicity, age, social status, or other trait.

perceptual field   The human range of recognition and organization of sensory input.

permissive parenting style   Baumrind's term for a manner of raising children that is nondemanding and noncontrolling and that allows children to develop according to their natural instincts.

personal relevance curriculum   Curriculum based on the belief that the goal of education is to support personally satisfying experiences for each student.

person-oriented family   A family unit focused on the development of individual children.

phonics   The letter–sound relationships of a language.

play-oriented curriculum   Curriculum for children that emphasizes the belief that children learn as they play with materials and other children.

position-oriented family   Manner of family functioning that is present- and object-oriented and that assigns roles according to position in the family.

postmodern family   Family of today that views parenting as a shared responsibility of father, mother, and care provider.

postnuclear family units   Family units that vary from the traditional mother–father–child units.

power brokers   Members of a community or group with enough influence and power to become major decision makers for that community or group.

predetermined curriculum   A course of study, established by a person or a group, that determines what students should learn and how they should proceed in the learning process.

Project Follow Through   U.S.-government-sponsored program that supports students after Head Start programs through kindergarten and the primary grades. (See **Head Start.**)

project-oriented curriculum   A curriculum of study that uses themes or projects as a means of presenting content and concepts.

resilient child (family)   Child or family demonstrating the ability to cope and manage in spite of debilitating environmental circumstances.

resource file   A professional's organized collection of plans, materials, and equipment to supplement units, projects, and daily activities.

resources and referral programs   Community agencies that support the development and improvement of child care and assist parents in finding appropriate and affordable care for their children.

restricted language code A manner of speaking that is syntactically simple and direct and that has concrete meanings.

role expectation Behavioral expectation for an individual that depends on status or function within the family, peer group, school, or community.

Scholastic Aptitude Test (SAT) Norm-referenced exam for high-school students. Often used by colleges and scholarship boards to determine the ability for advanced study.

school-identified disability Learning difficulty or problem identified after a child enters school.

scope and sequence chart List of important skills for children's achievement, arranged on two dimensions: (1) the broad extent of the skill and (2) the order in which a skill or set of related skills is learned.

secular education Education in which there is no religious or spiritual training.

self-fulfilling prophecy The concept that expectations of others shape and reinforce one's behavior such that the expectations are eventually met. Also known as the Pygmalion effect.

servant–leader interns College-age students who pledge to serve and help in Freedom Schools (sponsored by Children's Defense Fund) and learn the techniques of working and advocating for children.

service agency Organization within a community that provides the health, education, transportation, protection, or communication services necessary to the community's citizens.

SES Acronym for **socioeconomic status**.

sexism Prejudice based on gender.

sexual energy Freudian concept that human behavior and energy is derived from the primal sex drive.

signage Public information signs.

significant other (adult) The person in a child's life who is particularly important to the child. This relationship exists independently of any biological or formal social relationship between child and adult.

single-parent family A family unit consisting of one parent, either mother or father, and children, and no other adults.

site-based management A procedure for managing schools in which organizational and educational decisions for children at a particular school should be made by persons at that school.

skills ladder A careful ordering of the skills needed for a particular task.

social agencies Broad grouping of community offices and institutions that administer human services, governmental benefits, or counseling. (See **service agencies**.)

social capital The amount of human connections and relationships that results in learning.

social climate The attitudes, feelings, and relationships that people within a community maintain toward one another.

social network Parallel relationships developed among individuals in a community that foster communication and a sense of belonging.

social reconstructionist curriculum Curriculum based on the thesis that the goals of education are to effect social change. Students learn social needs and values and how to use these concepts in critical thought processes.

social setting A place, such as a home, a school, or a community, where interactive events between or among individuals happen naturally.

socioeconomic factors The social relationships and financial developments that exist in a family or community.

socioeconomic status (SES) The economic and social level to which one belongs because of wealth, occupation, and educational background.

special-interest group Group with a narrow purpose or agenda organized to influence others to accept their point of view.

sponsored independence parenting style Clark's term, similar to Baumrind's **authoritative style**, describing a manner of raising children. Indicates a rational, receptive, and warm but demanding style.

stages of development Distinct steps in the growth process that individuals pass through from infancy through adulthood.

stakeholder Person who stands to gain or profit from selected activities and programs in a school or community.

standardized test Test with scientifically chosen items, given under similar conditions, that enables persons to be compared to a group standard. Tests may be either criterion referenced or norm referenced.

Structured English Immersion (SEI) Program where bilingual children are taught all subjects in English, receiving special English-language assistance as needed and using their own language only to clarify concepts.

subfamily A family cluster living with other adults or families in which the parent in the cluster is not the central figure in the household.

subsidized child care Care supported by government funding for families with financial need.

technological intelligence Those parts of human intelligence related to literacy and numeracy skills.

technologist curriculum A curriculum based on the notion that the primary goal of education is for students to master the basic skills of reading and computing in order to function in society.

theme-focused program A phase of curriculum, based on a particular theme, wherein important objectives are identified and activities are prepared so students acquire knowledge and skills relating to that theme.

time on task The actual amount of time a student is engaged in or attending to a particular assigned task.

Title I school School where students meet the poverty guidelines developed under Title I legislation.

traditional curriculum Curriculum based on the notion that the objective of education is for students to acquire knowledge in subject-matter disciplines and specified fields of study. Similar to **academic curriculum**.

transactional process of development The process whereby multiple facets of the environment (people, objects, symbols) unleash the child's genetic potential to produce varied behaviors. Children's reactions and behaviors in turn affect new actions or movements from the environment.

transcultural Extending across cultures or involving more than one culture.

transmitter of knowledge A person who has information (understandings, insights) and passes this information directly on to another.

transracial Encompassing the physical features or interests of two or more races.

underclass The part of the population limited in opportunity and resources and locked into a cycle of poverty and despair.

undocumented immigrants Persons who enter another country illegally to set up residency but lack any legal certification of their status.

unit of study Part of a curriculum based on a particular theme, around which learning activities are organized. Similar to **theme-focused program**.

universal pre-K Public education for children ages 3–5.

unstructured learning events Incidental and self-selected experiences in which children become interested and involved, and learning results.

upper class The most economically advantaged group of a population; often wealth is inherited.

upper working-class The population group represented by skilled laborers who are financially able to cope but severely affected by economic depressions.

voucher plan Plan whereby parents receive certificates indicating the financial support for their children's education. Parents have the right to select a school and use the certificate to pay the cost of education.

War on Poverty President Lyndon B. Johnson's War on Poverty became the byword for legislation aimed at helping disadvantaged populations overcome the effects of poverty.

Weblogs Internet programs on particular topics set up by individuals whereby others can contribute

welfare reform measures (See **welfare-to-work program**.)

welfare-to-work program Welfare Reform Act of 1996, requiring welfare parents to seek education and employment or lose benefits.

well baby clinic Health clinic or hospital program where parents can, without cost, bring their children for regular checkups and discussions regarding ways to provide a healthy environment.

whole-language program Curriculum practice emphasizing the totality of language, presuming that children should learn to read the same way they learn to speak, that is, holistically with respect to their environment. Reading, writing, speaking, and listening are all aspects of language learned in conjunction with all experiences.

Women, Infants, and Children (WIC) A government program that provides health checks, counseling, and food stamps for families below the poverty level.

writing to read A strategy for teaching reading in combination with writing.

zone of proximal development Vygotsky's label for the distance between a child's ability to perform a task independently and his or her ability to perform it under guidance.

REFERENCES

Adams, D. B. (2001). The quest for quality child care. In J. C. Westman (Ed.), *Parenthood in America: Undervalued, underpaid, under siege* (pp. 150–157). Madison: University of Wisconsin Press.

Adelman, H. S., & Taylor, L. (2002). Building comprehensive multifaceted and integrated approaches to address barriers to student learning. *Childhood Education, 78*(5), 261–273.

Administration for Children and Families. 2000. *Head Start Bulletin, Issue #69.* Washington D.C.: U.S. Department of Health and Human Services. Also available from Web site: http://www.headstartinfo.org.

Afterschool Alliance. (2002). *Afterschool alliance poll.* Retrieved August 10, 2003, from http://www.afterschoolalliance.org

Aldridge, J., & Kirkland, L. (2006). Issues related to children's literature and genre selection. *Focus on Elementary, 19*(1), 1–5.

Alexander. A. (2001). The meaning of television in the American family. In J. Bryant & J. A. Bryant (Eds.), *Television and the American family* (2nd ed., pp. 273–287). Mahwah, NJ: Lawrence Erlbaum.

Alexander, B. (2003). *The state of the nation's housing: 2003.* Cambridge, MA: Joint Center for Housing Studies for Harvard University.

Allen, K. R., Fine, M. A., & Demo, D. H. (2000). An overview of family diversity: Controversies, questions and values. In D. Demo, K. Allen, & M. Fine (Eds.), *Handbook of family diversity* (pp. 1–14). New York: Oxford University Press.

Almeida, D. M., & McDonald, D. A. (2005). The national story: How Americans spend their time on work, family, and community. In J. Heymann & C. Beem (Eds.), *Unfinished work: Building equality and democracy in an era of working families* (pp. 180–206). New York: The New Press.

American Academy of Pediatrics, Task Force on Children and Television. (1990). *Children, adolescents and television.* Elk Grove Village, IL: Author.

American Anthropological Association. (2002). *AAA statement on race.* Retrieved August 30, 2003, from http://www.aaanet.org/stmts/racepp.htm

American Family Traditions. (2006). Statistics for 2005. Retrieved February 8, 2006 from http://www.americanfamilytraditions.com

American Library Association. (2005). Censorship Basics. Retrieved January 23, 2006, from www.ala.org/ala/oif/basics/censorshipbasics/

Ames, B. D., & Farrell, P. (2005). An ecological approach: A community-school strategy for health promotion. *Journal of Family and Consumer Sciences, 97*(2), 29–34.

Anderson, C. (2003). The diversity, strength, and challenges of single-parent households. In F. Walsh (Ed.), *Normal family processes: Growing diversity and complexity* (3rd ed., pp. 121–152). New York: Guilford Press.

Anderson, K. J., & Cavallaro, K. (2002). Parents or pop culture? Children's heroes and role models. *Childhood Education, 78*(3), 161–168.

Andreasen, M. (2001). Evolution in the family's use of television: An overview. In J. Bryant & J. A. Bryant (Eds.), *Television and the American family* (2nd ed., pp. 3–30). Mahwah, NJ: Lawrence Erlbaum.

Annie E. Casey Foundation. (2005). *Kids Count data book: State profiles of child well-being.* Baltimore: Author. Also retrieved June 2006 from http://www.Kidscount.org

Anstine-Templeton, R., & Johnston, M. A. (2004). Helping children with learning disabilities succeed. In D. B. Hiatt-Michael (Ed.), *Promising practices connecting schools to families of children with special needs* (pp. 57–78). Greenwich, CT: Information Age Publishing.

Apple, M. W. (1995). *Education and power* (2nd ed.). New York: Routledge.

Arce, E. (1999). Family-centered communities benefit young children: What policies enhance the developing child? In E. Arce (Ed.), *Perspectives: Early childhood education* (pp. 136–137). Boulder, CO: Coursewise.

Arendell, T. (1997). A social constructionist approach to parenting. In T. Arendell (Ed.), *Contemporary parenting: Challenges and issues. Vol. 9. Understanding families* (pp. 1–45). Thousand Oaks, CA: Sage.

Aronson, S. (2002). *Healthy young children: A manual for programs.* Washington, DC: National Association for the Education of Young Children.

Bailyn, B., Dalleck, R., Davis, D., Donald, D., Thomas, J., & Wood, G. S. (2000). *The great republic: A history of the American people* (6th ed.). Lexington, MA: Heath.

Ball, R.A.H. (2006). Supporting and involving families in meaningful ways. *Young Children, 61*(1), 10–11.

Banks, J. A. (1996). *Multicultural education, transformative knowledge, and action: Historical and contemporary perspectives.* New York: Teachers College Press.

Banks, J. A. (2002). *Teaching strategies for ethnic studies* (7th ed.). Boston: Allyn & Bacon.

Banks, J. A., & McGee-Banks, C. A. (Eds.). (2005). *Multicultural education: Issues and perspectives* (5th ed.). Hoboken, NJ: John Wiley.

Barbour, C., Barbour, N., & Hildebrand, J. (2001, April). *Building a grandparent curriculum.* Paper presented at the conference of the Association for Childhood Education International, Toronto, Ontario, Canada.

Barbour, N. (1989). A naturalistic study of young children's problem solving skills. Paper presented at Association for Childhood Education International Research Forum, Indianapolis, IN, April 5, 1989.

Bardige, B. (2005). *At a loss for words: How America is failing our children and what we can do about it.* Philadelphia: Temple University Press.

Barfield, R. (2002). *Real-life homeschooling.* New York: Fireside.

Bartholomae, S., & Fox, J. (2005). Economic stress and families. In P. C. McKenry & S. J. Price (Eds.), *Families and change: Coping with stressful events and transitions* (pp. 205–225). Thousand Oaks, CA: Sage.

Bartolome, L. I., & Macedo, D. P. (1997). Dancing with bigotry: The poisoning of racial and ethnic identities. *Harvard Educational Review, 67*(2), 222–246.

Baumrind, D. (1966). Effects of authoritative parental control on child behavior. *Child Development, 37,* 387–407.

Baumrind, D. (1968). Authoritarian vs. authoritative parental control. *Adolescence, 3,* 255–272.

Baumrind, D. (1995). *Child maltreatment and optimal caregiving in social contexts.* New York: Garland.

Beaty, J. J. (2006). *Observing development of the young child* (6th ed.). Upper Saddle River, NJ: Merrill/Prentice Hall.

Benson, P. (1997). *All kids are our kids.* San Francisco: Jossey-Bass.

Bergen, D., Reid, R., & Torelli, L. (2001). *Educating and caring for very young children: The infant/toddler curriculum.* New York: Teachers College Press.

Berger, B. (2002). *The family in the modern age: More than a lifestyle choice.* New Brunswick, NJ: Transactions Publishers.

Berger, E. H. (2004). *Parents as partners in education: Families and schools working together* (6th ed.). Upper Saddle River, NJ: Merrill/Prentice Hall.

Berk, L. E. (2005). Why parenting matters. In S. Olfman (Ed.), *Childhood lost: How American culture is failing our kids* (pp. 19–54). Westport, CT: Praeger.

Berlin, I. (1998). *Many thousands gone: The first two centuries of slavery in North America.* Cambridge, MA: Belknap/Harvard University Press.

Berns, R. M. (2006). *Child, family, school, community: Socialization and support* (6th ed.). Belmont, CA: Wadsworth Publishing.

Bernstein, B. (1972). A sociolinguistic approach to socialization with some reference to educability. In J. Gumperz & D. Hymes (Eds.), *Directions in sociolinguistics* (pp. 465–497). New York: Holt, Rinehart & Winston.

Bettelheim, B. (1976). *The uses of enchantment.* New York: Knopf.

Bianchi, S. M., & Casper, L. M. (2000). American families. *Population Bulletin, 55*(4), 3–43.

Bianchi, S. M., & Spain, D. (1996). Women, work and family in America. *Population Bulletin, 47*(2), 2–47.

Bigner, J. J. (2002). *Parent–child relations: An introduction to parenting* (6th ed.). Upper Saddle River, NJ: Merrill/Prentice Hall.

Bigner, J. J. (2006). *Parent–child relations: An introduction to parenting* (7th ed.). Upper Saddle River, NJ: Merrill/Prentice Hall.

Black, J. K., & Puckett, M. B. (2005). *The young child: Development from prebirth through age eight* (4th ed.). Upper Saddle River, NJ: Merrill/Prentice Hall.

Blank, H. (1997). Child care in the context of welfare reform. In S. B. Kamerman & A. J. Kahn (Eds.),

Child care in the context of welfare "reform" (pp. 1–44). New York: Columbia University School of Social Work, Cross-National Studies Research Program.

Bloom, J. (1992). *Parenting our schools: A hands-on guide to education reform.* Boston: Little, Brown.

Bogenschneider, K., & Corbett, T. (2004). Building enduring family policies in the 21st century: The past as prologue? In M. Coleman & L. H. Ganong (Eds.), *Handbook of contemporary families: Considering the past, contemplating the future* (pp. 451–468). Thousand Oaks, CA: Sage.

Bookman, A. (2004), *Starting in our own backyards: How working families can build community and survive the new economy.* New York: Routledge.

Borkowski, J. G., Ramey, S. L., & Stile, C. (2002). Parenting research: Translations to parenting practices. In J. G. Borkowski, S. L. Ramey, & M. Bristol-Power (Eds.), *Parenting and the child's world* (pp. 365–386). Mahwah, NJ: Erlbaum.

Bornstein, M. H. (2001). Refocusing on parenthood. In J. C. Westman (Ed.), *Parenthood in America: Undervalued, underpaid, under siege* (pp. 5–20). Madison: University of Wisconsin Press.

Bornstein, M. H. (2002). Parenting infants. In M. H. Bornstein (Ed.), *Handbook of parenting: Vol. 1. Children and parenting* (2nd ed., pp. 3–43). Mahwah, NJ: Lawrence Erlbaum.

Bossard, J., & Boll, E. (1949). Ritual in family living. *American Sociological Review, 14,* 526–530.

Boyd-Franklin, N. (2003). Race, class, and poverty. In F. Walsh (Ed.), *Normal family processes: Growing diversity and complexity* (3rd ed., pp. 260–279). New York: Guilford.

Bradley, R. H. (2002). Environments and parenting. In M. H. Bornstein (Ed.), *Handbook of parenting: Vol. 2. Biology and ecology of parenting* (2nd ed., pp. 281–314). Mahwah, NJ: Lawrence Erlbaum.

Brazelton, T. B., & Greenspan, S. I. (2000). *The irreducible needs of children: What every child must have to grow, learn, and flourish.* Cambridge, MA: Perseus.

Bredekamp, S., & Rosegrant, T. (1995). *Reaching potential: Appropriate curriculum and assessment for young children* (Vol. 2). Washington, DC: National Association for the Education of Young Children.

Bronfenbrenner, U. (1979). *The ecology of human development: Experiment by nature and design.* Cambridge, MA: Harvard University Press.

Bronfenbrenner, U. (1986). Ecology of the family as a context of human development: Research perspectives. *Developmental Psychology, 22,* 723–742.

Bronfenbrenner, U. (1993). The ecology of cognitive development: Research models and fugitive findings. In R. H. Wozniak & K. W. Fisher (Eds.), *Development in context: Activity and thinking in specific environments* (pp. 3–24). Hillsdale, NJ: Lawrence Erlbaum.

Bronfenbrenner, U. (1995). Developmental ecology through space and time: A future perspective. In P. Moen, G. H. Elder, & K. Luscher (Eds.), *Examining lives in context* (pp. 619–648). Washington, DC: American Psychological Association.

Bronfenbrenner, U. (2001). Growing chaos in the lives of children, youth and families: How can we turn it around? In J. Westman (Ed.), *Parenthood in America: Undervalued, underpaid, under siege* (pp. 197–210). Madison: University of Wisconsin Press.

Bronfenbrenner, U. (2005). The social ecology of human development. In U. Bronfenbrenner (Ed.), *Making human beings human: Bioecological perspectives on human development* (pp. 27–40). Thousand Oaks, CA: Sage.

Bronfenbrenner, U., & Crouter, A. (1982). Work and family through time and space. In S. B. Kammerman & C. D. Hayes (Eds.), *Families that work: Children in a changing world* (pp. 39–83). Washington, DC: National Academy Press.

Bronfenbrenner, U., Moen, P., & Garbarino, J. (1984). Child, family, and community. In R. D. Parke (Ed.), *Review of child development research: Vol. 7. The family* (pp. 283–328). Chicago: University of Chicago Press.

Bronfenbrenner, U., & Weiss, H. (1983). *Beyond policies without people: An ecological perspective on child and family policy.* New York: Cambridge University Press.

Brouillette, L. (2002). *Charter schools: Lessons in school reform.* Mahwah, NJ: Lawrence Erlbaum.

Bruer, J. T. (1999). *The myth of the first three years: A new understanding of early brain development and life-long learning.* New York: Free Press.

Bruer, J. T. (2002, October). *A rational approach to education: Integrating behavioral, cognitive, and brain science.* Address at Oxford University, Oxford, England.

Buchwald, A. (1994). *Leaving home: A memoir.* New York: Putnam.

Byrnes, J. P. (2001). *Minds, brains and learning: Understanding the psychological and educational relevance of neuro scientific research.* New York: Guilford.

Bulkley, K. E., & Wohlstetter, P. (2004). *Taking account of charter schools: What's happened and what's next?* New York: Teachers College Press.

Bullock, H. A. (1967). *A history of Negro education in the South from 1619 to the present.* Cambridge, MA: Harvard University Press.

Burchinal, M. R., Roberts, J. E., Riggins, R., Jr., Zeisel, S. A., Neebe, E., & Bryant, D. (2000). Relating quality of center-based child care to early cognitive and language development longitudinally. *Child Development, 71,* 339–357.

Burnette, S. (1998). Book 'Em! Cops and librarians working together. *American Libraries, 29*(2), 48–50.

Burtless, G., & Smeeding, T. M. (2001). The level, trend and composition of poverty. In S. H. Danziger & R. H. Haverman (Eds.), *Understanding poverty* (pp. 27–68). New York: Russell Sage Foundation.

Butler, J. (2004). *Undoing gender.* New York: Routledge.

Butler, R. D. (1976). Black children's racial preference: A selected review of literature. *Journal of Afro-American Issues, 4*(2), 168–171.

Cadwell, L. (2003). *Bringing learning to life: The Reggio approach to early childhood education.* New York: Teachers College Press.

Cadwell, L. B. (1997). *Bringing Reggio Emilia home: An innovative approach to early childhood education.* New York: Teachers College Press.

Calfee, C., Wittwer, F., & Meredith, M. (1998). *Building full-service schools.* San Francisco: Jossey-Bass.

Campbell, F. A., & Ramey, C. T. (1995). Cognitive and school outcomes for high-risk African American students in middle adolescence: Positive effects of early intervention. *American Educational Research Journal, 32,* 743–772.

Carnegie Corporation. (1994). *Starting points. Meeting the needs of our youngest.* New York: Author. Also retrieved August 10, 2003, from http://www.carnegie.org/starting_points/startpt1.html

Carnegie Forum on Education and the Economy. (1986). *A nation prepared: Teachers for the 21st century.* New York: Carnegie Corporation.

Carper, J. C. (2000). Pluralism to establishment to dissent: The religious and educational context of home schooling. *Peabody Journal of Education, 75*(1), 8–19.

Casper, L. M., & Bianchi, S. M. (2002). *Continuity and change in the American family.* Thousand Oaks, CA: Sage.

Cassebaum, A. (2003). Revisiting Summerhill. *Phi Delta Kappan, 84,* 575–578.

Center for Education Reform. (2003). *Charter report flawed: California Research Group offers baseless criticism* [Press release]. Retrieved August 12, 2003, from http://edreform.com/press/2003/pace.htm

Center for Education Reform. (2006). Charter Schools. Retrieved July 1, 2006, from http://www.edreform.com

Center for Mental Health Services. (2003). *Bullying is not a fact of life.* Washington DC: Department of Health and Human Services. Also available from http://www.mentalhealth.samhsa.gov

Chadwick, K. G. (2004). *Improving schools through community engagement.* Thousand Oaks, CA: Corwin Press.

Cherlin, A. J., & Furstenberg, F. (1992). *The new American grandparent: A place in the family, a place apart.* Cambridge, MA: Harvard University Press.

Cherry, L. (1982). *A river ran wild.* San Diego, CA: Harcourt Brace.

Child Welfare League of America. (2003). *Family foster care fact sheet.* Retrieved June 11, 2003, from http://www.cwla.org

Childrens Defense Fund. (2000). The state of America's children 2000: A report from the Childrens Defense Fund. Boston: Beacon Press.

Children's Defense Fund. (2001). *The state of America's children: A report from the Children's Defense Fund.* Washington, DC: Author.

Children's Foundation. (2003). *2003 Family child care licensing study.* Washington, DC: Author.

Childrens Defense Fund. (2005a). Child Care Basics, April 2005. Retrieved April 9, 2006, from http://www.childrensdefense.org

Childrens Defense Fund. (2005b). *The state of America's children 2005.* Washington DC.: Childrens Defense Fund.

Childrens Defense Fund. (2006). *CDF Freedom Schools.* Retrieved May 21, 2006 from http://www.freedomschools.org/programs/

Chrisman, K., & Couchenour, D. (2002). *Healthy sexuality development: A guide for early childhood educators and families.* Washington, DC: National Association for the Education of Young Children.

Christie, J. F., Vukelich, C., & Enz, B. (2006). *Teaching language and literacy: Preschool through the elementary grades* (3rd ed.). Boston: Allyn & Bacon.

Clark, R. M. (1983). *Family life and school achievement: Why poor Black children succeed or fail.* Chicago: University of Chicago Press.

Clarke-Stewart, K. A., Allhusen, V. D., & Clements, D. C. (1995). Nonparenting caregiving. In M. H. Bornstein (Ed.), *Handbook of parenting: Vol. 3. Status and social conditions of parenting* (pp. 141– 175). Mahwah, NJ: Lawrence Erlbaum.

Clay, J. W. (1991). *Becoming literate: The construction of inner control.* Portsmouth, NH: Heinemann.

Cochran, M., & Davila, V. (1992). Societal influences on children's peer relationships. In R. D. Parke & G. W. Ladd (Eds.), *Family–peer relationships: Modes of linkage* (pp. 191–214). Hillsdale, NJ: Lawrence Erlbaum.

Cochran, M., & Niegro, S. (2002). Parenting and social networks. In M. H. Bornstein (Ed.), *Handbook of parenting: Vol. 4. Social conditions and applied parenting* (2nd ed., pp. 123–148). Mahwah, NJ: Lawrence Erlbaum.

Cochran, M., & Walker, S. (2005). Parenting and personal social networks. In L. Luster & L. Okogaski (Eds.), Parenting: An ecological perspective (2nd ed., pp. 235–272). Mahwah, NJ: Lawrence Erlbaum.

Cohen, S. (1974). *A history of colonial education, 1607–1776.* New York: Wiley.

Cohen, S. (2001). *Championing child care.* New York: Columbia University Press.

Coleman, J. S. (1966). *Equality of educational opportunity.* Washington, DC: U.S. Government Printing Office.

Coleman, J. S. (1991). *Policy perspectives: Parental involvement in education.* Washington, DC: U.S. Department of Education, Office of Educational Research and Improvement.

Coles, R. (1997). *The moral intelligence of children.* New York: Random House.

Coles, R. L. (2006). *Race and family: A structural approach.* Thousand Oaks, CA: Sage Publications.

Colfax, J. D., & Colfax, M. (1992). *Hard times in paradise.* New York: Warren.

Collins, R. C. (1984, April). *Head Start: A review of research with implications for practice in early childhood education.* Paper presented at the annual meeting of the American Educational Research Association, New Orleans, LA. (ERIC Document Reproduction Service No. ED245833)

Comer, J. P. (1980). *School power: Implications of an intervention project.* New York: Free Press.

Comer, J. P. (1988). *Maggie's American dream: The life and times of a Black family.* New York: New American Library.

Comer, J. P. (1997). *Waiting for a miracle: Why schools can't solve our problems and how we can.* New York: Penguin Putnam.

Comer, J. P., Ben-Avie, M., Haynes, N., & Joyner, E. T. (Eds.). (1999). *Child by child: The Comer process for change in education.* New York: Teachers College Press.

Comer, J. P., & Haynes, N. M. (1991). Parent involvement in schools: An ecological approach. *Elementary School Journal, 91,* 271–277.

Comer, J. P., Haynes, N. M., & Joyner, E. T. (1996). The school development program. In J. P. Comer, N. M. Haynes, E. T. Joyner, & M. Ben-Avie (Eds.), *Rallying the whole village: The Comer process for reforming education* (pp. 1–27). New York: Teachers College Press.

Committee on Family and Work Policies. (2003). *Working families and growing kids: Caring for children and adolescents: 2003.* Washington DC: Institute of Medicine.

Community Update. (2002, July/August). *Secretary Paige focuses on supplemental services.* Retrieved August 16, 2003, from http://www. NoChildLeftBehind.gov

Coontz, S. (1999). Introduction. In S. Coontz (Ed.), *American families: A multicultural reader* (pp. ix– xxxii). New York: Routledge.

Coontz, S. (2000). *The way we never were: American families and the nostalgia trip.* New York: Basic Books.

Coontz, S. (2005). *Marriage, a history: From obedience to intimacy, or how love conquered marriage.* New York: Viking.

Copple, C., & Bredekamp, S. (2005). *Basics of developmentally appropriate practice.* Washington, DC: National Association for the Education of Young Children.

Cornell, C. E. (1993). Language and culture monsters that lurk in our traditional rhymes and folktales. *Young Children, 48*(6), 40–46.

Cremin, L. A. (1961). *The transformation of the school: Progressivism in American education, 1876–1957.* New York: Knopf.

Cremin, L. A. (1982). *American education: The national experience, 1783–1876.* New York: Harper & Row.

Cross, W. E. (1987). Black identity: Rediscovering the distinction between personal identity and reference group orientation. In M. B. Spencer, G. Brookins, & W. Allen (Eds.), *Beginnings: The social and affective development of Black children* (pp. 155–171). Mahwah, NJ: Lawrence Erlbaum.

Cruickshank, D. (1990). *Research that informs teachers and teacher educators.* Bloomington, IN: Phi Delta Kappa Educational Foundation.

Cruickshank, D. R., Jenkins, D. B., & Metcalf, K. K. (2002). *The act of teaching* (3rd ed.). New York: McGraw-Hill.

Cryer, D., & Clifford, R. M. (Eds.). (2003). *Early childhood education and care in the USA.* Baltimore: Brookes.

Cutler, W. W. (2000). *Parents and schools: The 150-year struggle for control in American education.* Chicago: University of Chicago Press.

Damon, W. (1988). *The moral child: Nurturing children's natural moral growth.* New York: Free Press.

Daniels, E. (2002). *Family literacy parties.* Washington, DC: Children's Resources International.

Danzberger, J. P., & Gruskin, S. J. (1993). *Project abstracts: Educational Partnerships Program. Programs for the improvement of practice.* Washington, DC: Office of Educational Research and Improvement.

D'Arcangelo, M. (2003). On the mind of a child: A conversation with Sally Shaywitz. *Educational Leadership, 60*(7) 6–10.

Davis, T. J. (2006). *Race relations in America: A reference guide with primary documents.* Westport, CT: Greenwood Press.

De Carvalho, M. E. P. (2001). *Rethinking family–school relations: A critique of parental involvement in schooling.* Mahwah, NJ: Lawrence Erlbaum.

Deckard, S. (1996). *Home schooling laws and resource guide for all fifty states* (9th ed.). Ramona, CA: Vision.

DeGaetano, G. (2005). The impact of media violence on developing minds and hearts. In S. Olfman (Ed.), *Childhood lost: How American culture is failing our kids* (pp. 89–106). Westport, CT: Praeger.

Demarris, K. P., & LeCompte, M. D. (1998). *How schools work: A sociological analysis of education.* New York: Longman.

de Ramirez, L. L. (2006). *Voices of diversity: Stories, activities and resources for the multicultural classroom.* Upper Saddle River, NJ: Prentice Hall.

Derman-Sparks, L. (1989). *Anti-bias curriculum: Tools for empowering young children.* Washington, DC:

National Association for the Education of Young Children.

Desmond. R. (2001). Free reading. In D. G. Singer & J. L. Singer (Eds.), *Handbook of children and the media* (2nd ed., pp. 29–45). Thousand Oaks, CA: Sage.

DeVita, C. J. (1995). The United States at mid-decade. *Population Bulletin, 50*(4), 2–42.

DeVita, C. J., & Mosher-Williams, R. (2001). *Who speaks for America's children?* Washington, DC: Urban Institute.

Dewey, E. (1919). *New schools for old: The regeneration of the Porter School.* New York: E. P. Dutton.

Dewey, J. (1910). *How we think.* New York: D. C. Heath.

Dewey, J. (1944). *Democracy and education.* New York: Macmillan. (Originally published 1916.)

Dewey, J. (1975). *Interest and effort in education.* Edwardsville: Southern Illinois University Press. (Original work published 1913.)

Dickey, C. (2003, September 8). Not silly kid stuff. *Newsweek, 162*(10), E22–E24.

Diffily, D. (2004). *Teachers and families working together.* Boston: Allyn & Bacon.

Dilworth, M. E., & Brown, C. E. (2001). Consider the difference: Teaching and learning in culturally rich schools. In V. Richardson (Ed.), *Handbook of research on teaching* (4th ed., pp. 643–667). Washington DC: American Educational Research Association.

Dimidijian, V. J. (2001). Helping vulnerable families give their children an even start toward school success. *Childhood Education, 77,* 379–395.

Dinkmeyer, D., McKay, G. D., & Dinkmeyer, J. (1997). *Parenting young children: Systematic training for effective parenting (STEP) of children under six.* Circle Pines, MN: American Guidance Service.

Dodson, L., & Bravo, E. (2005). When there is not time or money: Work, family, and community lives of low-income families. In J. Heymann & C. Beem (Eds.) *Unfinished work: Building equality and democracy in an era of working families.* New York: The New Press.

Doll, R. C. (1995). *Curriculum improvement: Decision making and process* (9th ed.). Boston: Allyn & Bacon.

Douville-Watson, L., & Watson, M. A. (2002). *Infants and toddlers: Curriculum and teaching* (5th ed.). Albany, NY: Delmar.

Dowd, N. E., Singer, D. G., & Wilson, R. F. (Eds.) (2005). *Handbook of children, culture and violence.* Thousand Oaks, CA: Sage.

Dowling, J. E. (2004). *The great brain debate: Nature or nurture*. Washington DC: The National Academies Press.

Dryfoos, J. D. (1998). *Full-service schools: A revolution in health and social services for children, youth and families*. San Francisco: Jossey-Bass.

Dryfoos, J. D. (2003). A community school in action. *Reclaiming Children and Youth, 11*(4), 203–205.

Dryfoos, J. G., Quinn, J., & Barkin, C. (2005). *Community schools in action*. New York: Oxford University Press.

Duarte, G., & Rafanello, D. (2001). The migrant child: A special place in the field. *Young Children, 56*(3), pp. 26–34.

Duffey, J. (1998). Home schooling: A controversial alternative. *Principal 77*(5), 23–26.

Dunn, K., & Frazier, E. R. (1990). *Teaching styles*. Reston, VA: National Association of Secondary School Principals.

Dunn, R., & Dunn, K. (1999). *Complete guide to the Learning Styles Inservice Program*. Upper Saddle River, NJ: Prentice Hall.

Durkin, D. D. (1966). *Children who read early*. New York: Teachers College Press.

Eccles, J., Wigfield, A., Harold, R., & Blumenfeld, P. (1993). Age and gender differences in children's self and task perceptions during elementary school. *Child Development, 64*, 830–847.

Eddowes, E. A., & Hranitz, J. R. (1989). Educating children of the homeless. *Childhood Education, 65*(4), 197–200.

Edmiaston, R. K., & Fitzgerald, L. (2000). How Reggio Emilia encourages inclusion. *Educational Leadership, 58*(1), 66–69.

Education Commission of the States. (1996). *Bridging the gap between neuroscience and education. Summary of the workshop cosponsored by Education Commission of the States and the Charles A. Dana Foundation*. Denver, CO: Author.

Edwards, C. P., Gandini, L., & Forman, G. (1998). *The hundred languages of children: The Reggio Emilia approach* (2nd ed.). Greenwich, CT: Ablex.

Edwards, J. O., Derman-Sparks, L., & Ramsey. P. G. (2006). *What if all the kids are white?: Anti-bias multicultural education with young children and families*. New York: Teachers College Press.

Eisner, E. W. (2002). *The educational imagination: On the design and evaluation of school programs* (3rd ed.). Upper Saddle River, NJ: Merrill/Prentice Hall.

Eitzen, D. S., & Zinn, M. B. (2005). *Globalization: The transformation of social worlds*. Belmont, CA: Wadsworth Publishing.

Eley, M. A. (2002). Making the homeschooling connection. *Educational Leadership, 59*(7), 54–56.

Elkin, F., & Handel, G. (1989). *The child and society* (5th ed.). New York: Random House.

Elkind, D. (1994). *Ties that stress: The new family imbalance*. Cambridge, MA: Harvard University Press.

Elkind, D. (1995). School and family in the postmodern world. *Phi Delta Kappa, 77*, 8–14.

Elkind, D. (2001). *The hurried child: Growing up too fast too soon* (3rd ed.). New York: Basic Books.

Epstein, J. (1999). *School and family partnerships: Preparing educators and improving schools*. Boulder, CO: Westview Press.

Epstein, J. L. (2001). *School, family and community partnerships: Preparing educators and improving schools*. Boulder, CO: Westview Press.

Epstein, J. L., Sanders, M. G., Simon, B., Salina, K., Jansorn, N., & Van Voorhis, F. (2002). *Schools, family and community partnerships: Your handbook for action* (2nd ed.). Thousand Oaks, CA: Corwin Press.

Erera, P. I. (2002). *Family diversity: Continuity and change in the contemporary family*. Thousand Oaks, CA: Sage.

Erickson, F. (2005). Culture in society and in educational practices. In J. A. Banks & C. A. McGee-Banks (Eds.), *Multicultural education: Issues and perspectives* (5th ed., pp. 31–60). Hoboken, NJ: John Wiley.

Erikson, E. (1963). *Childhood and society*. New York: Norton.

Essa, E. L., & Murray, C. I. (1999). Sexual play: When should you be concerned? *Childhood Education, 75*(4), 231–234.

Evans, E. (1975). *Contemporary influences in early childhood education* (2nd ed.). New York: Holt, Rinehart & Winston.

Evans, R. (1996). *The human side of school change*. San Francisco: Jossey-Bass.

Evans, R. (2004). *Family matters: How school can cope with the crisis in child rearing*. San Francisco: Jossey-Bass.

Even Start. (1999). *Even Start*. Retrieved August 2, 2003, from http://www.ed.gov/legislation/ESEA/sec1201.html

Falvey, M. A. (2005). *Believe in my child with special needs: Helping children achieve their potential in school*. Baltimore: Paul H. Brookes.

Fass, P. S., & Mason, M. A. (Eds). (2000). *Childhood in America*. New York: New York University Press.

Ferri, D., & Amick, S. (2002). San Diego's 6 to 6: A community's commitment to out-of-school time. In G. Noam & B. Miller (Eds.), *Youth development and after-school time: A tale of many cities*. San Francisco: Wiley Periodicals.

Fine, M. A., Ganong, H., & Demo, D. H. (2005). Divorce as a family stressor. In P. C. McKenry & S. J. Price (Eds.), *Families and change: Coping with stressful events and transitions* (pp. 227–252). Thousand Oaks, CA: Sage.

Fine, M. J. (1993). Current approaches to understanding family diversity. *Family Relations, 43*(3), 235–237.

Fine, M. J., & Lee, S. W. (2001). *Handbook of diversity in parent education: The changing faces of parenting and parent education*. San Diego, CA: Academic Press.

Fisch, S. M. (2004). *Children's learning from educational television: Sesame Street and beyond*. Mahwah, NJ: Lawrence Erlbaum.

Fisch, S. M., & Truglio, R. T. (Eds.). (2001). *"G" is for growing: Thirty years of research on children and Sesame Street*. Mahwah, NJ: Lawrence Erlbaum.

Fraenkel, P. (2003). Contemporary two-parent families: Navigating work and family challenges. In F. Walsh (Ed.), *Normal family processes: Growing diversity and complexity* (3rd ed., pp. 61–95). New York: Guilford.

Frankel, E. (2004). Supporting inclusive care and education for young children with special needs and their families: An international perspective. *Childhood Education, 80*(6), 310–316.

Fredriksen-Goldsen, K. I., & Scharlach, A. E. (2001). *Families and work: New directions in the twenty-first century*. New York: Oxford University Press.

Fried, R. L. (2001). *The passionate learner: How teachers and parents can help children reclaim the joy of learning*. Boston: Beacon Press.

Fried, R. L. (2005). *The game of school: Why we all play it, how it hurts kids, and what it will take to change it*. San Francisco: Jossey-Bass.

Froebel, F. (1889). *The education of man*. New York: D. Appleton. (Original work published 1826.)

Fuller, B. (2003). *Policy analysis for California education (PACE). Charter schools and inequality: National disparities in funding, teacher quality and student support*. Retrieved August 21, 2003, from http://www.edreform.com/press/2003/pace.htm

Fuller, M. L., & Olsen, G. (1998). *Home–school relations: Working successfully with parents and families*. Boston: Allyn & Bacon.

Futrell, M. H., Gomez, J., & Bedden, D. (2003). Teaching the children of a new America: The challenge of diversity. *Phi Delta Kappan, 84*, 381–385.

Gabe, T. (2003). *Trends in welfare, work, and the economic well-being of female-headed households with children*. New York: Novinka Books.

Galinsky, E. (1987). *The six stages of parenthood*. Reading, MA: Addison-Wesley.

Galinsky, E., Howes, C., & Kontos, S. (1995). *The family child care training study: Highlights of the findings*. New York: Families and Work Institute.

Galinsky, E., Howes, C., Kontos, S., & Shinn, M. (1994). *The study of children in family child care and relative care: Highlights of the findings*. New York: Families and Work Institute.

Galle, O., Gove, W., & McPherson, J. (1972). Population density and pathology: What are the relationships for men? *Science, 176*, 23–30.

Gallego, M. A., & Cole, M. (2001). Classroom cultures and cultures in the classroom. In V. Richardson (Ed.), *Handbook of research on teaching* (4th ed., pp. 951–997). Washington, DC: American Educational Research Association.

Gandara, P., Maxwell, J.J., Garcia, E., Asato, J., Gutierez, K., & Stritikus, T., et al. (1999). *The initial impact of Proposition 227*. Davis, CA: University of Linguistic Minority Institute.

Gander, E. M. (2003). *On our minds: How evolutionary psychology is reshaping the nature-versus-nurture debate*. Baltimore: Johns Hopkins University Press.

Gandini, L. (1993). Fundamentals of the Reggio Emilia approach to early childhood education. *Young Children, 49*(1), 4–8.

Gandini, L. (1997). Foundations of the Reggio Emilia approach. In J. Hendrick (Ed.), *First steps toward teaching the Reggio way* (pp. 14–25). Upper Saddle River, NJ: Merrill/Prentice Hall.

Gandini, L, Hill, L., Cadwell, L., & Schwall, C. (Eds). (2005). *In the spirit of the studio: Learning from the atelier of Reggio Emilia*. New York: Teachers College Press.

Garbarino, J. (1999). *Lost boys: Why our sons turn violent and how we can save them*. New York: Free Press.

Garbarino, J., & Abramowitz, R. H. (1992). The family as a social system. In J. Garbarino (Ed.), *Children and families in the social environment* (2nd ed., pp. 71–98). New York: De Gruyter.

Garbarino, J., Dubrow, N., Kostelny, K., & Pardo, C. (1998). *Children in danger: Coping with the consequences of community violence* (2nd ed.). San Francisco: Jossey-Bass.

Gardner, H. (1983). *Frames of mind. The theory of multiple intelligences.* New York: Basic Books.

Gardner, H. (1993). *Multiple intelligencies: The theory in practice.* New York: Basic Books.

Gardner, H. (1999). *The disciplined mind: What all students should understand.* New York: Simon & Schuster.

Gardner, S. (1993). Failure by fragmentation. In S. Thompson (Ed.), *Whole child, whole community* (pp. 11–17). Boston: Institute for Responsive Education.

Geen, R. (Ed.). (2005). *Kinship care: Making the most of a valuable resource.* Washington, DC: Urban Institute Press.

Gelles, R. J., & Cavanaugh, M. M. (2005). Violence, abuse, and neglect in families and intimate relationships. In P. C. McKenry & S. J. Price (Eds.), *Families and change: Coping with stressful events and transitions* (pp. 129–154). Thousand Oaks, CA: Sage.

Gelnaw, A. (2005). Belonging: Including children of gay and lesbian parents and all children in your program. *Child Care Information Exchange, 163,* 42–45.

Gentile, D. A., & Walsh, D. A. (2002). A normative study of family media habits. *Applied Developmental Psychology, 23,* 157–178.

Gersten, J. C. (1992). Families in poverty. In M. E. Procidano & C. B. Fisher (Eds.), *Contemporary families: A handbook for school professionals* (pp. 137–158). New York: Teachers College Press.

Giambo, D., & Szecsi, T. (2005). Parents can guide children through the world of two languages. *Childhood Education, 81*(3), 164–165.

Giovanni, D. (2001). Traces of childhood: A child's diary. In L. Gandini & C. Edwards (Eds.), *The Italian approach to infant/toddler care* (pp. 146–152). New York: Teachers College Press.

Giroux, H. A. (1978). Developing educational programs: Overcoming the hidden curriculum. *The Clearing House, 52*(4), 148–152.

Goetz, E. (2003). *Clearing the way: Deconcentrating the poor in urban America.* Washington, DC: Urban Institute.

Goertz, M. E. (2001). Redefining government roles in an era of standards-based reform. *Phi Delta Kappan, 83*(1), 62–66.

Goff, P. (2004). Diversity and religion. In P. Goff & P. Harvey (Eds.), *Themes in religion and American culture* (pp. 327–360). Chapel Hill, NC: University of North Carolina Press.

Goffman, E. (1967). *Interaction ritual: Essays on face-to-face behavior.* New York: Harper & Row.

Goleman, D. (1995). *Emotional intelligence.* New York: Bantam Books.

Gollnick, D. M., & Chinn, P. (2006). *Multicultural education in a pluralistic society* (7th ed.). Upper Saddle River, NJ: Merrill/Prentice Hall.

Gonzalez-Mena, J. (2006). *The young child in the family and the community* (4th ed.). Upper Saddle River, NJ: Merrill/Prentice Hall.

Good, L. (2005/06). Using digital photography in early childhood. *Childhood Education 82* (2), 79–85.

Good, T. L., & Brophy, J. E. (1986). School effects. In M. C. Wittrock (Ed.), *Handbook of research on teaching* (3rd ed., pp. 570–604). Upper Saddle River, NJ: Prentice Hall.

Good, T. L., & Brophy, J. E. (2002). *Looking in classrooms* (9th ed.). Boston: Allyn & Bacon.

Good, T. L., & Early, M. (Eds). (2000). *American education: Yesterday, today and tomorrow: 99th yearbook of the National Society for the Study of Education. Part II.* Chicago: University of Chicago Press.

Gorder, C. (1996). *Home schools: An alternative. You do have a choice!* (4th ed.). Tempe, AZ: Blue Bird.

Gordon, T. (2000). *Parent effectiveness training: The proven approach for raising responsible children.* New York: Crown.

Gorman, J. C. (2004). *Working with challenging parents of students with special needs.* Thousand Oaks, CA: Corwin Press.

Gormick, J. C., & Meyers, M. K. (2005). Supporting a dual-earner/dual-career society. In J. Heymann & C. Beem (Eds.). *Unfinished work: Building equality and democracy in an era of working families* (pp. 371–408). New York: New York Press.

Gorsuch, R. L. (1976). Religion as a major prediction of significant human behavior. In W. J. Donaldson, Jr. (Ed.), *Research in mental health and religious behavior* (pp. 206–221). Atlanta, GA: Psychological Studies Institute.

Green, C., & Oldendorf, S. B. (2005). Teaching religious diversity through children's literature. *Childhood Education, 81*(4), 209–218.

Greenberg, D., Sadofsky, M., & Lempka, J. (2005). *The pursuit of happiness: The lives of Sudbury Valley Alumni*. Framingham, MA: Sudbury Valley School Press.

Greenberg, P. (1990). Head Start—Part of a multi-pronged antipoverty effort for children and their families. Before the beginning: A participant's view. *Young Children, 45*(6), 40–73.

Greene, S. M., Anderson, E., Hetherington, E. M., Forgatch, M. S., & DeGarmo, D. S. (2003). Risk and resilience after divorce. In F. Walsh (Ed.), *Normal family processes: Growing diversity and complexity* (3rd ed., pp. 96–120). New York: Guilford Press.

Greenfield, P. M., & Suzuki, L. K. (2001). Culture and parenthood. In J. C. Westman (Ed.), *Parenthood in America: Undervalued, underpaid, under siege* (pp. 20–33). Madison: University of Wisconsin Press.

Greenspan, S., & Salmon, J. (2001). *The four-thirds solution: Solving the child-care crisis in America*. Cambridge, MA: Perseus Press.

Gronlund, G., & Engel, B. (2001). *Focused portfolios: A complete assessment for the young child*. St. Paul, MN: Redleaf Press.

Gunter, B., Harrison, J., & Wykes, M. (2003). *Violence on television: Distribution form, context and themes*. Mahwah, NJ: Lawrence Erlbaum.

Gutek, G. L. (2005). *Historical and philosophical foundations of education: A biographical introduction* (4th ed.). Upper Saddle River: Merrill/Prentice Hall.

Gutrel, F. (2003, September 8). Overloaded? Today's kids are tech addicts. *Newsweek, 162*(10), E4–E8.

Haberman, M. (1992). Creating community contexts that educate: An agenda for improving education in inner cities. In L. Kaplan (Ed.), *Education and the family* (pp. 27–40). Boston: Allyn & Bacon.

Haddock, S. A., Zimmerman, T. S., & Lyness, K. P. (2003). Changing gender norms: Transitional dilemmas. In F. Walsh (Ed.), *Normal family processes: Growing diversity and complexity* (3rd ed., pp. 301–336). New York: Guilford.

Hafner, K. (2002, October 31). Making the Web child-safe. *The New York Times*, p. E4.

Hagan, J. L. (1998). The new welfare law is tough on work. *Families in Society, 79*, 596–605.

Hamilton, S. F, Hamilton, M. A., & Pittman, K. (2004). Principles for youth development. In S. F. Hamilton & M. A. Hamilton (Eds.), *The youth development handbook: Coming of age in American communities* (pp. 3–22). Thousand Oaks, CA: Sage.

Hammer, T. J., & Turner, P. H. (2000). *Parenting in contemporary society* (4th ed.). Boston: Allyn & Bacon.

Hanhan, S. F. (2003). Parent–teacher communication: Who's talking. In G. Olsen & M. L. Fuller (Eds.), *Home–school relations: Working successfully with parents and families* (pp. 111–133). Boston: Allyn & Bacon.

Hansen, K. V. (2005). *Not-so-nuclear families: Class, gender, and networks of care*. New Brunswick, NJ: Rutgers University Press.

Hanson, M. J., & Lynch, E. W. (2004). *Understanding families: Approaches to diversity, disability, and risk*. Baltimore: Paul H. Brookes.

Harrington, M. (2000). *Care and equality: Inventing a new family politics*. New York: Routledge.

Harris, A. (2004). *All about the girl*. New York: Routledge.

Harris, J. (2002). Beyond the nurture assumption. Testing hypotheses about the child's environment. In J. G. Borkowski, S. L. Ramey, & M. Bristol-Power (Eds.), *Parenting and the child's world* (pp. 3–20). Mahwah, NJ: Erlbaum.

Harris, J. R. (1998). *The nurture assumption*. New York: Free Press.

Hart, B., & Risley, T. R. (1995). *Meaningful differences in the everyday experience of young American children*. Baltimore: Paul H. Brookes.

Hart, B., & Risley, T. R. (1999). *The social world of children learning to talk*. Baltimore: Paul H. Brookes.

Hart, B., & Risley, T. R. (2003). The early catastrophe: The 30 million word gap by age 3. *American Educator, 27*(1), 5–9.

Hartman, A. (2003). Family policy: Dilemmas, controversies, and opportunities. In F. Walsh (Ed.), *Normal family processes: Growing diversity and complexity* (3rd ed., pp. 635–662). New York: Guilford.

Hartup, W. W. (1983). Peer relations. In P. H. Mussen (Ed.), *Handbook of child psychology: Vol. 4. Socialization, personality, and social development* (pp. 103–196). New York: Wiley.

Hatch, J. A. (2005). *Teaching in the new kindergarten*. Clifton Park, NY: Thomson Delmar Learning.

Hayslip, B., & Patrick, J. H. (2006). *Custodial grandparenting: Individual, cultural and ethnic diversity*. New York: Springer Publishing.

Head Start Bureau. (2006). U.S. Department of Health & Human Services, President Bush's Proposal for Head Start, 2003. Retrieved April 21, 2006, from http://www.acf.hhs.gov/programs/hbs

Heath, S. D. (1983). *Ways with words: Language, life, and work in communities and classrooms.* New York: Cambridge University Press.

Helburn, S. & Bergman, B. (2002). *America's child care problem: The way out.* New York: Palgrave/St. Martin's.

Heleen, O. (1990). Schools reaching out: An introduction. *Equity and Choice, 6*(3), 5–9.

Helm, J. (1994). Family theme bags: An innovative approach to family involvement in the school. *Young Children, 49*(4), 48–52.

Helms, H. M., & Demo, D. (2005). Everyday hassles and family stress. In P. McKenry & S. J. Price (Eds.), *Families and change: Coping with stressful events and transitions* (3rd ed., pp. 405–435). Thousand Oaks, CA: Sage.

Hendrick, J. (Ed.). 1997. *First steps toward teaching the Reggio way.* Upper Saddle River, NJ: Merrill/Prentice Hall.

Hendrick, J. (Ed.). (2004). *Next steps toward teaching the Reggio way: Accepting the challenge to change.* Upper Saddle River, NJ: Merrill/Prentice Hall.

Henniger, M. L. (2004). *Teaching young children: An introduction* (2nd ed.). Upper Saddle River, NJ: Merrill/Prentice Hall.

Hernandez, D. J. (2005), Changes in the demographics of families over the course of American history. In J. Heymann & C. Beem (Eds.), *Unfinished work: Building equality and democracy in an era of working families* (pp. 13–35). New York: The New Press.

Hesse, P., & Lane, F. (2003). Media literacy starts young: An integrated curriculum approach. *Young Children., 58*(6), 20–27.

Hetherington, E. M., & Kelly, J. (2002). *For better or worse: Divorce reconsidered.* New York: Norton.

Hetherington, E. M., & Stanley-Hagan, M. M. (2002). Parenting in divorced and remarried families. In M. Bornstein (Ed.), *Handbook of parenting: Vol 3. Being and becoming a parent* (pp. 287–316). Mahwah, NJ: Lawrence Erlbaum.

Heward, W. L. (2006). *Exceptional children: An introduction to special education* (8th ed.). Upper Saddle River, NJ: Merrill/Prentice Hall.

Heward, W. L., Cavanaugh, R. A., & Ernsbarger, S. C. (2005). Educational equality for students with disabilities. In J. A. Banks & C. A. Banks (Eds.), *Multicultural education: Issues and perspectives* (pp. 317–349). Hoboken, NJ: John Wiley & Sons.

Hewlett, S. A., & West, C. (2005). The war against parents. In S. Olfman (Ed.), *Childhood lost: How American culture is failing our kids* (pp. 57–88). Westport, CT: Praeger Publishers.

Heymann, J. (2005). Inequalities at work and at home: Social class and gender divides. In J. Heymann & C. Beem (Eds.), *Unfinished work: Building equality and democracy in an era of working families* (pp. 89–121). New York: The New Press.

Hiatt-Michael, D. B. (2004). Connecting schools to families of children with special needs. In D. B. Hiatt-Michael (Ed.), *Promising practices connecting schools to families of children with special needs* (pp. 1–14). Greenwich, CT: Information Age Publishing.

Hill, E. (1967). *Evan's corner.* New York: Holt.

Hill-Clark, K. (2005). Families as educators: Supporting literacy development. *Childhood Education, 82,* 46–47.

Hirsch, B. J. (2005). A place to call home: After-school programs for urban youth. Washington, DC: American Psychological Association.

Hofferth, S. L. (1991). *National child care survey, 1990.* Washington, DC: Urban Institute.

Hoge, D. R. (1996). Religion in America: The demographics of belief and affiliation. In E. P. Shafranske (Ed.), *Religion and the clinical practice of psychology* (pp. 21–41). Washington, DC: American Psychological Association.

Holmbeck, G. N., Paikoff, R., & Brooks-Gunn, J. (1995). Parenting adolescents. In M. Bornstein (Ed.), *Handbook of parenting Vol: 1. Children and parenting* (pp. 91–118). Mahwah, NJ: Lawrence Erlbaum.

Hong, E., & Milgram, R. M. (2000). *Homework: Motivation and learning preference.* Westport, CT: Bergin & Garvey.

Horgen, K. B. (2005). Big food, big money, big children. In S. Olfman (Ed.), *Childhood lost: How American culture is failing our kids* (pp. 123–135). Westport, CT: Praeger.

Hrabowski, F. A., Maton, K. I., & Greif, G. L. (1998). *Beating the odds: Raising academically successful African American males.* New York: Oxford University Press.

Hrabowski, F. A., Maton, K. I., Greene, M., & Greif, G. L. (2002). *Overcoming the odds: Raising academically successful African American young women.* New York: Oxford University Press.

Hurd, T. L., Lerner, R. M., & Barton, C. E. (1999). Integrated services: Expanding partnerships to meet the needs of today's children and families. *Young Children, 54*(2), 74–81.

Hymowitz, K. S. (2002). Parenting: The lost art. *American Educator 25*(1), 4–9.

Individuals with Disabilities Education Act. (1997, March 12). Assistance to States for the Education of Children with Disabilities and the Early Intervention Program for Infants and Toddlers with Disabilities. 34 C.F.R., 300 & 303, Vol. 64, No. 48.

Institute of Medicine. (2006). Child obesity in the United States: Facts and figures, 2006. Washington DC.: Institute of Medicine. Retrieved January 20, 2006 from http://www.iom.edu

Ispa, J. M., Thornburg, K. R., & Fine, M. A. (2006). *Keepin' on: The everyday struggles of young families in poverty.* Baltimore: Paul H. Brookes.

Jacobs, J. W. (2004). *All you need is love and other lies about marriage.* New York: Harper Collins.

Jacobs, K. (2004). Parent and child together time. In B. H. Wasik (Ed.), *Handbook of family literacy* (pp. 193–221). Mahwah, NJ: Lawrence Erlbaum.

Janosik, E., & Green, E. (1992). *Family life: Process and practice.* Boston: Jones & Bartlett.

Jencks, C., Smith, M. S., Acland, H., Bane, M. J., Cohen, I., Gintis, H., et al. (1972). *Inequality: A reassessment of family and schooling in America.* New York: Harper & Row.

Jenkins, E. J., & Bell, C. C. (1997). Exposure and response to community violence among children and adolescents. In J. Osofsky (Ed.), *Children in a violent society* (pp. 9–31). New York: Guilford.

Johnson, E. A., & Mappin, M. J. (2005). *Ecological education and environmental advocacy.* New York: Cambridge University Press.

Jones, K. (1988). *Interactive learning events: A guide for facilitators.* New York: Nichols.

Joshi, A. (2005). Understanding Asian Indian families: Facilitating meaningful home–school relations. *Young Children, 60*(3), 75–78.

Joyce, B., & Weil, M. (1996). *Models of teaching* (5th ed.). Boston: Allyn & Bacon.

Joyce, B., Weil, M., & Calhoun, E. (2003). *Models of teaching* (7th ed.). Boston: Allyn & Bacon.

Kagan, S. L. (1993). Home–school linkages. In S. L. Kagan, D. R. Powell, B. Weisbourd, & E. F. Zigler (Eds.), *America's family support programs: Perspectives and prospects* (pp. 160–181). New Haven, CT: Yale University Press.

Kamerman, S. B. (2005a). Early childhood education and care in advanced industrialized countries: Current policy and program trends. *Phi Delta Kappan, 87*(3), 193–195.

Kamerman, S. B. (2005b). Europe advanced while the United States lagged. In J. Heymann & C. Beem (Eds.), *Unfinished work: Building equality and democracy in an era of working families* (pp. 309–347). New York: The New Press.

Karcher, M. J., Brown, B. B., & Elliot, D. W. (2004). Enlisting peers in developmental interventions: Principles and practices. In S. F. Hamilton & M. A. Hamilton (Eds.), *The youth development handbook: Coming of age in American communities* (pp. 193– 214). Thousand Oaks, CA: Sage.

Karpowitz, D. H. (2001). American families in the 1990s and beyond. In M. J. Fine & S. W. Lee (Eds.), *Handbook of diversity in parent education* (pp. 3–14). San Diego, CA: Academic Press.

Katz, L. G., & Chard, S. C. (2000). *Engaging children's minds: The project approach.* Norwood, NJ: Ablex Publishing.

Katz, P. A. (1976). The acquisition of racial attitudes in children. In P. A. Katz (Ed.), *Towards the elimination of racism* (pp. 125–154). New York: Pergamon.

Kerman, K. (1990). Home schooling day by day. In A. Pedersen, P. O'Mara (Eds.), *Schooling at home: Parents, kids, and learning* (pp. 175–182). Santa Fe, NM: Muir.

Kidwell, C. S., & Swift, D. W. (1976). Indian education. In D. W. Swift (Ed.), *American education: A sociological view* (pp. 329–390). Boston: Houghton Mifflin.

Kieff, J., & Wellhousen, K. (2000). Planning family involvement in early childhood programs. *Young Children, 55*(3), 18–25.

Kieff, J. E., & Casbergue, R. M. (2000). *Playful learning and teaching: Integrating play into preschool and primary programs.* Boston: Allyn & Bacon.

Kinch, A. F., & Schweinhart, L. J. (1999). Making child care work for everyone. *Young Children, 54*(1), 68–73.

Kochenderfer, R., Kanna, E., & Kiyosaki, R. (2002). *Homeschooling for success: How can parents create a superior education for their child?* New York: Warner.

Koralek, D. (2002). Professionalism leads to quality in family child care. *Young Children, 57*(1), 8.

Kostelnik, M. J., Soderman, A. K., & Whiren, A. P. (2004). *Developmentally appropriate curriculum: Best practices in early childhood education.* Upper Saddle River, NJ: Merrill/Prentice Hall.

Kozol, J. (1991). *Savage inequalities: Children in America's schools.* New York: Crown.

Kralovec, E., & Buell, J. (2000). *The end of homework: How homework disrupts families, overburdens children and limits learning.* Boston: Beacon.

Kumove, L. (1966). *A preliminary study of the social implications of high-density living conditions.* Toronto, Ontario, Canada: Social Planning Council of Metropolitan Toronto.

Kyle, D. W., McIntyre, E., Miller, K. & Moore, G. (2007). *Reaching out: Strategies and tips for connecting with families.* Thousand Oaks, CA: Corwin.

Ladd, G. W., & Pettit, G. S. (2002). Parents and children's peer relationships. In M. Bornstein (Ed.), *Handbook of parenting: Vol. 4. Applied and practical parenting* (2nd ed., pp. 377–409). Mahwah, NJ: Lawrence Erlbaum.

Lancaster, P. E. (2001). Parenting children with learning disabilities. In M. J. Fine & S. W. Lee (Eds.), *Handbook of diversity in parent education* (pp. 233– 253). San Diego, CA: Academic Press.

Lareau, A. (2003). *Unequal childhoods: Class, race, and family life.* Berkeley, CA: University of California Press.

Larzelere, R. E. (2001). Combining love and limits in authoritative parenting. In J. C. Westman (Ed.), *Parenthood in America: Undervalued, underpaid, under siege* (pp. 81–89). Madison: University of Wisconsin Press.

Lazar, I. (1977). *The persistence of preschool effects: A long-term follow-up of fourteen infant and preschool experiments.* Washington, DC: Administration for Children, Youth, and Families.

Lazzara, K. C., & Poland, S. (2001). Managing crisis: Intervention skills for parents. In M. J. Fine & S. W. Lee (Eds.), *Handbook of diversity in parent education: The changing faces of parenting and parent education* (pp. 339–372). San Diego, CA: Academic Press.

Leach, P. (1994). *Children first: What our society must do—And is not doing—For our children today.* New York: Knopf.

Leach, P. (1997). *Children first.* New York: Random House.

Lee, H., & Ostrowsky, M. (2004). Toward successful collaboration: Voices from families of children with developmental delays and disabilities. In D. B. Hiatt-Michael (Ed.), *Promising practices connecting schools to families of children with special needs* (pp. 101–128). Greenwich, CT: Information Age Publishing.

Lee, S. W., & Guck, T. P. (2001). Parenting chronically ill children. In M. J. Fine & S. W. Lee (Eds.), *Handbook of diversity in parent education* (pp. 277– 298). San Diego, CA: Academic Press.

Lerner, J. W., Lowenthal, B., & Egan, R. W. (2003). *Preschool children with special needs: Children at risk and children with disabilities.* Boston: Allyn & Bacon.

Lerner, R. M., & Benson, P. L. (Eds.). (2003). *Developmental assets and asset-building communities: Implications for research, policy, and practice.* New York: Kluwer Academic/Plenum Publishers.

Letiecq, B. L., Anderson, E. A., & Koblinsky, A. (1998). Social support of homeless and house mothers: A comparison of temporary and permanent housing arrangements. *Family Relations, 47,* 415–421.

Levin, D. (2005). So sexy, so soon: The sexualization of childhood. In S. Olfman (Ed.), *Childhood lost: How American culture is failing our kids* (pp. 137–153). Westport, CT: Praeger.

Levine, S., & Ion, H. W. (2002). *Against terrible odds: Lessons in resilience from our children.* Boulder, CO: Bull Publishing.

Lewis, R. B., & Doorlag, D. (2006). *Teaching special students in general education classrooms* (7th ed.). Upper Saddle River, NJ: Merrill/Prentice Hall.

Lichter, D. T., & Crowley, M. L. (2002). Poverty in America: Beyond welfare reform. *Population Bulletin, 57*(2), 3–34.

Lightfoot, S. L. (1978). *Worlds apart: Relationships between schools and families.* New York: Basic Books.

Lilly, E., & Green, C. (2004). *Developing partnerships with families through children's literature.* Upper Saddle River, NJ: Merrill/Prentice Hall.

Lim, S. (2003). Parent involvement in education. In G. Olsen & M. L. Fuller (Eds.), *Home school relations: Working successfully with parents and families* (2nd ed.). Boston: Allyn & Bacon.

Lin, H. (2002, November 16). Making the Net child-safe. *The New York Times,* p. 25.

Lindner, E. (2003). *Yearbook of American and Canadian churches, 2002.* Nashville, TN: Abingdon.

Lindsey, E. W. (1998). The impact of homelessness and shelter life on family relationships. *Family Relations, 47*(3), 243–252.

Lines, P. (2001, July). *Home school in the United States: 1999.* Washington, DC: U.S. National Center for Educational Statistics.

Liston, D. P., & Zeichner, K. (1996). *Reflective teaching: An introduction.* Mahwah, NJ: Lawrence Erlbaum.

Liverman, C. T., Kraak, V. I., & Koplan, J. (Eds.) 2005. *Preventing childhood obesity: Health in the balance.* Washington DC.: National Academies Press.

Lombardi, J. (2003). *Time to care: Redesigning child care to promote education, support families, and build communities.* Philadelphia: Temple University Press.

Long, N. (2004). e-Parenting. In M. S. Hoghughi & N. Long (Eds.), *Handbook of parenting: Theory and research for practice* (pp. 369–380). Thousand Oaks, CA: Sage.

Louv, R. (2005). *Last child in the woods: Saving our children from nature-deficit disorder.* Chapel Hill, NC: Algonquin Books.

Lovell, J., & Kluger, J. (1994). *Lost moon: The perilous voyage of Apollo 13.* Boston: Houghton Mifflin.

Lynn-Garbe, C., & Hoot, J. L. (2004/05). Weighing in on the issue of childhood obesity. *Childhood Education 81*(2), 70–78.

MaCauley, D. (1980). *The new how things work.* Boston: Houghton Mifflin.

Maccoby, E. E., & Martin, J. (1983). Socialization in the context of family: Parent–child interaction. In P. H. Mussen (Ed.), *Handbook of child psychology: Socialization, personality and social development* (4th ed., pp. 1–102). New York: Wiley.

Maeroff, G. I. (1998). Altered destinies: Making life better for schoolchildren in need. *Phi Delta Kappan, 79,* 424–432.

Magnuson, K. A., & Duncan, G. J. (2002). Parents in poverty. In M. H. Bornstein (Ed.), *Handbook of parenting: Vol. 4. Social conditions and applied parenting* (2nd ed., pp. 95–122). Mahwah, NJ: Lawrence Erlbaum.

Mahood, H. R. (2000). *Interest groups in American national politics.* Upper Saddle River, NJ: Prentice Hall.

Mallett, D. (1995) *Inch by inch: The garden song.* New York: HarperCollins.

Marcus, G. F. (2004). *The birth of the mind: How a tiny number of genes creates the complexities of human thought.* New York: Basic Books.

Mardell, B. (2002). *Growing up in child care: A case for quality early childhood education.* Portsmouth, NH: Heinemann.

Marsh, C., & Willis, G. (2003). *Curriculum: Alternative approaches, ongoing issues* (3rd ed.). Upper Saddle River, NJ: Merrill/Prentice Hall.

Maslow, A. H. (1970). *Motivation and personality* (Rev. ed.). New York: Norton.

Mason, M. A. (1998). The modern American stepfamily: Problems and possibilities. In M. A. Mason, A. Skolnick, & S. D. Sugarman (Eds.), *All our families: New policies for a new century* (pp. 95–116). New York: Oxford University Press.

Mass, Y., & Cohan, K. A. (2006). Home connections to learning: Supporting parents as teachers. *Young Children, 61*(1): 54–55.

Mayer, S. (1997). *What money can't buy: Family income and children's life chances.* Cambridge, MA: Harvard University Press.

Mbugua, T., Wadas, J., Casey, M. A., & Finnerty, J. (2004). Authentic learning: Intercultural, international, and intergenerational experiences in the elementary classroom. *Childhood Education, 80*(5), 237–245.

McChesney, R. W. (1999). *Rich media, poor democracy: Communication politics in dubious times.* Urbana: University of Illinois Press.

McCormick, L., Wong, M., and Yogi, L. (2003). Individualization in the inclusive preschool: A planning process. *Childhood Education, 79*(4), 212–217.

McDermott, D. (2001). Parenting and ethnicity. In M. J. Fine & S. W. Lee (Eds.), *Handbook of diversity in parent education* (pp. 73–96). San Diego, CA: Academic Press.

McDevitt, T. M., & Ormrod, J. E. (2002). *Child development and education.* Upper Saddle River, NJ: Merrill/Prentice Hall.

McFalls, J. A., Jr. (1998). Population: A lively introduction. *Population Bulletin, 53*(3), 3–47.

McGoldrick, M. (2003). Culture: A challenge to concepts of normality. In F. Walsh (Ed.), *Normal family processes: Growing diversity and complexity* (3rd ed., pp. 235–259). New York: Guilford Press.

McGroder, S. M. (2000). Parenting among low income African American single mothers with preschool age children: Patterns, predictors as developmental correlates. *Child Development, 71*(3), 752–771.

McKenry, P. C., & Price, S. J. (Eds.). (2005). *Families and change: Coping with stressful events and transitions.* Thousand Oaks, CA: Sage.

McNeil, J. D., & Darby, J. (2005). *Curriculum: A comprehensive introduction* (6th ed.). New York: John Wiley.

Mediavilla, C. (2001). *Creating the full-service homework center in your library.* Chicago: American Library Association.

Meier, D. (2002a). *In schools we trust: Creating communities of learning in an era of testing and standardization.* Boston: Beacon Press.

Meier, D. (2002b). Standardization versus standards. *Phi Delta Kappan, 84,* 190–198.

Meier, D. (2003). Becoming educated: The power of ideas. *Principal Leadership 3*(7), 16–19.

Meier, D., & Wood, G. (2004). *Many children left behind: How the No Child Left Behind Act is damaging our children and our schools.* Boston: Beacon Press.

Melton, J. G. (2002). *Encyclopedia of American religions* (7th ed.). Detroit, MI: Gale Research.

Meringoff, L. K. (1980). Influence of the medium on children's story comprehension. *Journal of Educational Psychology, 72*(2), 240–249.

Mitchell, C. J., & Spencer, L. M. (1997). *21st-Century community learning centers program.* Washington, DC: U.S. Department of Education, Office of Educational Research and Improvement.

Monroe, L. (1997). *Nothing's impossible: Leadership lessons and stories from the front.* New York: Time Books.

Moriarty, M. L., & Fine, M. J. (2001). Educating parents to be advocates for their children. In M. Fine & S. W. Lee (Eds.), *Handbook of diversity in parent education: The changing faces of parenting and parent education* (pp. 315–336). San Diego, CA: Academic Press.

Morris, J. E. (2002). A "community bonded" school for African American students, families, and community. *Phi Delta Kappan 84*(3), 230–234.

Morrison, G. S. (2006). *Fundamentals of early childhood education* (4th ed.). Upper Saddle River, NJ: Merrill/Prentice Hall.

Morse, S. C. (1997). *Unschooled migrant youth: Characteristics and strategies to serve them.* Washington, DC: Superintendent of Documents. (Gov. Doc. ED 1.310/2:405158).

Mukhopadhyay, C., & Henze, R. C. (May 2003). How real is race: Using anthropology to make sense of human diversity. *Phi Delta Kappan, 84,* 669–678.

Murphy, J., & Shiffman, C. D. (2002). *Understanding and assessing the charter school movement.* New York: Teachers College Press.

Murray, J. P. (1997). Media violence and youth. In J. D. Osofsky (Ed.), *Children in a violent society* (pp. 72–97). New York: Guilford Press.

Naisknov, A. (2002, June 16). Charter schools share ideas. *Boston Globe,* p. E6.

Narvaez, A., Feldman, J., & Theriot, C. (2006). Virtual pre-K: Connecting, home, school, and community. *Young Children, 61*(1), 52–53.

National Adoption Information Clearinghouse. (2004). *Adoption.* Washington DC: Author. Also retrieved August 29, 2006, from http://www.childwelfare.gov

National Alliance to End Homelessness. (2006). Family Homelssness. Retrieved June 20, 2006, from http://www.endhomelessness.org/back/Familiesfacts.pdf

National Association for Family Child Care. (2003). *The quality standard for NAFCC accreditation* (3rd ed.). Washington DC: Author.

National Association for the Education of Young Children. (1998). *Accreditation criteria and procedures of the National Association for the Education of Young Children.* Washington, DC: Author.

National Association of Child Care Resource and Referral Agencies (NACCRRA). (2006). Child care in America. Retrieved April 10, 2006, from http://www.nrex.org

National Center for Children in Poverty (NCCP). (2006). http://www.nccp.org/press.html. Accessed Sept. 1, 2006.

National Center for Missing & Exploited Children. (2006). Current figures. Retrieved January 24, 2006, from http://www.missingkids.com

National Commission on Excellence in Education. (1983). *A nation at risk: The imperative for educational reform.* Washington, DC: U.S. Government Printing Office.

National Commission on Migrant Children. (1992). *Invisible children: A portrait of migrant education in the United States* (Supt. of Documents, Stock No. 022–003–01173–1). Washington, DC: Author.

National Head Start Association. (2006). Update on Head Start reauthorization. Retrieved May 16, 2006, from http://www.nhsa.org

National Institute of Child Health & Human Development (NICHD). Early Child Care Research Network. (2000) The relation of child care to cognitive and language development. *Child Development, 71*(4), 960–980.

National Institute of Child Health and Human Development Early Child Care Research Network. (1997). Child care in the first year of life. *Merrill–Palmer Quarterly, 43,* 340–360.

National Institute on Media and the Family. (2006). Focus on families. Retrieved June 2, 2006, from http://www.mediafamily.org

National Research Council. (2002). *Minority students in special and gifted education.* Washington, DC: National Academy Press.

Neill, A. S. (1960). *Summerhill.* New York: Hart.

Neito, S. (2002). *Language, culture and teaching: Critical perspectives for a new century.* Mahwah, NJ: Erlbaum.

Neugebauer, R. (2005). The U.S. military child care system: A model worth replicating. *Exchange, 161,* 31–32.

Neuman, S. B. (1995). *Myth of the TV effect.* Norwood, NJ: Ablex.

Neuman, S. B. (1997). Television as a learning environment: A theory of synergy. In J. Flood, S. Brice-Heath, & D. Lapp (Eds.), *Handbook of research on teaching literacy through the communicative and visual arts* (pp. 15–23). New York: Simon & Schuster.

New, R. (1998). Theory and praxis in Reggio Emilia: They know what they are doing, and why. In C. Edwards, L. Gandini, & G. Forman (Eds.), *The hundred languages of children: The Reggio Emilia approach—Advanced reflections* (pp. 261–285). Greenwich, CT: Ablex.

New, R. (2001). Quando o'e figli [Where there are children]. Observations in an Italian Early Childhood Program. In L. Gandini & C. P. Edwards (Eds.), *Bambini: The Italian approach to infant/toddler care* (pp. 210–216). New York: Teachers College Press.

New, R. S. (2003). Reggio Emilia: New ways to think about schooling. *Educational Leadership, 60*(7), 34–39.

Newberger, J. J. (1997). New brain development research: A wonderful window of opportunities to build public support for early childhood education. *Young Children, 52*(4), 4–10.

Newman, L. A. (2004). A national study of parent involvement in education of youth with disabilities. In D. B. Hiatt-Michael (Ed.). *Promising practices connecting schools to families of children with special needs* (pp. 25–40). Greenwich, CT: Information Age Publishing.

Noam, G. G., & Miller, B. M. (Eds.). (2002). *Youth development and after-school time: A tale of many cities.* San Francisco: Jossey-Bass.

Noddings, N. (2002). *Educating moral people: A caring alternative to character education.* New York: Teachers College Press.

Noddings, N. (2005). *Happiness and education.* New York: Cambridge University Press.

Notar, E. E. (1992). They come with stories. *Childhood Education, 68*(3), 131–133.

Ogbu, J. U. (1994). Racial stratification and education in the United States: Why inequality persists. *Teachers College Record, 96*(2), 265–298.

O'Hare, W. P. (1992). America's minorities: The demographics of diversity. *Population Bulletin, 47*(4), 2–40.

Okagaki, L., & Luster. T. (2005). Research on parental socialization of child outcomes. in T. Luster & L. Okagaki (Eds.), *Parenting: An ecological perspective* (2nd ed., pp. 377–401). Mahwah, NJ: Lawrence Erlbaum.

Oladele, F. (1999). Passing the spirit. *Educational Leadership, 56*(4), 62–65.

Olfman, S. (2005a), Introduction. In S. Olfman (Ed.), *Childhood lost: How American culture is failing our kids* (pp. i–xiv). Westport, CT: Praeger.

Olfman, S. (2005b), Where do the children play? In S. Olfman (Ed.), *Childhood lost: How American culture is failing our kids* (pp. 203–216). Westport, CT: Praeger Publishers.

Olsen, G., & Fuller, M. L. (Eds.), (2003). *Home–school relations: Working successfully with parents and families* (2nd ed.). Boston: Allyn & Bacon.

Opie, I. A., & Opie, P. (1969). *Children's games in street and playgound: Chasing, catching, seeking, hunting, racing, duelling, exerting, daring, guessing, acting, pretending.* Oxford, UK: Clarendon.

Orpinas , P., & Horne, A. M. (2006). *Bullying prevention: Creating a positive school climate and developing social competence.* Washington, DC: American Psychological Association.

Orr, D. (2004). *Earth in mind: On education, environment, and the human prospect.* Washington, DC: Island Press.

O'Shea, M. R. (2005). *From standards to success: A guide for school leaders.* Alexandria, VA: Association for Supervision and Curriculum Development.

Osofsky, J. D. (1998). Children as invisible victims of domestic and community violence. In G. W. Holden,

R. Geffner, & E. N. Jouriles (Eds.), *Children exposed to marital violence* (pp. 95–120). Washington, DC: American Psychological Association.

Ovando, C. J. (2005). Language diversity and education. In J. A. Banks & C. A. McGee Banks (Eds.), *Multicultural education: Issues and perspectives* (5th ed. pp. 289–313). Hoboken, NJ: John Wiley.

Paik, H. (2001). The history of children's use of electronic media. In D. G. Singer & J. L. Singer (Eds.), *Handbook of children and the media* (pp. 7–27). Thousand Oaks, CA: Sage.

Pann, K. M., & Crosbie-Burnett, M. (2005). Remarriage and recoupling: A stress perspective. In P. C. McKenry & S. J. Price (Eds.), *Families and change: Coping with stressful events and transitions* (pp. 253–284). Thousand Oaks, CA: Sage Publications.

Paratore, J. R. (2001). *Opening doors, opening opportunities: Family literacy in an urban community.* Boston: Allyn & Bacon.

Parke, R. D. (1990, Fall). Family–peer systems: In search of a linking process. *Developmental Psychology, 5,* 20–29.

Pattnaik, J. (2003). Learning about the "other": Building a case for intercultural understanding among minority children. *Childhood Education, 79*(4), 204–211.

Pavao, J. M. (1998). *The family of adoption.* Boston: Beacon Press.

Peisner-Feinberg, E. S., Burchinal, M. R., Clifford, R. M., Culkin, M. L., Howes, C., Kagan, S. L., et al. (1999). *The children of the cost, quality, and outcomes study go to school: Technical report.* Chapel Hill: Frank Porter Graham Child Development Center, University of North Carolina.

Perry, D. G. (1987, Fall). How is aggression learned? *School Safety,* 23–25.

Piaget, J. (1967). *Six psychological studies.* New York: Random House.

Piburn, D. E. (2006). Gender equality for a new generation: Expect male involvement in ECE. *Exchange, 168,* 18–22.

Pica, R. (2006). Physical fitness and the early childhood curriculum. *Young Children, 61*(3), 12–19.

Pinar, W. F. (2004). *What is curriculum theory?* Mahwah, NJ: Lawrence Erlbaum.

Pinker, S. (2002). *The blank slate: The modern denial of human nature.* New York: Viking.

Pinnell, G. S. (1996). Ways to look at the foundation of children's language. In B. M. Power & R. Hubbard

(Eds.), *Language development: A reader for teachers* (pp. 146–155). Upper Saddle River, NJ: Merrill/Prentice Hall.

Pipher, M. (1996). *The shelter of each other: Rebuilding our families.* New York: Ballantine Books.

Pipher, M. (2002). *The middle of everywhere: The world's refugees come to our town.* New York: Harcourt.

Patrikakou, E. N., Weisberg, R. P., Redding, S., & Walber, H. J. (Eds.). (2005). *School–family partnerships for children's success.* New York: Teachers College Press.

Popin, M. (1990). *The active parenting discussion program.* Marietta, GA: Active Parenting.

Population Reference Bureau. (2006). Immigration: Shaping and reshaping America, 2003. Washington, DC: Author. Retrieved August 16, 2006 from http://www.prb.org

Poussaint, A. F. (2006). Understanding and involving African American Parents. *Young Children, 61*(1), 48.

Powers, J. (2005). *Parent-friendly early learning: Tips and strategies for working well with families.* St. Paul, MN: Redleaf Press.

Presser, H. B. (2003). *Working in a 24/7 economy: Challenges for American families.* New York: Russell Sage Foundation.

Proctor, P. (1984). Teacher expectations: A model for school improvement. *Elementary School Journal, 84,* 469–481.

Prothrow-Stith, D., & Spivak, H. (2003). *Murder is no accident: Understanding and preventing youth violence in America..* New York: John Wiley.

Puckett, M. B., & Black, J. K. (2005). *The young child: Development from prebirth through age eight* (4th ed.). Upper Saddle River, NJ: Merrill/Prentice Hall.

Pulliam, J. D., & Van Patten, J. (2007). *History of education in America* (9th ed.). Upper Saddle River, NJ: Lawrence Prentice Hall.

Quint, S. (1994). *Schooling homeless children: A working model for America's public schools.* New York: Teachers College Press.

Raden, A. (2003). Universal access to prekindergarten: A Georgia case study. In A. J. Reynolds, M. C. Wang, & H. J. Walberg, *Early childhood programs for a new century* (pp. 71–114). Washington, DC: CWLA Press.

Rafanello, D. (2004). Child care for families who are homeless: A model of comprehensive early childhood services. *Child Care Information Exchange, 156*, 58–63.

Rainwater, L., & Smeeding, T. M. (2004). Single-parent poverty, inequality, and the welfare state. In D. P. Moynihan, T. M. Smeeding, & L. Rainwater (Eds.), *The future of the family* (pp. 96–115). New York: Russell Sage Foundation.

Ramirez-Smith, C. (1995). Stopping the cycle of failure: The Comer model. *Educational Leadership, 52*(5), 14–19.

Ramsey, P. G. (1987). Young children's thinking about ethnic differences. In J. S. Phinney & M. J. Rotheram (Eds.), *Children's ethnic socialization: Pluralism and development* (pp. 56–72). Newbury Park, CA: Sage.

Ramsey, P. G. (2004). *Teaching and learning in a diverse world: Multicultural education for young children* (3rd ed.). New York: Teachers College Press.

Rankin, B. (1998). Curriculum development in Reggio Emilia: A long-term curriculum project about dinosaurs. In C. Edwards, L. Gandini, & G. Forman, (Eds.), *The hundred languages of children: The Reggio Emilia approach—Advanced reflections* (pp. 215–237). Greenwich, CT: Ablex.

Ray, B. (1997, May/June). Home education across the United States. *Home School Court Report, 13*(3), 11–16.

Ray, B. D. (2000a). Homeschooling for individual's gains and society's common good. *Peabody Journal of Education, 75*(1, 2), 272–293.

Ray, B. D. (2000b). Homeschooling: The amelioration of negative influence on learning? *Peabody Journal of Education, 75*(1, 2), 71–106.

Ray, B. D. (2002). Customization through homeschooling. *Educational Leadership, 59*(7), 50–55.

Ray, J. A., & Shelton, D. (2004). E-pals: Connecting with families through technology. *Young Children, 59*(3), 30–34.

Reich, R. (2002). The civic perils of homeschooling. *Educational Leadership, 59*(7), 56–59.

Reppucci, N. D., Britner, P. A., & Woolard, J. L. (1997). *Preventing child abuse and neglect through parent education.* Baltimore: Paul H. Brookes.

Reyna, V. F. (2005). The No Child Left Behind act and scientific research: A view from Washington, D.C. In J. S. Carlson & J. R. Levin (Eds.), *The No Child Left Behind legislation* (pp.1–27). Greenwich, CT: Information Age Publishing.

Rich, D. (1992). *Megaskills: In school and life—The best gift you can give your child.* Boston: Houghton Mifflin.

Rich, J. M. (1997). *Foundations of education: Perspectives on American education.* Upper Saddle River, NJ: Prentice Hall.

Rideout, V., Vanderwater, E., & Wartella, E. (2003). *Zero to six: Electronic media in the lives of infants, toddlers, & preschoolers. A Kaiser Family Report.* Menlo Park, CA: The Kaiser Family Foundation.

Ridley, M. (2003a). *Nature via nurture: Genes, experience and what makes us human.* New York: Random House.

Ridley, M. (2003b). What makes you who you are? *Time, 161*(22), 54–63.

Riley, R. W. (1995). Reflections on Goals 2000. *Teachers College Record, 96*, 380–389.

Rinaldi, C. (1998). Projected curriculum constructed through documentation—Progottazione: An interview with L. Gandini. In C. Edwards, L. Gandini, & G. Forman (Eds.), *The hundred languages of children: The Reggio Emilia approach—Advanced reflections* (2nd ed.). Greenwich, CT: Ablex.

Robinson, J. D., & Godbey, G. (1999). *Time for life: The surprising way Americans use their time* (2nd ed.). University Park: Penn State University Press.

Romanowski, M. H. (2001). Teaching migrant students: The voices of classroom teachers. *Rural Education, 23*(1), 31–38.

Rose, L. C., & Gallup, A. M. (2006). The 38th annual Phi Delta Kappa/Gallup Poll of the public's attitude toward the public schools. *Phi Delta Kappan, 88*, 41–66.

Rosenthal, R., & Jacobson, L. (1968). *Pygmalion in the classroom.* New York: Holt, Rinehart & Winston.

Rowe, D. C. (1994). *The limits of family influence: Genes, experience and behavior.* New York: Guilford Press.

Rubin, H. (2002). *Collaborative leadership: Developing effective partnerships in communities and schools.* Thousand Oaks, CA: Corwin.

Rupp, R. (1998). *The complete home learning resource book.* New York: Three Rivers Press.

Sacks, P. (2005). "No child left": What are schools for in a democratic society? In S. Olfman (Ed.), *Childhood lost: How American culture is failing our kids* (pp. 185–202). Westport, CT: Praeger.

Sadker, D., & Sadker, M. (2005a). Gender bias: From colonial america to today's classrooms. In J. A. Banks and C. A. McGee-Banks (Eds.), *Multicultural education: Issues and perspectives* (pp. 135–163). Hoboken, NJ: John Wiley.

Sadker, M. P., & Sadker, D. M. (2005b). *Teachers, schools and society* (7th ed.). New York: McGraw-Hill.

Salend, S. J. (2001). *Creating inclusive classrooms: Effective and reflective practices* (4th ed.). Upper Saddle River, NJ: Merrill/Prentice Hall.

Salzstein, H. D. (1976). Social influence and moral development: A perspective on the role of parents and peers. In T. Lickona (Ed.), *Moral development and behavior: Theory, research, and social issues* (pp. 241– 252). New York: Holt, Rinehart & Winston.

Sameroff, A., Seifer, R., Barocas, R., Zax, M., & Greenspan, S. (1987). Intelligence quotient scores of four-year-old children: Social–environmental risk factors. *Pediatrics, 79,* 343–350.

Sanders, M. G. (2006). *Building school-community relationships: Collaborations for school success.* Thousand Oaks, CA: Corwin Press.

Sanderson, S. K. (1995). *Social transformations: A general theory of historical development.* Cambridge, MA: Blackwell.

Sateran, S. S. (2001). *Going to school in colonial America.* Mankato, MN: Capstone Press.

Saul, W., & Newman, A. R. (1986). *Science fare: An illustrated guide and catalog of toys, books, and activities for kids.* New York: Harper & Row.

Scanzoni, J. (2004). Household diversity: The starting point for healthy families in the new century. In M. Coleman & L. H. Ganong (Eds.), *Handbook of contemporary families: Considering the past, contemplating the future* (pp. 3–22). Thousand Oaks, CA: Sage.

Scarf, M. (1997). *Intimate worlds: How families thrive and why they fail.* New York: Ballantine Books.

Scarf, M. (1999). *Intimate worlds: Life inside the family.* Collingdale, NY: Diane.

Scarr, S. (1998). American child care today. *American Psychologist, 53,* 95–108.

Schlossman, S. (1976). Before Home Start: Notes towards a history of parent education in America, 1897–1929. *Harvard Educational Review, 46,* 436–467.

Schorr, J. (2002). *Hard lessons: The promises of an inner city charter school.* New York: Ballantine Books.

Schott, J. C. (1989). Holy wars in education. *Educational Leadership, 47*(2), 61–66.

Schuman, David. (2004). *American schools, American teachers: Issues and perspectives.* Boston: Allyn & Bacon.

Schwartz, L. L., & Kaslow, F. W. (1997). *Painful partings: Divorce and its aftermath.* New York: Wiley.

Schweinhart, L. J., & Weikart, D. P. (1997). *Lasting differences: The High/Scope preschool curriculum comparison study through age 23* (Monographs of the High/Scope Educational Research Foundation, 12). Ypsilanti, MI: High/Scope.

Sclafani, J. D. (2004). *The educated parent: Recent trends in raising children.* Westport, CT: Praeger.

Scully, P. (2003). Time out from tension: Teaching young children how to relax. *The Journal of Early Education and Family Review, 10*(4), 22–29.

Scully, P., Seefeldt, C., & Barbour, N. H. (2003). *Developmental continuity across the preschool and primary grades: Implications for teachers* (2nd ed.). Olney, MD: Association for Childhood Education International.

Seefeldt, C., & Barbour, N. (1998). *Early childhood education: An introduction* (4th ed.). Upper Saddle River, NJ: Merrill/Prentice Hall.

Sheldon, S. B., & Epstein, J. L. (2002). Improving student behavior and school discipline with family and community involvement. *Education and Urban Society, 35*(1), 4–26.

Sheldon, S. B., & Epstein, J. L. (2005). Involvement counts: Family and community partnerships and mathematics achievement. *Journal of Educational Research, 98*(4), 196–206.

Shoop, R. J., & Dunklee, D. R. (1992). *School law for the principal: A handbook for practitioners.* Boston: Allyn & Bacon.

Side, R. (2006). *Unsung heroines: Single mothers and the American dream.* Berkeley, CA: University of California Press.

Sigel, I. E., Dreyer, A. S., & McGillicuddy-DeLisi, A. V. (1984). Psychological perspectives of the family. In R. D. Parke (Ed.), *Review of child development research: Vol. 7. The family* (pp. 42–79). Chicago: University of Chicago Press.

Silber, J. (1989). *Straight shooting: What's wrong with America and how to fix it.* New York: Harper & Row.

Simmons, L. L. (2004). Historical antecedents, legal issues, and government policies related to family involvement for children with special needs. In D. B. Hiatt-Michael (Ed.), *Promising practices connecting schools to families of children with special needs* (pp. 15–24). Greenwich, CT: Information Age Publishing.

Singer, D. G., & Singer, J. L. (2001). Introduction: Why a handbook on children and media? In D. G. Singer & J. L. Singer (Eds.), *Handbook of children and the media* (pp. vi–xxii). Thousand Oaks, CA: Sage.

Singer, D. G., & Singer, J. L. (2005). *Imagination and play in the electronic age.* Thousand Oaks, CA: Sage.

Siris, K. (2001). Using action research to alleviate bullying and victimization in the classroom. (Doctoral dissertation, Hofstra University.)

Siris, K., & Osterman, K. (2004). "Interrupting the cycle of bullying and victimization in the elementary classroom. *Phi Delta Kappan, 86*(4), 288–291.

Sleeter, C. E., & Grant, C. A. (2006). *Making choices for multicultural education: Five approaches to race, class, and gender* (5th ed.). New York: Wiley.

Small, M. L., & Newman, K. (2001). Urban poverty after *The Truly Disadvantaged:* The rediscovery of the family, the neighborhood, and culture. *Annual Review of Sociology, 27,* 23–45.

Sonenstein, F. L., Gates, G., Schmidt, S. & Bolshun, N. (2002). *Primary child care arrangements of employed parents.* Washington DC: Urban Institute.

Spaggiari, S. (1998). The community–teacher partnership and its expansion in the governance of the schools. In C. Edwards, L. Gandini, & G. Forman (Eds.), *The hundred languages of children: The Reggio Emilia approach—Advanced reflections* (pp. 99–113). Greenwich, CT: Ablex.

Sparling, J. (2004). Earliest literacy: From birth to age three. In B. H. Wasik (Ed.), *Handbook of family literacy* (pp. 45–56). Mahwah, NJ: Lawrence Erlbaum.

Spewock, T. S. (1991). Teaching parents of young children through learning packets. *Young Children, 47*(1), 28–30.

Stanford, B. H., & Yamamoto, K. (Eds.). (2001). *Children and stress: Understanding and helping.* Olney, MD: Association for Childhood Education International.

Steglin, D. A. (2005). Making the case for play policy: Research-based reasons to support play-based environments. *Young Children, 60*(2), 76–85.

Stein, C. B., Jr. (1986). *Sink or swim: The politics of bilingual education.* Westport, CT: Greenwood.

Steinberg, L. (1991). Authoritative parenting and adolescent adjustment across various ecological niches. *Journal of Research in Adolescence, 1,* 19–36.

Steinberg, L., & Silk, J. S. (2002). Parenting adolescents. In M. H. Bornstein (Ed.), *Handbook of parenting: Volume 1, Children and parenting* (pp. 103–133). Mahwah, NJ: Lawrence Erlbaum.

Sternberg, R. J. (1997). The concept of intelligence and its role in life-long learning and success. *American Psychologist, 52,* 1030–1037.

Stevens, M. L. (2001). *The kingdom of children: Culture and controversy in the homeschooling movement.* Princeton, NJ: Princeton University Press.

Stewart, V., & Kagan, S. L. (2005). A new world view: Education in a global era. *Phi Delta Kappan, 87*(3), 241–244.

Stiggins, R. J. (2005). *Student-involved classroom assessment* (4th ed.). Upper Saddle River, NJ: Merrill/Prentice Hall.

Stille, A. (1998, June 11). The betrayal of history. *New York Review of Books, 45*(10), pp. 8–11. Also retrieved May 4, 2003, from http://www.nybooks.com

Strasburger, V. C., & Wilson, B. J. (2002). *Children, adolescents, and the media.* Thousand Oaks, CA: Sage.

Strohmaier, P. (2004). The Iraq war on children's TV. *Television, 17,* 18–23.

Strom, R., & Strom, S. (1997). Building a theory of grandparent development. *Journal of Aging and Human Development, 9,* 255–285.

Studer, J. R. (1993/1994). Listen so that parents will speak. *Childhood Education, 70*(2), 74–76.

Sugrue, T. J. (1999). Poor families in an era of urban transformation: The underclass family in myth and reality. In S. Coontz (Ed.), *American families: A multicultural reader* (pp. 243–258). New York: Routledge.

Surr, J. (2004). Who is accredited? What and how the states are doing on best practices in child care. *Child Care Exchange, 156,* 14–19.

Swick, K. J. (1999). Empowering homeless and transient children and families: An ecological framework for early childhood teachers. *Early Childhood Education Journal, 26*(3), 195–201.

Swick, K. J. (2004). The dynamics of families who are homeless: Implications for early childhood education. *Childhood Education, 80*(3), 116–120.

Swiniarski, L., & Breitborde, M. L. (2003). *Educating the global village: Including the child in the world* (2nd ed.). Upper Saddle River, NJ: Merrill/Prentice Hall.

Swisher, R., & Whitlock, J. (2004). How neighborhoods matter for youth development. In S. F. Hamilton & M. A. Hamilton (Eds.), *The youth development handbook: Coming of age in American communities* (pp. 216–237). Thousand Oaks, CA: Sage.

Szasz, M. C. (1988). *Indian education in the American colonies, 1607–1783.* Albuquerque: University of New Mexico Press.

Tabors, P. O., & Snow, C. E. (2001). Young children and early literacy development. In S. Neuman & D. K. Dickinson (Eds.), *Handbook of early literacy research* (pp. 159–178). New York: Guilford Press.

Tao, F., Khan, S., & Arriola, C. (1997). *Special analysis of migrant education: Even Start Projects 1995–1996 program year.* Washington, DC: U.S. Department of Education, Office of Educational Research and Improvement. (ERIC Document Reproduction Service No. ED417921.)

Taylor, K. W. (1981). *Parents and children learn together.* New York: Teachers College Press.

Taylor, R. L. (2000). Diversity within African American families. In D. Demo, K. Allen, & M. Fine (Eds.), *Handbook of family diversity* (pp. 232–257). New York: Oxford University Press.

Teachman, J. D. (2000). Diversity of family structure: Economic and social influences. In D. Demo, K. Allen, & M. Fine (Eds.), *Handbook of family diversity* (pp. 32–58). New York: Oxford University Press.

Terzi, N., & Cantorelli, M. (2001). Parma: Supporting the work of teachers, through professional development, organization and administrative support. In L. Gandini & C. P. Edwards (Eds.), *Bambini: The Italian approach to infant–toddler care* (pp. 78–89). New York: Teachers College Press.

The Teaching Home. (2002). *Educational approaches and methods.* Retrieved May 3, 2003, from http://www.teachinghome.com

Thomas, R. M. (2001). *Recent theories of human development.* Thousand Oaks, CA: Sage.

Thornburgh, D., & Lin, H. S. (Eds.). (2002). *Youth, pornography and the Internet.* Washington, DC: National Academy Press.

Tiedt, P. L., & Tiedt, I. M. (2001). *Multicultural teaching: A handbook of activities, information and resources.* Reading, MA: Allyn & Bacon.

Tomlin, A. M. (1998). Grandparents' influences on grandchildren. In M. E. Szinovacz (Ed.), *Handbook on grandparenthood* (pp. 161–171). Westport, CT: Greenwood.

Travers, P. D., & Rebore, R. W. (2000). *Foundations of education: Becoming a teacher* (4th ed.). Boston: Allyn & Bacon.

Trawick-Smith, J. (2006). *Early childhood development: A multicultural perspective* (4th ed.). Upper Saddle River, NJ: Merrill/Prentice Hall.

Turnbull, A., Turnbull, R., & Wehmeyer. M. (2007). *Exceptional lives: Special education in today's schools* (5th ed.). Upper Saddle River, NJ: Merrill/Prentice Hall.

U.S. Bureau of the Census. (1998a). *Current population report: P20–497–1998.* Washington, DC: Author.

U.S. Bureau of the Census. (1998b). *Statistical abstract of the United States: 1998* (118th ed.). Washington, DC: Author.

U.S. Bureau of the Census. (2001). *Current population report* (pp. 20–52). Washington, DC: Author.

U.S. Bureau of the Census. (2002a). *Current population report: P20–537–2000.* Washington, DC: Author.

U.S. Bureau of the Census. (2002b). *Statistical abstract of the United States: 2002* (122nd ed.). Washington, DC: Author.

U.S. Bureau of the Census. (2004a). *Statistical abstract of the United States: 2004* (124th ed.). Washington DC: Author.

U.S. Bureau of the Census. (2004b). U.S. interim projections by age, sex, race, and hispanic origin. Retrieved June 4, 2006, from http://www.census.gov/lpc/www/usinterimproj/

U.S. Bureau of the Census. (2005). *Statistical abstract of the United States: 2005* (125th ed.). Washington DC: Author.

U.S. Census Bureau News. (2006). Census Bureau releases population estimates for states and counties, August 4, 2006. Washington D.C.: U.S. Bureau of the Census, U.S. Department of Commerce.

U.S. Department of Agriculture (USDA), Center for Nutrition Policy and Promotion. (2006). Retrieved June 5, 2006, from www.mypyramid.com

U.S. Department of Education. (1991). *America 2000: An education strategy.* Washington, DC: Author.

U.S. Department of Education. (1993a). *Goals 2000: Educate America.* Washington, DC: Author.

U.S. Department of Education. (1993b). *National Education Goals.* Gov. Doc. ED 1.2:G 53/5. Washington, DC: Author.

U.S. Department of Education. (2002). Twenty-fourth annual report to Congress on the implementation of the Individuals with Disabilities Education Act. Washington, D.C.: Author.

U.S. Department of Education. (2003). The nation's report card. *The Achiever, 2*(1), 2–3.

U.S. Department of Education. (2003). President Bush's proposal for Head Start. Retrieved April 15, 2006 from http://www.headstartinfo.org

U.S. Department of Education (2004a). *Individuals with Disabilities Education Act (IDEA) data (Table AA3)*. Washington, DC: Author.

U.S. Department of Education. (2004b). *Successful charter schools*. Washington, DC: Office of Innovation and Improvement, U. S. Department of Education.

U.S. Department of Education. (2006). National Coalition for Parent Involvement in Education (NCPIE) Reports. Retrieved July 1, 2006, from http://www.ncpie.org

U.S. Department of Labor Bureau of Labor Statistics. (2005). Women in the Labor Force: A data book. Accessed April 10, 2006, from http://www.bls. gov

Urban Institute. (2002). *Homeless Americans*. Washington, DC: Author. Also retrieved August 10, 2003, from http://www.nationalhomeless.org/numbers. html

Urban Institute. (2007). Child-care expenses of America's families. Retrieved January 30, 2007, from http://www.urban.org

Uttal, L. (2002). *Making care work: Employed mothers in the new childcare market*. New Brunswick, NJ: Rutgers University Press.

Valente, W. D., & Valente, C. M. (2005). *Law in the schools* (6th ed.). Upper Saddle River, NJ: Merrill/Prentice Hall.

Van Evra, J. (2004). *Television and child development* (3rd ed.). Mahwah, NJ: Lawrence Erlbaum.

Vandell, D. L., & Pierce, K. M. (2003). Child care quality and children's success at school. In A. J. Reynolds, M. C. Wang, & H. J. Walberg (Eds.), *Early childhood programs for a new century* (pp. 115–139). Washington, DC: CWLA Press.

Vanourek, G. (2005). *State of the charter movement 2005: Trends, issues & indicators*. Washington, DC.: National Alliance for Public Charter Schools.

Vosler, N. R. (1996). *New approaches to family practice: Confronting economic stress*. Thousand Oaks, CA: Sage.

Voss, M. M. (1993). "I just watched": Family influences on one child's learning. *Language Arts, 70,* 632–641.

Vygotsky, L. S. (1978). *Mind in society*. Cambridge, MA: Harvard University Press.

Wade, S. M. (2004). Parenting influences on intellectual development & educational achievement. In M. A. Hoghughi & N. Long (Eds.), *Handbook of parenting: Theory and research for practice* (pp. 198–212). Thousand Oaks, CA: Corwin Press.

Wagner, T. (2003). Reinventing American schools. *Phi Delta Kappan, 84,* 665–668.

Walberg, H. J. (1984). Improving the productivity of America's schools. *Educational Leadership, 41*(8), 19–27.

Walker, L. J., & Taylor, J. H. (1991). Family interaction and the development of moral reasoning. *Child Development, 62,* 264–283.

Waller, P. L., & Crawford, K. (2001). Education advocacy for the nation's invisible population—The migrant community. *Delta Kappa Gamma Bulletin, 68*(1), 24–27.

Wallerstein, J., Lewis, J., & Blakeslee, S. (2000). *The unexpected legacy of divorce*. New York: Hyperion.

Wallerstein, J. S. (2001). The challenges of divorce for parents and children. In J. C. Westman (Ed.), *Parenthood in America: Undervalued, underpaid, under siege* (pp. 127–139). Madison: University of Wisconsin Press.

Walsh, F. (2002). Family resilience: Strengths forged through adversity. In F. Walsh (Ed.), *Normal family processes: Growing diversity and complexity* (pp. 399–423). New York: Guilford Press.

Walsh, M. (2002, June 5). Home school enrollment surge fuels "cottage" industry. *Education Week, 21*(39), 8.

Wang, M. C., & Walberg. H. J. (2001). Epilogue. In M. C. Wang & H. J. Walberg (Eds.), *School choice or best systems: What improves education*. Mahwah, NJ: Lawrence Erlbaum.

Warren, M. R. (2005). Communities and schools: A new view of urban education reform. *Harvard Educational Review, 75*(2), 133–173.

Wartella, E., & Gray, G. E. (2004). Raising a world-wise child and the power of media: The impact of television on children in intercultural knowledge. *Phi Delta Kappan, 86*(3), 222–224.

Webb, L. D., Metha, A., & Jordan, K. F. (2007). *Foundations of American education* (5th ed.). Upper Saddle River, NJ: Merrill/Prentice Hall.

Weber, E. (1969). *The kindergarten.* New York: Teachers College Press.

Weikart, D. P. (2004). Head Start and evidence-based educational models. In E. Zigler & S. Styfco (Eds.), *The Head Start debates* (pp. 143–159). Baltimore: Paul H. Brookes.

Weikart, D. P., & Hohmann, M. (2002). *Educating young children: Active learning practices for preschool and child care programs* (2nd ed.). Ypsilanti, MI: High/Scope Press.

Weinberg, M. (1977). *A chance to learn: A history of race and education in the United States.* New York: Cambridge University Press.

Weldin, D. J., & Tumarkin, S. R. (1999). More power in the portfolio process. *Childhood Education, 75*(2), 90–96.

Werner, E. E. (1999). *Through the eyes of innocents: Children witness World War II.* Boulder, CO: Westview Press.

Werner, E. E., & Smith, R. (2001). *Journeys from childhood to midlife: Risk, resilience, and recovery.* Ithaca, NY: Cornell University Press.

Werner, E. E., & Smith, R. S. (1992). *Overcoming the odds: High-risk children from birth to adulthood.* Ithaca, NY: Cornell University Press.

Werts, M., Culatta, R., & Tompkins, J. (2007). *Fundamentals of special education: What every teacher needs to know.* Upper Saddle River, NJ: Prentice Hall.

Westinghouse Learning Corporation–Ohio University. (1969). *The impact of Head Start.* Springfield, VA: U.S. Department of Commerce, Clearinghouse for Federal Scientific and Technical Information.

Westman, J. C. (2001). Growing together: Parenthood as a developmental experience. In J. C. Westman (Ed.), *Parenthood in America: Undervalued, underpaid, under siege* (pp. 34–46). Madison: University of Wisconsin Press.

Whitman, W. (1855). *Leaves of grass.* New York: Andrew & James Rome.

Wilson, P. P., & Leslie, R. (2001). *Premier events: Library programs that inspire elementary school patrons.* Englewood, CO: Libraries Unlimited.

Winn, M. (2002a). *The plug-in drug: Television, computers and family life.* New York: Penguin Books.

Winn, M. (2002b). What television chases out of life. *American Educator, 26*(2), 40–45.

Withers, Anne. (2006). Personal communication from Office of Head Start Bureau on April 20, 2006.

Wohl, F. (1997). A panoramic view of work and family. In S. Parasuraman & J. H. Greenhaus (Eds.), *Integrating work and family: Challenges and choices for a changing world* (pp. 15–24). Westport, CT: Quorum Books.

Wohlstetter, P., & Smith, J. (2006). Improving schools through partnerships. *Phi Delta Kappan, 86,* 464–467.

Wood, J. (2002). *Adapting instruction to accommodate students in inclusive settings* (4th ed.). Upper Saddle River, NJ: Merrill/Prentice Hall.

Woolfolk, A. E. (2000). *Educational psychology* (8th ed.). Boston: Allyn & Bacon.

Wortham, S. (2006). *Early childhood curriculum: Developmental bases for learning and teaching* (4th ed.). Upper Saddle River, NJ: Merrill/Prentice Hall.

Wright, M. A. (1998). I'm chocolate, you're vanilla: Raising healthy Black and biracial children in a race-conscious world. San Francisco: Jossey-Bass.

Wynter, L. (2002). *American skin: Pop culture, big business, and the end of White America.* New York: Crown.

Yamaguchi, B. J., Strawser, S., & Higgins, K. (1997). Children who are homeless: Implications for educators. *Intervention in School and Clinic, 33*(2), 90–97.

Zelizer, V. A. (1994). *Pricing the priceless child: The changing social value of children.* Princeton, NJ: Princeton University Press.

Zigler, E., & Styfco, S. J. (Eds.), (2004). *The Head Start debates.* Baltimore: Paul H. Brookes.

NAME INDEX

SUBJECT INDEX